Communications in Computer and Information Science 1586

More information about this series at https://link.springer.com/bookseries/7899

Xingming Sun · Xiaorui Zhang · Zhihua Xia ·
Elisa Bertino (Eds.)

Advances in Artificial Intelligence and Security

8th International Conference
on Artificial Intelligence and Security, ICAIS 2022
Qinghai, China, July 15–20, 2022
Proceedings, Part I

 Springer

Editors
Xingming Sun 🆔
Nanjing University of Information Science
and Technology
Nanjing, China

Zhihua Xia 🆔
Jinan University
Guangzhou, China

Xiaorui Zhang 🆔
Nanjing University of Information Science
and Technology
Nanjing, China

Elisa Bertino 🆔
Purdue University
West Lafayette, IN, USA

ISSN 1865-0929   ISSN 1865-0937 (electronic)
Communications in Computer and Information Science
ISBN 978-3-031-06766-2   ISBN 978-3-031-06767-9 (eBook)
https://doi.org/10.1007/978-3-031-06767-9

This Springer imprint is published by the registered company Springer Nature Switzerland AG
The registered company address is: Gewerbestrasse 11, 6330 Cham, Switzerland

Preface

The 8th International Conference on Artificial Intelligence and Security (ICAIS 2022), formerly called the International Conference on Cloud Computing and Security (ICCCS), was held during July 15–20, 2022, in Qinghai, China. Over the past seven years, ICAIS has become a leading conference for researchers and engineers to share their latest results of research, development, and applications in the fields of artificial intelligence and information security.

We used the Microsoft Conference Management Toolkit (CMT) system to manage the submission and review processes of ICAIS 2022. We received 1124 submissions from authors in 20 countries and regions, including the USA, Canada, the UK, Italy, Ireland, Japan, Russia, France, Australia, South Korea, South Africa, Iraq, Kazakhstan, Indonesia, Vietnam, Ghana, China, Taiwan, Macao, etc. The submissions cover the areas of artificial intelligence, big data, cloud computing and security, information hiding, IoT security, multimedia forensics, encryption and cybersecurity, and so on. We thank our Technical Program Committee (TPC) members and external reviewers for their efforts in reviewing papers and providing valuable comments to the authors. From the total of 1124 submissions, and based on at least three reviews per submission, the Program Chairs decided to accept 166 papers to be published in three LNCS volumes and 168 papers to be published in three CCIS volumes, yielding an acceptance rate of 30%. This volume of the conference proceedings contains all the regular, poster, and workshop papers.

The conference program was enriched by a series of keynote presentations, and the keynote speakers included Q.M. Jonathan Wu and Brij B. Gupta, amongst others. We thank them for their wonderful speeches.

There were 68 workshops organized in ICAIS 2022 which covered all the hot topics in artificial intelligence and security. We would like to take this moment to express our sincere appreciation for the contribution of all the workshop chairs and participants. We would like to extend our sincere thanks to all authors who submitted papers to ICAIS 2022 and to all TPC members. It was a truly great experience to work with such talented and hard-working researchers. We also appreciate the external reviewers for assisting the TPC members in their particular areas of expertise. Moreover, we want to thank our sponsors: ACM, ACM SIGWEB China, the University of Electronic Science and Technology of China, Qinghai Minzu University, Yuchi Blockchain Research Institute, Nanjing Normal University, Northeastern State University, New York University, Michigan State University, the University of Central Arkansas, Dublin City University,

Université Bretagne Sud, the National Nature Science Foundation of China, and Tech Science Press.

April 2022
                                          Xingming Sun
                                          Xiaorui Zhang
                                          Zhihua Xia
                                          Elisa Bertino

Organization

General Chairs

Yun Q. Shi	New Jersey Institute of Technology, USA
Weisheng Ma	Qinghai Minzu University, China
Mauro Barni	University of Siena, Italy
Ping Jiang	Southeast University, China
Elisa Bertino	Purdue University, USA
Xingming Sun	Nanjing University of Information Science and Technology, China

Technical Program Chairs

Aniello Castiglione	University of Salerno, Italy
Yunbiao Guo	China Information Technology Security Evaluation Center, China
Xiaorui Zhang	Engineering Research Center of Digital Forensics, Ministry of Education, China
Q. M. Jonathan Wu	University of Windsor, Canada
Shijie Zhou	University of Electronic Science and Technology of China, China

Publication Chair

Zhihua Xia	Jinan University, China

Publication Vice Chair

Ruohan Meng	Nanjing University of Information Science and Technology, China

Publicity Chair

Zhaoxia Yin	Anhui University, China

Workshop Chairs

Baowei Wang	Nanjing University of Information Science and Technology, China
Lingyun Xiang	Changsha University of Science and Technology, China

Organization Chairs

Genlin Ji	Nanjing Normal University, China
Jianguo Wei	Qinghai Minzu University and Tianjin University, China
Xiaoyu Li	University of Electronic Science and Technology of China, China
Zhangjie Fu	Nanjing University of Information Science and Technology, China
Qilong Sun	Qinghai Minzu University, China

Technical Program Committee

Saeed Arif	University of Algeria, Algeria
Anthony Ayodele	University of Maryland Global Campus, USA
Zhifeng Bao	Royal Melbourne Institute of Technology, Australia
Zhiping Cai	National University of Defense Technology, China
Ning Cao	Qingdao Binhai University, China
Paolina Centonze	Iona College, USA
Chin-chen Chang	Feng Chia University, Taiwan
Han-Chieh Chao	National Dong Hwa University, Taiwan
Bing Chen	Nanjing University of Aeronautics and Astronautics, China
Hanhua Chen	Huazhong University of Science and Technology, China
Xiaofeng Chen	Xidian University, China
Jieren Cheng	Hainan University, China
Lianhua Chi	IBM Research Center, Australia
Kim-Kwang Raymond Choo	University of Texas at San Antonio, USA
Ilyong Chung	Chosun University, South Korea
Martin Collier	Dublin City University, Ireland
Qi Cui	Nanjing University of Information Science and Technology, China
Robert H. Deng	Singapore Management University, Singapore
Jintai Ding	University of Cincinnati, USA

Alex Liu	Michigan State University, USA
Guangchi Liu	Stratifyd Inc., USA
Guohua Liu	Donghua University, China
Joseph Liu	Monash University, Australia
Quansheng Liu	University of South Brittany, France
Xiaodong Liu	Edinburgh Napier University, UK
Yuling Liu	Hunan University, China
Zhe Liu	Nanjing University of Aeronautics and Astronautics, China
Daniel Xiapu Luo	Hong Kong Polytechnic University, Hong Kong
Xiangyang Luo	Zhengzhou Science and Technology Institute, China
Tom Masino	TradeWeb LLC, USA
Nasir Memon	New York University, USA
Noel Murphy	Dublin City University, Ireland
Sangman Moh	Chosun University, South Korea
Yi Mu	University of Wollongong, Australia
Elie Naufal	Applied Deep Learning LLC, USA
Jiangqun Ni	Sun Yat-sen University, China
Rafal Niemiec	University of Information Technology and Management, Poland
Zemin Ning	Wellcome Trust Sanger Institute, UK
Shaozhang Niu	Beijing University of Posts and Telecommunications, China
Srikant Ojha	Sharda University, India
Jeff Z. Pan	University of Aberdeen, UK
Wei Pang	University of Aberdeen, UK
Chen Qian	University of California, Santa Cruz, USA
Zhenxing Qian	Fudan University, China
Chuan Qin	University of Shanghai for Science and Technology, China
Jiaohua Qin	Central South University of Forestry and Technology, China
Yanzhen Qu	Colorado Technical University, USA
Zhiguo Qu	Nanjing University of Information Science and Technology, China
Yongjun Ren	Nanjing University of Information Science and Technology, China
Arun Kumar Sangaiah	VIT University, India
Di Shang	Long Island University, USA
Victor S. Sheng	Texas Tech University, USA
Zheng-guo Sheng	University of Sussex, UK
Robert Simon Sherratt	University of Reading, UK

Yun Q. Shi	New Jersey Institute of Technology, USA
Frank Y. Shih	New Jersey Institute of Technology, USA
Guang Sun	Hunan University of Finance and Economics, China
Jianguo Sun	Harbin University of Engineering, China
Krzysztof Szczypiorski	Warsaw University of Technology, Poland
Tsuyoshi Takagi	Kyushu University, Japan
Shanyu Tang	University of West London, UK
Jing Tian	National University of Singapore, Singapore
Yoshito Tobe	Aoyang University, Japan
Cezhong Tong	Washington University in St. Louis, USA
Pengjun Wan	Illinois Institute of Technology, USA
Cai-Zhuang Wang	Ames Laboratory, USA
Ding Wang	Peking University, China
Guiling Wang	New Jersey Institute of Technology, USA
Honggang Wang	University of Massachusetts-Dartmouth, USA
Jian Wang	Nanjing University of Aeronautics and Astronautics, China
Jie Wang	University of Massachusetts Lowell, USA
Jin Wang	Changsha University of Science and Technology, China
Liangmin Wang	Jiangsu University, China
Ruili Wang	Massey University, New Zealand
Xiaojun Wang	Dublin City University, Ireland
Xiaokang Wang	St. Francis Xavier University, Canada
Zhaoxia Wang	Singapore Management University, Singapore
Jianguo Wei	Qinghai Minzu University and Tianjin University, China
Sheng Wen	Swinburne University of Technology, Australia
Jian Weng	Jinan University, China
Edward Wong	New York University, USA
Eric Wong	University of Texas at Dallas, USA
Shaoen Wu	Ball State University, USA
Shuangkui Xia	Beijing Institute of Electronics Technology and Application, China
Lingyun Xiang	Changsha University of Science and Technology, China
Yang Xiang	Deakin University, Australia
Yang Xiao	University of Alabama, USA
Haoran Xie	Education University of Hong Kong, China
Naixue Xiong	Northeastern State University, USA
Wei Qi Yan	Auckland University of Technology, New Zealand

Aimin Yang	Guangdong University of Technology, China
Ching-Nung Yang	National Dong Hwa University, Taiwan
Chunfang Yang	Zhengzhou Science and Technology Institute, China
Fan Yang	University of Maryland, USA
Guomin Yang	University of Wollongong, Australia
Qing Yang	University of North Texas, USA
Yimin Yang	Lakehead University, Canada
Ming Yin	Purdue University, USA
Shaodi You	Australian National University, Australia
Kun-Ming Yu	Chung Hua University, Taiwan
Shibin Zhang	Chengdu University of Information Technology, China
Weiming Zhang	University of Science and Technology of China, China
Xinpeng Zhang	Fudan University, China
Yan Zhang	Simula Research Laboratory, Norway
Yanchun Zhang	Victoria University, Australia
Yao Zhao	Beijing Jiaotong University, China
Desheng Zheng	Southwest Petroleum University, China

Organization Committee

Xianyi Chen	Nanjing University of Information Science and Technology, China
Qi Cui	Nanjing University of Information Science and Technology, China
Zilong Jin	Nanjing University of Information Science and Technology, China
Yiwei Li	Columbia University, USA
Yuling Liu	Hunan University, China
Zhiguo Qu	Nanjing University of Information Science and Technology, China
Huiyu Sun	New York University, USA
Le Sun	Nanjing University of Information Science and Technology, China
Jian Su	Nanjing University of Information Science and Technology, China
Qing Tian	Nanjing University of Information Science and Technology, China
Qi Wang	Nanjing University of Information Science and Technology, China
Lingyun Xiang	Changsha University of Science and Technology, China

Zhihua Xia	Nanjing University of Information Science and Technology, China
Lizhi Xiong	Nanjing University of Information Science and Technology, China
Leiming Yan	Nanjing University of Information Science and Technology, China
Tao Ye	Qinghai Minzu University, China
Li Yu	Nanjing University of Information Science and Technology, China
Zhili Zhou	Nanjing University of Information Science and Technology, China

Contents – Part I

Contents – Part II

Big Data

Cloud Computing and Security

Multimedia Forensics

Contents – Part III

Information Hiding

IoT Security

Artificial Intelligence

A Target Extraction Algorithm Based on Polarization Image Attention Mechanism

Jian Zhou[1], Fengchang Fei[2(✉)], Zhuping Wang[3], and Cong Nie[1(✉)]

[1] Xi'an Modern Control Technology Research Institute, Xi'an, People's Republic of China
abbqq_15986@163.com

[2] College of Modern Economics and Management, Jiangxi University of Finance and Economics, Nanchang, People's Republic of China
ffcbox@163.com

[3] Xi'an Institute of Electromechanical Information Technology, Xi'an, People's Republic of China

Abstract. Polarization images can highlight the reflection attribute of the target and enhance the display effect of the target boundary on the images. More comprehensive target attributes can be obtained from images taken from multiple polarization angles. However, the number of polarization images is limited at present, and it is difficult to carry out effective research on the premise of small samples. Therefore, based on the polarization images, we give full play to the advantages of polarization images, improve the traditional neural network, and introduce the visual attention model to focus on the salient region. Based on the structural similarity between hyperspectral images and polarization images, twin convolution neural network is constructed to carry out the research of transfer learning in order to learn the network parameters in the case of small samples, and finally realize the target extraction.

Keywords: Polarization · Attention mechanism · Transfer learning · Polarization extraction

1 Introduction

Polarization means that the vibration direction is asymmetric to the propagation direction. It is the most obvious sign that the shear wave is different from other longitudinal waves. Images with different polarization angles can show different effects and have unique imaging advantages[1, 2]. Sarkar et al. [3] designs polarization sensors to realize material classification. Gruev et al. [4] designs the polarization imager from the perspective of hardware. Huang et al. [5] puts forward a new idea of designing polarization imager. Yang et al. [6] analyzes the characteristics of polarization images and natural images and proposes a fusion algorithm. Van et al. [7] analyzes from a biological point of view and guides the development of polarization. Zhang et al. [8] constructs the PCNN polarization image fusion system. Zhang et al. [9] realizes image fusion based on curvelet change. Haining et al. [10] carries out analysis from the feature level to realize polarization image fusion. Zhang et al. [11] constructs a wavelet transform to realize polarization

X. Sun et al. (Eds.): ICAIS 2022, CCIS 1586, pp. 3–16, 2022.
https://doi.org/10.1007/978-3-031-06767-9_1

image enhancement. Zhang et al. [12] establishes a model from the perspective of energy to realize infrared polarization image processing. Ming et al. [13] establishes a model from the perspective of deep learning to fuse image features. Li et al. [14] carries out target detection on the basis of infrared polarization. Inspired by the idea of polarization filtering, Calisti et al. [15] proposes the rotating polarization enhancement to realize image enhancement. Zhu et al. [16] improves the image enhancement features of toggle operator. Wang et al. [17] realizes the polarization image feature enhancement based on global information. Zhang et al. [18] introduces the idea of multi-size to realize target detection in polarized images. Xie et al. [19] realizes the polarization image enhancement based on two scale gradient filtering. Jiang et al. [20] uses NSST to realize visible polarization image mixing. Wang et al. [21] uses NSCT and CNN to realize polarization image fusion.

To sum up, main problems of target extraction based on polarization images are: 1) It is limited to explore polarization image features by constructing a depth model. 2) The feature region of focused polarization images is insufficient, which can result in limited feature extraction. 3) Due to the limited number of polarized images, how to carry out research in the case of small samples is an important problem.

Based on the above shortcomings, a new polarization image target extraction algorithm is proposed in this paper. 1) The existing deep learning network structure is optimized to effectively prevent the loss of feature information caused by nonlinear activation during network channel compression, and the features of polarized images are fully explored. 2) An attention selection mechanism is proposed to simulate the visual focus area and extract the target area. 3) Through twin convolution neural network, the relationship between spectral image features and polarization image features is established to realize small sample transfer learning.

2   Algorithm

In the framework of deep learning, a feature extraction model is constructed to explore features of polarized images. An attention mechanism is introduced to focus on key areas to realize feature extraction. The relationship between spectral images and polarization images is constructed to realize sample transfer learning. The specific process is shown in Fig. 1.

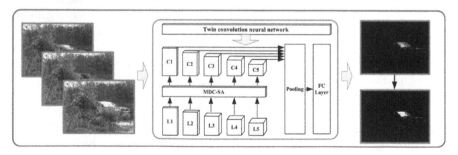

Fig. 1. The algorithm flow chart.

2.1 Feature Extraction Network

Fast R-CNN uses VGG to extract features, which unifies the suggestion box generation, target classification and boundary box into the network for training, and realizes the end-to-end detection task. The corresponding loss function is

$$L(P, T) = \frac{\lambda}{N_{cls}} \sum_i L_{cls}(p_i, p_i^*) + \frac{1 - \lambda}{N_{reg}} \sum_i p_i^* L_{reg}(t_i, t_i^*) \tag{1}$$

where L is the total loss function. p_i is the probability that the i-th border is the foreground. p_i^* is that the border is a positive sample or a negative sample. t_i^* is the coordinates of the real box. L_{cls} is the classification loss. L_{reg} is the regression loss. N_{cls} is the normalized weight of classification loss. N_{reg} is the normalized weight of regression loss. λ is the balance factor of classification loss and regression loss.

The adopted convolution neural network has a large number of parameters. In order to realize practical application, we introduce the Deep separable convolution (DS-Conv), which can achieve the effect similar to the traditional convolution when the parameters are reduced.

ResNet uses multi-scale information to construct the function $F(x) = H(x)\text{-}x$. When $F(x) = 0$, $H(x) = x$. The network is simplified and easy to train. We adopt multi-layer ResNet network structure to enhance the ability of feature expression, and introduce the identity shortcut connection to connect the network. The number of feature graphs is reduced by 1×1 convolution. The convergence of the network is speed up and the cost of training time is reduced.

DS-Conv is used to replace the traditional convolution in ResNet50. The traditional convolution structure is shown in Fig. 2. M convolution kernels are convoluted with all channels of input data. All convolution results are output after fusion, and the output dimension is M. DS-Conv consists of Depthwise Convolution and Pointwise Convolution. DS-Conv convolutes all channels of input data, and then linearly connects the intermediate output results by point-by-point convolution to obtain the M-dimensional output results.

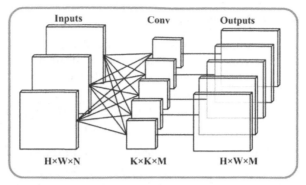

(a) Traditional convolution network

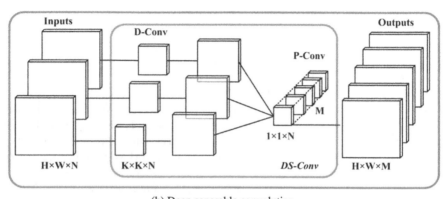

(b) Deep separable convolution

Fig. 2. Convolution network structure.

When the input data is $H \times W \times N$, there are M convolution cores with the size of k $\times$ k and the sliding step size of 1. The ratio of depth separable convolution to traditional convolution parameters is:

$$R = \frac{R_{Ds-Conv}}{R_{T-Conv}} = \frac{k \times k \times N + N \times M}{k \times k \times N \times M} = \frac{1}{M} + \frac{1}{k^2} \quad (2)$$

The amount of DS-Conv parameters is greatly reduced. When the number of output vector channels is large, the DS-Conv parameters are about $1/k^2$ of T-Conv. Deep separable convolution can split the traditional convolution structure and decouple the channel and spatial correlation. Because the number of channels cannot be changed in the process of deep convolution, the negative value of the activation function is 0, resulting in the loss of feature information. Therefore, we introduce the idea of ResNet, use channel expansion to reduce the loss of feature information, and construct the inverse ResNet structure, as shown in Fig. 3.

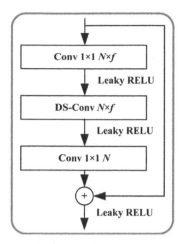

Fig. 3. Inverse ResNet structure.

The expansion factor f ($f = 2$) is introduced into R-ResNet, and input and utilization of N-dimensional data 1×1 convolution realizes the expansion of the number of channels, which outputs $N \times f$ channels. It effectively prevents the loss of feature information caused by nonlinear activation during network channel compression.

2.2 Attention Mechanism

In order to select salient feature regions and improve the ability of network feature expression, a model is constructed based on the idea of attention module

$$J = s\{c[Gap(f'), Gmp(f')]\}$$
$$f' = F[f, d_{conv2}(f), d_{conv4}(f)]$$

(3)

where J is the output feature diagram. c is the core with 7×7 convolution. Gap is the global average pooling. GMP is the global maximum pooling. s(.) is the activation function. d_{conv2} and d_{conv4} are the void convolution with a factor of 2 and 4. F (.) is the up sampling. The specific structure is shown in Fig. 4:

After introducing the attention model, the detail information is better highlighted. At the same time, down sampling fusion is used to increase the interaction between shallow and deep features, and then pay attention to cyberspace information.

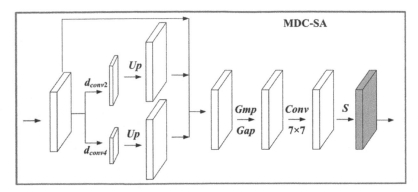

Fig. 4. Multiscale spatial attention module.

Because Gcnet integrates Non-local Block in the network, it can effectively model the global context information and maintain the lightweight characteristics of SENet. We introduce the Global Context module into the feature extraction network based on the idea of Gcnet to capture the dependencies between channels and realize the context modeling, as shown in Fig. 5. Context modeling is a multi-channel attention mechanism, and the corresponding format is expressed as follows:

$$z_i = F\{x_i, W_3\delta[AE]\}, \quad AE = W_2 \sum_{j=1}^{N_p} \frac{x_j \exp(W_1 x_j)}{\sum_{m=1}^{N_p} \exp(W_1 x_m)} \tag{4}$$

where AE is the context module and δ is the conversion module, which is used to obtain the relationship between channels. Our global context module consists of feature extraction, feature transformation and feature fusion. The attention weight is obtained through W_c, and the global features are captured by attention pooling to realize context modeling. W_t is used to realize feature transformation, normalization and improve feature generalization ability. Global context features are aggregated by adders.

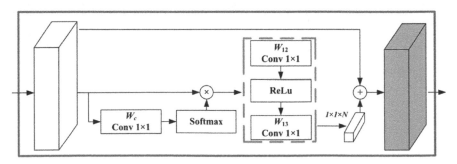

Fig. 5. Global context module.

2.3   Semi Supervised Transfer Learning

Due to the particularity of polarization image data, few data cannot meet the needs of practical application. Therefore, we introduce the idea of transfer learning to learn the knowledge of target domain with the help of marked source domain knowledge in order to reduce the difference between them and realize knowledge transfer learning (Fig. 6). The key of transfer learning is that the source task domain is similar to the target task domain.

Because hyperspectral images and polarization images have strong data structure and similarity. We use hyperspectral images to effectively avoid the occurrence of negative migration.

The embedding function g passes through a convolution neural network, which is composed of an initial convolution layer and a full connection layer. The twin network includes training source domain and target domain. Network parameters are shared in both branches. The source domain branch uses additional full connection layer modeling to build the loss function.

$$L_{total}(f) = \alpha L_c(f) + \beta L_s(f) + \gamma L_D(f)$$
$$\alpha + \beta + \gamma = 1 \tag{4}$$

$$\begin{cases} L_C(f) = E\left[f(X), Y\right] \\ L_S(f) = \sum_{i=1}^{\upsilon} d\left(p\left(g\left(X_i^s\right)\right), p\left(g\left(X_i^t\right)\right)\right) \\ L_D(f) = \sum_{i=1}^{c}\sum_{j=1}^{c} k\left(p\left(g\left(X_i^s\right)\right), p\left(g\left(X_i^t\right)\right)\right) \end{cases} \tag{5}$$

where L_c is the classification loss function. L_s is the loss function of similar samples. L_D is the loss function of different samples. $E[.]$ is the statistical expectation. $d(.)$ is the spatial distance measurement function. $k(.)$ is a spatial similarity measure function. α, β, γ are weights. The established network structure is as follows. It is mainly divided into feature extraction, classification and similarity calculation. In the part of feature extraction, the branch structure of twin convolution network is consistent. The input source domain images and target domain images are mapped to the feature space, and the distance between samples is measured by Euclidean distance. The distance between similar samples in two adjacent domains is shortened by L_s, and the distance between different samples is enlarged by L_D.

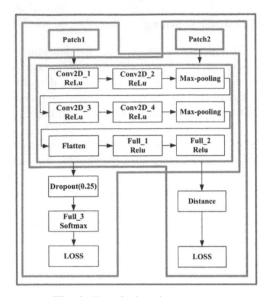

Fig. 6. Transfer learning structure.

3   Experiment and Result Analysis

The experiment uses visible light polarization camera to collect data, and the image resolution is 1280 × 960, collect data every 5 degrees of polarization. The experiment is written by Python in Linux environment. The specific display is shown in Fig. 7.

3.1   Image Information Statistics

The variance of images taken at different azimuth and pitch angles of the scene is counted to show the amount of image information (Fig. 8). It can be seen that the response curve is concave, and the curve shows a downward trend at the beginning, reaches the minimum value, when the polarization angle is about 19. Then it shows an upward trend. It can be seen from the horizontal angle curve that the image information is the largest at 0° and the image information at 135° is the smallest. From the vertical angle curve, the information is the largest at 45° and the smallest at 20°. Through the above analysis, it can be summarized as follows: for this group of data, the amount of information decreases first and then increases with the increase of angle. The vertical direction shows an upward trend with the increase of angle.

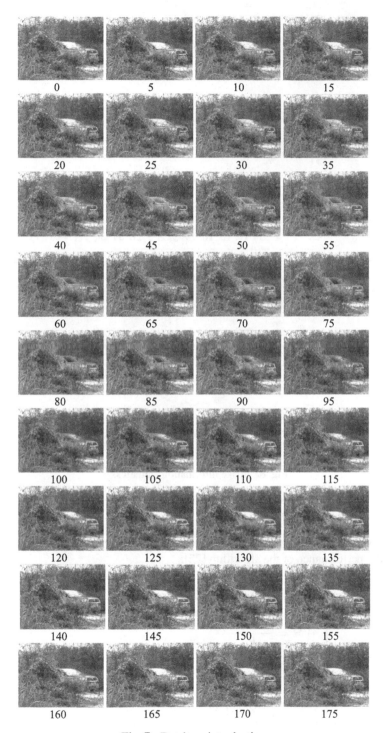

Fig. 7. Database introduction.

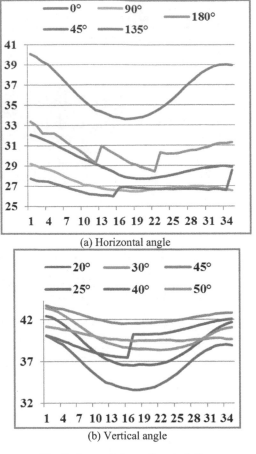

(a) Horizontal angle

(b) Vertical angle

Fig. 8. Image information statistics.

3.2   Target Extraction Result Statistics

In order to verify the performance of the proposed algorithm, we introduce indicators to measure the performance of the algorithm [22]:

$$
\begin{cases}
AOM = \dfrac{R_s \cap R_g}{R_s \cup R_g} \\[2mm]
AVM = \dfrac{R_s - R_g}{R_s} \\[2mm]
AUM = \dfrac{R_g - R_s}{R_g} \\[2mm]
CM = \dfrac{1}{3}\{AOM + (1 - AVM) + (1 - AUM)\}
\end{cases}
\tag{6}
$$

where R_g is the gold standard and R_s is the segmentation result of the algorithm. AOM and CM are directly proportional to the segmentation result, and AVM and AUM are inversely proportional to the segmentation result.

The target extraction results are shown in Table 1. Ref [11] analyzes the information composition of polarization images from the perspective of wavelet, but this method is not universal and the effect is not good. Ref [19] analyzes the characteristics of polarization images, constructs gradient enhancement model, highlights the characteristics of target boundary and realizes target extraction, which has a certain effect. Ref [12] analyzes the target composition from the perspective of energy, and the target detection rate has been improved. Ref [20] constructs the depth feature of network learning to realize target extraction and further improve the effect of target recognition. However, the problem of feature information loss caused by nonlinear activation in network channel compression is not overcome. The proposed algorithm optimizes the existing network structure, improves the traditional ResNet structure, realizes better feature extraction, and the algorithm result is the best.

Table 1. Comparison of image segmentation algorithms.

Algorithm	AOM	AVM	AUM	CM
Wavelet	0.63	0.45	0.37	0.60
Gradient enhancement	0.67	0.39	0.32	0.65
Energy	0.70	0.32	0.29	0.70
CNN	0.72	0.28	0.25	0.73
Ours	0.75	0.25	0.20	0.77

3.3   Network Performance of Transfer Learning

In order to measure the transfer learning performance, we introduce Sensitivity, Specificity and Accuracy to evaluate it [24]:

$$
\begin{cases}
Sen = \dfrac{TP}{TP + FN} \\[2mm]
Spe = \dfrac{TN}{TN + FP} \\[2mm]
Acc = \dfrac{TP + TN}{TP + FN + TP + FN}
\end{cases}
\tag{7}
$$

where TP is True Positive. FP is False Positive. FN is False Negative. TN is True Negative.

The results of different tranfer networks are compared, as shown in Table 2. Alexnet uses Relu as the activation function to solve the gradient dispersion problem when the network is deep, and speeds up the training speed. During training, dropout is used to avoid over fitting of the model, and maximum pooling is used to avoid the fuzzy effect of average pooling. The LRN layer is proposed to create a competition mechanism for the activities of local neurons, so that the value with larger response becomes relatively larger, inhibit other smaller neurons, and enhance the generalization ability of the model. Googlenet uses the idea of NiN for reference and adopts 1×1 conv to maintain the spatial dimension and reduce the depth, that is, reduce the number of channels, and 1×1 conv can also enhance nonlinearity for your network. The horizontal convolution kernel arrangement design enables multiple convolution kernels of different sizes to obtain the information of different clusters in the image. The computational capability is widened to avoid the problem of deep training gradient dispersion. In the face of the huge difference of information location by InceptionV3, it is difficult to select the appropriate convolution kernel size for convolution operation. Very deep networks are easier to over fit, and it is very difficult to transmit gradient updates to the whole network. Simply stacking large convolution layers consumes computing resources. To solve this problem, a dense component is proposed to approximate the optimal local sparse solution, and some results are obtained. VGG Net has a simple structure. The whole network uses the same convolution kernel size (3×3) and maximum pool size (2×2). The combination of finite small filter (3×3) convolution layer is better than that of a large filter $(5 \times 5$ or $7 \times 7)$. It is verified that the performance can be improved by deepening the network structure. However, VGG consumes more computing resources and uses more parameters, resulting in more memory consumption. The proposed algorithm uses DS-Conv instead of the traditional convolution in ResNet50 to increase the computational performance of the algorithm, and input and utilization of N-dimensional data 1×1 convolution realizes the expansion of the number of channels, which outputs $N \times f$ channels. It effectively prevents the loss of feature information caused by nonlinear activation during network channel compression. The effect is the best.

Table 2. Performance of different transfer learning algorithms.

Algorithm	Sen	Spe	Acc
Alexmet	67%	68%	65%
Googlenet	71%	70%	69%
Inception-V3	75%	79%	72%
VGG	78%	81%	76%
Ours	81%	85%	82%

3.4 Effect Display of Target Extraction

We select polarization images taken in different scenes and show the effect through the algorithms. In Fig. 9, the vehicle is hiding in the grassland environment. The polarization response is strong due to the strong reflection of the area where the glass is located, and the algorithm effect is obvious. In Fig. 9-b, there is no target in the grassland environment, but very few leaf surfaces have strong reflective areas, so there is some false detection. It can be seen that our algorithm can effectively focus on the target area due to the introduction of attention mechanism, and build a feature extraction network, which has achieved good results.

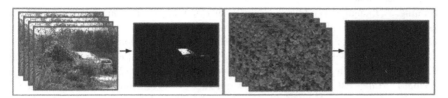

Fig. 9. Target extraction effect of polarization images.

4 Conclusion

In view of the difficulty of target detection in a specific environment, the advantage of polarization imaging is given full play to construct a target extraction algorithm. The existing network structure is improved, and DS-Conv is proposed to replace the traditional convolution to improve the computational performance of the algorithm. The expansion factor is added to effectively prevent the loss of characteristic information caused by nonlinear activation during network channel compression. The attention mechanism is introduced to focus on key areas. Twin convolution neural network is proposed to realize small sample transfer learning. The results show that the algorithm can realize target detection. The AOM reaches 75%, and the subsequent research on target recognition will be further improved and carried out.

References

1. Hossain, I., Samsuzzaman, M., Hoque, A., Baharuddin, M.H., Binti, N.: Polarization insensitive broadband zero indexed nano-meta absorber for optical region applications. Comput. Mater. Continua **71**(1), 993–1009 (2022)
2. Tian, Q., Cao, M., Chen, S., Yin, H.: Structure-exploiting discriminative ordinal multi-output re-gression. IEEE Trans. Neural Netw. Learn. Syst. **32**(1), 266–280 (2021)
3. Sarkar, M., Bello, D.S.S.S.S., Hoof, C.V., Theuwissen, A.: Integrated polarization analyzing CMOS image sensor for material classification. IEEE Sens. J. **11**(8), 1692–1703 (2010)
4. Gruev, V., Spiegel, J.V.D., Engheta, N.: Dual-tier thin film polymer polarization imaging sensor. Opt. Express **18**(18), 19292–19303 (2010)
5. Huang, K.C., Chang, C.L., Wu, W.H.: Novel image polarization method for measurement of lens decentration. IEEE Trans. Instrum. Meas. **60**(5), 1845–1853 (2011)
6. Yang, F.B., Li, W.W., Lin, S.Z., Wang, F.Y.: Study on fusion of infrared polarization and intensity images. Infrared Technol. **33**(5), 262–266 (2011)
7. Spiegel, J.V.D., Wu, X., Zhang, M., Engheta, N.: Polarization image sensors: learning from biology to make the invisible visible. In: 2012 IEEE International Conference on Electron De-vices and Solid State Circuit (EDSSC), pp. 1–3 (2012)

8. Zhang, S., Yuan, Y., Su, L., Hu, L., Liu, H.: Polarization image fusion algorithm based on improved PCNN. In: 2013 International Conference on Optical Instruments and Technology: Optoelectronic Imaging and Processing Technology, International Society for Optics and Photonics, vol. 9045, p. 90450B (2013)

9. Zhang, D.X., Wang, H.H., Xue, F.: Fusion of polarization image based on curvelet transform. Appl. Mech. Mater. **536**, 111–114 (2014)

10. Haining, Y., Liangmei, H., Zhiguo, F.: Fusion method for polarization images based on analysis of features. J. Appl. Opt. **36**(2), 220–226 (2015)

11. Zhang, D., Yuan, B., Zhang, J.: Research on fusion algorithm of polarization image in tetrolet domain. In: Sixth International Conference on Electronics and Information Engineering, vol. 9794, p. 97941Q. International Society for Optics and Photonics (2015)

12. Zhang, L., Yang, F.B., Ji, L., Yuan, H., Dong, A.: A categorization method of infrared polarization and intensity image fusion algorithm based on the transfer ability of difference features. Infrared Phys. Technol. **79**, 91–100 (2016)

13. Ming, Y., Jiyong, P., Yuanyuan, W., Puhong, D.: Image fusion algorithm based on nonsubsampled dual-tree complex contourlet transform and compressive sensing pulse coupled neural network. J. Comput. Aided Des. Comput. Graph. **28**, 411–419 (2016)

14. Li, X., Huang, Q.: Target detection for infrared polarization image in the background of desert. In: 2017 IEEE 9th International Conference on Communication Software and Networks (ICCSN), pp. 1147–1151 (2017)

15. Calisti, M., Carbonara, G., Laschi, C.: A rotating polarizing filter approach for image enhancement. OCEANS 2017-Aberdeen, pp. 1–4 (2017)

16. Zhu, P., Ding, L., Ma, X., Huang, Z.: Fusion of infrared polarization and intensity images based on improved toggle operator. Opt. Laser Technol. **98**, 139–151 (2018)

17. Zhang, J.H., Zhang, Y., Shi, Z.: Long-wave infrared polarization feature extraction and image fusion based on the orthogonality difference method. J. Electron. Imaging **27**(2), 23021 (2018)

18. Wang, X., Sun, J., Xu, Z., Chang, J.: Polarization image fusion algorithm based on global in-formation correction. In: Proceedings of the 2nd International Conference on Image and Graphics Processing, pp. 98–104 (2019)

19. Zhang, J., Zhou, H., Wei, S., Tan, W.: Infrared polarization image fusion via multi-scale sparse representation and pulse coupled neural network. In: International Society for Optics and Photonics, vol. 11338, p. 113382A. International Society for Optics and Photonics (2019)

20. Xie, F., Chen, J.: A new polarized image fusion algorithm based on two-scale guided filtering. In: 2020 Asia-Pacific Signal and Information Processing Association Annual Summit and Conference, pp. 1150–1155 (2020)

21. Jiang, Z., Han, Y., Ye, F., Ren, S., Zhai, H., Hu, Z.: A visible polarization image fusion algo- rithm based on NSST transform. In: International Society for Optics and Photonics, vol. 11567, p. 115671V. International Society for Optics and Photonics (2020)

22. Wang, S., Meng, J., Zhou, Y., Hu, Q., Wang, Z., Lyu, J.: Polarization image fusion algorithm Using NSCT and CNN. J. Russ. Laser Res. **42**(4), 443–452 (2021)

23. Qiu, S., Luo, J., Yang, S., Zhang, M., Zhang, W.: A moving target extraction algorithm based on the fusion of infrared and visible images. Infrared Phys. Technol. **98**, 285–291 (2019)

24. Shujaat, M., Aslam, N., Noreen, I., Ehsan, M.K., Qureshi, M.: Intelligent and integrated framework for exudate detection in retinal fundus images. Intel. Autom. Soft Comput. **30**(2), 663–672 (2021)

Fidelity-Preserved Reversible Data Hiding in JPEG Images Based on Adaptive Position Selection

Zhen Yue[1], Hua Ren[2]([✉]), Ming Li[3], Cun-liang Liang[1], Ben-zhai Hai[1], and Rui-ping Li[1]

[1] Faculty of Education, Henan Normal University, Xinxiang 453007, Henan, China
[2] Beijing Key Lab of Intelligent Telecommunication Software and Multimedia, School of Computer, Beijing University of Posts and Telecommunications, Beijing 100876, China
renhuahtu@163.com
[3] College of Computer and Information Engineering, Henan Normal University, Xinxiang 453007, China

Abstract. Reversible data hiding (RDH) in JPEG images has gained considerable attention from scholars in recent years. However, it is not easy for JPEG images to exploit the pixel redundancy for RDH design like uncompressed images. In this paper, we propose a fidelity-preserved RDH in JPEG images. The proposed scheme embeds the secret data using the histogram shifting method after considering different distortion costs of non-zero AC coefficients at different positions. Accord-ing to the block entropy obtained by summing the squares of all pixels of each 8×8 block, the quantified DCT blocks are divided into the smoothed blocks and texture blocks, and the obtained smoothed blocks are sorted in ascending order. The AC coefficients with values 1 and/or -1 in the smoother blocks are used for the embedding, the non-zero AC coefficients are shifted toward the right or the left at most by one, and the others remain invariant. Experiment results have verified the effectiveness of the proposed method.

Keywords: Reversible data hiding · Block division · JPEG · Histogram shifting

1 Introduction

Reversible data hiding (RDH) [1,2], as one particular type of data hiding, is always a core means for content-protected applications where true fidelity is needed, such as medical and military image processing. By concealing secret data into cover images imperceptibly, one can extract the embedded data without any error, and recover the original cover image perfectly. The existing RDH schemes typically can be classified into three types: lossless compression [3,4], difference expansion [5], and histogram shifting (HS) [6]. The lossless compression-based methods compressed the redundancy characteristics of the original carriers loss-lessly to provide the space for the em-bedding process. The difference expansion-based methods divided adjacent two pixels into one pair, and each pair carried one bit of the secrecy streams. The histogram shifting-based approaches selected peak pixels to carry secrecy and shifted the other pixels close to the peak position toward the left or right direction to vacate the space. Although the existing RDH methods have achieved significant breakthroughs in terms of visual quality and embedding capacity, the limitation of the application is apparent because only the uncompressed images can be the original carriers. Com-pared with exist-ing uncompressed images, the compressed images that possess less redundancy are broadly transmitted on the Internet. Thus, it is quite essential but hard to conceal secrecy into compressed images reversibly. Among different formats of the compressed images, the joint photograph experts group (JPEG) format is of widespread popularity when transmitted [4,7]. In this light, developing RDH in JPEG images has practical application value in real life.

The existing methods regarding RDH in JPEG images can be divided into four categories: modifying the quantization table [7,8], modifying the Huffman table [9–11], modifying the quantized DCT coefficients [12–18], and RDH in the encrypted JPEG images [19,20]. The quantization table modification-based method [8] must perform a preprocessing process before embedding. Some ele-ments of the quantization table are divided by an integer, and the correspond-ing quantized coefficients are multiplied by the same integer to create the space for embedding. A higher visual quality of the marked image accompanies an evident increase in the file size. The Huffman table modification-based methods [9–11] modified the Huffman table by building the mapping between the variable length codes (VLC). Such methods provided higher visual quality and almost unchanged file size, yet with a low embedding rate, even for a 512×512 image carrying only hundreds of bits. The quantized DCT coefficients-based modifica-tion methods [12–21] modified DCT coefficient values to hide secret messages, and the used quantization table was invariant throughout the embedding. The embedding rate of DCT coefficient modification methods is substantial with cer-tain file sizes.

Recently, Huang et al. [13] have presented a novel DCT coefficient modification-based RDH scheme in JEPG images. The scheme utilizes a block selection strategy for selecting the smoothed block and the texture block. The zero AC coefficients in each block remain invariant, and only AC coefficicnts with the values 1 and -1 are used to carry secret messages. The zero AC coeffi-cients determine the block positions used for the embedding, making correct data extraction and perfect image restoration available. Wedaj et al. [14] improved the method [13] by considering the coefficient distributions and the position modification cost. Unfortunately, the scheme [14] altered the quantization table during embedding. The improvement version [15] utilized all quantized non-zero AC coefficients to embed secret messages. However, the visual quality of the marked JPEG image is poor, and the Huffman table must be modified to preserve the file size of the final image. Xiao et al. [17] presented a variant of [13] based on multiple two-dimensional histograms, which effectively insured higher visual quality. Based on this trait, they then presented an improvement version with multiple histogram modification in JPEG images [18]. Yao et al. [19] introduced a dynamic allocation method to arrange the embedding bits rationally to implement less distortion in dual JPEG image. Xuan et al. [20] just utilized minimum entropy and histogram-pair to improve the method [13]. Four thresholds, including embedding amplitude threshold, fluctuation threshold, lower frequency threshold, and higher frequency threshold, were considered during embedding. The target frequencies used for embedding might brought multiple shifts when embedding capacity increases, whereas the image distortion and file size are satisfactory. Unfortunately, the method did not consider the coefficient distributions and the modification cost of the AC coefficients position, only manually determining the embedding interval $[T_L, T_H]$, where T_L and T_H represent lower threshold and upper threshold, respectively.

Based on the above discussion, we detail an improvement version based on the method [20]. First, we utilize the block entropies obtained by summing the squares of all pixels of each 8×8 block for generating the smoothed blocks and the texture blocks. After sorting the smoothed blocks in ascending order according to the obtained entropy values, the blocks with lower entropies have priority over the blocks with higher entropies during the embedding. In addition, enlightened by the method [14], the improvement also considers two other aspects: the coefficient distributions and the modification cost of the position. In other words, we calculate the distortion cost in each non-zero AC position by considering all of the obtained smoothed blocks and select non-zero AC coefficients at positions with lower distortions to preferably embed. Compared with the method [20], the main contributions of the proposed scheme are summarized below.

- We sort the obtained smoothed blocks in ascending order according to the obtained entropy values. Thus, we can preferably hide the secret messages into the blocks with smaller entropies.
- Among all the smoothed blocks of the embedded secret bits, we consider the distortion cost in each position of one block and preferably choose non-zero AC coefficients at the positions with lower distortions for embedding the secret bits.

The rest parts of the paper are organized as follows. Section 2 briefly describes the previous arts. The proposed method is elaborated in Sect. 3. Experiment results are given in Sect. 4 to show the effectiveness of the proposed method. Finally, the paper is concluded in Sect. 5.

2 Previous Arts

2.1 Overview of JPEG Compression Standard

Joint photograph experts group (JPEG) as a widely used image format is a lossy compression format. The unimportant data of the original image is missing when compressed, and thus the compressed image is distorted. The existing JPEG encoder consists of three components, namely DCT, quantizer, and entropy encoder. Figure 1 shows the main steps of JPEG compression. The original image is processed into a series of sized 8×8 image blocks, and each block is transformed from spatial domain to frequency domain using a two-dimensional DCT function. These obtained DCT coefficients are quantized and rounded to the nearest integer according to the quantization table. The quantized coefficients are re-arranged in zigzag scanning order and pre-processed using the differential pulse code modulation (DPCM) and run-length en-coding (RLE). The symbol string is Huffman-coded to obtain the final compressed bit streams. After pre-pending the header, someone can generate the final JPEG image.

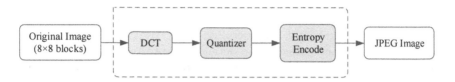

Fig. 1. Block diagram of JPEG encoder.

Mathematical definitions of 8×8 DCT transformation and inverse DCT are formulated as follows:

$$F(u,v) = c(u)c(v) \sum_{x=0}^{7} \sum_{y=0}^{7} f(x,y) cos\frac{(2x+1)u\pi}{16} cos\frac{(2y+1)u\pi}{16} \tag{1}$$

$$f(x,y) = \sum_{x=0}^{7} \sum_{y=0}^{7} c(u)c(v)F(u,v) cos\frac{(2x+1)u\pi}{16} cos\frac{(2y+1)v\pi}{16} \tag{2}$$

where:

$$c(u) = \begin{cases} \frac{1}{2\sqrt{2}}, & if\ u = 0 \\ 1, & otherwise \end{cases} \tag{3}$$

During compression, the DCT coefficients of each 8×8 block are quantized based on a quantization table. Figure 2 shows an example of DCT block quantization. Figure 2(a) represents the zigzag scanning sketch, Fig. 2(b) is the corresponding position distribution in each 8×8 block, and Fig. 2(c) shows the final quantized DCT coefficients obtained by divided each DCT coefficient with the quantization table as follows.

$$C_q(u,v) = Inter Round\frac{F(u,v)}{q(u,v)} \tag{4}$$

In Eq. 4, $f(x,y)$ denotes the pixel value at block position (x,y), $c(u) = c(v)$, $u,v = 0,1,\cdots,7$, $F(u,v)$ and $C_q(u,v)$ denote the original DCT coefficient and the quantified DCT coefficient at block position of the u-th row and the v-th column, respectively. $q(u,v)$ denotes the corresponding step of quantification table $\mathbf{Q}$. As shown in Fig. 2, the first coefficient of the quantized block is the DC coefficient, which keeps invariant during the embedding. Except for the first DC coefficient, the remaining ones are the AC coefficients. By remaining the zero AC coefficients invariant, the proposed method shifts the AC coefficients larger than 1 and less than -1 to vacate the room, and uses the AC coefficients with values 1 and -1 for the embedding.

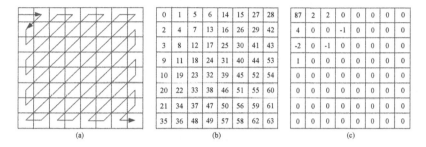

Fig. 2. An example of DCT block. (a) Scanning order; (b) zigzag order; (c) quantized block.

2.2 Overview of Xuan et al. Method

Xuan et al. [20] have presented a novel histogram-based RDH in JEPG images recently. In the method, the minimum entropy is applied to select the smoothed blocks of the embedding process, and the histogram pairs of the smoothed blocks is used to carry the secret message bits. Let us denote the embedding threshold as T, the secrecy messages as b, the quantized AC coefficients as x, the marked quantized coefficients as x', and the embedding interval as $[T_L, T_H]$. In each block, not all non-zero AC coefficients hide the secret bits, but only the non-zero AC coefficient values that fall into the range of $[T_L, T_H]$ hide the secrecy information. The detail of the embedding process is

$$x' = \begin{cases} x + sign(x) \times b, \ if \ |x| = |T| \\ x + sign(x), \qquad others \end{cases} \tag{5}$$

where

$$sign(x) = \begin{cases} 1, & if \ x > 0 \\ 0, & if \ x = 0 \\ -1, if \ x < 0 \end{cases} \tag{6}$$

The extraction is the reverse of the embedding. The details of the data extraction and image recovery are as follows.

$$b = \begin{cases} 0, if \ |x'| = |T| \\ 1, if \ |x'| = |T| + 1 \end{cases} \tag{7}$$

$$x = \begin{cases} x', & if \ |x'| = |T| \\ x' - sign(x'), & if \ |x'| >= |T+1| \end{cases} \tag{8}$$

The embedding threshold T is an embedding sequence, which can be expressed by

$$[T, -T, T-1, -T+1, ..., 2, -2, 1, -1, 0] \ for \ T > 0 \tag{9}$$

$$[T, -T-1, T+1, -T-2, T+2, ..., 2, -2, 1, -1, 0] \ for \ T < 0 \tag{10}$$

The embedding threshold T relies on a given payload size, and a larger payload leads to more histogram pairs to participate in the data embedding. The non-zero AC coefficients carry the secret bits. For example, assume two histogram pairs as $[0, -1]$ and $[1, 0]$, the embedding threshold T as 1. Xuan et al. [20] firstly embed a part of the payload into the AC coefficients with the value 1, and then embed the remaining into the AC coefficients with the value -1. The embedding process is implemented accord-ing to the arranged sequence of Eq. 5 and Eq. 6. However, two issues are non-negligible. One is that the method [20] only uses the minimum entropy to obtain the smoothed blocks, and it does not include an entropy-based block order which can preferably choose these blocks with smaller entropies to embed. The other is that the method does not consider the distortion cost on each coefficient position in each block. Although selecting the embedding interval $[T_L, T_H]$ to embed can reduce certain embedding distortion, it is not the best choice.

3   The Proposed Method

In this section, a novel RDH scheme in JPEG images is proposed to achieve fidelity preservation of protected images. In the following, we detail the minimum entropy-based block selection and block order, AC coefficient position selection and position order, the data embedding, and the data extraction and restoration successively.

3.1   Minimum Entropy-Based Block Selection and Block Order

Suppose that an original image is divided into a series of equal-size $n \times n$ blocks. If the block size n is 8, there are a total of 4096 blocks for a sized 512×512 image. The entropy E under Gaussian distribution is defined as follows.

$$E = \ln \sqrt{2\pi e \sigma^2} \tag{11}$$

$$\sigma^2 = \frac{1}{n^2} \sum_{i=1}^{n} \sum_{j=1}^{n} (I(i,j) - \mu)^2 \tag{12}$$

where e denotes a natural constant, $I(i,j)$ is the pixel value in the i-th row and the j-th column, n is set as 8 when taking usual JPEG compression, and represents the mean value of one block. Next, a fluctuation value F measures the smoothness of each coefficient block:

$$F = \frac{1}{n^2 - 1}(\sum_{i=1}^{n}\sum_{j=1}^{n} x(i,j)^2 - x(1,1)^2) \tag{13}$$

where $x(i,j)$ is the coefficient value in the i-th row and the j-th column, $x(1,1)$ is the DC coefficient value. Since only AC coefficients are utilized to measure the block smoothness, the first DC coefficient should not be included. The computation of the smoothness of each block in the transform domain by using Eq. 13 is exactly equal to that in the spatial domain by using Eq. 12. In other words, we can have

$$F = \frac{1}{n^2 - 1}(\sum_{i=1}^{n}\sum_{j=1}^{n} x(i,j)^2 - x(1,1)^2) = \frac{1}{n^2}\sum_{i=1}^{n}\sum_{j=1}^{n}(I(i,j) - \mu)^2 = \sigma^2 \tag{14}$$

Thus, instead of exploiting AC coefficients to classify the smoothed block and the texture block, the pixels variance of one block is utilized in the spatial domain. For a given threshold T_F, only the blocks smaller than T_F are selected for embedding, whereas the blocks larger than T_F are skipped. After all entropies of smoothed blocks are obtained, we sort the entropies in ascending order to preferably choose the blocks with smaller entropies for data embedding.

3.2   AC Coefficient Position Selection and Position Order

In this section, we consider the AC coefficient position selection and position order before embedding, and we will not modify the used quantization table. The purpose of selecting the AC coefficient positions is to find the positions with smaller distortion costs when considering the coefficient distributions. The core of position order is to preferably embed secret messages into non-zero AC coefficients at positions with smaller distortion costs.

To select smaller distortion-causing position, the shiftable AC coefficients, the em-beddable AC coefficient, and the quantization table are used to calculate a metric called embedding efficiency η_i for each position $i \in \{1, 2, 3, \cdots, 63\}$.

$$\eta_i = \sum_{n=1}^{N_1} \frac{E(i,n)}{(S(i,n) + E(i,n)/2) \times Q_i^2} \tag{15}$$

where $E(i,n) \in \{0,1\}$ means that the AC coefficient at position i of the n-th block is embeddable 1 or not 0, $S(i,n) \in \{0,1\}$ denotes the AC coefficient at position i of the n-th block is shiftable 1 or not 0, Q_i denotes the quantization table entry at position i, and $N_1 \in [0, 4096]$ represents the total number of the smoothed block depending on the threshold T_F. According to Eq. 15, one can easily know that $E(i,n)$ actually computes the total embedding capacity at position i, and $S(i,n) + E(i,n)/2$ computes the total modified amount at position i (assuming the payload is pseudo-random, approximately half of the embeddable will cause modification), i.e., the total distortion. Thus, the best position to embed will have the largest embedding efficiency, and vice versa. Once all embedding efficiencies are calculated for 63 positions, the values will be sorted from the highest to the lowest. For example, if the positions (4,9,14,3,2,7) are determined for embedding, the secret message bits will be successively hide into the positions (2,3,4,7,9,14) to ensure perfect data extraction. It is quite different from the method [20], which selects continuous embedding position to modify, such as (4,5,6,7,8,9).

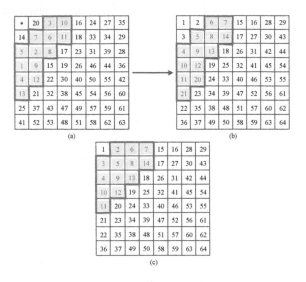

Fig. 3. Comparison on location selection for data embedding of our scheme and [20]. (a) Priority selection of embedding location for our scheme; (b) the corresponding selected embedding region; (c) the selected embedding region for [20].

Table 1. Various PSNRs for embedding data into Lena under quality factor QF = 80.

Lena		Xuan et al. method [20]	Proposed method
PL (bpp)	T_F	PSNR (dB)	PSNR (dB)
0.01	22	54.32	54.56
0.02	70	50.44	50.52
0.03	150	48.13	48.23
0.04	220	46.26	46.73
0.05	1200	44.49	44.54

To describe the effectiveness of this strategy easily, Fig. 3 shows a comparison on location selection for data embedding of our scheme and [20]. The proposed method adopts the entropy sorting strategy, whereas the scheme [20] manually selects the fixed embedding area. Figure 3(a) is the priority selection of embedding location according to AC coefficient position selection. The priorities marked with red color region are the final selected priorities for data embedding. Figure 3(b) is the selected coefficient region of our scheme according to the priority in Fig. 3(a), and Fig. 3(c) is the manually selected region of the scheme [20]. Depending on these two ways used for ours and the scheme [20], The PSNR results under different embedding rates are listed in Table 1, where PL means the embedded payload. The results imply our sorting strategy outperforms the manually selected fixed region [20]. In our scheme, only the lower entropies are used for data embedding, which leads to lower visual distortion for the directly decrypted image. The manually selected fixed region [20] may contain the unexpected modified coefficients, thus incurs a worse result, even under various embedding rates.

For histogram shifting-based RDH in JPEG images, some side information should be processed to ensure true reversibility. The side information of the proposed method includes the size of the secret messages, the length of the threshold T_F, and the position map information. The maximum payload size needed to transmit is $\log(W \times H)$, where W and H are the weight and the height of an image. For an image sized 512×512, the maximum length needed to be recorded should be 18 bits. The thresh-old TF is exploited to select the smoothed blocks. The maximum length of the value is 13 bits. The binary position map (the value 1 is embeddable and the value 0 is not embeddable) records the embedding positions. Since there are a total of 63 AC coefficient positions in 8×8 blocks, the size of the binary position map should be 63 bits. To sum up, the total size of side information is 94 bits, which can be embedded in the first 94 LSBs of the DC coefficients. The original 94 LSBs of the DC coefficients are collected and regarded as a part of the payload to facilitate the perfect recovery of these selected DC coefficients.

3.3   Embedding, Extraction and Restoration

The proposed method embeds secret message bits into these AC coefficients with the values 1 and -1. Non-zero AC coefficients close to the AC coefficients with the values 1 and -1 are shifted to vacate the room. All zero AC coefficients are invariant during the embedding. The following depicts the embedding algorithm of the proposed method.

$$x' = \begin{cases} x + sign(x) \times b, \, if\, |x| = 1 \\ x + sign(x), \quad\ others \end{cases} \tag{16}$$

$$sign(x) = \begin{cases} 1, & if\, x > 0 \\ 0, & if\, x = 0 \\ -1, & if\, x < 0 \end{cases} \tag{17}$$

where x and x' denote the quantized non-zero AC coefficients and the marked quantized non-zero AC coefficients, $b \in \{0,1\}$ denotes the secret messages to be embedded, and $sign(\bullet)$ denotes a sign function. According to Eq. 16 and Eq. 17, we can embed secret messages into the AC coefficients with the values 1 and -1.

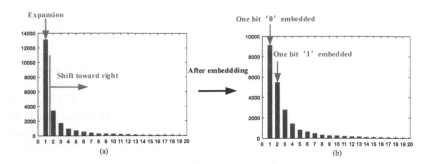

Fig. 4. Local details of histogram of the non-zero AC coefficients of the Lena image. (a) the original histogram; (b) the shifted histogram.

In the following, we take an example to explain the histogram shifting-based embedding process. Suppose the quality factor QF = 80, T_F = 300, the selected embedding position as (10,9,6,11,4,8,5,13,12,7,14,20,21,3,19,15,18,17,25). Figure 4 shows the local details of the histogram shifting process, where the ordinate axes represent the statistic amount on the above-specified positions and the horizontal axes represent different non-zero AC coefficients on the selected positions. Figure 4(a) shows the original histogram of the non-zero AC coefficients in image Lena, and Fig. 4(b) shows the corresponding shifted histogram. We can see that a majority of the AC coefficients gather in the value 1, which indicates the amount of the secret messages embedded.

When needed to extract the embedded secret messages and restore the original coefficients, the following formulas can be carried out.

$$b = \begin{cases} 0, \, if \, |x'| = 1 \\ 1, \, if \, |x'| = 2 \end{cases} \tag{18}$$

$$x = \begin{cases} x', & if \, |x'| = 1 \\ x' - sign(x'), \, if \, |x'| >= 2 \end{cases} \tag{19}$$

Data Embedding Steps. In the embedding process, AC coefficients with the values −1 and 1 are modified to hide secret messages.

Step 1: Divide the original image into a series of equal-size non-overlapping 8 × 8 blocks, and there are total 4096 blocks for an image sized 512 × 512. Perform DCT quantization on each block, and obtain the quantized AC coefficients.

Step 2: Scan the total 4096 blocks from left to right from top to bottom. For each selected DCT coefficient block, use Eq. 14 to compute the entropy F, if $F > T_F$, obtain all smoothed blocks. And, sort the obtained entropies of all blocks from the low-est to the highest.

Step 3: Select non-zero AC coefficients at positions with lower distortion cost according to Eq. 15, and sort the corresponding positions from the highest to the lowest.

Step 4: Embed the message length L (represented by l_1, 18 bits), the threshold T_F (represented by l_2, 13 bits), and the position map (represented by l_3, 63 bits) into the first 94 LSBs of the DC coefficients.

Step 5: Encrypt and shuffle the secret message using a pseudo-random sequence, and embed the encrypted secret message into the AC coefficients with the value 1 and -1 according to Eq. 16.

Step 6: After all secret messages are embedded, entropy-encode the obtained coefficients to get the marked JPEG file.

Extraction and Restoration Steps. Step 1: Entropy-decode the marked JPEG file to obtain the quantized DCT coefficients.

Step 2: Extract the message length L, the threshold T_F, and the position map from the first 94 LSBs of the DC coefficients.

Step 3: Scan the total 4096 blocks from left to right from top to bottom. For each selected DCT coefficient block, use Eq. 14 to compute the entropy F, if $F > T_F$, obtain all smoothed blocks. And, sort the obtained entropies of all blocks from the low-est to the highest.

Step 4: Extract the secret messages according to the position map from all sorted smoothed blocks according to Eq. 18, and restore the original coefficients according to Eq. 19.

Step 5: After extracting all secret messages, inversely shuffle and decrypt the extracted secret messages to recover the original secret messages. Entropy-encode the restored coefficients again to obtain the original JPEG file.

4   Experiment Results and Analyses

In our experiments, the secret messages are generated randomly, and the JPEG images are compressed with the optimal Huffman table using the IJG toolbox [22]. All of our experiments are based on the compressed JPEG images, and the obtained four compressed images (QF = 80) are shown in Fig. 5.

4.1   Effectiveness of the Proposed Method

In order to illustrate the effectiveness of the proposed method, the PSNR results and the file size of the marked images separately with QF = 70, 80, 90 under different embedding capacities are listed in Table 2. As expected, with the increase of payload bits, the PSNR value is correspondingly decreased. What is more, the PSNR values are increased with the growth of quality factor QF. The reason is straightforward because a larger QF will have a higher visual quality. In addition, PSNRs of the marked images are still acceptable when the payload size becomes 16000 bits, thus the proposed method is satisfactory.

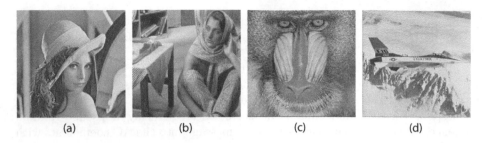

(a)   (b)   (c)   (d)

Fig. 5. Four compressed JPEG images. (a) Lena; (b) Barbara; (c) Baboon; (d) Airplane.

Besides, the threshold T_F of the proposed method determines the total number of the selected smoothed blocks. The smoothed blocks ensure the preferentially selected positions for embedding. Therefore, the settings of the threshold affect the PSNR values and file size of marked images. Figure 6 presents the PSNR values and file size of the marked Lena under three payloads by setting different T_F values. As seen in Fig. 6, when keeping the same payload bits, the PSNR values are decreased with the increase of T_F, whereas there will remain almost stable if the threshold T_F is large enough. Moreover, as for the embedding of the same payload, the file size of the marked Lena will become fluctuant within a small range when the T_F becomes larger. Thus, we suggest setting the threshold T_F into the scope [20,450] to a better PSNR value and preservation of file size.

Table 2. PSNR results and file size separately with QF = 70, 80, 90 under different embedding capacity.

Image	QF	PL (bits)					
		6000	8000	10000	12000	14000	16000
Lena	70	48.04,6976	45.84,10272	44.40,12256	42.79,16128	41.51,19488	40.14,22888
	80	50.90,6928	49.15,9000	47.21,12104	46.11,14560	44.93,18232	43.86,22112
	90	54.87,6600	53.35,9072	52.06,11336	50.83,13856	49.93,16560	48.98,20088
Barbara	70	46.38,7712	44.33,10840	42.63,13936	41.11,17560	39.95,20880	38.76,24112
	80	49.43,6920	47.20,10272	45.65,13208	44.07,17096	42.80,20232	41.42,24336
	90	53.56,6976	52.00,9992	50.40,13000	49.09,16208	47.80,20216	46.68,23280
Baboon	70	45.23,7792	43.37,10392	41.80,13768	40.41,16816	39.17,20712	37.99,23304
	80	47.03,7480	45.24,10400	43.57,13672	42.12,17168	40.74,21704	39.83,24168
	90	49.63,8552	47.74,12016	45.88,16744	44.24,22128	43.39,25032	42.47,28816
Airplane	70	48.40,6520	45.96,10024	43.94,12960	42.20,16128	40.56,19632	39.14,22648
	80	51.09,6576	49.29,9032	47.16,12080	45.74,15696	44.41,18600	42.91,21832
	90	55.22,7240	53.60,8936	52.30,11672	51.23,14256	50.28,16888	49.01,20480

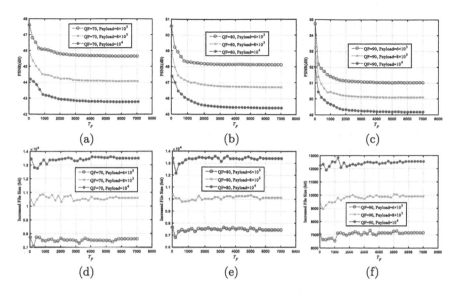

Fig. 6. PSNR values and file size of the marked Lena under three payloads by setting different T_F values. (a, d) PSNRs and file size of marked Lena with QF = 70; (b, e) PSNRs and file size of marked Lena with QF = 80; (c, f) PSNRs and file size of marked Lena with QF = 90.

4.2   Comparisons

Since the proposed method is an improvement version based on the method [20], the proposed method is compared with the method [20]. Tables 3, 4, 5, 6 show the comparison results under quality factor QF = 70 and QF = 80. The total selected position number of our method is consistent with the length of the embedding interval $[T_L, T_H]$ of the Xuan et al. method. The compressed images containing Lena, Barbara, Baboon, Airplane, are considered under the assumptions of the same T_F and the same payload size.

Note that in Tables 3, 4, 5, 6, parameters PL, FS, and Rate performance represent the embedded payload, the increased file size to the original JPEG image (in bits), and the rate of increased file size to the payload, respectively. The first column also lists the original JPEG size with byte representation. From which, we can observe that for different QFs, the original JPEG sizes with the same image are different. Moreover, with the increase of embedded payload bits, the PSNR values of different images with QF = 70 are always lower than QF = 80, and the two comparison methods show consistency in this trend. In addition, from Tables Tables 3, 4, 5, 6, we can observe that the PSNR results obtained by the proposed method are better than that of Xuan et al. [20]. This is because the non-zero coefficients at the positions with smaller distortion costs are always preferentially selected to modify for embedding in our method; on the contrary, Xuan et al. method [20] only makes the modifications on the non-zero AC in the given embedding interval $[T_L, T_H]$. The FS and rate performance of the marked JPEG images in our method are not entirely better than that of the Xuan et al. method, because the proposed method always preferentially selects the non-zero coefficients at positions with smaller distortion costs to modify, which ensures the visual quality of marked JPEG images but does not always ensure the embedding capacity. In other words, the non-zero coefficients at positions with smaller distortion costs do not con-currently signify that the total embedding numbers in these positions are higher.

Table 3. Comparison results with Lena.

	PL (bpp)	T_F	PL (bits)	Xuan et.al method [20]			Proposed method		
				PSNR (dB)	Inc. FS (bits)	Rate (%)	PSNR (dB)	Inc. FS (bits)	Rate (%)
QF=70 (original JPEG size 29294 bytes)	0.01	20	2621	51.37	3384	29	**52.71**	3464	32
	0.02	30	5243	47.59	6712	28	**48.73**	**6360**	**21**
	0.03	80	7864	45.08	10,096	28	**46.07**	**9720**	24
	0.04	300	10,486	43.06	14,088	34	**43.70**	**13,592**	30
	0.05	300	13,107	39.69	17,880	36	**42.05**	**17,840**	**36**
QF=80 (original JPEG size 37937 bytes)	0.01	22	2621	54.32	2776	6	**54.56**	3120	19
	0.02	70	5243	50.44	5824	11	**50.52**	5960	14
	0.03	150	7864	48.13	9560	22	**48.23**	9648	23
	0.04	220	10,486	46.26	13,512	29	**46.73**	**12,856**	**23**
	0.05	1200	13,107	44.49	17,536	34	**44.54**	17,680	35

Table 4. Comparison results with Barbara.

	PL (bpp)	T_F	PL (bits)	Xuan et.al method [20]			Proposed method		
				PSNR (dB)	Inc. FS (bits)	Rate (%)	PSNR (dB)	Inc. FS (bits)	Rate (%)
QF=70 (original JPEG size 38880 bytes)	0.01	40	2621	50.74	3368	29	**51.71**	**3240**	**24**
	0.02	65	5243	46.7	6656	27	**47.26**	7424	42
	0.03	265	7864	42.42	10,520	34	**44.31**	**10,376**	32
	0.04	420	10,486	41.09	14,504	38	**42.32**	14,576	39
	0.05	450	13,107	39.55	18,560	42	**39.64**	19,616	50
QF=80 (original JPEG size 48335 bytes)	0.01	22	2621	53.03	3360	28	**54.28**	**2944**	**12**
	0.02	50	5243	48.94	7624	45	**50.38**	**6288**	**20**
	0.03	170	7864	46.37	10,920	39	**47.31**	**10,048**	**28**
	0.04	210	10,486	42.75	16,040	53	**45.27**	**14,248**	**36**
	0.05	250	13,107	40.4	19,456	48	**42.23**	19,608	50

Table 5. Comparison results with Baboon.

	PL (bpp)	T_F (bits)	PL (bits)	Xuan et.al method [20]			Proposed method		
				PSNR (dB)	Inc. FS (bits)	Rate (%)	PSNR (dB)	Inc. FS (bits)	Rate (%)
QF=70	0.01	70	2621	48.78	3224	23	**49.9**	**3064**	17
(original JPEG size	0.02	220	5243	44.46	6880	31	**45.41**	**6528**	25
62536 bytes)	0.03	200	7864	42.21	10,472	33	**43.43**	**10,128**	29
	0.04	300	10,486	40.29	15,264	46	**41.45**	**14,168**	35
	0.05	360	13,107	38.52	19,208	47	**39.4**	**18,544**	41
QF=80	0.01	190	2621	50.25	3400	30	**50.41**	**2832**	8
(original JPEG size	0.02	200	5243	46.66	6872	31	**47.2**	**6360**	21
78677 bytes)	0.03	430	7864	44.02	11,304	44	**44.31**	**11,424**	45
	0.04	440	10,486	41.35	15,192	45	**42.89**	**14,440**	38
	0.05	360	13,107	39.16	17,552	34	**41.47**	**18,792**	43

Table 6. Comparison results with Airplane.

	PL (bpp)	T_F (bits)	PL (bits)	Xuan et.al method [20]			Proposed method		
				PSNR (dB)	Inc. FS (bits)	Rate (%)	PSNR (dB)	Inc. FS (bits)	Rate (%)
QF=70	0.01	22	2621	51.41	3400	30	**52.6**	**2720**	4
(original JPEG size	0.02	40	5243	47.2	6944	32	**48.96**	**6016**	15
30636 bytes)	0.03	50	7864	44.34	10,584	35	**46.09**	**9624**	22
	0.04	150	10,486	42.11	14,240	36	**43.43**	**13,664**	30
	0.05	320	13,107	39.48	18,096	38	**41.07**	**18,136**	38
QF=80	0.01	14	2621	54.01	3080	18	**54.93**	**3288**	25
(original JPEG size	0.02	40	5243	50.7	6304	20	**51.38**	**6144**	17
38344 bytes)	0.03	120	7864	47.92	9512	21	**48.52**	**9224**	17
	0.04	270	10,486	45.92	13,384	28	**46.32**	**13,000**	24
	0.05	470	13,107	44.18	17,904	37	**44.51**	**17,728**	35

In addition, we compare the PSNR values and the increased file size under different embedding capacity with the methods [13,14,20]. Figure 7 shows the comparison results of different embedding capacity with QF = 70. Figure 8 shows the comparison results of different embedding capacity with QF = 80. Huang et al. method [13] originally uses non-zero AC coefficients with the values -1 and 1 to carry secret bits as well as other non-zero coefficients to vacate room for embedding, and the zero AC coefficients are used to select smoothed blocks. The improvement method [20] adopts histogram-pair based to embed secret messages into a given embedding interval $[T_L, T_H]$. If two histogram pairs $[0,-1]$ and $[1, 0]$ are used to carry secret messages, the method [20] firstly embeds a part of the payload into the AC coefficients with the value 1, subsequently embeds the remaining part of payload into the AC coefficients with the value -1. Therefore, we compare the three state-of-the-art methods [13,14,20] in the following. As seen, the PSNR values of the proposed method are larger than the other three methods [13,14,20], and the file sizes of the marked images are al-most less than the methods [13,14,20]. In particular, these advantages will become more obvious when the compression rate is lower (compared with QF = 70 and QF = 80). It is because the proposed method always embeds the secret messages into the non-zero AC coefficients with the values 1 and -1 with lower distortion cost.

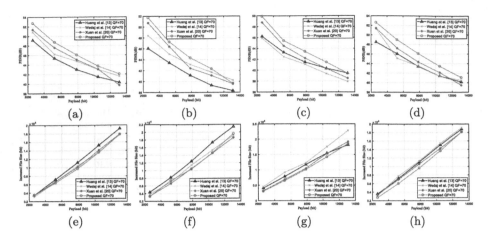

Fig. 7. Comparisons of different embedding capacity with QF = 70. (a, e) Lena; (b, f) Barbara; (c, g) Baboon; (d, h) Airplane.

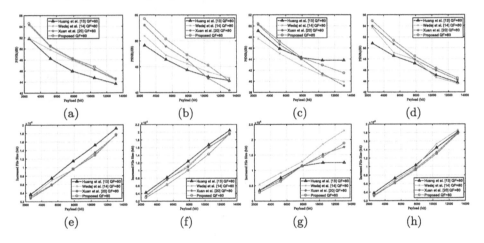

Fig. 8. Comparisons of different embedding capacity with QF = 80. (a, e) Lena; (b, f) Barbara; (c, g) Baboon; (d, h) Airplane.

5 Conclusion

In this paper, an improvement of the work [20] is proposed. In the process of block selection, we first obtain the entropy value of each block then use it to sort the smooth blocks in ascending order. In the position selection of smoothed blocks, instead of the fixed embedding selection utilized by [20], the distributions of embeddable, unchangeable and shiftable coefficients and the modification cost of the position in each block are considered. Thus, the proposed method can preferentially embed the secret messages into these 1 and −1 coefficients with lower distortion cost. Experiments have verified that the proposed method is better than the method [20], especially when the compression rate QF is lower. However, this proposed method evenly divides the whole image into 8×8 blocks and does not consider the intra-block structural characteristics, which may limit the embedding capacity. In the future, we will consider using adaptive block selection strategy to divide the image into blocks of different sizes, such that the characteristics of the compressed image can be fully exploited.

Acknowledgements. We thank all the appending authors for their contributions to this article.

Funding Statement. This work is supported by the National Natural Science Foundation of China (No. 61602158), the Science and Technology Research Project of Henan Province (No. 212102210413). Start-up grant for doctoral research at Henan Normal University (QD2021096).

Conflict of Interest. The authors declare that they have no conflicts of interest to report regarding the present study.

References

1. Chung, K.L., Huang, Y.H., Chang, P.C., Mark, H.Y.: Reversible data hiding-based approach for intra-frame error concealment in H.264/AVC. IEEE Trans. Circ. Syst. Video Technol. **20**(11), 1643–1647 (2010)
2. Ren, H., Niu, S.: Separable reversible data hiding in homomorphic encrypted domain using POB number system. Multimedia Tools Appl. **81**(2), 2161–2187 (2021). https://doi.org/10.1007/s11042-021-11341-w
3. Fridrich, J., Goljan, M., Du, R.: Lossless data embedding-new paradigm in digital watermarking. EURASIP J. Adv. Signal Process. **2002**(2), 185–196 (2002)
4. Fridrich, J., Goljan, M., Du, R.: Lossless data embedding for all image formats. SPIE Secur. Watermarking Multimedia Contents IV **4675**, 572–583 (2002)
5. Tian, J.: Reversible data embedding using a difference expansion. IEEE Trans. Circ. Syst. Video Technol. **13**(8), 890–896 (2003)
6. Ni, Z.C., Shi, Y.Q., Ansari, N., Su, W.: Reversible data hiding. IEEE Trans. Circ. Syst. Video Technol. **16**(3), 354–362 (2006)
7. Chang, C.C., Lin, C.C., Tseng, C.S., Tai, W.L.: Reversible hiding in DCT-based compressed images. Inf. Sci. **177**(13), 2768–2786 (2007)
8. Wang, K., Lu, Z.M., Hu, Y.J.: A high capacity lossless data hiding scheme for JPEG images. J. Syst. Softw. **86**(7), 1965–1975 (2013)
9. Qiu, Y.Q., He, H., Qian, Z.X.: Lossless data hiding in JPEG bitstream using alternative embedding. J. Vis. Commun. Image Represent. **52**, 86–91 (2018)
10. Zhang, C., Ou, B., Tian, H.W., Qin, Z.: Reversible data hiding in JPEG bitstream using optimal VLC mapping. J. Vis. Commun. Image Represent. **71**, 1–12 (2020)
11. Zhang, C., Ou, B., Tang, D.: An improved VLC mapping method with parameter optimization for reversible data hiding in JPEG bitstream. Multimedia Tools Appl. **79**(27), 19045–19062 (2020)
12. Nikolaidis, A.: Reversible data hiding in JPEG images utilizing zero quantized coefficients. IET Image Process. **9**(7), 560–568 (2015)

13. Huang, F.J., Qu, X., Kim, H.J., Huang, J.W.: Reversible data hiding in JPEG images. IEEE Trans. Circ. Syst. Video Technol. **26**(9), 1610–1621 (2016)
14. Wedaj, F.T., Kim, S., Kim, H.J., Huang, F.: Improved reversible data hiding in JPEG images based on new coefficient selection strategy. EURASIP J. Image Video Process. **2017**(1), 1–11 (2017). https://doi.org/10.1186/s13640-017-0206-1
15. Liu, Y., Chang, C.C.: Reversible data hiding for JPEG images employing all quantized non-zero ac coefficients. Displays **51**, 51–56 (2018)
16. Xuan, G., Li, X., Shi, Y.Q.: Histogram-pair based reversible data hiding via searching for optimal four thresholds. J. Inf. Secur. Appl. **39**, 58–67 (2018)
17. Xiao, M.Y., Li, X.L., Zhao, Y.: Reversible data hiding for JPEG images based on multiple two-dimensional histograms. IEEE Signal Process. Lett. **28**, 1620–1624 (2021)
18. Xiao, M.Y., Li, X.L., Ma, B., Zhang, X.P., Zhao, Y.: Efficient reversible data hiding for JPEG images with multiple histograms modification. IEEE Trans. Circ. Syst. Video Technol. **31**(7), 2535–2546 (2021)
19. Yao, H., Mao, F.Y., Qin, C.A., Tang, Z.J.: Dual-JPEG-image reversible data hiding. Inf. Sci. **563**, 130–149 (2021)
20. Xuan, G., Li, X., Shi, Y.Q.: Minimum entropy and histogram-pair based JPEG image reversible data hiding. J. Inf. Secur. Appl. **45**, 1–9 (2019)
21. Hou, D., Wang, H., Zhang, W., et al.: Reversible data hiding in JPEG image based on DCT frequency and block selection. Signal Process. **148**, 41–47 (2018)
22. Independent JPEG Group. http://www.ijg.org/. Accessed 12 Jan 2020

Research on Image Multi-feature Extraction of Ore Belt and Real-Time Monitoring of the Tabling by Sema ntic Segmentation of DeepLab V3 +

Huizhong Liu[1,2,3](✉) and Keshun You[1]

[1] School of Mechanical and Electrical Engineering, Jiangxi University of Science and Technology, Ganzhou 341000, China
liuhuizhong@jxust.edu.cn
[2] Jiangxi Mining and Metallurgical Mechanical and Electrical Engineering Technology Research Center, Ganzhou 341000, China
[3] China-Zim International Minerals Corporation, Mt Pleasant, 04-304618 Harar, Zimbabwe

Abstract. The image segmentation technology of ore belt through deep learning image processing is the key to realize the automation and intelligence of the Tabling. In order to extract richer and more effective ore belt image features from the ore belt of the Tabling, a deep learning semantic segmentation model of DeepLab v3 + is constructed. Only 100 small samples of data are used for training. In the last iteration, the training accuracy and loss can be optimized, and it takes less time than other deep learning algorithms. The segmentation quality of the ore belt image is evaluated, and the MIOU, PA and FRP value have reached considerable indicators. the geometric characteristics of the ore belt image and the grade and recovery of the beneficiation concentrate are used for establishing Convolutional Neural Network Regression model (CNNR), which can realize the mapping relationship between the ore belt image and the concentrate grade and recovery rate, the corresponding processing index can be learned only by image processing technology and data modeling, and real-time monitoring of the process of the Shaking table Concentrator, which lays a foundation for the realization of the intelligent control of the Shaking table Concentrator.

Keywords: The ore belt image of the shaking table concentrator · Deep learning semantic segmentation model of Decplab V3 + · Convolutional neural network regression model · Real-time monitoring · Intelligent control of the shaking table concentrator

1 Introduction

Shaking table Concentrator is a widely-used flow film gravity beneficiation equipment, especially in the beneficiation of tungsten ore and tin ore, which is irreplaceable. Nowadays the number of applications of Shaking table Concentrator in beneficiation production is enormous, and according to incomplete statistics, which reach hundreds of

X. Sun et al. (Eds.): ICAIS 2022, CCIS 1586, pp. 35–49, 2022.
https://doi.org/10.1007/978-3-031-06767-9_3

thousands Sets [1][2]. The separation process of the Tabling is as follows: When the slurry is fed to the Tabling surface, the particles in the slurry are loosened and stratified under the action of the lateral flushing water and the reciprocating motion of the Tabling surface. The mineral particles with large specific gravity enter the lower layer due to the high sedimentation speed. On the contrary, the mineral particles with a small specific gravity are in the upper layer. Because the heavy minerals in the lower layer are in contact with the bed surface, they are more affected by the differential action of the bed surface, mainly doing longitudinal movement, while the upper mineral particles are more affected by the horizontal flushing water. with lateral movement, so the light and heavy mineral grains after stratification gradually move in different directions, and finally the grain group spreads out in a fan shape on the surface of the Tabling. Mineral particles with different specific gravities are distributed in different positions. Because of the color difference between them, a unique Tabling's ore zone is formed [3, 4].

In the past, the operation and control of the Shaking table Concentrator was achieved by experienced Tabling technicians. First, the worker judges the processing state of the Tabling and whether the interception position of the concentrate is reasonable by observing the distribution of the ore belt of the Tabling, and corresponding adjustments are made for the position of the concentrate intercepting plate and the volume of horizontal flushing water to achieve The purpose of controlling the grade of concentrate. Because everyone's experience and technology are different, it is easy to cause errors in the interception of the concentrate, resulting in fluctuations in the grade of the concentrate, therefore there is no guarantee that the Tabling be in the best operating state.

In recent years, the use of machine vision and image processing technology instead of manual identification of the ore belt of the Shaking table Concentrator, and then realize the automatic interception of concentrate, which has made certain progress, and proposed an intelligently optimized color image threshold segmentation algorithm [5][6], using krill optimization algorithm and improved firefly optimization algorithm to get the best image segmentation threshold; image recognition and processing technology are used by BGRIMM(Beijing General Research Institute of Mining and Metallurgy) to identify and analyze the ore belt, realize the automatic access of the Shaking table Concentrator [7–9]. The conventional image processing technology can only detect the coordinate information of the mineral separation point of the shaker, and cannot obtain the real-time grade and recovery data during the separation process of the Tabling, nor can it determine the status of the separation process, because it can only detect The location of the target point, the acquired image feature is single, and other feature information cannot be obtained. In recent years, deep learning has been increasingly applied to the identification and classification of minerals, and has achieved good results [10, 11]. With the continuous development of deep learning convolutional neural networks and machine vision technology, advanced deep learning models and machine vision algorithms have been more and more widely used in the industry, which also provides a strong support for automation of mineral processing.

Aiming at the defects of the existing recognition technology of ore belt image, the deep learning semantic segmentation algorithm with DeepLab v3 + is used to segment the target ore belt. In addition to obtaining the location information of the mine belt, it can also obtain the points, lines and plane of the ore belt image, noodles and other rich and meaningful features. After obtaining these features, a deep learning Convolutional Neural Network Regression model is constructed by the input of image feature information and the output of concentrate grade and recovery rate. The concentrate grade and recovery rate are predicted by the constructed machine learning model. The feasibility of constructing a real-time state monitoring and intelligent control system of the Tabling discussed by the model.

2 Materials and Method

A video of the ore belt of the multi-stage Tabling separation process was collected from the production of a tungsten ore dressing plant in Ganzhou of china. Finally, a representative video of about 1 min was selected as the experimental data for the deep learning semantic segmentation model.

2.1 Acquisition and Production of Data Sets

Video Frame Drawing. Video files used as experimental data have more ad-vantages, such as data continuity and representativeness than a large number of images taken separately as experimental data. However, it is difficult to train deep learning semantic segmentation models by the video files, so it is necessary to extract frames from the video files into images, and obtain one image data every 10 frames, which can obtain about 200 image data. 100 images are used as the training set, 50 images as the verification set, and 50 images as the test.

Training Set Data Label Making. It is time-consuming for the deep learning semantic segmentation model to spend time on the pre-processing of the image data and make it into the input data of the model. The original training set image size is 1280*720 and needs to be resized to a size of 700*395. Then a mask label made on the image.

Label Image Conversion Ground Truth Image. large amount of data are required for manual annotation for supervised training in Deep learning semantic segmentation [12, 13], The image Labeler tool that comes with Matlab is used to make a mask label for the image, automatically generated a Label image, and then saved as a Ground Truth image, with the original training image as the input, and the corresponding Ground Truth image as the training output. As shown in Fig. 1.

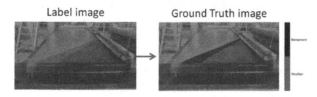

Fig. 1. The effect of converting Labe image to Ground Truth image.

2.2 Construction of Semantic Segmentation Model by Deep Learning

Semantic segmentation is usually used to classify each pixel of an image, such as through pixel-level decision tree classification and deep convolutional neural network classification [14]. At present, deep learning become gradually the best classification method in machine learning, and it is also the first popular image segmentation algorithm [15]. Deep learning semantic segmentation model are developed from the FCN [14] to Seg-Net [15], Unet [16] and Dilated Convolutions [18], from DeepLab (v1&v2) [19, 20], RefineNet [21] and PSPNet [22] to Large Kernel Matters [23] and DeepLab v3 [24] in Fig. 2, The score in the data set VOC2012 has been continuously improved, as shown in Table 1.

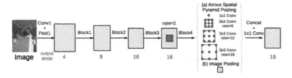

Fig. 2. DeepLab v3 model structure.

Table 1. Comparison of deep learning semantic segmentation models.

Deep learning model	IOU /% (VOC2012)
FCN	67.2
SegNet	59.9
Dilated convolutions	75.3
DeepLab (v1&v2)	79.7
RefineNet	84.2
PSPNet	85.4
Large kernel matters	83.6
DeepLab v3	85.7

DeepLab as an excellent deep learning model for image semantic segmentation, which aims to assign semantic labels (such as human dogs, cats, etc.) to each pixel of the input image. As shown in Table 2, DeepLab v1 combines deep convolutional neural networks and Atrous Convolution is used for semantic segmentation. DeepLab v2 is based on the optimization of DeepLab v1 and with Atrous Spatial Pyramid Pooling (ASPP) to effectively segment objects, multi-scale perforated convolution cascade or parallel are used in DeepLab v3 to capture multi-scale background, and optimizes the segmentation of ASPP through image features. DeepLab v3 is extended to DeepLab v3 +, adding a simple and efficient decoder module to improve segmentation qualities.

The DeepLab v3 + as an advanced deep learning semantic segmentation model and the model's architecture have improved. In order to integrate multi-scale information, the commonly used Encoder-Decoder for semantic segmentation is introduced [25]. In the Encoder-Decoder architecture, the resolution of features extracted by the encoder can be arbitrarily controlled, and the accuracy and time-consuming are balanced through the hole convolution. In addition, the Xception module is used in the semantic segmentation task, and the Depthwise Separable Convolution is used in the ASPP and Decoding module to improve the operating speed and robustness of the Encoder-Decoder network.

Table 2. Comparison of deep learning semantic segmentation models.

	DeepLab v1	DeepLab v2	DeepLab v3	DeepLab v3 +
Backbone network	VGG-16	RestNet	RestNet	Xception
Module	Atrous Conv	Atrous Conv	Atrous Conv	Atrous Conv
	CRF	CRF	--	--
	--	ASPP	ASPP +	ASPP +
	--	--	--	Encoder-Decoder

2.3 Train and Prediction of DeepLab V3 + model

The DeepLab v3 + deep learning semantic segmentation model is trained in Matlab R2020b programming environment, and training parameters are seted and related training data sorted out. The software and hardware used in the experiment are shown in Table 3.

The prepared data set and 100 color images of are prepared for model training, the initial learning rate is seted to 0.0001, MaxEpochs to 20, and MiniBatchSize to 8. $L2$ regularization is used to prevent overfitting, and the model automatically enhances the image before training.

$$L = E_{in} + \lambda \sum_j w_j^2 \qquad (1)$$

where L is the training loss, E_{in} is the sample training error that the regularization term is not contained, λ is the regularization parameter, and is the training weight. The model that needs to be trained is a deep learning model that performs two classifications of pixels. The image is divided into a target area where ore belt area marked as StopSign and a background area where marked as Background to achieve the effect of segmentation.

The model was trained on a single GPU, because only 100 sets of data were trained, and the maximum number of rounds was seted to 20. When the training reached the last round, the maximum iteration reached 240 times, which only took 8 min and 52 s. The changes in the accuracy and loss of the last round of training are shown in Table 4, and the visualization results of the entire training are shown in Fig. 3. It can be seen that the training accuracy of 100 sets of data can reach 99.43% in the last iteration. It can be seen that the training accuracy of 100 sets of data can reach 99.43% in the last iteration. As shown in Fig. 4, the trained model has a excellent prediction effect on the test sets.

Table 3. Software and hardware for deep learning semantic segmentation model training.

Laboratory equipment	GT62VR 7RE
Device memory	256gSSD and 1T
CUDA	8g,GTX1070
Equipment storage	16g
Programming environment	Matlab R2020b
Operating environment	DeepLearn Tool

Table 4. Training results for round 20.

Round	Iteration	Train time	Batch accuracy	Batch loss	Learning rate
20	230	8 m 32	99.32%	0.0155	$4 \times 10-5$
20	232	8 m 36	99.37%	0.0142	$4 \times 10-5$
20	234	8 m 40	99.43%	0.0160	$4 \times 10-5$
20	236	8 m 44	99.37%	0.0133	$4 \times 10-5$
20	238	8 m 48	99.31%	0.0159	$4 \times 10-5$
20	240	8 m 52	99.35%	0.0146	$4 \times 10-5$

Fig. 3. Visualization of the training process.

Fig. 4. Result of DeepLab v3 + semantic segmentation model prediction.

2.4 Evaluation of the Results

Semantic segmentation is currently widely used in many fields such as automatic driving scene analysis and medical image segmentation. At present, the most commonly used evaluation indicators in semantic segmentation are Mean Inetersection Over UnioN (*MIOU*), Pixel Accuracy (*PA*) and False Positive Rate (*FPR*). In order to better understand and calculate each evaluation index, it is necessary to construct a confusing matrix as shown in Fig. 5. True Positive (*TP*) indicates that the prediction result is a positive example, the actual value is also a positive example, and the prediction is correct, False Negative(*FP*) indicates that the predicted result is a negative example, the actual value is a positive example, and the prediction is wrong., False Negative (*FN*) indicates that the predicted result is a negative example, the actual value is positive, and the prediction is wrong, True Negative (*TN*) indicates that the predicted result is a negative example, the actual value is also a negative example, and the prediction is correct, The relationship between the elements of the confusion matrix is shown in Fig. 6.

The *MIOU* is a standard evaluation index for image segmentation problems, which calculates the overlap ratio of the intersection of two sets and their union. In this problem, the calculation is the intersection ratio between the real segmentation and the segmentation predicted by the model. This ratio can be redefined as the number of divided by the total number (including *TP*, *FP*, *FN* and *TN*).

$$MIOU = \frac{1}{k+1} \sum_{i=0}^{k} \frac{p_{ii}}{\sum_{j}^{k} p_{ij} + \sum_{j}^{k} p_{ij} - p_{ii}} \tag{2}$$

where $p_{ii} = TP + TN$, $p_{ij} = FP + FN$, The confusion matrix can be expressed as:

$$MIOU = \frac{TP}{TP + FP + FN} \tag{3}$$

where *PA* is the ratio of the number of correctly classified pixels to the number of all pixels.

$$PA = \frac{\sum_{i=0}^{k} p_{ii}}{\sum_{i=0}^{k} \sum_{j=0}^{k} p_{ij}} \tag{4}$$

The confusion matrix can be expressed as:

$$PA = \frac{TP + TN}{TP + FP + TN + FN} \tag{5}$$

The False Positive Rate (*FRP*) can be expressed as a confusion matrix:

$$FPR = \frac{FP}{TP + FP + FN} \tag{6}$$

As shown in Fig. 7, by performing a pixel-level intersection operation between the Ground Truth image and the predicted result image, In the end, the *MIOU* value of 0.985, *PA* value of 0.993, and *FPR* value of 0.003 through calculations are obtained, where the value of *MIOU* is exceeded the 0.857 performance in the VOC2012, and the comprehensive evaluation effect is excellent.

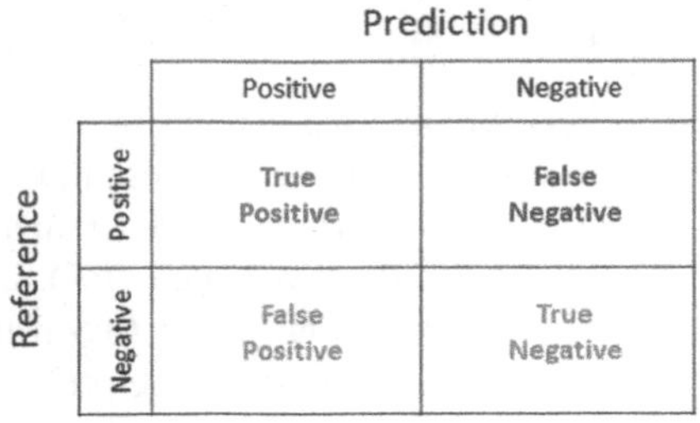

Prediction

		Positive	Negative
Reference	Positive	True Positive	False Negative
	Negative	False Positive	True Negative

Fig. 5. Schematic diagram of comparison between segmentation results and true values.

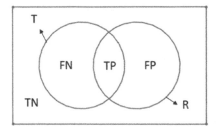

Fig. 6. Schematic diagram of comparison between segmentation results and true values.

Fig. 7. The left side is Ground Truth, the right side is the prediction result.

3 Real-Time Monitoring and Intelligentization of Tabling

3.1 Modeling the Relationship Between Image Features and Indexes of Tabling Processing

There have been established corresponding mathematical models (logistic regression models, etc.) to analyze some of the effects of Tabling's operating parameters on the separating state, or construct neural network models to predict the indexes of Tabling and other related gravity separation processes [26][27], which proves that it is feasible to build a mathematical model related to the separating state of the Tabling through the machine learning method of data modeling, and it is also an significant way to realize the automatic control and parameter optimization of the Tabling separating process.

Each image data corresponds to a different value of concentrate grade and recovery rate. Separately assay the concentrate slurry under each image, and test the value of grade and recovery rate. The separating indexes corresponding to each frame of image obtained can be carried out. The previously trained DeepLab v3 + deep learning semantic segmentation model is used to predict the image features, and extract the multi-scale geometric features of the points, lines, and plane of the ore belt image.

As shown in Fig. 8, five characteristic values, r, θ, l_1, l_2, l_3, are extracted from the segmented target area, where A_1 is the area of the ore belt, A_2 is the area of the background, the ratio of A_1 and A_2 is r, the angle between the left and right boundary lines of the ore belt is θ, The length of the left boundary line of the ore belt is l_2, The length of the right boundary line of the ore belt is l_3, The distance between the intersection of the left boundary line and the bottom boundary line of the ore belt and the left boundary line of the Shaking Table Concentrator is l_1。

After these image features are extracted, the indicators (concentrate grade and recovery rate) under the corresponding separating state of the frame image need to be analyzed by assay. The trained deep learning semantic segmentation model can be used to detect ore belts on the videos taken in real time during separating processes of Shaking Table Concentrator.

r, θ, l_1, l_2, l_3
concentrate grade(%) , recovery rate(%)

Fig. 8. Correspondence between image features and separating indicators.

In order to realize the real-time detection of the indicators in the state of the beneficiation shaking table, the relationship between the image characteristics of the ore belt and the corresponding grade and recovery rate is studied. A machine learning model with multiple inputs of r, θ, l_1, l_2, l_3 and multiple outputs of concentrate grade and recovery rate is established.

And a Convolutional Neural Network Regression model (CNNR) is constructed, as shown in Fig. 9. The input layer is the geometric feature value of the ore belt image of deep learning semantic segmentation. The original input data is two-dimensional data of 5*1, which needs to be expanded into four-dimensional input data of 5*1*1*n to adapt to the format of CNNR input data, where n is the number of sample, the network form of a only single sample is shown in Fig. 9, then sixteen 3*3 convolution kernels are used to perform feature convolution operations. In order to ensure the size of after convolution is same as the input size, the filling method of Same is utilized for convolution, and the step size of convolution is one.

As shown in Fig. 10, After the convolution operation, it is calculated by three fully connected layers, and the activation function of ReLU is used to accelerate the training convergence. Finally, a regression layer is added at the end of the network to calculate

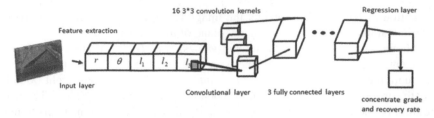

Fig. 9. Regression model of convolutional neural network.

the loss of the entire training and predict the value of concentrate grade and recovery rate. By constructing a deep learning Convolutional Neural Network Regression model, the real-time monitoring of the Shaking Table Concentrator and the evaluation of the separatting state can be realized.

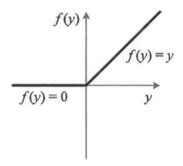

Fig. 10. ReLU activation function.

3.2   Conception of Real-Time Monitoring and Intelligent System

In order to monitor the separating state of the Shaking Table Concentrator in real time and automatically adjust various operating parameters (stroke, rush time, slope angle of Tabling, feed water flow, feed concentration, etc.), and to monitor the fluctuation of various parameters in real time, In the environment of Matlab R2020b, a set of real-time monitoring and intelligent system for the separating status of the Shaking Table Concentrator was designed. The system consists of camera debugging interface, mine belt detection and sorting status monitoring system interface, as shown in Fig. 11 and Fig. 12.

The system's debugging interface is designed to facilitate the first installation of the system for camera debugging, and to adjust the camera to the best position so that the sharpness of the captured ore belt image is minimally affected by light. The detection interface of the tabling ore belt is specially designed here to visually analyze the detection effect of the ore belt. Considering the complexity of the actual surface imaging of the ore belt of Shaking Table Concentrator, the detection of the ore belt can be interfered by the fluctuation in the lighting environment of the beneficiation plant affect. As a result, the detection and extraction of the wrong geometric feature values of the ore belt can be caused by drastic changes in light intensity. Therefore, when this designed system is puted into use in the actual beneficiation plant, the lighting environment needs to be controlled to be more stable.

The deep learning semantic segmentation of DeepLab v3 + and the deep learning convolutional neural network of CNNR method are applied in the design of the real-time monitoring system interface of the separating status of Shaking Tabling Concentrator, and the trained DeepLab v3 + deep learning learning semantic segmentation model and CNNR convolutional neural network regression, which can detect the fluctuation of ore belt in real time, and monitor the grade and recovery value of the corresponding frame of video. The design of the intelligent control mode interface of the system is embedded with the automatic control program, which can continuously adjust the parameters of the Tabling through the negative feedback system according to the seted optimal grade and recovery rate value. This interface is designed to record real-time monitor of the fluctuations in parameters. The real-time monitoring function and intelligent control mode of this system are the keys to real-time monitoring and intelligent realization of the beneficiation shaker sorting process. The internal relationship between the various systems is shown in Fig. 13.

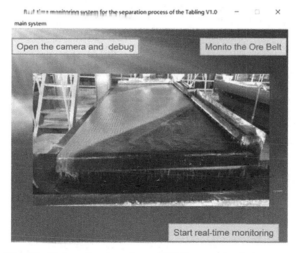

Fig. 11. Debugging interface of Tabling monitoring system.

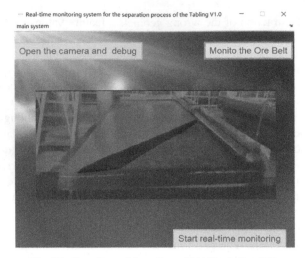

Fig. 12. Interface of detection of Tabling's Ore Belt.

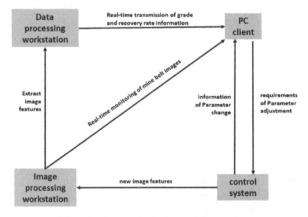

Fig. 13. Internal relations of the system

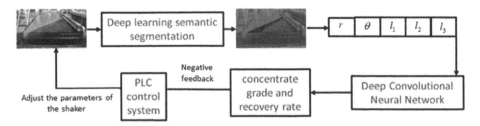

Fig. 14. Feedback system intelligent Tabling negative.

4   Conclusions

A deep learning semantic segmentation of DeepLab v3 + is constructed, and the features of ore belt images in the process of shaking table concentrator are extracted. Not only can the location information of mineral interception be obtained, but also more meaningful ore belt image features can be obtained. These acquired multi-scale ore belt image features can not only provide corresponding coordinate positions for achieving the automatic interception of minerals in the separating processing of the Shaking Table Concentrator, but also provide corresponding data support for realizing the indexes' monitoring of the separating processing of the Shaking Table Concentrator.

The extracted ore belt image features, are fully utilized as model's inputs, and the concentrate grade and recovery rate in the process of Shaking Table Concentrator as outputs, and a machine learning model of deep learning Convolutional Neural Network Regression model is constructed. In order to realize the mapping relationship between the ore belt image and the concentrate grade and recovery rate in the processing.

As shown in Fig. 14, Deep learning semantic segmentation algorithm is applied to segment and feature extraction of real-time ore belt images, and the extracted multi-scale geometric features inputed into the deep learning regression model, the corresponding concentrate grade and recovery rate can be predicted to achieve monitoring of Tabling separating Process. According to the monitoring results of the grade and recovery rate, the process parameters such as the feeding concentration of the Shaking Tabling Concentrator and the operating parameters such as stroke, rush time, slope angle of the Tabling, and the position of mineral interception are automatically adjusted, therefore the Feedback system of the intelligent Tabling is preliminarily conceived, which is of great significance to the realization of intelligent Tabling and the realization of unmanned, high-efficiency and green concentrator.

Acknowledgement. The authors sincerely appreciate the data and technical support provided by related companies and researchers, and especially thanks to Fund Project of Talent Project and Jiangxi Province Key Research and Development Project for all kinds of help and patient guidance during his work.

Fund Statement. Talent Project: Jiangxi Province Double Thousand Plan" Innovative Talent Project (JXSQ2018101046); Jiangxi Province Key Research and Development Project (20212BBE53026).

References

1. Liu, H.: Application progress and prospects of gravity separation equipment in metal ore beneficiation in my country. Non-Ferrous Met. (Miner. Process. Part) **1**, 18–23 (2011)
2. Abaka-Wood, G.B., Quast, K., Zanin, M., Addai-Mensah, J., Skinner, W.: A study of the feasibility of upgrading rare earth elements minerals from iron-oxide-silicate rich tailings using Knelson concentrator and Wilfley shaking table. Powder Technol. **344**, 897–913 (2019)
3. Li, Y.: The sorting principle of shaker. China Science and Technology Expo **16** (2013)
4. Zhang, X., Kang, Ji.: New exploration and practice of gravity beneficiation. In: Proceedings of the National Mine Beneficiation Production, Technological Innovation and Beneficiation Technology of Complex and Refractory Ores

5. He, L., Huang, S.: An efficient krill herd algorithm for color image multilevel thresholding segmentation problem. Appl. Soft Comput. J. **89**, 106063 (2020)
6. Ali, U., Mahmood, M.T.: Defocus blur segmentation using local binary patterns with adaptive threshold. Comput. Mater. Continua **71**(1), 1597–1611 (2022)
7. Liu, L., Li, Q., Wu, T., et al.: The design and application of the automatic ore access device of the shaker Gold **39**(10), pp. 48–51 (2018)
8. Yang, W., He, Q., Lan, X., et al.: Development and application of intelligent inspection robot for mineral processing shaker. Non-Ferrous Met. (Miner. Process. Part) **05**, 102–106 (2020)
9. Wang, H., Dong, L., Song, W., Zhao, X., Xia, J.: Improved u-net-based novel segmentation algorithm for underwater mineral image. Intell. Autom. Soft Comput. **32**(3), 1573–1586 (2022)
10. Wang, L., Chen, S., Jia, M., et al.: Deep learning-based image recognition and beneficiation method of wolframite. Chin. J. Nonferrous Met. **30**(05), 1192–1201 (2020)
11. Li, C.: Design of an Automatic Ore Access System Based on Vision. Kunming University of Science and Technology (2020)
12. Luo, Y., Zheng, L.: Taking a closer look at domain shift: Category-level adversaries for semantics consistent domain adaptation (2019). arXiv:1809.09478
13. Kang, S., Choi, J.: Unsupervised semantic segmentation method of user interface component of games. Intell. Autom. Soft Comput. **31**(2), 1089–1105 (2022)
14. Naz, J., Khan, M.A., Alhaisoni, M., Song, O., Tariq, U.: Segmentation and classification of stomach abnormalities using deep learning. Comput. Mater. Continua **69**(1), 607–625 (2021)
15. Zhang, G., Ge, Y., Dong, Z., Wang, H., Zheng, Y., Chen, S.: Deep high-resolution representation learning for cross-resolution person re-identification. IEEE Trans. Image Process. **30**, 8913–8925 (2021)
16. Long, J., Shelhamer, E., Darrell, T.: Fully convolutional networks for semantic segmentation. In: Proceedings of the IEEE Conference on Computer Vision and Pattern Recognition, pp. 3431–3440 (2015)
17. Badrinarayanan, V., Kendall, A., Cipolla, R.: A deep convolutional encoder-decoder architecture for image segmentation. IEEE Trans. Pattern Anal. Mach. Intell. **39**(12), 2481–2495 (2017)
18. Ronneberger, O., Fischer, P., Brox, T.: U-net: Convolutional networks for biomedical image segmentation. In: Proceedings of the International Conference on Medical Image Computing and Computer-Assisted Intervention, pp. 234–241. Springer, Cham (2015)
19. Rajaragavi, R., Rajan, S.P.: Optimized u-net segmentation and hybrid res-net for brain tumor MRI images classification. Intell. Autom. Soft Comput. **32**(1), 1–14 (2022)
20. Yu, F., Koltun, V.: Multi-scale context aggregation by dilated convolutions (2015). arXiv: 1511.07122
21. Chen, L.C., Papandreou, G., Kokkinos, I., et al.: Semanticimage segmentation with deep convolutional nets and fully connected crfs (2014). arXiv:1412.7062
22. Chen, L.C., Papandreou, G., Kokkinos, I., et al.: Deeplab: Semantic image segmentation with deep convolutionalnets, atrous convolution, and fully connected crfs. IEEE Trans. Pattern Anal. Mach. Intell. **40**(4), 834–848 (2017)
23. Lin, G., Milan, A., Shen, C., Reid, I.: Refinenet: Multi-path refinement networks for high-resolution semantic segmentation. In: Proceedings of the IEEE Conference on Computer Vision and Pattern Recognition, pp. 1925–1934 (2017)
24. Zhao, H., Shi, J., Qi, X., et al.: Pyramid scene parsing net-work. In: Proceedings of the IEEE Conference on Computer Vision and Pattern Recognition, pp. 2881–2890 (2017)
25. Peng, C., Zhang, X., Yu, G., Luo, G., Sun, J.: Large kernel matters-improve semantic segmentation by global convolutional network. In: Proceedings of the IEEE Conference on Computer Vision and Pattern Recognition, pp. 4353–4361 (2017)

26. Chen, L.C., Papandreou, G., Schroff, F., et al.: Rethinking atrous convolution for semantic image segmentation (2017). arXiv:1706.05587
27. Chen, L.C., Zhu, Y., Papandreou, G.,et al.: Encoder-decoder with atrous separable convolutionfor semantic image segmentation (2018). arXiv:1802.02611
28. Manser, R.J., Barley, R.W., Wills, B.A.: The shaking table concentrator-the influence of operating conditions and table parameters on mineral separation-the development of a mathematical model for normal operating conditions. Miner. Eng. 4(3), 369–381 (1991)
29. Panda, L., Tripathy, S.: Performance prediction of gravity concentrator by using artificial neural network-a case study. Int. J. Min. Sci. Technol. 24(4), 461–465 (2014)

A Reinforcement Learning-Based Method to Coordinated Multi-energy Optimization

Feng Jing[1], Xudong Wang[2(✉)], Ning Yu[3], Wei Chen[2], Xiaojun Sun[2], and Jinyue Xia[4]

[1] State Grid OF Shanxi Branch, Taiyuan 030021, China
[2] Shanxi Yitong Gird Protection, Co.Ltd, Taiyuan 030021, China
`1928879373@qq.com`
[3] State Grid Shanxi Electric Power Company Information and Communication Branch., Taiyuan 030021, China
[4] International Business Machines Corporation (IBM), Armonk, NY 100014, USA

Abstract. Aiming at the current problems of emission reduction and reliability to be optimized in multi-energy co-optimization related research results, a multi-energy co-optimization method in integrated energy system based on reinforcement learning is proposed. With the objective function of lowest total system cost, highest reliability and highest emission reduction rate, and the constraints of reliability, heat balance, equipment operation, energy storage and demand response, a multi-energy collaborative optimization model is constructed. The objective model is solved by a reinforcement learning algorithm, which uses the fast optimization performance of reinforcement learning to gradually approach the theoretical optimal solution, dynamically maintains the optimal solution size according to the adaptive grid density method, and optimizes the diversity of the optimal solution set by adaptive chaos optimization, and finally selects the best update particle for the state space by the optimal solution selection scheme. The algorithm stops when the conditions of optimal solution or maximum number of iterations are met, and the optimal solution is output to obtain a multi-energy collaborative optimization scheme that meets the target model. The experiments show that this method can effectively improve the system reliability and has strong robustness in emission reduction and environmental protection.

Keywords: Integrated energy systems · Multi-energy · Synergistic optimization

1 Introduction

As one of the key material bases for the progress of human society, energy plays an important role in economic development and national security. Among them, the study of multi-energy synergistic planning and regulation in integrated energy systems will have innovative effects on the reconstruction of energy production and energy production paradigms, and fully enrich the overall construction of integrated energy systems and the coverage of the energy Internet [3], thus promoting the green and ecological development of energy, and providing support for efficient energy use and energy conservation and emission reduction. In view of the practical significance of multi-energy optimization in integrated energy [4], many excellent results have been presented.

In this paper, we propose an innovative approach to apply deep reinforcement learning algorithms to parametric optimization problems. Combining the characteristics of the parameter optimization problem, the state, action space and payoff function are defined. The value network of neural network structure is constructed, and the structure and activation function of the neural network are determined by experimental analysis. Then the training and optimization process corresponding to the parameter optimization problem was designed according to the deep reinforcement learning algorithm. Again, the deep reinforcement learning algorithm [6] was implemented to optimize the structural parameter optimization problem for large motors. The results show that the optimization results of the deep reinforcement learning algorithm are better than those of the genetic algorithm and the particle swarm algorithm [1]. The training time of the deep reinforcement learning algorithm is much longer than that of the first two algorithms, but the trained value network can greatly reduce the optimization time when used in the optimization process. However, deep reinforcement learning also has the disadvantages of long training time and strong dependence on parameter structure, which need to be used in suitable scenarios.

1. A deep reinforcement learning parameter optimization model is established, and by analyzing and studying the characteristics of parameter optimization problems and deep reinforcement learning algorithms, an innovative method of applying deep reinforcement learning algorithms to parameter optimization problems is proposed.
2. The proposed deep reinforcement learning parameter optimization method is verified in a real wind turbine structure parameter optimization problem, and the traditional genetic algorithm and particle swarm algorithm are used to optimize the same problem, and the optimization results are compared to prove the superiority of the proposed algorithm.

2   Related Work

Weichun Xiao et al. [14] pointed out the current situation of the increasing abundance of various devices in the integrated energy system, and proposed to treat the operators of the district energy as the main body, design and build a dual-side system operation model through the multi-energy complementarity of the integrated energy system on the system side and the user side, and adjust the distribution factors of the energy conversion equipment to achieve the effective improvement of the multi-energy demand matching of the system, but the reliability of this method is low. Xu Hang et al. [15] pointed out that an industrial park is a typical integrated energy system, and applied the energy gradient to the integrated energy system for multi-energy regulation and optimization. However, the practical application cost of this method is high; Wang et al. [13] pointed out that the integrated energy system as the core of the integrated energy internet is one of the key ways to manage ecological pollution, and took the integrated energy system of the community as the target object of the study, and proposed to build a user coordination model including shared energy storage and combined heat and power supply, and scientifically redistribute the overall cost according to the daily consumption of users [9, 10], but the emission reduction rate of this method is limited. However, the emission reduction rate of this method is limited [5]. In order to better realize the cooperative optimization of integrated energy sources, reduce energy consumption costs, enhance system reliability, and improve emission reduction rates, we propose a multi-energy cooperative optimization method based on the chaotic frog-jumping algorithm, which gradually approaches the theoretical optimal solution by using the fast optimization performance of reinforcement learning. The optimal solution size is dynamically maintained based on the adaptive grid density method [1], and the optimal solution selection scheme is used to select the best updated particles for the frog population. The optimal solution [6] is obtained when the optimal solution is obtained or the maximum number of iterations is satisfied, and the multi-energy co-optimization solution is obtained in accordance with the objective model.

3 Multi-energy Synergy Optimization

3.1 Optimization Objectives

Considering the practical needs of multi-energy co-optimization, the multi-energy co-optimization model is constructed based on the basic structure of the integrated energy system as illustrated in Fig. 1

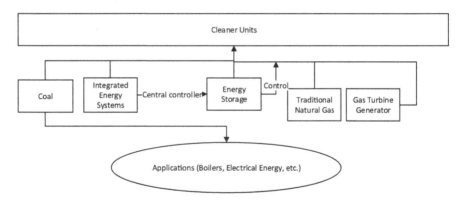

Fig. 1. Basic structure of integrated energy system.

In the integrated energy system, the integrated energy system is for the whole social energy market and power supply market, for the current customers have electricity, natural gas, heating and other energy sources, through the control of big data to convert them into interactive energy to provide security, where coal and thermal power generation is non-renewable energy generation with volatility, intermittency and uncertainty, and wind power generation near the consumption of renewable energy generation, etc. The overall integrated energy supply covering the city and town area. The overall integrated energy system covering the town is a bottom-up [2], customer-centered structure, and the customer side has various forms of energy such as gas, cooling, and heat, in addition to electricity, and therefore requires an integrated multi-energy response. The following aspects are the main objective functions for the construction.

Minimum Total System Cost. In the process of multi-energy system optimization, the total cost $C_{total,T}$ in the total number of periods T of the energy dispatch cycle is composed according to the production operation and maintenance costs and compensation fees for clean units and net power purchase from the grid during the cycle, then there is shown in Eq. (1):

$$
\begin{aligned}
C_{total,T} = \sum_{t=1}^{T} \sum_{\mu \in U} W_{u,t} c_u + \sum_{t=1}^{T} \sum_{a \in U} (\lambda_{a,t}^0 P_{a,t}^0 + \lambda_{a,t}^\mu P_{a,t}^\mu) \\
+ \sum_{t=1}^{T} (C_{purc,t} - D_{sale,t})
\end{aligned}
\tag{1}
$$

where U represents the set of equipment in the integrated energy system, $W_{u,t}$ represents the energy supplied by equipment u in time t, and C_u represents the cost per unit of energy supplied by u. A represents the set of clean units, $P_{a,t}^0$ represents the shortage of unit a due to over-dispatch, and represents the sum of the value of available electricity and demand dispatched electricity at a fixed time t. $\lambda_{a,t}^0$ represents the compensation factor of unit a during over − dispatch, $P_{a,t}^u$ represents the shortage of unit a due to under-dispatch, and represents the difference between the value of available electricity and demand dispatched electricity. $\lambda_{a,t}^u$ represents the compensation coefficient in the under-dispatch process of unit a. Where $P_{a,t}^u$ is specifically expressed as $P_{a,t}^u$, $C_{purc,t}$ represents the purchased power in time t, and $D_{sale,t}$ represents the revenue from the sale of power in time t.

Maximum System Reliability. The Loss of Power Supply Probability (LPSP) [9] is the proportion of the system's power shortage in the rated cycle range to the total system power demand for that cycle. LPSP is the reliability factor of the power supply and is calculated by introducing the type of power source included in the integrated energy system as:

$$
LPSP(T) = \frac{\left[\sum_{t=1}^{T} - \left(\sum_{t=1}^{T} W_{gas,t} + \sum_{t=1}^{T} W_{PV,t} + \sum_{t=1}^{T} W_{wind,t} + \sum_{t=1}^{T} W_{grid,t} - \sum_{t=1}^{T} W_{sell,t} \right) \right]}{\sum_{t=1}^{T} W_{load,t}}
\tag{2}
$$

In Eq. (2), $W_{load,t}$ represents $W_{gas,t}$, $W_{PV,t}$, $W_{wind,t}$, $W_{grid,t}$ of the integrated energy system at time t, representing the electricity generated by gas units and photovoltaic and wind turbines and the electricity purchased from the main grid at time t, $W_{sell,t}$ representing the total electricity sold to the main grid at time t.

Maximum System Abatement Rate. The abatement rate in an integrated energy system is the pollution reduction rate of the system compared to conventional natural gas cogeneration and is expressed as Eq. (3):

$$
E_T = \frac{\left(L_{S,T} - \sum_{t=1}^{T} \sum_{u \in U} P_{u,t} - \sum_{t=1}^{T} P_{i,t} \lambda_g \right)}{L_{S,T}}
\tag{3}
$$

3.2 Constraints

When the overall reliability of the power supply is a certain level, the cost and energy consumption will be increased at the cost of further improvement. In the light of the current macro trend, it is not the best choice to simply pursue the highest level of system power supply. In summary, in the process of considering the power balance, it is not necessary to require that the sum of unit output and main grid purchase must be greater than or equal to the load, but to optimize the reliability level as the target. However, according to the relevant national regulations [18], a lower limit is designed for the reliability of power supply, and the LPSP cannot be higher than the upper limit if the relevant indicators are integrated.

$$LPSP(t) \leq \overline{LPSP} \tag{4}$$

In Eq. (4), LPSP represents the upper limit of LPSP.

Heat Balance Constraint. The constraint contains two parts of heat and cold balance, and its physical concept is that the heat obtained from each heat source is converted into heat and cold load respectively after considering the equipment efficiency and related losses. The expression of the heat balance constraint is:

$$Q_t^{heat} = Q_{recly,t}^{heat}\eta_{recly} + Q_{gas,t}^{heat}\eta_{gas} + Q_{solar,t}^{heat}\eta_{solar} \tag{5}$$

In Eq. (5), $Q_{recly,t}^{heat}$, $Q_{gas,t}^{heat}$, $Q_{solar,t}^{heat}$ represent the waste heat recovery heat and gas combustion heat and solar heat collection heat in time t, $Q_{recly,t}^{heat}$ represents the heat load in time t, η_{recly}, η_{gas}, η_{solar} represents the utilization rate of waste heat and gas and solar heat.

The Cold Equilibrium Constraint. The expression for the cold equilibrium constraint is shown in Eq. (6), $Q_{absor,t}^{cool}$ represents the photothermal heat captured by the absorbed form of the chiller at time t, $W_{elec,t}^{cool}$ represents the total power consumption of the electric chiller at time t, and η_{absor}, η_{elec} represents the efficiency of the two chillers.

$$Q_t^{cool} = Q_{absor,t}^{cool}\eta_{absor} + W_{elec,t}^{cool}\eta_{elec} \tag{6}$$

Equipment Operating Constraints. PV unit operation: the upper limit of PV unit output in the integrated energy system is the value of a certain time period. The upper limit of PV unit output in an integrated energy system is the product of the total radiant energy of local solar energy, the total area of solar panels, and the solar conversion efficiency for a certain time period, and is less than the rated power value of the unit [1, 16, 17]. In the scheduling process, if necessary, the PV unit output is lowered by using the abandoned light, however, it must be guaranteed that its output is higher than the minimum limit. In summary there are shown in Eq. (7, 8):

$$P_{PV}(t) = \min(P_{capa}, \eta_{PV}) \tag{7}$$

$$P_{PV} \leq P_{PV}(t) < \overline{P}_{PV}(t) \tag{8}$$

where $P_{PV}(t)$ represents the operating power of the PV unit at time t, P_{Pcapa} represents the rated installed capacity of the PV unit, η_{PV} represents the solar energy conversion efficiency, S_{PV} represents the solar panel areas, and P_{PV}, $\overline{P}_{PV}(t)$ represents the minimum and maximum power generation values of the PV unit.

The internal combustion engine unit of natural gas: the unit should be in the middle of the upper and lower limits during the power output, and the rate of power change of the unit will be constrained by the climbing rate. Then there are:

$$
\begin{aligned}
P\_{gas} &\leq P_{gas}(t) < \overline{P}_{gas}(t) \\
P_{gas}(t) - P_{gas}(t-1) &\leq U_{gas}\Delta t \\
P_{gas}(t) - P_{gas}(t-1) &\geq -D_{ngas}\Delta t
\end{aligned} \tag{9}
$$

where $P_{wind}(t)$ represents the total power generated by the wind turbine at time t, $P\_{wind}(t)$, $\overline{P}_{wind}$ represents the minimum and maximum power generated by the wind turbine, $v(t)$ is the PV function, P_{rate} represents the rated output powerly value of the turbine, v_{in}, v_{out} represents the cut-in and cut-out wind speed v_{rate} represents the rated wind speed.

Refrigeration unit: absorption form of refrigeration machines with electric refrigeration machine power value must be positive, while not exceed the upper limit of power, then there are:

$$
\begin{aligned}
0 &\leq P_{cold}^{inso}(t) < P_{cold}^{inso}(t) \\
0 &\leq P_{cold}^{elec}(t) < \overline{P}_{cold}^{elec}(t)
\end{aligned} \tag{10}
$$

Total cooling power value and maximum power value for absorption chillers and electric chillers at time t.

4 Collaborative Optimization of Multiple Energy Sources Based on RL

The process of exploring the environment to find the optimal action in the deep reinforcement learning algorithm is similar to the process of searching for the optimal solution in the parametric optimization problem. The method of using value networks in deep reinforcement learning algorithms[8, 11, 12] to accumulate the experience of exploring in the environment by an intelligent body can be borrowed for accumulating the experience of searching for optimal solutions in parametric optimization problems, which is the core idea of this paper.

In this paper, we propose a deep reinforcement learning parameter optimization method to solve the parameter optimization problem of complex products[1], as shown in Fig. 2. In the following, we will take the optimization of large wind turbine structure parameters as an example, and introduce in detail how to define the state, action space and payoff function in the optimization problem, and how to design the training and optimization process and construct the value function, the detailed process is shown below.

State Space. When deep reinforcement learning is applied in the control domain, its state space is generally discrete-valued and easily defined, while the state in a parametric optimization problem can be every solution and the solution space is generally continuous.

$$S = (x_1,x_2,x_3,...,x_{10}) \tag{11}$$

In a multi-energy coordinated parametric optimization problem, a state refers to a combination of a set of parametric variables, each of which has a constraint given by the designer and cannot be exceeded. There are 10 dimensions of variables in this problem, where the first dimension is slotted variables are nominal variables with 6 values, and the full state space is the range of all feasible solutions, which is a continuous space. Therefore, the state is defined as a vector of length 10 to represent the dimensions of the 10-dimensional variables.

This discrete definition of the action space is actually a discretization of the state space, each variable is discretized into 100 value points between its own upper and lower bounds, so that the overall state space actually has 13 states, and if multiplied by the action of each state, there are 3 state action pairs, which is a large number and difficult to record using a table-type value function, so It is still necessary to approximate the value function of the neural network structure.

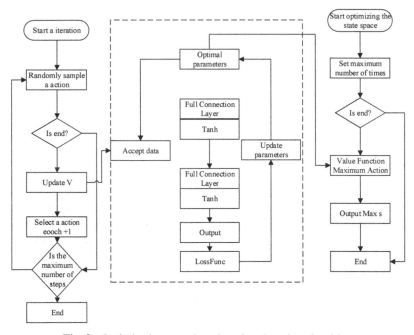

Fig. 2. Optimized process based on deep learning algorithm.

Action Space. In this problem, the action space is defined as discrete 38 values, where actions 1 and 20 represent a decrease or increase of 1 for slotted variables, respectively, actions 219 represent a decrease of 0.01 for other dimensional variables, and actions 2138 represent an increase of 0.01 for other dimensional variables 219, which will not be changed when a variable is out of bounds after an action change. This method of discrete definition of action space actually discrete the state space as well. Each variable is discretized into 100 value points between its own upper and lower bounds, so that the overall state space actually has 13 states, and if multiplied by the action of each state, there are 3 state action pairs, which is a large number and difficult to record using a tabular value function, so it still needs to be approximated by the value function of the neural network structure.

Loss Function. The mean-square error (MSE) is chosen as the loss function and is calculated as follows: where n is the number of samples, y_i is the predicted value, and $\hat{y}_i$ is the actual value.

$$MSE = \frac{1}{n} \sum_{i=1}^{n} (y_i - \hat{y}_i)^2 \tag{12}$$

There are two evaluation metrics, one is the correctness, which can be defined as the size of the loss function in the function fitting problem, divided into validation sample loss function and test sample loss function; the second is the training time, the same training 100 times[1], compare the training time and results.

4.1   Neural Network Structure

The general structure of a fully connected neural network is shown in the Fig. 3 The input x is calculated by the weights and bias of the first layer, and then the output value to the second layer is calculated by the activation function, and the last layer is the output layer, which outputs the predicted value and compares it with the actual value, and changes the weights of the neurons in each layer by some optimization methods (e.g. stochastic gradient descent) to reduce the loss function and achieve the purpose of function fitting.

Reward Function. The return function is relatively easy to define in this problem, and the intuition is the total cost. Since reinforcement learning tends to look for states with greater returns, and the total price is smaller, the calculated price takes the opposite number, i.e., a negative number. Each state, i.e., a set of dimensions, can be calculated by the calculation module for each material weight and output performance index under the program, and if the performance index does not meet the design requirements, the current state is considered infeasible and falls into the end point; if the performance is satisfied, the payoff function is defined as the opposite of the total price obtained for each material. Therefore, when calculating the payoff function for each state, two values are returned through the calculation module, a Boolean value indicating whether the performance is satisfied or not, and the total price. If the first value is unsatisfied then it is considered to fall into the end point and directly ends this exploration; if the first value is satisfied then the payoff function is returned as the opposite of the second value.

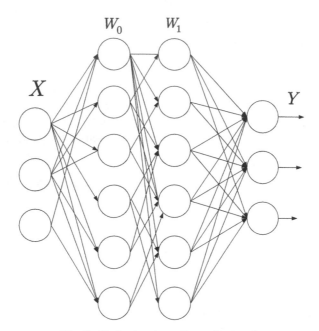

Fig. 3. Basic structure of neural network.

5   Experimental Results and Analysis

A correlation test was conducted to verify the effectiveness of a multi-energy collaborative optimization approach in an integrated energy system based on reinforcement learning algorithms. A pilot project of an integrated energy system in an industrial park in a city was selected, in which 15 lower-tier customer plants and 1 uppertier integrated energy provider were installed. The basic data are: 2 gas turbines, 4 wind turbines, 2 photovoltaic units, 5 solar hot water boilers, 3 absorption chillers and 2 electric chillers.

The data from the tests were transferred to MATLAB software for simulation, mainly for the power generation of wind turbines, energy storage and other physical quantities of the turbine constraints. According to the requirement of power balance, the reliability of power supply is designed as a lower limit value, which must be less than or equal to the load, that is to say, the reliability constraint target is optimized by using the electrical load as the measurement index. The difference between the original load and the optimized load after the test is shown in Fig. 4.

The analysis of Fig. 4 shows that there is a significant change before and after the optimization of the electrical load, and there is a significant trend to reduce the original load compared with the optimized load, and the balance of the electrical load is stronger.

However, assuming that some of the theoretical optimal solutions are not stored in the state set, it is necessary to introduce an adaptive chaos optimization method when screening the particles in the state set in order to match the optimal solutions, and the equipment fuel consumption and regular maintenance costs are the main sources of production operation and maintenance costs, among which, the clean unit compensation costs In this process, the parameters of the optimization model need to be adaptive to

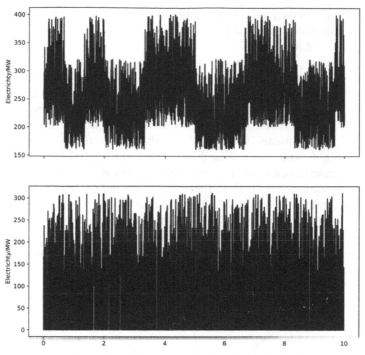

Fig. 4. Comparison before and after electric load optimization.

meet the requirements of the time period. Therefore, the adaptive capability is tested and compared with the adaptive capability of literature [14], literature [15] and literature [13].

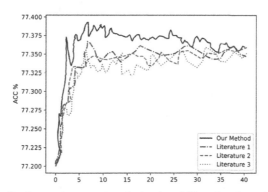

Fig. 5. Comparison results of adaptive ability of each method.

As can be seen from the above Fig. 5, assuming that 100 optimal solution particles are not stored centrally, these 100 particles will be optimized adaptively. In the comparison results between the adaptive capability of this method and those of literature [14], literature [15] and literature [13], the adaptive accuracy of each method fluctuates to different degrees with the increase of the number of particles, and the least fluctuation of this method indicates that the adaptive accuracy of this method is the highest. The adaptive accuracy of this method is the highest, and it can adjust the over-dispatching and under-dispatching situations according to the electromechanical groups in different time periods to realize the energy consumption and cost control of electromechanical groups, and the reliability of its cooperative optimization scheme has been proved[7].

The objective model proposed in the multi-energy collaborative optimization method based on reinforcement learning algorithm contains indicators such as optimal solution selection, and the constraints are compatible with the objective function. The results are shown in Fig. 6. The objective model proposed in the multi-energy collaborative optimization method based on the reinforcement learning algorithm contains indicators such as optimal solution selection, and the constraints and the objective function also have the characteristics of conformity. The grid density mechanism can adjust the set uniformity to some extent, and the following tests are conducted to compare the grid density mechanism of this paper with those of literature [14], literature [15], and literature [13]. The Pareto optimal solution selection scheme makes the smaller the D_k' grid in the Archive set, the higher the probability of being elected to solve the multi-objective optimization problem.

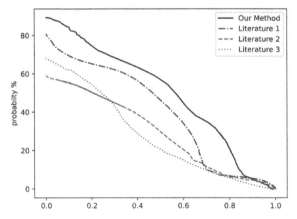

Fig. 6. Grid density mechanism test results of each method

6   Conclusion

The proposed method is based on reinforcement learning algorithm for co-optimization of multi-energy systems. The objective function is the lowest total cost and the highest reliability of the system, and the chaotic frog-hopping algorithm is introduced to solve the objective function and obtain the best solution for multi-energy co-optimization. Compared with the traditional methods, the proposed method can effectively solve the problems of energy load and system emission reduction with high reliability and high control ability of cost and energy consumption, but the dynamic characteristics of the system operation should be analyzed according to the system dynamic model before control.

References

1. Bai Hongkun, Y.S., Li, H.: Optimal planning of multi-energy stations considering carbon-trading cost. J. Electric Power Sci. Technol. **34**(1), 11–19 (2019)
2. Saraereh, O.A., Ali, A.: Beamforming performance analysis of millimeter-wave 5g wireless networks. Comput., Mater. Continua **70**(3), 5383–5397 (2022)
3. Jiang, Y., Xun, J.: Comprehensive energy coordinated optimal scheduling. Considering Human Comfort Flexible Load Power Autom. Equipment **12**(8), 254–260 (2019)
4. Asiri, Y.: Short text mining for classifying educational objectives and outcomes. Comput. Syst. Sci. Eng. **41**(1), 35–50 (2022)
5. Liu, M., Zhang, W.: Multidisciplinary modeling and collaborative optimization of mars global remote sensing probe. Spacecraft Recovery Remote Sens. **38**(5), 57–67 (2017)
6. Vinayagam, P., Anandan, P., Kumaratharan, N.: Image denoising using a nonlinear pixel-likeness weighted-frame technique. Intell. Autom. Soft Comput. **30**(3), 869–879 (2021)
7. Alrajhi, H.: A generalized state space average model for parallel dc-to-dc converters. Com-put. Syst. Sci. Eng. **41**(2), 717–734 (2022)
8. Ke, H.D.S., Chunxiao, L.: Multi-Energy cooperative optimization model of factory IES considering multi-model of ice storage. Electric Power Constr. **38**(12), 12–19 (2017)
9. Dan, M.Z.W., Hongjio, J.: Distributed energy station selection and constant volume planning based on configuration-operation collaborative optimization. Power Autom. Equipment **3**(8), 152–160 (2019)
10. Keerthana, G., Anandan, P., Nachimuthu, N.: Robust hybrid artificial fish swarm simulated annealing optimization algorithm for secured free scale networks against malicious attacks. Comput., Mate. Continua **66**(1), 903–917 (2021)
11. Jun, G.W.W., Shuai, L.: Coordinated planning of multi-district integrated energy system combining heating network model. Autom. Electric Power Syst. **40**(15), 17–24 (2016)
12. Wang, Q., Xin, L., Wu, J.: Comprehensive optimization including user behavior analysis for supply and demand sides ofIES-MEC. Electric Power Autom. Equipment **37**(6), 179–185 (2017)
13. Wang, S., Xue, G.: Synergic optimization of community energy internet considering the shared energy storage. Electric Power **51**(8), 77–84 (2018)
14. Wei, C., Xiao, C., Wang, Y.: Optimization of regional multi-energy system operation considering bilateral cooperation between system and uses. Modern Electric Power **36**(1), 65–74 (2019)
15. Xu, H., He, Z.: Multi-energy cooperative optimization of integrated energy system in plant considering stepped utilization of energy. Autom. Electric Power Syst. **42**(14), 123–130 (2018)
16. Yu, B., Lu, X.: Optimal dispatching method of integrated community energy system. Electric Power Constr. **37**(1), 70–76 (2016)
17. Yu, X., Chen, S.: A brief review to integrated energy system and energy internet. Trans. China Electrotechnical Soc. **31**(1), 1–13 (2016)
18. Zhou, M., Liu, R.: An adaptive adjustment method of line protection setting based on data-driven. Power Syst. Prot. Control **2017**(24), 50–56 (2017)

Real-Time Domestic Garbage Detection Method Based on Improved YOLOv5

Shengqi Kan[1]([✉]), Wei Fang[1,2], Jiayi Wu[1], and Victor S. Sheng[3]

[1] School of Computer and Software, Engineering Research Center of Digital Forensics, Ministry of Education, Nanjing University of Information Science and Technology, Nanjing 210044, China
`201983290107@nuist.edu.cn`
[2] State Key Laboratory of Severe Weather, Chinese Academy of Meteorological Sciences, Beijing 100081, China
[3] Department of Computer, Texas Tech University, Lubbock, TX 79409, USA

Abstract. With the substantial improvement of people's living standards, the amount of domestic garbage is increasing rapidly, and intelligent waste classification has become an urgent need in modern society. In this paper, we propose a real-time garbage detection model based on the improved YOLOv5 (you only look once version 5) algorithm. Firstly, mosaic data enhancement is introduced to enrich the background of the detection object and improve the robustness of the network. Secondly, Distance-IOU Non-Maximum Suppression is used to replace the traditional Non-Maximum Suppression to improve the suppression effect of prediction boxes. Finally, the network is further optimized from the aspect of activation function. The experimental results show that among the four versions of YOLOv5, their mean average precision(mAP) all reach more than 84%, The improved YOLOv5x has the best recognition effect, whose mAP reaches 89.4%, which is 2.1% higher than that of YOLOv5x and 5.3% higher than that of YOLOv5s.

Keywords: Garbage classification · Object detection · Yolov5 · Mosaic · DIOU-NMS

1 Introduction

In the era of intelligent science and technology, people's lives are heading in a more convenient and intelligent direction. The enormous amount of household garbage not only stands in the way of sustainable development, but leads to serious environmental degradation as well. Garbage classification and orderly processing suggest improved efficiency of garbage disposal, multiple utilization of available resources and sustainable development of human society. Therefore, countries all over the world have promulgated corresponding laws and regulations to promote the implementation of waste classification. Hence, it can be seen that garbage classification has become an unresolved issue in nations around the world.

© The Author(s), under exclusive license to Springer Nature Switzerland AG 2022
X. Sun et al. (Eds.): ICAIS 2022, CCIS 1586, pp. 62–74, 2022.
https://doi.org/10.1007/978-3-031-06767-9_5

1.1 Related Work

In 2012, AlexNet [1] set off increasing research into deep learning. Subsequently, the emergence of VGG-Net [2, 3], DenseNet [4], ResNet [5] and other classification networks [6] has greatly improved the speed and accuracy of object detection. Ke et al. [7] employed VGG-Net to describe the synchronization dynamics captured in the correlation matrix, and automatically identified the captured state of Electroencephalogram. Budhiman et al. [8] applied deep learning to medicine by proposing a model of melanoma cancer classification based on ResNet50. Until now, there have been two categories of object detector on the basis of deep learning: two-stage object detector and one-stage object detector. The core principle of the two-stage algorithm is that it generates a series of region proposals, and classifies them through convolutional neural networks. Representative networks are RCNN [9], Fast RCNN [10] and its variant Faster RCNN [11, 12]. On the basis of Fast RCNN network, some scholars improve the detection accuracy of cloth defects by means of depth residual network. The one-stage algorithm directly generates the category probability and position coordinate value of the object, and obtains the final result only after a single detection. YOLO (You only look once) and SSD [13] are widely used in Object Detection among the one-stage algorithm. YOLOv1 [14] divides the input image into S × S grid, and each grid predicts an object, which leads to a poor performance in dense targets detection. In 2016, YOLO9000 [15, 16] was proposed, introducing batch normalization and anchor box mechanism. It not only solves the limitations of YOLOv1, but also improves the speed compared with the two-stage algorithm. YOLOv3 [17–19] refers to the residual block in ResNet network and constructs DarkNet-53 structure. YOLOv4 [20] tries to combine different methods in the field of deep learning, such as using Mish activation function to improve the generalization ability of the network. Moreover, YOLOv4 creates CSP structure consisting of convolution layer and multiple residual blocks. Liu et al. [21] combined ResNet and DenseNet to construct RD-Net to obtain more semantic information. Li et al. [22] introduced the depthwise separable convolution into YOLOv4 to reduce the parameters of the indoor scene model. Zheng et al. [23] added an adaptive path aggregation network to enable YOLOv4 to fuse more location information and semantic information. He et al. [24] proposed Dynamic-ReLU to replace the Mish activation function in YOLOv4 and found that the modification of activation function can improve the detection accuracy without increasing the depth and width of network.

Traditionally, garbage classification mainly relies on manual labor. With the rapid development of automatic equipment and image recognition technology, it provides a scheme for solving the tricky problem of garbage classification with the help of deep learning. Aiming at the speed and accuracy of garbage classification and detection, scholars at home and abroad have made various improvements on deep learning. Adedeji et al. [25] transferred the extracted features to the SVM classifier based on ResNet network, but the detection effect of multiple garbage data sets is not good, whose precision is 87%. Cenk et al. [26] constructed RecycleNet on foundation of DenseNet121, and proposed the skip connections inside dense blocks, optimizing the total amount of parameters and reaching 81% precision. Ning et al. [27] combined shallow features with deep features in YOLOv2, and its precision reached 84.98% on the self-built data set. However, the recognition effect is poor in similar object. Ying et al. [28] used a tiny YOLOv2 network with fewer parameters, and performed well in real-time detection, with the precision of 89.1%. Wu zipei [29] used Generalized Intersection over Union instead of traditional Intersection over Union (IOU) to solve the poor performance of small targets detection by YOLOv3. The precision of the improved YOLOv3 algorithm is 84.02%, which can meet the application requirements in the actual scene. Ying Wang et al. [30] overcome the problem of false regional detection by using region proposal network and ResNet network to train Faster RCNN. However, the complex network structure results in long detection time and is not suitable for real-time detection.

1.2 Main Work

Although the deep learning algorithm has achieved great results in garbage classification, there are still some aspects that remain to be improved.

1) a high error rate in the detection of small target objects.
2) difficulties of adapting to complex backgrounds and multi-objective scenes.
3) the inefficient performance of real-time garbage detection.

In this paper, the data set is composed of nine kinds of household garbage obtained from the network. In view of the speed and accuracy of domestic waste detection, this paper makes a pre-experiment based on four versions of YOLOv5, and further improves the model with the best pre-experimental effect. Traditional Non-Maximum Suppression (NMS) is replaced by Distance Intersection over Union Non-Maximum Suppression (DIOU-NMS), taking the center distance between prediction boxes and real boxes as a factor to modify the suppression effect of prediction boxes in overlapping area. At the same time, ACON-C dynamically controls activation function: non-linear or linear, which enhances the effect of object detection. Experiments show that the improved model has a great performance in garbage detection, meeting the real-time requirements, and can be further applied to industrial production.

2 YOLOv5 Algorithm

YOLOv5 modifies its structure, more flexible and faster than YOLOv3 and YOLOv4. Its network structure can be divided into four parts: Input, Backbone, Neck and Head. The whole model structure is shown in Fig. 1.

The input-images are randomly scaled, cropped and arranged by Mosaic data enhancement, strengthening the robustness of the network. For different sorts of data sets, the adaptive calculation of anchor box iteratively updates the initial anchor box to obtain the best anchor box.

The backbone network consists of the Focus structure and the CSP structure. Taking YOLOv5x as an example, 608 * 608 * 3 image is input to the Focus structure. Through the slicing operation, it first becomes a 304 * 304 * 12 feature map, and then becomes a 304 * 304 * 32 feature map after 32 convolution operations. According to the network idea of CSPNet, YOLOv5 creates two CSP structures as shown in Fig. 2. CSP1_X is applied to Backbone and CSP2_X structure is applied to Neck. SPP is the spatial pyramid

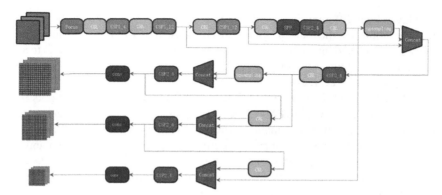

Fig. 1. YOLOv5x network structure diagram.

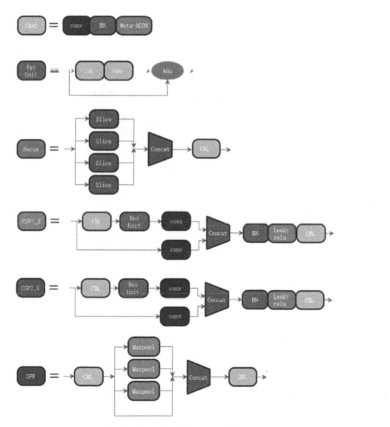

Fig. 2. Main model structure diagram.

pooling layer. Four different sizes of 1*1, 5*5, 9*9 and 13*13 are used for the maximum pooling operation, and the four sub-results are concatenated. The 1*1 convolution model is used several times to integrate the information of different channels and also to adjust the depth on the original structure of the picture, thus accomplishing the function of dimension increase or decrease.

Like YOLOv4, the Neck of YOLOv5 also adopts feature pyramid networks (FPN) and path aggregation networks (PAN). The deep feature map carries stronger semantic features and weak location information, while the shallow feature map carries strong location information and weak semantic features. FPN transfers the deep semantic features to the shallow ones, and thus enhancing semantic expression on multiple scales. On the contrary, PAN transmits the positioning information from the shallow layer to the deep layer, which enhances the multi-scale positioning capability. They complement each other and overcome their respective limitations, thus improving the feature extraction ability of the model.

Head is the output layer of YOLOv5, which outputs three feature maps of different scales, and improves the target recognition accuracy of large, medium and small target.

3 Improvement of YOLOv5 Network Model

3.1 Diou-Nms

In the traditional NMS algorithm, IOU is the only factor considered to measure the level of overlapping area between the bounding box and ground truth in object detection.

$$IOU = \frac{|area(pre) \cap area(gt)|}{|area(pre) \cup area(gt)|} \tag{1}$$

As shown in Fig. 3, pre represents the bounding box, gt represents ground truth and area represents the area of the detection box. The high value of IOU means that the high accuracy of prediction, as is shown by the coincidence degree between the bounding box and ground truth. As shown in Fig. 5, when the overlapping area between cups is small, the traditional NMS algorithm has an excellent effect of detection. However, in the case of occlusion of cups, multiple detection frames of two adjacent cups are deleted to only one frame, resulting in numerous missed detection.

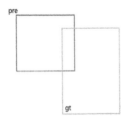

Fig. 3. IOU.

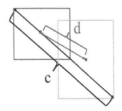

Fig. 4. DIOU-NMS.

Therefore, aiming at the problem of missed detection caused by the dense placement of target objects, DIOU-NMS is used to replace the traditional NMS algorithm. Compared with the traditional NMS algorithm, DIOU-NMS considers not only IOU, but also

Fig. 5. NMS algorithm detection diagram.

Fig. 6. DIOU-NMS algorithm detection diagram.

the center distance between the two frames. If the center distance of two frames is far enough, DIOU-NMS may consider them as different objects and remain original boxes. The formula is defined as follows:

$$l_i = \begin{cases} l_i, IOU - R_{DIOU}(M, B_i) < \varepsilon, \\ 0, IOU - R_{DIOU}(M, B_i) \geq \varepsilon. \end{cases} \tag{2}$$

In Fig. 4, the blue rectangle and the yellow rectangle respectively represent M and B_l. According to formula (3), ρ represents the center point distance d, and c represents the minimum diagonal length of the circumscribed rectangle of the two target detection frames. R_{DIOU} represents the square ratio of d and c.

$$R_{DIOU} = \frac{\rho^2(pre, gt)}{c^2} = \frac{d^2}{c^2} \tag{3}$$

Comparing Fig. 5 and Fig. 6, we can see that DIOU-NMS is better than traditional NMS in dense object detection. DIOU-NMS algorithm recognizes 10 cups, while NMS algorithm only shows 7 detection frames, and its recognition effect is poor because NMS does not make any detection for the target object with serious occlusion.

3.2 ACON-C Activation Function

Initially, the activation function of SiLU is adopted in the YOLOv5 model, as is shown in formula(4). It can be seen from the derivative function $f'(x)$ of SiLU that gradient explosion may occur when neuron $x \rightarrow +\infty$.

$$f(x) = x \cdot \sigma(x) \tag{4}$$

$$f'(x) = f(x) + \sigma(x)(1 - f(x)) \tag{5}$$

$$\sigma(x) = \frac{1}{1+e^{-x}} \tag{6}$$

[31] explored the smoothing approximation principle based on Swish function and ReLU function, applied it to the Maxout activation function and get Smooth Maximum S_β, as is shown in formula (7). Eventually, the team proposed a new activation function: ACON activation function.

$$S_\beta(x_1 x_2 \ldots x_n) = \frac{\sum_{i=1}^n x_i e^{\beta x_i}}{\sum_{i=1}^n e^{\beta x_i}} \tag{7}$$

ACON series activation functions have three versions: ACON-A, ACON-B, ACON-C. ACON-C activation function is widely used in ACON series, and its formula is as follows:

$$f_{ACON-C}(x) = (p_1 - p_2)x \cdot \sigma(\beta(p_1 - p_2)x) + p_2 x \tag{8}$$

$$\frac{d}{dx}f_{ACON-C}(x) = \frac{(p_1-p_2)\left(1+e^{-\beta(p_1 x - p_2 x)}\right) + \beta(p_1-p_2)^2 e^{-\beta(p_1 x - p_2 x)}x}{\left(1+e^{-\beta(p_1 x - p_2 x)}\right)^2} + p_2 \tag{9}$$

$$\lim_{x \to \infty} \frac{d}{dx}f_{ACON-C}(x) = p_1 \tag{10}$$

$$\lim_{x \to -\infty} \frac{d}{dx}f_{ACON-C}(x) = p_2 \tag{11}$$

Where p_1 and p_2 are two learnable parameters adaptively adjusting activation function. When $x \rightarrow \infty$, the gradient of ACON-C is p_1. When $x \rightarrow -\infty$, the gradient of ACON-C is p_2. The two parameters p_1 and p_2 are used to control the upper and lower limits of the first derivative function, which is beneficial to select better activation function. Parameter β dynamically determines the linearity or nonlinearity of activation function. According to formula(7), when $\beta \rightarrow 0$, the activation function is linear; When $\beta \rightarrow +\infty$, the activation function is nonlinear.

Inspired by [31, 32], this paper improves the activation function in the convolution module CBL with ACON-C, and proposes the basic structure of a new CBAC, as shown in Fig. 7.

Fig. 7. CBAC structure diagram.

4 Experiments

4.1 Data Set

The data set of this paper mainly comes from Internet, including 9 categories of items such as cup, mask, battery, medicine and so on. However, collected images contain many images with no target images, which does no benefit to the research on garbage detection. After deleting those data regarded as background pictures, 1101 high-quality garbage pictures are made data sets, as is shown in Fig. 8.

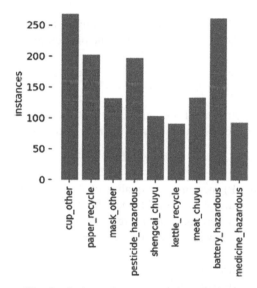

Fig. 8. Garbage data set made by ourselves.

1101 pieces of pictures are preprocessed and manually labeled with LabelImg, thus generating Pascal VOC format of data sets. Finally, each category is equally divided into training set and validation set according to the proportion of 8:2. The total number of training sets and validation sets is 881 and 220 respectively.

4.2 Experiment Environment

In this paper, Pytorch deep learning framework is used to build, train and test YOLOv5 model. Graphics Processing Unit (GPU) accelerates computer graphics computing capacity based on Compute Unified Device Architecture(CUDA). Table 1 is specific experimental environment.

Table 1. Experimental environment.

Configuration	Version
System	Windows10
GPU	GeForce RTX 2080 Ti
CPU	AMD Ryzen 7 3800X 8-Core
Python	3.8
Pytorch	1.9
CUDA	10.0

4.3 Experiment Environment

In this paper, precision(P), recall(R) and mAP are selected as the evaluation indexes of garbage detection.

P refers to the proportion of all correctly identified objects (TP) to all actually retrieved objects (TP + FP). Precision represents the prediction accuracy in the positive sample results.

$$p = \frac{TP}{TP+FP} \tag{12}$$

R refers to the proportion of all correctly identified objects (TP) to all objects (TP + FN) that should be retrieved. Recall measures the recognition ability of the classifier.

$$R = \frac{TP}{TP+FN} \tag{13}$$

Average precision(AP) measures the quality of detecting one class, and mAP is the quality of detecting multiple classes. The definition of mAP first appeared in Pascal visual objects classes (VOC) competition. There are two calculation methods: mAP@0.5 and mAP@0.5:0.95, both depending on AP. This paper selects mAP@0.5 as one of the evaluation indicators.

mAP@0.5 is the mean value of AP@0.5 of all classes, AP@0.5 defined as the mean value of precision of n positive samples when the IOU threshold is 0.5, as is shown in formula(15).

$$AP@0.5 = \frac{1}{n}\sum_{i=1}^{n}\frac{1}{n}P_1 + \frac{1}{n}P_2 + \ldots + \frac{1}{n}P_n \tag{14}$$

$$mAP@0.5 = \frac{1}{N}\sum_{i=1}^{N}AP@0.5_i \tag{15}$$

From the analysis of detection effect, it can be observed that both YOLOv5s and YOLOv5x have excellent functionality to identify the household garbage in the picture. Taking the medicine picture in Fig. 9 as an example, YOLOv5s can detect medicine with a precision of 70%. At the same time, YOLOv5x enlarges the width and depth of the network model, which obtains higher fine-grained features and more rich and complex features extracted from images, improving the precision of recognition greatly. Figure 10 shows the recognition performance of the same picture reaches 92% in precision. Compared with YOLOv5s, YOLOv5x has improved the recognition precision of any other categories. Table 2 clearly demonstrates that the mAP improves gradually with the increase of network depth and width among the four versions of traditional YOLOv5. Furthermore, the mAP of YOLOv5x and its accuracy is improved by 2.5 percentage points and 5.4 percentage points respectively in comparison to the mAP of YOLOv5s.

Fig. 9. Detection effects of YOLOv5s.

Fig. 10. Detection effects of YOLOv5x.

In this paper, the traditional NMS algorithm is improved with DIOU-NMS. The dataset contains numerous dense targets, such as cups, batteries, etc. The traditional NMS algorithm eliminates the prediction boxes of adjacent objects, losing numerous target information. DIOU-NMS considers the overlapping area of objects, which greatly improves the detection performance of dense targets. Compared the performance of DIOU-NMS with NMS under YOLOv5x with 0.25 confidence threshold and 0.45 DIOU, the former mAP is 1.4% higher than that of the latter, reaching 88.7%. It can be seen that DIOU-NMS algorithm improves the accuracy of garbage detection and classification compared with traditional NMS.

Based on the YOLOv5x + DIOU-NMS, SiLU activation function in the convolution module is replaced by the ACON-C. Compared with the SiLU activation function, ACON-C can adaptively activate neurons and dynamically control the linear or nonlinear ability of the function. Table 2 shows that Precision、Recall and mAP of our model all have been improved to a certain extent, which are the highest among the six models. Precision is 92.6%, Recall is 87.3%, and mAP reaches 89.4%. Table 3 shows the accuracy of each garbage under the improved YOLOv5x algorithm. A large number of experiments show that ACON activation functions adaptively activates neurons and control the linearity or nonlinearity of the activation function which improves model's generalization

Table 2. Comparison of results of detection models.

Model	Precision (%)	Recall (%)	mAP@0.5 (%)
YOLOv5s	80.8	81.3	84.1
YOLOv5m	80.5	81.9	85.6
YOLOv5l	92.3	82.4	86.6
YOLOv5x	86.2	85.1	87.3
YOLOv5x + DIOU-NMS	90.1	83.4	88.7
Ours	92.6	87.3	89.4

Table 3. Precision comparison of different garbage types.

Category	Precision (%)
Cup_other	88.1
Paper_recycle	74.2
Mask_other	90.4
Pesticide_hazardous	99.5
Shengcai_chuyu	90.8
Kettle_recycle	99.5
Meat_chuyu	82.5
Battery_hazardous	85.1
Medicine_hazardous	94.5

and transfer performance, obtaining excellent performance in deep learning detection and classification.

5 Conclusion

This paper proposes a garbage classification detection model based on yolov5x. Firstly, DIOU-NMS is used instead of traditional NMS, where the center distance between prediction frame and real frame is taken as a factor, to improve the suppression effect of prediction boxes in overlapping areas. At the same time, ACON-C activation function is used to dynamically learn the linearity or nonlinearity of the activation function, which enhances the effect of target detection. The experimental results show that the improved YOLOv5x is improved on precision, recall and mAP, with high detection accuracy and good robustness. In the future, we will expand the data set, increase the types of garbage into model detection, and continue to study how to improve the detection accuracy while meeting the needs of real-time detection.

Acknowledgement. This work was supported by "Automatic Garbage Classification System Based on DenseNet" in National training program of innovation and entrepreneurship for undergraduates.

References

1. Krizhevsky, A., Sutskever, I., Hinton, G.: Imagenet classification with deep convolutional neural networks. Adv. Neural. Inf. Process. Syst. **25**, 1097–1105 (2012)
2. Simonyan, K., Zisserman, A.: Very deep convolutional networks for large-scale image recognition. arXiv preprint arXiv:1409.1556 (2014)
3. Buvana, M., Muthumayil, K., Kumar, S.S., Nebhen, J., Alshamrani, S.S.: Deep optimal vgg16 based covid-19 diagnosis model. Comput., Mater. Continua **70**(1), 43–58 (2022)
4. Huang, G., Liu, Z., Maaten, L.V.D.: Densely connected convolutional networks. In: Proceedings of the IEEE Conference on Computer Vision and Pattern Recognition, pp. 4700–4708 (2017)
5. He, K., Zhang, X., Ren, S.: Deep residual learning for image recognition. In: Proceedings of the IEEE Conference on Computer Vision and Pattern Recognition, pp. 770–778 (2016)
6. Jeslin, T., Linsely, J.A.: Agwo-cnn classification for computer-assisted diagnosis of brain tumors. Comput., Mater. Continua **71**(1), 171–182 (2022)
7. Ke, H., Chen, D., Li, X.: Towards brain big data classification: Epileptic EEG identification with a lightweight VGGNet on global MIC. IEEE Access **6**, 14722–14733 (2018)
8. Budhiman, A., Suyanto, S., Arifianto, A.: Melanoma cancer classification using ResNet with data augmentation. In: 2019 International Seminar on Research of Information Technology and Intelligent Systems (ISRITI), IEEE, pp. 17–20 (2019)
9. Girshick, R., Donahue, J., Darrell, T.: Rich feature hierarchies for accurate object detection and semantic segmentation. In: Proceedings of the IEEE Conference on Computer Vision and Pattern Recognition, pp. 580–587 (2014)
10. Girshick, R.: Fast r-cnn. In: Proceedings of the IEEE International Conference on Computer Vision, pp. 1440–1448 (2015)
11. Ren, S., He, K., Girshick, R.: Faster r-cnn: Towards real-time object detection with region proposal networks. In: Advances in Neural Information Processing systems vol. **28**, pp. 91–99 (2015)
12. Ushasukhanya, S., Karthikeyan, M.: Automatic human detection using reinforced faster-rcnn for electricity conservation system. Intell. Autom. Soft Comput. **32**(2), 1261–1275 (2022)
13. Liu, W., Anguelov, D., Erhan, D.: Single shot multibox detector. In: European Conference on Computer Vision. Springer, Cham, pp. 21–37 (2016)
14. Redmon, J., Divvala, S., Girshick, R.: You only look once: Unified, real-time object detection. In: Proceedings of the IEEE Conference on Computer Vision and Pattern Recognition, pp. 779–788 (2016)
15. Redmon, J., Farhadi, A.: YOLO9000: better, faster, stronger. In: Proceedings of The IEEE Conference on Computer Vision and Pattern Recognition, pp. 7263–7271 (2017)
16. Murthy, C.B., Hashmi, M.F., Muhammad, G., Alqahtani, S.A.: Yolov2pd: an efficient pedestrian detection algorithm using improved yolov2 model. Comput., Mater. Continua **69**(3), 3015–3031 (2021)
17. Redmon, J., Farhadi, A.: Yolov3: An incremental improvement. arXiv preprint arXiv:1804.02767 (2018)
18. Wang, Y.M., Jia, K.B., Liu, P.Y.: Impolite pedestrian detection by using enhanced YOLOv3-Tiny. J. Artif. Intell. **2**(3), 113–124 (2020)

19. Liu, Q., Lu, S., Lan, L.: Yolov3 attention face detector with high accuracy and efficiency. Comput. Syst. Sci. Eng. **37**(2), 283–295 (2021)
20. Bochkovskiy, A., Wang, C.Y., Liao, H.Y.M.: Yolov4: Optimal speed and accuracy of object detection. arXiv preprint arXiv:2004.10934 (2020)
21. Liu, J., Zhang, Y., Li, Z., Zhao, Y., Ran, X., Cui, Z., Niu, M.: Head detection based on rdm-yolov3. Laser & Optoelectronics Progress, 1–15 (2021)
22. Li, W., Yang, C., Jiang, L., Zhao, Y.: Indoor scene target detection based on improved yolov4 algorithm. Laser & Optoelectronics Progress, 1–19 (2021)
23. Wei, Z., Xiaohui, Y., Zhongbin, R.L., Cong, W., Hefeng, W.: Chao: Real time detection method of key components of yolov4 transmission line based on improvement. Sci., Technol. Eng. **21**(24), 10393–10400 (2021)
24. He, G., Hu, W., Tang, H.: Study on the headgear and seat of the thangka image based on the improved yolov4 algorithm. In: 2020 5th International Conference on Information Science, pp. 153–157 (2020)
25. Adedeji, O., Wang, Z.: Intelligent waste classification system using deep learning convolutional neural network. Procedia Manuf. **35**, 607–612 (2019)
26. Bircanog˘lu, C., Atay, M., Bes¸er, F.: RecycleNet: intelligent waste sorting using deep neural networks. In: 2018 Innovations in Intelligent Systems and Applications (INISTA), IEEE, pp. 1–7 (2018)
27. Ning, K., Dongbo, Z., Yin, F.: Garbage detection and classification of intelligent sweeping robot based on visual perception. Chin. J. Image Graph **24**(8), 1358–1368 (2019)
28. Liu, Y., Ge, Z., Lv, G.: Research on automatic garbage detection system based on deep learning and narrowband internet of things. J. Phys: Conf. Ser. **1069**, 12032 (2018)
29. Zipei, W.: Recognition and classification system of bottles for garbage classification. M.S. dissertation, Hebei University of Engineering (2020)
30. Wang, Y., Zhang, X.: Autonomous garbage detection for intelligent urban management. In: MATEC Web of Conferences, EDP Sciences, vol. 232, p. 01056 (2018)
31. Ma, N., Zhang, X., Liu, M.: Activate or not: learning customized activation. In: Proceedings of the IEEE/CVF Conference on Computer Vision and Pattern Recognition, pp. 8032–8042 (2021)
32. Biswas, K., Kumar, S., Banerjee, S.: SAU: Smooth activation function using convolution with approximate identities. arXiv preprint arXiv:2109.13210 (2021)

Research on Epidemic Spreading Model Based on Double Groups

Weirui Qiao[1], Bolun Chen[1,2($\boxtimes$)], Wenxin Jiang[1], Xiaoyan Wang[1], and Xue Xu[1]

[1] Department of Computer Science, Huaiyin Institute of Technology, Huaiyin 223003, China
chenbolun1986@163.com
[2] Institute of Informatics, University of Zurich, 8050 Zurich, Switzerland

Abstract. In recent years, Corona Virus Disease 2019 (COVID-19), as a highly contagious disease worldwide, poses a serious threat to public health. It is necessary to scientifically predict the development of the epidemic and to study and judge the situation of the epidemic. Based on the Susceptible-Exposed-Infectious-Recovered (SEIR) model, this paper divides the population according to infectivity and considers the impact of double groups on the spread of the new coronavirus COVID-19. In the propagation model, important factors such as the incubation period, average healing days, and recovery rate are introduced, and its stability is analyzed and simulated. In the end, the experimental results prove that the model is stable and can achieve the desired expected effect. The research results provide a theoretical basis for the accurate simulation of the spread of the epidemic in the population, and have important research value and practical significance for improving the prevention and control strategy of the epidemic .

Keywords: COVID-19 · Epidemic spread · SEIR model · Double-group classification

1 Introduction

Since the World Health Organization announced the new crown pneumonia pandemic on March 11, 2020, in just 10 months, the new crown pneumonia has spread to seven continents, and nearly 2.1 million people have died from the new coronavirus. So far, more than 230 million COVID-19 cases have been confirmed globally. This poses a huge threat to global public health. The available data show that the COVID-19 epidemic will show different symptoms in different groups, with clinical manifestations as asymptomatic cases, mild cases (such as dry cough and fever) and severe cases (such as pneumonia) [1, 2]. And patients with different symptoms have different degrees of impact during the spread of the COVID-19 epidemic.

There is no clear standard for how to reasonably divide the population. However, the data of the epidemic so far show that there are obvious differences in the data of the epidemic among people of different ages, different genders, and different immune status. For example, in terms of age, according to a study by Russell T W and others, the severity of symptoms and their clinical results are related to the age of the population

X. Sun et al. (Eds.): ICAIS 2022, CCIS 1586, pp. 75–85, 2022.
https://doi.org/10.1007/978-3-031-06767-9_6

[3]. According to related articles, the COVID-19 epidemic occurred in the earliest stage, and the cases were mainly elderly, but as the epidemic progressed, the number of young cases gradually increased [4, 5]. In terms of gender, the study by Onder G et al. showed that in Italy, the deaths caused by COVID-19 were mainly elderly male patients with multiple comorbidities [6].

At present, there are relatively few studies on the spread of double groups of viruses. Therefore, this article studies the transmission process of the new crown epidemic based on the division of groups of people. On the basis of the traditional SEIR model, a variety of group mechanisms have been added, and factors such as rehabilitation of recovered persons have been added to construct a brand-new double-layered epidemic transmission model.

2   Current Research Status at Home and Abroad

2.1   Propagation Model Based on Statistical Analysis

In the research of using statistical models to predict, Babukarthik et al. proposed to use the Genetic Deep Learning Convolutional Neural Network (GDCNNN) method to complete the classification task of the new coronary pneumonia population, the normal population and the population of other pneumonia diseases in the data set [7]. Based on observations of reported infections in China, combined with liquidity data, networked dynamic meta-population models, and Bayesian inference, Li et al. inferred key epidemiological characteristics related to the new coronavirus, including the proportion of undocumented infections and their infections sex [8]. Zhang et al. respectively used polynomial regression and Long Short Term Memory Networks (LSTM) analysis to predict the effects of epidemic prevention and control policies in various countries on epidemic control and economic recession [9]. Shwet et al. proposed an ARIMA-LSTM hybrid model based on deep learning to predict the outbreak of COVID-19 [10]. Sultana et al. proposed to predict various COVID-19 outbreaks through Machine Learning classifiers such as Linear regression, Multi-Layer Perception, and Vector Auto Regression [11]. Aldhyani et al. proposed to predict coronaviruses through deep learning algorithm and Holt-trend model [12]. Hamadneh et al. proposed an Artificial Neural Network (ANN) model to estimate and predict the number of COVID-19 cases [13].

2.2   Propagation Model Based on Statistical Analysis

Compared with the prediction of statistical models, the creation of dynamic models to predict the spread of the epidemic is more widely used in the field of scientific research. The construction of general dynamic models can be roughly divided into three types: the propagation model based on Susceptible-Infectious-Recovered (SIR) improvement, the propagation model based on SEIR improvement, and the dynamic propagation model created by combining some mathematical ideas.

In the research on the transmission model based on SIR improvement, Adekola et al. tested the SIR, SEIR and SEIAR models. The results emphasized that these models can better simulate the dynamics of disease transmission and help decision makers make accurate decisions, thereby reducing the transmission rate of the disease [14]. Fanelli et al. used the Susceptible-Infectious-Recovered-Dead (SIRD) model to compare and evaluate the evolution of the COVID-19 epidemic in China, Italy, and France, and clarify the spread of the epidemic [15]. Chen et al. proposed a time-dependent SIR model to track the propagation speed and recovery rate of the model at time t [16].

In terms of the research on the improved transmission model based on SEIR, Zhao et al. considered the impact of the isolation strategy on the spread of the virus, and constructed a Susceptible-Exposed-Infected-Quarantined-Removed (SEIQR) model, combined with the time step, through population migration data to predict the development of the epidemic [17]. Yang et al. established a Susceptible-Exposed-Infectious-Recovered-Dead (SEIRD) model for the spread of the new coronavirus in China to simulate the relationship between the migrant population and confirmed patients in Wuhan [18]. Yang et al. improved the traditional SEIR model and considered the inflow and outflow of susceptible population and exposed population over time on the basis of the original model [19]. Liu et al. established a two-layer network model that couples epidemics and individual behaviors based on the SEIR model and game theory. By calculating the basic reproduction number, the existence and stability of the positive equilibrium point in the behavioral dynamics model are analyzed [20].

In addition, some scholars combined mathematical ideas to construct related dynamic transmission models. Kong et al. used the negative binomial distribution transfer function to construct a new SEIR model in a closed population, which takes into account the natural birth, death, and population contact rate of the population [21]. Chen et al. constructed the Bats-Hosts-Reservoir-People (BHRP) transmission network model [22]. Hua et al. built an improved IC model algorithm to simulate the spread of nodes in social networks [23].

3   Model Definition and Stability Analysis

The model proposed in this article not only considers the impact of human gender or age differences on the transmission results during the spread of the epidemic, but also considers the antibodies in the resisters (the populations of infected individuals who will have antibodies in their bodies after treatment) The effect of changes over time on model propagation. That is to say, the antibodies in the human body will gradually decrease with time. Once it drops to a certain level, when the individual comes into contact with the virus-carrying people again, it will be again with another probability, which is the rejuvenation rate we proposed. Become an infected individual. Figure 1 is a schematic diagram of the DSEIRS model, and the model parameters are shown in Table 1.

It can be seen from the figure that our model is divided into upper and lower layers, and each layer has its own population. Although the two layers do not intersect in the figure, there is a close connection between the two layers. The latent and infected persons on the first floor will not only affect the people on the other floor, but also affect the people on the other floor. In this article, we define the two layers of the model as two types of people. There is no limit to the way the people can be divided. They can be divided into males and females in terms of gender, and can also be divided into people aged 0–60 and people over 60 and many more. In this article, these two groups of people

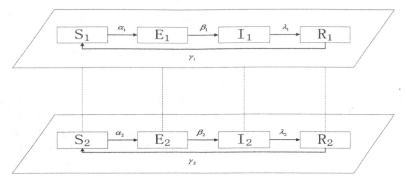

Fig. 1. DSEIRS model diagram.

Table 1. DSEIRS model descriptions of parameters.

Symbol	Explain
α_{11}	Probability of infection of a latent person to a susceptible person who is susceptible to infection
α_{12}	Probability of infection of infected people to susceptible people who are easily infected
α_{21}	Probability of infection of a latent person to a susceptible person who is not easily infected
α_{22}	Probability of infection of an infected person to a susceptible person who is not easily infected
β_1	Probability of a latent person who is easily infected into an infected person
β_2	Probability of a latent person who is not easily infected into an infected person
λ_1	Probability that the infected people who are easily infected will be cured
λ_2	Probability of cured people who are not easily infected
γ_1	Re-infected rate of resisters who are susceptible to infection
γ_2	Re-infected rate of resisters who are not susceptible to infection
r	Number of people contacted per person per day
N	Total people

are collectively called the people who are susceptible to infection and the people who are not easily infected. In addition, in the setting of parameters, we also introduced the incubation period, infection rate, recovery rate and other parameters.

The differential equation corresponding to the model is as follows:

$$\frac{dS_1}{dt} = -\frac{\alpha_{11}S_1(E_1 + E_2)r}{N} - \frac{\alpha_{12}S_1(I_1 + I_2)r}{N} + \gamma_1 R_1 \qquad (1)$$

$$\frac{dE_1}{dt} = \frac{\alpha_{11}S_1(E_1 + E_2)r}{N} + \frac{\alpha_{12}S_1(I_1 + I_2)r}{N} - \beta_1 E_1 \qquad (2)$$

$$\frac{dI_1}{dt} = \beta_1 E_1 - \lambda_1 I_1 \qquad (3)$$

$$\frac{dR_1}{dt} = \lambda_1 I_1 - \gamma_1 R_1 \qquad (4)$$

$$\frac{dS_2}{dt} = -\frac{\alpha_{21} S_2 (E_1 + E_2) r}{N} - \frac{\alpha_{22} S_2 (I_1 + I_2) r}{N} + \gamma_2 R_2 \qquad (5)$$

$$\frac{dE_2}{dt} = \frac{\alpha_{21} S_2 (E_1 + E_2) r}{N} + \frac{\alpha_{22} S_2 (I_1 + I_2) r}{N} - \beta_2 E_2 \qquad (6)$$

$$\frac{dI_2}{dt} = \beta_2 E_2 - \lambda_2 I_2 \qquad (7)$$

$$\frac{dR_2}{dt} = \lambda_2 I_2 - \gamma_2 R_2 \qquad (8)$$

Here $t \geq t_0$ is the number of time steps, each step represents one day, t_0 is the start date of the epidemic, S_1 is the number of susceptible persons in the vulnerable population at time t, and E_1 is the latent person in the vulnerable population at time t. I_1 is the number of people who are susceptible to infection at time t, and R_1 is the number of people who are vulnerable to infection (that is, those who have recovered from treatment after being discovered and have virus antibodies) at time t. S_2 is the number of susceptible people in the easily infected population at time t. E_2 is the number of latent people in the easily infected population at time t. I_2 is the number of infected persons in the susceptible population at time t, and R_2 is the number of resisters in the susceptible population at time t. At time $t = 0$, $S_1 = N_1 - 1$, $S_2 = N_2$, $I_1 = 1$, $I_2 = 0$.

The specific propagation rules of the model are as follows:

- When the latent person comes into contact with the susceptible persons of the first and second groups of people, they will turn into a latent person with the probability of α_{11} and α_{21} respectively.
- When the infected person comes into contact with the susceptible persons of the first and second groups of people, they will turn into latent persons with the probability of α_{12} and α_{22} respectively.
- The latent persons of different groups of people will become infected with the probability of β_1 and β_2 respectively, which means that the latent persons have passed their respective incubation periods.
- People who enter the infection stage will turn into resisters with the probability of λ_1 and λ_2 after isolation treatment. People who enter this stage already have virus antibodies in their bodies and it is difficult to be infected again.
- After a period of time, the antibodies in the resisters will gradually decrease. When the antibodies are reduced to a certain level and contact with the latent or infected again, they will regain the yang with the probability of γ_1 and γ_2.

Use 4-character indent on the first line of each new paragraph. Use single line spacing, three pounds after segment. Use 3 pt spacing after the paragraph. All levels of headings should use 12 pt spacing before the paragraph, 3 pt after the paragraph.

4   Experiment

Table 2. Initial values of parameters.

Parameter symbol	Initial value
α_{11}	0.04
α_{12}	0.06
α_{21}	0.03
α_{22}	0.05
β_1	1/10
β_2	1/16
λ_1	0.1
λ_2	0.2
γ_1	0.00002
γ_2	0.00001
r	20
N	100000

In this experiment, we assume that the virus is spreading in a closed area, the number of people in this area is fixed, there is no entry and exit of outsiders, and no births and deaths. The initial value settings of each parameter in the model are shown in Table 2. After that, we will change the value of each parameter, conduct experiments, and compare the effects of each parameter on various groups of people and populations, and analyze them in detail. For each parameter change in the experiment, we have done two different experiments. For convenience, we use 1 and 2 to represent the two categories of people. In each experiment, we only change a certain parameter 4 times, and the values of the remaining parameters remain the same as the initial values.

4.1   The Impact of the Incubation Rate β_1/β_2 on the Spread of the Epidemic

The influence of the latency rate β_1/β_2 on the two groups of people and their respective 4 populations is shown in Fig. 2–3. Figure 2 is the impacts caused by parameter β_1, and Fig. 3 is the impacts caused by parameter β_2. The size of β_1 and β_2 is the reciprocal of the incubation period of the two groups of people. The longer the incubation period, the smaller the parameter value. Conversely, the shorter the incubation period, the larger the parameter value.

Regarding the influence of parameter β_1, it can be seen from the figure Fig. 2. When the parameters decrease, the latent, infected, and resistant of the first group of people change significantly. Among them, the peak of the latent curve becomes larger, and the time required to reach the peak becomes longer but rises. The speed is similar, but from

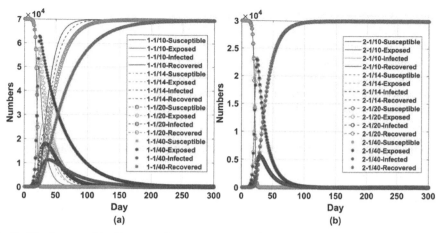

Fig. 2. The impact of lurking rate β_1 on two groups of population. (a) Changes in the 1 types population (b) Changes in the 2 types population.

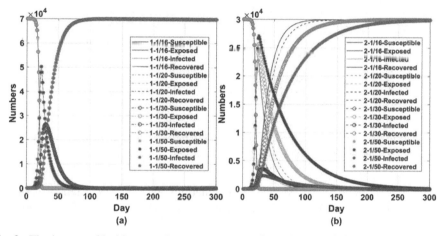

Fig. 3. The impact of lurking rate β_2 on two groups of population. (a) Changes in the 1 types population (b) Changes in the 2 types population.

the peak to the steady state, the time becomes longer and the descending speed becomes smaller. The peak of the infected person's curve decreased, but the time required to reach the peak did not change significantly, but the time required for the subsequent stage of the curve became longer, resulting in a gentle decline. The resister curve becomes flatter, and the time required to reach a steady state is longer. As the incubation period increases, the parameter β_1 decreases, and the curve of the above three populations changes more obviously in the experimental results. The four population curves of the susceptible and the 2 types of population did not change significantly.

Regarding the influence of parameter β_2, the influence caused by parameter β_2 is mainly concentrated on the latent, infected, and resistant persons of the 2 types of population, but not on the curve of the 4 populations of the 1 population and the susceptible persons of the 2 population. Cause a greater impact. Comparing the influence caused by parameter β_1, it can be seen that it is just relative. This happens because the parameter β_1 is directly related to the type 1 population, and the parameter β_2 is directly related to the change of the type 2 population. This can be seen from the dynamic formula.

4.2   The Impact of γ_1/γ_2 Recovery Rate on the Spread of the Epidemic

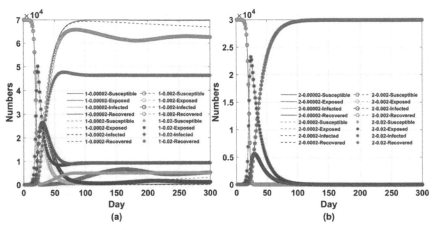

Fig. 4. The impact of Re-infected rate γ_1 on two groups of population. (a) Changes in the 1 types population (b) Changes in the 2 types population.

The effect of γ_1/γ_2 on the two types of populations and their 4 populations is shown in Fig. 4–5. Figure 4 shows the influence caused by parameter γ_1, and Fig. 5 shows the influence caused by parameter γ_2.

Regarding the influence of parameter γ_1, it can be seen from Fig. 4 that the change of the curve only occurs in the first group of people. The curve of the susceptible person changes mainly in about 25 days. When the probability of re-yang is 0.00002, the curve is already stable at this time, but when the probability is expanded by 10 times, the value does not reach equilibrium after falling to 0, but the value is slowly rising. When the probability expands to 100 times, the subsequent stage of the curve rises first, then drops at about 170 days, and becomes stable after the time reaches about 230 days. When the probability is expanded to 1000 times, the speed of the curve rises greatly, and then it reaches equilibrium after 80 days. The change of the lurker is also in the subsequent plateau phase. When the parameter is the initial value, the curve reaches a plateau at 60 days. After the parameter value is expanded by 10 times, the curve does not change significantly. When expanded to 100 times, the number of lurkers slowly approached 0 but did not reach 0. After about 110 days, the value began to slowly rise. When the parameter value is expanded by 1000 times, the curve has undergone a big change.

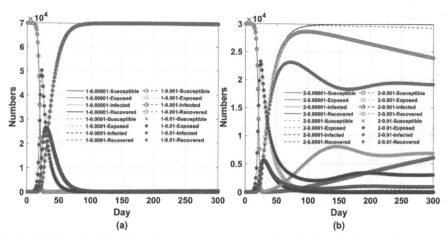

Fig. 5. The impact of Re-infected rate γ_2 on two groups of population. (a) Changes in the 1 types population (b) Changes in the 2 types population.

In the subsequent stage, the number of people first drops and then rises and becomes stable in about 100 days, and the value in a stable state is above 8000.The change of the infected person's curve is similar to that of the latent person, except that the value of the final plateau is different. The resister curve also changes in the final stable stage. As the parameter value changes, it first reaches a certain peak, then drops, and then rises to a new stable state, but the resister curve is changed by 10 times the parameter value. Decrease slowly, and it will take a long time to reach a steady state later than the set time range. The change of 100 times the parameter value will rise slowly, and the time to reach a stable state will also exceed the set area. When it is changed by 1000 times, whether it is a decline or a rebound in the subsequent stage, the speed becomes faster and the time used becomes shorter. It can be clearly seen that the curve finally reaches a new steady state, and the value of the steady state decreases.

5 Summary

During the spread of the COVID-19 epidemic, different groups of people often have different symptoms, and patients with different symptoms often have different degrees of impact during the spread of the epidemic. Based on the original SEIR model, this paper divides the population reasonably, and fully considers the influence of double groups during the spread of the epidemic. In addition, it also proposes the concept of rehabilitation of recovered patients and integrates it into the model. Then, build the DSEIRS model, and analyze and simulate the stability of the model. In addition, in terms of dividing the population, according to the results shown by the statistics of the epidemic so far, this article believes that it is an effective and reasonable way to divide the population by age, gender, and different immune status. The experimental results show that the model can reach a stable state under the condition of reasonable parameters. It has important research value and practical significance in accurately simulating the spread of the COVID-19 epidemic and improving epidemic prevention and control strategies.

Acknowledgment. This research was supported in part by the National Natural Science Foundation of China under grant No. 61602202, the Natural Science Foundation of Jiangsu Province under contract No. BK20160428, and the Natural Science Foundation of Education Department of Jiangsu Province under contract No. 20KJA520008. Six talent peaks project in Jiangsu Province (Grant No.XYDXX-034) and China Scholarship Council also supported this work.

References

1. Pan, Y., Zhang, D., Yang, P., Poon, L.L., Wang, Q.: Viral load of SARSCOV-2 in clinical samples. Lancet. Infect. Dis **20**(4), 411–412 (2020)
2. Huang, C., et al.: Clinical features of patients infected with 2019 novel coronavirus in Wuhan, China. The Lancet **395**(10223), 497–506 (2020)
3. Russell, T.W., et al.: Estimating the infection and case fatality ratio for coronavirus disease (COVID-19) using age-adjusted data from the outbreak on the diamond princess cruise ship, February 2020. Euro. Surveill. **25**(12), 2000256 (2020)
4. Chen, N., et al.: Epidemiological and clinical characteristics of 99 cases of 2019 novel coronavirus pneumonia in Wuhan, China: A descriptive study. The Lancet **395**(10223), 507–513 (2020)
5. Li, Q., et al.: Early transmission dynamics in Wuhan, China, of novel coronavirus-infected pneumonia. N. Engl. J. Med. (2020)
6. Onder, G., Rezza, G., Brusaferro, S.: Case-fatality rate and characteristics of patients dying in relation to COVID-19 in Italy. JAMA **323**(18), 1775–1776 (2020)
7. Babukarthik, R., Adiga, V.A.K., Sambasivam, G., Chandramohan, D., Amudhavel, J.: Prediction of COVID-19 using genetic deep learning convolutional neural network (GDCNN). IEEE Access **8**, 177647–177666 (2020)
8. Li, R., et al.: Substantial undocumented infection facilitates the rapid dissemination of novel coronavirus (SARS-COV-2). Sci. **368**(6490), 489–493 (2020)
9. Zhang, Y., Sun, J.: A COVID-19 epidemics trend prediction algorithm based on LSTM. In: Proceedings of the 2021 IEEE 4th International Conference on Computer and Communication Engineering Technology (CCET), pp. 252–256. IEEE (2021)
10. Shwet, K., Mishra, P.K.: A hybrid deep learning model for COVID-19 prediction and current status of clinical trials worldwide. Comput. Mater. Continua **66**(2), 1896–1919 (2021)
11. Sultana, J., Singha, A.K., Siddiqui, S.T., Nagalaxmi, G., Sriram, A.K., Pathak, N.: COVID-19 pandemic prediction and forecasting using machine learning classifiers. Intell. Autom. Soft Comput. **32**(3), 1007–1024 (2022)
12. Aldhyani, T.H., Alrasheed, M., Alzahrani, M.Y., Ahmed, H., et al.: Deep learning and holt-trend algorithms for predicting COVID-19 pandemic. Comput. Mater. Continua **67**(2), 2141–2160 (2021)
13. Hamadneh, N.N., Khan, W.A., Ashraf, W., Atawneh, S.H., Khan, I., Hamadneh, B.N.: Artificial neural networks for prediction of COVID-19 in saudi arabia. Comput. Mater. Continua **66**(3), 2787–2796 (2021)
14. Adekola, H.A., Adekunle, I.A., Egberongbe, H.O., Onitilo, S.A., Abdullahi, I.N.: Mathematical modeling for infectious viral disease: The COVID-19 perspective. J. Public Aff. **20**(4), e2306 (2020)
15. Fanelli, D., Piazza, F.: Analysis and forecast of COVID-19 spreading in China, Italy and France. Chaos, Solitons Fractals **134**, 109761 (2020)
16. Chen, Y.C., Lu, P.E., Chang, C.S., Liu, T.H.: A time-dependent sir model for COVID-19 with undetectable infected persons. IEEE Trans. N. Sci. Eng. **7**(4), 3279–3294 (2020)

17. Zhao, Y., He, Y., Zhao, X.: COVID-19 outbreak prediction based on seiqr model. In: Proceedings of the 2020 39th Chinese Control Conference (CCC), pp. 1133–1137. IEEE (2020)
18. Yang, H., et al.: Population migration, confirmed COVID-19 cases, pandemic prevention, and control: Evidence and experiences from China. J. Public Health **2020**, 1–7 (2020)
19. Yang, Z., et al.: Modified seir and ai prediction of the epidemics trend of COVID-19 in China under public health interventions. J. Thorac. Dis. **12**(3), 165 (2020)
20. Liu, M., Zhang, R., Xie, B.: Modeling and analyzing the propagation of COVID-19 in Wuhan based on game theory: Quarantine or not? (2020). DOI: https://doi.org/10.21203/rs.3.rs-113997/v1
21. Kong, L., Wang, J., Han, W., Cao, Z.: Modeling heterogeneity in direct infectious disease transmission in a compartmental model. Int. J. Environ. Res. Public Health **13**(3), 253 (2016)
22. Chen, T.M., Rui, J., Wang, Q.P., Zhao, Z.Y., Cui, J.A., Yin, L.: A mathematical model for simulating the phase-based transmissibility of a novel coronavirus. Infect. Dis. Poverty **9**(1), 1–8 (2020)
23. Hua, Y., Chen, B., Yuan, Y., Zhu, G., Li, F.: An influence maximization algorithm based on the influence propagation range of nodes. J. Internet of Things **1**(2), 77 (2019)

Application Prospect of High-Precision Map Mode and Pure Vision Mode in Automatic Driving

Bojing Cheng, Hongye Liu[✉], Ying Wang, and Yongchao Liu

Hunan Automotive Engineering Vocational College, Zhuzhou 412000, China
283948152@qq.com

Abstract. With the introduction of NiO's Pilot Navigation (NOP), autonomous driving is becoming increasingly important, because Tesla's Autopilot navigation (NoA) is a purely visual mode, while NoP needs high-precision map support. In max et al., high-precision maps are not necessarily required in an environment of autonomous driving technology close to L3. L3 autonomous driving is achieved in pure vision mode. This paper analyzes and forecasts autonomous driving technology based on high-precision maps and pure vision. The conclusion is that the future of self-driving cars must be inextricably linked to a variety of multiple fusion technologies such as vision, radar, and high-precision maps.

Keywords: High-precision map · Pure vision · Automatic driving

1 Introduction

Autonomous driving has four key research areas: environment perception, path planning, decision control, and positioning and navigation. In the L2 assisted driving stage, environmental perception and decision-making control are the most discussed parts, and the role of navigation is not too much related to assisted driving [1].

However, once it reaches the level of L3 and above autonomous driving, the autonomous driving map becomes a necessary option. It is not only the basis of path planning, which provides basis for positioning, decision-making, and new traffic dynamics information for autonomous driving [2], but also becomes another guarantee in addition to the intelligent system of the car in the harsh environment or when the vehicle fails [3].

NIO, the second company in the world to implement pilot assistance functions, has adopted the integration of high-precision maps and the NIO Pilot assisted driving system. However, Tesla, the world's first to implement pilot assistance functions, did not use high-precision maps. Elon Musk's attitude towards high-precision maps provided by suppliers has never been considered enthusiastic.

X. Sun et al. (Eds.): ICAIS 2022, CCIS 1586, pp. 86–94, 2022.
https://doi.org/10.1007/978-3-031-06767-9_7

2 The Significance of High-Precision Maps in Autonomous Driving

The high and precision of high-precision maps are reflected in two aspects. On the one hand, the absolute coordinate accuracy is high, and on the other hand, the information is richer. Traditional navigation maps usually have an accuracy of about meter or 10 m, while the accuracy of high-precision maps can reach sub-meter or even higher [4]. Traditional navigation maps usually only provide road network structure information and rough geometric point locations. In addition to this information, the high-precision map also contains lane information (lane line location, type, lane direction, lane traffic restriction information, etc.), traffic sign information, and location information of traffic lights, overpasses, gantry, etc. (see Fig. 1).

Fig. 1. High-precision map overlaid with semantic landmark layer.

If you use the analogy of manual driving, the autonomous driving map is the route in the brain's memory, and the high-precision positioning is the human perception of spatial location. High-precision positioning has a certain function overlap with single-car environment perception such as cameras, radars, and lidars. Therefore, most mainstream solutions use high-precision maps as "long-distance sensors" to provide "a priori" for path planning. Intelligence is used as a "decision" for on-the-spot execution, and data fusion analysis of the two is carried out.

3 Application and Limitation Analysis of High-Precision Maps in Autonomous Driving

Cadillac Super Cruise is the first assisted driving system that links the assisted driving system with a high-precision map. At that time, Cadillac's assisted driving system was based on the Mobileye Q3 platform, which was consistent with the hardware level of

Tesla's Autopilot 1.0, and its high-precision map collected 130,000 miles in the United States (the total mileage of US highways exceeded 170,000 miles) (see Fig. 2).

However, due to the limitations of the electrical and electronic architecture at the time, the two systems of assisted driving and high-precision maps did not form a good integration at that time. The high-precision map requires an additional Wi-Fi hotspot through the in-vehicle Internet to be updated online, and it is not integrated into its own data gateway. In other words, the Super Cruise at the time was an "external" system for the entire vehicle [5].

Fig. 2. Cadillac based on mobileye Q3 platform.

Therefore, the role of high-precision maps for assisted driving systems was not very obvious in the first generation of Super Cruise. What is really useful is the strict supervision on whether the driver maintains eyeballs on Super Cruise, which is also one of the reasons why many Tesla owners at that time blindly trusted Autopilot and were distracted to cause accidents.

On the NIO NOP and the latest enhanced version of Super Cruise, the upgrade of the electronic and electrical architecture and the stronger level of intelligent computing power for bicycles have allowed the role of high-precision maps as "further sensors" to be brought into full play.

The high-precision map achieves lane-level accuracy and can reflect geographic information such as road slope, curvature, and surrounding obstacles that cannot be reflected by ordinary maps (see Fig. 3). It can enable vehicles to have stronger global path planning capabilities: vehicles can achieve autonomy on specific road sections Change lanes and overtake to maintain a faster average speed, automatically get on and off highways or urban express road ramps and perform active speed control (see Fig. 4).

However, the current high-precision map also has its limitations. First of all, the high-precision map collection is slow to update and the collection cost is high, and there are problems with data map format exchange specifications, data interconnection standards, and car networking scenes. Therefore, the current high-precision maps for vehicles are basically offline maps. On the other hand, in accordance with national regulations, high-precision maps cannot cover all scenes. For example, the NOP of NIO cannot be used within Beijing's Fifth Ring Road. In addition, areas related to national security cannot be used for civilian purposes or can only show some elements.

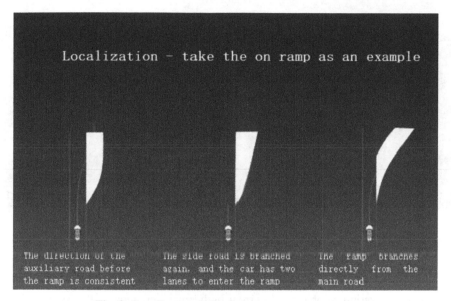

Fig. 3. Localization - take the on ramp as an example.

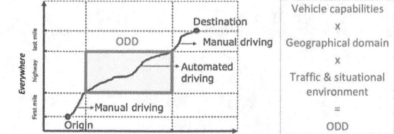

Fig. 4. Advantages of system based on high-precision map.

Therefore, at least at this stage, the use conditions and application scenarios of the integration of high-precision maps and assisted driving systems are relatively harsh. Therefore, neither Cadillac nor NIO defines the integration of high-precision maps and assisted driving systems as L3 autonomous driving, but as a functional upgrade of the current L2 assisted driving system (see Fig. 5).

Fig. 5. NIO car cabe.

4 Autonomous Driving Solution Based on Pure Vision

Because of the various problems of current high-precision maps, in theory, if a single car is smart enough, it can weaken the demand for high-precision maps to a certain

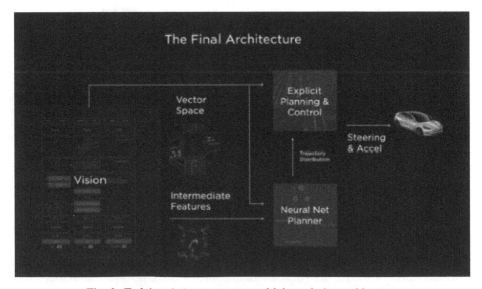

Fig. 6. Tesla's existing autonomous driving solution architecture.

extent. For example, Tesla has always insisted on using visual perception to reduce its dependence on navigation accuracy (see Fig. 6).

On the Tesla car, eight cameras are used as visual input (see Fig. 7). The image information is first mapped to the same vector space (Vector Space), complements each other, and obtains their intermediate features, and then they are incorporated into the neural network. The network planner obtains the planned path, and finally the planning control algorithm obtains the steering or acceleration/deceleration signal based on the above input.

For the lack of memory problems that may appear in the neural network of the video, Tesla also takes the kinematics parameters into consideration, and at the same time uses time or road conditions as a reference.

Therefore, it is ensured that only the features and parameters of the region of interest are input, rather than large-scale unfiltered data.

Currently, Tesla, Mobileye and Baidu Apollo Lite are the most mature solutions for pure vision autonomous driving. At present, the pure visual perception frameworks of the three companies are not completely the same, and the differences in perception frameworks directly lead to different computing power required for decision-making. To some extent, this is evidence that the pure visual route is still in its early stages [6]. The Table 1 gives a summary of the pure vision solutions in automatic driving.

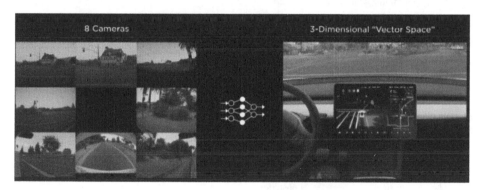

Fig. 7. Vision based autopilot system of Tesla.

The main purpose of businesses choosing pure visual solutions is to reduce costs. But the advantages of the high-precision map solution are clear at a glance. In fact, Tesla is also silently doing another thing-building its own high-precision maps. It uses various sensors in the car, and Tesla owners around the world jointly draw a high-precision map that belongs to Tesla only [7]. In the autonomous driving map industry, this "crowdsourcing model" should actually have a very important position, especially when the high-precision map collection cost is high and the update cycle is long. The acquisition mode has greater advantages [8].

Tesla first mentioned this matter when musk said Tesla wanted to "avoid potholes on the road". When Tesla owners passing through a place will avoid the same place, and Tesla's visual system also recognizes that it is a pothole on the road, the background system will mark it on the map. When other Tesla pass here, they will automatically

Table 1. List of pure vision solutions in automatic driving.

Brand	Front view camera		Side view camera		Rear view camera	Independent look around camera	Chip computing power
Apollo Lite	Wide field of vision Short focal length	1	Lateral anterior	2	1	2	< 30 Tops
	Middle field of vision Medium focal length	1	Lateral posterior	2			
	Narrow field of vision Long focal length	1					
FSD	Wide field of vision Short focal length	1	Lateral anterior	2	1	2	< 30 Tops
	Middle field of vision Medium focal length	1	Lateral posterior	2			
	Narrow field of vision Long focal length	1					
Mobileye SuperVision	Wide field of vision Short focal length	1	Lateral anterior	2	1	4	48 Tops
	Middle field of vision Medium focal length	-	Lateral posterior	2			
	Narrow field of vision Long focal length	1					

avoid it (see Fig. 8). This is in fact an upgrade of Tesla's automatic driving system, machine learning, big data backhaul and re feedback mechanism [9].

In the high-precision map crowdsourcing mode, there are currently no unified regulations on the types of data collected, accuracy, and data transmission standards. This is why the collection of high-precision maps can still only be carried out by a few qualified companies. However, Tesla does not care about these issues, and what it does is only to

Fig. 8. The simulation program tests the edge condition.

meet its own needs. Moreover, Tesla's style has always been to do it first, talk about it, and change it later [10].

Therefore, Tesla just insists not to use the high-precision maps provided by the supplier, but it uses the crowdsourcing model to draw high-precision maps to improve its own perception, but in fact it applies the idea of high-precision maps (see Fig. 9).

Fig. 9. Screenshot of Tesla FSD user video.

5   Conclusion

Is it necessary to use high-precision maps for autonomous driving? This matter is currently inconclusive. Everyone chooses their own technical routes based on their actual conditions.

High-precision maps make the perception system more powerful. If Tesla's pure visual perception technology can reach perfection, it does not require high-precision maps. Just like human driving, pure vision and traditional navigation can realize autonomous driving.

However, under current technical conditions, pure vision technology is definitely far from meeting the requirements of autonomous driving.

Of course, high-precision maps also have their limitations. Such as coverage rate, update rate and so on. But these can all be solved through crowdsourced maps.In fact, although Tesla did not buy a high-precision map from a graphic company, it is not sure whether it has used many Tesla cars to collect the road information collected by each car in real time, and generate its own pseudo-high-definition map on the server side. Fine map.

Therefore, based on the current development trend, the strategy of perception system + high-precision map will approach true autonomous driving faster than pure vision.

Acknowledgement. This research is supported by Natural Science Foundation of Hunan Province (2021JJ60005).

References

1. Wang, X., She, X., Bai, L., Qing, Y., Jiang, F.: A novel anonymous authentication scheme based on edge computing in internet of vehicles. Comput. Mater. Continua **67**(3), 3349–3361 (2021)
2. Gong, C., Yang, X., Huangfu, W., Lu, Q.: A mixture model parameters estimation algorithm for inter-contact times in internet of vehicles. Comput. Mater. Continua **69**(2), 2445–2457 (2021)
3. Chen, Z., Yan, L., Yin, S., Shi, Y.: Vehicle license plate recognition system based on deep learning in natural scene. J. Artif. Intell. **2**(4), 167–175 (2020)
4. Guo, J., Liu, Y., Li, S., Li, Z., Kherbachi, S.: Game-oriented security strategy against hotspot attacks for internet of vehicles. Comput. Mater. Continua **68**(2), 2145–2157 (2021)
5. Liu, Q., Xiang, X., Qin, J., Tan, Y., Tan, J., Luo, Y.: Coverless steganography based on image retrieval of DenseNet features and DWT sequence mapping. Knowl.-Based Syst. **192**(5), 105375–105389 (2020)
6. Ramakrishnan, U., Nachimuthu, N.: An enhanced memetic algorithm for feature selection in big data analytics with mapreduce. Intell. Autom. Soft Comput. **31**(3), 1547–1559 (2022)
7. Selvi, U., Pushpa, S.: Machine learning privacy aware anonymization using mapreduce based neural network. Intell. Autom. Soft Comput. **31**(2), 1185–1196 (2022)
8. Cui, G.R., Li, H., Zhang, Y.C., Bu, R.J., Kang, Y.: Weighted particle swarm clustering algorithm for self-organizing maps. J. Quantum Comput. **2**(2), 85–95 (2020)
9. Li, L., Wei, Y., Zhang, L., Wang, X.: Efficient Virtual Resource Allocation in Mobile Edge Networks Based on Machine Learning. J. Cyber Secur. **2**(3), 141–150 (2020)
10. Malik, M., Nandal, R., Dalal, S., Jalglan, V., Le, D.: Driving pattern profiling and classification using deep learning. Intell. Autom. Soft Comput. **28**(3), 887–906 (2021)

An Automatic Construction Technology of Chinese Knowledge Graph for Teaching Plan

Ling Zhang[1]([mail]) [iD] and Wentao Hou[2]

[1] Nanjing Vocational College of Information Technology, 99 Wenlan Road, Xianlin College Community, Nanjing, Jiangsu, People's Republic of China
597436779@qq.com
[2] S University of Waterloo, 200 University Avenue West, Waterloo, ON N2L3G1, Canada

Abstract. With the wide application of knowledge in the field of education, the demand for automatic knowledge graph construction based on educational data is becoming more and more urgent. The existing construction technology of educational Chinese knowledge graph has some problems, such as easy omission of knowledge points, low accuracy of knowledge point relationship, manual participation and so on. This paper puts forward the automatic construction technology of Chinese knowledge graph based on educational teaching plan. The automatic generation of Chinese knowledge graph based on educational teaching plan is aimed to improve teaching efficiency. This paper studies the knowledge graph technology based on teaching plan in the computer field. It automatically extracts knowledge points and the relationship between knowledge points, allocates the relationship weight according to the relationship rules, and generates the knowledge graph based on teaching plan.

Keywords: Knowledge graph · Teaching plan · HMM · Transformer

1 Introduction

Information overload has become a more and more serious problem in the process of information acquisition because the rapid development of information technology and the explosive growth of information. To solve this problem, Knowledge Graph is widely used as a systematic method to reveal the potential relationship between rich knowledge sources and can describe many kinds of entities and relationships among these entities in the real world. Knowledge Graph contains lots of triples, which contain nodes composed of entities and edges composed of relationships between entities. Now Knowledge Graph has been applied in various fields, from the initial Google search engine to the current chat robot, intelligent medical treatment, big data risk control, adaptive education and recommendation system, securities investment. Its popularity in various research fields is also increasing year by year.

At present, researchers have made various achievements in the automatic construction of English knowledge graph. However, due to the differences between Chinese and English, the automatic construction scheme of English knowledge graph is difficult to be

X. Sun et al. (Eds.): ICAIS 2022, CCIS 1586, pp. 95–105, 2022.
https://doi.org/10.1007/978-3-031-06767-9_8

directly applied to Chinese knowledge graph. The main reasons are that there is no basis for segmentation between Chinese phrases (such as spaces), Chinese Polyphonic words and the need for context to determine the meaning of words, which makes it difficult for computers to recognize meaningful words or phrases. Although some progress has been made in the research of Chinese knowledge graph, compared with other languages, the processing of Chinese text is still facing a more difficult situation. Therefore, the automatic construction of Chinese knowledge graph still has great challenges.

2   Research Status of Knowledge Graph in the Field of Education

In the field of education, with the rise of smart classroom, there are more and more research on Smart Education Based on Knowledge Graph. Accordingly, the application demand of Knowledge Graph also increases. Personalized path recommendation plays an important role in improving students' academic performance. However, the recent research on personalized path recommendation only considers the learning status of students, and does not consider the relationship between knowledge points. Article [1] proposed a method to improve personalized path recommendation by using the prerequisite dependency between students' learning status and knowledge points. The research is based on Knowledge Graph, and the experiment shows that the method of personalized recommendation based on the combination of students' learning state and knowledge map has achieved good results. Similarly, article [2] believes that most recommendation algorithms lack consideration of the content and structure of curriculum knowledge points, so it proposes an exercise recommendation algorithm based on Knowledge Graph, the algorithm uses tracking technology as an evaluation method to judge learners' ability to master knowledge points. The above research is based on Knowledge Graph.

2.1   Knowledge Annotation

In terms of annotation, semantic knowledge base is a knowledge base containing semantic annotation words and has been successfully used to a lot of natural language processing tasks. Article [3] pointed out that the existing semantic knowledge base only contains a few languages, which greatly limits the popularization and use of semantic knowledge base. In order to solve this problem, this paper proposes to build a unified semaphore knowledge base for multiple languages based on the multilingual encyclopedia dictionary Babel net: firstly, a data set is constructed as the seed of the multilingual semaphore knowledge base. On this basis, the semaphore prediction task of Babel net synonym set is proposed and formally defined for the first time, it aims to expand the seed data set into an available knowledge base; Then, two simple and effective models are proposed, which make use of different synonym sets; Finally, carry out quantitative and qualitative analysis to explore the important factors and difficulties in the task.

2.2   Knowledge Extraction

In terms of knowledge extraction, Chris quirk and other scholars pointed out that with the growth of the demand for structured knowledge, people have great interest in relationship extraction. The existing remote supervision methods do not explore the relationship extraction of cross sentences, but only extract the relationship expressed in single sentences. Even in the research of supervised learning, the extraction of cross sentence relationship has not been fully explored in article [4]. In this paper, it is the first time to use remote supervision to realize cross sentence relationship extraction. The core of the proposed method is a graph representation. This method can combine dependency and discourse relations, so as to provide a unified way to simulate the relationship within and between sentences. Extracting features from multiple paths in the graph improves the accuracy and robustness in the face of language variation and error analysis. Through remote supervision, this method extracts about 64000 different instances from about 1 million full-text PubMed Central. The accuracy of this method is increasing more than twice.

Aiming at the problem of cross sentence N-ary relationship extraction, article [5] proposed a graph based short-term memory network (LSTM) relationship extraction framework graph state LSTM. The core of the framework is a document graph. The graphical LSTM framework provides a unified way to explore different relationships, including dependencies within and between sentences, such as sequential relationships, syntactic relationships and textual relationships. This simplifies the processing of complex relationships and makes multi task learning related to relationships possible. The paper tested the framework on medical data sets to verify the effectiveness of graphical LSTM framework.

Article [6] pointed out that in the current research on N-ary relationship extraction across sentences, the typical method is to represent the input as a document graph and integrate the dependencies within and between various sentences. Although this method can use the edge of the graph to model rich language knowledge, important information may be lost in the segmentation process. Therefore, a graph state LSTM model is proposed. The graphical LSTM model uses parallel state to model each word. The advantage of the model is to retain the original graph structure and increase the computing speed by increasing parallelization. Extracting relational triples from unstructured text is the key to building large-scale knowledge graph. However, there are few existing research results on solving the problem that multiple relational triples in the same sentence share the same entity. Wei and other scholars Proposed a new cascaded binary markup framework casrel for relational triples extraction. The framework models the relationship as a function that maps the subject in the sentence to the object, and solves the overlap problem in article [7]. Experiments show that when casrel framework uses randomly initialized Bert encoder in the coding module, its performance has exceeded the most advanced methods, which shows the powerful function of the new label framework.

2.3 Entity Alignment

In terms of entity alignment, article [8] proposed a cross language entity alignment method, which aims to match entities with the same semantics in different language knowledge bases. The author believes that the knowledge graphs of different languages may have the same ontology division, which may be helpful for entity alignment, so a vector model based on trans C is proposed. Firstly, the model uses trans C and parameter sharing model to map all entities and relationships in the knowledge map to the shared low dimensional semantic space based on a set of aligned entities; then, the re initialization and soft alignment strategies are used iteratively to improve the performance of entity alignment. Experimental results show that compared with the benchmark algorithm, the model can effectively fuse ontology information and achieve better results. Fan and other scholars believe that these works not only do not make effective use of the attribute information of the graphs, but also have a negative impact on the overall model because of the great differences in the attributes of the same entity in different languages. Attention networks, which provide node level and semantic level attention mechanisms, these methods still do not consider the impact of different attributes in article [9]. Therefore, a cross language entity alignment method based on graph convolution network is proposed. By designing an attribute vector for the training of GCN (graph convolutional networks), it is found that GCN can learn the information of feature vector and attribute vector at the same time. Experiments show that this method is the best GCN alignment model.

2.4   Graph Generation

In terms of graph generation, Qiu and other scholars proposed that many current graph representation learning methods train a model for a domain or a graph, that is, these trained models are not suitable for new data outside the domain in article [10], so they designed an unsupervised graph comparison coding model GCC to capture the global topological features between different graphs. Article [11] designed the pre training task of GCC as a local subgraph structure to distinguish different points in different graphs, and used comparative learning to learn some inherent and transferable structural representations. The overall idea of GCC is to use different graphs to supervise and learn the model, so as to obtain the pre trained model, and fine tune the trained model for practical work. In the above research, advanced methods for knowledge map generation are proposed, and good results are obtained in experiments.

3   Automatic Construction of Knowledge Graph of Teaching Plan

This chapter mainly introduces the automatic construction process of Knowledge Graph of teaching plan.

3.1   Raising Questions

Teaching plan plays an important role in college teaching. It is recognized that teachers prepare it according to the content system of the course, and the knowledge difficulty involved is in line with the knowledge level of college students. At present, there are two main reasons why educational knowledge graphs cannot be used on a large scale. On the one hand, most of the existing generation technologies of educational knowledge graphs are semi-automatic generation technologies, which need more human intervention and consume human resources. On the other hand, in the existing work, the data sets used in the generation of educational knowledge graphs include teaching videos, Web links and student behavior data. It is difficult to obtain and extract relevant data and there is a data threshold.

In order to solve the above problems and promote the large-scale use of educational knowledge graph, this paper proposes an automatic generation technology of educational knowledge map based on teaching materials (KG-TF). This technology uses the teaching materials used in college teaching to generate the educational knowledge graph through natural language processing, which effectively reduces the labor cost and realizes the automatic generation of educational knowledge graph. Moreover, it is relatively easy to obtain the data set of college teaching materials and reduce the data threshold. This technology can be effectively applied to various disciplines.

3.2 Implementation Process

The implementation process of generating knowledge graph based on teaching plan used in this paper includes three parts. The main implementation process of this paper is shown (see Fig. 1).

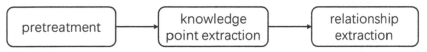

Fig. 1. Implementation process of KG-TP.

(1) Pretreatment. In order to facilitate sorting and reading, the teaching plan is usually arranged in tabular form according to units, and there are non-knowledge points such as course code, total class hours, teaching methods, evaluation methods, student activities, annotations and so on. The content of the teaching plan mentioned above cannot play a positive role in extracting relevant knowledge point information from the teaching plan. On the contrary, because its complexity will affect the accuracy of subsequent processes, it is necessary to preprocess the corresponding irrelevant parts in the teaching plan and simplify the text information in the teaching plan to ensure the accuracy of subsequent operations.

(2) Knowledge point extraction. This part includes word segmentation, annotation and knowledge point extraction. On the one hand, the knowledge point extraction part needs to segment the preprocessed teaching plan output in step (1), divide it into several tag sequences, label each tag with knowledge points, and label and distinguish the knowledge points from non-knowledge points in the teaching plan text, By training the three-layer connected hidden Markov model, a prediction model for textbook knowledge point extraction is obtained. On the other hand, the trained three-layer interconnected hidden Markov model is used to label the label sequence. The extraction of knowledge points depends on the quality and quantity of knowledge points in the training set. The use of high-quality labeling training set can effectively improve the quality of knowledge point extraction.

(3) Relationship extraction. This section uses the transformer framework to implement relationship extraction. This part takes the teaching plan text and the knowledge point pairs extracted in step (2) as the input, predicts the relationship between the knowledge

point pairs in the teaching plan based on the context attention mechanism, obtains the triplet representing the sequence of knowledge points, and finally combines all the predicted knowledge points to obtain the educational knowledge graph generated based on the teaching plan.

4   Implementation

Before extracting knowledge points, we need to preprocess the teaching plan text. Because most of the teaching plans are arranged in the form of tables, and there are non-knowledge points such as curriculum code, total class hours, teaching methods, evaluation methods, student activities and annotations, this paper first removes the non-knowledge points and extracts the table contents to form an unformatted teaching plan text. This process greatly reduces the text content to be processed in formal work.

4.1   Extracting Knowledge Point Entities

Word segmentation is the first core task of knowledge graph construction. Unlike English sentences, each word is divided by spaces. It is difficult to define the boundary of phrases in Chinese. Although the word is the smallest unit in Chinese, the semantic expression in the text takes the phrase as the smallest unit. Therefore, when dealing with Chinese text, we need to segment the text and divide the phrases in the whole sentence. The

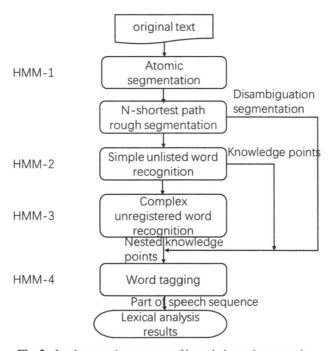

Fig. 2. Implementation process of knowledge point extraction.

work in this part of this paper uses the method proposed in paper 11. In addition, the vocabulary in the dictionary is not only the basis for word segmentation of the text, but also an important basis for extracting keywords. The quality of the dictionary will directly affect the quality of the final knowledge graph. Firstly, this paper introduces the dictionary, uses the special dictionary in the field of electronic computer, and simplifies and supplements the dictionary to make the words contained more accurate. The paper proposed a method to integrate word segmentation, ambiguous word segmentation and part of speech tagging into a whole algorithm system. The algorithm system is based on hierarchical hidden Markov model. The implementation process of the algorithm system is shown (see Fig. 2).

Firstly, the input text is atomic segmented in the preprocessing stage, that is, the input text content is segmented into atomic unit sequence. Atomic unit sequence is the smallest word segmentation unit. Atomic units can be recombined in the word segmentation process, but cannot be split. Using the method of n-shortest path rough segmentation, the best n rough segmentation results for disambiguation can be obtained; After the rough classification result set is obtained, the common non nested knowledge points and more complex nested knowledge points are identified by the bottom hidden Markov

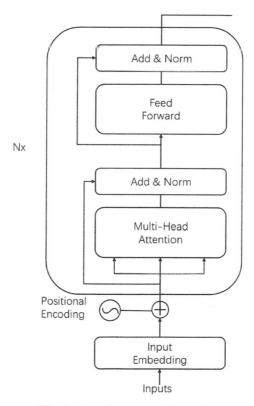

Fig. 3. Transformer model encoder.

model and the high-level hidden Markov model respectively; Finally, the results of word segmentation are labeled.

4.2   Extract the Relationship Between Knowledge Points and Entities

In this paper, the transformer model in Deep KE3 is used to extract the relationship between key concepts based on the relationship between knowledge points extracted from teaching materials. The architecture of encoder in transformer model is shown (see Fig. 3).

In the process of extracting the relationship between knowledge points, the word vector is processed first, and the word vector is used as the input. Then the text and key concept information are encoded through the encoder part of the model, the multi head attention module is used to repeatedly extract the important features in the text, and the output and input of the self-attention layer are spliced and regularized through the superposition residual network. The stacked multi-layer attention mechanism makes the extraction of key information in sentences more effective. Finally, the result is connected with the full connection layer, and then the final classification result of the relationship between knowledge points and entities is obtained.

4.3   Relationship Extraction Rules

This paper studies the teaching plan with significant hierarchical structure for the teaching purpose of electronic computer. The structure of this kind of teaching plan is shown (see Fig. 4). In this paper, the hierarchical structure of teaching plan is divided into four kinds: upper and lower level relationship, key and difficult relationship, same level relationship and interlayer relationship. The key and difficult relationship belongs to the upper and lower level relationship, but the weight is greater.

Upper and lower level relationship: that is, the relationship between two entities at adjacent levels. For example, if entity a is in the first layer and entities E and F are in the second layer, entity A and entity E (or F) belong to the upper and lower level relationship. For two entities with upper and lower level relationship, there is a prerequisite relationship between them. In this paper, the weight between entities with upper and lower level relationship is assigned as 1.

Key and difficult relationship: the key and difficult points are important parts of the chapter, which need to be explained by teachers and mastered by students. Therefore, the key and difficult points are extracted in this paper. The key and difficult points belong to the superior and subordinate relations with the second and third levels. In this paper, the weight of the key and difficult points is assigned as 0.8.

Same level relationship: that is, the relationship between entities at the same level. For example, entities A and B are in the first level and belong to the same level relationship. Similarly, entities E and F belong to the same level relationship. For two entities at the same level, because they appear under the same heading, it is defined that there is a weak prerequisite relationship between them, a small weight value is given, and the former entity is defined as the precursor entity of the latter entity. In this paper, the weight between entities with upper and lower level relationship is assigned as 0.3.

Hierarchical relationship: that is, the relationship between entities in two non-adjacent levels. For example, entities A and D are located in the first and third layers respectively, belonging to the compartment relationship. This paper does not judge the entities with this relationship.

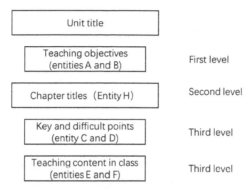

Fig. 4. Schematic diagram of teaching plan level.

The specific assignment rules of different hierarchical relationships are shown in Table 1.

Table 1. Table captions should be placed above the tables.

Relationship description	Relationship example	Weight value
Upper and lower level relationship	A < -H	1
Key and difficult relationship	H < -C	0.8
Same level relationship	E < -F	0.3
Hierarchical relationship	A < -E	无

5 Testing and Summary

Using the method of this paper, a knowledge graph is constructed for the teaching plan of Natural Language Processing (See Fig. 5).

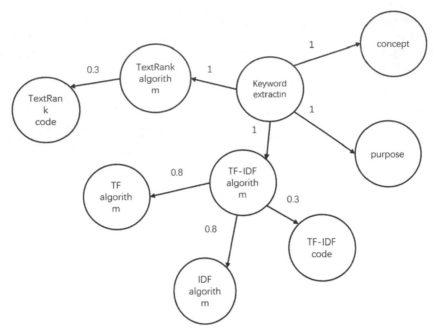

Fig. 5. Part of Knowledge Graph based on Teaching Plan.

Figure 5 is a partial knowledge map of the keyword extraction algorithm in unit 4. Firstly, preprocess the teaching plan text, remove the content of non-knowledge points, extract entities, extract entity relationships and assign values. Through the experiments, the method proposed in this paper can realize the automatic construction of Chinese knowledge map of teaching plan.

Acknowledgement. This paper is supported by Jiangsu provincial colleges of Natural Science General Program (No.20KJB520019, Ling Zhang).

References

1. Lv, P., Wang, X.X., Xu, J.: Utilizing knowledge graph and student testing behavior data for personalized exercise recommendation. In: Proceedings of the The ACM TURC 2018 Conference (SIGCSE China), pp. 53–59 (2018)
2. Hu, H.: Research on recommendation of personalized exercises based on knowledge graph. Master Dissertation, Sichuan Normal University, China (2019)
3. Qi, F., Chang, L., Sun, M.: Towards building a multilingual sememe knowledge base: Predicting sememes for BabelNet synsets. In: Proceedings of the AAAI Conference on Artificial Intelligence, vol. 34, pp. 8624–8631 (2020)
4. Chris, Q., Hoifung, P.: Distant supervision for relation extraction beyond the sentence boundary. In: Proceedings of the 15th Conference of the European Chapter of the Association for Computational Linguistics, pp. 1171–1182 (2017)

5. Peng, N., Hoifung, P.: Cross-sentence n-ary relation extraction with graph LSTMs. Assoc. Comput. Linguist. **5**(1), 101–115 (2017)
6. Song, L., Zhang, Y., Wang, Z.: N-ary relation extraction using graph state LSTM. In: Proceedings of the Conference on Empirical Methods in Natural Language Processing, pp. 2226–2235 (2018)
7. Wei, Z., Su, J., Wang, Y.: A novel cascade binary tagging framework for relational triple extraction. In: Proceedings of the 58th Annual Meeting of the Association for Computational Linguistics, pp. 1476–1488 (2019)
8. Kang, S., Ji, L., Li, Z.: Iterative cross-lingual entity alignment based on trans C. ICE Trans. Inf. Syst. **103**(5), 1002–1005 (2020)
9. Xiong, F., Gao, J.: Entity alignment for cross-lingual knowledge graph with graph convolutional network. In: Proceedings of the Conference on Empirical Methods in Natural Language Processing, pp. 349–357 (2018)
10. Qiu, J., Chen, Q., Dong, Y.: GCC: Graph contrastive coding for graph neural network pretraining. In: Proceedings of the 26th ACM SIGKDD Conference on Knowledge Discovery and Data Mining, pp. 1150–1160 (2020)
11. Liu, Q.: Chinese Lexical Analysis Using Cascaded Hidden Markov Model. J. Comput. Res. Dev. **41**(8), 1421–1429 (2004)

Research on Cloud Office Resource Allocation Algorithm Based on Correction Weight PSO

Guozhen Wang[1], Chun Wang[2], Tong Gan[3(✉)], and Jiahang An[4]

[1] KylinSoft Corporation, No. 9. Beisihuanxi Road, Yingu Building, Haidian District, Beijing 100083, People's Republic of China

[2] Beijing Jingneng Information Technology Co., Ltd., Building 3, Yard 32, Jinfu Road, Shijingshan District, Beijing 100043, People's Republic of China

[3] Beijing Metro Consultancy Corporation Ltd., Beijing 100071, China
alanshearer@126.com

[4] School of Computer and Communication Engineering, University of Science and Technology Beijing, Beijing 100083, China

Abstract. With the development of science and technology, cloud computing technology has changed people's office methods. People begin to use cloud services to realize remote collaborative office, which can save costs and improve work efficiency. However, users' demand for cloud office is increasing, and their requirements for cloud office services are becoming higher. Aiming at the problem of uneven resource allocation of cloud office services, this paper proposes a cloud resource allocation algorithm CWPSO based on weight correction. This algorithm improves the problem of fixed weight of PSO algorithm in the process of particle update, so that the algorithm can search the target faster. Simulation results show that the performance of the resource allocation strategy obtained by the proposed algorithm is improved by 6.08% in terms of processing time.

Keywords: Cloud office · PSO · Resource allocation

1 Introduction

With the development of modern technology, people's office style has changed greatly. Cloud office is an emerging office mode. With the development of Internet and cloud computing technology, the number of users of cloud office software is increasing rapidly, and the number of users using cloud office technology will exceed 1 billion worldwide [1, 2]. In particular, affected by the epidemic this year, both companies and universities have begun to apply cloud office technology to achieve remote synchronization. However, as the number of cloud office users increases, users have higher requirements for cloud office technology [3]. On the one hand, users want to synchronize content more quickly and efficiently, so they need lower delay; On the other hand, with the increase of business, service providers hope to realize user needs in a lower cost way, so more efficient resource allocation is needed [4]. In the future, the way people cooperate to complete tasks will change greatly. Different from the traditional offline interaction mode, each

X. Sun et al. (Eds.): ICAIS 2022, CCIS 1586, pp. 106–117, 2022.
https://doi.org/10.1007/978-3-031-06767-9_9

person uploads their tasks to the cloud computing devices for processing. The advantage of this is that it can not only reduce the cost of physical devices, but also greatly improve the processing efficiency of work tasks [5].

Sharmin et al. proposed a new algorithm combining PSO and GA algorithm to achieve load balancing of cloud computing infrastructure and efficient resource management [6]. Wang et al. proposed a dynamic hierarchical resource allocation algorithm for collaborative tasks of multiple cloud nodes. The algorithm uses fuzzy pattern recognition to dynamically divide tasks and nodes into different levels according to computing power and storage factors. The algorithm uses dynamic hierarchy to reduce communication traffic in the process of resource allocation [7]. Bano et al. Introduced the concept of fog computing and proposed a cloud computing platform, which uses remote servers to residential areas, provides their services efficiently through the Internet, manages energy consumption by reducing the time and cost of end users, connects to the fog edge, and uses different load balancing and optimization technologies to efficiently allocate resources to intelligent residential areas. They proposed a random load balancing algorithm for reliable and efficient task scheduling to overcome the delay rate and cost of users in cloud computing environment [8]. The algorithm proposed by Tiwari et al. can effectively minimize the response and migration time, maximize the reliability and throughput, and ensure the effective utilization of virtual machine resources [9].

Although many studies have solved the problem of resource allocation in cloud computing, in the future cloud office scenario, the mapping relationship between users and tasks is not simple one-to-one. Many times, a user will submit multiple tasks, which will be a new challenge to the optimization strategy of the system [10, 11]. In addition, using more efficient algorithms to solve the problem of resource allocation is also an important research direction in cloud office scenarios.

In this paper, we propose a cloud office resource allocation algorithm based on correction weighted particle swarm optimization. The main work can be divided into the followings:

1) Cloud office task model: office tasks have several typical characteristics, such as inconsistent task volume, large number of office users, processing time constraints, etc. How to convert complex cloud office tasks into mathematical models is of great help to solve the problem of cloud office resource allocation. This paper establishes a cloud office task model from the aspects of users, task volume, cloud computing resources processing efficiency and processing time, and uses the proposed resource allocation algorithm to solve the problem and obtains satisfactory results.
2) Cloud office resource allocation algorithm: particle swarm optimization algorithm has the advantage of fast convergence, but this algorithm is easy to produce local optimal solution. Obviously, this is not the most appropriate result of the resource allocation algorithm. Based on the particle swarm optimization algorithm, this paper uses the thinking of modifying the weight to improve the weight update process in the algorithm iteration, and adds the correction parameters to make the weight update closer to the optimal solution.

The remainder of this paper is organized as follows. In Section II, we introduce the cloud office service architecture and PSO algorithm. Section III establish cloud office task model and algorithm improvement. In Section IV, we evaluate the performance of improved algorithm. Finally, Section VI concludes this paper.

2 Related Work

2.1 Cloud Office Services

Cloud office service is a new office mode. Figure 1 shows the service mode of cloud office. Different staff directly access the cloud through the client or web page, and use the cloud computing resources to complete the corresponding tasks. The working mode of Cloud office is showed in Fig. 1. Cloud office services have the following advantages [12, 13]:

1) Reduce costs. Cloud office is to open the virtualized hardware settings to users in the form of leasing on the basis of cloud computing. In the traditional working mode, to complete a multi person collaborative task between staff, it is necessary to equip each person with a high-performance equipment, or multiple people use a high-performance equipment at the same time. These two working modes cannot guarantee the requirements of efficiency and cost at the same time. Cloud office services provide convenience for these users. They can rent high-performance computing resources at a cheap price and provide permissions to multiple users at the same time. Now, when users are performing collaborative tasks, they only need to input tasks to the cloud to realize remote collaborative work, so as to reduce cost investment.
2) Improve efficiency. Cloud office is an open and secure collaborative service mode. When the cloud receives requests from different tasks, these tasks will be allocated to different virtual machines for separate processing [14]. Cloud office service supports real-time online work of multiple people, which means that a user can view the task progress of other users at any time to facilitate real-time communication. The open service mode can reduce redundant labor in task processing. Cloud office service allocates tasks to different virtual machines through algorithms for synchronous processing, completes tasks in the shortest time and feeds back to users, which will improve the efficiency of the whole project.
3) Energy saving and environmental protection [15]. In the traditional working mode, each user is equipped with a high-performance computer to ensure work efficiency. However, the energy consumption of high-performance computers is also huge, which will produce a lot of excessive waste of power resources. In addition, replacing computers will also produce a large number of waste parts. Although the environmental protection department has a way to recycle these metals, it will still have a certain impact on the environment. Cloud office service only needs an ordinary computer to complete the task, and the energy consumption will be greatly reduced.

The cloud office market has great potential. In the face of the needs of more and more users, the cloud office service is also further improved. Many users have put forward a large number of software function requirements. They are no longer satisfied with the IaaS resources provided on the cloud. Instead, they need software services that are available out of the box and quickly provided on demand to meet their direct business needs.

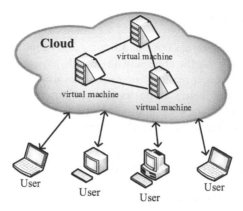

Fig. 1. Cloud office.

2.2 Particle Swarm Optimization

Particle swarm optimization (PSO) algorithm is a classical intelligent optimization algorithm [16]. It has the advantages of fast convergence speed and low complexity in dealing with optimization problems. It has good applications in many fields such as Internet of vehicles, Internet, deep learning and so on. Inspired by the predation behavior of birds, the creation of particle swarm optimization algorithm will transfer information between different individuals in the process of looking for food, so as to help each bird correct the target in the direction close to the food. Each information transfer is equivalent to an information iteration in the algorithm. Through continuous information sharing and correction, the birds will search the target food in the effective area, that is, the optimal solution in the optimization problem.

According to the above principles, within the effective range, each particle of the particle swarm can be regarded as a bird, and each particle has the potential to find the optimal solution. The optimization process is to express the distance between the bird and the food through the fitness function. In particle swarm optimization, each particle has three independent attributes: position, speed and fitness value. These attributes play a key role in whether the particle can find the optimal solution.

We use the parameter $X_i = (x_{i1}, x_{i2}, \cdots, x_{iD})^T$ to describe the position, which represents the position of a d-dimensional particle I in the solution space. Similarly, the particle speed can be expressed by $V_i = (V_{i1}, V_{i2}, \cdots, V_{iD})^T$, and the fitness value is a function f reflecting the current advantages and disadvantages of the particle. Without an iteration, the position and velocity of the particles will be redefined [17]:

$$V_{id}^{o+1} = \omega V_{id}^o + c_1 r_1 (P_{id}^o - X_{id}^o) + c_2 r_2 (P_{gd}^o - X_{gd}^o) \tag{1}$$

$$X_{id}^{o+1} = X_{id}^o + V_{id}^{o+1} \tag{2}$$

where ω is the inertia weight of particles, indicating the speed of each particle's speed update. P_i and P_g represent the individual extremum and group extremum of particles respectively, which are used to correct the speed update. c_1 and c_2 are nonnegative constants, called acceleration factors; r_1 and r_2 are random numbers distributed in the interval [0,1].

Particle swarm optimization has obvious advantages. The initial particles have strong randomness. At the same time, the algorithm has simple structure and fast convergence speed. However, the convergence speed of particle swarm optimization algorithm is limited by the setting of parameters. If the deviation of parameter setting is large, it may not converge quickly and appear local optimal solution. In this paper, we will optimize the weight parameters to improve the overall performance of the algorithm.

3 Cloud Office Resource Optimization Algorithm

3.1 Cloud Office Service Model

In the cloud data center, the information submitted by users is stored in a specific buffer in the form of workflow, which is composed of multiple tasks [18]. The resource management of cloud data center is to allocate the workflow to the virtual machine through some reasonable resource allocation methods, so as to reduce the completion time of workflow and save costs. The cloud service resource allocation diagram is shown in Fig. 2.

Cloud office needs to provide services to multiple users at the same time. n user sets are defined as $User = \{U_1, U_2 \ldots, U_n\}$. In the cloud office scenario, each user will deploy multiple tasks at the same time. The l task group of the i-th user is represented by $Task_{il} = \{R_{i1}, R_{i2}, \ldots, R_{il}\}$. Each task is independent of each other, expressed as $Task_n = \{Task_1, Task_2, \ldots Task_i, \ldots, Task_n\}$. These tasks will be allocated to different

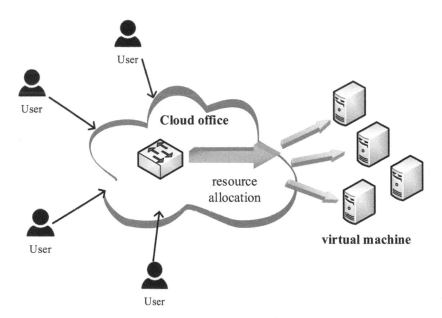

Fig. 2. Cloud office task allocation.

resource pools for processing. In order to minimize the cost and improve the system stability, each virtual machine can only process one task at the same time. Here, it is assumed that a total of k virtual machines provide computing services, which is defined as xs. Each different virtual machine has different processing capabilities, so our goal is to allocate these tasks to the appropriate virtual machine for processing, so as to obtain the optimal resource allocation strategy.

Because the number of tasks to be deployed by each user is different, but each task is independent, the task collection of each user can be assigned to different virtual machines. The tasks of all users can be merged, which are represented by $Task_m = \{R_1, R_2, \ldots, R_m\}$, where m is the total number of tasks, and the task quantity of the m-th task is represented by $Task - Volume_m$.

The key index to evaluate the performance of resource allocation strategy is the efficiency of processing tasks, that is, the processing time of a single task. The processing time of a single task is expressed as:

$$T'_{solve-m} = \frac{Task - Volume_m}{E_k} \tag{3}$$

where E_k is the task processing speed of virtual machine k. In the actual task processing process, there are still some unstable factors, such as temperature and power fluctuation, which will affect the performance of computing resources. Therefore, in the process of computing time, it is also necessary to add random interference to thse computing power, which will be more in line with the real cloud office scene. The processing time of a single task after adding interference is expressed as:

$$T_{solve-m} = \frac{Task - Volume_m}{(E_k + \varphi_k)} \tag{4}$$

where φ_k indicates the interference in virtual machine k. Thus, it can be obtained that the processing time of the k-th virtual machine after processing the assigned task is:

$$T_{Vk} = \sum_{i=1}^{q} T_{solve-i} \tag{5}$$

where q represents the number of tasks assigned to the virtual machine. Cloud office services provide virtualized computing resources for working user groups. Therefore, the overall performance should focus on the time required to complete all tasks:

$$T_{all} = \max(T_{Vk}), k = 1, 2, \ldots, k \tag{6}$$

So far, it is clear that the goal we need to optimize is the shortest processing time.

$$f(k) = \min[\max(T_{Vk})] \tag{7}$$

3.2 Correction Weight PSO (CWPSO)

In the later stage of PSO iteration [16], the particle position is very close to the target position. In order to avoid the particle speed missing the target position too fast and increase redundant calculation, the more iterations, the smaller the range of speed change. If the value of the initial weight is too small, the particles will fall into the local optimal position, so they cannot correctly search the global optimal solution. Therefore, our goal is to make the particles traverse the effective range and obtain excellent convergence speed by modifying the change of weight.

The process of cloud office service resource allocation using CWPSO is shown in Fig. 3. It is mainly divided into the following steps:

1) Generate initialization population. In order to make the particles traverse the complete search range as much as possible, at the beginning of the algorithm, we generate the first batch of particles in a random way, update their position and speed based on the initial position of these particles, and search the position of the optimal solution in space.
2) Calculate the fitness value. Fitness value is an intuitive index to evaluate the position of each particle, so how to calculate the fitness value is the key of this algorithm. In Sect. 3.1, we have obtained the calculation formula of task completion time index. Our goal is to improve the efficiency of cloud office service. Therefore, the smaller the processing time, the smaller the fitness value, indicating the better performance of the algorithm. Use o to represent the current number of iterations, and the fitness

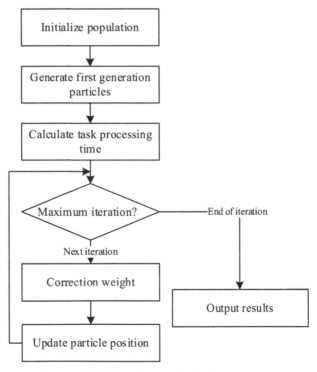

Fig. 3. CWPSO optimizes cloud office resources.

function is expressed as:

$$f(o) = \min[\max(T_{Vo})] \tag{8}$$

3) Update particle position and velocity. According to the formula (1), the speed and position of particles in the next iteration can be updated. In this process, the setting of parameters has a great impact In the traditional PSO, parameters are fixed and need to be adjusted many times to improve the performance of the algorithm. PSO algorithm is easy to fall into local optimization in the later stage of convergence, which is mostly caused by incorrect parameter setting. In this paper, in order to improve the performance of the algorithm and avoid the difficulty of correcting the weight for many times, we make an active correction to the weight when updating each iteration. This correction is evaluated according to the previous iteration results, so as to control to speed up or slow down the particle speed. The inertia weight update method as follow.

$$\omega'_o = \omega_{o-1}\alpha_o \tag{9}$$

where α_o is the correction coefficient, which is expressed as

$$\alpha_o = \begin{cases} \dfrac{|T_{v-1} - T_{0-2}|}{|T_{o-1} - T_{\min}|} & T_{o-1} > T_{\min} \\ 1 & T_{o-1} = T_{\min} \end{cases} \tag{10}$$

Only when the number of iterations is higher than 2, the correction mechanism will be punished. The speed update can be further expressed as:

$$V_{id}^{o+1} = \omega_{o-1}\alpha_o V_{id}^o + c_1 r_1 (P_{id}^o - X_{id}^o) + c_2 r_2 (P_{gd}^o - X_{gd}^o) \tag{11}$$

There are also correction coefficients in PSO algorithm. According to the individual extreme value and group extreme value generated in each iteration, the speed is corrected by weight $c_1 r_1$ and $c_2 r_2$. However, this correction is rigid and fixed, because at the beginning of the iteration, the group needs to rely on divergent individuals to judge the target position, but at the end of the iteration, the group extreme value has a greater effect on individuals approaching the target, and the relationship between groups and individuals cannot be fixed. We redefine the determination of these two coefficients in the improved algorithm, and the speed update is further expressed as:

$$V_{id}^{o+1} = \omega_{o-1}\alpha_o V_{id}^o + \frac{c_1 r_1}{o}(P_{id}^o - X_{id}^o) + c_2 r_2 \cdot \frac{o_{\max}}{o_{\max} - o + 1}(P_{gd}^o - X_{gd}^o) \tag{12}$$

where $o_{\max}$ represents the maximum number of iterations.

4) End of iteration. When the algorithm reaches the maximum number of iterations, it means that the particle swarm optimization process is over. At this time, the position of the optimal particle is the optimal solution sought by the algorithm.

4 Simulation Verification

The algorithm proposed in this paper modifies the parameter weight on the basis of PSO algorithm. This process does not change the overall iteration mode of PSO algorithm, so the time complexity is still $O(N * D)$. Although the time complexity is the same, the algorithm proposed in this paper optimizes the speed update mechanism and can reach the convergence limit of the algorithm at a faster speed.

We want to verify that the CWPSO algorithm proposed in this paper has faster convergence speed and better performance. In this section, we set up another two algorithms PSO and EPSO for comparison. EPSO algorithm introduces the information entropy model into the particle swarm optimization algorithm, and according to the characteristics of aggregation in the particle swarm search process, then optimizes the search process in stages. In the first stage, the difference of entropy generated by particle iteration is introduced into the particle swarm optimization algorithm, and then the inertia weight value in the algorithm is adjusted appropriately; In the second stage, the inertia weight is reset at an appropriate time by using the information of the change of the direct value of particle swarm optimization; In the third stage, a truncation strategy is adopted to reduce invalid iterations. Compared with PSO algorithm, EPSO algorithm not only improves the solution accuracy of particles, but also speeds up the convergence speed of particles. At the same time, due to the timely adjustment and reset of the algorithm, the efficiency of the algorithm is improved. First, we need to agree on the original parameters of the algorithm. The parameter settings are shown in the table below Table 1:

In this simulation, we choose to set the initial weight parameters. In order to more comprehensively verify the performance of the algorithm, we set the task volume between 200–1000 to verify the performance of the algorithm for different tasks. In addition, we test the performance of CWPSO algorithm under different population numbers.

Table 1. Parameter setting.

Parameter	Value
$c_1 、 c_2$	1.4,1.5
$r_1 、 r_2$	1.5,1.4
ω	0.5
iterations	100
Task-volume	[200,1000]
Population number	100 、 200 、 300

Firstly, we compare the convergence speed of CWPSO and PSO algorithm. In Fig. 4, we can intuitively see that CWPSO completes the convergence faster than PSO. The optimal value is 114ms after 18 iterations of CWPSO and 121ms after 22 iterations of PSO. The difference between the optimal values is because we added random interference during modeling, so the difference between the optimal values converged at a single time does not mean that the results obtained by PSO algorithm are bad, which needs to be verified many times later. After we modify the parameter weight, the convergence speed of CWPSO is faster in the early stage and more gentle in the later stage. The simulation results meet our expectations for the algorithm. Next, through comparative experiments, we verify the impact of different population numbers and tasks on the performance of the algorithm.

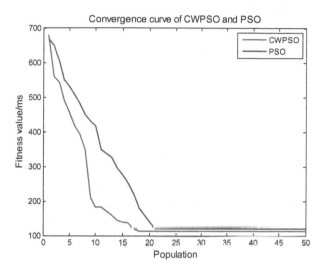

Fig. 4. Convergence curve of algorithm.

Figure 5 shows the performance of the three algorithms when dealing with different tasks. The population of the algorithms is fixed to 100. It is obvious that the cloud office resource allocation strategy obtained by CWPSO algorithm has good performance. Compared with PSO algorithm, the task processing time is reduced by 6.08%. Compared with EPSO algorithm, the performance is further improved, but when the amount of tasks increases, the performance difference between the two algorithms is not significant.

Figure 6 shows the performance of the three algorithms with different population numbers. When the population is 100 and 200, the CWPSO algorithm proposed in this paper has good performance, which shows that when the population is small, the CWPSO algorithm can better approach the optimal solution. However, when the population reaches 300, the performance of CWPSO decreases. We analyze that the reason for this result is that the speed of CWPSO algorithm is too fast in the early stage of convergence. If the population size is too large, some particles will fall into the local optimal solution. However, the smaller the population, the lower the complexity of the algorithm and the lower the loss of computing resources. Therefore, CWPSO also has good performance in reducing resource consumption.

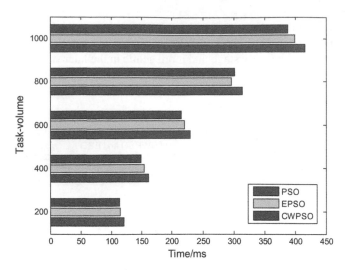

Fig. 5. Time of different tasks volume.

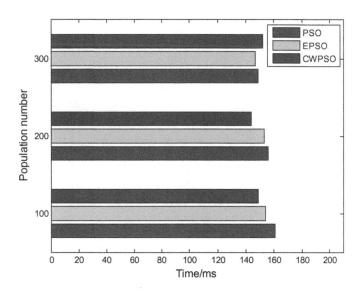

Fig. 6. Time of different population number.

5   Conclusion

Aiming at the problem of uneven resource allocation in cloud office services, this paper proposes CWPSO algorithm to optimize the allocation strategy between virtual machine resources and tasks. Firstly, according to the task processing flow of cloud office users, we establish a cloud office task resource allocation model. Secondly, based on this model, the improved CWPSO algorithm is used to optimize the resource allocation strategy, and the efficiency of the algorithm is improved by modifying the selection of weight value in the particle velocity update mechanism. Finally, through simulation, the convergence speed of CWPSO algorithm is 6.08% higher than that of PSO algorithm, and the processing speed of resource allocation strategy is also improved.

References

1. Tolsdorf, J., Dehling, F., Feth, D.: Benutzerfreundlicher datenschutz in cloud-basierten office-paketen. Datenschutz und Datensicherheit-dud **45**(1), 33–39 (2021)
2. Bhatia, M., Sood, S.K.: Exploring temporal analytics in fog-cloud architecture for smart office healthcare. Mobile Networks Appl. **24**(4), 1392–1410 (2019)
3. Masdari, M., Khoshnevis, A.: A survey and classification of the workload forecasting methods in cloud computing. Clust. Comput. **23**(4), 2399–2424 (2019). https://doi.org/10.1007/s10 586-019-03010-3
4. Sharkh, M.A., Kanso, A., Shami, A., Öhlén, P.: Building a cloud on earth: A study of cloud computing data center simulators. Comput. Netw. **108**, 78–96 (2016)
5. Sun, P.J.: Research on the trade-off between privacy and trust in cloud computing. IEEE Access **7**, 10428–10441 (2019)
6. Sheuly, S.S., Bankarusamy, S., Begum, S., Behnam, M.: Resource allocation in industrial cloud computing using artificial intelligence algorithms. In: Proceedings of the SCAI, pp. 128–136 (2015)
7. Wang, Z.J., Su, X.X.: Dynamically hierarchical resource-allocation algorithm in cloud computing environment. J. Supercomput. **71**(7), 2748–2766 (2015)
8. Bano, H., Javaid, N., Tehreem, K., Ansar, K., Zahid, M., Nazar, T.: Cloud computing based resource allocation by random load balancing technique. In: Proceedings of the International Conference on Broad- Band and Wireless Computing, Communication and Applications, pp. 28–39. Springer (2018)
9. Tiwari, P.K., Joshi, S.: Dynamic management of resources in cloud computing. Int. J. Softw. Innovation, IJSI **8**, 65–81 (2020)
10. Chuka-Maduji, N., Anu, V.: Cloud computing security challenges and related defensive measures: A survey and taxonomy. SN Comput. Sci. **2**(4), 1–17 (2021)
11. Kushwah, G.S., Ranga, V.: Optimized extreme learning machine for detecting DDoS attacks in cloud computing. Comput. Secur. **105**, 102260 (2021)
12. Zhu, Y., Wu, W., Wu, L., Wang, L., Wang, J.: SmartPrint: A cloud print system for office. In: Proceedings of the IEEE 9th International Conference on Mobile Ad-hoc and Sensor Networks, pp. 95–100 (2013)
13. Shah, S.D.A., Gregory, M.A., Li, S.: Cloud-native network slicing using software defined networking based multi-access edge computing: A survey. IEEE Access **9**, 10903–10924 (2021)
14. Jeong, Y.S., Park, J.H.: High availability and efficient energy consumption for cloud computing service with grid infrastructure. Comput. Electr. Eng. **39**(1), 15–23 (2013)
15. Elmroth, E., Leitner, P., Schulte, S., Venugopal, S.: Connecting fog and cloud computing. IEEE Cloud Comput. **4**(2), 22–25 (2017)
16. Khennak, I., Drias, H.: An accelerated PSO for query expansion in web information retrieval: Application to medical dataset. Appl. Intell. **47**(3), 793–808 (2017). https://doi.org/10.1007/s10489-017-0924-1
17. Fu, Y.Y., Wu, C.J., Chien, T.L., Ko, C.N.: Integration of PSO and GA for optimum design of fuzzy PID controllers in a pendubot system. Artif. Life Robot. **13**(1), 223–227 (2008)
18. Ye, K.Z., Htun, K.M., Htet, Z., Maung, S.M.: Officer profile management system using by cloud computing services. In: Proceedings of the Conference on Complex, Intelligent, and Software Intensive Systems, pp. 832–841. Springer (2018)

Analysis of Wind Speed Characteristics During Typhoon Rammasun: A Case Study of Qinzhou, Guangxi

Mingxuan Zhu[1], Aodi Fu[1], Wenzheng Yu[1(✉)], Xin Yao[1], and Hanxiaoya Zhang[2]

[1] School of Geographical Sciences, Nanjing University of Information Science and Technology, Nanjing 210044, China
ywzheng519@126.com
[2] Faculty of Science, The University of Auckland, Auckland 1010, New Zealand

Abstract. The gust coefficients of different wind speeds at different heights were analyzed by using the data of Qinzhou station and wind tower, and the extrapolation function was constructed to restore the 10-min average maximum wind speeds at 80 m height of wind tower during Rammasun landing. Then the wind shear index of each height was calculated based on the lidar data, and the average maximum wind speed within 10 min at each height during typhoon landing was obtained, and the air density was corrected with the results. The results show that the maximum wind speeds of different heights in ten minutes are 30.5 m/s, 30.9 m/s, 31.4 m/s, 31.9 m/s, 32.6 m/s, 33.4 m/s and 35.1 m/s, respectively. The average maximum wind speed in ten minutes at different heights of the wind tower was corrected, and the extreme values were 28.6 m/s, 29.2 m/s, 29.6 m/s, 30.1 m/s, 30.6 m/s, 31.2 m/s, 32.2 m/s, 33.5 m/s.

Keywords: Typhoon Rammasun · Gust factor · Wind shear index

1 Introduction

Wind shear index and gust coefficient are two important indexes to reflect typhoon intensity. Wind shear index represents the speed of wind speed changing with height, which plays an important role in estimating wind power generation and evaluating wind energy resources [1–3]. Based on the wind speed data of 356 m weather tower in Shenzhen, Zhang Qing et al. analyzed and concluded that the wind profile index of horizontal wind near the ground in Shenzhen decreased with the increase of height and wind speed during the landing of Typhoon "Manksteen". Yang Rui et al. analyzed the influence of wind shear effect on blade structure of wind turbine based on the layering model of 5WM horizontal axis wind turbine blade, and concluded that wind shear effect would have an impact on blade modal frequency and blade tip deformation [4, 5]. Gustiness coefficient is a measure of wind sudden and is an important basis for evaluating engineering structure design [6, 7]. Based on 10 min wind speed data of meteorological stations from 2011 to 2013, Yang Mingji analyzed the gust coefficient characteristics of cold air, tropical cyclone and strong convective gale on land and offshore in Zhejiang Province, and concluded that the gust coefficient on offshore sea was less than 1.5. Wen Lin studied the relationship between gust factor and average wind speed, observation height and gust time interval under different underlying surface conditions by using the observation data of four-layer ultrasonic anemometer of typhoon [8, 9].

Threat mason is logged in guangxi province since the founding of new China and the influence of the typhoon, the most destructive researchers based on coefficient of wind shear index and gust Rammasun study interlaminar fold [10, 11]. situated ho-fai wong, etc. Based on the wind profile index, and turbulence intensity, gust coefficient using threat mason during login Xuwen county, Guangdong province town in the west wind observation data, The relationship between wind profile index and rough length, turbulence intensity and gust coefficient and different strong wind regions is obtained by analyzing the strong wind characteristics near the formation of "Rammasun" [12]. Won etc. Based on the index of wind shear, turbulence intensity, gust coefficient and wind direction, using Rammasun Guangdong Xuwen landing situated during the mighty wind observation data, points the wind cutting table index such as spatial and temporal variations of four parameters, it is concluded that wind shear index compared to the long under the trimming index change of the typhoon, gust coefficient and turbulent intensity decreases with the increase of the height, the wind clockwise [13–15].The above studies provide theoretical and methodological support for analyzing the characteristics of typhoon Rammasun landing in Qinzhou, Guangxi.

In this paper, the gust coefficients of wind speeds at different levels in each height of the wind tower were analyzed based on the data of Qinzhou Wind tower in Guangxi province in 2017, 2018 and 2019 and the data of Qinzhou Station in 2014. The extrapolation function was constructed to restore the 10-min average maximum wind speed at 80 m height of the wind tower during Rammasun's landing. Then the wind shear index of each height was calculated based on the lidar data, and the average maximum wind speed within 10 min at each height during typhoon landing was obtained, and the air density was corrected with the results.

2 Research Methods

2.1 Gust Factor

In the process of strong wind, gust variation is often one of the important causes of wind disasters, and gust factors are usually used to represent the gust characteristics of wind [16, 17]. Gust factor is defined as the ratio of maximum wind speed to the corresponding 10 min average wind speed. In this study, the ratio of the maximum wind speed within 10 min to the corresponding average wind speed within 10 min was used as the gust factor for 10 min:

$$T = \frac{v_{max}}{\overline{v}} \tag{1}$$

where, T is gust factor; v_{max} is maximum wind speed (m/s); $\overline{v}$ stands for 10 min average wind speed (m/s).

2.2 Wind Shear Index

In the process of strong wind, gust variation is often one of the important causes of wind disasters, and gust factors are usually used to represent the gust characteristics of wind [16–21]. Gust factor is defined as the ratio of maximum wind speed to the corresponding 10 min average wind speed. In this study, the ratio of the maximum wind speed within 10 min to the corresponding average wind speed within 10 min was used as the gust factor for 10 min:

$$T = \frac{v_{max}}{\bar{v}} \tag{2}$$

where, T is gust factor; v_{max} is maximum wind speed (m/s); $\bar{v}$ stands for 10 min average wind speed (m/s).

The exponential formula is:

$$\alpha = \frac{\log_{10}(\frac{v_2}{v_1})}{\log_{10}(\frac{z_2}{z_1})} \tag{3}$$

where, α is the wind shear index; z_1 is the known height, m; z_2 is the height of wind speed after change, m; v_1 is the wind speed at height z_1, m/s; v_2 is the wind speed at height z_2, m/s.

3 Analysis of Wind Speed Characteristics of Typhoon Rammasun

3.1 Analysis of Gust Coefficient of Wind Tower

The gust coefficient was constructed based on the 2017–2019 hourly average wind speed data of the wind tower and the corresponding 10-min average maximum wind speed. The results are as shown in Table 1.

Although there are many data of wind speed above 10 m/s in wind tower, there are few data above 15 m/s, so only the gust coefficients of wind level 6 and wind level 7 can be constructed. At the same time, the gust coefficient of wind tower 6 wind at 80 m is 1.098, and that of wind tower 7 wind at 80 m is 1.074, both of which are relatively small. According to the theory, the higher the wind speed is, the smaller the gust coefficient should be and greater than 1. Therefore, the function with extreme value of 1 is constructed and extrapolated within the interval of [1,1.074] to ensure the accuracy. After segmented statistics (10–11 m/s; 11–12 m/s; 12–13 m/s, 13–14 m/s, 14–15 m/s, 15–16 m/s), and construct function extrapolation:

$$Y = \left(1 + \frac{a}{x}\right) \tag{4}$$

The fitting result of SPSS is:

$$Y = 1 + \frac{0.919}{X} \tag{5}$$

The equation (R = 0.66) was used to restore the 10-min maximum average wind speed at the height of 80 m of the wind tower during Rammasun's landing, as shown in the figure below, where the extreme wind speed was 29.8 m/s Fig. 1:

Table 1. Gust coefficient statistics corresponding to different wind speed grades.

Wind speed level		Level 6	Level 7
Corresponding to the time	Start	2017/7/12 8: 00	2017/10/15 23: 00
	End	2019/3/23 22: 00	2018/12/12 4: 00
Gust coefficients at all heights (Unit:m/s)	80	1.098	1.074
	70	1.079	1.067
	50	1.083	——
	30	1.069	——
	10	1.097	——
	Average	1.084	1.071

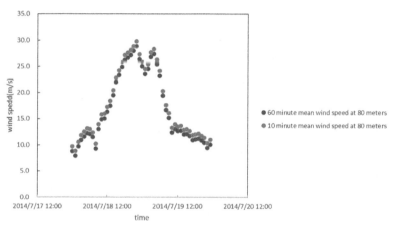

Fig. 1. Restoration of 10-min maximum wind speed at 80 m height of wind tower during Rammasun landing.

3.2 Analysis of Wind Shear Index Based on Lidar

Using lidar data, the data series with the velocity above 10 m/s in the observed value at 80 m height are extracted, and the corresponding shear index at 90 m height is calculated by the equation:

$$Y = \frac{\ln \frac{v_{90}}{v_{80}}}{\ln \frac{z_{90}}{z_{80}}} \qquad (6)$$

The same work was successively done for 100 m, 110 m, 120 m, 140 m, 150 m and 200 m, and the scatter diagram of shear index was obtained as follows Fig. 2:

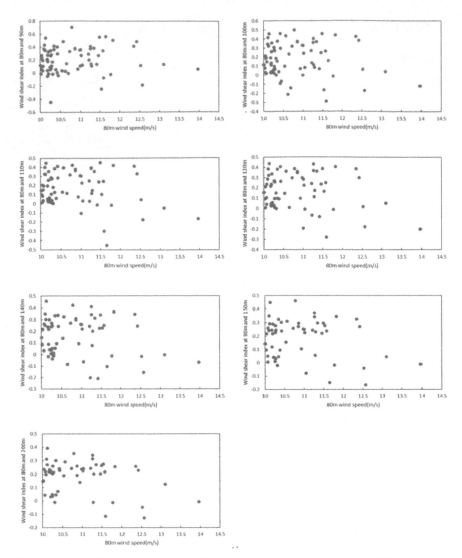

Fig. 2. Scatter diagram of wind shear index changing with wind speed at different heights.

According to the above statistics, the wind shear indices at different heights are shown in Table 2:

Table 2. Average wind shear index at different heights.

Height (m)	80 m and 90 m	80 m and 100 m	80 m and 110 m	80 m and 120 m
Wind shear index	0.203	0.173	0.169	0.173
Height (m)	80 m and 140 m	80 m and 150 m	80 m and 200 m	
Wind shear index	0.162	0.185	0.181	

The wind shear index was used to restore the 10-min mean maximum wind speed at different heights during Rammasun landing. As shown in Fig. 3, extreme values of wind speed at 90 m–200 m height are 30.5 m/s, 30.9 m/s, 31.4 m/s, 31.9 m/s, 32.6 m/s, 33.4 m/s and 35.1 m/s respectively:

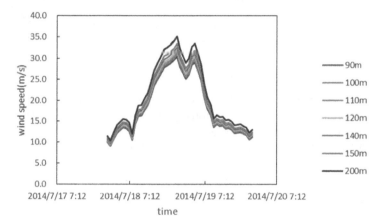

Fig. 3. Average 10-min maximum wind speeds at different heights during Rammasun's landfall.

3.3 Air Density Correction

Conversion formula for air density at different heights:

$$\rho_z = \rho_h e^{-0.0001(z-h)} \tag{7}$$

Formula for calculating surface air density based on meteorological data from meteorological stations:

$$\rho_z = \frac{1.276 \times 10^{-3}}{1 + 3.66 \times 10^{-3}T}(P - 0.378E) \tag{8}$$

$$E = f \times E_0 \tag{9}$$

$$E_0 = 6.11\exp(17.269T)/(T + 273.16 - 35.86) \tag{10}$$

After calculating other height densities, the wind speed correction formula is as follows:

$$v_0 = v\sqrt{\frac{\rho}{\rho_0}} \tag{11}$$

The surface air density during the transit was obtained from the weather station data during the transit of Rammasun and then converted to the table of air density at different altitudes, as shown in the following table Table 3:

Table 3. Air density tables at different altitudes during the transit of Rammasun.

Air density *	Surface	80 m	90 m	100 m	110 m	120 m	140 m	150 m	200 m
7.18	1.136	1.127	1.126	1.125	1.124	1.123	1.120	1.119	1.114
7.19	1.140	1.131	1.130	1.129	1.128	1.127	1.124	1.123	1.118

* Unit: kg/m3

During the period from July 18th to July 19th, the 10-min average wind speed at different heights calculated in 4.3 was restored to the wind speed at standard air density, as shown in the figure below, where the extreme wind speed at 90 m–200 m height was: 28.6 m/s, 29.2 m/s, 29.6 m/s, 30.1 m/s, 30.2 m/s, 31.2 m/s, 32.2 m/s, 33.5 m/s Fig. 4.

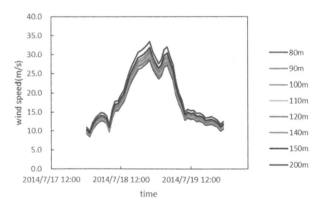

Fig. 4. 10-min mean maximum wind speeds at different heights of wind towers during Rammasun landfall (Air density correction)

4 Conclusion

(1) The gust coefficients of each section are calculated by dividing wind speed of wind measuring tower in 2017, and the functional relationship between gust coefficients and wind speed is established according to the mechanism, and the equation is obtained by fitting: $Y = 1 + \frac{0.919}{X}$, equation correlation coefficient R = 0.66, moderate correlation, but because the gust coefficient varies between 1.074–1, the lack of precision of the model has little influence on the final calculation results. The gust coefficient around the tower during Rammasun landing was restored by the equation, and the average maximum wind speed of the tower at 80 m height in ten minutes was calculated.

(2) Based on the wind tower 80 m, using lidar data, the shear coefficients of 90 m, 100 m, 110 m, 120 m, 140 m, 150 m and 200 m were 0.203, 0.173, 0.169, 0.173, 0.162, 0.185 and 0.181, respectively. According to this, the average maximum wind speed in ten minutes at different heights during Rammasun landing was restored, and the extreme values were 30.5 m/s, 30.9 m/s, 31.4 m/s, 31.9 m/s, 32.6 m/s, 33.4 m/s and 35.1 m/s, respectively.

(3) Using the conventional monitoring data of Qinzhou meteorological station, such as temperature, relative humidity and atmospheric pressure, the air density data at different heights during The landing of Rammasun in Qinzhou area were calculated, and the 10-min average maximum wind speed at different heights of the wind tower was modified accordingly, and the extreme values were: 28.6 m/s, 29.2 m/s, 29.6 m/s, 30.1 m/s, 30.2 m/s, 31.2 m/s, 32.2 m/s, 33.5 m/s.

Acknowledgement. This work was supported by the National Natural Science Foundation of China "Study on the Second Tibet Plateau Scientific Expedition and Research Program (STEP) under grant number 2019QZKK0804, and the dynamic mechanism of grassland ecosystem response to climate change in Qinghai Plateau" under grant number U20A2098. "

References

1. Xu, B.Q., Wu, T.T., Li, W.H.: Screening of calculation methods for wind shear exponent. Trans. Chin. Soc. Agric. Eng. **30**(16), 188–194 (2014)
2. Hu, B.: Analysis of gust factor associated with typhoons on Zhejiang coast. J. Trop. Meteorol. **33**(06), 841–849 (2017)
3. Song, X.Q., Wang, F.H., Xi, P.: Three-beam methodology and observations of wind profiling with doppler lidar. Periodical of Ocean Univ. Chin. **50**(04), 136–144 (2020)
4. Zhang, Q., Lu, C., Long, H., Tan, M.Y., Xiang, D.: Analysis of the vertical characteristics of horizontal wind near the surface of shenzhen during the visit of typhoon mangkhut. Guangdong Meteorol. **43**(04), 6–10 (2021)
5. Yang, R., Quan, P., Zhang, K.K.: Analysis of influence of wind shear effect on structural performance of wind turbine blades. Mach. Des. Manuf. **05**, 172–175 (2021)
6. Yu, H., Yan, Y.L.: Experimental study on wind load of enclosure structure of Hanling Art Museum. Build. Struct. **50**(S1), 234–238 (2020)

7. Feng, S., Huang, H.C., Xie, Z.N.: Estimation method of extreme wind pressure on long-span roof and its application. J. Build. Struct. **42**(05), 10–18 (2021)
8. Zhou, F., Jiang, L.L., Tu, X.P.: Near-surface gust factor characteristics in several disastrous winds over Zhejiang province. J. Appl. Meteorol. Sci. **28**(1), 119–128 (2017)
9. Lin, W., Fang, P.Z., Lei, X.T.: Study on the converting coefficients of maximum wind speed with different averaging periods for landfall typhoons. J. Trop. Meteorol. **32**(1), 42–50 (2016)
10. Huang, H.H., Chen, W.C., Zhi, S.Q., Wang, B.L.: Analysis on severe wind characteristics during typhoon Rammasun landing process based on the observation at wind tower. Meteorol. Mon. **47**(02), 143–156 (2021)
11. Lv, X.Y., Xu, Y.L., Huang, H.Q.: Analysis on environmental factors of the extremely rapid intensification of typhoon "Rammasun"(1409) in the northern. South China Sea. Mar. Forecasts **38**(03), 1–10 (2021)
12. Wang, H.L., Wu, X.Q., Huang, Z.H., Cai, Y.F., Zhang, C.H.: Study on the boundary layer wind variation characteristics of super-typhoon Rammasun during landing on Xuwen County. J. Trop. Meteorol. **34**(03), 297–304 (2018)
13. He, L., Bai, H., Ouyang, D., Wang, C., Wang, C.: Satellite cloud-derived wind inversion algorithm using GPU. Comput. Mater. Continua **60**(2), 599–613 (2019)
14. He, L., Cai, Z., Ouyang, D., Wang, C., Jiang, Y.: A revised satellite cloud-derived wind inversion algorithm based on computer cluster. Comput. Mater. Continua **64**(01), 373–388 (2020)
15. Maheswari, R.U., Umamaheswari, R.: Wind turbine drivetrain expert fault detection system: Multivariate empirical mode decomposition based multi-sensor fusion with bayesian learning classification. Intell. Autom. Soft Comput. **26**(03), 479–488 (2020)
16. Liu, J., Chen, Y.Z.: A preliminary analysis of the characteristics of strong winds of shenzhen as affected by typhoon mangkhut (1822). Guangdong Meteorology **41**(05), 11–14 (2019)
17. Chen, W.C., Song, L.L., Zhi, S.Q.: Analysis on gust factor of tropical cyclone strong wind over different underlying surfaces. Sci. Chin. (Series E) **41**(11), 1449–1459 (2011)
18. Zhang, C.X., Wang, Y.R., Huang, Z.Q., Li, Z.N., Wang, C.Q.: Field measurement study on wind structure characteristics of specific topography under typhoon Maria. J. Nat. Disasters **28**(04), 100–110 (2019)
19. Sabiha, N.A., Alkhammash, H.I.: Ferroresonance overvoltage mitigation using surge arrester for grid-connected wind farm. Intell. Autom. Soft Comput. **31**(02), 1107–1118 (2022)
20. Hussain, D., Soother, K., Kalwar, I.H., Memon, T.D., Memon, Z.A.: Stator winding fault detection and classification in three-phase induction motor. Intell. Autom. Soft Comput. **29**(03), 869–883 (2021)
21. El-Bshah, A., Al-Wesabi, F.N., Al-Kustoban, A.M., Alamgeer, M., Nemri, N.: Resource assessment of wind energy potential of mokha in yemen with weibull speed. Comput. Mater. Continua **69**(01), 1123–1140 (2021)

An MR Image Segmentation Method Based on Dictionary Learning Preprocessing and Probability Statistics

Yihua Song[1], Chen Ge[2(✉)], Xia Zhang[1], Ningning Song[3], Wentao Hou[4], and Zuojian Zhou[1]

[1] Nanjing University of Chinese Medicine, Nanjing 210003, China
[2] Shandong Vocational and Technical University of Engineering, Jinan 276500, China
gechen1993@163.com
[3] Nanjing First Hospital, Nanjing 210003, China
[4] University of Waterloo, Waterloo, ON N2L 3G1, Canada

Abstract. Segmentation of brain MR images can help clinicians to extract regions of interest. At present, there are many studies on brain MR image segmentation, especially in deep learning methods. However, deep learning methods requires a very large quantity of datasets. With the popularity of deep learning, dictionary learning has been revived again. As a traditional machine learning segmentation method, dictionary learning requires less sample size, has high segmentation efficiency, and can describe the image well. This paper mainly proposes an MR image segmentation method based on posterior probability. The process of medical image acquisition is accompanied by the generation of noise which is limited by factors such as the equipment environment. We use the powerful classification function of the naive Bayes model to classify the noise data and sample label data in the images, and then provide the classification results to the dictionary learning sparse matrix for sparse expression. We achieve the effect of noise reduction and denoising through mathematical methods to improve the signal-to-noise ratio of medical image data. After getting the denoised image, we adopt region growth combined with the softmax function method to classify the pixels. The results of this paper provide technical support for the subsequent image segmentation, detection and other computer-assisted clinical diagnosis, so as to improve the efficiency of automated clinical diagnosis for clinical application.

Keywords: Posterior probability · Dictionary learning · Bayes model · Denoising

1 Introduction

The prevention and treatment of brain diseases is a common challenge faced by all mankind [1, 2]. MR imaging is widely used in brain imaging because of its unique imaging method that is very effective on the soft tissue of the organism [3, 4]. MR imaging of brain tissues can be effectively used for quantitative analysis of brain lesions

X. Sun et al. (Eds.): ICAIS 2022, CCIS 1586, pp. 127–136, 2022.
https://doi.org/10.1007/978-3-031-06767-9_11

and various brain tissues. For example, for some brain degenerative diseases, such as Alzheimer's syndrome, analyzing hippocampus tissue through MR imaging can give clinically effective data references, and brain tissue segmentation is one of the prerequisite methods for brain tissue analysis [5, 6]. However, due to the complexity of brain tissue and quality of images, brain MR image preprocessing has always been a difficult and hot spot in the field of medical image analysis [7–9].

In terms of MR image denoising, quantities of approaches have been presented, including statistics-based method and pixel feature-based method et al. [10–14]. In recent years, dictionary learning has been applied to medical imaging fields. Dictionary learning is a feature extraction method, the core idea is to use the least resources to express the most meaning [15, 16]. We can express unlimited content with only the limited words stored in the dictionary, and the dictionary in it provides the basis for our emotional expression. Therefore, from a theoretical perspective, dictionary learning is to use limited features to express more core content in the sample data.

Wang et al. [17] proposed a novel algorithm based on the 4-frame parallel dictionary learning and dynamic total variation for the real-time MRI reconstruction. Ravishankar et al. [18] proposed a k-space highly undersampled MRI image reconstruction based on dictionary learning, and then, Ma et al. [19] introduced a dictionary learning method for the Poisson image deblurring. Afterwards, Zhang et al. [20] studied a tensor-based dictionary learning method for the spectral CT reconstruction. The above works demonstrated the advantages and feasibility of dictionary learning in the medical imaging and processing.

As of today, the preliminary study on the probability statistics in the MR imaging preprocessing has been accomplished. For example, Based on statistical knowledge, the sample data can be classified more accurately Zhu et al. [21] presented a new denoising method using deep image prior. According to the existing classification application scenarios, it can be concluded that the naive Bayes method has high classification accuracy. This mathematical method combines the prior probability and posterior probability in probability statistics. It not only effectively avoids the interference of subjective factors on the classification results in the classification process, but also has a high generalization ability, which reduces the over-fitting of the classification to a certain extent. Based on this, researches have done a lot of work on image denoising.

Liu et al. [22] proposed an image denoising algorithm using two-dimensional empirical mode. In this algorithm, the Bayesian maximum posterior probability is used to derive the threshold from the model. Zhuo et al. [23] proposed a novel method to estimate the probability density of wavelet coefficients based on the Bayesian maximum posterior probability. Then the noise variance and the standard deviation of the wavelet coefficients of the offspring is calculated, so that the denoising algorithm has adaptive capabilities. Yang et al. [24] applied adaptive contourlet hidden Markov model (HMM)-pulse-coupled neural network (PCNN) in the sparse representation model to achieve image denoising. Kataoka et al. [25] proposed a discrete Markov random fields and the fast Fourier transform- based method to denoise images, where Bayesian approach is utilized to create the posterior probability distribution of the denoised image for inferring the original image.

In recent years, there have been many segmentation methods for brain tissue images, among which multi-atlas segmentation is the representative. This method is based on the prior knowledge of the image label, and the original image and the image to be segmented are registered to obtain the mapping between the target area and the label image, and the segmentation result is obtained [26]. It is widely used in brain tissue segmentation. Although the multi-atlas segmentation method can effectively use prior knowledge, the results of registration and label fusion have a greater impact on the segmentation effect. Lotjonen et al. [27] Introduces a fast and robust multi-atlas registration method to segment brain mr images. After the atlas registration, the graph cut method and the maximum expectation algorithm are used to perform subsequent processing on the data. in recent years, with the popularity of deep learning, dictionary learning methods have returned to the attention of researchers. Because deep learning requires too much sample data, the sparse representation based on dictionary learning and sparse representation has received renewed attention in image processing.

However, the offset field and noise that are widely present in MR images still exist, and the imbalance of tissue samples in the brain tissue brings a great deal difficulties to the segmentation. The existing image denoising methods have the disadvantages of poor effect, complex process and low accuracy [28–30]. In order to solve this problem, this paper uses the posterior probability of the naive Bayes method to classify the noise data and effective feature data in the medical image data. And dictionary learning sparse matrix can remove the redundant noise data in the image, and keep the label data in the image as much as possible. We develop a dictionary learning method combined softmax function to classify the pixels into different categories to achieve tissues segmentation in MR images. More details of the proposed method are introduced in the following chapters. The flowchart of the proposed strategy is shown as Fig. 1.

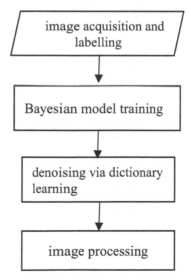

Fig. 1. Flowchart of the proposed method.

2 Method

We use the posterior probability classification of the naive Bayes model to classify the noise data and sample label data in the image data more accurately. The preliminary classification results are input into the dictionary learning sparse matrix. At this stage, we use the self-learning sparse expression function of dictionary learning to reduce or

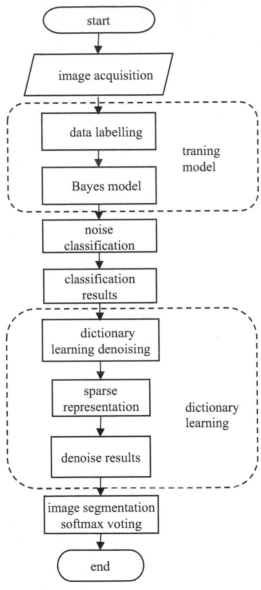

Fig. 2. Details of the proposed approach.

remove the noise data in the image. The following flowchart demonstrates more details about the presented method (Fig. 2).

The algorithm is mainly consists of the following steps.

1. Data collection. The data sources of medical images are diverse. The acquisition of multi-source image data can be directly obtained through CT and MR scans, which are used as raw data for subsequent processing and analysis.
2. Data labeling. Data labeling requires the participation of specialists. The labelImg tool is utilized to label the label data noise data and sample label data for label calibration, and the mapping relationship of the category labels is stored in the yaml file.
3. Bayesian model training. The Bayesian classification mathematical method is used to subdivide the labeled label data. Then the parameters are fixed after training through the corresponding model file, which is regarded as the basis for later classification.
4. Denoising. The classification results are imported into the dictionary learning sparse matrix for noise reduction. Based on the sparse expression function of the sparse matrix, we denoise the classification results.
5. Segmentation of the denoised image. Based on the previous preprocessing stafe, we adopt the region growing algorithm to segment the MR images on brain tissues.

2.1 Bounding Box

Bounding box technique is to establish a bounding box [31] of the target area in the process stage to approach or extract the main target, ignoring the non-target area. According to the prior knowledge, the overall brain MR images are far bigger than the ROI.

Therefore, bounding box are extracted to improve computational efficiency by mapping label image to the corresponding original images in this paper. Suppose there are label images in the dataset, we detect a rectangular boundary covering all the non-zero pixels expressed as (ximin, ximax), (yimin, yimax) in each label image. Therefore, bounding box is from min(ximin), i = 1,...,n to max(ximax), i = 1,...,n, and from min(yimin), i = 1,...,n to max(yimax), i = 1,...,n.

2.2 Data Labelling

The collected data can be directly scanned from CT, MR and other equipment, and the data obtained here is the original data. we adopt an open source tool labelImg for data labeling. By manually labeling the target points in the image, the mapping relationship between the image and the label data can be generated. The mapping relationship is saved in a yaml file. The further model training is performed by reading the yaml file.

2.3 Bayesian Model Training

The Naive Bayes method simplifies some processes of the Bayesian method, and makes certain assumptions for the classified sample data, so that the sample data can be applied to the Naive Bayes method on the basis of mutual independence. Therefore, in the process of sample data analysis, the fairness of the data is guaranteed, and the naive

Bayes method reduces the complexity of Bayesian classification. At the same time, it can effectively improve the generalization of the Bayesian model in the classification process in real scenes.

In this process, the Bayesian classification mathematical method is used to subdivide the labeled data, and the parameters after training are solidified through the corresponding model file, which is used as the basis for later classification.

The model of the Bayesian classification mathematical method can be expressed as follows:

$$Classify(f_1, \ldots\ldots, f_2) = \arg \max_c p(C = c) \prod_{i=1}^{n} p(F_i = f_i | C = c) \tag{1}$$

where i indicates the sample label, f indicates the sample data set, $p(C = c)$ indicates posterior probability and $p(F_i = f_i | C = c)$ represents independent probability distribution, n indicates the number of samples, C indicates the categorical variables and F_i indicates the scaling factor.

2.4   Dictionary Leaning Denoising

Dictionary learning is a feature extraction method, and its core idea is to express the most meaning with the least resources. The dictionary can be used to reduce the dimensionality of the sample data, and the most basic features can be extracted in this way (Fig. 3).

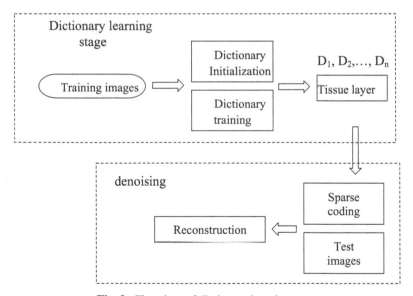

Fig. 3. Flowchart of dictionary learning stage.

The classification result of the previous step is used as the input for noise reduction in the subsequent dictionary learning sparse matrix: In this step, the noise and sample label data in the original data have been classified more accurately, so only the sparse expression of the sparse matrix is needed here. Function performs a noise reduction process on the noise data in the image.

$$\mathbf{X} = \left(\lambda\mathbf{I} + \sum_{s=1}^{S} E_s^T E_s\right)^{-1} \left(\lambda\mathbf{Z} + \sum_{s=1}^{S} E_s^T \mathbf{D}\alpha_s\right) \tag{2}$$

where X and I represents the sparse expression result image and the output image after Bayesian classification, respectively, and S indicates the number of divided patches from images, E_s^T indicates transpose matrix of image path matrix, E_s indicates extracting image path matrix, Z represents noisy image data, D represents sparse representation matrix and α_s represents the sparse expression signal data of the patch image.

2.5 Segmentation

There are many segmentation algorithms, considering the segmentation accuracy and efficiency, therefore, the region growing algorithm is selected. The region growing method is a traditional image segmentation method that aggregates pixels with similar attributes.

This method first needs to specify a set of seed points (the seed point can be a single pixel or a small area), and then judge the pixels in the neighborhood of the seed point according to a predefined growth criterion. If the similarity between the neighboring pixel and the seed pixel meets the growth criterion, the neighboring pixel is calibrated as the target, and the neighboring pixel is taken as the new seed point, and the above search and judgment process is repeated until all the pixels meet the conditions are included.

We expect to get the probability value of the pixel category in the region growing process, here the Softmax function is introduced. Softmax assigns a probability value to the results of each organization's output classification, indicating the possibility of belonging to each category. Suppose we divide the segmented regions into n parts, including background, accumbens, amygdala, caudate, hippocampus, pallidum, putamen, thalamus etc., which are mutually exclusive. The definition of the Softmax function is given below:

$$s_i = \frac{e^{C_i}}{\sum_{j=1}^{T} e^{C_j}} \quad T \quad indicates \quad classes \tag{3}$$

where C_i denotes the ith category error in the objects to be segmented. This method omits labeling for images and implements pixel level segmentation using unsupervised learning classification.

3   Experimental Results

In order to verify the denoising method with the dictionary learning proposed in this paper, an MR imaging experiment on MR images from MICCAI2012 Multi-Atlas Labeling Challenge is conducted. Each atlas image contains a label image and the corresponding original image, our method are not limited with labeling images notwithstanding.

All image are skull-stripped and intensity normalized. 20 atlas images (after bounding box) are picked out from the dataset randomly as testing dataset to evaluate this method. Due to most of the non-ROIs being excluded, the size of each original image reduces from 256 * 256 * 280 around to 80 * 80 * 80. The smaller size of sample data and more accurate regions to be segmented will improve the computation and dictionary learning accuracy significantly. Figure 4 shows the original image and denoising results.

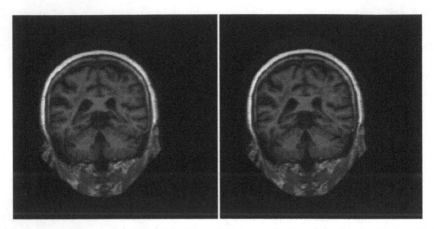

Fig. 4. Comparisons results. The original brain MR image (left) and the denoised image (right).

Compared with the existing methods, the algorithm in this article is based on the image denoising method of naive Bayes posterior probability and dictionary learning sparse matrix. Compared with the existing methods, the algorithm in this article is based on the image denoising method of naive Bayes posterior probability and dictionary learning sparse matrix, and then provide the classification results to the dictionary learning sparse matrix for sparse expression.

4   Conclusion

In this article, we propose an image denoising method based on Naive Bayes posterior probability and dictionary learning sparse matrix. Firstly, we use the precise posterior probability of Naive Bayes and the denoising effect of the dictionary learning sparse matrix to classify the noise and label data of the given medical image data to obtain the preprocessed classification results. Then, take the classification results as the input of the dictionary learning sparse matrix, we adopt the expression function of the dictionary learning sparse matrix to reduce the noise and noise of the noise data. On the one hand, the method proposed in this paper is a denoising method for medical image data, which combines the naive Bayes model and the dictionary learning sparse matrix, and has a relatively effective effect on improving the signal-to-noise ratio of image data. On the other hand, this method has certain clinical medical significance, especially in the process of computer-aided diagnosis. Therefore, the processing results in this article provides more information for later observation and analysis of medical clinical data.

Because of the complexity of MR imaging and brain imaging mode and variety of brain tissues, the brain MR image processing has been faced with various challenges. In summary, Experiments show that this method can provide technical support for computer-assisted clinical diagnosis such as image registration, fusion, recognition and detection, so as to improve the efficiency of automated clinical diagnosis in hospitals.

Funding Statement: This research was funded by Natural Science Foundation of the Higher Education Institutions of Jiangsu Province, China, grant number 20KJB520030.

Conflicts of Interest:. The authors declare that they have no conflicts of interest to report regarding the present study.

References

1. Muthaiyan, R., Malleswaran, D.M.: An automated brain image analysis system for brain cancer using shearlets. Comput. Syst. Sci. Eng. **40**(1), 299–312 (2022)
2. Kurian, S.M., Devaraj, S.J., Vijayan, V.P.: Brain tumour detection by gamma denoised wavelet segmented entropy classifier. Comp. Mater. Contin. **69**(2), 2093–2109 (2021)
3. Guo, Y., Cui, Z., Li, X., Peng, J., Hu, J.: Mri image segmentation of nasopharyngeal carcinoma using multi-scale cascaded fully convolutional network. Intell. Auto. Soft Compu. **31**(3), 1771–1782 (2022)
4. Renukadevi, T., Saraswathi, K., Prabu, P., Venkatachalam, K.: Brain image classification using time frequency extraction with histogram intensity similarity. Comput. Syst. Sci. Eng. **41**(2), 645–460 (2022)
5. Jin, K., Wang, S.: Image denoising based on the asymmetric Gaussian mixture model. Journal of Internet of Things **2**(1), 1–11 (2020)
6. Rajaragavi, R., Rajan, S.P.: Optimized u-net segmentation and hybrid res-net for brain tumor mri images classification. Intell. Auto. Soft Compu. **32**(1), 1–14 (2022)
7. Alshathri, S.I., Vincent, D.J., Hari, V.S.: Denoising letter images from scanned invoices using stacked autoencoders. Comp. Mater. Contin. **71**(1), 1371–1386 (2022)
8. Gong, P., Liu, J., Lv, S.: Image denoising with gan based model. J. Info. Hid. Priva. Protec. **2**(4), 155–163 (2020)
9. Huang, Y., Zheng, F., Cong, R.: Multi-task coherent modality transferable gan for 3d brain image synthesis. In: IEEE Transactions on Image Processing, p. 1 (2020)
10. Chen, Z., Fu, Y., Xiang, Y.: A novel MR image denoising via LRMA and NLSS. Signal Process. **185**, 108109 (2021)
11. Xu, L., Wei, Y.: Pyramid deep dehazing: an unsupervised single image dehazing method using deep image prior. Opt. Laser Technol. **148**(3), 107788 (2022)
12. Gong, K., Han, P., Fakhri, G.E.: Arterial spin labeling MR image denoising and reconstruction using unsupervised deep learning. NMR Biomed. **2019**(1), e4224 (2019)
13. Yu, H., Ding, M., Zhang, X.: Laplacian eigenmaps network-based nonlocal means method for mr image denoising. Sensors **19**(13), 2918 (2019)
14. Sun, Z., et al.: MR images denoising for Rician noise using curvelet transform and variance stabilizing transformation. J. Liaon. Nor. Univ. (Natural Science Edition) (2019)
15. Yan, R., Shao, L., Liu, Y.: Nonlocal hierarchical dictionary learning using wavelets for image denoising. IEEE Trans. Image Process. **22**(12), 4689–4698 (2013)

16. Li, H., Wang, Y., Yang, Z.: Discriminative dictionary learning-based multiple component decomposition for detail-preserving noisy image fusion. IEEE Trans. Instrum. Meas. **69**(4), 1082–1102 (2020)
17. Wang, Y.: Real-time dynamic MRI using parallel dictionary learning and dynamic total variation. Neurocomputing **238**(C), 410–419 (2017)
18. Ravishankar, S., Bresler, Y.: MR image reconstruction from highly undersampled k-space data by dictionary learning. IEEE Trans. Med. Imaging **30**(5), 1028 (2011)
19. Ma, L., et al.: A Dictionary learning approach for poisson image deblurring. IEEE Trans. Med. Imaging **32**(7), 1277 (2013)
20. Zhang, Y.: Tensor-based dictionary learning for spectral ct reconstruction. IEEE Trans. Med. Imaging **36**(1), 142–154 (2016)
21. Zhu, Y., Pan, X., Lv, T., Liu, Y., Li, L.: DESN: An unsupervised MR image denoising network with deep image prior. Theoret. Comput. Sci. **880**, 97–110 (2021)
22. Liu, P., Jia, J., Li, C., Ying, A.: Image denoising algorithm based on fast and adaptive bidimensional empirical mode decomposition. Computer Science **046**(011), 260–266 (2019)
23. Zhuo, D.: Design of noise control algorithm for CT images of pulmonary tumor based on Bayesian rough set. Biomedical engineering research **2019**(3) (2019)
24. Yang, G., Lu, Z., Yang, J., Wang, Y.: An adaptive contourlet HMM–PCNN model of sparse representation for image denoising. IEEE Access **7**, 88243–88253 (2019)
25. Kataoka, S.: Yasuda: bayesian image denoising with multiple noisy images. The Review of Socionetwork Strategies **13**(2), 267–280 (2019)
26. Heckemann, A.R., Hajnal, A., Aljabar, A., Rueckert, A.: Hammers: automatic anatomical brain mri segmentation combining label propagation and decision fusion. Neuroimage **33**(1), 115–126 (2006)
27. Jyrki, M.P., et al.: Fast and robust multi-atlas segmentation of brain magnetic resonance images. Neuroimage **49**(3), 2352–2365 (2010)
28. Shi, D., Yang, W., Li, J.: Infrared image denoising algorithm based on adaptive dictionary learning. In: MIPPR 2011: Multispectral Image Acquisition, Processing, and Analysis, vol. 8002, pp. 429–433. SPIE (2011)
29. Rubinstein, R., Peleg, T., Elad, M.: Analysis K-SVD: A dictionary-learning algorithm for the analysis sparse model. IEEE Trans. Signal Process. **61**(3), 661–677 (2013)
30. Su, K., et al.: Image denoising based on learning over-complete dictionary. In: 2012 9th International Conference on Fuzzy Systems and Knowledge Discovery, pp. 395–398. IEEE (2012)
31. Shimizu, A.: Probabilistic atlas-guided eigen-organ method for simultaneous bounding box estimation of multiple organs in volumetric ct images. Medi. Imag. Technol. **24**(3), 191–200 (2006)

D2D Resource Allocation Problem in Full - Load Cellular Networks

Haimin Yi[1], Xiaoli He[1], Lun Li[3]([✉]), Yu Song[2], Hongwei Li[1], Zhen Zeng[1], and Xiaodong Yin[1]

[1] School of Computer Science, Sichuan University of Science and Engineering, Zigong 643000, China
[2] Department of Network Information Management Center, Sichuan University of Science and Engineering, Zigong 643000, China
[3] China Mobile Group Sichuan Company Limited, Zigong Branch, Zigong 643000, China
1940215403@qq.com

Abstract. With the increasing demand of local service load, how to improve resource utilization is an important problem. D2D (Device-to-Device) communication is considered to be an effective solution. The letter allows users in close proximity to communicate directly without passing through the base station.D2D communication technology has improved user experience, reduced delay and reduced power consumption and other potential advantages. However, cellular users will be disturbed when D2D users reuse channel resources, resulting in complex interference environment in the cell, so how to allocate resources and interference management of D2D users is an urgent problem to be solved. Aiming at the cellular network scenario, this paper studies the wireless resource allocation algorithm of D2D communication in cellular network, which reduces the interference of D2D users to cellular users and improves the total throughput of cell.

Keywords: D2D · Resource allocation · Interference · Multiplex

1 Introduction

In the cellular network of D2D users (DU), users who are close to each other can establish D2D direct links under the control of base stations to realize direct data transmission between users, instead of relying on the relay forwarding mode of base stations. The short distance of D2D communication link can use less transmitting power to meet communication requirements, thus improving system resource utilization efficiency and throughput. However, the data transmission in D2D multiplexing mode will inevitably introduce the same frequency interference between DU and cellular users (CU). Excessive interference will affect the throughput of the system and the user's communication quality of service, making the cellular network unable to obtain performance gain. Aiming at the resource allocation problem of DU, DU interference problem is the main problem to be solved by DU access to the cellular network. In order to coexist between D2D communication and the cellular network, reduce the interference caused by the

X. Sun et al. (Eds.): ICAIS 2022, CCIS 1586, pp. 137–148, 2022.
https://doi.org/10.1007/978-3-031-06767-9_12

same frequency of DU reuse CU, and design a reasonable resource allocation algorithm to control DU interference is the study of the key to improve system performance.

DU can reuse the spectrum resources of cellular uplink or downlink. Due to cellular network uplink frequency resource utilization ratio is usually lower than downward spectrum resource utilization, spectrum capacity improvement space is opposite bigger, and BS has more powerful signal processing ability, the interference can be eliminated by a series of interference technique to avoid, therefore, this chapter considers only DU multiplexing cellular network uplink establish direct communication link.

In this chapter, a D2D communication resource allocation algorithm that the further interference reduction filtering algorithm based on candidate links, and the resource allocation process is divided into two stages: CU candidates and DU selecting the least interference to CU. Under the requirement of ensuring the throughput, the DU selects itself to reuse the least interference to the candidate CU, which not only meets the service experience of the DU and reduces the interference to the reused CU.

1.1 Related Work

Please In recent years, D2D, as one of the key technologies of 5G, has been studied by many scholars. The literature [1] combine full-duplex communication and D2D, further study of FD and gain access to the premise of, is deduced under the specified workload, an average coverage probability, the sum throughput, total maximum throughput of key parameters such as the enclosed expression, deduce FD model can improve the D2D auxiliary in low flow conditions of the underlying cellular network performance. The literature [2] investigates an enhanced hybrid spectrum access scheme based on non-switching spectrum switching. The scheme is superior to single interleaving and hybrid interleaving underlying spectrum access strategies in terms of spectrum efficiency, throughput and EDDT. The literature [3] studied the D2D resource allocation problem under the perfect channel, assuming that the cellular network is under full load, all the link resources in the network are occupied by cellular users, and BS has the CSI of all communication link feedback and converted the MINLP problem to be solved into three subproblems. The results also show that the performance in the network transmission rate is better than the random resource allocation algorithm, greedy inspired algorithm. The literature [4] using outdated channel information as input and use the unsupervised approach in depth study on the D2D system of power allocation problem is studied, and the supervised algorithm breaks through the conventional power allocation algorithm can achieve the subprime limit, the simulation results show that the algorithm performance is beyond the conventional power allocation algorithm performance. The literature [5] proposed a D2D communication resource allocation algorithm based on user rate demand, which enables D2D users to reuse cellular downlink resources. This allocation process is divided into two stages: guaranteed rate demand and excess resource allocation. The division of these two stages can effectively reduce the interference of D2D users to cellular users. Moreover, it shows good system fairness under uniform and non-uniform distribution conditions. The literature [6] In order to solve the problem of co-channel interference, an algorithm based on graph shading is proposed. The main idea is to use the weighted prioritization of specification resources to enable multiple D2D users to reuse a single cellular user resource. The literature [7] argues that efficient power control can reduce the negative impact of interactions, enabling better D2D communication. It proposes two power control schemes, Power Control Scheme 1 (PCS1) and Power Control Scheme 2 (PCS2) to minimize interference and provide performance analysis. The literature [8] reducing interference in cellular networks by changing the number of antennas. The literature [9] proposes a joint algorithm for time scheduling and power control. Its core idea is to maximize the number of resources allocated that meet the service quality requirements in each scheduling cycle, and the algorithm also effectively improves the resource allocation. The literature [10] proposes a two-tier segment-based device-to-device (S-D2D) caching method that significantly reduces the startup and playback delays experienced by video-on-demand (VoD) users in the network.

1.2 Contribution

In this paper, we assume that the cellular network is at full load and D2D users only reuse cellular users' uplink. In this environment, our goal is to maximize the total throughput in the network and reduce the influence of D2D users on cellular users. The specific steps are as follows:

First of all, according to the problem modeling, the solved problem is the MINLP problem that cannot be solved in polynomial time, so the problem is transformed into two small problems, namely candidate link selection and further interference reduction screening.

Finally, the simulation results of candidate link selection and further interference reduction screening prove that the proposed solution can get a better result.

1.3 Organization of the Paper

The rest of this paper is organized as follows. Section 2 establishes system model, including scene model, channel model and problem model. Section 3 presents a solution and some pseudocode. Section 4 shows the simulation results. Section 5 conclusion.

2 System Model and Problem Description

2.1 System Model

The wireless cellular network model of D2D communication mode is added, and this model also reflects the actual scene. Two DU terminals within a range of distance can exchange data with each other without transit through BS. To improve throughput and reduce cellular interference by DU, only one DU is allowed to reuse one CU, and a CU can only be reused by one DU. There are two interference links in the model, one is the interference caused by the DU sender and the interference caused by the CU sender to the DU receiver. It is assumed that the BS can receive the CSI of all the communication link feedback in the network during operation. As shown in the Fig. 1. M pairs DU and N CU users share the communication resources of the cellular system in the cell. In this paper, the influence of the downlink is not considered for the time being, because the frequency spectrum resource utilization of the uplink is lower than that of the downlink, so the case of the uplink is given priority. In the following, the set = {1,2, 3, ..., i, ...} and = {1,2, 3, ..., j, ...} to represent the set of CU and DU respectively.

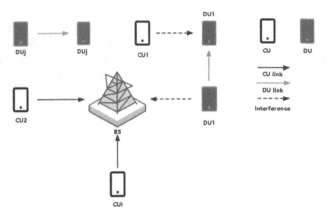

Fig. 1. System model.

From Fig. 1, the SINR of the DU and the CU at multiplexing can be expressed as:

$$\xi_i^c = \frac{P_i^c g_i^c}{\sigma_N^2 + \sum_{j \in D} \rho_{i,j} P_j^d g_{j,i}^d} \tag{1}$$

$$\xi_j^d = \frac{P_j^d g_j^d}{\sigma_N^2 + \sum_{i \in C} \rho_{i,j} P_i^c g_{i,j}^c} \tag{2}$$

ξ_i^c and ξ_j^d represents the SINR of CU with D2D, $\rho_{i,j}$ is a two-indicator function representing the link multiplexing relationship of CU and D2D.

The results of assignment are as follows:

$$\rho_{i,j} = \begin{cases} 1, \text{The DU j multiplicates the link resource of the CU i} \\ 0, \text{Other circumstances} \end{cases} \tag{3}$$

P_i^c represents the transmission power of CU, P_j^d represents the transmission power of DU, g_i^c represents the link transmission gain between CU and BS, g_j^d represents the link transmission gain between D2D transmitter and the receiver, $g_{i,j}^c$ represents the link gain between CU and D2D receiver, and $g_{j,i}^d$ represents the link transmission gain between D2D transmitter and BS. σ_N^2 indicates the link noise power. According to the above definition, when the DU multiplicities the link resources of the CU, the transmission rate of the DU and the CU is expressed as respectively:

$$T_{i,j}^c = B_c * \log_2\left(1 + \xi_i^c\right) \tag{4}$$

$$T_{j,i}^d = B_c * \log_2\left(1 + \xi_j^d\right) \tag{5}$$

$T_{i,j}^c$ represents the transmission rate when the CU is multiplicated and $T_{j,i}^d$ represents the transmission rate of the DU.

The transmission rate when the CU is not multiplicated is:

$$T_i^c = B_c * \log_2\left(1 + \frac{P_i^c g_i^c}{\sigma_N^2}\right) \tag{6}$$

B_c represents the transmission link bandwidth.

2.2 Power Distribution and Path Loss

The user's transmit power uses a standard simplified formula for 3GPP already standardized uplink open loop power [11] as follows:

$$P_f = \min\{P_{\max}, P_0 + \alpha * PL\} \tag{7}$$

$P_{\max}$ is the maximum emission power of the CU and the DU, defined as 24 dbm, the parameters set by the cell BS or the user according to the interference level, α is defined as the path loss compensation coefficient, and the path loss between the users is PL. From previous studies as well as existing standardized documentation, setting E to C performs best for the system throughput in this case.

The path loss model used for CU and D2D to BS refers to the ITU-R standardized micro-urban model [12], where the signal transmission in wireless channels accounts only for large-scale fading including path loss and shadow fading. In cities, the signal transmission obstacle between BS and users is very small, so the LOS model is adopted. Path loss model between the user and the BS:

$$PL_{user-BS} = 32.4 + 21\log(d) + 20\log(f) \tag{8}$$

The d represents the distance from CU or D2D to BS in m, the carrier frequency used by the system is f, and the model is only applied to the path loss between CU and BS, and D2D and BS. In cities, the signal transmission barriers between users and users are relatively large, so the NLOS model is adopted. Path loss model between the user and the BS:

$$PL_{user-user} = 22.7 + 36.7\log(d) + 26\log(f) \tag{9}$$

The d represents the distance between users in m, the carrier frequency f, and the model is only applied to the path loss between the CU and DU, the D2D transmitter and the D2D receiver.

Receiving power of CU:

$$P_{j-CU} = P_{f-CU} - PL_{user-BS} - WGN - NEN \tag{10}$$

In the equation, P_{f-CU} is the transmit power of the cellular user, $PL_{user-BS}$ is the path loss of CU to BS, WGN is the Gaussian random noise, and NEN is the base station noise index.

Receiving power of D2D:

$$P_{j-D2D} = P_{f-D2D} - PL_{user-BS} - WGN - NUE \qquad (11)$$

In the equation, P_{f-D2D} is the transmit power of cellular users, $PL_{user-BS}$ is the path loss of DU to BS, WGN is the Gaussian random noise, and NUE is the base station noise index.

2.3 Problem Description

Therefore, in order to exert the advantages of D2D communication in the cellular network as much as possible, the optimization goal of maximizing the total data transmission rate in the network next transforms the link sharing and power distribution problem of D2D communication into the following optimization problem:

$$\max_{\rho_{i,j}} \sum_{i \in C} \sum_{j \in D} \left(T_{i,j}^c + \rho_{i,j} T_{j,i}^d \right), \qquad (12)$$

$$\text{s. t.} \sum_{j \in D} \rho_{i,j} \le 1, \rho_{i,j} \in \{0, 1\}, \forall i \in C, \qquad (13)$$

$$\sum_{i \in C} \rho_{i,j} \le 1, \rho_{i,j} \in \{0, 1\}, \forall j \in D, \qquad (14)$$

$$P_i^c \le P_{\max}^c, \forall i \in C, \qquad (15)$$

$$P_j^d \le P_{\max}^d, \forall j \in D, \qquad (16)$$

Equation (13) means that each DU can only share link resources with at most one CU, and Eq. (14) means that the CU can only share link resources with at most one DU. Equation (15) represents the maximum transmission power of CU, Eq. (16) represents the maximum transmission power of DU, Eq. (15) and (16) can guarantee that the transmission power of CU and DU can be limited to a certain range.

Equations (12)–(16) is difficult to solve in polynomial time, so we convert the problem into two subproblems to solve it.

3 Design of the D2D Link Sharing Algorithm Based on Throughput and Interference Reduction

3.1 Link Candidates

The content of this section is to increase the total transmission rate in the network and reduce the interference caused to the CU, so that the DU that can maximize the transmission rate can preferentially occupy the link resources of the CU. By analyzing the Eqs. (1) and (2), it can be seen that when the value of power is fixed, the size of the throughput is related to the gain of the link, that is, the link transmission gain between CU and BS and the link transmission gain between D2D transmitter and the receiver are proportional to the throughput, the link transmission gain between D2D transmitter and BS and the link transmission gain between D2D transmitter and BS is inversely proportional to throughput, so you can get a priority equation for D2D filtering CU.

$$\theta_i^j = \frac{g_i^c * g_j^d}{g_{i,j}^c * g_{j,i}^d} \tag{17}$$

θ_i^j represents the link gain coefficient of the CU and DU within the network, which can help the DU select the CU. The preferential selection of DU in the network makes the largest CU shared link resources of B and can better improve the total rate of the communication system.

The algorithm steps are as follows. Initialize the DU within the network with CU, $D_{j,i}$ represents the candidate link of DU, D represents the DU set, and C represents the CU set (Table 1).

Table 1. Link candidate pseudocode.

(1) **Initialize:**$D_{j,i}, D, E = C,$
(2) **for all** j $\in$ D and i $\in$ E, calculate $(i^*, j^*) = \underset{j \in D, i \in E}{\arg \max}\, \theta_i^j$, Get the DU j^* and CU i^* that maximize θ_i^j in the current set
(3) if number $(D_{j^*,i})$ < Maximum number of candidates
(3) set $\rho_{i^* j^*} = 1$, Indicates that i^* was selected
(4) $D_{j^*,i^*} = \{j^*, i^*\}$, The CU i^* was added to the candidate link of the DU j^*
(5) $E = E\backslash\{i^*\}$, Remove i^* from the collection
(6) **end for**

3.2 Further Interference Screening

In the previous section, how to select the appropriate set of communication links for DU has been solved. Next, this section will solve how to select the set of candidates for DU and share the least interference to CU, which can make the communication quality of CU less poor.

Here, IoT (Interference over Thermal) is used to characterize the interference caused by the CU by the D2D user transmitter, and IoT is used to indicate the interference of CU, the candidate link of DU selects the CU with minimum IoT for link sharing (Table 2).

$$I_{IoT} = \frac{P_j^d g_{j,i}^d + \sigma_N^2}{\sigma_N^2} \tag{18}$$

Table 2. Further interference with the filtering of the pseudocode.

(1) **Initialize** $I_{j,i}$
(2) **for** $D_{j,i}$, calculate $\left(i^*, j^*\right) = \underset{j,i \in D_{j,i}}{\arg\min}\, I_{IoT}^{j^*}$, The i^* with the smallest I_{IoT} in the candidate i of j^* was obtained
(3) $I_{j^*,i^*} = \{j^*, i^*\}$, Add i^* and j^* to the final collection of shared links
(4) **end for**

4 Simulation Results and Analysis

4.1 Simulation Parameters and Simulation Process

This section will demonstrate the designed algorithm in the MATLAB simulation platform to verify the performance of the candidate link-based further interference reduction screening algorithm proposed in this paper through a series of simulation analyses. Simulation scenario, communication link. The simulation scenario is a separately distributed cellular cell with a network coverage radius of 500 m, and the cellular users and D2D users are randomly distributed in the cell, assuming that the cellular users occupy all the spectrum resources, the D2D users can only communicate by sharing resources with the cellular users, and the cellular users and D2D users can transmit data at the same time. The parameter settings of this system refer to the 3GPP protocol. This simulation uses a system-level platform, which can only calculate SINR and throughput by assigning parameters to the user, use these values to simulate a realistic model, and compare the performance of other algorithms. The path loss model in this simulation only considers the large-scale fading model.

In order to better reflect the performance of the algorithm proposed in this paper, the further interference reduction screening algorithm based on the candidate link proposed in this paper is compared with the random resource allocation algorithm [13], in this algorithm, DU randomly selects CU and its multiplex link resources, and the power is also the same as the power allocation method used in this paper, that is, the open-loop power control method.

The parameters of the system simulation are shown in the following table (Table 3):

Table 3. Simulation parameters.

Parameters	Value
Simulation scenario	Urban area
Transmission link bandwidth	180 kHz

(continued)

Table 3. (*continued*)

Parameters	Value
Cell radius	500 m
CU numbers	50
D2D number	10
CU maximum transmit power	24 dBm
DU maximum transmit power	24 dBm
Noise power spectral density	−154 dBm/Hz
Path loss model (user-BS)	$32.4 + 21 \log(d) + 20 \log(f)$
Path loss model (user-user)	$22.7 + 36.7 \log(d) + 26 \log(f)$
Carrier frequency	1 GHz

4.2 Influence of Channel Fading on D2D Communication Performance

Figure 2 depicts the model diagram in the simulation, with the black flag representing BS, the green flag representing the CU, and the red flag representing the DU, where the CU and DU are randomly distributed.

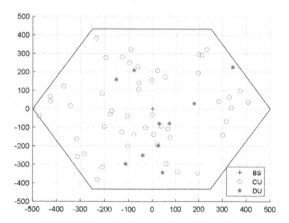

Fig. 2. User distribution simulation plot.

Figure 3 depicts the cumulative distribution function of the network transmission rates of different algorithms. Wherein the number of DU in the network is 10. The total rate in the system is determined by the CU that is not multiplexed and the CU and DU that reuse the same channel. From the figure, it can be concluded that the further interference reduction screening algorithm based on candidate links in this paper has a significant improvement in network transmission rate compared with the random resource allocation algorithm, and the algorithm in this paper has higher performance than random resource allocation algorithms in throughput.

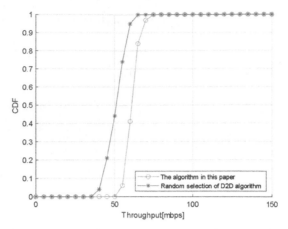

Fig. 3. Network transmission rate cumulative distribution function curve.

Figure 4 depicts the cumulative distribution function of the transmission rates of du networks of different algorithms. Where the number of DU in the network is 10. It can be concluded from the figure that the DU network transmission rate based on the candidate link further interference reduction screening algorithm proposed in this paper is better than the random resource allocation algorithm. The results show that the further interference reduction filtering algorithm based on the candidate link in this paper can reduce the channel interference to the CU and assign a more reasonable communication link to the DU, thereby improving the communication performance.

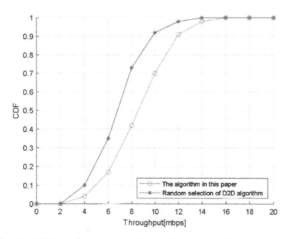

Fig. 4. DU transfer rate cumulative distribution function curve.

5   Conclusion

D2D communication users can reuse the channels of cellular users, thus improving the overall transmission rate of the region and improving the system throughput. This paper studies how to improve network performance through D2D communication in full load networks and proposes a further interference reduction screening algorithm based on candidate links. The algorithm consists of two parts: link candidate and further interference screening. In the link candidate, a throughput equation is obtained through the allocation of fixed power. According to this equation, D2D users can be selected as cellular users, thus improving the overall throughput in the network. Further interference screening, that is, D2D users select the candidate link that causes the least interference to cellular users for reuse, so as to reduce the interference to cellular users. In addition, this paper analyzes the throughput performance and SINR performance of D2D in the network through simulation and compares the performance with that of an existing classical algorithm. Simulation results show that the proposed further interference reduction filtering algorithm based on candidate links can improve the access speed of D2D users and the overall throughput of the system.

Acknowledgement. The authors would like to thank the anonymous reviewers for their selfless reviews and valuable comments, which have improved the quality of our original manuscript.

Funding Statement: This work was partially supported by the National Natural Science Foundation of China (No.61876089, No. 61771410), by the Talent Introduction Project of Sichuan University of Science & Engineering (No. 2020RC22), by the Zigong City Key Science and Technology Program (No. 2019YYJC16), by the Teaching Reform Research Project of Sichuan University of Science & Engineering (JG-2121), by the Enterprise Informatization and Internet of Things Measurement and Control Technology Sichuan Provincial Key Laboratory of universities (No.2020WZY01).

Conflicts of Interest:. The authors declare that they have no conflicts of interest to report regarding the present study.

References

1. Du, C., Zhang, Z., Wang, X., An, J.: Optimal duplex mode selection for D2D-aided underlaying cellular networks. IEEE Trans. Veh. Technol. **69**(3), 3119–3134 (2020)
2. Du, C., Zhang, Z., Wang, X.: Optimal duplex mode selection for D2D-aided underlaying cellular networks. IEEE Trans. Veh. Technol. **69**(3), 3119–3134 (2020)
3. Tian, C.S.: Research on key technology of resource allocation for device-to-device communications underlaying cellular networks. Ph.D. Thesis. Jilin University (2020)
4. Shi, J.: The research on D2D power control based on deep. M.S. Thesis. University of Electronic Science and Technology of China (2021)
5. Wang, X.: Research on resource allocation algorithm for device-to-device communications in cellular networks. Ph.D. Thesis. Jilin University (2020)

6. Hamid, A.K., Al-Wesabi, F.N., Nemri, N., Zahary, A., Khan, I.: An optimized algorithm for resource allocation for d2d in heterogeneous networks. Comp. Mater. Contin. **70**(2), 2923–2936 (2022)
7. Ahamad, R.Z., Javed, A.R., Mehmood, S., Khan, M.Z., Noorwali, A.: Interference mitigation in d2d communication underlying cellular networks: towards green energy. Comp. Mater. Contin. **68**(1), 45–58 (2021)
8. Bashir, S., Khan, I., Al-Wesabi, F.N., Nemri, N., Zahary, A.: An optimized algorithm for d2d-mimo 5g wireless networks. Comp. Mater. Contin. **68**(3), 3029–3044 (2021)
9. Al-Wesabi, F.N., Khan, I., Alamgeer, M., Al-Sharafi, A.M., Choi, B.J.: A joint algorithm for resource allocation in d2d 5g wireless networks. Comp. Mater. Contin. **69**(1), 301–317 (2021)
10. Anjum, N., Yang, Z., Khan, I., Kiran, M., Wu, F.: Efficient algorithms for cache-throughput analysis in cellular-d2d 5g networks. Comp. Mater. Contin: **67**(2), 1759–1780 (2021)
11. 3GPP TR 36.213 V9.1.0.: Universal Terrestrial Radio Access (E-UTRA). Physical layer procedures (2010)
12. Series, M.: Guidelines for evaluation of radio interface technologies for IMT-2020. ReportITU 2412–0 (2017)
13. Belleschi, M., Fodor, G., Penda, D.: D: Benchmarking practical RRM algorithms for D2D communications in LTE advanced. Wireless Pers. Commun. **82**(2), 883–910 (2015)

Study on the Transmission Characteristics and the Longest Transmission Distance of 0.1–1 Terahertz Wave in the Atmosphere

Xiaodong Yin[1], Xiaoli He[1(✉)], Yu Song[2], Weijian Yang[1], Zhen Zeng[1], Hongwei Li[1], and Haimin Yi[1]

[1] School of Computer Science, Sichuan University of Science and Engineering, Zigong 643000, China
hexiaoli_suse@hotmail.com
[2] Department of Network Information Management Center, Sichuan University of Science and Engineering, Zigong 643000, China

Abstract. Terahertz wave has broad application prospects in the field of communication, but terahertz communication also has its limitations, because terahertz wave attenuation in the atmosphere is relatively strong, especially the existence of water vapor in the atmosphere will cause strong absorption of terahertz wave. In this article, the low frequency attenuation characteristics of the terahertz wave in the standard atmospheric conditions are studied and simulation, mainly study the absorption of oxygen and water vapor in the atmosphere to transmit signal attenuation characteristics, according to the simulation diagram, select a few special frequency plus gaussian white noise in different distance of analog transmission test, and oversee the distortion of the original signal, The longest feasible transmission distance of this frequency signal is obtained, which lays a foundation for better utilization of terahertz communication.

Keywords: Terahertz wave · Complex refractive index · Attenuation rate

1 Introduction

Terahertz wave refers to the electromagnetic wave with a frequency of 0.1–10 THz and a wavelength of 3 mm–0.03 mm, between microwave and infrared, compared with light waves, terahertz waves are composed of tiny particles during propagation. The scattering factor has a smaller influence on molecules [1], and compared with microwave, Terahertz wave has the characteristics of strong penetration, high bandwidth and high transmission efficiency, which make terahertz in future communication, radar market to achieve better use prospects [2]. The physical properties of terahertz determine the great attenuation of terahertz wave in space, so terahertz technology, terahertz slot antenna, terahertz multimode horn antenna design and terahertz paraboloid four feed antenna design are also particularly important in terahertz communication system [3].

X. Sun et al. (Eds.): ICAIS 2022, CCIS 1586, pp. 149–159, 2022.
https://doi.org/10.1007/978-3-031-06767-9_13

However, when the terahertz wave propagates in the atmosphere, it is mainly affected by the strong absorption effect of gas molecules in the atmosphere, leading to the transmission of the signal. When the signal decays rapidly, it cannot reach the expected transmission distance. The transmission attenuation of terahertz wave caused by dust and cloud weather should not be ignored. Domestic research of THZ wave transmission characteristics relative to the abroad should start later [4], and the early stage of the domestic condition of experiment, the lack of production and propagation of THZ wave, detector devices such as instruments and experimental conditions of immature, cause the spectrum in the band in a "blank" range of atmospheric absorption lines of various molecules are relatively small, The e study focuses on the terahertz space transmission characteristics [5]. Therefore, the study of atmospheric transmission attenuation rate of terahertz has important scientific research value for the wide application scenarios of terahertz technology.

2   Transmission Characteristics of Terahertz Wave in Atmosphere

Exploring the transmission window of terahertz wave in the atmosphere is an important step in terahertz wireless communication. Compared with microwave and optical bands, various molecules in the atmosphere have a strong absorption effect on terahertz band, especially oxygen and water vapor in the air, which makes the application of terahertz wave in wireless communication system a congenital bottleneck. The non resonant continuous absorption model of dry air and water vapor and dust, In order to better develop high-speed communication in wireless communication system, it is necessary to explore the transmission characteristics and laws of terahertz wave (Fig. 1).

2.1   Absorption Model of Oxygen and Water Vapor and Solution

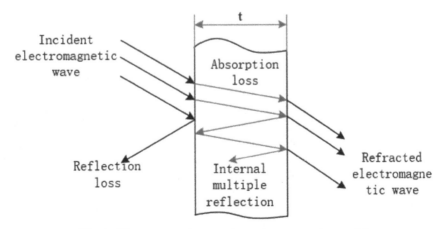

Fig. 1. Electromagnetic wave absorption attenuation model.

The essence of terahertz wave is an electromagnetic wave. The absorption effect of the atmosphere on electromagnetic waves depends not only on the oxygen molecules and water vapor molecules in the air, but also on the changes of atmospheric temperature, humidity, pressure and other environments. In order to better study the absorption and attenuation characteristics of terahertz, firstly, considering the essential electromagnetic wave, the expression of electromagnetic wave field strength in the atmosphere [6] is:

$$E = E_0 \times \exp[jk_0L(N \times 10^6 + 1)] \tag{1}$$

Here E_0 represents the initial field strength of the electromagnetic wave, and E_0 represents the complex refractive index of the atmosphere. L is the distance that the electromagnetic wave has transmitted, and K_0 is the propagation constant in vacuum. Here, N is usually decomposed into dispersion term $N(f)$ and frequency independent term N_0

$$N = N_0 + N(f) \tag{2}$$

Here N_0 is a real number, and $N(f)$ can also be decomposed into an imaginary part $N''(f)$ and a real part $N'(f)$

$$N(f) = N'(f) - jN''(f) \tag{3}$$

The absorption attenuation rate of the atmosphere to terahertz($\gamma/dB \cdot Km^{-1}$) is determined by the imaginary part of the atmospheric complex refractive index $N(f)$. The expression is

$$\gamma = \gamma_d + \gamma_w = 0.182fN''(f) \tag{4}$$

Here, γ_d represents the attenuation rate of oxygen, γ_w represents the attenuation rate of water vapor, f represents the signal frequency (GHz) propagating in the atmosphere, and the expression of $N''(f)$ can be expressed as

$$N''(f) = N_L''(f) + N_d''(f) + N_w''(f) \tag{5}$$

Here, $N_L''(f)$ represents the absorption spectrum of oxygen and water vapor to terahertz, $N_d''(f)$ represents the absorption spectrum of non resonant dry air to terahertz, and $N_w''(f)$ represents the continuous absorption spectrum of water vapor to terahertz. The $N_L''(f)$ expression is

$$N_L''(f) = \sum_{i=1}^{44} S_i F_i(f) + \sum_{j=1}^{30} S_j F_j(f) \tag{6}$$

According to HITRAN database, 44 oxygen absorption lines below 1 THz and 30 water vapor absorption lines can be obtained. Here, S_i represents the intensity of the i-th oxygen linear absorption spectrum, $F_i(f)$ represents the corresponding spectral shape function of the i-th oxygen absorption spectrum, S_j represents the intensity of the j-th water vapor linear absorption spectrum, and $F_j(f)$ represents the corresponding spectral shape function of the i-th water vapor absorption spectrum.The spectral shape function is expressed as

$$F_i(f) = \frac{f}{f_i}(\frac{A}{X} + \frac{B}{Y}) \tag{7}$$

where the expressions A, B, X and Y are

$$A = \gamma_i - \delta_i(f - f_i) \tag{8}$$

$$X = (f_i - f)^2 + \gamma_i^2 \tag{9}$$

$$C = \gamma_i - \delta_i(f + f_i) \tag{10}$$

$$Y = (f_i + f)^2 + \gamma_i^2 \tag{11}$$

Here, γ_i represents the i-th line width of the spectral line, f_i represents the i-th absorption spectral line frequency, f is the transmitted terahertz wave frequency, and δ_i represents the i-th overlap correction factor. In Eqs. (6) to (11), the expressions of S_i, γ_i and δ_i of oxygen and water vapor are respectively

$$S_{iO_2} = 10^{-7}a_1 P\theta^3 \exp[(a_2(1 - \theta)] \tag{12}$$

$$\gamma_{iO_2} = 10^{-4}a_3(P\theta^{0.8-a_4} + 1.1e\theta) \tag{13}$$

$$\delta_{iO_2} = 10^{-4}(a_5 + a_6\theta)P\theta^{0.8} \tag{14}$$

$$S_{iH_2O} = 10^{-1}b_1 e\theta^{3.5} \exp[(b_2(1 - \theta)] \tag{15}$$

$$\gamma_{iH_2O} = 10^{-4}b_3(P\theta^{b_4} + b_5 e\theta^{b_6}) \tag{16}$$

$$\delta_{iH_2O} = 0 \tag{17}$$

where e and θ The expression for is

$$e = \frac{\rho T}{216.7} \tag{18}$$

$$\theta = \frac{300}{T} \tag{19}$$

In Eqs. (12) to (19),where P is the atmospheric pressure, t is the absolute temperature and E is the water vapor pressure, ρ Is the water vapor density, a_1-a_6 is the absorption spectrum coefficient of oxygen, and b_1-b_6 is the absorption spectrum coefficient of water vapor, which is taken from HITRAN spectral parameter database.Finally, the linear absorption spectrum of oxygen and water vapor to terahertz wave can be obtained by calculating formula (6).It can be seen from Fig. 2, Fig. 3 and Fig. 4 that there are several high peaks in the absorption effect of oxygen on terahertz wave, the absorption of water vapor to terahertz wave shows an upward trend as a whole, and the absorption effect of oxygen is mainly in the low band, and the absorption effect of water vapor to terahertz wave is mainly in the high band.

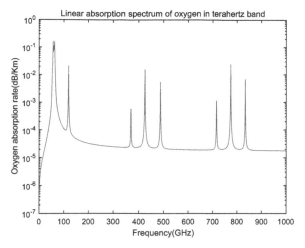

Fig. 2. Linear absorption spectrum of oxygen in terahertz band.

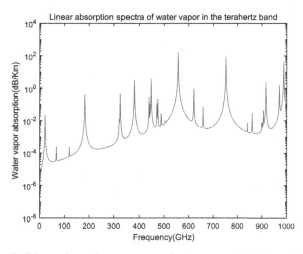

Fig. 3. Linear absorption spectrum of water vapor in terahertz band.

2.2 Non Resonant Continuous Absorption Model of Dry Air and Water Vapor and Solution

The expressions of $N_d''(f)$ and $N_w''(f)$ in Eqs. (5) are

$$N_w''(f) = 10^{-7}(3.57e\theta^{7.5} + 0.113P)fe\theta^3 \tag{20}$$

$$N_d''(f) = \frac{S_d f}{\gamma_0[1 + (\frac{f}{\gamma_0})^2]} + a_p f P^2 \theta^{3.5} \tag{21}$$

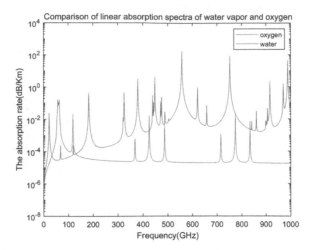

Fig. 4. Comparison of linear absorption spectra of water vapor and oxygen.

where the expressions of S_d, γ_0 and a_p are

$$S_d = 6.14 \times 10^{-5} P\theta^2 \tag{22}$$

$$\gamma_0 = 5.6 \times 10^{-4}(P + 1.1e)\theta \tag{23}$$

$$a_p = 1.4 \times 10^{-12}(1 - 1.2 \times 10^{-5} f^{1.5}) \tag{24}$$

Through the Eqs. (20) to (24) and (4) (5), and setting the temperature is 288 K, the atmospheric pressure to 101.5 kPa and the water vapor density to 7.5 g/m^3, an attenuation diagram of 0.1–1 THz wave transmission in the atmosphere can be calculated finally (Fig. 5).

According to the transmission attenuation of terahertz wave in the atmosphere in relevant literature [7], the simulation is carried out and compared with the transmission model in this paper. As can be seen from Fig. 7, in the frequency band of 0.1 THz to 1 THz, the attenuation rate of terahertz wave in relevant papers is generally higher than that in this paper. The different experimental results may be that the attenuation models are different, or the parameters of the atmospheric molecular absorption models may have different values at different times, and whether the weather changes or not affect the experimental results to a great extent.

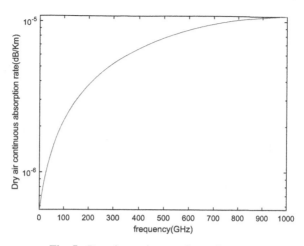

Fig. 5. Dry air continuous absorption rate.

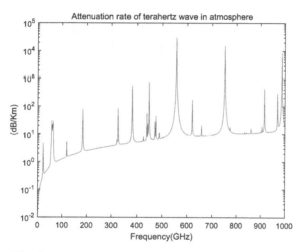

Fig. 6. Attenuation rate of terahertz wave in atmosphere.

3 Simulation of Terahertz Wave Transmission Distance

From the above attenuation model of terahertz wave in the atmosphere,Several absorption peaks reached the maximum attenuation effect around 380 GHz, 448 GHz, 557 GHz, 752 GHz and 988 GHz respectively. At 752 GHz, the attenuation rate reaches 15388 dB/Km. At 557 GHz, the attenuation rate reaches 29499 dB/Km. At 0.1 THz, the attenuation rate is as low as 1.2 db/km, up to around 191 GHz, 390 GHz, 654 GHz, 816 GHz, 941 GHz At a trough, the attenuation rate of 941 GHz is only 12.19 dB/km. In order to make better use of terahertz wave, The test will be carried out at a frequency with high frequency and low attenuation rate. In order to build a terahertz communication system, we choose the ambient pressure of standard atmospheric pressure, Set

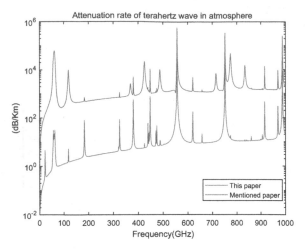

Fig. 7. Attenuation rate comparison.

atmospheric pressure $P = 101.3\,\text{kPa}$, Absolute temperature $T = 288k$, water vapor density $\rho = 7.5\,\text{g/m}^{-3}$. The terahertz frequency used for the test is $f = 941$ GHz, the amplitude is 1 V, and the signal strength of Gaussian white noise is g = 10 mV. Here, the transmission distances of 1000 m, 4000 m and 8000m will be tested respectively [8].

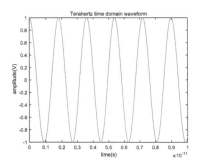

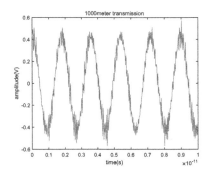

Fig. 8. Terahertz time domain waveform.   **Fig. 9.** 1000 m transmission.

It can be seen from Figs. 8, 9, 10 and 11 that the terahertz waveform transmitting 941 GHz frequency changes slightly after 1000 m, but does not affect the data sampling. The original signal can be restored. The waveform transmitting 2000 m has obvious changes, but the first original signal can be restored through amplifiers and other equipment. When transmitting 4000 m, the signal power attenuates too much, The original signal is mixed with Gaussian white noise, resulting in a very low signal-to-noise ratio, resulting in the final signal distortion and unable to restore the signal to be transmitted. The above shows that it is feasible for 941 GHz high-frequency terahertz wave to transmit 2000 m in the atmosphere [9].

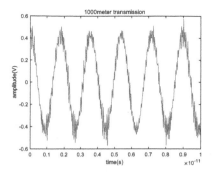
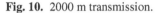

Fig. 10. 2000 m transmission.

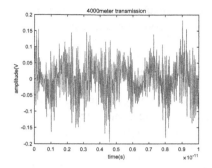

Fig. 11. 4000 m transmission.

As can be seen from Fig. 6, the transmission attenuation of 557 ghz has reached 29499db / km. Under the same environmental conditions. The transmission of terahertz wave in 557 ghz band is simulated. It can be seen from Fig. 12 that under the transmission condition of 557 ghz band, the original signal can be almost obtained by sampling and quantizing the waveform after transmission of 0.5m and 1m. However, the waveform after transmission of 1.5m has begun to be seriously distorted, so it is impossible to judge the waveform of the initial original signal, and the error rate of sampling judgment is very high. Therefore, it can be concluded that there is no problem for 557 ghz band to transmit within 1m in the atmosphere. If the transmission distance exceeds 1.5m, the signal is almost distorted and the original signal cannot be recovered. Although the attenuation rate of terahertz wave is generally positively correlated with frequency, there are also some special frequency bands. Obviously, the frequency of 941 ghz is

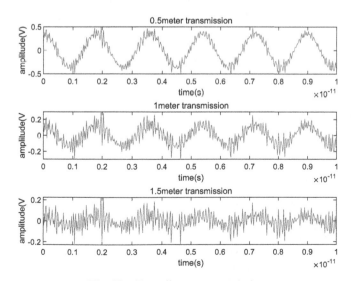

Fig. 12. Short distance transmission.

higher than 887 ghz and the transmission distance is longer, which is more suitable for communication transmission.

4   Conclusion

This paper mainly studies the transmission characteristics of 0.1-1Tz terahertz wave in the atmosphere, mainly the absorption of terahertz wave by water vapor, oxygen and dry air in the atmosphere. The simulation results show that the transmission attenuation rate increases as the frequency increases, but there are several special frequency ranges around these frequencies, The obvious increase of atmospheric absorption effect leads to a high attenuation around these frequencies. For example, the attenuation rate of 557 ghz is more than 2000 times that of 941 ghz. The corresponding 941 ghz can transmit 2000 m, while 557 can only transmit 1m. Therefore, the high frequency band here is more suitable for user communication. However, in the real environment, at different altitudes, there are different complex refractive indexes of electromagnetic waves. If longitudinal signal transmission is carried out, it will have a great influence and it may also face various complex effects of wind, rain, lightning, weather and temperature. If the influence of weather change and transmission direction is considered, an attenuation of terahertz waves with different frequencies will be calculated more accurately.

Acknowledgement. The authors would like to thank the anonymous reviewers for their selfless reviews and valuable comments, which have improved the quality of our original manuscript.

Funding Statement: This work was partially supported by the National Natural Science Foundation of China (No.61876089, No. 61771410), by the Talent Introduction Project of Sichuan University of Science & Engineering (No. 2020RC22), by the Zigong City Key Science and Technology Program (No. 2019YYJC16), by the Teaching Reform Research Project of Sichuan University of Science & Engineering (JG-2121), by the Enterprise Informatization and Internet of Things Measurement and Control Technology Sichuan Provincial Key Laboratory of universities (No.2020WZY01).

Conflicts of Interest:. The authors declare that they have no conflicts of interest to report regarding the present study.

References

1. Alsharif, M.H., Albreem, M.A.M., Solyman, A.A.A., Kim, S.: Toward 6g communication networks: terahertz frequency challenges and open research issues. Comp. Mater. Contin. **66**(3), 2831–2842 (2021)
2. Wanke, M.C., Mangan, M.A., Foltynowicz, R.J.: Atmospheric propagation of terahertz radiation. Sandia National Laboratories (2005)
3. Saraereh, O.A., Al-Tarawneh, L., Ali, A.: A: Design and analysis of a novel antenna for thz wireless communication. Intell. Auto. Soft Compu. **31**(1), 607–619 (2022)

4. Wang, J.: Study on attenuation characteristics of THz wave propagation in the atmosphere. Nanjing University of information engineering (2017)
5. Zhao, G.: New progress in terahertz science and technology. Foreign Elec. Measure. Technol. **33**(02), 1–6 (2014)
6. Huang, G.: Study on terahertz wave transmission characteristics. Xi'an University of Electronic Science and technology (2010)
7. Xu, W.: Study on attenuation characteristics of terahertz wave in the atmosphere. Tianjin University (2014)
8. Liu, H.: Research and design of terahertz wireless communication system. University of Electronic Science and technology (2014)
9. Yang, T., Huang, D., Chen, M., Zhang, F., Chen, X.: Study on signal distortion of parametric acoustic source demodulation. Chinese J. Sci. Instru. **34**(08), 1771–1778 (2013)

Research on Diabetic Retinal Fundus Screening Model Based on Conditional Generative Adversarial Nets

Chenxi Huang[1], Jin Qi[1(✉)], Song Xu[1], and Lei Wang[2]

[1] School of Internet of Things, Nanjing University of Posts and Telecommunications, Nanjing 210003, China
qijin@njupt.edu.cn
[2] RWTH Aachen University, 52056 Aachen, Germany

Abstract. Retinal fundus screening is of great significance to the diagnosis of diabetes. However, the existing methods have various problems in retinal blood vessel segmentation and exudate detection, such as insufficient blood vessel segmentation, weak anti-noise ability, strict requirements on the number of data sets and so on. Meanwhile, an assessment of new medicinal symbolisms stays complex [1]. Aiming at the defects of existing methods for screening diabetic fundus, this paper proposes a method for screening diabetic fundus based on generative confrontation network. In view of the high-resolution characteristics of medical images and the small number of retinal images with calibration maps, the Generative Adversarial Nets is introduced into the retinal fundus screening model, and PatchGAN is introduced into the discrimination network to realize high-resolution image generation. In order to reduce the prediction error in noisy images, a method is proposed to modify the prediction results at pixel level according to the prediction results of exudate probability distribution. The experimental result show that the accuracy of vessel segmentation and exudate detection is 98.75% and 98.62%, respectively.

Keywords: Conditional Generative Adversarial Nets · Retinal vascular segmentation · Eyeground exudate detection · Medical image processing

1 Introduction

Retinopathy (DR), as the most typical microvascular complication in diabetes mellitus, it leads toward irreversible vision loss [2]. has attracted wide attention in medical industry and academia. Traditional retinal screening methods are restricted by low awareness rate and screening rate, which makes it difficult to ensure the eye health of patients. Therefore, how to achieve reliable and timely retinal fundus detection through efficient and accurate fundus exudate detection and blood vessel extraction has become a great challenge in the medical field [3].

In order to achieve accurate and efficient fundus screening, some researchers have tried to extract blood vessels by vessel segmentation. These techniques are divided into

X. Sun et al. (Eds.): ICAIS 2022, CCIS 1586, pp. 160–172, 2022.
https://doi.org/10.1007/978-3-031-06767-9_14

different categories such as: pattern recognition, supervised and unsupervised machine learning, mathematical morphology, model tracking, adaptive filtering, and multiscalar approaches [4]. Computer-Aided Diagnosis (CAD) models have been developed to diagnose the disease in an automated manner [5]. References [6–8] respectively put forward retinal vessel segmentation methods based on threshold method, vessel segmentation based on morphology and vessel segmentation based on region growing method. However, the above studies have not considered the different quality of retinal images, low background contrast and many noises. In order to solve this problem, Niemeijer et al. realized hard exudate detection by using supervised machine learning method combined with KNN classifier [9]. Akram et al. used Bayesian classifier to divide exudate and non-exudate areas [10], Osareh et al. realized exudate extraction by using support vector machine (SVM) and MLP classifier respectively [11]. However, the above machine learning methods have the limitation of not accurately extracting all features, and can not achieve satisfactory results in retinal images of different quality. In order to get rid of the limitations of traditional machine learning methods, some researchers consider using deep learning methods to screen diabetic retina. Prentasic et al. used convolution neural network to segment the color fundus image and extract exudate [12], Melinsca et al. proposed to extract retinal blood vessels using deep convolution neural network [13], Benson et al. proposed a vessel segmentation method based on vector field divergence for diseased retina images [14]. However, due to the lack of retinal image data sets at present, the above methods have the problem of information loss. To solve the above problems, Son et al. realized retinal blood vessel extraction by using Generative Confrontation Network (GANs) [15]. However, when solving the training value of GAN in actual images, this method is unstable. Therefore, in view of the shortcomings of the existing methods and the realistic background that there are few retinal data sets with calibration maps, this paper proposes an automatic detection method of retinal hard exudate based on condition-generated countermeasure network, which realizes retinal blood vessel segmentation and hard exudate detection.

The main contributions of this paper are as follows: (1) In view of the high-resolution characteristics of medical images and the small number of retinal images with calibration maps, the Generative Adversarial Nets is introduced into the retinal fundus screening model, and PatchGAN is introduced into the discrimination network to realize high-resolution image generation; (2) Aiming at the problems of low exudate contrast and unclear edge in the original retina image, a variety of image processing algorithms are combined reasonably to solve the problem of uneven illumination, correct the over-dark overexposed image, highlight the details of blood vessels and exudates, and cover up the optic disc to eliminate the bright edge area, thus effectively improving the efficiency and accuracy of model training. (3) In order to reduce the prediction error in noisy images, a method is proposed to correct the prediction results at pixel level according to the prediction results of exudate probability distribution.

2   Problem Description

2.1   Model Structure

The fundus screening model based on conditional Generative Adversarial Nets proposed in this paper is composed of generation network and discrimination network, and the model structure is shown in Fig. 1. Firstly, the preprocessed retina image (a) and expert calibration map (b) are paired and input into the generating network (g), which generates the predicted image G(a) with the same specification as the expert calibration map by learning the mapping relationship between retina image and expert calibration map, and then discriminates the generated image by the discriminating network, which discriminates between the input image pairs {a,b} and {a,G(a)} by learning. Finally, through the trained generation network, the blood vessels and exudates of retinal fundus images can be predicted and analyzed, so as to achieve the goal of diabetic retinal fundus screening.

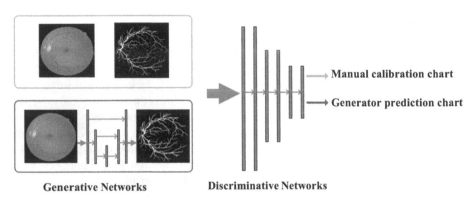

Generative Networks   Discriminative Networks

Fig. 1. Retinal fundus screening model based on Generative Adversarial Nets.

2.2   Generate Network

Generation Network (G) is used to learn the mapping relationship between the original image and the expert calibration image. The purpose of g is to learn the distribution of real samples and maximize the generation of generated samples that are close to the real samples. In this model, U-net [16] network is used as generator network g.. The network is improved on FCN. There is no full connection layer, and the input and output are all images. Only a few training pictures can be used to complete the training and obtain higher segmentation accuracy.

In addition, this model introduces the idea of conditional Generative Adversarial Nets, uses a kind of GAN with conditional constraints, and introduces conditional variable b into the modeling of both the generation model g and the discriminant model d. in the generation model, the prior input noise p(c) and conditional information b form a joint hidden layer representation, and additional information y is used to add constraints to the model, which can guide the data generation process.

In order to constrain the difference between the generated retina prediction image and the expert calibration map, this paper introduces the K1 distance as the constraint condition of the conditional generation countermeasure network [17]:

$$K_{K1}(G) = Q_{a,b,c}[||b - G(a, c)||_1] \tag{1}$$

the objective function of the whole cGANs is:

$$G^* = \arg \min_G \left[\max_D K_{cGAN}(G, D) \right] + \lambda K_{K1}(G) \tag{2}$$

The λ is the regular coefficient (set as 0.1 in the experiment).

2.3 Discriminant Network

Because the common GAN discriminator can only judge the whole image by mapping the input into a real number, it can not reflect the details of retinal image, and the details such as blood vessel structure and exudate structure need to be strictly judged in retinal image processing. Therefore, this paper uses PatchGAN discriminator to realize the discrimination network, which can minimize the probability of discrimination errors by discriminating whether the training samples come from real samples or generated samples. In this paper, PatchGAN maps the input to a matrix A of N × N, the A_ij represents the probability that each patch is a true sample, and the output of the discriminator is the mean of the A_ij. PatchGAN can only judge whether the matrix of N × N is true or false, so it can distinguish high-frequency information well.

In the discriminant network, let the input preprocessed retina image be a, and the output retina prediction image of the generative network G be a $G(a)$, and the expert calibration map be b. For the input b of the discriminant network D, the output of the $D(b)$ is a real number between the $0 \sim 1$, which is used to judge the probability that the input data is an expert calibration map. Let P_x and P_g represent the distribution of expert calibration map and the distribution of predicted image respectively, and the objective function of discriminant network D is expressed as [17]:

$$K_{cGAN}(C, D) = Q_{a \sim Pr}[\log D(a, b)] + Q_{a \sim Pr}[\log(1 - D(a, G(a, c)))] \tag{3}$$

In order to restrict the difference between the generated image and the real image, the K1 distance is introduced as the constraint condition of the conditional Generative Adversarial Nets:

$$K_{K1}(G) = Q_{a,b,c}[||b - G(a, b)||_1] \tag{4}$$

The objective function of the whole cGANs is:

$$G^* = \arg \min_G \left[\max_D K_{cGAN}(G, D) \right] + \lambda K_{K1}(G) \tag{5}$$

Among them, λ is taken as the regularization coefficient (set as 0.1 in the experiment).

3 Solution Method

In the previous section, we established a retina fundus screening model based on Conditional Generative Adversarial Nets, which corresponds to the pretreatment of original fundus photos, the gradient problem of optimizing learning rate, and the optimization of exudate prediction results. In order to solve the above problems, this paper firstly comprehensively uses various algorithms such as gray-scale transformation, gamma transformation, homomorphic filtering, CLAHE, optic disc masking, etc. in the best order to solve the preprocessing problem of fundus photos, then introduces an Adame algorithm which can replace the traditional random gradient descent process to optimize the gradient problem in model training, and finally optimizes the exudate results through the prediction results of probability distribution level.

3.1 Discriminant Network

The preprocessing of retina will first eliminate noise and highlight details, and then based on the preprocessed image, complete data set expansion and area masking. For the three problems, namely, blood vessel segmentation map, pixel-level exudate prediction and probability distribution exudate prediction, the same noise elimination and detail highlighting scheme can be adopted, but different data set expansion and area masking are needed.

Data Set Expansion and Regional Concealment. In view of the three applications of vessel segmentation, pixel-level exudate prediction and probability distribution exudate prediction, this paper adopts two different data set expansion schemes. In this paper, segmentation expansion is used for blood vessel segmentation and pixel-level exudate detection, while rotation expansion is used for probability distribution exudate detection. For the application of blood vessel segmentation, there is no need to mask the optic disc, but the exudate detection needs to mask the optic disc first to avoid being predicted as regional exudate.

Preparation of Blood Vessel Segmentation Data Set. The fundus image provided by the public data set DRIVE is selected for the blood vessel segmentation data set. Firstly, the initial color retina image is preprocessed according to the above process, and the preprocessed image with clear blood vessel edge is obtained. The size of the preprocessed image is 1024*1024 pixels, and each preprocessed image and calibration image is averagely divided into 16 sub-images with 256*256 pixels. At the same time, the data set is expanded, and the expanded image is provided to the generator.

Preparation of Exudate Detection Data Set. In this model, the morphological dilation operation is used to eliminate blood vessels in the image after masking the optic disc, and the kernel s is convolved with the image F to calculate the maximum value of pixels in the area covered by the kernel S [18]:

$$E = F \oplus S \qquad (6)$$

In which F is the original image, and S is the convolution kernel.

Noise Elimination and Detail Highlighting. In order to improve the problem of uneven illumination, Clara et al. proposed to enhance the brightness of YIQ color space to improve the problem of uneven illumination, and then transformed the image into RGB color model. The method is as follows [19]:

$$Y_{mod} = \rho T + \varsigma U + \sigma Z \tag{7}$$

In order to compress the brightness range and enhance the contrast, the homomorphic filtering algorithm is used to further process the gray channel image as follows:

$$\odot(u, v) = (y_H - y_L) \odot_{hp} (u, v) + y_L \tag{8}$$

Finally, the limited contrast adaptive histogram equalization (CLAHE) algorithm is used to divide the image into several regions to further enhance the contrast and highlight the details [14]. Firstly, CDF estimation is carried out on the region to approximately transform the gradient density function into a uniform density function [20]:

$$y_{i,j} = \frac{(N-1)}{M} * \sum_{k=0}^{n} \delta_{i,j} (e); n = 1,2,3, \dots, N-1 \tag{9}$$

For each quadrant of a region, the mapping function is calculated based on its four closest regions:

$$P_n = \frac{s}{r+s} \left(\frac{b}{a+b} f_{i-1,j-1}(P_o) + \frac{b}{a+b} f_{i,j-1}(P_o) \right) + \frac{s}{r+s} \left(\frac{b}{a+b} f_{i-1,j}(P_o) + \frac{b}{a+b} f_{i,j}(P_o) \right) \tag{10}$$

The new gray level of pixel is obtained by the following formula:

$$P_n = \frac{s}{r+s} \left(f_{i,j-1}(P_o) \right) + \frac{s}{r+s} \left(f_{i,j}(P_o) \right) \tag{11}$$

Because the shape of optic disc is similar to exudate, it will affect the detection of exudate, so it is necessary to cover the optic disc. Through observation, it is found that the blood vessels are densest in the center of the optic disc, and the center point of the optic disc can be determined by combining the blood vessel distribution information and the image gray information. The formula is as follows [21]:

$$D_O(m, n) = D_{BV'}(m, n) - 1.2 D_{G'}(m, n) \tag{12}$$

Among them, the $D_{G'}$ is the image after the mean filtering of the green channel image D_G.

Firstly, the average gray value of pixels in an N × M sliding window (step size is 1) is calculated (recorded as $D_{BV'}$). After many experiments, when n is set at 60 pixels and m is set at 25 pixels, the effect is best. Find out the minimum value of and process it. D_O is the processed picture. At this time, the center pixel of the window is the center position of the optic disc. Finally, taking the center position of the optic disc as the center point, the Hoff circle detection algorithm is used to detect the boundary of the optic disc and cover up the optic disc to avoid interference to the subsequent detection.

3.2 Optimization of Model Training Gradient

In order to optimize the training gradient in fundus screening model, this paper uses Adam optimization algorithm to optimize the gradient direction of learning rate [22]. Calculate the gradient of t time step:

$$gr_t = \nabla_\theta J(\alpha_{t-1}) \tag{13}$$

Let the exponential decay rate $\gamma_1 = 0.9$, m_0 be initialized to 0, and calculate the exponential moving average of the gradient according to the gradient as follows:

$$m_t = \gamma_1 m_{t-1} + (1 - \gamma_1)gr_t \tag{14}$$

Let the exponential decay rate $\gamma_2 = 0.999$, v_0 be initialized to 0, and calculate the exponential moving average of gradient square as follows:

$$v_t = \gamma_2 v_{t-1} + (1 - \gamma_2)gr_t^2 \tag{15}$$

In order to prevent m_t and v_t from deviating to 0, the gradient mean m_t and gradient square v_t are corrected respectively:

$$\widehat{m_t} = m_t/\left(1 - \gamma_1^t\right) \tag{16}$$

$$\widehat{v_t} = v_t/\left(1 - \gamma_2^t\right) \tag{17}$$

and then, update the learning rate as:

$$\alpha_t = \alpha_{t-1} - \beta * \widehat{m_t}/\left(\sqrt{\widehat{v_t}} + \delta\right) \tag{18}$$

3.3 Correction and Solution of Exudate Prediction Results

After training pixel-level data sets and probability distribution data sets respectively, two models which can be used for pixel-level evaluation and probability distribution prediction are obtained. For the same test image, two models are used to predict, and the probability distribution prediction graph is used to modify the pixel-level prediction graph.

In the prediction result of probability distribution, the probability that the pixel is exudate is represented by gray value. The higher the gray level, the higher the probability of exudation. Firstly, according to a set threshold Z, the prediction result of exudate probability distribution is set to 0. Then the probability distribution map is binarized, and the region with gray value of 255 is not only the region with higher probability of exudate. The binarized image and the pixel-level predicted image are transformed into a matrix and intersected, and the new matrix obtained is the corrected pixel-level predicted result.

The pixel point set in the pixel-level calibration graph is $\{p_1, p_2, p_3 \ldots, p_n\}$, the pixel point set in the probability distribution graph is $\{d_0, d_1, d_2, \ldots, d_n\}$, the modified pixel point set is $\{m_0, m_1, m_2, \ldots, m_n\}$, and the threshold value is n. The revised formula is as follows:

$$m_n = p_n \cap (d_n > n) \tag{19}$$

4 Experiment and Analysis

4.1 Data Preparation and Operation Environment

In the training and testing of this model, the data sets of DIARETDB1 and e-ophtha EX are divided into a training set and a testing set according to the ratio of 9:1. All the color retinal images of training samples and testing samples in the database are preprocessed to highlight details and reduce noise, and then each pair of images is cut or rotated to realize data amplification. Finally, the image sub-blocks used for training are input into the model in pairs for training.

4.2 Evaluation Criteria

Pixel-level evaluation criteria are used for vessel segmentation, while the evaluation criteria for exudate detection can be divided into pixel-level evaluation and image-level evaluation. Pixel-level evaluation criteria evaluate the accuracy of prediction results of each pixel. The image-level evaluation method is to classify the images according to certain classification rules and judge the classification accuracy of the predicted images.

Pixel Level Evaluation. Intersection of Union (Iou) is to calculate the ratio of intersection and union of prediction diagram and calibration diagram, and to measure the accuracy of prediction by calculating the ratio of overlapping parts in prediction diagram and calibration diagram. The pixel-level evaluation steps of blood vessel segmentation map and pixel-level exudate prediction map are as follows: first, the predicted image is binarized, then each line of the image is taken as an array to calculate the Iou value, and then the Iou accuracy of the image is obtained by averaging the Iou values of each line [23].

$$Iou = \frac{Card\left(d \,|\, d \in Predict \cap e \in GroundTruth \cap (0 < |d - e| < n)\right)}{Card\left(Predict \cup GroundTruth\right)} \quad (20)$$

Evaluation of Image Classification Accuracy. The principle of image level evaluation standard needs to formulate certain classification rules first, and then classify the prediction map and calibration map according to the classification rules, and then compare whether the classification of prediction map and calibration map is the same. Because this study only analyzes the index of hard exudate, this grading is only used to verify that the exudate recognition ability of this model is sufficient to meet the accuracy requirements of grading function. For all prediction maps and calibration maps, calculate whether the classification of each group of maps is accurate, and then count the proportion of prediction maps with accurate classification. For the probability distribution prediction chart, the percentage of points with probability greater than 0 (gray value greater than 0) in the probability distribution of exudate is divided into ten levels according to the step length of 10%, and the calculation method is the same as above.

4.3 Analysis of Results

Pixel Level Evaluation. The training results of blood vessel segmentation test set are shown as Fig. 2. It can be seen from the prediction results of the blood vessel segmentation model that the main body of the blood vessel is clear and accurate, and compared with the calibration chart, only the terminal small blood vessels are not fully recognized or are not clear enough. Because the identification and calibration of terminal tiny blood vessels are highly subjective, the number of terminal blood vessels calibrated by different experts is not the same, and the overall prediction effect will not be affected if the difference of terminal blood vessels is very small.

The average accuracy of the prediction results of the test set is 98.75% based on the IoU pixel evaluation standard. Compared with the traditional machine learning method and convolution neural network method, the results as shown in Table 1.

Analysis of Exudate Detection Results. We can conclude from Fig. 3 that, on the test set, the average accuracy of pixel-level exudate prediction of this model is 98.62%. The main purpose of the probability distribution exudate prediction is to correct the prediction of pixel-level exudate. Because each pixel means the probability value of exudate, it is of no practical significance to evaluate the predicted results of probability distribution at pixel level alone. In addition, the accuracy of the two exudate models in image-level evaluation is 100%, which indicates that the exudate detection at present can replace manual discrimination in the task of fundus image classification, and has excellent accuracy. The exudate detection accuracy of different methods is shown in Table 2:

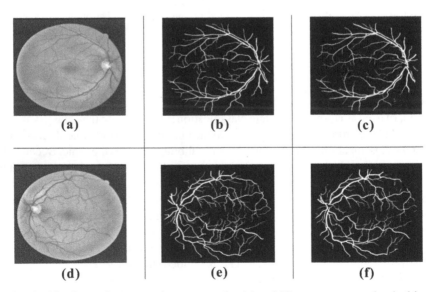

(a)   (b)   (c)

(d)   (e)   (f)

Fig. 2. The blood vessel segmentation test samples (a) and (d) are preprocessed retinal images, (b) and (e) are expert calibration maps, and (c) and (f) are prediction results.

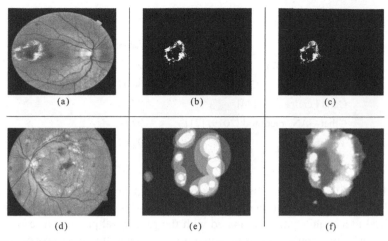

Fig. 3. The blood vessel segmentation test sample diagrams (a) and (d) are preprocessed retinal images, (b) are pixel-level exudate calibration diagrams, and (c) are pixel-level prediction diagrams. (e) is the calibration chart of probability distribution, and (f) is the prediction chart of probability distribution.

Table 1. Comparison of accuracy of retinal vessel segmentation by different methods.

Methods	Accuracy/%
Hoover [24]	91.58
Jiang et al. [25]	92.12
Benson [14]	94.74
Soares et al. [26]	94.66
HED(2015) [27]	90.54
DRIU(2016) [28]	91.65
CNN(2016) [29]	94.28
This paper	98.75

Table 2. Comparison of accuracy of different methods in extracting retinal hard exudate.

Methods	Accuracy/%
Akram et al. (2012) [10]	97.54
Xiao et al. (2015) [30]	93.7
UsmaanAkram et al. [31]	97

(continued)

Table 2. (*continued*)

Methods	Accuracy/%
T. Jaya et al. [32]	93
Imanietal (2016) [33]	80.32
Carla Pereira et al. [34]	87.72
Other GANs medthod (2019) [21]	97.8
This paper	98.62

In addition, after using probability distribution exudate prediction results to correct the pixel-level exudate prediction results, the accuracy of the prediction results obtained is improved to a certain extent compared with the pixel-level prediction results alone. For images with less noise, there is no obvious change in accuracy. However, for noisy images, the accuracy is improved by about 0.32%.

To sum up, this model has good performance in vessel segmentation and exudate detection tasks. Both exudate detection models have achieved very good detection accuracy in two public databases (DIARETDB1 and e-ophtha EX). Compared with traditional machine learning methods, this model has great advantages in accuracy. Compared with convolution neural network, which has been widely used in recent years, this model can achieve better training effect on smaller data sets while improve the accuracy to a certain extent.

5   Conclusion

This paper proposes an effective exudate detection method and blood vessel segmentation method, which is based on the Conditional Generative Adversarial Nets, for retinal fundus images. The results show that both the vascular segmentation method and hard exudate detection method proposed in this paper outperform existing methods in terms of accuracy and have better robustness for lesioned retinal images with different types of lesion, which have certain clinical reference and application value. However, considering the retinal image preprocessing process, this paper eliminates the bright edge area of the image, which may cause some exudates in the bright edge area to be ignored. The diabetic retinopathy classification task was highly critical due to noisy, saturated, and limited data [2]. The next step is to try to find a more effective method to preprocess the retinal image to keep more details of exudates.

References

1. Zia, F., et al.: A multilevel deep feature selection framework for diabetic retinopathy image classification. Comput. Mater. Contin. **70**, 2261–2276 (2022)
2. Nawaz, F., Ramzan, M., Mehmood, K., Khan, H.U., Khan, S.H., Bhutta, M.R.: Early detection of diabetic retinopathy using machine intelligence through deep transfer and representational learning. Comput. Mater. Contin. **66**, 1631–1645 (2021)

3. Hong, T., Yang, J.: Translational medicine research on diabetes prevention and treatment in China: opportunities and challenges. Chin. J. Diabetes Mellit. **9**(12), 729–731 (2017)
4. Escorcia-Gutierrez, J., et al.: A feature selection strategy to optimize retinal vasculature segmentation. Comput. Mater. Contin. **70**(2), 2971–2989 (2022)
5. Nguyen, P.T., Huynh, V.D.B., Vo, K.D., Phan, P.T., Yang, E., Joshi, G.P.: An optimal deep learning based computer-aided diagnosis system for diabetic retinopathy. Comput. Mater. Contin. **66**(3), 2815–2830 (2021)
6. Hoover, A.D., Kouznetsova, V., Goldbaum, M.: Locating blood vessels in retinal images by piecewise threshold probing of a matched filter response. IEEE Trans. Med. Imaging **19**(3), 203–210 (2000)
7. Yu, H., Wang, X.: Retinal vessels segmentation based on hessian enhancement and morphological scale space. Comput. Appl. Softw. **33**(8), 200–205 (2016)
8. Cheng, M., Huang, X.Y., Huang, S.H.: Directional region growing algorithm and its applications in vessel segmentation. J. Image Graph. **1**, 44–49 (2011)
9. Niemeijer, M., Ginneken, B.V., Russell, S.R., Suttorp-Schulten, M.S., Abramoff, M.D.: Automated detection and differentiation of drusen, exudates, and cotton-wool spots in digital color fundus photographs for diabetic retinopathy diagnosis. Invest. Ophthalmol. Vis. Sci. **48**(5), 2260–2267 (2007)
10. Akram, M.U., Tariq, A., Anjum, M.A., Javed, M.Y.: Automated detection of exudates in colored retinal images for diagnosis of diabetic retinopathy. Appl. Opt. **51**(20), 4858–4866 (2012)
11. Osareh, A., Mirmehdi, M., Thomas, B., Markham, R.: Comparative exudate classification using support vector machines and neural networks. In: International Conference on Medical Image Computing and Computer-Assisted Intervention, pp. 413–420 (2002)
12. Prentašić, P., Lončarić, S.: Detection of exudates in fundus photographs using convolutional neural networks. In: 2015 9th International Symposium on Image and Signal Processing and Analysis (ISPA), pp. 188–192 (2015)
13. Melinscak, M., Prentasic, P., Loncaric, S.: Retinal vessel segmentation using deep neural networks. In: VISAPP, vol.1, pp. 577–582 (2015)
14. Lam, B.S.Y., Yan, H.: A novel vessel segmentation algorithm for pathological retina images based on the divergence of vector fields. IEEE Trans. Med. Imaging **27**(2), 237–246 (2008)
15. Son, J., Park, S.J., Jung, K.H.: Retinal vessel segmentation in fundoscopic images with generative adversarial networks, arXiv preprint arXiv:1706.09318 (2017)
16. Ronneberger, O., Fischer, P., Brox, T.: U-Net: convolutional networks for biomedical image segmentation. In: Medical Image Computing and Computer-Assisted Intervention - MICCAI 2015. pp. 234–241 (2015)
17. Goodfellow, I., et al.: Generative adversarial networks. In: Communications of the ACM, vol. 63, no. 11, pp. 139–144 (2014)
18. Haralick, R.M., Sternberg, S.R., Zhuang, X.: Image analysis using mathematical morphology. IEEE Trans. Pattern Anal. Mach. Intell. **9**(4), 532–550 (1987)
19. Sánchez, C.I., Hornero, R., López, M.I., Aboy, M., Poza, J., Abásolo, D.: A novel automatic image processing algorithm for detection of hard exudates based on retinal image analysis. Med. Eng. Phys. **30**(3), 350–357 (2008)
20. Reza, A.M.: Realization of the contrast limited adaptive histogram equalization (CLAHE) for real-time image enhancement. J. VLSI Sig. Process. Syst. Signal Image Video Technol. **38**(1), 35–44 (2004)
21. Long, S., Chen, J., Huang, X., Chen, Z.: Hard exudates detection method based on generative adversarial networks in color fundus images. Chin. J. Biomed. Eng. **38**(2), 157–165 (2019)
22. Kingma, D.P., Ba, J.: A method for stochastic optimization, arXiv preprint arXiv:1412.6980 (2014)

23. Rezatofighi, H., Tsoi, N., Gwak, J., Sadeghian, A., Reid, I., Savarese, S.: Generalized intersection over union: a metric and a loss for bounding box regression. In: Proceedings of the IEEE/CVF Conference on Computer Vision and Pattern Recognition, pp. 658–666 (2019)
24. Zhang, H., Jiang, Q., Yu, Y., Zheng, X.: Based on retinal vessel model to segment the image and to detect the vessels. Acta Electron. Sin. 6 (1999)
25. Jiang, X., Mojon, D.: Adaptive local thresholding by verification-based multithreshold probing with application to vessel detection in retinal images. IEEE Trans. Pattern Anal. Mach. Intell. 25(1), 131–137 (2003)
26. Soares, J.V., Leandro, J.J., Cesar, R.M., Jelinek, H.F., Cree, M.J.: Retinal vessel segmentation using the 2-D Gabor wavelet and supervised classification. IEEE Trans. Med. Imaging 25(9), 1214–1222 (2006)
27. Xie, S., Tu, Z.: Holistically-nested edge detection. In: Proceedings of the IEEE International Conference on Computer Vision, pp. 1395–1403 (2015)
28. Maninis, K.K., Pont-Tuset, J., Arbeláez, P., Gool, L.V.: Deep retinal image understanding. In: International Conference on Medical Image Computing and Computer-Assisted Intervention, pp. 140–148 (2016)
29. Liskowski, P., Krawiec, K.: Segmenting retinal blood vessels with deep neural networks. IEEE Trans. Med. Imaging 35(11), 2369–2380 (2016)
30. Xiao, Z.: Hard exudates detection method based on background-estimation and SVM classifier. Chin. J. Biomed. Eng. 34(6), 720–728 (2015)
31. Akram, M.U., Khalid, S., Tariq, A., Khan, S.A., Azam, F.: Detection and classification of retinal lesions for grading of diabetic retinopathy. Comput. Biol. Med. 45, 161–171 (2014)
32. Jaya, T., Dheeba, J., A, N.: Singh: detection of hard exudates in colour fundus images using fuzzy support vector machine-based expert system. J. Digit. Imaging 28(6), 761–768 (2015)
33. Imani, E., Pourreza, H.R.: A novel method for retinal exudate segmentation using signal separation algorithm. Comput. Methods Programs Biomed. 133, 195–205 (2016)
34. Pereira, C., Gonçalves, L., Ferreira, M.: Exudate segmentation in fundus images using an ant colony optimization approach. Inf. Sci. 296, 14–24 (2015)

One-Hot Coding Similarity of Vehicle Routing Particle Swarm Optimizer

CHao He[1,2,3], Zhi Li[1,2,3], Shoubao Su[1,2,3,4(✉)], Liukai Xu[2,3,4], and Chishe Wang[2,3(✉)]

[1] School of Computer, Jiangsu University of Science and Technology, Zhenjiang 212003, China
sushowbo@163.com
[2] Jiangsu Key Laboratory of Data Science and Smart Software, Jinling Institute of Technology, Nanjing 211169, China
wangcs@163.com
[3] Provincial Engineering Research Center of Digital Technology for Industrial Economic, Jinling Institute of Technology, Nanjing 211169, China
[4] School of Computer, Nanjing University of Posts and Telecommunications, Nanjing 210003, China

Abstract. Aiming at the real-time problem of vehicle routing planning, an improved particle swarm optimization method, called AVSPSO, is proposed in this paper. In the method, the path similarity of vehicle routing is calculated by adopting based on the One-Hot coding vector and by improving the constraint processing through the combination of coding mode and fixed penalty, in which dynamically adjust the inertia weight through the evolution state is to balance the ability of local mining and global development of particles. Experimental results on two practical cases of vehicle routing optimization problems and comparisons with other methods have shown that the proposed method is feasible and stable with better performances.

Keywords: One-Hot coding · Path similarity · Vehicle routing · Particle swarm optimization

1 Introduction

With the rapid development of the logistics industry, it has brought great convenience to life, and the logistics delivery cost has gradually become a key problem. To reduce the cost of logistics delivery is to solve the problem of route planning (VRP). Path planning problem (VRP) [1] is a constrained optimization problem, which is an important problem in combinatorial optimization, especially in the field of supply chain management. Many variants of VRP have been proposed, most of which come from real life problems. Scholars try to find the most suitable algorithm to solve their problems [2–4]. A variant of VRP is capacity vehicle routing problem (CVRP), which aims to minimize the total distance traversing all customers under capacity constraints.

As a heuristic intelligent algorithm, particle swarm optimization (PSO) can efficiently solve the vehicle routing problem. Different modeling and performance requirements can generate many types of path planning problems, so the solution strategy is

X. Sun et al. (Eds.): ICAIS 2022, CCIS 1586, pp. 173–187, 2022.
https://doi.org/10.1007/978-3-031-06767-9_15

diverse and targeted. For example, Qing et al. [5] proposed a full load demand splitting vehicle routing strategy based on particle swarm optimization algorithm, and continuously optimized the delivery route through particle swarm optimization algorithm. The experimental results show that this method can greatly reduce the distance of the delivery route. Xie [6] introduced Levy flight and reverse flight mechanism in particle swarm optimization algorithm to solve the path planning problem with time window, and in order to solve the incompatibility problem between particles in continuous space and driving scheme in discrete space, the sorting method was used to map and encode particles and driving scheme. Ou et al. [7] proposed a coordinate representative particle swarm optimization algorithm to solve the open vehicle routing problem with time windows considering third-party logistics. Compared with other optimization algorithms, the result is better.

In recent years, particle swarm optimization has been developed by combining the concept of particle swarm optimization with other meta heuristic methods or introducing new mechanisms. There is a class of particle swarm optimization improved by a feedback system adaptive algorithm, which is called adaptive particle swarm optimization (APSO). The feedback strategy should be easy to calculate and can successfully guide particles [8]. Inertia weight and acceleration coefficient have the greatest impact on the performance of particle swarm optimization algorithm. By properly adjusting inertia weight and acceleration coefficient, particle swarm optimization algorithm can be started with a small particle swarm size or the maximum number of iterations [9]. The standard strategy of setting control parameters is based on time, using linear or nonlinear functions [10]. In order for particles to explore effectively in the search space, the control parameters need to be determined based on the feedback state of the captured particle state, rather than following the predefined trajectory [11]. Among them, Manjula et al. [12] used an adaptive strategy to dynamically adjust the inertia weights; Shoukat et al. [13] made the control parameters of the PSO dynamic and the initialization chaotic for better exploration and exploitation to support the search for global solutions. In addition, it is also practical to use velocity vector as feedback parameter. Mojtaba et al. [14] used the recent change of velocity vector in the direction to adjust the control parameters. The direction refers to the current particle's approach or alienation to the historical optimal position of the individual. This strategy promotes more randomness, thus increasing the diversity of the population. Isiet et al. [15] used the fitness value of particles at each time as the feedback parameter to weigh the proportion between the current global search and local search.

Aiming at the real-time problem of vehicle path planning, the evolutionary state is designed. The similarity of vehicle path is calculated by using the independent heat coding vector. The adaptive inertia weight particle swarm optimization algorithm (AVSPSO) is proposed. The feasibility and stability of the algorithm are verified by two practical schemes.

2 Vehicle Routing Problem

2.1 Vehicle Routing Problem

When we order anything online, we want to get it at a lower price, a greater discount and a faster delivery speed. In this case, a kind of vehicle routing problem (VRP) is generated. In the real world, this problem exists in multi-disciplinary fields, such as logistics, distribution, production, economics and so on. With the rapid development of logistics industry, it has brought great convenience to life, and the logistics cost has gradually become a key problem. Path planning problem is a constrained optimization problem. Its basic idea is to dispatch multiple vehicles carrying goods from the warehouse (starting point) and return to the starting point halfway to traverse all customer locations and minimize the cost. That is to say, given the demand location, demand quantity and vehicle load and other information, and then under the constraints of the constraints, the path planning problem can be solved, Find the minimum cost delivery route.

2.2 Components of VRP

Component analysis is an effective method to consolidate knowledge. It can not only efficiently and effectively store, classify and analyze statistics, but also expand and build knowledge [16].

Decide to Manage Components. Supply chain management is an effective way to integrate customers, manufacturers, warehouses and vehicles. It ensures that products are produced and distributed in the right quantity, in the right place and at the right time, thus minimizing system costs while meeting service level requirements. Therefore, the integration of different functions of decision-making, such as procurement, inventory control, outsourcing, positioning warehouse, production planning and distribution management, is the practice followed by more and more companies. Service type decision is a strategic level decision, each customer must be served once, and only once. However, profits may be related to customer service. In this case, a subset of service customers must be determined to maximize the objective function, including the total profit collected. This variant of VRP is called profit VRP.

Warehouse. In the classic VRP, a single warehouse is used, which may be very limited in practice. Therefore, in a real application, there are usually multiple warehouses, and vehicles may have different starting and final positions. Customers may need to be assigned to the appropriate warehouse. Warehouses may have different characteristics in terms of quantity, location and capacity, which may affect the total cost.

Load Sharing. In the classic VRP, each customer is served by only one car. At the same time, each car has the possibility to visit the same customer many times. When multiple products have to be delivered to customers, intermediate level segmentation should also be determined. In this case, multiple visits to the same customer may occur, with each product delivered during a unique visit.

Vehicles. Vehicles with different characteristics can better meet customers' needs related to physical constraints, environmental concerns, specific logistics equipment or demand changes. The primary characteristics of the vehicles considered here relate to the types of vehicles available during the planning period. One of the most important characteristics is the capacity limit of the vehicle. The most common capacity limitation in logistics transportation is expressed by weight, volume or number of pallets. Several capacity constraints can be considered at the same time.

Time Related Restrictions. Time window constraint requires that each customer's service must start and end in a given time window. In the case of hard time window, vehicles are allowed to arrive before the specified time window, waiting for customers to be free, but late arrival is not allowed. If it is a soft time window, starting the service after the allowed time window will be punished. It leads to taking into account the delivery time between customer locations, customer service time and handling time.

Objective Function. Goals can be diverse. The most common goals include minimizing some or all of these criteria: total delivery distance, total time, total delivery overhead, or maximizing quality of service. When multiple goals are determined, different goals often conflict. Therefore, the appropriate algorithm must ensure that there is a certain trade-off between the two.

2.3 Mathematical Model of the Capacity Vehicle Routing Problem

Capacity vehicle routing problem [17] (CVRP) is a kind of various vehicle routing problems. The goal is to minimize the total distance of traversing all customers under capacity constraints. The basic requirements are as follows: 1) a single warehouse, and the warehouse is both the starting point and the ending point; 2) Each vehicle has a limited capacity, which must deliver materials without exceeding the capacity limit; 3) Each vehicle can only be delivered once at most; 4) Each customer has and can only be served by one car.

CVRP is expressed as a directed complete graph, defined as $G = (V, A)$. V is the set of customers, denoted by $V = \{c_0, c_1, \ldots, c_n\}$. $A = \{< c_i, c_j > | c_i, c_j \in V, i \neq j\}$ denotes the path between customer clients. The warehouse is denoted as c_0 and the initial demand ($q_0 = 0$), $c_1 \ldots n$ are denoted as customers and the number of demands per customer is q_i. The depots are the departure and return points for all vehicles. The route is defined as the path of the vehicle passing through the customer on the way plus the path on the way back. In addition, customers may not make repeat visits using the same vehicle for each visit. Each vehicle has a loading capacity $Q_i (i = 1 \ldots N)$, and each load must not exceed it carrying capacity. The distance (d_{ij}) or dispatch time (t_{ij}) for each path is calculated using the Euclidean distance and is expressed as $\sqrt{\sum_{i=0}^{n} (c_i - c_j)^2}$.

The mathematical expression of CVRP is defined as:

$$\text{Minimize } F(x) = \sum_{k=1}^{K} \sum_{i=0}^{N} \sum_{j=0}^{N} d_{ij} x_{ijk}. \tag{1}$$

$$\text{S.t } x_{ijk} = \begin{cases} 1, & \text{If vehicle k passes through path } <c_i, c_j> \\ 0, & \text{Otherwise} \end{cases}. \tag{2}$$

$$\sum_{j=1}^{N} x_{0jk} = \sum_{i=1}^{N} x_{i0k} = 1, \, k \in \{1, 2, \ldots, K\}. \tag{3}$$

$$\sum_{j=0,j\neq i}^{N} x_{ijk} = \sum_{j=0,j\neq i}^{N} x_{jik} \leq 1, \, i \in \{1, 2, \ldots, N\}, k \in \{1, 2, \ldots, K\}. \tag{4}$$

$$\sum_{k=1}^{K} \sum_{i=0,i\neq j}^{N} x_{ijk} = 1, \, j \in \{1, 2, \ldots, N\}. \tag{5}$$

$$\sum_{k=1}^{K} \sum_{j=0,j\neq i}^{N} x_{ijk=1}, \, i \in \{1, 2, \ldots, N\}. \tag{6}$$

$$\sum_{i=0}^{N} q_i \sum_{j=0,j\neq i}^{N} x_{jik} \leq Q, \, k \in \{1, 2, \ldots, K\}. \tag{7}$$

Equation (1) represents the objective of minimizing the CVRP, i.e., the total distance from the vehicle to visit all customers; Eq. (2) defines the path c_{ij} for the kth vehicle, as shown in x_{ijk}; Eqs. (3) and (4) represent each vehicle departing from the warehouse, passing each customer one at a time, and then returning to the depot; The vehicles are defined in Eqs. (5) and (6) to access each client node once.; The formula (7) indicates that each vehicle can carry a load that exceeds its capacity Q; Constraints (3)–(6) define that the customer cannot be served by the vehicle more than once, and that each route must start and end from the warehouse; Eq. (7) defines the capacity of the vehicle.

3 PSO for Vehicle Routing Problem

3.1 Particle Swarm Optimization (PSO)

PSO simulates cluster phenomenon, each particle in the group occupies a certain position in d-dimensional search space, which also represents the potential solution of the problem. For particle I ($i = 1, 2 \ldots N$), position Xi is expressed as:

$$X_i = (x_{i1}, x_{i2}, \ldots, x_{iD}). \tag{8}$$

The optimal position of each particle so far is denoted as *Pbest_i*:

$$Pbest_i = (pbest_{i1}, pbest_{i2}, \ldots, pbest_{iD}). \tag{9}$$

The velocity of a particle is expressed as:

$$V_i = (v_{i1}, v_{i2}, \ldots, v_{iD}). \tag{10}$$

Each particle in the particle swarm has an individual optimal position (*pbest*), which is the optimal solution obtained so far. In addition, the position of the optimal particle among all particles is recorded as the global optimum (*gbest*). Each particle updates its position based on its distance from *pbest* and *gbest*. The velocity of particle i in the particle swarm is updated by the following equation.

$$V_{iD} = \omega * (v_{iD}) + c_1 * r_1 * (P_{iD} - X_{iD}) + c_2 * r_2 * (P_{gD} - X_{iD}). \quad (11)$$

where V_{iD} is the updated velocity of the particle and v_{iD} is the current velocity of the particle; X_{iD} denotes the current position of the particle, ω denotes the inertia weight. c_1 denotes the cognitive factor and c_2 denotes the social factor. P_{iD} denotes the individual optimal position of each particle and P_{gD} denotes the global optimal solution. r_1, r_2 are random values in the interval [0, 1].

Here, r_1, r_2 are used to maintain population diversity. ω is the inertia factor, which is mainly used to balance the exploration and exploitation process, but also controls the effect of previous velocities on new velocities; The cognitive factor c_1 and the social factor c_2 drive the particles to move through the historically optimal positions of the particles themselves and the positions of the optimal particles in the particle swarm. The following equation represents the position update of particle i in the population:

$$X_{id} = X_{id} + V_{id}. \quad (12)$$

3.2   The Encoding Methods

Since the solution of the vehicle routing problem is discrete and the operator of the particle swarm algorithm is continuous, it is necessary to construct an encoding for the vehicle routing problem to be applicable to the particle swarm algorithm. In this paper, the encoding method of the solution set is first rounded and then sorted, and the specific scheme is as follows:

Define the number of vehicles as m, the number of customers as n, and a particle of the particle swarm as $X = (x_1, x_2, \ldots, x_n)$, $x_i \in [1, m]$, The i position of the particle indicates the i customer, whose size does not exceed the size of the number of vehicles. The particle X is first rounded to each position, and the integer obtained corresponds to the vehicle number, i.e., it is dispatched by the vehicle with this integer number. Then subtract the corresponding integer from each position of the particle to get $Y = (y_1, y_2, \ldots, y_n)$, $y_i \in [0, 1)$. Finally, customers dispatched by the same vehicle are divided into the same group, and the dispatch order of vehicles is determined according to the corresponding Y size in the same group from largest to smallest, following the principle that the smaller the Y value is, the more priority is given to dispatch.

Suppose the number of vehicles is 2, the number of customers is 5, and a particle of the particle swarm is $X = (1.23, 2.95, 1.36, 1.91, 2.55)$, Rounding X yields $(int)(X) = (1, 2, 1, 1, 2)$, And then subtract X from its integer code, Get $Y = (0.23, 0.95, 0.91, 0.55)$. Then sort by vehicle grouping to obtain $X_1 = (1.23, 1.36, 1.91)$, $X_2 = (2.55, 2.95)$, The following table shows the exact process (Tables 1 and 2).

Table 1. Before grouping.

CSR No.	1	2	3	4	5
X	1.23	2.95	1.36	1.91	2.55
$Int(X)$	1	2	1	1	2
Y	0.23	0.95	0.36	0.91	0.55

Table 2. After sorting in groups.

CSR No.	1	2	3	4	5
X_1	1.23	2.95	1.36	1.91	2.55

According to the description in the above table, we can get the customers served by each vehicle with their order of priority, Vehicle 1:0 → 1 → 3 → 4 → 0, Vehicle 2:0 → 5 → 2 → 0.

3.3 Constraint Processing

For the constraint treatment of the mathematical model of the vehicle path problem, its constraint Eqs. (3), (4), (5) and (6) equations can be solved by the coding method. The rounding operation of the coding method ensures that each customer can only be served by one vehicle and that each vehicle can only serve the same customer at most once. The sorting operation determines the first and last customer served by each vehicle, and these two customers construct paths with the warehouse, which determines that each vehicle starts and ends from the warehouse. For constraint Eq. (7), the fixed penalty method is used, and a larger penalty value is added to the fitness for the violation of the constraint.

3.4 Particle Swarm Optimization Algorithm for Adaptive Vehicle Routing Particle

In order to solve the problem of vehicle path optimization in which the PSO algorithm is easy to be premature and dependent on the initial control parameters [18], a vehicle distance grouping-based particle swarm optimization (AVSPSO) is proposed.

Vehicle Path Similarity. Based on the encoding of particles, the unique thermal encoding is used to encode the vehicle information in the particles, which is used to measure the path similarity between each particle. Assume that customer j in particle i is delivered by the k vehicle out of *m*vehicles, using the unique heat code as:

$$(One - Hot)_{ij} = (o_{j1}, o_{j2}, \ldots, o_{jk}, \ldots, o_{jm}). \qquad (13)$$

where all are 0 except $o_{jk} = 1$ (indicating that customer j is delivered by the k vehicle). It is not difficult to find that the above encoding lacks the order information, i.e., the order that customer j occupies in the k vehicle delivery route. For all customers in particle i form the 0–1 set as in Eq. (14).

$$(One - Hot)_i = ((One - Hot)_{i0}, (One - Hot)_{i1}, \ldots, (One - Hot)_{iN}). \tag{14}$$

In the PSO algorithm, each particle defines the similarity by the cosine between its unique thermal encoding vectors, and the similarity between particle i and particle j can be determined by Eq. (15):

$$S_{ij} = cos((One - Hot)_i, (One - Hot)_j). \tag{15}$$

where $S_{ij} \in [0, 1]$ and larger values indicate that the paths are more similar.

Adaptive Strategies Based on Evolutionary State Feedback. Isiet et al. [15] designed the evolutionary state (ES_{iD}) of particle i based on its individual optimum, global optimum and its current fitness at the current iteration as follows.

$$ES_{iD} = \frac{f(P_{iD}) - f(P_{gD})}{f(X_{iD})}. \tag{16}$$

where, $f(P_{iD})$ represents the individual optimal fitness value in the current iteration, $f(P_{gD})$ represents the global optimal fitness value, and $f(X_{iD})$ represents the current fitness value. It can be seen that the value of ES_{iD} is between [0,1], and its size describes the location structure among individual optimal location, global optimal location and current location. Inspired by this, the evolutionary state based on vehicle path similarity is proposed, which is described as follows.

$$ES_{iD} = S_{xp} - S_{xg}. \tag{17}$$

where, S_{xp} denotes the path similarity between the individual optimal position and the current particle position at the current iteration, and S_{xg} denotes the path similarity between the global optimal position and the current particle position. The value of ES_{iD} is between the interval $[-1,1]$, and when ES_{iD} is positive, it reflects that the current particle position is more similar to the individual optimal position and less similar to the global optimal position; when ES_{iD} is negative, the current particle position is more similar to the global optimal position and less similar to the individual optimal position. When the value of ES_{iD} is close to 0, it shows that the current particle position is similar to the individual optimal position and the global optimal position. Accordingly, the control parameters of the improved algorithm in the paper are designed as follows.

Inertia Weights ω. Since the inertia weight controls the influence of the previous velocity on the current velocity, when the value is taken as large, the particle exploration is strong, generally at the beginning of the algorithm search, while when the value is small, it facilitates the local search, corresponding to the end of the algorithm. It is verified that the decreasing strategy for ω facilitates the algorithm to search for better solutions. Therefore, based on the evolutionary state, the improvement of ω is as follows.

$$\omega_{iD} = \frac{1}{1 - e^{-1.3863 * |ES_{iD}|}}. \tag{18}$$

where $|ES_{iD}| \in [0, 1]$, ω_{iD} is a formula decreasing on the value domain $[0.5, 0.8]$, taking absolute values for the evolutionary state, larger reacts to the algorithm in the exploration period, ω_{iD} takes larger values; smaller reacts to the algorithm in the stable period, ω_{iD} takes larger values.

Acceleration Coefficient c_1, c_2. The acceleration coefficient describes the memory of the historical location information. When c_1 takes a larger value, it is beneficial to local search, and when c_2 takes a larger value, it is beneficial to global search. Therefore, according to $|ES_{iD}|$, c_1, c_2 are improved as follows.

$$
c_{1i} = \begin{cases} c_{max} - \frac{(c_{max}-c_{min})*(max_k-k)}{max_k}, & \text{If } ES_{iD} > 0.1 \\ \frac{c_{max}+c_{min}}{2}, & \text{If } |ES_{iD}| \le 0.1 \\ \frac{(c_{max}-c_{min})*(max_k-k)}{max_k} + c_{min}, & \text{If } ES_{iD} < -0.1 \end{cases} \tag{19}
$$

$$
c_{2i} = \begin{cases} \frac{(c_{max}-c_{min})*(max_k-k)}{max_k} + c_{min}, & \text{If } ES_{iD} > 0.1 \\ \frac{c_{max}+c_{min}}{2}, & \text{If } |ES_{iD}| \le 0.1 \\ c_{max} - \frac{(c_{max}-c_{min})*(max_k-k)}{max_k}, & \text{If } ES_{iD} < -0.1 \end{cases} \tag{20}
$$

where, c_{max}, c_{min} denote the upper and lower bounds of acceleration coefficients. max_k is the total number of iterations, and k is the current iteration number.

4 Experimental Results and Analysis

In this section, two cases are selected and several intelligent algorithms are compared to analyze the performance of AVSPSO algorithm through statistical methods. The statistical performance considered includes the optimal function value, the worst function value, the mean function value, the standard deviation and the average number of iterations to find the global optimal. The population size of all optimization algorithms is set to 30, the number of iterations is 1000, and the upper and lower bounds of speed are set to the upper and lower limits of the number of vehicles designed.

In this paper, the experimental test and comparative analysis of all cases are written in Python 3.7 on win10 system. All constrained optimization problems are independently run for 50 times to analyze and evaluate the statistical performance of the algorithm.

4.1 Case 1

The optimization path is solved for logistics dispatch optimization of one warehouse, 20 customers and 4 vehicles. The maximum capacity of each vehicle is 15 kg. Table 3 describes the customer location (unit km), and the warehouse location is (3 km, 14 km).

The algorithms used for comparison are particle swarm optimization (PSO), a particle swarm optimization algorithm based on dynamic neighbor and mutation factor (DNMPSO) [19], semi-autonomous particle swarm global optimization algorithm based on gradient information and diversity control (SAPAO) [20] and particle swarm optimization algorithm based on adaptive control parameters (UAPSO) [15, 21, 22]. Table 4 shows the statistical performance comparison of AVSPSO algorithm with other methods. As shown in the table, the AVSPSO algorithm performs better than the comparison method in obtaining the optimal solution, the worst solution, the mean value and the standard deviation. In terms of finding the global optimal average number of iterations, AVSPSO algorithm has more iterations than PSO algorithm and SAPSO algorithm, but less than DNMPSO algorithm and UAPSO algorithm. Figure 1 depicts the convergence curve of AVSPSO algorithm and other methods in finding the optimal solution. As shown in the figure, the optimization ability of AVSPSO algorithm is not different from SAPSO and UAPSO in the early stage, but only on the convergence curve of UAPSO algorithm in the middle stage, and is better than all other methods in the late stage. According to the data and convergence curve in the table, AVSPSO algorithm has the best comprehensive performance in solving the problem of case 1. Figure 2 shows the AVSPSO algorithm in solving case 1 to get the optimal f(x) = 86.123351 of the specific vehicle allocation and path.

Table 3. AAA 20 customer locations and demands.

No.	1	2	3	4	5	6	7	8	9	10
x	4	15	19	12	10	5	1	6	8	16
y	6	11	13	8	10	10	10	15	19	16
Dem and q	1	1	1	2	1	1	2	1	2	2
No.	11	12	13	14	15	16	17	18	19	20
X	15	2	9	5	8	9	15	15	10	1
Y	15	5	9	13	10	8	5	19	5	7
Dem and q	1	2	1	2	1	1	1	1	1	1

Table 4. Statistical performances of AVSPSO compared with other methods on case 1.

Method	Best	Worst	Mean	Std	Mean-steps
PSO	98.049754	166.040687	133.220000	1.33E + 01	721.56
DNMPSO	102.215466	152.623239	128.073085	1.06E + 01	805.74
SAPSO	101.218524	141.684828	122.396789	8.58E + 00	626.88
UAPSO	96.675764	135.358436	116.022923	8.58E + 00	866.56
AVSPSO	86.123351	118.156093	100.325097	8.31E + 00	805.22

4.2 Case 2

For the logistics delivery optimization problem of one warehouse, 35 customers and 5 vehicles, the optimal path is solved. The maximum capacity of each vehicle is limited

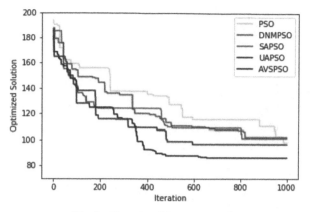

Fig. 1. Five algorithms on case 1.

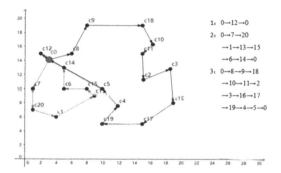

Fig. 2. A optimum solution obtained from AVSPSO.

to 13 kg. Table 5 describes the location of customers (unit km), and the location of warehouse is (15.31 km, 12.61 km).

The algorithms used for comparison include particle swarm optimization (PSO), a particle swarm optimization algorithm based on dynamic neighbor and mutation factor (DNMPSO), semi-autonomous particle swarm optimization global optimization algorithm based on gradient information and diversity control (SAPAO) and particle swarm optimization algorithm based on adaptive control parameters (UAPSO). The statistical performance comparison between AVSPSO algorithm and other methods is given in Table 6. As shown in the table, the AVSPSO algorithm performs better than the comparison method in obtaining the optimal solution, the worst solution and the mean value. In terms of standard deviation, AVSPSO algorithm is slightly inferior to DNMPSO algorithm and SAPSO algorithm. In terms of finding the global optimal average number of iterations, AVSPSO algorithm has more iterations than PSO algorithm, SAPSO algorithm and UAPSO algorithm, but less than DNMPSO algorithm, which shows that AVSPSO algorithm has better search ability in the later stage. Figure 3 depicts the convergence curve of AVSPSO algorithm and other methods in finding the optimal solution. As shown in the figure, the optimization ability of AVSPSO algorithm is general in the

Table 5. Customer locations and demand list.

No.	1	2	3	4	5	6	7	8	9	10
x	12.9	18.43	16.11	2.51	15.9	4.38	10.79	8.63	13.23	14.18
y	8.5	2.77	16.48	6.77	11.13	10.07	7.17	8.3	1.6	4.4
Dem and q	0.43	1.44	0.65	1.59	0.69	1.26	0.35	0.68	2.4	1.02
No.	11	12	13	14	15	16	17	18	19	20
x	6.75	15.17	2.16	12.19	7.86	0.92	12.28	13.87	7.28	10.01
y	16.8	1.64	8.27	2.63	0.72	2.59	19.7	14.59	4.6	14.37
Dem and q	0.45	2.71	1.99	2.22	2.16	2.36	2.63	2.42	1.33	2.42
No.	21	22	23	24	25	26	27	28	29	30
x	6.88	4.1	5.53	0.94	12.94	21.8	8.46	19.74	10.61	11.8
y	8.84	14.64	4.6	12.93	7.58	6.05	10.51	14.3	17.66	6.67
Dem and q	0.98	1.94	2.43	0.48	1.01	1.3	1.36	2.41	0.72	1.69
No.	31	32	33	34	35					
x	13.07	5.22	10.01	4.24	17.2					
y	2.46	9.27	11.05	15.8	10.6					
Dem and q	0.9	2.29	1.45	1.47	1.19					

early stage, and is greater than that of all other directions in the middle stage, because its optimal function value drops the fastest, and the convergence speed is only slightly lower than that of SAPSO algorithm in the late stage. According to the data and convergence curve in the table, AVSPSO algorithm has the best comprehensive performance, and SAPSO algorithm has the second. Figure 4 shows the AVSPSO algorithm in solving case 2 to get the optimal $f(x) = 197.301399$ of the specific vehicle allocation and path.

Table 6. Statistical performances of AVSPSO compared with other methods on case 2.

Methods	Best	Worst	Mean	Std	Mean-steps
PSO	294.880233	399.211260	347.233592	2.33E + 01	312.90
DNMPSO	234.246423	301.009859	266.888806	1.53E + 01	910.24
SAPSO	213.110429	278.363470	240.702353	1.37E + 01	764.76
UAPSO	216.391120	286.997129	250.445415	2.14E + 01	696.72
AVSPSO	197.301399	267.068494	236.959434	1.68E + 01	830.8

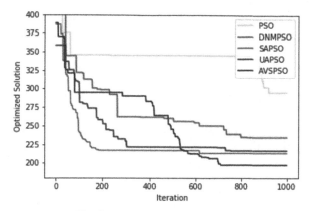

Fig. 3. Five algorithms on case 2

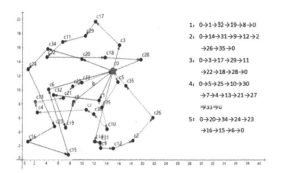

Fig. 4. A optimum solution obtained from AVSPSO

5 Conclusion

Aiming at the real-time problem of vehicle path planning, the vehicle path similarity calculation method based on the unique hot coding vector is adopted, and the constraint processing is improved by combining the coding method and fixed penalty. The particle swarm optimization algorithm (AVSPSO) with dynamically adjusting inertia weight in evolutionary state is proposed to balance the local mining and global development ability of particles. By solving two practical cases of vehicle routing optimization problem and comparing with other four similar methods (PSO, DNMPSO, SAPSO, UAPSO), the experimental results show that the proposed algorithm has better performance, feasibility and stability. AVSPSO algorithm is an improved swarm intelligence algorithm based on the original PSO algorithm, which can be better adapted to solve the vehicle routing problem, has the ability to explore a better path, thus reducing the total cost, and has a certain practical value.

Acknowledgement. The work is partially supported by the Scientific Research Foundations and the Virtual Experimental Class Projects of Jinling Institute of Technology (Nos.JIT-rcyj-201505, D2020005), the National Natural Science Foundation of China (Nos.61375121,41801303), the

Natural Science Foundation of Jiangsu Province (No. BK200170116), and sponsored by the Funds for Jiangsu Provincial Sci-Tech Innovation Team of Swarm Computing and Smart Software led by Prof S.B. Su.

References

1. Asghari, M., Mirzapou, S.M.J.: Green vehicle routing problem: a state-of-the-art review. Int. J. Prod. Econ. **231**(2), 107899 (2020)
2. Zarandi, M.H.F., As, A.A.S., Sotudian, S.: A state-of-the-art review of intelligent scheduling. J. Artif. Intell. Rev. **53**(3), 501–593 (2018)
3. Li, J., Pardalos, P.M., Sun, H.: Iterated local search embedded adaptive neighborhood selection approach for the multi-depot vehicle routing problem with simultaneous deliveries and pickups. J. Expert Syst. Appl. **42**(7), 3551–3561 (2014)
4. Qiu, Y.Z., Wang, L., Xu, X.: Formulations and branch-and-cut algorithms for multi-product multi-vehicle production routing problems with startup cost. J. Expert Syst. Appl. **98**(3), 1–10 (2018)
5. Marinakis, Y., Marinaki, M., Migdalas, A.: A multi-adaptive particle swarm optimization for the vehicle routing problem with time windows. J. Inf. Sci. **481**, 311–329 (2019)
6. Xue, Y., Wang, Y., Liang, J.Y.: A self-adaptive mutation neural architecture search algorithm based on blocks. IEEE Comput. Intell. Mag. **16**(3), 67–78 (2021)
7. Mehlawat, M.K., Gupta, P., Khaitan, A.: A hybrid intelligent approach to integrated fuzzy multiple depot capacitated green vehicle routing problem with split delivery and vehicle selection. J. IEEE Trans. Fuzzy Syst. **28**(6), 1155–1166 (2019)
8. Ou, T., Cheng, C., Lai, C.H.: A coordination-based algorithm for dedicated destination vehicle routing in B2B e-commerce. J. Comput. Syst. Sci. Eng. **40**(3), 895–911 (2022)
9. Weng, Z., Tang, K.J., Li, W.Z.: Research on application of vehicle routing problem using an enhanced particle swarm optimization. J. Chongqing Univ. Posts Telecommun. (Natural Science Edition) **32**(05), 891–897 (2020)
10. Yang, J.C., Li, S.X., Cai, Z.Y.: Research and development of path planning algorithm. J. Control Eng. **24**(7), 1473–1480 (2017)
11. Isiet, M., Gadala, M.: Self-adapting control parameters in particle swarm optimization. J. Appl. Soft Comput. J. **83**, 105653 (2019)
12. Schranz, M., Caro, G.A.D., Schmickl, T.: Swarm intelligence and cyber-physical systems: concepts, challenges and future trends. J. Swarm Evol. Comput. **60**(2), 100762 (2020)
13. Manjula, A., Kalaivani, L., Gengaraj, M.: PSO based torque ripple minimization of switched reluctance motor using FPGA controller. J. Intell. Autom. Soft Comput. **29**(2), 451–465 (2021)
14. Shoukat, A., Mughal, M.A., Gondal, S.Y.: Optimal parameter estimation of transmission line using chaotic initialized time-varying pso algorithm. J. Comput. Mater. Contin. **71**(1), 269–285 (2022)
15. Wang, L.L., Gui, J.S., Deng, X.H.: Routing algorithm based on vehicle position analysis for internet of vehicle. J. IEEE Internet Things J. **7**(12), 11701–11712 (2020)
16. Taherkhani, M., Safabakhsh, R.: A novel stability-based adaptive inertia weight for particle swarm optimization. Appl. Soft Comput. **38**, 281–295 (2016)
17. Isiet, M., Gadala, M.: Self-adapting control parameters in particle swarm optimization. J. Appl. Soft Comput. **83**, 105653 (2019)
18. Lahyani, R., Khemakhem, M., Semet, F.: Rich vehicle routing problems: from a taxonomy to a definition. J. Eur. J. Oper. Res. **241**(1), 1–14 (2015)

19. Luo, Y.: Multiple strategies of particle swarm optimization and its application in vehicle routing problem. D. Jiangnan University (2018)
20. Su, S.B., Li, Z., He, C.: Constrained fractional-order PSO with self-adaptive neighbors and differential mutators. J. Chongqing Univ. **43**(11), 84–98 (2020)
21. Xue, Y., Zhu, H., Liang, J.Y.: Adaptive crossover operator based multi-objective binary genetic algorithm for feature selection in classification. Knowl.-Based Syst. **227**(5), 1–9 (2021)
22. Santos, R., Borges, G., Santos, A.: A semi-autonomous particle swarm optimizer based on gradient information and diversity control for global optimization. J. Appl. Soft Comput. **69**, 330–343 (2018)

Detection Method of Potholes on Highway Pavement Based on Yolov5

Qian Gao[1,3,4], Pengyu Liu[1,2,3,4(✉)], Shanji Chen[2], Kebin Jia[1,3,4], and Xiao Wang[1,3,4]

[1] The Information Department, Beijing University of Technology, Beijing 100124, China
liupengyu@bjut.edu.cn
[2] School of Physics and Electronic Information Engineering, Qinghai Minzu University, Xining 810000, China
[3] Beijing Laboratory, Advanced Information Network, Beijing 100124, China
[4] Beijing Key Laboratory, Computational Intelligence and Intelligent Systems, Beijing 100124, China

Abstract. Pavement pothole detection is very important for highway maintenance and safety management. Aiming at the problems of low detection accuracy and low efficiency due to the characteristics of various shapes, different scales, and complex background environment of current pavement potholes, this paper proposed a highway pavement pothole detection method based on YOLOv5. First, a pothole image dataset containing multiple scene types was established. Then, based on the adaptive anchor frame adjustment strategy, the YOLOv5 model was improved to complete the design of the pavement pothole detection network, which solved the problem of low detection accuracy caused by large changes in the target scale during the network training process. By modifying the classification network, the output dimension is reduced, the amount of calculation is reduced, and the detection speed is accelerated. Finally, with the help of transfer learning ideas, the model is trained and learned, and the method of rotation, cropping and other methods are used for data enhancement, which solved the problem of training overfitting caused by insufficient dataset. The experimental results show that the proposed method has a detection accuracy of 93.99% for pavement potholes, which is 3.6% higher than the original YOLOv5 model, and the average detection time on a single test image is 12.78 ms, which is reduced by 4.14 m.

Keywords: Pavement pothole · Yolov5 · Adaptive anchor frame adjustment · Transfer learning

1 Introduction

As an important part of the modern comprehensive transportation system, highways play a pivotal role in promoting and restricting the development of the national economy. With the continuous improvement of highway construction and the continuous increase of highway mileage, the problem of highway maintenance has become increasingly prominent. Affected by natural disasters and increasing traffic load and other factors, the road surface has diseases of different shapes and sizes, which leads to the deterioration of the road surface and causes huge traffic safety hazards. Pavement disease is one of the main indicators to measure the quality of pavement. Pavement disease detection is the key to timely maintenance and repair of pavement, and has important guiding significance for highway maintenance decision-making.

Highway pavements can be divided into cracks, surface diseases and deformations according to the types of damage. Common types of pavement diseases include cracks, potholes, and ruts. Among them, potholes are the most common and difficult to detect type of pavement diseases, and are also the main type of surface diseases [1]. Traditional pavement pothole detection is mainly based on manual survey and on-board detection system. Manual observation is time-consuming and laborious, inefficient, and the evaluation standards are not uniform; on-board detection system equipment is expensive and data transmission is difficult. Therefore, research on effective pavement pothole detection technology and rapid and accurate detection of pavement potholes is of great significance for improving the detection efficiency of pavement disease and improving the quality of road maintenance.

In recent years, the rapid development of image processing technology and deep learning technology in video analytics [2], disease diagnosis [3–5], event detection [6] and other fields has brought the possibility of automated and intelligent detection of pavement potholes. Using the combination of deep learning technology and image processing technology, automatic feature extraction, analysis and processing of pavement pothole images can realize timely detection and identification of pavement potholes, thereby improving the level of automatic detection of road pavement diseases and improving the maintenance efficiency of the highway department. The research of road pothole detection technology based on deep learning has received extensive attention from scholars in the industry, and it is also a very challenging task in current computer vision.

2 Related Work

The pavement pothole detection technology based on deep learning mainly relies on the powerful feature extraction capabilities of convolutional neural networks to continuously perform feature learning and feature classification from a large amount of data, which can achieve better detection accuracy and speed [7, 8]. Currently, there are two main categories of road pothole detection technologies based on deep learning: pavement pothole detection technologies based on semantic segmentation and pavement pothole detection technologies based on object detection.

Pavement pothole detection technology based on semantic segmentation [9, 10], pixel-level classification of the image through the segmentation network, can depict the rough shape of the pavement pothole, but it is easily disturbed by background information, and the pixel-level labeling cost is usually huge. Pavement pothole detection technology based on object detection [11], a series of detections are obtained through the detection network, and then the target in the detections is identified and classified through the classification network. The location and category of the target can be output at the same time, with faster detection accuracy and speed, and it is widely favored by the industry.

Object detection algorithms based on deep learning are mainly divided into two categories, two-stage detectors based on candidate regions and one-stage detectors based on no-candidate regions [12]. Among the two-stage detectors, representative networks include R-CNN [13], Fast R-CNN [14], Faster R-CNN [15], and FPN [16]. The candidate frames are first generated through methods such as sliding windows, and then convolutional neural networks are used for classification and coordinate regression. Higher detection accuracy, but slower detection speed. The most classic one-stage detector is the YOLO series network. YOLOv1 [17] creatively proposed to treat the object detection task as a regression problem. It combines the generation of candidate frames and classification regression into one network, which greatly reduced the complexity of network calculations. Faster detection speed, but the detection accuracy is not high. Later, YOLOv2 [18] and YOLOv3 [19] were published successively, which improved YOLOv1 from many aspects such as training data, network structure and anchor point processing, which improved the detection accuracy to a certain extent while ensuring the detection speed. The YOLOv4 [20] algorithm adds modules such as spatial pyramid pooling SPP [21] and cross-stage partial connection CSP on the basis of YOLOv3, and at the same time improved the detection accuracy and speed. The latest updated version of YOLOv5 adds the Focus structure on the basis of YOLOv4, which enhances the feature capabilities of the network, and adds positive samples in training, which speeds up the training, and the detection accuracy and speed have been greatly improved [22].

Based on the above analysis, in order to realize the real-time detection of pavement potholes and further improve the detection accuracy, this paper proposed a highway pavement pothole detection method based on YOLOv5.

3   Method

In this section, we introduce in detail the highway pavement pothole detection method based on the YOLOv5 model. It mainly includes three parts: dataset, network structure and evaluation index.

3.1   Dataset

The dataset is established. We collected available image data by downloading open source dataset, web crawlers, and shooting with handheld devices, and filter the collected image data to eliminate poor-quality and unusable images, and only keep good quality, clearly visible image. Standardize the format of the filtered images and use the labeling tool to label them to generate a label file in VOC format for model training. Figure 1 shows the label file in VOC format. The label file mainly stores the data information used for model training, including the object category name: pothole and the bounding box coordinates (xmin, ymin, xmax, ymax).

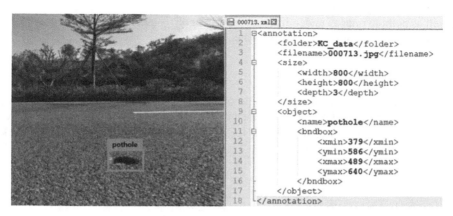

Fig. 1. Label file in VOC format.

Dataset expansion. The deep learning model requires a large amount of training data as support, but the actual collected data has problems such as limited quantity and low quality, which greatly limits the performance of the model. Therefore, we use data enhancement methods, such as flipping, rotation, and other operations to expand the dataset, so as to obtain more and higher-quality training data, and improve the generalization and robustness of the model to a certain extent.

Dataset description. The established pavement pothole dataset contains 9655 images, a total of 20500 pothole samples, the image format is JPEG format, and the image size is uniformly 800 × 800. Figure 2 shows some examples of images in the road pothole dataset. The dataset covers a variety of scene types, such as pavement images under different scene types such as (a) sunny days, (b) rainy days, and (c) shadow interference,

Fig. 2. Examples of images in the dataset.

as well as pothole images under different pavement types such as (d) asphalt pavement, (e) sand and gravel pavement, and (f) cement pavement.

3.2 Network Structure

Based on the YOLOv5 model, the design of the pavement pothole detection network structure is completed. The network structure mainly includes five parts: Input Image, Backbone, Neck, Prediction and Output Image, as shown in Fig. 3 below, the network structure is introduced in detail.

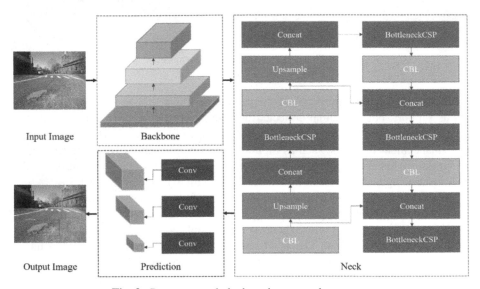

Fig. 3. Pavement pothole detection network structure.

The first part of the network is input, the input is the road pothole image to be detected, which is preprocessed before being sent to the network. Here, in order to better adapt to the pit targets of different scales, we adjust the image resolution size of the network input from $640 \times 640 \times 3$ to $608 \times 608 \times 3$.

The second part of the network is Backbone, the Focus structure is added to the CSPNet module structure. The CSPNet [23] module is used to extract image features, and the Focus structure is used to slice the image. The combination of the two enhances the feature extraction ability of the convolutional neural network, while reducing the computational bottleneck and memory cost.

The third part of the network is Neck, which adopts the FPN + PAN structure. FPN adopts the top-down feature pyramid structure to transfer the strong semantic features of the high-level to the low-level, which enhances the semantic information. PAN adds a bottom-up pyramid structure behind FPN, which further supplements FPN. It transfers the strong positioning features of the low-level to the high-level, which enhances the positioning information, thereby strengthening the network's ability to integrate features of different scales.

The fourth part of the network is Precision, after the previous series of feature extraction and calculation operations, three feature maps of specific sizes are obtained through convolution operations, the sizes are respectively $80 \times 80 \times 3$, $40 \times 40 \times 3$ and $20 \times 20 \times 3$.

The fifth part is the Output, which is mainly to post-process the detection results. The detection frames with a confidence score greater than the threshold 0.5 are selected by NMS and sent to the classification network, and the classification network performs feature recognition and classification of the targets in the detection frame. In the pavement pothole detection problem, only one category of potholes needs to be detected and identified, so we modified the classification network to adjust the filter output dimension of the last layer to $3 \times (5 + 1) = 18$. By reducing the output dimension, the amount of network parameters and calculation overhead are reduced, and the detection accuracy and speed are improved. Finally, visualize information such as the detection frame and target category on the image, and output an intuitive visualized result map.

3.3 Evaluation Metrics

We use the precision, recall and mAP (mean average precision) in object detection to evaluate the performance of the model.

IoU (Intersection-over-Union) [24], as shown in Fig. 4, which is used to measure the degree of overlap between the predicted frame and the real frame, and the precision and recall are based on the evaluation of the IoU. In the object detection task, if the IoU value of the predicted frame and the real frame output by the model is greater than the set threshold (usually 0.5), we consider that the model prediction is correct.

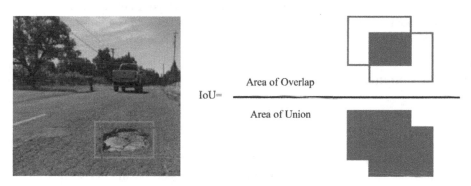

Fig. 4. IoU calculation method.

Precision, abbreviated P [25], which refers to the ratio of model predictions as positive samples (TP) and that are true positive samples to all model predictions as positive samples that contains true positive samples and false positive samples (FP).

$$Precision = \frac{TP}{TP + FP} \tag{1}$$

Recall, abbreviated R, which refers to the ratio of positive samples (TP) predicted by the model and that are true positive samples to all positive samples that contains true positive samples and false negative samples (FN).

$$Recall = \frac{TP}{TP + FN} \tag{2}$$

F1-Score [26] is the weighted harmonic average of precision and recall. Precision and recall are a pair of contradictory metrics. Generally speaking, when the precision is high, the recall value tends to be low; when the precision value is low, the recall value tends to be high. When the classification confidence is high, the precision is high; when the classification confidence is low, the recall is high. Therefore, in order to be able to comprehensively consider these two indicators, the concept of F1-Score was proposed to evaluate the comprehensive performance of the model. The core idea of F1-Score is to improve precision and recall as much as possible, but also hope that the difference between the two is as small as possible. It is especially suitable for the two classification problems of pavement potholes studied in this paper.

$$F1 - Score = 2 \times \frac{P \times R}{P + R} \tag{3}$$

AP (Average accuracy). The average prediction accuracy of a certain type of object in the dataset, that is, the average value of the accuracy, is calculated by averaging the precision value on the PR curve.

$$AP = \int_0^l (P \times R) dr \tag{4}$$

mAP, which calculates the average AP value of all categories on the dataset. It is the most important evaluation index in the object detection task and is used to evaluate the overall performance of the model.

4 Experiment

In this section, we introduced the details of the experiment; compared the performance evaluation indicators of the original YOLOv3, YOLOv4 and YOLOv5 models on the pavement pothole test set images; compared the method in this paper with the original YOLOv5 model on the pavement potholes. The performance comparison on the test set verified the effectiveness of the method in this paper. Finally, the results of the visualization of the test set images are displayed.

4.1 Experimental Details

Dataset division. The dataset is divided according to the ratio of 8:1:1 and used for model training, verification, and testing. Among them, there are 7723 training images, including 16244 pothole samples; 966 verification images, including 2024 pothole samples; 966 test images, including 2111 pothole samples.

The unified size of all input training, verification and test data is 608 × 608, which is convenient for model evaluation; batch training images are spliced through random flip, geometric distortion, illumination distortion, image occlusion, random cropping, and matting. Enrich training data samples.

Experimental configuration. The hardware configuration is NVIDIA GeForce RTX 3060, Intel(R)Xeon(R)CPU E5–2680 v4 @ 2.40GHz, memory size 29G, video memory size 12G. The software configuration is python3.7.4, torch1.9.0 + cuda111. Using adaptive moment estimation (Adam) optimizer instead of stochastic gradient descent (SGD) to train the network. Some experimental parameter settings refer to Table 1.

Table 1. Experimental parameter settings.

Parameter	Value
Batch_size	16
Epochs	100
Img_size	608
Learning_rate	1e–3
Learning_rate_decay_step	1
Weight_decay	5e–4
Momentum	0.937

4.2 Experimental Results

Quantitative Evaluation. In order to verify the effectiveness of the YOLOv5 model in pavement pothole detection, we use the same parameters to train the pothole dataset with YOLOv3, YOLOv4 and YOLOv5 models, respectively. And after each round of training, four indicators of precision, recall, mAP@0.5 (IoU threshold is 0.5) and mAP@0.5:0.95 (IoU threshold is from 0.5 to 0.95, step size is 0.05) are evaluated on the test set. The evaluation result is shown in Fig. 5.

As can be seen from the figure, the result curves of the YOLOv5 model on the four evaluation indicators Precision, Recall, mAP@0.5 and mAP@0.5:0.95 are significantly better than YOLOv3 and YOLOv4. In the initial stage of training, the evaluation result curves of the three models have risen rapidly; as the training epoch increases, the evaluation result curves of various indicators begin to gradually slow down; when the training epoch reaches 90, the evaluation result curves of the three models are basically Keep it stable; when the training epoch reaches 100, the model stops learning, at this time all evaluation indicators reach the maximum. Refer to Table 2 for detailed data.

It can be seen from the table that the YOLOv5 model has achieved the best results in all evaluation indicators on the test set. The details are as follows: The precision index is 2.67% and 4.31% higher than the YOLOv3 and YOLOv4 models, respectively; the recall index is 13.15% and 6.87% higher than the YOLOv3 and YOLOv4 models, respectively; in the mAP@0.5 evaluation, the YOLOv5 model is 8.87 higher than the YOLOv3 and YOLOv4 models, respectively % And 6.98%; in the mAP@0.5:0.95 evaluation, it is

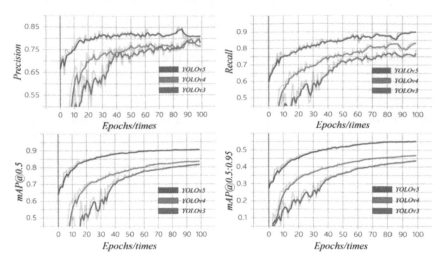

Fig. 5. Precision, recall, mAP@0.5 and mAP@0.5:0.95 evaluation results of YOLOv3, YOLOv4 and YOLOv5 on the test set.

Table 2. Comparison of various evaluation indicators of three models on the test set.

Model	Precision/%	Recall/%	mAP@0.5/%	mAP@0.5:0.95/%
YOLOv3	78.26	76.97	81.52	43.61
YOLOv4	76.62	83.25	83.41	46.76
YOLOv5	80.93	90.12	90.39	55.16

11.55 and 8.4% higher than the YOLOv3 and YOLOv4 models, respectively. Obviously, the above results verify the effectiveness of the YOLOv5 model in the detection of pavement potholes.

Model improvements. In the pavement pothole detection problem, due to the large uncertainty in the scale of the pothole in the image, the anchor frame set by the original YOLOv5 model cannot meet the needs of accurate detection of the pothole. Therefore, in order to enable the YOLOv5 model to better adapt to the learning of targets such as pits, we adopt an adaptive anchor frame adjustment strategy based on the Kmeans algorithm to regenerate anchor frames of three scales suitable for the pit training data set. The settings are as follows: (61, 52), (72, 125), (126, 69) are used to detect small targets; (127, 210), (200, 115), (213, 342) are used to detect medium-sized targets and (308, 185), (445, 313) and (559, 569) are used to detect large targets. We have also modified the final output layer of the classification network to reduce the dimensionality of the output and reduce the amount of calculation, thereby improving the detection accuracy and speed to a certain extent. The five evaluation indicators of Precision, Recall, F1-Score, mAP and the average detection time on a single test image are used to evaluate the test results before and after the model adjustment. Refer to Table 3 for detailed data.

Table 3. Evaluation of the test results before and after the adjustment of the YOLOv5 model.

Model	Precision/%	Recall/%	F1-Score/%	mAP/%	Time/ms
YOLOv5	80.93	90.12	85.28	90.39	16.92
YOLOv5_adj	83.78	92.77	88.05	93.99	12.78

It can be seen from Table 3 that the performance of YOLOv5_adj in various evaluation indicators is significantly better than that of YOLOv5. The details are as follows: Precision index increased by 2.85%, Recall index increased by 2.65%, F1-Score index increased by 2.77%, mAP index increased by 3.6%, and the average detection time on a single test image was only 12.78ms, reduced 4.14ms, which verified the effectiveness of the method in this paper.

Qualitative Evaluation. In order to better show our experimental results, we selected some representative images in the test set, and performed predictions and visual displays on these images by loading the best model weight files obtained from training.

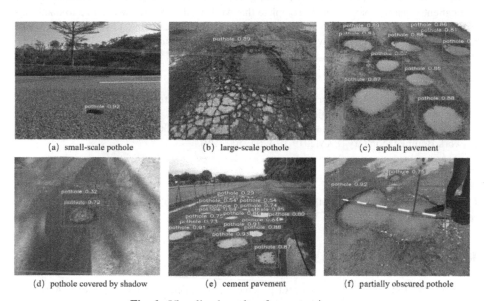

(a) small-scale pothole   (b) large-scale pothole   (c) asphalt pavement

(d) pothole covered by shadow   (e) cement pavement   (f) partially obscured pothole

Fig. 6. Visualized results of some test images.

As shown in Fig. 6, our method can accurately detect (a) small-scale pothole, (b) large-scale pothole, and (f) partially obscured pothole with high confidence; for multiple potholes in (c) asphalt pavement and (e) cement pavement, our method also achieved better detection results. However, there are some failure cases, such as (d) pothole covered by shadows. Although our method can also detect the target, there will be false detections. This is because the shadow interference results in low boundary pixel values of the pits in the image, and it is difficult to distinguish the detailed information of the contours.

5   Conclusion

This paper introduces in detail the detection method of highway pavement potholes based on YOLOv5, and has achieved good detection results. First, a large-scale pothole dataset containing multiple scene types is established, which contains 9655 images and 20,500 pothole samples in total. Then, based on the YOLOv5 model, the pavement pothole detection network structure was designed, including input size adjustment, classifier modification, and adaptive anchor frame adjustment strategy. Finally, a detailed comparative experiment verifies the availability of the dataset and the effectiveness of the method in this paper. In future work, we will continue to collect a large amount of available data and conduct research on the accurate detection of pits under shadow interference.

Acknowledgement. In the process of writing this paper, I received a lot of support and help. First of all, I would like to thank my supervisor, Liu Pengyu. Her expertise in formulating research questions and methods has benefited me a lot. Your profound insights and timely feedback on pavement pothole detection research prompted me to sharpen my thinking and take my work to the next level. Secondly, I would like to thank my teammate, Wang Xiao, his excellent cooperation and patient support prompted me to complete this work well. Finally, I would like to thank my friend Zhang Xue for her support. She provided some additional help and suggestions for my research, at the same time, allowed me to relax and rest well outside of the research. In short, thanks for their help!

Funding Statement: This paper is supported by the following funds: Basic Research Program of Qinghai Province under Grants No. 2021-ZJ-704, National Key R&D Program of China (2018YFF01010100), Beijing Natural Science Foundation (4212001), and Advanced information network Beijing laboratory (PXM2019_014204_5000 29).

Conflicts of Interest:. The authors declare that they have no conflicts of interest to report regarding the present study.

References

1. Cao, W., Liu, Q., He, Z.: Review of pavement defect detection methods. IEEE Access **8**, 14531–14544 (2020)
2. Palanisamy, P.N., Malmurugan, N.: FPGA implementation of deep leaning model for video analytics. Comput. Mater. Continu. **71**(1), 791–808 (2022)
3. Kanthavel, R., Dhaya, R.: Prediction model using reinforcement deep learning technique for osteoarthritis disease diagnosis. Comput. Syst. Sci. Eng. **42**(1), 257–269 (2022)
4. Ahmed, S., Alhumam, A.: Analyzing the implications of covid-19 pandemic: saudi arabian perspective. Intell. Autom. Soft Comput. **27**, 835–851 (2021)
5. Chea, N., Nam, Y.: Classification of fundus images based on deep learning for detecting eye diseases. Comput., Mater. Continu. **67**(1), 411–426 (2021)
6. Anitha, G., Priya, S.B.: Vision based real time monitoring system for elderly fall event detection using deep learning. Comput. Syst. Sci. Eng. **42**(1), 87–103 (2022)

7. Mandal, V., Mussah, A.R., Adu-Gyamfi, Y.: Deep learning frameworks for pavement distress classification: a comparative analysis. In: 2020 IEEE International Conference on Big Data (Big Data), pp. 5577–5583 (2020)
8. Rastogi, R., Kumar, U., Kashyap, A.: A comparative evaluation of the deep learning algorithms for pothole detection. In: 2020 IEEE 17th India Council International Conference (INDICON), pp. 1–6 (2020)
9. Su, Y.J., Wang, M.Q.: Improved CV models for highway pavement disease image segmentation. Jisuanji Gongcheng/Comput. Eng. 37(10) (2011)
10. Fan, R., Wang, H., Wang, Y.: Graph attention layer evolves semantic segmentation for road pothole detection: a benchmark and algorithms. IEEE Trans. Image Process. 30, 8144–8154 (2021)
11. Dharneeshkar, J., Aniruthan, S.A., Karthika, R.: Deep Learning based Detection of potholes in Indian roads using. In: 2020 International Conference on Inventive Computation Technologies (ICICT), pp. 381–385 (2020)
12. Xiao, Y., et al.: A review of object detection based on deep learning. Multimedia Tools Appl. 79(33–34), 23729–23791 (2020)
13. Girshick, R., Donahue, J., Darrell, T.: Rich feature hierarchies for accurate object detection and semantic segmentation. In: Proceedings of the IEEE Conference on Computer Vision and Pattern Recognition, pp. 580–587 (2014)
14. Girshick, R.: Fast r-cnn. In: Proceedings of the IEEE International Conference on Computer Vision, pp. 1440–1448 (2015)
15. Ren, S., He, K., Girshick, R.: Faster r-cnn: Towards real-time object detection with region proposal networks. Adv. Neural. Inf. Process. Syst. 28, 91–99 (2015)
16. Lin, T.Y., Dollár, P., Girshick, R., He, K., Hariharan, B., Belongie, S.: Feature pyramid networks for object detection. In: Proceedings of the IEEE Conference on Computer Vision and Pattern Recognition, pp. 2117–2125 (2017)
17. Redmon, J., Divvala, S., Girshick, R., Farhadi, A.: You only look once: Unified, real-time object detection. In: Proceedings of the IEEE conference on computer vision and pattern recognition, pp. 779–788 (2016)
18. Redmon, J., Farhadi, A.: YOLO9000: better, faster, stronger. In: Proceedings of the IEEE conference on computer vision and pattern recognition, pp. 7263–7271 (2017)
19. Redmon, J., Farhadi, A.: Yolov3: an incremental improvement. arXiv:1804.02767 (2018)
20. Bochkovskiy, A., Wang, C.Y., Liao, H.Y.M.: Yolov4: optimal speed and accuracy of object detection. arXiv:2004.10934 (2020)
21. He, K., Zhang, X., Ren, S.: Spatial pyramid pooling in deep convolutional networks for visual recognition. IEEE Trans. Pattern Anal. Mach. Intell. 37, 1904–1916 (2015)
22. Zhou, F., Zhao, H., Nie, Z.: Safety helmet detection based on YOLOv5. In: IEEE International Conference on Power Electronics, pp. 6–11 (2021)
23. Wang, C.Y., Liao, H.Y.M., Wu, Y.H. Chen, P.-Y., Hsieh, J.-W.: CSPNet: A new backbone that can enhance learning capability of CNN. In: Proceedings of the IEEE/CVF Conference on Computer Vision and Pattern Recognition Workshops, pp. 390–391 (2020)
24. Zhou, D., et al.: IOU loss for 2d/3d object detection. In: 2019 International Conference on 3D Vision (3DV), pp. 85–94. IEEE (2019)
25. Norton Wise, M. (ed.): The Values of Precision. Princeton University Press (1997)
26. Chicco, D., Jurman, G.: The advantages of the Matthews correlation coefficient (MCC) over F1 score and accuracy in binary classification evaluation. BMC Genomics 21(1), 1–13 (2020)

Further Understanding Towards Sparsity Adversarial Attacks

Mengnan Zhao[1], Xiaorui Dai[1], Bo Wang[1(✉)], Fei Yu[1], and Fei Wei[2]

[1] School of Information and Communication Engineering, Dalian University of Technology, Dalian, Liaoning 116087, China
bowang@dlut.edu.cn
[2] Department of Electrical Engineering, Arizona State University, Tempe, AZ 85281, USA

Abstract. The emergence of adversarial attacks validated the vulnerability of neural networks. Recently, highly sparse adversarial examples gradually attracted the attention of researchers for their ability in explaining what the neural networks have learned from datasets. For further understanding the sparsity adversarial attacks, we propose two different white-box techniques, the BPs, and binary fitting. BPs generates adversarial examples by validating the existence of adversarial samples in a top-down way, that is, decreasing the upper border of tempered pixel positions step by step. Additionally, the binary fitting method approximates the $\mathcal{L}_0$ distance to search for the optimal adversarial example considering the 0-norm function is non-convex. Experimental results illustrate that the proposed methods exhibit superior or competitive performance to the state-of-the-art attacks.

Keywords: Neural networks · Sparse adversarial examples · BPs · The binary fitting method

1 Introduction

Deep neural networks (DNNs) have achieved amazing performance in extensive vision tasks such as image classification [12,15,29] and object detection [11,18]. However, recent researches [10,30] illustrate that well-trained models may give wrong decisions to craft adversarial examples, whereas only tiny perturbations are added to these examples, The vulnerability of DNNs limits its applications in critical fields, such as the self-driving system [16,36], the forensic task [8,37]. Adversarial examples, especially samples generated by the sparse adversarial attack [3,6,25], are attracting attention from researchers, as they are helpful to understand deep learning. For instance, the modified pixel positions in sparsity adversarial attacks show great influence on model predictions than the rest positions.

Recent studies have introduced the adversarial attack to various tasks, e.g. object detection [34], neural language processing [4]. According to the access degree to the target model, attack methods are categorized into white-box attacks that allow attackers to utilize all model information and black-box attacks that only classification results

---

M. Zhao and X. Dai—Contributed equally to this work.

X. Sun et al. (Eds.): ICAIS 2022, CCIS 1586, pp. 200–212, 2022.
https://doi.org/10.1007/978-3-031-06767-9_17

are available. Additionally, several norm functions are adopted to measure the distance between benign samples and adversarial examples considering various requirements, $\mathcal{L}_0$, $\mathcal{L}_1$, and $\mathcal{L}_2$. The adversarial examples constrained by $\mathcal{L}_2$ norm [2,5] that measures the overall disturbance in the attack process show better human imperceptible performance. Highly sparse adversarial examples ($\mathcal{L}_0$ norm [26]) are valuable for their ability in explaining the model and imperceptible spot-like disturbances. In this work, we aim at improving the performance of white-box sparsity adversarial attacks.

We construct two sparsity adversarial attacks. These attacks tend to modify the smallest image pixels to successfully attack the model. The paper has the following contributions. 1) Based on the C&W attack, we propose BPs, which decrease its possibility of falling into the local minimum value. Motivated by (Project Gradient Descent) PGD attack [22], BPs have added the batch searching, initial perturbation, and multiple strides to $\mathcal{L}_0$ attack. 2) Compared with search-based attacks such as C&W attack, the attacks based on the gradient propagation are more powerful in explaining the model. Therefore, following several formulas in $\mathcal{L}_0$, we construct the approximate function of $\mathcal{L}_0$. Based on this, we design several loss functions to realize the sparsity adversarial attack. For instance, $\mathcal{L}_{C+P}$ separates the size and position of the perturbation into two vectors and then constrains each vector by the approximate function. 3) The proposed sparsity adversarial attacks outperform or are competitive to previous attacks.

The paper is organized as the following. The BPs attack is derived in part Sect. 3.2. In part Sect. 3.3, we first give several formulae of $\mathcal{L}_0$ and then describe how the binary fitting method (BFM) realizes the sparsity adversarial attack. In the fourth part, we compare the BPs and BFM with the state-of-the-art attacks, where also include the ablation analysis for various constraints.

2   Related Work

2.1   Attacking Methods

Adversarial attacks are categorized into the white-box attack and the black-box attack based on the accessibility of the attacked model. Specifically, white-box attacks make an assumption that attackers can access all knowledge about the attacked model. For instance, model architectures, model weights, and selected hyper-parameters. Inversely, black-box attacks mean attackers know nothing about attacked models unless classification results. Whether it is the white-box attack or the black-box attack, perturbations added to the benign samples are imperceptible to humans. Gradient and iteration attack [16] is the most commonly used attack mode. We have listed several common adversarial attacks in the following subsection.

Goodfellow et al. [10] proposed the Fast Gradient Sign Method (FGSM). FGSM only modifies pixels once for each sample according to the direction of gradient backward. Therefore, FGSM is useful for untargeted attacks even though it cannot guarantee a successful attack. Since the attack difficulty of FGSM towards un-targeted and targeted attack intention, [16] proposed the Basic Iteration Methods (BIM). Based on FGSM, BIM realizes the attack by multi-step optimization. Meanwhile, BIM restricts the max scope of perturbations for better visualization performance. Besides, [9] introduced momentum iteration to generate adversarial examples considering the convergence speed. Sarkar et al. [28] designed the *UPSET* and *ANGRI* methods that attack multiple classifiers simultaneously for improving the generalization performance of attacks. Carlini and Wagner (C&W) attack [3] obtained the crafted adversarial perturbations by limiting different norm functions. Generative Adversarial Networks(GAN) was used to generate adversarial examples [7], which learned the distribution of adversarial examples generated by FGSM and establish a generation model, thus generating corresponding adversarial examples in batches.

For special tasks like semantic segmentation and object detection, Xie et al. [34] adopted the Dense Adversary Generation (DAG) to design adversarial examples. [31] proposed the targeted adversarial attack for black-box audio systems. Ruiz et al. [27] first consider defeating the deepfake generator by adding the perturbations to the benign samples. After attacking, the facial manipulation system outputs the disrupted sample instead of the expected manipulated image. Y. Wang et al. [33] proposed an adversarial attack method for face recognition, which fool face recognition both digital domain and physical domain. [35] proposed a character level text adversarial sample generation model. Via finding important keywords and using five interference strategies, The model made the emotion of the sentences to change for artificial intelligence systems without influencing people to read and understand.

2.2 Defense Methods

Considering the application scenarios, defense methods are divided into active defense and passive defense. The former is proposed to prevent the generation of adversarial examples while the latter is adopted to detect the generated adversarial examples. Gradient mask and adversarial training are the most common methods of active defense. Networks after crafted processings lose their gradient backward information,e.g. the distillation network. Both [10] and [13] generated adversarial samples in the training stage and use them as training data in the training process. Experimental results show adversarial training increases the network robustness to various adversarial attacks. [32] proposed an adversarial joint model, MDJM-ADV, for dialog systems to predict domain, intent, and entity using a single LSTM cell to reduce the risk of downstream error propagation that is present in the typical pipelined approach Since the prediction for the bounding box is not very accurate, [21] indicated that standard detectors would not be fooled by physical adversarial stop signs.

The passive defense includes various detection methods, such as image reconstruction, which plays the role in the testing phase. [1] proposed a deep image restoration model that eliminates the perturbation of adversarial examples, the recovered original examples can be classified correctly. Metzen et al. [24] assigned the detector for the trained classification network to distinguish the adversarial examples from benign samples. Similarly, lu et al. [20] extracted the binary threshold output from each ReLU layer as the features to train the adversarial detector. The task of image reconstruction means to transform the adversarial examples to clean images, while should not affect the normal classification performance. However, the existing methods seem only to break the crafted correlations between the pixel of the adversarial example, such as Magnet [23]. The researchers first determine whether the inputs are adversarial examples and then introduce the Gaussian noise to disrupt the crafted adversarial distribution.

3   Proposed Methods

3.1   Background

Given a trained network S, a specific distance metric $\| \cdot \|_0$, inputs $\mathbf{I}$ and a radius D, the norm ball $\mathcal{B}(S, \mathbf{I}, \| \cdot \|_0, D)$ is a solution for $\mathcal{L}_0$ attack such that $\mathcal{B}(S, \mathbf{I}, \| \cdot \|_0, D)$ $= \{\mathbf{I}' = \emptyset| \; \| \; \mathbf{I}' - \mathbf{I} \;\|_0 \leq D\}$. The optimal value D_{op} of D means that no adversarial example is possible for perturbation of less than D_{op} pixels change, which is also called the least pixel attack.

By adding tiny perturbations σ to benign samples $\mathbf{I}$, the well-trained models, such as the classification network, will be deceived. The targeted attack based on $\mathcal{L}_0$ norm is expressed as,

$$\min_{\sigma} \mathcal{L}_0 = \mathcal{L}\{ S(\mathbf{I} + \sigma) = \ell | \theta_S \} + \alpha \cdot \| \sigma \|_0 \tag{1}$$

where S denotes the target model, such as the trained classification network, with fixed parameters θ_S. $\mathcal{L}$ and ℓ represents the loss function and expected targets. α is the hyper-parameter that is used to balance the attack rate and perturbation degree, which is assigned by ablation experiments.

Following the C&W attack, we introduce the variable $\mathbf{w}$ that within infinite range to calculate perturbations σ, which eliminates the problem introduced by limiting pixel values of adversarial examples $\mathbf{I}'$ to [0,1].

$$\sigma = \frac{1}{2}(\tanh(\mathbf{w}) + 1) - \mathbf{I}, -1 \leq \tanh(\mathbf{w}) \leq 1$$

Actually, adversarial examples are iteratively updated, which are separated into the pixel value map and pixel position map.

$$\mathbf{I}'_i = \left[\frac{\tanh\left(\mathbf{w} + t'_{i-1}\right) + 1}{2} \right] \cdot P_i + (1 - P_i) \cdot \mathbf{I} \tag{2}$$

where $t'_{i-1} = \arctanh\left(\mathbf{I}'_{i-1} \cdot 2. - 1\right)$, i and P_i denote the ith attack and the binary vector that measures the tampered pixel positions. $\sum P_i$ is fixed in each iterative attack and $\sum P_i \geq \sum P_{i+1}$, where $\sum P_i$ describes how many pixels can be modified in the ith attack. The termination goal of the iteration for $\mathcal{L}_0$ attack is set to

$$\min_{\sigma} \mathcal{L}_0 < 0.001 \text{ or } S\left(\mathbf{I}'_i\right) = \ell$$

3.2   BPs Method

BPs is a kind of search-based attack, which introduces batch processing, initial perturbation, and multi-strides. The search-based attack means to iteratively decrease the value of radius D until it cannot find adversarial examples.

Given benign samples $\mathbf{I}$, the initial perturbations, such as the normal distribution perturbation $n_k = \text{Noise}(\mathbf{I}, \mu, \delta)$ $n_k \in [0, 1]$, a batch of image points are expanded from one image point $\mathbf{I}$, $\mathbf{R}_0 = \{\mathbf{I}, \ldots, \mathbf{I}\} + \{0, n_{0,1}, \ldots, n_{0,b}\}$ $\forall_{j=0}^{b} \mathbf{R}_{0,j} \in [0, 1]$. μ and δ are the mean and standard deviation of the noise.

Each sample in $\mathbf{R}_0$ denotes one potential optimization direction. To find the image points that contribute to affecting the model decision, we modify the termination goal of each iteration to

$$\exists_{j \in [0,b]} \mathcal{S} \left(\mathbf{R}'_{i,j} \right) = \ell$$

Since a batch of image points do not share the same optimization step, image points that initially reach the optimization criterion will be destroyed by the optimization process of the remaining image points. Therefore, we set a static process to decrease the P_i.

$$sp = [st_0, st_1, \cdots, st_m] \quad st_i \geq st_j \, when \quad i \geq j$$

$$\sum P_i \geq \sum P_{i-1} - sp[i]$$

Note that $|sp| \geq H \cdot W \cdot c$, $H \times W \times c$ denotes the image shape. The BPs obtains the potential optimal adversarial examples of the sparsity adversarial attack when it meets

$$\exists_{j \in (0,b)} \mathcal{S} \left(\mathbf{R}'_{t,j} \right) = \ell, \forall_{j \in (0,b)} \mathcal{S} \left(\mathbf{R}'_{>t,j} \right) \neq \ell$$

Here $\sum P_t$ is the maximum radius of D. We set multiple strides to validate the reliability of D.

$$\sum P_i \geq \sum P_{i-1} - sp_k[i] \quad k \in \Omega$$

$$\forall_{i \in [0,m]} sp_k[i] < sp_t[i] \quad when \quad k < t$$

This setting considers the case that, the optimization process cannot find the adversarial example with P_{i-1}, but successfully generates adversarial examples with P_i, where $\sum P_{i-1} > \sum P_i$. Finally, we express the termination goal as

$$\exists_{k \in \Omega} \exists_{j \in (0,b)} \mathcal{S} \left(\mathbf{R}'_{i,j} \right) = \ell$$

Although we can better generate sparsity adversarial examples by setting multiple strides, the consumption of time is impractical. Therefore, we set $sp = stride$ ($st\_0 = st\_1 = \cdots = st\_m$), $\max(k) = 3$, and $stride_k \in (2,3,5)$ for both the targeted attack and untargeted attack.

3.3 Binary Fitting Method

The search-based attack spends time to validate the potential possibility of the sparsity adversarial attack on each P_i. Next, we use the optimization strategy to determine the location and size of perturbation. Same as the search-based attack, we separate perturbations into two vectors.

Before the detailed description, we first understand the conditions of the $\mathcal{L}_0$ attack. Given the adversarial example, the tampered positions are located by the difference between the benign sample and the adversarial example.

$$|\mathbf{I}' - \mathbf{I}| > 1. \, or \, \mathbf{I}' \neq \mathbf{I} \quad \mathbf{I} \in [0., 255.] \tag{3}$$

Based on Eq. (2), $\| \sigma \|_0$ is expressed as

$$\| \mathbf{I}'_i - \mathbf{I} \|_0 = \| \left\{ \left[\frac{\tanh \left(\mathbf{w} + t'_{i-1} \right) + 1}{2} \right] - \mathbf{I} \right\} \cdot P_i \|_0$$

Properties. For convenience, we denotes $\mathbf{C} = \left\{ \left[\frac{\tanh(\mathbf{w}+t'_{i-1})}{2} \right] - \mathbf{I} \right\}$ and $\mathbf{P} = P_i \cdot \mathbf{C}$

and $\mathbf{P}$ are the size and location of perturbations, respectively. Different from other norm functions, 0-norm function only calculates the number of 0 (For image pixels, calculate the number of $|\mathbf{I}'_i - \mathbf{I}| < 1$.). Therefore, $\| \sigma \|_0$ satisfies the following properties. The **upper border** of the $\| \sigma(w) \|_0$

$$
\begin{aligned}
\| \sigma(w) \|_0 &= \| \mathbf{C} \cdot \mathbf{P} \|_0 \\
&= \| \mathbf{C} \|_0 + \| \mathbf{P} \|_0 - \| \mathbf{C} + \mathbf{P} \|_0 \\
&\leq \| \mathbf{C} \|_0 + \| \mathbf{P} \|_0
\end{aligned}
$$

Meanwhile, the **lower border** of $\| \sigma(w) \|_0$ is expressed as

$$
\| \mathbf{C} \cdot \mathbf{P} \|_0 \geq \max\{\| \mathbf{C} \|_0, \| \mathbf{P} \|_0\}
$$

We use Pro_1 and Pro_2 to denote the upper border and the lower border of the $\| \sigma(w) \|_0$. Pro_1 and Pro_2 are unconditioned conclusions. In addition, when both $\| \mathbf{C} \|_0$ and $\| \mathbf{P} \|_0$ are greater than 0, we have

$$
Pro_3 \quad \| \mathbf{C} \|_0 \cdot \| \mathbf{P} \|_0 \geq \| \mathbf{C} \cdot \mathbf{P} \|_0
$$

Any value in $\mathbf{C}$ and $\mathbf{P}$ to 0 can decrease the value of the 0-norm function.

Fitting. The variable $\mathbf{P}$ should be an optional binary vector since we denote it as positions of $\mathcal{L}_0$ attack. However, it is well-known that the 0-norm function is an NP-hard problem, and $\mathcal{L}_0$ loss is discontinuous. Therefore, the optimal point cannot obtain by the forward-backward process. Many works are proposed to solve $\mathcal{L}_0$ task in the search mode, which are not determined by the internal information of the model, such as the gradient and logit. However, larger perturbations are set in advance, e.g. directly changing the value of any selected pixel (normalized) to 0 or 1.

For such cases, we introduce the following function to replace the 0-norm function

$$
\max_{\mathbf{w}} \| \sigma(\mathbf{w}) \|_0 = \max_{\mathbf{w}} \| \mathbf{C} \cdot \mathbf{P} \|_0
$$

$$
\Rightarrow \min_{\mathbf{w}} \sum \left\{ 1 - \frac{1}{\exp(\beta \cdot \mathbf{C}_{i,j,k} \cdot \mathbf{P}_{i,j,k})} \right\} \quad \mathbf{P} \in R_{H \times W \times c}
$$

We denote $C(\mathbf{T}_{i,j,k})$ as $\frac{1}{\exp(\beta \cdot \mathbf{T}_{i,j,k})} - 1$ and use $C(\cdot)$ to replace $\| \cdot \|_0$. β is a hyperparameter to better fit the 0-norm function. $C(\mathbf{P}_{i,j,k}) = 0$ only when $\mathbf{P}_{i,j,k} \to 0$.

Next, we prove that $\| \mathbf{T} \|_0$ can be replaced by $C(\mathbf{T})$. For Pro_2,

$$
C(\mathbf{C} \cdot \mathbf{P}) \geq \max\{C(\mathbf{C}), C(\mathbf{P})\}
$$

$$
\Leftrightarrow \max\left\{ \frac{1}{\exp(\beta \cdot \mathbf{C}^2)}, \frac{1}{\exp(\beta \cdot \mathbf{P}^2)} \right\} \leq \frac{1}{\exp(\beta \cdot \mathbf{C}^2 \cdot \mathbf{P}^2)}
$$

$$
\Leftrightarrow \mathbf{P}^2 \leq 1, st. \; \| \mathbf{P} \|_0 \leq \| \mathbf{C} \|_0 \; or
$$

$$
\mathbf{C}^2 \leq 1, st. \; \| \mathbf{C} \|_0 \leq \| \mathbf{P} \|_0
$$

$\max\{\| \mathbf{C} \|_0, \| \mathbf{P} \|_0\} = \| \mathbf{P} \|_0$, since $\mathbf{P}$ denotes the modified positions. For $\mathbf{C} = \frac{\tanh(\mathbf{w}+t')+1}{2} - \mathbf{I}$, its value is limited to [-1,1]. Therefore, Pro_2 is an unconditioned expression. For Pro_3,

$$\sum C(\mathbf{C} \cdot \mathbf{P}) \leq \sum C(\mathbf{C}) \cdot \sum C(\mathbf{P})$$

Pro_3 always holds since $C(\mathbf{C} \cdot \mathbf{P}) \leq 0$ and $C(\mathbf{C}) \cdot C(\mathbf{P}) \geq 0$. Combine the Pro_2 and Pro_3, we have $\max\{C(\mathbf{C}), C(\mathbf{P})\} \leq C(\mathbf{C}\cdot\mathbf{P}) \leq 0$. Thus, the function $C(\mathbf{P}\cdot\mathbf{C}) \leq C(\mathbf{C}) + C(\mathbf{P})$ is possibly holds, $C(\mathbf{P} \cdot \mathbf{C}) = C(\mathbf{C}) + C(\mathbf{P})$ only when the value of β (the default value is 10) is large enough. For Pro_1,

$$C(\mathbf{C} \cdot \mathbf{P}) \leq C(\mathbf{C}) + C(\mathbf{P})$$

$$\Leftrightarrow 0 \leq (\frac{1}{\exp(\beta \cdot \mathbf{C}^2)} - \frac{1}{\exp(\beta \cdot \mathbf{P}^2 \cdot \mathbf{C}^2)})+$$
$$(\frac{1}{\exp(\beta \cdot \mathbf{P}^2)} - 1)$$

Available Loss Function. To decrease the number of tampered image pixels, we construct the constraint as,

$$\min_{\mathbf{w},\mathbf{P}} \mathcal{L}_{\mathbf{C}\cdot\mathbf{P}} = -\sum_{i=1}^{b} C(\mathbf{C}_i \cdot \mathbf{P}_i)$$

Next, several $\mathcal{L}_0$ attacks are realized by separating the perturbation to the pixel value map and pixel position map.

$$\min_{\mathbf{w}} \mathcal{L}_{\mathbf{C}} = -\sum_{i=1}^{b} C(\mathbf{C}_i), \quad \min_{\mathbf{P}} \mathcal{L}_{\mathbf{P}} = -\sum_{i=1}^{b} C(\mathbf{P}_i)$$
$$\min_{\mathbf{w},\mathbf{P}} \mathcal{L}_{\mathbf{C}+\mathbf{P}} = \mathcal{L}_{\mathbf{P}} + \gamma \cdot \mathcal{L}_{\mathbf{C}}$$

Normally, the value of $\|\mathbf{P}\|_0$ is much greater than the value of $\|\mathbf{C}\|_0$. Therefore, we use γ ($\gamma \leq 1$) to show the different contributions of the $\mathbf{C}$ and $\mathbf{P}$. $\mathcal{L}_{\mathbf{C}}$, $\mathcal{L}_{\mathbf{P}}$, and $\mathcal{L}_{\mathbf{C}+\mathbf{P}}$ are both lower constraints of $\mathcal{L}_{\mathbf{C}\cdot\mathbf{P}}$, that is, if *case* is a optimal solution of $\mathcal{L}_{\mathbf{C}}$ (or $\mathcal{L}_{\mathbf{P}}$, $\mathcal{L}_{\mathbf{C}+\mathbf{P}}$), then *case* is also a optimal solution of $\mathcal{L}_{\mathbf{C}\cdot\mathbf{P}}$. On the contrary, $\mathcal{L}_{\|\mathbf{C}\|_0\cdot\|\mathbf{P}\|_0}$ is the upper border of the $\mathcal{L}_{\mathbf{C}\cdot\mathbf{P}}$, which cannot guarantee the optimal value of $\mathcal{L}_{\mathbf{C}\cdot\mathbf{P}}$.

$$\min_{\mathbf{w},\mathbf{P}} \mathcal{L}_{\|\mathbf{C}\|_0\cdot\|\mathbf{P}\|_0} = \mathcal{L}_{\mathbf{C}} \cdot \mathcal{L}_{\mathbf{P}}$$

The overall loss function, $\mathcal{L}_0$ in Eq. (1), is constructed by replacing the $\| \sigma \|_0$ with the above-mentioned constraints such as $\mathcal{L}_{\mathbf{C}+\mathbf{P}}$.

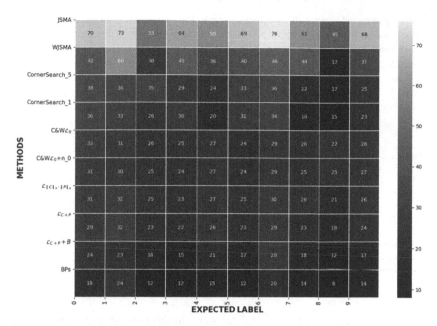

Fig. 1. The value denotes how many pixels have been modified. The X-axis denotes the targeted attack goals (10 classes, 0–9). Y-axis is the sparse attack method used in this paper. The T in CornerSearch$_T$ means the search stride. The maximum perturbable pixels in CornerSearch are set to 100. Similar to PGD (projected gradient descent) attack, we introduce the initial perturbation (the normal distribution perturbation) to the benign sample which is expressed as $+n_0$. In the same way, +B denotes the model with batch processing.

4   Experiments

4.1   Settings

In our experiments, all data comes from the public datasets CIFAR-10 [14] and MINIST [17]. We implement the prepared model by using Tensorflow®. Without the special statement, we set the batch size to 128 when training the model (the default model used in C&W attack) and to 32 in the attacking process. The initial value of the learning rate is set to 0.01 in the training and attacking process. The code is available at https://github.com/Dlut-lab-zmn/Least_pixel_attack.

4.2   Evaluation of Targeted Attack Ability

We compare the proposed sparse adversarial attacks with state-of-the-art methods: Carlini-Wagner $\mathcal{L}_0$-attack [3], JSMA [25], WJSMA [19] and CornerSearch [6]. In this section, for the targeted attack, we randomly select 500 images (50 images in each class) from the testing set for targeted attacks. Each sample has 10 attack targets (0–9). Therefore, for each attack, we will generate 4500 adversarial examples. To visually compare various attack methods, we provide the confusion matrix that records the experiment

Table 1. Comparison of various of $\mathcal{L}_0$ targeted attack. Each sample has 10 attack targets. For the C&W attack, we set the search iteration to 1000. n_0 denotes the normal distribution perturbation. For CornerSearch, the upper limit of the allowed number of pixel changes is 100. Please note that CornerSearch can not always succeed in the attack. In BFM, we assign the optimization iterations to 2000, γ to 0.4 for MNIST, and 1. for CIFAR. The search iteration for BFM and $\mathcal{L}_{C+P}+B$ is 512. ** and ** are the 1st and 2nd best results. The codes for the comparison methods are given in the reference.

		JSMA		CornerSearch	C&W		BPs	Binary Fitting Method (BFM)			
	Metrics	JSMA	WJSMA	Stride = 5	$\mathcal{L}_0$	$\mathcal{L}_0+n_0$		$\mathcal{L}_{C \cdot P}$	$\mathcal{L}_{||C||_0 \cdot ||P||_0}$	$\mathcal{L}_{C+P}$	$\mathcal{L}_{C+P}+B$
Dataset	Type	Bottom-up		Top-down	Bottom-up		Top-down	Optimize-based mode			
MNIST	AR	46.85	96.64	49.82	97.93	98.62	**100.0**	96.69	92.76	98.1	**100.0**
	Pixel (mean)	63.84	39.6	29.52	27.82	26.7	**14.88**	110.6	26.68	24.77	19.38
	Per (mean)	49.1	33.32	17.24	16.95	18.72	**11.88**	12.47	14.52	14.56	12.24
	Time (s)	0.32	**0.25**	4.19	5.14	5.58	10.5	4.95	4.84	4.5	5.74
CIFAR	AR	99.62	100	79.15	99.11	99.71	100	100	77.78	98.88	100
	Pixel (mean)	68.25	42.53	43.27	27.58	32.29	**5.34**	642.8	127.4	25.51	14.24
	Per (mean)	63.17	38.19	27.91	9.78	14.72	**4.16**	11.38	3.07	4.76	4.44
	Time(s)	5.32	2.92	7.057	4.67	7.83	24.8	4.67	4.51	4.37	6.63

results on the MNIST dataset in Fig. 1. The value in this confusion matrix denotes the average modified pixels that need to generate adversarial examples. We observe from Fig. 1 that the model performs poor recognition ability for digit 8, but is robust for digits 1 and 6.

In Table 1, we report the attack rate of each method, which is the fraction of correctly classified samples that can be successfully attacked. *Pixels(Mean)* denotes the number of pixels that need to modify to misclassify the network for each attack. To better illustrate the perturbation, we adopt the Eq. (4) to calculate *Pixels(mean)* instead of Eq. (5), which also measures the difference for different channel, such as when evaluation on the CIFAR dataset for the CornerSearch method, 43.27 for Eq. (5) and 14.44 for Eq. (4).

$$Pixels(Mean) = \sum \{|\mathbf{I}' - \mathbf{I}| \geq 1.\} \quad \mathbf{I} \in [0., 255.] \tag{4}$$

$$Pixels(Mean) = \sum \{\max(|\mathbf{I}' - \mathbf{I}|, c) \geq 1.\} \mathbf{I} \in [0., 255.] \tag{5}$$

The average value of the size of perturbations for all adversarial examples is denoted as *Per(Mean)*. *Time* denotes the average time consumption for generating each targeted adversarial example. The sparsity adversarial attacks are categorized into three types according to different search modes, top-down, bottom-up, and optimize-based mode. Top-down attacks such as C&W gradually reduce the number of pixels ($\sum P_i \leq \sum P_{i-1}$) that can be modified. Conversely, bottom-up attacks such as JSMA tend to modify more pixels to affect the classification decision step by step. The pixel positions of the optimize-based method will be changed following the optimization process.

We observe from Table 1 that initial perturbations are not efficient in improving the targeted attack rate, e.g., the results of $\mathcal{L}_0$ and $\mathcal{L}_0 + n_0$. Additionally, BPs achieves the state-of-the-art attack performance, namely, BPs only modifies half of the pixels than the best baseline while maintaining a similar attack rate. The significant attack performance of BPs benefits from batch processing and multiple strides. The former provides multiple initialization directions, and the latter increases the probability of obtaining the optimal solution.

$\mathcal{L}_{C\cdot P}$ performs worse attack performance than other sparsity constraints. In our opinion, that is because $C(\mathbf{T})$ is only the fitting version of $\| \mathbf{T} \|_0$, many pixels are constrained towards 0 but are not really equal to 0. Therefore, many pixels are modified for generating adversarial examples, but the size of perturbation is still small. For instance, not all $C(\mathbf{T})$ meets Pro_1 in $\| \mathbf{T} \|_0$. The $\mathcal{L}_{C+P}$ is helpful because both $\mathbf{C}$ and $\mathbf{P}$ are limited to tiny values for invalid positions. Similar to BPs, the batch processing for $\mathcal{L}_{C+P}$ that offers multiple optimization directions has successfully improved the attack rate.

For both targeted and untargeted attacks, the bottom-up attacks tend to spend less time than the top-down attacks. The more vulnerable the sample, the greater the time difference. However, we cannot observe this situation in a targeted attack since the low attack rate of bottom-up methods. For the bottom-up attack, the running time is controlled by the maximum search steps.

Table 2. Comparison of various of $\mathcal{L}_0$ untargeted attack. For C&W attack, we set the search iteration to 1000. We assign the optimization iteration of the attack with batch processing to 512.

Dataset	Metrics	CornerSearch Stride = 5	C&W $\mathcal{L}_0$	$\mathcal{L}_0$+n$_0$	BPs	BFM $\mathcal{L}_{C+P}$+B
MNIST	AR	100.0	100.0	100.0	100.0	100.0
	Pixel (mean)	7.54	19.75	15.21	**5.80**	10.51
	Per (mean)	7.39	13.23	13.29	**4.97**	6.74
	Time (s)	**1.05**	4.32	4.64	14.73	5.61
CIFAR	AR	100.0	100.0	100.0	100.0	100.0
	Pixel (mean)	**5.44**	15.76	19.31	8.20	9.41
	Per (mean)	3.86	6.14	8.92	2.25	**1.74**
	Time (s)	**0.69**	4.45	4.96	28.87	7.21

4.3 Evaluation of Untargeted Attack Ability

In this subsection, we compare the performance of the untargeted attack between our methods (BPs attack and BFM attack) and existing attacks (CW) attack and CornerSearch method). We randomly select 1000 images from the testing set as the dataset. All of them are correctly classified. Thus we need to generate 1000 adversarial examples for each attack. The experiment results are given in Table 2. As we can see, the initial perturbation improve untargeted attack performance in the MNIST dataset. However, this conclusion is not valid in CIFAR since we use Eq. (4) and Eq. (5) to count the tampered points. Apart from that, our method generates adversarial examples with fewer pixels changed, but this improvement comes at the cost of time. For instance, in the

CIFAR dataset, the corner search method only needs 0.69 s to generate one adversarial example, but the BFM need 7.21 s. Therefore, BPs and BFM will be more useful for targeted attack tasks, the high attack rate, and the necessary time consumption.

5   Conclusion

In this paper, we propose two white-box sparsity adversarial attacks, BPs and BFM. Both attacks tend to search for the most influential pixels that affect the model decision. Extensive experiments show that our methods outperform or are competitive with previous works. Since the attack efficiency of these two white-box sparsity adversarial attacks is at the cost of time, we recommend that BPs and BFM be used for a targeted attack task.

Acknowledgement. This work is supported by the National Natural Science Foundation of China (No. U1936117, No. 62106037, No. 62076052), the Science and Technology Innovation Foundation of Dalian (No. 2021JJ12GX018), the Fundamental Research Funds for the Central Universities (DUT21GF303, DUT20TD110, DUT20RC(3)088), and the Open Project Program of the National Laboratory of Pattern Recognition (NLPR) (No. 202100032).

References

1. Ali, K., Quershi, A.N., Arifin, A.A.B., Bhatti, M.S., Sohail, A., Hassan, R.: Deep image restoration model: a defense method against adversarial attacks. CMC-Comput. Mater. Continua **71**(2), 2209–2224 (2022)
2. Carlini, N., Wagner, D.: Adversarial examples are not easily detected: bypassing ten detection methods. In: Proceedings of the 10th ACM Workshop on Artificial Intelligence and Security, pp. 3–14 (2017). https://github.com/carlini/nn_robust_attacks
3. Carlini, N., Wagner, D.: Towards evaluating the robustness of neural networks. In: 2017 IEEE Symposium on Security and Privacy (SP), pp. 39–57. IEEE (2017)
4. Chen, H., Zhang, H., Chen, P.Y., Yi, J., Hsieh, C.J.: Attacking visual language grounding with adversarial examples: a case study on neural image captioning. arXiv preprint arXiv:1712.02051 (2017)
5. Croce, F., Hein, M.: A randomized gradient-free attack on ReLU networks. In: Brox, T., Bruhn, A., Fritz, M. (eds.) GCPR 2018. LNCS, vol. 11269, pp. 215–227. Springer, Cham (2019). https://doi.org/10.1007/978-3-030-12939-2_16
6. Croce, F., Hein, M.: Sparse and imperceivable adversarial attacks. In: Proceedings of the IEEE International Conference on Computer Vision, pp. 4724–4732 (2019). https://github.com/fra31/sparse-imperceivable-attacks
7. Deng, B., Ran, Z., Chen, J., Zheng, D., Yang, Q., Tian, L.: Adversarial examples generation algorithm through DCGAN. Intell. Autom. Soft Comput. **30**(3), 889–898 (2021)
8. Ding, X., Chen, Y., Tang, Z., Huang, Y.: Camera identification based on domain knowledge-driven deep multi-task learning. IEEE Access **7**, 25878–25890 (2019)
9. Dong, Y., et al.: Boosting adversarial attacks with momentum. In: Proceedings of the IEEE Conference on Computer Vision and Pattern Recognition, pp. 9185–9193 (2018)
10. Goodfellow, I.J., Shlens, J., Szegedy, C.: Explaining and harnessing adversarial examples. arXiv preprint arXiv:1412.6572 (2014)
11. He, K., Gkioxari, G., Dollar, P., Girshick, R.: Mask R-CNN. IEEE Trans. Pattern Anal. Mach. Intell. **42**(2), 386–397 (2020)

12. He, K., Zhang, X., Ren, S., Sun, J.: Deep residual learning for image recognition. In: Proceedings of the IEEE Conference on Computer Vision and Pattern Recognition, pp. 770–778 (2016)
13. Huang, R., Xu, B., Schuurmans, D., Szepesvári, C.: Learning with a strong adversary. arXiv preprint arXiv:1511.03034 (2015)
14. Krizhevsky, A., Hinton, G., et al.: Learning multiple layers of features from tiny images (2009)
15. Krizhevsky, A., Sutskever, I., Hinton, G.E.: ImageNet classification with deep convolutional neural networks. In: Advances in Neural Information Processing Systems, pp. 1097–1105 (2012)
16. Kurakin, A., Goodfellow, I., Bengio, S.: Adversarial examples in the physical world. arXiv preprint arXiv:1607.02533 (2016)
17. LeCun, Y., Cortes, C., Burges, C.: MNIST handwritten digit database (2010)
18. Lin, T., Goyal, P., Girshick, R., He, K., Dollar, P.: Focal loss for dense object detection. IEEE Trans. Pattern Anal. Mach. Intell. **42**(2), 318–327 (2020)
19. Loison, A., Combey, T., Hajri, H.: Probabilistic Jacobian-based saliency maps attacks. arXiv: abs/2007.06032 (2020). https://github.com/probabilistic-jsmas/probabilistic-jsmas
20. Lu, J., Issaranon, T., Forsyth, D.: SafetyNet: detecting and rejecting adversarial examples robustly. In: 2017 IEEE International Conference on Computer Vision (ICCV), pp. 446–454 (2017)
21. Lu, J., Sibai, H., Fabry, E., Forsyth, D.: Standard detectors aren't (currently) fooled by physical adversarial stop signs. arXiv preprint arXiv:1710.03337 (2017)
22. Madry, A., Makelov, A., Schmidt, L., Tsipras, D., Vladu, A.: Towards deep learning models resistant to adversarial attacks, June 2017
23. Meng, D., Chen, H.: MagNet: a two-pronged defense against adversarial examples. In: Proceedings of the 2017 ACM SIGSAC Conference on Computer and Communications Security, pp. 135–147 (2017)
24. Metzen, J.H., Genewein, T., Fischer, V., Bischoff, B.: On detecting adversarial perturbations. In: ICLR 2017: International Conference on Learning Representations 2017 (2017)
25. Papernot, N., McDaniel, P., Jha, S., Fredrikson, M., Celik, Z.B., Swami, A.: The limitations of deep learning in adversarial settings. In: 2016 IEEE European Symposium on Security and Privacy (EuroS&P), pp. 372–387. IEEE (2016), https://github.com/RobertoFalconi/BlackBoxAttackDNN
26. Ruan, W., Wu, M., Sun, Y., Huang, X., Kroening, D., Kwiatkowska, M.: Global robustness evaluation of deep neural networks with provable guarantees for the hamming distance. In: International Joint Conference on Artificial Intelligence (2019)
27. Ruiz, N., Bargal, S.A., Sclaroff, S.: Disrupting deepfakes: adversarial attacks against conditional image translation networks and facial manipulation systems. arXiv: abs/2003.01279 (2020)
28. Sarkar, S., Bansal, A., Mahbub, U., Chellappa, R.: UPSET and ANGRI: breaking high performance image classifiers. arXiv preprint arXiv:1707.01159 (2017)
29. Simonyan, K., Zisserman, A.: Very deep convolutional networks for large-scale image recognition. arXiv preprint arXiv:1409.1556 (2014)
30. Szegedy, C., et al.: Intriguing properties of neural networks. arXiv preprint arXiv:1312.6199 (2013)
31. Taori, R., Kamsetty, A., Chu, B., Vemuri, N.: Targeted adversarial examples for black box audio systems. In: 2019 IEEE Security and Privacy Workshops (SPW), pp. 15–20. IEEE (2019)
32. Uprety, S.P., Jeong, S.R.: Adversarial training for multi domain dialog system. Intell. Autom. Soft Comput. **31**(1), 1–11 (2022)

33. Wang, Y., Zhang, C., Liao, X., Wang, X., Gu, Z.: An adversarial attack system for face recognition. J. Artif. Intell. **3**(1), 1 (2021)
34. Xie, C., Wang, J., Zhang, Z., Zhou, Y., Xie, L., Yuille, A.: Adversarial examples for semantic segmentation and object detection. In: Proceedings of the IEEE International Conference on Computer Vision, pp. 1369–1378 (2017)
35. Xu, H., Du, C., Guo, Y., Cui, Z., Bai, H.: A generation method of letter-level adversarial samples. J. Artif. Intell. **3**(2), 45 (2021)
36. Yuan, X., He, P., Zhu, Q., Bhat, R.R., Li, X.: Adversarial examples: Attacks and defenses for deep learning. arXiv preprint arXiv:1712.07107 (2017)
37. Zhao, M., Wang, B., Wei, F., Zhu, M., Sui, X.: Source camera identification based on coupling coding and adaptive filter. IEEE Access **8**, 54431–54440 (2020)

MRDA-Net: Multiscale Residual Dense Attention Network for Image Denoising

Jianhu Zhu[1], Cheng Yao[1(✉)], Yibin Tang[1], Yuan Gao[1], Lin Zhou[2], and Hongmei Hu[3]

[1] College of Internet of Things Engineering, Hohai University,
Changzhou 213022, China
`yaoc@hhu.edu.cn`
[2] School of Information Science and Engineering, Southeast University,
Nanjing 210096, China
[3] Medizinische Physik, Carl von Ossietzky Universität Oldenburg and Cluster
of Excellence "Hearing4all", Küpkersweg 74, 26129 Oldenburg, Germany

Abstract. Deep learning methods have become prevalent in image denoising. Existing deep-learning approaches can mainly be divided into two categories: encoder-decoder and high-resolution models, wherein high-resolution models have superior resolution capabilities in detail description and restoration. In this study, we propose a network, namely, multi-scale residual dense attention network, that takes advantage of the context and attention information of images. Specifically, a residual dilated dense module containing dilated dense convolutional layers is employed to enlarge the receptive field of the proposed network. Then, we train such module to learn multi-scale features of images. A feature aggregation module is sequentially designed with dual attention blocks, yielding multi-scale feature maps effectively. We aggregate the multi-scale maps by a concatenation operation. Finally, a simple convolutional layer is adopted to generate residual images. With the residual learning strategy, clean images are obtained implicitly. During the experiment tests, we firstly carry out ablation studies to demonstrate the function of each proposed module. Then, blind and non-blind denoising procedures are carried out. Additionally, the total parameters are considered for analyzing the complexity of the proposed network. Comprehensive experiments show our method is better than several selected state-of-the-art denoising ones by the measure of PSNR and SSIM.

Keywords: Attention mechanism · Deep-learning · Dense connection · Dilated convolution · Image denoising · Multi-scale feature

1 Introduction

As there exist various noises in the process of image generation, storage, and transmission, the task of image denoising to restore a clear image from its noisy

X. Sun et al. (Eds.): ICAIS 2022, CCIS 1586, pp. 213–230, 2022.
https://doi.org/10.1007/978-3-031-06767-9_18

observation follows a model $y = x + n$, where an assumption is that n is additive white Gaussian noise (AWGN) with standard deviation of σ.

To date, image denoising has evolved from model-based methods to deep-learning-based ones. In past decades, model-based methods have achieved tremendous success. In early studies, they involved a filtering process that aimed to remove noise by calculating the value of each pixel in local areas or patch groups such as linear filtering [2,39], non-linear filtering [28,35,44] and graph filtering [32]. These methods are effective in removing noises but unable to exploit the statistical information of the entire image. Later, model-based methods recover denoised image by modeling image prior such as non-local self-similarity [15,23,43], sparse models [4,5,7,21,40,41] and low-rank models [3,9,42] and others [20,24,36]. For example, the sparse models based on K-SVD [11] method used the sparse representations to restore target images by training dictionaries. However, the over-complete dictionary in sparse coding may cause instability of image restoration. In the block matching and three-dimensional collaborative filtering (BM3D) [13] method, similar image patches were stacked together and jointly filtered in the 3-D transform domain. BM3D shows promising denoising results but its performances deteriorate when the noise is complex. Generally, model-based methods rely on the internal prior information of noisy images, thus they are flexible and robust for solving various kinds of noise. However, most of them are constrained by handcrafted models and suffer from the fact that they are time-consuming in the denoising process.

Nowadays, increasing deep-learning-based methods are proposed to overcome the above issues. They can learn the potential structure of image from training and preserve more details in denoising [8,33,47,48]. Zhang et al. proposed a DnCNN [47] model for image denoising, which introduced residual learning [14] and batch normalization [19] to speed up the training process and boost the denoising performance. The DnCNN dealt with gaussian noises at a certain level as well as an unknown level. It is difficult to measure the noise level of real noisy images in application. Thus unknown noise level denoising i.e. blind-denoising is necessary. The recent development of blind denoising methods, for example, the blind real image denoising network (RIDNet) [1] and the convolutional blind denoising network (CBDNet) [11], show excellent blind-denoising performance. Especially, Noise2Noise [22] and Neighbor2Neighbor [18] are more attractive because they do not require noisy-clean image pairs which are challenging and expensive to collect.

Inspired by recent work in [45], the deep-learning-based image restoration network can be divided into two categories: encoder-decoder and high-resolution. The encoder-decoder models can learn rich contextual information by multiple image scale transformations such as downsampling operations. In detail, they smooth the input images firstly then the smoothed images are multiply downsampled to obtain a series of reduced images. By combining these spatial-resolution reduced images, sufficient contextual information is learned for clean images reconstruction. Nevertheless, contiguous downsampling operations lead to the loss of fine spatial details which are extremely hard to recover in the next stage. For example, the residual dense neural network (RDUNet)[19] used strided convolution in the subsampling operation to recover local contrast information lost by downsampling. In [10], to preserve more details and textures, a dilation selective block with attention mechanism was embedded in the U-Net [30] which contains symmetric sampling operations.

On the other hand, high-resolution models choose another way to deal with the denoising problem such that they recover images with more details. Specifically, they first map the input to multi-channel features. Then they learn these features in convolutional layers without downsampling-like operations. The features at each layer share the same spatial position with the target pixel. Therefore, local details can be exquisitely rebuilt without downsampling-based loss. However, there exist some issues in high-resolution models. Therefore, various strategies were proposed to ameliorate these issues. In [26,34,50], researchers built a very deep network by increasing the network depth or width to learn high-level features of input images. However, as the network deepens, the extracted features become more advanced, and a large number of low-level features corresponding to edge and detail information are lost [12]. High-resolution models seldom leverage contextual information for their limited network receptivity. Therefore, some methods employed multi-kernel traditional or dilated convolution operations to enlarge the receptive field [12,37,38]. Nevertheless, they increased the computational burden. In addition, all features in convolution operations share equal significances without the consideration of the cross-feature relationships, which is unbeneficial to establish a broad contextual correlation between input and output information. Thus, the dense connection was added to encourage feature reuse, which enriches contextual information of different convolution layers [17,31,50]. Besides, attention mechanism was also widely used, some remarkable attentions, namely, spatial and channel attentions [37,46], are adopted for image denoising. For example, dual attention has been successfully used to supervise multiscale sampled images, yielding improved image restoration [45].

In this paper, we propose an efficient high-resolution network called Multiscale Residual Dense Attention Network (MRDA-Net) for image denoising. The main contributions of this study are:

1) We combine dilated convolution, dense connection and attention strategies with the high-resolution network. In detail, dilated convolution and dense connection are utilized together in the residual dilated dense (RDD) module. It not only enlarges the receptive field of the network but also learns rich context information for feature extraction. The attention-based feature aggregation (FA) module acts as a filter which goes through useful information, and aggregates multi-scale feature maps adaptively. 2) We reinterpret the function of dilated convolution and view it as a complex downsampling operation. Therefore, multiscale feature analysis can be conducted in the proposed network. 3) Experiments demonstrate that our MRDA-Net outperforms several state-of-the-art model-based and deep-learning methods in both blind and non-blind image denoising. In addition, ablation studies show the adopted strategies have effects on the network.

The remainder of this paper is organized as follows. In Sect. 2, additional related work is briefly reviewed. Section 3 introduces the proposed method. In Sect. 4, extensive experiments are conducted to evaluate MRDA-Net. Finally, concluding remarks are given in Sect. 5.

2   Related Work

In this section, we briefly review and discuss the three attractive strategies, including dilated convolution, dense connection, and attention mechanism for image denoising.

2.1   Dilated Convolution

Dilated convolution is a useful tool for enlarging the receptive field of networks [42,47]. It covers a feature area with a certain checkerboard pattern, where a scale factor s is defined to describe its sampling interval for the checkerboard pattern. As a result, dilated convolution has s times more receptive fields than in traditional convolution. When feature maps are downsampled, the noise is also removed very efficiently. Therefore, we reinterpret dilated convolution from a new perspective as shown in Fig. 1. We treat the dilated convolution as a complex operation that includes downsampling, convolution, and aggregation steps. More specifically, a downsampling step casts the input features into each feature slice in terms of the given checkerboard pattern. Then, a traditional convolution operation is performed on these slices to obtain their local features. These local features are sequentially aggregated to form the final output features that share the same size as the input features. Because dilated convolution implicitly adopts a downsampling operation, it naturally generates multiscale features and thus has an advantage in learning the contextual information of images. Therefore, we use dilated convolution to capture multiscale features at different layers for our MRDA-Net.

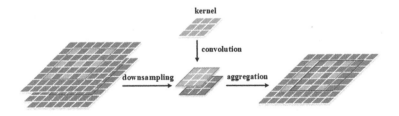

Fig. 1. Reinterpretation of dilated convolution.

2.2   Dense Connection

The Dense Convolutional Network (DenseNet) was first proposed in [17]. It was proposed for comparison with the Residual Network (ResNet) [14], and its experiment results showed that the DenseNet is superior to the ResNet in terms of improving the network. Meanwhile, the DenseNet has the advantages in various fields, that is, alleviating the vanishing-gradient problem, enhancing the propagation and reuse of features, and substantially reducing the number of parameters. The feed-forward propagation of features from layer to layer can be viewed as one state to another state. In the ResNet, feature propagation is completed by summation that creates a new state for the subsequent layers after it reads states of preceding layers. In contrast to ResNet, the concatenation in DenseNet directly combines the states of preceding layers with the state of current layer without creating a new state, which saves a lot of memory and computation. Therefore, dense connections strengthen feature propagation and encourage features reuse. It is known that the problem of vanishing-gradient may occur when the network is deep. The dense connection strengthens the transmission of the gradient in the process of feature feed-forward propagation, so that dense network alleviates the vanishing-gradient problem.

By fully employing the advantages of such propagation, image restoration methods using dense connections were successively proposed [31,50]. For example, in RDN [50], a Residual Dense Block (RDB) was proposed to extract a large number of local features. To adaptively learn the local features of each layer and stabilize the deep network training, the local features in RDB were fused by dense connections. Finally, global hierarchical features were learned by using global feature fusion. Therefore, both global and local features were well utilized, which gave rise to sufficient contextual information for image reconstruction. In our study, to avoid the problems of grid phenomenon and the excessive consumption of GPU memory caused by a large number of continuous use of dense connections, we adopt a different dense connection approach. The details will be described in Sect. 3.1.1.

2.3   Attention Mechanism

The attention mechanism is inspired by human visual attention to images and has been widely used in the field of image denoising in recent years. In deep learning, attention can be differentiated so that we can calculate the gradient through a neural network and learn the weight of attention through forward propagation and backward feedback. Attention is mainly divided into two kinds, namely, subnetwork-based attention and self-attention. Attention networks based on subnets generally focus on externally provided attention. In detail, this type of attention emphasizes obtaining features from different perspectives under the same background. If the attention selected is reasonable, it plays a role of attention as well as supervision used to correct the main network. Thus the main network can correctly learn the features we need. For example, a supervised attention module (SAM) was proposed in [46]. This module firstly provides ground-truth supervisory signals that are beneficial for progressive image restoration. Secondly, with the help of locally supervised predictions, attention maps were generated to suppress the less informative features and only allow the useful ones to propagate.

The self-attention network pays attention to the influence of different branches in the same network to guide the next stage of feature learning. In other words, it autonomously learns features among different stages of the network. For example, a dual attention unit (DAU) was proposed to suppress less useful features and only allows more informative ones to pass further in the network [45]. Compared with the self-attention network, the sub-network-based attention network increases the computational cost of training. However, it may not be able to optimize the performance of the network. In this paper, we take DAU as the basic unit of attention network and test the performance of networks for image denoising. The details will be described in Sect. 4.

3   Proposed Method

In this section, we first introduce the proposed denoising network MRDA-Net in detail. Then the implementation details of the training are described.

3.1   Network Structure

Our proposed MRDA-Net consists of four parts, as indicated in Fig. 2: a shallow feature preprocessing block (SFP), a residual dilated dense module (RDD), an attention-based feature aggregation module (FA), and a residual reconstruct block (RR). The shallow feature preprocessing block is composed of a convolution layer and a ReLU activation layer, where the convolution layer is used to convert input noisy images into 64 channels features. The ReLU activation layer aims to pre-activate the network, which offers significant error reductions for network training [29]. The RDD module cascades numerous (3 in this paper) RDD blocks into a feature-extraction stream which extracts features with different receptive field size. The FA module further enhances the extracted multi-scale feature maps and then aggregates them. Finally, a RR block using the residual learning strategy is adopted to restore clean images. In detail, a hyperbolic tangent function and a convolution layer are sequentially employed to generate a residual image for noise prediction. More detailed operations are explained as follows.

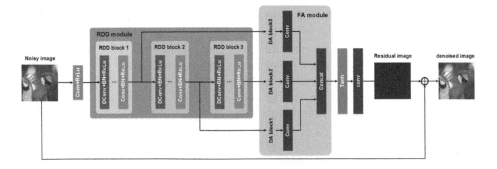

Fig. 2. Architecture of MRDA-Net.

Residual Dilated Dense Module. We first present the structure of the proposed Residual Dilated Dense (RDD) Block which illustrated in Fig. 3. The RDD Module contains 3 sequential RDD blocks, each of which is composed of several (7 in this paper) CBR units. Note that CBR refers to putting convolution, batch normalization, and ReLU layers into a unit. Similarly, DCBR refers to putting dilated convolution with dilated factor of 2, batch normalization, and ReLU layers into a unit. Through empirical analysis, we find that the RDD block of 7 convolution layers and the RDD module of 3 RDD blocks can obtain a better tradeoff between performance and efficiency.

The RDD block combines the dilated and traditional convolutions to enlarge the receptive field size. And the dense connections are adopted to fuse contextual information for improving denoising performance. In Fig. 3, we introduce a hybrid convolution model for avoiding the gridding phenomenon resulting from sequential dilated convolutions. There is no dense connection directly connecting two different dilated convolution layers in this model. Besides, dense connections between traditional convolutions are also reduced because directly fusing features from all the convolution layers can stack a huge amount of features. Then a global residual connection is added in the RDD Block for maintaining the initial feature nature. Therefore, the RDD block not only enlarges the receptive field size of the network but also learns rich contextual information of the features, which has the advantages of both encoder-decoder and high-resolution models.

Specifically, all convolutions in this study with 64 filters of size $3 * 3 * c$ (c represents the number of image channels, $c = 1$ for gray image and $c = 3$ for color image) are employed to generate 64 channels feature maps. The dilated convolutions with dilated factor of 2 have the same parameters as traditional convolutions, the batch normalization is used to speed up the training process and the ReLU have functioned as nonlinear activation. The blue arrow in Fig. 3 represents the concatenation operation.

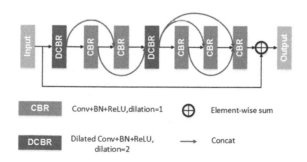

Fig. 3. Structure of RDD Block. (Color figure online)

Feature Aggregation Module. While the RDD module extracted multi-scale feature maps, we need a module to enhance and aggregate these feature maps. Motivated by the Dual Attention Unit (DAU) which suppresses less useful features and only allows more informative ones to pass further, we adopt DA block as the basic unit of attention mechanism. Each DA Block is followed by a traditional convolution layer for converting the multi-scale feature maps into 1 channel features that share the same size of the input noisy image. Then we aggregate the three features by a concatenation operation for residual learning.

The Dual Attention Block, as depicted in Fig. 4, is divided into three branches: spatial attention, channel attention, and local residual learning. The spatial branch is designed to exploit the inter-spatial dependencies of convolutional features [45]. The channel branch exploits the inter-channel relationships of the convolutional feature maps by applying squeeze and excitation operations [16]. And local residual learning is adopted to compensate for the useful information lost in the first two branches.

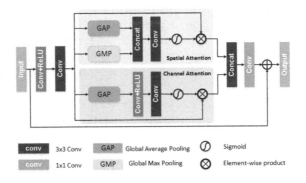

Fig. 4. Structure of DA Block.

3.2   Implementation

After constructing the network, we trained it to obtain the optimal network parameters. Given a clean image x_i and its paired noisy image y_i, we used the mean squared error as a loss function, which is represented as

$$L\left(\Theta\right) = \frac{1}{N} \sum_{i=1}^{N} \|R\left(y_i, \Theta\right) - \left(y_i - x_i\right)\|_F^2 \tag{1}$$

where Θ denotes the trainable network parameters, $R\left(y_i, \Theta\right)$ refers to the residual image derived from the noisy image y_i, and N is the number of training images.

In addition, we cropped approximately 1.3 million patches with a size of $50 * 50$ in each training epoch [33] and finished the training after 70 epochs. For each batch, 512 patches were used as the inputs. An Adam optimizer was employed to refresh the parameters at a learning rate of 0.001. Furthermore, we conducted our network in the PyTorch framework with NVIDIA GeForce RTX 3090 graphics card.

4   Experiment

In this section, we firstly introduce our experiment datasets. Then we evaluate the performance of our proposed method on several datasets and compare it with other state-of-the-art methods. To begin, ablation studies are performed to verify the superiority of the proposed several modules. Then we report our experimental results on Set12 and BSD68 datasets for Gray No-blind denoising. Finally, we test our method for Blind-denoising on Kodak24, McMaster, CBSD68, and Set12 datasets. To take the complexity of the network into the consideration, we test the total parameters of our network and compare it with several denoising networks.

4.1   Datasets

We employed BSD400 from the Berkeley segmentation database and Waterloo Exploration database (3,859 images) as training data for both color and gray image denoising [25,27]. For the test data, we used the CBSD68, Kodak24, and McMaster datasets for color image denoising, while using BSD68 and Set12 for gray image denoising [6,27,49]. Besides, DIV2K dataset was used when we test the total parameters of networks. In our experiments, all noisy images were generated using Gaussian noise.

4.2   Ablation Studies

As mentioned before, we know that the major determinants of our model are: 1) The dilated convolution enlarges the receptive field size. 2) The dense connection learns rich contextual information. 3) The Dual Attention Block enhances multi-scale feature maps.

The following are detailed explanations of several network variants:

- Variant A: There was no dense connection in the RDD block. All dilated convolutions were replaced with traditional convolutions. In the FA module, no DA block was added, only a traditional convolution was employed to aggregate multi-scale feature maps.
- Variant B: Based on Variant A, we replaced traditional convolution with dilated convolution in the RDD block as shown in Fig. 3.
- Variant C: Based on Variant A, we only added dense connections which are the same as Fig 3 to each RDD block.
- Variant D: In this case, the RDD block was identical to what have depicted in Variant A, but we added the DA block in FA Module.

A comparison of the denoising performances of these MRDA-Net variants is given in Table 1. Note that the test results were obtained on the BSD68 dataset at a noise level of 25. As Table 1 shows, Variant B and Variant C obtained an improvement of 0.04 and 0.05 dB than that of Variant A in PSNR, which revealed that the dilated convolution and the dense connections contributed to improving the denoising performance. That's because the dilated convolution enlarges the receptive field and the dense connections learn rich contextual information. Meanwhile, the improvement of Variant D in PSNR also indicated the positive effects of the attention-based DA block. The DA block suppresses less useful features and allows more informative ones to pass further, which enhanced the extracted feature maps and was conducive to better aggregating feature maps later.

Table 1. Denoising performance comparison with the MRDA-Net variants on the BSD68 dataset at a noise level of 25.

Model	Description	PSNR(dB)
MRDA-Net		**29.33**
Variant A	Without dilated Conv, dense connection, and DA block	**29.26**
Variant B	Only dilated Conv added	**29.30**
Variant C	Only dense connection added	**29.31**
Variant D	Only the DA block added	**29.29**

4.3 Non-blind Image Denoising

In this section, we first test the denoising performance of our method in terms of PSNR and SSIM analysis on Set12 and BSD68 Dataset. Then we compare ours with several competing denoising methods including classical model-based methods (BM3D, WNNM), deep-learning methods (DnCNN, FFDNet, ADNet, and BRDNet). Next, we give some denoising examples and analyze the results.

As shown in Table 2, the MRDA-Net achieves the best performance on noise levels of 15, 25 and 50, respectively. Specifically, bold and underlined numbers are used to denote the best and second denoising results in Table 2 and Table 3 respectively. The model-based methods (BM3D and WNNM) performed the worst because only the internal image prior information was used for image denoising. A large amount of external image prior information can be more conducive to the reconstruction of clean images, which explains why datasets-based deep learning has been widely used in image restoration in recent years.

The deep-learning methods (DnCNN, FFDNet, ADNet, and BRDNet) are the high-resolution models, which are comparable to our methods. The DnCNN and FFDNet methods yielded acceptable results for that the high-resolution models can extract features with more details. The ADNet employs an attention-guided strategy to recover clean images, thus it yielded superior results. By introducing dilated convolutions and batch renormalization, the BRDNet can learn contextual information with broader receptive field size and describe the distribution of a single patch sample, which provided it preferable results.

Table 2. Average PSNR (dB)/SSIM of various non-blind denoising methods for gray images.

σ	BM3D	WNNM	DnCNN	FFDNet	ADNet	BRDNet	MRDANet
Set12	PSNR/SSIM						
15	32.39/0.8949	32.70/0.8977	32.85/0.9025	32.74/0.9024	32.98/0.9075	33.03/0.9081	**33.09/0.9088**
25	29.95/0.8498	30.26/0.8552	30.43/0.8617	30.42/0.8631	30.58/0.8669	30.61/0.8674	**30.71/0.8691**
50	26.68/0.7651	27.05/0.7771	27.17/0.7828	27.30/0.7899	27.37/0.7885	27.45/0.7921	**27.57/0.7945**
BSD68	PSNR/SSIM						
15	31.07/0.8722	31.37/0.8764	31.74/0.8907	31.64/0.8902	31.74/0.8965	31.79/0.8975	**31.81/0.8975**
25	28.57/0.8017	28.83/0.8086	29.23/0.8279	29.19/0.8288	29.25/0.8344	29.29/0.8361	**29.33/0.8363**
50	25.62/0.6869	25.87/0.6982	26.24/0.7189	26.29/0.7239	26.29/0.7236	26.36/**0.7289**	**26.40**/0.7276

Figure 5 shows the denoising results of the gray images under various noise levels. We chose the results of the BM3D, WNNM, DnCNN, FFDNet, and ADNet methods to compare with ours. From the house pictures we can see that our method denoised more adequately, restored local details better, and had clearer edges and contours, which resulted from the more accurate prediction of multi-scale feature aggregation and residual learning strategy. Figure 6 shows the thermodynamic images of the multi-scale feature maps extracted from each RDD block during the training process, where "scale 1" represents the output of one RDD block, "scale 2" represents the output of two RDD blocks, and "scale 3" represents the output of three RDD blocks. Feature maps have different receptive fields and context information at different scales. In the figure "Scale 1", low-level features such as contours and edges are well restored. In the picture "Scale 2", there are many noise components, and the position of the image content is rough. The picture "Scale 3" contains different semantic information such as sky, grass, and man. After the network training, the noise components extracted by "scale 1" and "scale 2" are not sufficient, and "scale 3" will lose some local details. Therefore, multi-scale feature maps are first enhanced with DA blocks, and then aggregated to obtain the residual feature maps with more information.

4.4   Blind Image Denoising

The synthetic gray and color Gaussian noisy images include noisy images of certain noise levels and varying noise levels from 0 to 55. The noisy image with varying noise levels is called the image with blind noise. In this section, we evaluate our method for blind image denoising. Specifically, Set12 was used for gray blind-denoising, and CBSD68, Kodak24, and McMaster were used for Color ones. The DnCNN, ADNet, and Noise2Noise methods were compared with ours in terms of blind-denoising. Table 3 shows the results of the comparison, our methods achieved the best performance in PSNR value.

Table 3. Average PSNR (dB)/SSIM of different blind denoising methods on various datasets.

Noise level σ	DnCNN-B	ADNet-B	Noise2Noise	MRDA-Net-B
Set12	PSNR/SSIM			
15	32.67/0.9000	<u>32.77</u>/<u>0.9034</u>	32.15/0.8989	**32.99/0.9075**
25	30.35/0.8599	<u>30.46</u>/<u>0.8632</u>	30.12/0.8572	**30.65/0.8674**
50	27.18/0.7816	<u>27.33</u>/<u>0.7805</u>	27.04/0.7701	**27.52/0.7922**
BSD68	PSNR/SSIM			
15	33.90/0.9290	33.79/0.9584	<u>33.97</u>/**0.9652**	**35.28**/<u>0.9596</u>
25	31.24/0.8830	31.12/<u>0.9280</u>	<u>31.33</u>/**0.9386**	**32.66**/0.9273
50	27.95/0.7896	27.83/<u>0.8575</u>	<u>28.07</u>/**0.8772**	**29.37**/0.8528
kodak24	PSNR/SSIM			
15	34.48/0.9198	34.53/<u>0.9486</u>	<u>34.72</u>/**0.9511**	**34.87**/0.9440
25	32.02/0.8763	32.03/<u>0.9174</u>	<u>32.28</u>/**0.9219**	**32.39**/0.9074
50	28.83/0.7908	28.81/<u>0.8458</u>	<u>29.11</u>/**0.8575**	**29.23**/0.8280
McMaster	PSNR/SSIM			
15	33.45/0.9035	34.60/<u>0.9589</u>	<u>34.67</u>/**0.9576**	**35.02**/0.9450
25	31.52/0.8694	32.28/<u>0.9373</u>	<u>32.42</u>/**0.9398**	**32.73**/0.9174
50	28.62/0.7986	29.03/<u>0.8833</u>	<u>29.27</u>/**0.8911**	**29.58**/0.8596

Notes: We altered the names of certain blind denoising methods by adding a suffix "-B" (e.g., DnCNN-B).

We further analyze the table, the DnCNN-B method performed the worst because it directly cast noisy images into the network for its loss function calculation. Compare to DnCNN-B, an attention mechanism was introduced in ADNet-B to improve denoising performance. However, these two methods are simpler than our method and may not be robust enough to deal with blind noise. Benefit from similar statistical information of noise, Noise2Noise employed two kinds of noisy image pairs for training, thus superior SSIM performance has been obtained. While the PSNR performance of Noise2Noise is lower than our methods, it does not require clean image pairs. Our method benefited from broader receptive size and rich contextual information through RDD module, and the attention mechanism passed more useful information to aggregate multi-scale feature maps, which improved the performance of our network.

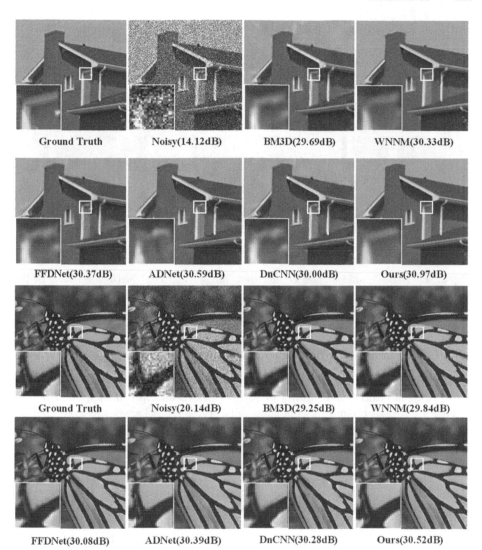

Fig. 5. Denoising performance for gray images on the Set12 dataset. The first and second sets of images (first two and last two rows, respectively) are named "House" and "Monarch," the noise levels of which are with traditional deviations of $\sigma = 50$ and $\sigma = 25$, respectively.

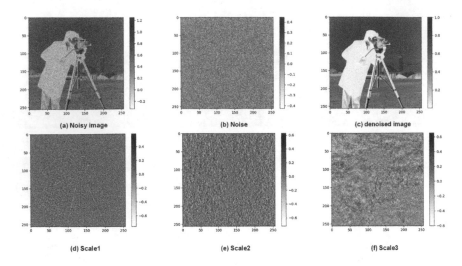

Fig. 6. Thermodynamic images of denoised image "Carmen" with noise level of 25. (a) Noisy. (b) Noise. (c) denoised image. (d) scale1-output of one RDD block. (e) scale2-output of two RDD blocks. (f) scale3-output of three RDD blocks.

4.5   Complexity of Network

In order to measure the complexity of the network, we measured the total parameters, runtime, and PSNR values of several networks. Specifically, the runtime represents the test time of denoising networks. We selected ten color super-resolution (SR) images with $1920 * 1080$ pixel from DIV2K dataset as the test dataset. Table 4 shows the results of our experiment.

Through comparison, we find that the amount of parameters of MRDA-Net is about three times that of ADNet and DnCNN. Meanwhile, the runtime of our network is about twice as long as ADNet and DnCNN. Therefore, we designed a lightweight network called MRDA-Net-L. All convolution layers of this network are replaced by depthwise separable convolution. We can see from Table 4 that the parameters of MRDA-Net-L are minimized and its runtime is the fastest. However, the PSNR values is still better than ADNet and DnCNN, which

Table 4. Comparison of the complexity of several methods at a noise level of 25.

Methods	Device	Runtime(s)	PSNR(dB)	Total Parameters(million)
CBM3D	CPU	22.6	28.86	–
ADNet	GPU	0.478	29.43	0.52
DnCNN	GPU	0.390	29.32	0.558
MRDA-Net	GPU	0.766	29.92	1.586
MRDA-Net-L	GPU	0.303	28.53	0.426

illustrates that our proposed Network is noticeably outperformed the existing representative deep-learning-based network.

5   Conclusion

In this paper, a deep convolutional neural network called MRDA-Net based on high-resolution models was proposed for image denoising. We first adopted dilated convolution for enlarging the network's receptive field and it can be regarded as similar as downsampling operation without disadvantage. The dense connections are added for fusing local contextual information in RDD blocks. Therefore, the latent noise information hidden in the noisy images can be extracted, which is useful to deal with complex denoising problems such as blind-denoising. In addition, an attention-based FA module is employed for enhancing and aggregating multi-scale feature maps extracted from the RDD module. Finally, the residual learning is adopted to separating noise from noisy observation. Experiments results showed that our method outperformed several state-of-the-art model-based and deep-learning methods in both blind and non-blind image denoising tests in terms of PSNR and SSIM values. In the future, we will investigate our method in more image restoration tasks such as super-resolution and image deblurring.

References

1. Anwar, S., Barnes, N.: Real image denoising with feature attention. In: Proceedings of the IEEE/CVF International Conference on Computer Vision, pp. 3155–3164 (2019)
2. Benesty, J., Chen, J., Huang, Y.: Study of the widely linear wiener filter for noise reduction. In: 2010 IEEE International Conference on Acoustics, Speech and Signal Processing, pp. 205–208. IEEE (2010)
3. Dong, W., Shi, G., Li, X.: Nonlocal image restoration with bilateral variance estimation: a low-rank approach. IEEE Trans. Image Process. **22**(2), 700–711 (2012)
4. Dong, W., Zhang, L., Shi, G., Li, X.: Nonlocally centralized sparse representation for image restoration. IEEE Trans. Image Process. **22**(4), 1620–1630 (2012)
5. Elad, M., Aharon, M.: Image denoising via sparse and redundant representations over learned dictionaries. IEEE Trans. Image Process. **15**(12), 3736–3745 (2006)
6. Franzen, R.: Kodak lossless true color image suite (2013). http://r0k.us/grapics/kodak/
7. Geng, T., Sun, G., Xu, Y., He, J.: Truncated nuclear norm minimization based group sparse representation for image restoration. SIAM J. Imaging Sci. **11**(3), 1878–1897 (2018)
8. Gong, P., Liu, J., Lv, S.: Image denoising with GAN based model. J. Inf. Hiding Priv. Protect. **2**(4), 155 (2020)
9. Gu, S., Zhang, L., Zuo, W., Feng, X.: Weighted nuclear norm minimization with application to image denoising. In: Proceedings of the IEEE Conference on Computer Vision and Pattern Recognition, pp. 2862–2869 (2014)
10. Guo, B., Song, K., Dong, H., Yan, Y., Tu, Z., Zhu, L.: Nernet: noise estimation and removal network for image denoising. J. Vis. Commun. Image Representation **71**, 102851 (2020)

11. Guo, S., Yan, Z., Zhang, K., Zuo, W., Zhang, L.: Toward convolutional blind denoising of real photographs. In: Proceedings of the IEEE/CVF Conference on Computer Vision and Pattern Recognition, pp. 1712–1722 (2019)
12. Guo, Y., Jia, X., Zhao, B., Chai, H., Huang, Y.: Multifeature extracting CNN with concatenation for image denoising. Sign. Process. Image Commun. **81**, 115690 (2020)
13. Gurrola-Ramos, J., Dalmau, O., Alarcón, T.E.: A residual dense u-net neural network for image denoising. IEEE Access **9**, 31742–31754 (2021)
14. He, K., Zhang, X., Ren, S., Sun, J.: Deep residual learning for image recognition. In: Proceedings of the IEEE Conference on Computer Vision and Pattern Recognition, pp. 770–778 (2016)
15. Hou, Y., Zhao, C., Yang, D., Cheng, Y.: Comments on image denoising by sparse 3-d transform-domain collaborative filtering. IEEE Trans. Image Process. **20**(1), 268–270 (2010)
16. Hu, J., Shen, L., Sun, G.: Squeeze-and-excitation networks. In: Proceedings of the IEEE Conference on Computer Vision and Pattern Recognition, pp. 7132–7141 (2018)
17. Huang, G., Liu, Z., Van Der Maaten, L., Weinberger, K.Q.: Densely connected convolutional networks. In: Proceedings of the IEEE Conference on Computer Vision and Pattern Recognition, pp. 4700–4708 (2017)
18. Huang, T., Li, S., Jia, X., Lu, H., Liu, J.: Neighbor2neighbor: self-supervised denoising from single noisy images. In: Proceedings of the IEEE/CVF Conference on Computer Vision and Pattern Recognition, pp. 14781–14790 (2021)
19. Ioffe, S., Szegedy, C.: Batch normalization: accelerating deep network training by reducing internal covariate shift. In: International Conference on Machine Learning, pp. 448–456. PMLR (2015)
20. Jin, K., Wang, S.: Image denoising based on the asymmetric gaussian mixture model. Internet of Things **2**(1), 11 (2020)
21. Lecouat, B., Ponce, J., Mairal, J.: Fully trainable and interpretable non-local sparse models for image restoration. In: Vedaldi, A., Bischof, H., Brox, T., Frahm, J.-M. (eds.) ECCV 2020. LNCS, vol. 12367, pp. 238–254. Springer, Cham (2020). https://doi.org/10.1007/978-3-030-58542-6_15
22. Lehtinen, J., Munkberg, J., Hasselgren, J., Laine, S., Karras, T., Aittala, M., Aila, T.: Noise2noise: Learning image restoration without clean data. arXiv preprint arXiv:1803.04189 (2018)
23. Li, S., Zhao, J., Zhang, H., Bi, Z., Qu, S.: A non-local low-rank algorithm for sub-bottom profile sonar image denoising. Remote Sens. **12**(14), 2336 (2020)
24. Li, X., Ye, C., Yan, Y., Du, Z.: Low-dose CTimage denoising based on improved WGAN-GP. J. New Media **1**(2), 75 (2019)
25. Ma, K., et al.: Waterloo exploration database: new challenges for image quality assessment models. IEEE Trans. Image Process. **26**(2), 1004–1016 (2016)
26. Mao, X., Shen, C., Yang, Y.B.: Image restoration using very deep convolutional encoder-decoder networks with symmetric skip connections. Adv. Neural Inf. Process. Syst. **29**, 2802–2810 (2016)
27. Martin, D., Fowlkes, C., Tal, D., Malik, J.: A database of human segmented natural images and its application to evaluating segmentation algorithms and measuring ecological statistics. In: Proceedings Eighth IEEE International Conference on Computer Vision. ICCV 2001, vol. 2, pp. 416–423. IEEE (2001)
28. Pitas, I., Venetsanopoulos, A.N.: Nonlinear digital filters: principles and applications, vol. 84. Springer Science & Business Media (2013)

29. Pleiss, G., Chen, D., Huang, G., Li, T., van der Maaten, L., Weinberger, K.Q.: Memory-efficient implementation of densenets. arXiv preprint arXiv:1707.06990 (2017)

30. Ronneberger, O., Fischer, P., Brox, T.: U-Net: Convolutional Networks for Biomedical Image Segmentation. In: Navab, N., Hornegger, J., Wells, W.M., Frangi, A.F. (eds.) MICCAI 2015. LNCS, vol. 9351, pp. 234–241. Springer, Cham (2015). https://doi.org/10.1007/978-3-319-24574-4_28

31. Song, Y., Zhu, Y., Du, X.: Dynamic residual dense network for image denoising. Sensors $19(17)$, 3809 (2019)

32. Tang, Y., Chen, Y., Jiang, A., Li, J., Kwan, H.K.: Guided intra-patch smoothing graph filtering for single-image denoising. Comput. Mater. Continua $69(1)$, 67–80 (2021)

33. Tian, C., Xu, Y., Li, Z., Zuo, W., Fei, L., Liu, H.: Attention-guided CNN for image denoising. Neural Netw. **124**, 117–129 (2020)

34. Tian, C., Xu, Y., Zuo, W., Du, B., Lin, C.W., Zhang, D.: Designing and training of a dual CNN for image denoising. Knowl.-Based Syst. **226**, 106949 (2021)

35. Tomasi, C., Manduchi, R.: Bilateral filtering for gray and color images. In: Sixth International Conference on Computer Vision (IEEE Cat. No. 98CH36271), pp. 839–846. IEEE (1998)

36. Vinayagam, P., Anandan, P., Kumaratharan, N.: Image denoising using a nonlinear pixel-likeness weighted-frame technique. Intell. Autom. Soft Comput. $30(3)$, 869–879 (2021)

37. Wang, Y., Wang, G., Chen, C., Pan, Z.: Multi-scale dilated convolution of convolutional neural network for image denoising. Multimedia Tools Appl. **78**(14), 19945–19960 (2019). https://doi.org/10.1007/s11042-019-7377-y

38. Wang, Y., Song, X., Gong, G., Li, N.: A multi-scale feature extraction-based normalized attention neural network for image denoising. Electronics $10(3)$, 319 (2021)

39. Weizheng, X., Chenqi, X., Zhengru, J., Yueping, H.: Digital image denoising method based on mean filter. In: 2020 International Conference on Computer Engineering and Application (ICCEA), pp. 857–859. IEEE (2020)

40. Wen, B., Ravishankar, S., Bresler, Y.: Structured overcomplete sparsifying transform learning with convergence guarantees and applications. Int. J. Comput. Vis. **114**(2), 137–167 (2015)

41. Xu, J., Zhang, L., Zhang, D.: A trilateral weighted sparse coding scheme for real-world image denoising. In: Proceedings of the European Conference on Computer Vision (ECCV), pp. 20–36 (2018)

42. Xu, J., Zhang, L., Zhang, D., Feng, X.: Multi-channel weighted nuclear norm minimization for real color image denoising. In: Proceedings of the IEEE International Conference on Computer Vision, pp. 1096–1104 (2017)

43. Xu, J., Zhang, L., Zuo, W., Zhang, D., Feng, X.: Patch group based nonlocal self-similarity prior learning for image denoising. In: Proceedings of the IEEE International Conference on Computer Vision, pp. 244–252 (2015)

44. Yang, R., Yin, L., Gabbouj, M., Astola, J., Neuvo, Y.: Optimal weighted median filtering under structural constraints. IEEE Trans. Sign. Process. **43**(3), 591–604 (1995)

45. Zamir, S.W., et al.: Learning enriched features for real image restoration and enhancement. In: Vedaldi, A., Bischof, H., Brox, T., Frahm, J.-M. (eds.) ECCV 2020. LNCS, vol. 12370, pp. 492–511. Springer, Cham (2020). https://doi.org/10.1007/978-3-030-58595-2_30

46. Zamir, S.W., et al.: Multi-stage progressive image restoration. In: Proceedings of the IEEE/CVF Conference on Computer Vision and Pattern Recognition, pp. 14821–14831 (2021)
47. Zhang, K., Zuo, W., Chen, Y., Meng, D., Zhang, L.: Beyond a gaussian denoiser: residual learning of deep CNN for image denoising. IEEE Trans. Image Process. **26**(7), 3142–3155 (2017)
48. Zhang, K., Zuo, W., Zhang, L.: FFDNet: Toward a fast and flexible solution for CNN-based image denoising. IEEE Trans. Image Proces. **27**(9), 4608–4622 (2018)
49. Zhang, L., Wu, X., Buades, A., Li, X.: Color demosaicking by local directional interpolation and nonlocal adaptive thresholding. J. Electron. Imaging **20**(2), 023016 (2011)
50. Zhang, Y., Tian, Y., Kong, Y., Zhong, B., Fu, Y.: Residual dense network for image restoration. IEEE Trans. Pattern Anal. Mach. Intell. **43**(7), 2480–2495 (2020)

Aspect-Level Sentiment Classification Based on Graph Attention Network with BERT

Jiajun Zou[1], Sixing Wu[2], Zhongliang Yang[3(✉)], Chong Chen[4], Yizhao Sun[5], Minghu Jiang[1], and Yongfeng Huang[3]

[1] School of Humanities, Tsinghua University, Beijing 100084, China
[2] North China Electric Power University, Beijing 100096, China
[3] Beijing National Research Center for Information Science and Technology.
Department of Electronic Engineering, Tsinghua University, Beijing 100084, China
yangzl15@tsinghua.org.cn
[4] North Automatic Control Technology Institute, Taiyuan 030006, China
[5] Multimedia Communications and Signal Processing,
Friedrich-Alexander-Universität Erlangen-Nürnberg, 91058 Erlangen, Germany

Abstract. With accelerated evolution of the internet, people can express their sentiments towards organizations, politics, products, events, etc. Analyzing these sentiments becomes very beneficial for businesses, government and individuals. To some extent, text sentiment analysis involves Internet content security. Aspect level sentiment classification aims to recognize the sentiment expressed towards a special target given a context sentence, which is more fine-grained than sentence level or document level sentiment analysis. Most previous works concentrate on the semantic information between the contexts and the aspect terms, but they ignore the structural information of the sentences. In this paper, we propose a new method based on Graph Attention Network (GAT) to deal with the complex connections among words in sentences through structural features. A lot of experiments are conducted on two datasets: Laptop and Restaurant from SemEval2014, the results show that our model outperforms other previous works, which confirms the effectiveness of taking sentence structural information into account.

Keywords: Aspect-level sentiment classification · Graph attention network · Deep learning · Natural language processing

1 Introduction

The development of the internet brings people into the era of information explosion, in which everyone can express his or her opinions, sentiments, emotions, appraisals and attitudes towards entities such as products, services, organizations, individuals, issues, events and topics through social media. Sentiment analysis aims to recognize these subjective information [21], which plays an

© The Author(s), under exclusive license to Springer Nature Switzerland AG 2022
X. Sun et al. (Eds.): ICAIS 2022, CCIS 1586, pp. 231–244, 2022.
https://doi.org/10.1007/978-3-031-06767-9_19

important role for businesses, government as well as individuals [1,12,13,25,31], and it has become one of the most active research field in Natural Language Processing (NLP) in the past 20 years. To some extent, text sentiment analysis involves Internet content security. According to Liu's point of view, we can divide sentiment analysis into document level sentiment analysis, sentence level sentiment analysis as well as aspect level sentiment analysis [21]. The researches on the first two tasks have reached satisfactory results in the past few years. However, just relying on these two methods alone, we cannot obtain rich subjective information, because they focus on the overall sentiment polarity of the whole document or sentence. In fact, people often express different sentiment towards aspects or entities in a sentence which are more fine-grained. Thus, we need aspect-level sentiment classification, and it has become a research hotspot in sentiment analysis field. The goal of aspect-level sentiment analysis is to identify the sentiment polarity of sentence with respect to the aspect targets [21], for instance, in sentence "I bought a mobile phone, its camera is wonderful but the battery life is short", through aspect-level sentiment analysis we can recognize that the sentiment polarity on the "camera" is positive and the sentiment on the "battery life" is negative. Because there are several mixed sentiments over the sentence, so it is more difficult for this task than the other two sentiment analysis tasks.

Intuitively, connecting aspects with their respective opinion words is the key to this task. Many works including traditional machine learning methods and deep learning models like Support Vector Machine (SVM) [37,38] and Long Short-Term Memory Neural Network (LSTM) [33,39,42] have achieved excellent results. However, due to the complexity of language structures, these methods sometimes fail to deal with it, with no learning the structural information well in sentences. There are some other efforts [8,32] taking the syntactic structures of a sentence into account and getting better results, which motivates many following researchers to adopt the same methods. How to learn these structural features well becomes an essential problem for this approach. Thanks for the powerful learning ability of Graph Neural Networks (GNNs) in characterizing graph structural features, some works [8,14,32,43,44] have used GNNs to tackle this problem. However, they need an external tool to obtain the structures such as dependency trees through dependency parsing, moreover, they sometimes could not get this correct structural information by these tools when the sentences are disordered. Thus, when transformed in GNNs, the deviations of the output in every layer may be magnified through edges with incorrect structural information, and make the last output of GNNs unsatisfactory.

In this paper, we design a model based on Graph Attention Network (GAT) [36] with Bidirectional Encoder Representation from Transformers (BERT) [6], which can capture structural properties in language [16]. And like other work [39], an attention mechanism [35] is adopted to pay attention to the interactions between aspects and the sentiment words. In the whole model, we directly put the outputs from attention module into GAT, we do not use extra tool to build dependency trees like other researches in addition to conducting controlled experiments. Experiments are conducted on two SemEval2014 datasets

[27], the results show that our model is superior to multiple models, proving our methodology to be feasible and effective.

This paper will be organized as follows: in Sect. 2, we will introduce some related works in this task. The proposed model will be explained in Sect. 3. The experiments and results are reported in Sect. 4. At last, conclusions are drew in Sect. 5.

2 Related Works

There have been a lot of works researching in aspect-level sentiment classification task. Earlier approaches take traditional machine learning models such as Support Vector Machine (SVM) [37,38], Maximum Entropy (ME) [29], Naive Bayes [26] and Conditional Random Field (CRF) [2,4] to detect the sentiment polarity of aspects. These methodologies are simple and have the limitations of representing the features of sentences thus needing to manually design supernumerary features like n-grams [5,17] and part of speech [19], which are tedious and time-consuming.

In recent years, deep learning methods have achieved remarkable or even surpassing human effects on many tasks including speech recognition, text classification, and image classification. Neural network models are excellent examples of deep learning [7] which are used to learn representations for aspects and contexts in this task without requiring manual feature engineering. Most of them are based on Long Short-Term Memory Neural Network (LSTM) [33,39,42], which is good at processing sequence signals, and several works adopt Convolution Neural Network (CNN) [11,28,41] to obtain feature maps from sentences. Attention mechanism [35] has also attracted many researchers in this task because it can enforce the model to pay more attention on important words related to the aspects and sentiment [3,9,20,30].

Although these above methods have achieved passable results, the architectures of these models themselves limit that they cannot effectively process the correlation features between the aspect terms and contexts within a sentence especially when the sentence is long or complex. Here are some examples:

1) Look at this specific sentence: "We ordered the special goat meat roll, that was so infused with bone, it was difficult to eat.", in this long sentence we can be sure that the "goat meat roll" is the aspect and the sentiment on it is negative, however, when it comes to this long sequence signals, especially there is an aspect separated away from its sentiment words, LSTM might suffer from this problem that it may be likely to lose the information during propagating the captured features word by word to the targets [8].

2) CNN can perceive multi-word features through local receptive fields which may be key to recognize the corresponding sentiment. But when there are several parts of the sentence deciding the sentiment of an aspect together, CNN may not be able to give an effective analysis on this. In sentence "The price of this computer is only slightly more expensive than the other", we can know it is positive to the "price", but CNN may emphasize the feature of "more expensive" and get a negative sentiment.

Fig. 1. The dependency analysis of a sentence.

3) If there are multi-aspects or multi-sentiment phrases in a sentence, attention mechanism could make wrong judgments about the relationships between sentiments and corresponding aspects. Still take the sentence in 1) as an example, attention mechanism could pay attention to "bone" rather than "goat meat roll", resulting unsatisfactory sentiment recognition.

In fact, there are relationships between the aspects and the sentiment words in a sentence represented through the structure information such as syntax feature. As shown in Fig. 1, the dependencies of the sentence have been drawn, we can easily find "difficult" and "goat meat roll" are closer in dependency, which gives us a possibility of effective solution to the task. Recently, Graph Neural Networks (GNNs) have been used for exploring to learn structural features from the dependency trees in many works [8,14,32,43,44], they propagate the information of nodes through edges and aggregate this information in a certain mechanism. However, the shortcomings cannot be ignored in these works: on the one hand, these methods must build the dependency matrix of words from the sentence by using external tools like spaCy[1] and StanfordNLP [24]. On the other hand, the dependencies of a sentence may not be well obtained through these tools, especially in a text with disorderly structures such as tweets, it will bring a lot of noise and make the deviations of the output magnified.

How to avoid these problems above is our purpose. We propose a new method based on GAT with BERT, as well as attention mechanism to tackle aspect-level sentiment classification task. Experimental results outperform other previous works and show that the proposed approach is effective and feasible.

3   The Proposed Method

In this section, we will first introduce the task definition of aspect level sentiment analysis, then the whole architecture of the proposed model will be described, the attention module and GAT module will be presented later. At last, we will introduce the output layer.

3.1   Task Definition

Given a sentence $s = \{w_1, w_2, ..., w_K\}$ consisting of K words, and $a = \{a_1, a_2, ..., a_m\}$ as the set of aspects where m is the number of aspects and every aspect $a_i = \{w_{i1}, w_{i2}, ..., w_{iN}\}$ is a subsequence of sentence s, which contains N words ($N \in [1, K]$), the purpose of this task is to predict the sentiment polarity of the sentence s corresponding to each aspect a_i.

---

[1] https://spacy.io/.

3.2 The Whole Architecture

The overall architecture of the proposed model is illustrated in Fig. 2. Inspired by the work of Ganesh Jawahar at el. [16], which shows that BERT can capture structural properties of the English language, we use BERT with different layers to obtain enough features of the input sentences as well as aspects, then an attention mechanism is applied to focus on the correlations between the words and aspect terms like other works. We no longer use additional tools to obtain the structural features such as dependency trees instead, we directly apply GAT to process the outputs from the attention module. In order to conduct a control experiment, we also use spaCy to obtain the dependency matrix of sentences which is treated as the edges-a part input of GAT. At last, a full connection layer and softmax function are used as a classifier to decide the sentiment polarity.

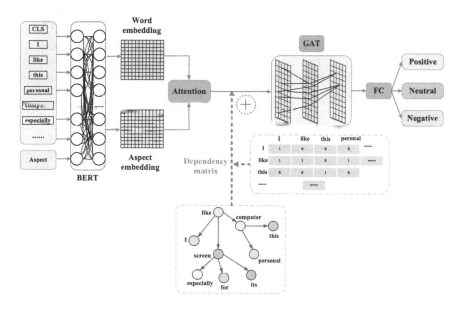

Fig. 2. The overall architecture of the proposed model.

3.3 Attention Module

The representations of sentences and aspects through BERT can be written as $H_s \in \mathbb{R}^{B \times L \times d_B}$ and $H_a \in \mathbb{R}^{B \times L \times d_B}$, respectively, where B is the batch size, L is the max length of sentence and aspects we pad, and d_B is the hidden size of BERT.

Then we adopt the attention mechanism to identify the important information with the influence from aspects on sentences. This module can obtain an attention vector as follows:

$$\alpha_i = \frac{exp(\gamma(H_s{}^i, H_a{}^i))}{\sum_{j=1}^{L} exp(\gamma(H_s{}^i, H_a{}^i))}, \tag{1}$$

where $\gamma(\cdot)$ is a score function to calculate the importance of $H_s{}^i$ according to $H_a{}^i$, and $i \in [1, L]$.

After computing the word attention weight, we can get final output of attention module by:

$$H_{att} = \sum_{i=1}^{L} \alpha_i H_s{}^i. \tag{2}$$

3.4   Graph Attention Network

GAT is a type of GNNs, if we take the words as nodes and the structural relations as edges, the feature of sentiment phrases from T hops away can be propagated to the aspect target nodes with a T-layer GAT network, the representations of nodes will be updated by aggregating neighborhood nodes representations denoted with N through multi-head attention: GAT is a type of GNN, if we take the words as nodes and the structural relations as edges, the feature of sentiment phrases from T hops away can be propagated to the aspect target nodes with a T-layer GAT network, the representations of nodes will be updated by aggregating neighborhood node representations denoted with $\mathcal{N}$ through multi-head attention:

$$h_{att_i}^{t+1} = ||_{m=1}^{M} \sum_{j \in \mathcal{N}_i} \alpha_{ij}^{tm} W_m^t h_j^t, \tag{3}$$

$$\alpha_{ij}^{tm} = attention(i, j), \tag{4}$$

where $h_{att_i}^{t+1}$ represents the hidden state of node i at $(t+1)$-th layer, $||_{m=1}^{M} x_i$ denotes the concatenation of vectors from x_1 to x_M, α_{ij}^{tm} is the attention coefficient of node i to its neighbor j computed by the m-th attention at layer t, W_m^t is a linear transformation matrix for the input states.

For brevity, we rewrite such feature propagation process as follows:

$$H_{t+1} = GAT(H_t, A, \Theta_t), \tag{5}$$

where $H_{t+1} \in \mathbb{R}^{B \times L \times d_G}$ is the output states of all nodes at layer t, $A \in \mathbb{R}^{B \times L \times L}$ represents the edges matrix, and Θ_t indicates model parameters of GAT at t-th layer. We set the dimension of the hidden state to d_G.

3.5   Sentiment Classification Layer

Before implementing the final sentiment classification decision, we average along the first dimension of the output from GAT, resulting a final representation: $\hat{H_{t+1}} \in \mathbb{R}^{B \times d_G}$.

We then fed the final output into a fully-connected layer, followed by a softmax normalization layer to yield a probability distribution over polarity decision space:

$$P = softmax(W\hat{H_{t+1}} + b), \tag{6}$$

where W, b are the weight matrix and bias for the linear transformation, respectively.

4   Experiment and Results

4.1   Dataset

We used two public sentiment analysis datasets to conduct experiments, which were the Laptop and Restaurant review datasets from SemEval2014 Task [27]. The statistics of them can be found in Table 1.

Table 1. Statistics of the dataset

Dataset		Positive	Neutral	Negative
Laptop14	Train	987	460	866
	Test	341	169	128
Restaurant14	Train	2164	633	805
	Test	728	196	196

4.2   Training and Parameters Setting

We minimize the cross-entropy loss with L_2 regularization to train our model:

$$loss = -\sum_{c \in C} I(y = c) log(P(y - c)) + \lambda ||\Theta||^2, \tag{7}$$

where C denotes the set of sentiment classes, $I(\cdot)$ is a indicator function, λ represents the L_2 regulation parameter and Θ is the parameters of the whole model.

The PyTorch implementation of BERT[2] was used in our experiments. We adopted output of the last f ($f \in [1, 6]$) layers of BERT as representations of sentences and aspect terms, the length of sentence and aspect we padded was 128 and batch size was 4. AdamW [22] was used as the optimizer, the learning rate was set to 5e–5, the coefficient of L_2 regularization was 1e–8. Moreover, we used 8 heads during multi-head attention in GAT module. The number of layers in GAT ranged from 1 to 5. In the controlled experiment, we used spaCy for dependency parsing, as well as an adjacent matrix of dimension 128×128 to save them, then the adjacent matrix was input to GAT. The dropout rate was 0.1. In sake of getting reliable results, we repeated each experiment 10 times, and finally took the average.

4.3   Models for Comparison

In order to show the effectiveness of our model, we compared it with a range of baseline methods, including: MemNet [34], an end-to-end memory network, captured the importance of every word. RAM [3] adopted a multiple-attention mech-

---

[2] https://github.com/huggingface/transformers.

238   J. Zou et al.

anism to obtain sentiment features separated by a long distance. A recurrent neural network was used as a nonlinear combiner for combining the results of attention mechanism. IAN [23] learnt the features of sentences and aspects respectively by using LSTM, interactive attentions between sentences and aspects were learnt. At last, the representations of them were generated respectively based on these attention vectors. AOA [15] utilized the idea of attention-over-attention from the field of machine translation to capture the interaction between aspects and sentences. BERT-FC [10] used BERT followed by a fully-connected layer and softmax to do classification with no consideration of any aspect information. AEN-BERT [30] applied attention-based encoder to model contexts and aspect terms, to form an attention encoder network. BERT-PT [40] treated aspect-level sentiment classification task as a machine reading comprehension problem: given an aspect as a question, the model output an answer to it.

4.4 Results and Analysis

The comparison results of overall performance are shown in Table 2, the results are the average of ten rounds of experiments. From the table, we can see that our model outperforms most of the baseline methods, the accuracy and Macro-F1 score of our model reach to 78.48%, 74.61% and 84.88%, 78.19% on the laptop and restaurant datasets, respectively. The results demonstrate the effectiveness of the proposed model in this task.

For the sake of verifying the influence of the components in our model, we conducted an ablation study. We removed the GAT module. The results are shown in Table 3, from which we can know that when GAT in the proposed model is removed, the performances will get more worse, this explains the importance of the component we designed.

In the purpose of exploring the influence on the results in the case of different layers of BERT, we changed the number of the layers and conducted a series of experiments for 10 times, the results are shown in Table 4 and Fig. 3. We can obviously see that the last layer output of BERT will produce the best results when we fix GAT with 2 layers. The reason for this phenomenon may be that

Table 2. Overall performance of different models on SemEval2014 dataset

Representation	Model	Laptop		Restaurant	
		Acc	Macro-F1	Acc	Macro-F1
BERT	AOA [10]	77.71	73.53	80.78	69.64
	IAN [10]	77.02	72.05	81.55	71.77
	MemNet [10]	76.93	72.11	84.04	76.15
	RAM [10]	77.3	72.9	83.11	74.35
	BERT-FC [10]	76.54	72.83	81.28	68.79
	AEN-BERT [10]	78.35	73.68	81.46	71.73
	BERT-PT [10]	78.07	**75.08**	**84.95**	76.96
	Our model	**78.48**	**74.61**	84.88	**78.19**

Table 3. An ablation study shows the effect of GAT

Composition change	Laptop		Restaurant	
	Acc	Macro-F1	Acc	Macro-F1
No GAT	78.2	74.38	84.74	78.11
Complete model	**78.48**	**74.61**	**84.88**	**78.19**

the deeper the BERT layer, the more dependencies it learns [16], which makes GAT take full advantage of dependency graph to propagate and aggregate the information in nodes. We also note that the results are competitive when we use the last 4 layers of BERT, we speculate it may be related to the structure of BERT itself.

Table 4. Results after changing the number of BERT output layers (Fixed GAT with 2 layers in 10 rounds of experiments)

Last layers of BERT		1	2	3	4	5	6
Laptop	Acc	**78.48**	78.17	77.93	78.43	78.06	78.09
	Macro-F1	**74.61**	74.20	74.13	74.51	74.07	73.96
Restaurant	Acc	**84.88**	84.73	84.32	84.84	84.29	84.62
	Macro-F1	**78.19**	77.56	77.34	77.82	77.33	77.64

We also changed the number of the GAT layers and conducted the same experiments as above; the results are shown in Table 5 and Fig. 4.

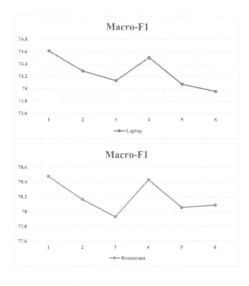

Fig. 3. The overall architecture of the proposed model.

As shown in Table 5 and Fig. 4, we can know that a two-layer GAT will obtain the best performance and increasing the GAT depth will not get more gains when we fixed BERT. One reason may be concerned with the structure of the sentence itself, namely the aspect terms may be connected to sentiment words through 2-hops. Another reason could be that with the increasing of GAT layers, the features in nodes are propagated to the whole graph, leading GAT not effectively using these structural features of sentences.

Table 5. Results after changing the number of GAT layers (Fixed BETR with the last 6 layers in 10 rounds of experiments)

Layers of GAT		1	2	3	4	5
Laptop	Acc	77.7	**78.48**	77.68	77.82	77.9
	Macro-F1	73.74	**74.61**	73.63	73.93	74.02
Restaurant	Acc	84.09	**84.88**	84.61	84.17	84.54
	Macro-F1	76.8	**78.19**	77.49	76.61	77.47

A controlled experiment was conducted, we adopted spaCy to get dependency matrices of contexts and used them as the edges, and the nodes are still served by the output of attention mechanism. The experimental results are shown in Table 6, which obviously present that using the dependency matrix will not improve the performance of the model but will bring make it worse. The reason

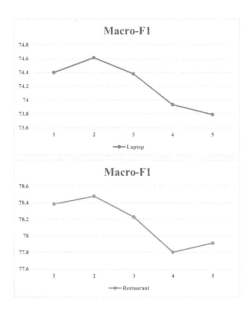

Fig. 4. The overall architecture of the proposed model.

for this phenomenon may be that adopting spaCy cannot analysis the dependency of review contexts with disordered structures well, and the noise is brought to the model, which impairs the judgment of sentiment polarity.

Table 6. A controlled experiment whether uses dependency matrix

Controlled	Variable	Original model	Using dependency matrices
Laptop	Acc	**78.48**	77.73
	Macro-F1	**74.61**	73.75
Restaurant	Acc	**84.88**	84.74
	Macro-F1	**78.19**	77.81

5   Conclusion

In this paper, we propose a novel model for aspect level sentiment classification based on GAT with BERT, which needs no external tools to analyze the structural features in sentences such as dependency of words, an attention mechanism is also used to focus on important information in contexts through aspect terms. Experiments on two SemEval2014 datasets show that our model outperforms most baseline methodologies, and an ablation study is also used to prove the feasibility of the proposed model. Exploring experiments with changing the number of layers in BERT or GAT show that the performances will get best with the last layer of BERT and a 2-layer GAT. In the future, other graph networks such as GCN [18] can be considered in this task.

Acknowledgements. Supported the National Key Research and Development Program of China (No.2018YFC1604000/2018YFC1604002).

References

1. Albahli, A.S., et al.: Covid-19 public sentiment insights: a text mining approach to the gulf countries. CMC-Comput. Mater. Continua, 1613–1627 (2021)
2. Brun, C., Perez, J., Roux, C.: Xrce at semeval-2016 task 5: feedbacked ensemble modeling on syntactico-semantic knowledge for aspect based sentiment analysis. In: Proceedings of the 10th International Workshop on Semantic Evaluation (SemEval-2016), pp. 277–281 (2016)
3. Chen, P., Sun, Z., Bing, L., Yang, W.: Recurrent attention network on memory for aspect sentiment analysis. In: Proceedings of the 2017 Conference on Empirical Methods in Natural Language Processing, pp. 452–461 (2017)
4. Chernyshevich, M.: Ihs r&d belarus: cross-domain extraction of product features using conditional random fields. In: Proceedings of the 8th International Workshop on Semantic Evaluation (SemEval 2014), pp. 309–313 (2014)
5. Cui, H., Mittal, V., Datar, M.: Comparative experiments on sentiment classification for online product reviews. In: AAAI. vol. 6, p. 30 (2006)

6. Devlin, J., Chang, M.W., Lee, K., Toutanova, K.: Bert: Pre-training of deep bidirectional transformers for language understanding. arXiv preprint arXiv:1810.04805 (2018)
7. Do, H.H., Prasad, P., Maag, A., Alsadoon, A.: Deep learning for aspect-based sentiment analysis: a comparative review. Expert Syst. Appl. **118**, 272–299 (2019)
8. Dong, L., Wei, F., Tan, C., Tang, D., Zhou, M., Xu, K.: Adaptive recursive neural network for target-dependent twitter sentiment classification. In: Proceedings of the 52nd Annual Meeting of the Association for Computational Linguistics (volume 2: Short papers), pp. 49–54 (2014)
9. Fan, F., Feng, Y., Zhao, D.: Multi-grained attention network for aspect-level sentiment classification. In: Proceedings of the 2018 Conference on Empirical Methods in Natural Language Processing, pp. 3433–3442 (2018)
10. Gao, Z., Feng, A., Song, X., Wu, X.: Target-dependent sentiment classification with Bert. IEEE Access **7**, 154290–154299 (2019)
11. Gu, X., Gu, Y., Wu, H.: Cascaded convolutional neural networks for aspect-based opinion summary. Neural Process. Lett. **46**(2), 581–594 (2017)
12. Hilal, A., Alfurhood, B., Al-Wesabi, F., Hamza, M., Al Duhayyim, M., Iskandar, H.: Artificial intelligence based sentiment analysis for health crisis management in smart cities. Comput. Mater. Continua, 143–157(2022)
13. Hnaif, A.A., Kanan, E., Kanan, T.: Sentiment analysis for Arabic social media news polarity. Intell. Autom. Soft Comput. **28**(1), 107–119 (2021)
14. Hou, X., Huang, J., Wang, G., Huang, K., He, X., Zhou, B.: Selective attention based graph convolutional networks for aspect-level sentiment classification. arXiv preprint arXiv:1910.10857 (2019)
15. Huang, B., Ou, Y., Carley, K.M.: Aspect level sentiment classification with attention-over-attention neural networks. In: Thomson, R., Dancy, C., Hyder, A., Bisgin, H. (eds.) SBP-BRiMS 2018. LNCS, vol. 10899, pp. 197–206. Springer, Cham (2018). https://doi.org/10.1007/978-3-319-93372-6_22
16. Jawahar, G., Sagot, B., Seddah, D.: What does Bert learn about the structure of language? In: ACL 2019–57th Annual Meeting of the Association for Computational Linguistics (2019)
17. Kim, S.M., Hovy, E.: Automatic identification of pro and con reasons in online reviews. In: Proceedings of the COLING/ACL 2006 Main Conference Poster Sessions, pp. 483–490 (2006)
18. Kipf, T.N., Welling, M.: Semi-supervised classification with graph convolutional networks. arXiv preprint arXiv:1609.02907 (2016)
19. Kouloumpis, E., Wilson, T., Moore, J.: Twitter sentiment analysis: the good the bad and the omg! In: Proceedings of the International AAAI Conference on Web and Social Media, vol. 5, no. 1, pp. 538–541 (2011)
20. Li, X., Bing, L., Li, P., Lam, W., Yang, Z.: Aspect term extraction with history attention and selective transformation. arXiv preprint arXiv:1805.00760 (2018)
21. Liu, B.: Sentiment Analysis: Mining Opinions, Sentiments, and Emotions. Cambridge University Press (2020)
22. Loshchilov, I., Hutter, F.: Fixing weight decay regularization in Adam (2018)
23. Ma, D., Li, S., Zhang, X., Wang, H.: Interactive attention networks for aspect-level sentiment classification. arXiv preprint arXiv:1709.00893 (2017)
24. Manning, C.D., Surdeanu, M., Bauer, J., Finkel, J.R., Bethard, S., McClosky, D.: The stanford corenlp natural language processing toolkit. In: Proceedings of 52nd Annual Meeting of the Association for Computational Linguistics: System Demonstrations, pp. 55–60 (2014)

25. Musleh, D.A., et al.: Twitter Arabic sentiment analysis to detect depression using machine learning. CMC-Comput. Mater. Continua **71**(2), 3463–3477 (2022)
26. Parkhe, V., Biswas, B.: Sentiment analysis of movie reviews: finding most important movie aspects using driving factors. Soft Comput. **20**(9), 3373–3379 (2015). https://doi.org/10.1007/s00500-015-1779-1
27. Pontiki, M., Galanis, D., Pavlopoulos, J., Papageorgiou, H., Androutsopoulos, I., Manandhar, S.: SemEval-2014 task 4: aspect based sentiment analysis. In: Proceedings of the 8th International Workshop on Semantic Evaluation (SemEval 2014), pp. 27–35. Association for Computational Linguistics, Dublin, Ireland (2014). https://doi.org/10.3115/v1/S14-2004,https://www.aclweb.org/anthology/S14-2004
28. Ruder, S., Ghaffari, P., Breslin, J.G.: Insight-1 at semeval-2016 task 5: Deep learning for multilingual aspect-based sentiment analysis. arXiv preprint arXiv:1609.02748 (2016)
29. Saias, J.: Sentiue: Target and Aspect Based Sentiment Analysis in Semeval-2015 Task 12. Association for Computational Linguistics (2015)
30. Song, Y., Wang, J., Jiang, T., Liu, Z., Rao, Y.: Attentional encoder network for targeted sentiment classification. arXiv preprint arXiv:1902.09314 (2019)
31. Suhail, K., et al.: Stock market trading based on market sentiments and reinforcement learning. CMC-Comput. Mater. Continua **70**(1), 935–950 (2022)
32. Sun, K., Zhang, R., Mensah, S., Mao, Y., Liu, X.: Aspect-level sentiment analysis via convolution over dependency tree. In: Proceedings of the 2019 Conference on Empirical Methods in Natural Language Processing and the 9th International Joint Conference on Natural Language Processing (EMNLP-IJCNLP), pp. 5683–5692 (2019)
33. Tang, D., Qin, B., Feng, X., Liu, T.: Effective lstms for target-dependent sentiment classification. arXiv preprint arXiv:1512.01100 (2015)
34. Tang, D., Qin, B., Liu, T.: Aspect level sentiment classification with deep memory network. arXiv preprint arXiv:1605.08900 (2016)
35. Vaswani, A., et al.: Attention is all you need. In: Advances in Neural Information Processing Systems, pp. 5998–6008 (2017)
36. Veličković, P., Cucurull, G., Casanova, A., Romero, A., Lio, P., Bengio, Y.: Graph attention networks. arXiv preprint arXiv:1710.10903 (2017)
37. Vicente, I.S., Saralegi, X., Agerri, R.: Elixa: A modular and flexible absa platform. arXiv preprint arXiv:1702.01944 (2017)
38. Wagner, J., Arora, P., Cortes, S., Barman, U., Bogdanova, D., Foster, J., Tounsi, L.: Dcu: Aspect-based polarity classification for semeval task 4 (2014)
39. Wang, Y., Huang, M., Zhu, X., Zhao, L.: Attention-based LSTM for aspect-level sentiment classification. In: Proceedings of the 2016 Conference on Empirical Methods in Natural Language Processing, pp. 606–615 (2016)
40. Xu, H., Liu, B., Shu, L., Yu, P.S.: Bert post-training for review reading comprehension and aspect-based sentiment analysis. arXiv preprint arXiv:1904.02232 (2019)
41. Xu, L., Lin, J., Wang, L., Yin, C., Wang, J.: Deep convolutional neural network based approach for aspect-based sentiment analysis. Adv. Sci. Technol. Lett. **143**, 199–204 (2017)
42. Yang, M., Tu, W., Wang, J., Xu, F., Chen, X.: Attention based LSTM for target dependent sentiment classification. In: Proceedings of the AAAI Conference on Artificial Intelligence, vol. 31 (2017)

43. Zhang, C., Li, Q., Song, D.: Aspect-based sentiment classification with aspect-specific graph convolutional networks. arXiv preprint arXiv:1909.03477 (2019)
44. Zhao, P., Hou, L., Wu, O.: Modeling sentiment dependencies with graph convolutional networks for aspect-level sentiment classification. Knowl.-Based Syst. **193**, 105443 (2020)

Design and Implementation of Teacher Workload Management System Based on JQuery Mobile

Yangyang Yi[1], Yiding Liu[1,2(✉)], and Ying Wang[1]

[1] Hunan Automotive Engineering Vocational College, Zhuzhou 412000, China
469930351@qq.com
[2] Jose Rizal University, 0900 Mandaluyong City, Metro Manila, Philippines

Abstract. Starting from the business needs of college teachers in workload filling, auditing and statistics, a set of teacher workload management system based on jQuery Mobile was researched and developed, aiming to improve the standardization of teachers and managers in workload management and improve workload statistics and management efficiency. Using jQuery Mobile + ThinkPHP to build the development environment, combined with SQL database technology, according to the workload management needs of hunan Automotive Engineering Vocational College teachers, the workload management system developed can run on Mobile devices and PC. To achieve efficient management of routine teaching other types of workload and projects and other aspects of data filling, summary, statistics, query. Taking Hunan Automobile Engineering Vocational College as an example, the teacher workload management system based on mobile devices was discussed. The platform built by the system could cooperate with teaching affairs Office, teaching departments, training center and teachers to work together. The system provides support for mobile devices. Users can make full use of their spare time and use the system at any time through their smart phones and tablets, which saves workload and transaction processing time and improves user experience.

Keywords: Mobile office · Workload management · JQuery mobile · ThinkPHP · Database

1 Introduction

Workload management is the management of the use of reasonable management means, statistical work completed in the data, teachers workload statistics is the quantity and quality of the work directly reflected. With the development of mobile Internet, users are more and more accustomed to using mobile phones for office work. Therefore, the development of software will be transferred to mobile devices in the future, and the development of App applications based on mobile devices is the general trend [1–3]. At present, smart phones have been fully popularized, more than 95% of teachers can install mobile phone application App, so the use of software management system in mobile devices and PC is the best solution [4, 5].

To sum up, the management mode of dealing with workload statistics based on office software has seriously hindered the development of management information of daily work of the college [6]. Therefore, the design and implementation of a teacher workload management system has its practical significance and application space [7, 8].

2   Technical Selection and Requirement Analysis

2.1   Framework to Choose

If the system is deployed on only one LAN and has many restrictions on upgrade and access, the B/S mode meets the actual requirements [9, 10]. Workload management system is the management of workload and other data, focusing on data flow control and data processing and display [11, 12]. Therefore, the background framework is ThinkPHP development framework [13]. The foreground view layer framework takes into account the compatibility of Android devices and Apple devices, and the most suitable framework is undoubtedly the jQuery Mobile framework compatible with all Mobile devices [14, 15].

2.2   System Modeling

System Role Analysis. There are seven basic roles that can be determined to use this system: full-time teachers of the college, part-time teachers of the college, director of teaching and research Office, teaching secretary of the department, teaching director of the department, workload auditor of the Teaching affairs Office, director of the training center, and system administrator. But not limited to these seven, can be dynamically expanded [16] (Fig. 1).

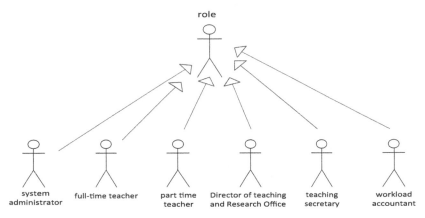

Fig. 1. System role division.

The main uses involved by a system administrator are shown in Fig. 2.

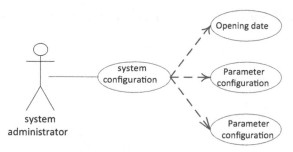

Fig. 2. System administrator use case diagram.

Major use case diagrams for full-time teachers (Fig. 3).

Fig. 3. Use case diagram of full-time teacher.

The main uses involved by the director of the teaching and Research section are shown in Fig. 4.

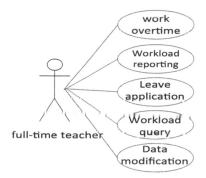

Fig. 4. Use case diagram of director of teaching and Research Section.

The main uses involved in departmental teaching secretary are shown in Fig. 5.

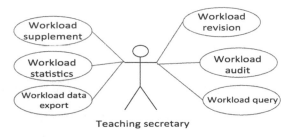

Fig. 5. Departmental teaching secretary use case diagram.

Use case diagram of director of training center (Fig. 6).

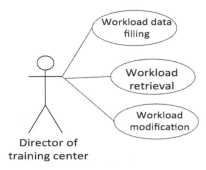

Fig. 6. The use case diagram of the director of the training center

Use case diagram of workload auditor of Academic Affairs Office (Fig. 7).

Fig. 7. Use case diagram of workload auditor of Teaching Affairs Office.

2.3 System Function Module Design

According to system analysis and design, the workload management system is divided into eight main functional modules [17]:

- Workload filling management.
- Workload review management.
- Workload retrieval and modification management
- Overtime leave management.
- Project management.
- Workload summary statistics.
- Graduation design workload statistics
- System management [18, 19] (Fig. 8).

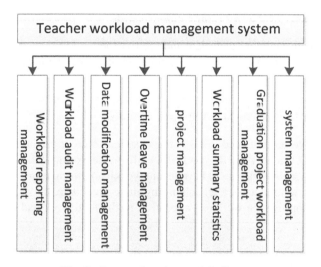

Fig. 8. System function module diagram.

3 Implementation Process and Results

The realization of the system from the expansibility and maintenance aspects of consideration, using the idea of hierarchical design to build a development framework. From the perspective of user experience, Query Mobile compatible with all Mobile devices is used to develop the Mobile version, and EasyUI is used to display the view of PC version [20].

3.1 Workload Management

This module is the core module of the system. The main realization of the user fill in the workload function. The system displays different menus for different roles. The role of teacher includes two sub-functions: teaching workload filling and other workload filling. For ease of operation, the mobile version presents both submodules as menu items [21–23].

3.2 Overtime Leave Management Module

Teacher role: can apply for overtime and leave.

Department Teaching director role: approve overtime and leave.
Delete overtime leave records [24, 25].

3.3 Workload Retrieval and Modification Module

The role of teachers can inquire, declare and modify the workload.
    The role of Teaching Secretary and Teaching Director can be logged in to retrieve the workload of all teachers in the department [26].

3.4 Graduation Design Workload Statistics Module

Teachers themselves do not need to fill in the workload data of graduation project, but after the director of teaching and Research office fills in the workload data and the department approves it, teachers can query the relevant workload information. The system also provides modification function, after submitting the correct data, the department teaching director can approve the workload allocation to the total workload of each teacher [27–29].

3.5 Workload Audit Module

The departmental teaching secretary checks the workload declarations submitted by all faculty members in the department [30].

3.6 Project Management Module

The department teaching director can create a project, designate a leader, modify the project, add project participants [31].

3.7 System Key Technology

The idea of Responsive Web Design is that the interface can be adjusted according to the application platform and screen size of mobile devices. The interface based on responsive design can automatically switch resolution and picture size for different mobile devices, improving user experience [32].

3.8 The System Test

As an essential part of the development process, software testing can effectively improve the quality of software. Detect software errors in functional implementation through testing. The system also needs to be tested for platform compatibility to verify whether the software can run on different mobile devices [33].

4 Usage and Summary

4.1 Use Effect

The statistics of teachers' satisfaction with the system are shown in the Fig. 9:

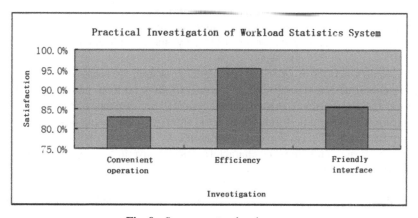

Fig. 9. Survey on teachers' usage.

The survey of the system used by the teaching secretary of the department is mainly reflected in data statistics and summary. Taking the monthly processing time cost as an example, the survey results are shown in the Fig. 10:

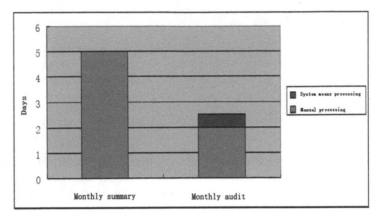

Fig. 10. Survey on the use of teaching secretaries.

4.2 Conclusion

The workload management of the business process of in-depth research, in the use of the system fully consider the use of various departments and convenience.

The view layer uses jQuery Mobile technology to realize the operation of the system on Mobile devices, and shows very good compatibility.

The control layer and model of background and database interaction use ThinkPHP framework, manage data operation in ORM way, the system is easy to expand and maintain.

All module functions of workload management system are realized [34].

A test case is designed to test the correctness of the workload management system, the time cost of the local code is tested using ThinkPHP performance debugging function, and the compatibility and performance of the system are tested using MTC. Finally, the operation and use of the system was investigated by different roles [35]. The results show that the system embodies the characteristics of convenient operation, time saving and complete functions.

Acknowledgement. This research is supported by Natural Science Foundation of Hunan Province (2021JJ60005).

References

1. Gao, L., Li, F.: The realization of college teacher workload management system based on ASP.NET technology. J. Zhongyuan Instit. Technol. **4**(18), 55–59 (2017)
2. Liu, F.: Design and implementation of workload management system for university teachers. J. Hebei N. Univ. (Nat. Sci. Edn.) **12**(6), 72–74 (2019)
3. Wang, M., Lu, Z.Q.: Research and implementation of MVC workload management system. Microcomput. Appl. **11**(30), 78–83 (2020)
4. Xu, R.C.: Improving the scientific research level of higher Vocational colleges by combining production, learning and research. J. Henan Inst. Eng.: Nat. Sci. Ed. **21**(1), 72–74 (2019)

5. Liu, G.Y., Zhang, G.P.: Implementation of WEB management system based on MVC pattern. J. East China Jiaotong Univ. **10**(2), 87–91 (2016)
6. Priyadharshini, T.C., Geetha, D.M.: Efficient key management system based lightweight devices in IoT. Intell. Autom. Soft Comput. **31**(3), 1793–1808 (2022)
7. Li, W.W.: Design and implementation of workload management system based on ASP.NET2.0. Comput. Appl. Softw. **8**(9), 163–165 (2014)
8. Zhang, Z.Q., Yan, L., Li, Y.F.: Implementation of dynamic query tree directory based on ASP.NET. Sci. Technol. Eng. **9**(29), 7286–7289 (2018)
9. Quan, G., Zhang, A.M.: Application of S many in web application development based on MVC framework. Sci. Technol. Inform. **2**(31), 36–39 (2018)
10. Alshammari, M., Nashwan, S.: Fully authentication services scheme for NFC mobile payment systems. Intell. Autom. Soft Comput. **32**(1), 401–428 (2022)
11. Lee, J., Park, S.: Mobile memory management system based on user's application usage pattern. Comput., Mater. Continu. **68**(3), 4031–4050 (2021)
12. Yao, D., Chen, Y.: Design and implementation of log data analysis management system based on Hadoop. J. Inform. Hiding Priv. Prot. **2**(3), 59–65 (2020)
13. Han, J., Wang, C., Miao, J., Lu, M., Wang, Y., Shi, J.: Research on electronic document management system based on cloud computing. Comput. Mater. Continu. **66**(3), 2645–2654 (2021)
14. Buraga, S.C., Amariei, D., Dospinescu, O.: An owl-based specification of database management systems. Comput. Mater. Continu. **70**(3), 5537–5550 (2022)
15. Ismail, S.N., Hamid, S., Ahmad, M., Alaboudi, A., Jhanjhi, N.: Exploring students engagement towards the learning management system (LMS) using learning analytics. Comput. Syst. Sci. Eng. **37**(1), 73–87 (2021)
16. Hamid, S., Ismail, S.N., Hamzah, M., Malik, A.W.: Developing engagement in the learning management system supported by learning analytics. Comput. Syst. Sci. Eng. **42**(1), 335–350 (2022)
17. Wang, M., Zhou, Z., Ding, C.: Blockchain-based decentralized reputation management system for internet of everything in 6G-enabled cybertwin architecture. J. New Media **3**(4), 137–150 (2021)
18. Palanisamy, P.N., Malmurugan, N.: FPGA implementation of deep leaning model for video analytics. Comput. Mater. Continu. **71**(1), 791–808 (2022)
19. Afzal, R., Murugesan, R.K.: Rule-based anomaly detection model with stateful correlation enhancing mobile network security. Intell. Autom. Soft Comput. **31**(3), 1825–1841 (2022)
20. Hsiao, S., Sung, W.: Using mobile technology to construct a network medical health care system. Intell. Autom. Soft Comput. **31**(2), 729–748 (2022)
21. Hassan, M.U., et al.: CNR: a cluster-based solution for connectivity restoration for mobile wsns. Comput. Mater. Continu. **69**(3), 3413–3427 (2021)
22. Naveed, Q.N., et al.: Evaluating and ranking mobile learning factors using a multi-criterion decision-making (MCDM) approach. Intell. Autom. Soft Comput. **29**(1), 111–129 (2021)
23. Moneera, A., et al.: Click through rate effectiveness prediction on mobile ads using extreme gradient boosting. Comput. Mater. Continu. **66**(2), 1681–1696 (2021)
24. Ahmad, I., et al.: Frequency reconfigurable antenna for multi standard wireless and mobile communication systems. Comput. Mater. Continu. **68**(2), 2563–2578 (2021)
25. Qian, J., Cheng, J., Zeng, Y., Tjondronegoro Dian, W.: Design of museum educational content based on mobile augmented reality. Comput. Syst. Sci. Eng. **36**(1), 157–173 (2021)
26. Farkh, R., Jaloud, K.A., Alhuwaimel, S., Quasim, M.T., Ksouri, M.: A deep learning approach for the mobile-robot motion control system. Intell. Autom. Soft Comput. **29**(2), 423–435 (2021)
27. Alsharif, M.H., et al.: Powering mobile networks with optimal green energy for sustainable development. Comput. Mater. Continu. **69**(1), 661–677 (2021)

28. Mehmood, G., Khan, M.Z., Fayaz, M., Faisal, M., Rahman, H.U., Gwak, J.: An energy-efficient mobile agent-based data aggregation scheme for wireless body area networks. Comput. Mater. Continu. **70**(3), 5929–5948 (2022)
29. Al-Khatib, M., Saif, W.: Improved software implementation for montgomery elliptic curve cryptosystem. Comput. Mater. Continu. **70**(3), 4847–4865 (2022)
30. Guan, Y., Choi, B.J.: Design, implementation and verification of topology network architecture of smart home tree. Comput. Mater. Continu. **68**(2), 2399–2411 (2021)
31. Kumar, T.M., Karthigaikumar, P.: Implementation of a high-speed and high-throughput advanced encryption standard. Intell. Autom. Soft Comput. **31**(2), 1025–1036 (2022)
32. Devi, S.S., Bhanumathi, V.: Reversible logic based mos current mode logic implementation in digital circuits. Comput. Mater. Continu. **70**(2), 3609–3624 (2022)
33. Mousa, G., Almaddah, A., Aly, A.A.: Design and implementation of wheel chair control system using particle swarm algorithm. Comput. Mater. Continu. **66**(2), 2005–2023 (2021)
34. Murugesh, V., et al.: Implementation of legendre neural network to solve time-varying singular bilinear systems. Comput. Mater. Continu. **69**(3), 3685–3692 (2021)
35. Sindhwani, M., Singh, C., Singh, R.: Implementation of k-means algorithm and dynamic routing protocol in VANET. Comput. Syst. Sci. Eng. **40**(2), 455–467 (2022)

A PSAO-Based Optimization Method for Integrated Energy Systems in Cities and Towns

Lei Ye[1], Liang Tang[2(✉)], Hongtao Qi[2], Ziyun Wang[3], Yuanjie Zheng[1], Pin Wang[1], Shikang Zhang[4], Huasheng Huang[1], and Jinyue Xia[5]

[1] State Grid Anhui Marketing Service Center, Hefei 230031, China
[2] State Grid Anhui Electric Power Co., Ltd, Hefei 230041, China
3300401945@qq.com
[3] State Grid Guzhen County Electric Power Supply Company, Bengbu 233700, China
[4] State Grid Huainan Panji District Electric Power Supply Company, Huainan 232000, China
[5] International Business Machines Corporation (IBM), New York, NY 10041-212, USA

Abstract. The optimal scheduling of urban energy systems is an important part of urban planning. For the characteristics of scenic power generation and urban energy supply system in China, a combined algorithm (PASO) with individual difference ant colony algorithm and particle swarm optimization algorithm is proposed to solve the mixed-integer nonlinear planning model for urban local integrated energy system (CCHP) and integrated energy system (IES) under both grid-connected and islanded operation. The simulation study is conducted for the dispatching of distributed power sources, and the economics of the dispatching scheme and the feasibility of the optimization algorithm is verified. The results show that the PASO algorithm is feasible for solving such problems, and the total annual operating cost of the integrated energy system in the town constructed in this paper is the lowest and the best in terms of the economy compared with the energy supply system using the traditional planning and configuration method. When the town IES is dispatched in the above way, the cost of supplying energy in isolated and grid-connected operation during summertime is reduced to 47% and 41% of that of a single supply, respectively; the cost of supplying energy in CCHP is 70.1%, 62.2% of the single supply in summer and 82% and 54% of the CCHP supply in winter, respectively.

Keywords: Town CCHP system · Town IES · PSO algorithm · ACO algorithm

1 Introduction

1.1 A Subsection Sample

With the rapid development of the national economy, energy and environmental ecological issues are receiving more and more attention from the state and society, and the need for industrial upgrading is very urgent. To avoid the continuous deterioration of the environment and to guarantee the people to use energy economically and reliably, it is

© The Author(s), under exclusive license to Springer Nature Switzerland AG 2022
X. Sun et al. (Eds.): ICAIS 2022, CCIS 1586, pp. 255–267, 2022.
https://doi.org/10.1007/978-3-031-06767-9_21

urgent to seek sustainable energy supply methods, and the regionally integrated energy system has been rapidly promoted and applied because it can realize the high efficiency and economy of comprehensive energy utilization by playing the respective advantages of multiple types of energy and equipment. In recent decades, distributed power generation system using new energy generation has been widely promoted, and its distinctive feature is that it is close to the customer side, and can use local renewable energy (solar, wind, etc.) and micro-combustion engine to meet the power load demand according to local conditions, and the energy utilization rate has been improved, and the technology has been rapidly developed [13]. Distributed power supply (DG) is close to the customer side, due to the strong support for CCHP systems around the world, research on CCHP systems has made great strides, the application of CH systems has also emerged, it has the advantages of high energy utilization, low cost and environmentally friendly, making CCHP systems have become an indispensable part of the study of energy supply systems [6].

Section 2 will introduce the related work on integrated energy, explore the feasibility of PS0-ACO algorithm in the optimization of urban integrated energy systems, present the existing problems, and introduce the combined algorithm of the ant colony and particle swarm optimization algorithm has been combined in Sect. 3 to investigate the principles of optimal scheduling of urban energy systems and the constraints and determine the economically optimal scheduling suitable for urban-type CCHP systems and IES in China strategies for urban-type CCHP systems and IES in China. Section 4 designs the experimental method and conducts experiments, Sect. 5 analyzes the experimental results and verifies the feasibility of the experiments, and Sect. 5 concludes with the future outlook and development.

2 Related Work

In the overview of the integrated energy system, Jia Hongjie et al. made a detailed introduction to the basic concept and main features of integrated energy, combined the experience of various countries in the world on the construction of this system and the actual situation of energy resources in China, discussed some problems that may be faced in the promotion of China's future integrated energy system from three aspects, namely, national, regional and terminal, and put forward constructive suggestions [4]. Peng K. et al. summarized the current development of integrated energy systems and the practical experience of demonstration projects at home and abroad, introduced the corresponding demonstration projects in IES, and made feasible suggestions for the development of IES in China, taking into account the domestic and international energy policies and the current situation [1].

The overall performance of urban integrated energy systems is closely related to their design planning and operation methods. The views on the benefit weights are also focused on due to the different demands of investors. The literature [2] uses indicators such as operating cost and payback period as the basis for system economic evaluation, while the literature [3] uses primary energy consumption and savings to reflect the energy use efficiency of the system. The literature [4] presents linear and nonlinear planning strategies for energy systems [5]. The literature [6] designed an online optimal operation strategy based on a linear planning approach and carried out integrated energy system planning based on a multi-time operation state. The literature [7] utilized a mixed-integer nonlinear model optimization approach to achieve the lowest system operation cost. The literature [8] minimizes the total energy consumption with the help of a mixed-integer linear model while considering the role played by elements such as energy price changes and CO_2 tax rates within the system. The literature [9] focuses on the impact of the technical parameters of the generating unit itself (e.g., electric cooling ratio, rated capacity) to integrate it with the economy and the environment to maximize the overall benefits.

Most of the integrated energy system planning techniques described in the above literature are single, not focusing on the allocation of more types of resources and systems, and the model and objective weights are not reasonably set. In this paper, we intend to explore the planning and optimal operation of regional integrated energy systems in-depth and to make the configuration of the constructed integrated energy systems more complete and comprehensive by incorporating more types of energy and multiple forms of energy conversion methods [9].

3 Regional Integrated Energy System Planning and Operation Optimization

A district integrated energy system is a whole that incorporates many different functional energy conversion devices, each of which has a direct or indirect effect on the whole system [10]. Therefore, in the process of building the whole system model, it is necessary to first complete individual mathematical modeling and analysis of each device in the system, and then use it as a basis for modeling and further optimization of the whole system.

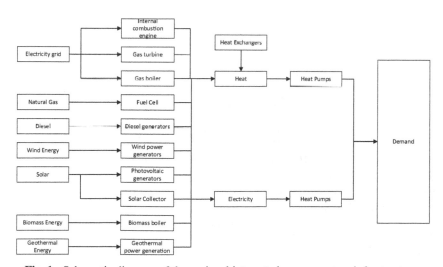

Fig. 1. Schematic diagram of the regional integrated energy system infrastructure.

Figure 1 shows the basic architecture of the regionally integrated energy system, which covers a large number and variety of energy production, conversion, or storage devices, corresponding to the end-load demand for heat, electricity, and cooling. Before constructing the basic architecture of the system, it is necessary to research the demand of the user side in advance, to clarify the climate, energy and resource conditions, as well as the existence of site constraints, etc., to make the basic architecture of the system more reasonable, and then further optimize it to the extent that it is compatible with the conditions here, and finally build the optimal integrated regional energy system. First, a general framework of the system is constructed based on basic data such as the energy status, equipment type, and capacity that the system can accept, and then the contents of this stage are used as input conditions for the next stage (taking into account prices, constraints, equipment parameters, etc.) to continue optimization until the optimal configuration and operation of the system are achieved.

3.1 Objective Function

Lowest Total System Cost. The total cost C_{total} of the municipal energy interconnection system consists of the investment cost C_{inve}, the production O&M cost C_{opma} and the net purchase cost to the grid C_{netp}.

$$C_{total} = C_{inve} + C_{opma} + C_{netp} \tag{1}$$

The system investment cost is shown in:

$$C_{inve} = C_{inde} + C_{inpe} = \sum_{i=1}^{I} M_i \cdot f_i \cdot \rho + \sum_{j=1}^{J} \sum_{i=1}^{I} C_{inpe}^{unit} \cdot L_{i,j} \cdot H_{i,j} \tag{2}$$

where C_{inde} is the equipment investment cost; C_{inpe} is the pipeline line cost; M_i is the unit price of equipment; f_i is the number of equipment; $L_{i,j}$ is the distance between equipment nodes; $H_{I,J}$ is a 0–1 variable; ρ is the capital recovery factor [15], and C_{inpe}^{unit} does the pipeline line unit cost?

Production O&M costs are shown in Eq. (3–5):

$$C_{opma} = C_{fuel} + C_{oper} \tag{3}$$

$$C_{oper} = C_{fixed} + C_{vari}^{unit}(Q_{total} - Q_{recly}) \tag{4}$$

$$C_{fuel} = C_{oper}^{hot} + C_{oper}^{cold} + C_{oper}^{power} + C_{oper}^{comib} \tag{5}$$

where: C_{fuel} is the fuel cost [16]; C_{oper} is the operation and maintenance cost; H is a 0–1 variable and H1 + H2 = 1; C_{vari}^{unit} is the unit variable cost; Q_{total} is the total supply of energy; Q_{recly} is the energy used for waste heat recovery; P(t) is the supply power; $\beta_m, X_m, \varphi_m, \gamma_m$ are the relevant parameters; f is the number of the corresponding co-generation unit. The net power purchase cost is shown in (6):

$$C_{netp} = C_{purc} - D_{sale} \tag{6}$$

where: C_{pure} is the cost of purchased electricity; D_{sale} is the revenue from selling electricity.

Highest System Energy-Saving Rate. The system energy savings rate mainly reflects the efficiency of energy storage and demand response in reducing and discarding system renewable power under highly informative dispatch.

$$\partial = \frac{1/\eta_{CCHP} - 1/\eta_{MEI}}{1/\eta_{CCHP}} = 1 - \frac{\eta_{CCHP}}{\eta_{MEI}} \tag{7}$$

$$\eta_{MEI} = \frac{G_{total} - (G_{cw} + G_{cp})}{\frac{G_{total}}{\eta_{CCHP}} - G_{cw}\lambda_{cw} - G_{cp}\lambda_{cp}} \tag{8}$$

Highest System Reduction Rate. The emission reduction rate of the system is equivalent to the pollutant emission reduction rate corresponding to the reduction of the amount of abandoned wind and electricity and the improvement of power generation efficiency

$$\ell = \frac{2\frac{(G_{cw}+G_{cp})}{\eta_{CCHP}} E_{gaco} - \frac{(G_{cw}+G_{cp})}{\eta_{MEl}} \cdot E_{eaco}}{\frac{G_{total}}{\eta_{CCHP}} \cdot E_{gaco}} \tag{9}$$

where: l is the emission reduction rate of energy interconnection system in energy cities and towns; E_{gaco} is the pollutant emission coefficient of natural gas cogeneration system; E_{eaco} is the pollutant emission coefficient of the urban energy interconnection system.

3.2 Constraints

System Energy Balance Constraint. Energy balance constraint is shown in Eq. (10, 11), where: $G_{total}(k)$ is the total power demand of the system in period K; $G_{self}(k)$ is the spontaneous self-consumption of the system in period K; $G_{pur}(k)$ refers to the electricity purchased from the power grid in period K; $G_{sell}(k)$ is the on-grid power in K periods; $G_{loss}(k)$ is the system power consumption in K period; $G_{gas}(k), G_{PV}(k), G_{wind}(k)$ is the power generation of gas, solar, and wind power units in period K; $P_{PV}(t)$, $P_{wind}(t)$ and $P_{gas}(t)$ corresponds to the generating power of PV unit, wind turbine unit, and gas turbine unit at time t.

$$G_{total}(k) = G_{self}(k) + G_{pur}(k) + G_{sell}(k) - G_{loss}(k) \tag{10}$$

$$G_{self}(k) + G_{sell}(k) = G_{gas}(k) + G_{PV}(k) + G_{wind}(k)$$
$$= \int_{t=1}^{k} P_{gas}(t) + \int_{t=1}^{k} P_{PV}(t) + \int_{t=1}^{k} P_{wind}(t) \tag{11}$$

Heat balance constraint is shown in Eq. (12–14), Where: Q_{recly} is the heat of waste heat recovery; Q_{gas} is the heat of gas combustion; Q_{solar} is the heat converted by solar energy; Q_{cold} is the heat used by the refrigeration unit; η_{cold} is the efficiency of the refrigeration unit; Q_{hot} is the heat used by the heat exchanger; η_{hot} is the efficiency of the heat exchanger; Q_{recly}^{gas} is the heat recovered from the waste heat of gas turbine (gas turbine); q_{gas} is the natural gas consumption of gas turbine; η_{gas} is the generation efficiency of a gas turbine; η_{recly} is the efficiency of heat recovery equipment.

$$Q_{recly} + Q_{gas} + Q_{solar} = \frac{Q_{cold}}{\eta_{cold}} H_1 + \frac{Q_{hot}}{\eta_{hot}} H_2 \tag{12}$$

$$H_1 + H_2 = 1 \tag{13}$$

$$Q_{\text{rely}}^{\text{gas}} = q_{\text{gas}} \cdot \left(1 - \eta_{\text{gas}}\right) \cdot \eta_{\text{recly}} \tag{14}$$

PV Unit Operation Constraints. PV unit operation constraints are shown in Eq. (15, 16), Where: $P_{PV}(t)$ is the electric power of PV unit at time t; P_{capa} is the rated installed capacity of PV unit; η_{PV} is the generation efficiency of PV unit; θ (k) is the local solar radiation; S_{PV} is the area of solar panel; P_{min}^{PV} and P_{max}^{PV} are the minimum and maximum generating power of PV unit respectively

$$P_{PV}(t) = \min\left\{P_{\text{capa}}, \theta(t) \cdot S_{PV} \cdot \eta_{PV}\right\} \tag{15}$$

$$P_{\min}{}^{PV} \leq P_{PV}(t) \leq P_{\max}{}^{PV} \tag{16}$$

Operation Constraints of the Natural Gas Internal Combustion Engine Unit. As shown in Eq. (17–19), Where: $P_{gas}(t)$ is the generating power of gas turbine at time t; P_{min}^{gas} and P_{max}^{gas} is the minimum and maximum generating power respectively; P_{min}^{wind}, U_{Pgas} and D_{Ngas} is the upward and downward climbing rate of the gas turbine.

$$P_{\min}^{\text{gas}} \leq P_{\text{gas}}(t) \leq P_{\max}^{\text{gas}} \tag{17}$$

$$P_{\text{gas}}(t) - P_{\text{gas}}(t-1) \leq U_{P\text{gas}} \cdot \Delta t \tag{18}$$

$$P_{\text{gas}}(t) - P_{\text{gas}}(t-1) \geq -D_{N\text{gas}} \cdot \Delta t \tag{19}$$

Demand Response Constraints. The demand-side load can be divided into a fixed load, random load, and transferable load [19]. Compared with the non-adjustability of fixed load and the unpredictability of random load, the transferable load is the load that users transfer the load from a certain period to other periods, which is adjustable. Using high-density information flow to reasonably schedule transferable load is an important means for energy interconnection microgrid systems to implement demand response. Transfer in and transfer out load capacity constraints are shown in Eq. (20–23):

$$R_j^T\left(t, t'\right) = X_j^T\left(t, t'\right) \Delta R_j^T \tag{20}$$

$$\sum_{j=1}^{N_t} R_j^T\left(t, t'\right) \leq R_{j,\max}^I(\Delta t) \tag{21}$$

$$\sum_{j=1}^{N_t} R_j^T\left(t, t'\right) \leq R_{j,\max}^o(\Delta t) = P_j^{Be}(\Delta t) \tag{22}$$

$$\Delta t = t' - t \tag{23}$$

3.3 Methods

Optimization Methods. The particle swarm optimization (PSO) algorithm corresponds the feasible solution of an optimization problem to a particle in the search space [11]. The particles search for the individual optimal particle and the global optimal particle at a certain speed for the current number of iterations, and through continuous iteration, sufficient competition, and cooperation, the search for the optimal solution in the search space is finally achieved. This algorithm can form a more reliable optimization effect by constantly iterating particle positions and speeds. It should be noted that the addition of weights and random coefficients can make the global search easier to complete based on the role of speed on iteration [12]. The traditional ant colony optimization (ACO) algorithm has self-organization characteristics and high generality but has the disadvantages of poor global search ability and slow search speed [14]. The ACO algorithm introduces individual differences in the population based on the ACO algorithm [15], which enhances the global search ability of the ACO algorithm, and because the ant individuals with multiple path selection strategies mixed collaboratively for path selection, premature convergence of the solution can be avoided.

PSAO Combination Algorithm. The ACO algorithm is slow at the beginning of the search due to the lack of pheromones and the long time to accumulate pheromones [16–19], while the PSO algorithm is a class of stochastic global optimization techniques that requires fewer parameters, but suffers from premature and local convergence problems. In this paper, we propose to combine the PSO algorithm and the ACO algorithm and use the optimization result of the PSO algorithm as the initial solution of the ACO algorithm, and further search to find the optimal solution. The specific flow chart of the PSAO algorithm is shown in Fig. 2. Considering that the wind power output, PV power output, and load power in Urban IES have certain randomness and fluctuation, and are more obviously influenced by season and climate [14], the simulation distinguishes four different scenarios such as winter and summer in isolated operation and grid-connected operation. That is, based on the energy demand of typical days in winter and summer under different operation scenarios, the optimal power dispatch of town ES is realized. In the practical application of the PSO algorithm, some parameters need to be adjusted: population size (number of individuals in the population) N, velocity limit of particle motion, position limit; acceleration factor and maximum number of iterations, inertia weight.

(1) The choice of population size N requires a trade-off between accuracy, stability, and running time. In general, if the focus is on reducing the running time, the population size can be set to about 40, and if the focus is on accuracy and stability, it can be set to 50–100 [17]. In this paper, the population size is taken as 80 and 100 for the simulation of the particle swarm algorithm.

(2) To prevent the blind search of particles, it is generally necessary to limit the position and velocity of particles in a certain interval. The position limit of the particle corresponds to the feasible solution domain, and the velocity limit is the refinement degree of the search, which is too large to easily jump out of the optimal solution and too small to easily fall into the local optimum. In this simulation, the upper

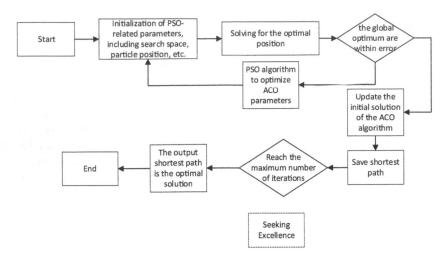

Fig. 2. PSO-IVACO algorithm flowchart.

and lower limits of the position are set to the upper and lower limits of the scenery combustion network and so on at this time, and the velocity limit is chosen as 1.05.

(3) In the PSO algorithm, if 0 is the loss of group diversity, which will lead to a rapid fall into the local optimum, if 0 is the loss of social information sharing, the convergence of the algorithm will be extremely slow, in order to balance the role of random factors, generally take [10]

(4) In the operation of the algorithm, a larger number of iterations is set first, and then a suitable number of iterations is selected by the successful convergence point in the graph of the fitness function to reduce the computing time and reduce the waste of computer resources.

4 Experimental Results and Analysis

4.1 Summer Optimization Results

By solving the optimization model, the synergistic operation strategy of the energy interconnection system in this energy town is shown in Figs. 4 and 5 for supplying the cold load and electric load in summer.

From Fig. 3 Optimization results of electric load supply in summer, it can be seen that the summer cooling load is supplied by two types of cooling methods: electric chillers and absorption chillers. During the daytime from 8:00 to 19:00, the light condition is good and the price of electricity in the area is higher during the peak and normal periods in summer. The optimization results for the electrical load are shown in Fig. 4. The summer electric load demand is supplied by energy storage (SE), distributed wind power (WT), grid purchased power (GR), gas-fired power (GT), and distributed photovoltaic (PV). The area is rich in available wind resources in summer, and during the night when the load demand is low, part of the electricity generated by wind is stored with energy storage equipment. 22:00–6:00 Electricity consumption decreases and gradually transitions to the valley hours, where wind power is consumed first and gas turbines are used to generate electricity and purchase electricity from the grid, and the price of electricity purchased from the grid is low in the early morning hours. In addition, this paper calculates a typical day in summer.

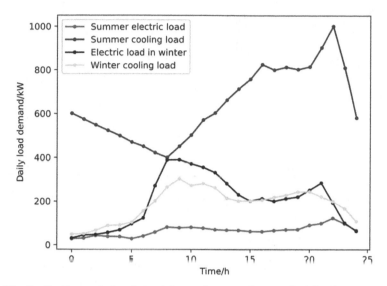

Fig. 3. Cooling and electric load demand curves of one typical day in summer.

To facilitate the comparison of the overall benefits of energy interconnection systems in energy towns, the PSAO algorithm is used to optimize the summer system costs and energy savings and emission reduction rates. Compared with the traditional DCCHP, the energy interconnection system of energy towns considering both supply and demand sides can reduce the system cost from 935,000 Yuan to 654,000 Yuan, which is 30.1% less, and the system energy-saving rate reaches 19.4% and emission reduction rate reaches 26.1%, so the system can realize energy saving and emission reduction while achieving economy. 3.2.2 Typical winter day optimization results.

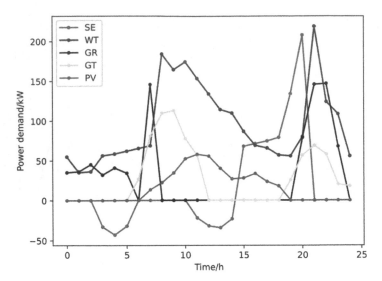

Fig. 4. Optimization results of electric load supply in summer.

4.2 Winter Optimization Results

Applying the same model and algorithm as above to the interconnected microgrid system for supplying thermal and electrical loads in winter is shown in Fig. 5.

As can be seen from Fig. 5, the unit output fluctuates with the light intensity during the daytime period from 6:00 to 18:00, and the energy storage characteristics of the natural gas hot water boiler can quickly increase the output during the morning and evening peak hours. In winter, the daytime is shorter and the light intensity is weaker. During the morning peak hours from 8:00 to 9:00, the output of PV power generation is increased slowly, and the power is released by energy storage, while a small amount of power is purchased from the grid to meet the demand. In the evening peak period after 17:00, we need to purchase electricity from both gas-fired power generation and the grid to fill the loading gap.

4.3 Convergence Verification

In order to verify the performance of the PSO-IVACO algorithm proposed in this paper, the IVACO algorithm, PSO algorithm, and IVACO-PSO algorithm are compared, and the optimization iterations of the three objective functions constructed in this paper are shown in Fig. 6. The number of iterations of the PSO algorithm is 29, which is better than the number of iterations of the IVACO algorithm (37), but the optimal solution of the IVACO algorithm is better than that of the PSO algorithm.

By fusing the two algorithms, the number of iterations of the PSO-IVACO algorithm is 33, and the optimal solutions of the opposite numbers of system cost, system energy-saving rate, and emission reduction rate are 654,000 yuan, 19.4%, and 26.1%, respectively, and the combined PSO-IVACO algorithm The combined PSO-IVACO algorithm has a slower convergence speed than the PSO algorithm, but it outperforms the

IVACO algorithm in terms of local optimality and the optimization result is better than the IVACO algorithm.

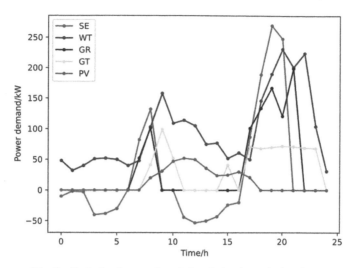

Fig. 5. Optimization results of electric load supply in winter.

5 Conclusion

In this paper, the PSAO algorithm is used to simulate the multi-energy cooperative combined operation strategy of a typical campus energy town energy interconnection system with typical daily loads in summer and winter. The energy supply calculation model with the total cost function as the objective function, the system cooling and heating loads, the operating capacity limits of each equipment, and the battery capacity as the main constraints is proposed for the constructed town IES. The results show that the cost of energy supply in the town IES is reduced to 47% and 41% of that of a single supply in summer and 70.1% and 62.2% of that of a CCHP supply in summer, respectively when the town IES is dispatched in the above way. In winter, the cost of supplying energy is reduced to 58% and 39% of that of a single supply, and 82% and 54% of that of CCHP. The system supply cost is reduced, and the fluctuation of wind power and PV output is smoothed out so that the system can enhance renewable energy consumption while achieving economy. In this paper, only the system steady-state is assumed as the premise of modeling, how to consider the steady-state and transient characteristics of the system, and how to establish a multi-level, multi-perspective, reflecting multi-state energy interconnection system optimization model of energy towns is the focus of future research.

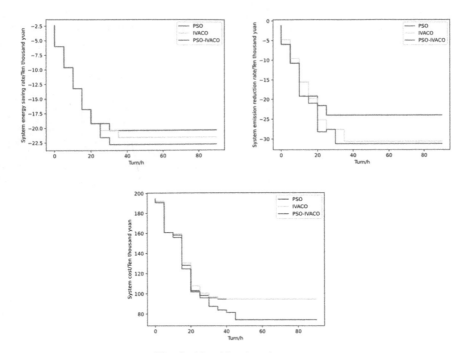

Fig. 6. Algorithm iteration process.

References

1. Ben, H.: Distributed combined cooling, heating, and power generation system and economic growth. Sino-Global Energy **2012**(2), 18–22 (2012)
2. Asiri, Y.: Short text mining for classifying educational objectives and outcomes. Comput. Syst. Sci. Eng. **41**(1), 35–50 (2022)
3. Dong, T.: Technical forms and key technologies on energy internet. Proc. CSEE **35**(14), 3482–3494 (2015)
4. Furlong, Z.: Energy-saving coordinated optimal dispatch of distributed combined cool, heat and power supply. Power System Technol. **36**(6), 8–14 (2020)
5. Keerthana, G., Anandan, P., Nachimuthu, N.: Robust hybrid artificial fish swarm simulated annealing optimization algorithm for secured free scale networks against malicious attacks. Comput. Mater. Contin. **66**(1), 903–917 (2021)
6. Cheng, C., Lin, D.: Based on compressed sensing of orthogonal matching pursuit algorithm image recovery. J. Internet Things **2**(1), 37–45 (2020)
7. Hong, W.: An integration scheme for DES/CCHP coordinated with power system. Autom. Electric Power Syst. **38**, 16–21 (2021)
8. Hu, Y.: Energy-analysis based comparative study of absorption refrigeration and electric compression refrigeration in CCHP systems. Appl. Therm. Eng. **2016**(93), 1228–1237 (2016)
9. Zheng, H., Shi, D.: A multi-agent system for environmental monitoring using boolean networks and reinforcement learning. J. Cyber Security **2**(2), 85–96 (2020)
10. Zcywjyzx, Q.: A novel operation strategy for CCHP systems based on minimum distance. Appl. Energy **128**, 325–335 (2014)
11. Saraereh, O.A., Ali, A.: Beamforming performance analysis of millimeter-wave 5g wireless networks. Comput. Mater. Contin. **70**(3), 5383–5397 (2022)

12. Qi, W.: The application on natural gas distributed energy system. Shanghai Gas **2012**, 24–30 (2012)
13. Ren, L.: Business models and market mechanisms of E-Net(2). Power System Technol. **39**(11), 3057–3063 (2015)
14. Yue, X.J.S.J., Bo, Z.: Two-layer optimal operation of district integrated energy system based on adjustable thermoelectric ratio model. Grid Technol. **40**(10), 2959–2966 (2016)
15. Xiao, P.: Individual variation ant colony optimization algorithm and its application. Application Research of Computers **25**(4), 1036–1038 (2008)
16. Yang, R.: Experimental study of a liquid dehumidification unit integrated in a CCHP system with varying operating condition. Energy Procedia **75**, 1178–1188 (2015)
17. Yuan, Z.: Development model, mechanism and key technology of energy internet based on complex adaptive system theory. Power System Technol. **40**(11), 3383–3390 (2016)
18. Zeng, M., Liu, D.: Generation-grid-load-storage coordinative optimal operation mode of energy internet and key technologies. Power System Technol. **40**(1), 114–124 (2016)
19. Zhuo, Z.: Analysis of energy internet key technologies. Science China **2014**(6), 702–713 (2014)

Applied Research on Cultivating Advanced Technical Engineering Talents Based on the Internet of Things+ Platform with Dual-Professional Teachers as the Guidance

Shengqian Ma[✉], Qianqian Song, Shuai Yue, Jiamei Wang, Chenyi Wang, Hongcheng Cong, Shengliang Xu, Haodong Wang, and Chao Han

School of Physics and Electronic Engineering, Taishan University, Taian 271000, Shandong, People's Republic of China
shqma@126.com

Abstract. In order to realize the smooth implementation of the transformation of the old and new kinetic energy, cultivate and bring up the engineering and technical talents with craftsman spirit, talent cultivation should go ahead, especially the innovative engineering and technical talents. Craftsman spirit is the spirit of pursuing excellence in creation, the spirit of keeping improving in quality, and the spirit of customer first in service. The main connotation of craftsman spirit includes four aspects: ingenuity, craftsmanship, craftsman spirit, craftsman line. We should build a three-dimensional innovation and entrepreneurship system of innovation methods-information technology-entrepreneurial resources-creative cases-competition practice-lean entrepreneurship, and form an innovation and entrepreneurship framework with industry characteristics. With curriculum system reform, training platform, science and technology competition, innovation and entrepreneurship as the main line School enterprise alliance as the core, gradually establish a more reasonable, more perfect practice mode, based on this mode, through the rich theoretical knowledge, create excellent engineering and technical personnel, use electronic engineer training and participate in various types of electronic design competition, gradually cultivate the professional quality of engineering and technical personnel, and achieve the goal of engineering and technical personnel by writing scientific papers. Through school enterprise cooperation and practical training, the practical application ability of solving specific problems in the work practice can explore a feasible way for the cultivation of college students in engineering science and technology.

Keywords: Internet of things+ platform · Dual-professional teachers · Advanced technical engineering talents · Six-in-one

1 Introduction

In 1998, the Massachusetts Institute of Technology (MIT) put forward the idea of the Internet of Things with Electronic Product Code (EPC) system. In 1999, the American

Auto-ID Center first proposed the concept of the Internet of Things. The Internet of Things uses sensor perception technology to obtain various parameter information of objects and environments, aggregates it on the information communication network through various wireless communication technologies, and transmits it to the back-end for data analysis and mining processing, and extracts valuable information to the decision-making layer. The Internet of things is a network that connects any item with the Internet for information exchange and communication by using radio frequency identification (RFID), sensors, infrared sensors, global positioning system, laser scanners and other information collection equipment according to the agreed protocol, so as to realize intelligent identification, positioning, tracking, monitoring and management. On November 17, 2005, the World Summit on the Information Society (WSIS) in Tunisia, the International Telecommunication Union (ITU) released the "ITU Internet Report 2005: Internet of Things", which officially put forward the concept of "Internet of Things". The report pointed out that the ubiquitous "Internet of Things" communication era is coming, and all objects in the world, from tires to toothbrushes, from houses to paper towels, can be actively exchanged through the Internet. Radio frequency identification technology (RFID), sensor technology, nanotechnology, and intelligent embedded technology will be more widely used. At present, China has formed a certain market scale, and Internet of things technology has been applied in public safety, urban management, environmental monitoring, energy conservation and emission reduction, traffic supervision and other fields. It is predicted that there will be hundreds of billions of sensor network terminals in China around 2035, and sensors will be everywhere in life in 2050. The Internet of Things has a wide range of uses, involving all aspects of life, such as intelligent transportation, environmental protection, public safety, smart home, industrial monitoring, agricultural production, food traceability and many other fields. Although the Internet of Things has not yet been widely used, there have been some successful cases that have achieved a substantial increase in management efficiency, and the application of the Internet of Things technology has broad prospects [1, 4–6].

The application field of the Internet of Things involves all aspects. The application in the field of infrastructure such as industry, agriculture, environment, transportation, logistics, and security has effectively promoted the intelligent development of these areas, making the limited resources more reasonable use and allocation, thereby Improve the efficiency and benefit of the industry. The application in home, medical and health, education, finance and service industry, tourism and other fields closely related to life has been greatly improved in terms of service scope, service mode and service quality, which has greatly improved people's quality of life; In terms of national defense and military fields, although it is still in the research and exploration stage, the impact of Internet of things applications can not be underestimated, ranging from satellite, missile, aircraft, submarine and other equipment systems to individual combat equipment. The embedding of Internet of things technology has effectively improved military intelligence, informatization and accuracy, and greatly improved military combat effectiveness. It is the key to future military reforms. For specific personnel as management objects, collect personnel identity, appearance area, residence time, and other relevant information of on-site personnel, such as body temperature, pulse, on-site video and other data: collect the above information of personnel in real time, realize change alarm according to the management rules dynamically set in the background, and configure the device according to the complexity of personnel, It also supports the interaction and control mode of Personnel Devices: it can help complete the real-time monitoring and control of people's on-site activities, and help managers realize the purpose of fine, intelligent and automatic management of a large number of personnel.

2 Review of Research at Home and Abroad

With the escalation of global competition, the more the times move forward, the importance of knowledge and talents becomes more prominent, and the status and role of education becomes more prominent. In the final analysis, the competition of comprehensive national strength in today's world is the competition of talents. Innovation and entrepreneurship are becoming more and more important, and innovative engineering and technical talents have also attracted great attention. American higher education has made diversified attempts in the field of innovation and entrepreneurship. Historically, most investors of American innovation companies have been centered on metropolises such as Silicon Valley, Boston, New York, New Jersey, Seattle, Washington and San Diego. Now, universities outside these regions are undergoing a new model of entrepreneurial ecosystem reform. There are hundreds of universities and colleges in the United States that are carrying out short-term or long-term entrepreneurial projects. Short-term projects aim to increase the value of education for students, while long-term projects better help local economic growth through local entrepreneurship. American universities and government departments have done a lot of work in five areas: providing entrepreneurial courses and degree programs, providing experience learning, promoting learning through competition, establishing a joint space for innovation and entrepreneurship, and entrepreneurship education in community colleges.

Since the early 1990s, Germany has put forward the idea of "combining theory with practice", promoted applied scientific research, and paid full attention to the transformation of scientific achievements into production products. Manufacturing, these products have extremely high technological content and unit output value. The entrepreneurship education models of British universities are mainly divided into two categories: one is the entrepreneurship education model dominated by business schools, and the other is the University led education model. Taiwan has set up an interdisciplinary cluster creative entrepreneurship credit program to improve the quality of curriculum education, implement the "creative teacher growth project", train "double specialized and multifunctional" teachers through multiple channels, implement creative teaching plans, promote students to improve their thinking intelligence and problem-solving ability, and implement the "creative student cultivation plan", so that students can train their creative entrepreneurship ability Measures to focus on the construction of innovation and entrepreneurship education support system and provide strong guarantee for innovation and Entrepreneurship Education [7, 8].

In his speech at the Central Talent Work Conference on September 27, 2021, Xi Jinping pointed out that in the course of a century of struggle, our party has always attached importance to cultivating talents, uniting talents, leading talents, and achieving talents, uniting and supporting talents from all walks of life to contribute to the cause of the party and the people. It is necessary to create a large-scale team of young scientific and technological talents, focus on the policy of cultivating national strategic talents on young scientific and technological talents, and support young talents to take the lead and play the leading role. It is necessary to train a large number of outstanding engineers, and strive to build a team of engineers who love the party and serve the country, are dedicated to their work, have outstanding technological innovation capabilities, and are good at solving complex engineering problems. It is necessary to mobilize the enthusiasm of universities and enterprises to achieve deep integration of production, education and research. General Secretary Xi Jinping delivered an important speech at the National Education Conference, "Education is the country's major plan and the party's major plan." Education is related to the development of the country and the future of the nation. Especially for the country and the nation, education is beneficial to the present and future. It is the socialist builders and successors to train, and who to train is the primary issue of education. The development of the times calls for artisans, and social progress needs artisans. General secretary Xi Jinping pointed out in the "three session of science and technology": "Throughout the history of human development, innovation has always been an important force in the development of a country and a nation, and also an important force in promoting the progress of human society. This hard-won is inseparable from the hard work of hundreds of millions of people and hundreds of millions of market entities, and the contribution of mass entrepreneurship and innovation is also indispensable. A large number of market players have established and become active, their innovation ability has been continuously improved, and new driving forces have accelerated growth, providing strong support for stabilizing employment and the overall economic situation. More people shine with mass entrepreneurship and innovation and create wealth through struggle. Entrepreneurship goes to the public, innovation comes from the masses, and converges into a surging force to promote economic development".

In the context of Premier Li Keqiang's call for "Mass Entrepreneurship and Innovation" and the nation's vigorous efforts to promote citizen innovation and entrepreneurship, colleges and universities across the country have followed up with active actions to carry out education and teaching reforms to enhance college students' innovation and entrepreneurship capabilities; In the government work report on March 5, 2016, it was mentioned that enterprises are encouraged to develop personalized customization and flexible production, cultivate a craftsman spirit of excellence, increase varieties, improve quality, and create brands. Since 2016, the Shanghai Federation of trade unions has implemented the plan of training and selecting thousands of Shanghai craftsmen. In the past three years, 280 "Shanghai craftsmen" have been selected, setting off a climax of striving to be craftsmen and learning craftsmen. In May 2018, the Shandong Provincial People's government issued the "opinions on the transformation of new and old kinetic energy to support talents". It pointed out that we should fully implement the spirit of general secretary Xi Jinping's inspection of important speeches and important instructions in Shandong and closely focused on the overall layout of "five in one" and the strategic layout of "four comprehensives", firmly grasped the goal orientation of being at the forefront, adhered to the principle of the party managing talents, and gathered talents from all over the world. In order to speed up the construction of a strong province with talents, reform and innovate the system and mechanism to adapt to the law of talent growth and stimulate the vitality of talent development, implement a more active, open and effective talent policy, strive to build a career platform to give full play to the role of talents and realize the value of talents, and comprehensively build a career platform where everyone is eager to become talents, everyone works hard to become talents and everyone can become talents The ecological environment in which everyone gives full play to their talents, so that all kinds of excellent talents can be attracted, retained and used well. Give full play to the supporting and leading role of talents in the transformation of old and new kinetic energy, create innovation advantages, industrial advantages and development advantages with talent advantages, and provide strong talent guarantee and intellectual support for accelerating the strategic transformation of Shandong from large to strong and realizing innovative development, sustainable development and leading development.

In September 2019, after the 18th meeting of the Standing Committee of the 13th Hangzhou Municipal People's Congress, it was decided that starting from 2019, September 26 each year will be established as the "Craftsman's Day", which is the first in the country according to law. The "Craftsman's Day" established will fully support the cultivation of a craftsman culture, encourage the growth of the team of skilled craftsmen, adapt to the technological revolution and industrial transformation, and promote the transformation of industrial development momentum. Novel coronavirus pneumonia was held in March 17, 2020 by the Shandong provincial Party committee and the provincial government. The mobilization meeting of the "key task tackling year" in the province has mentioned that since the outbreak of the new crown pneumonia, under the firm leadership of the Party Central Committee with Comrade Xi Jinping as the core, under the leadership of general secretary Xi Jinping, he has worked hard with the party members and cadres and the masses of the whole province. Our province, like the whole country, has shown a positive trend in epidemic prevention and control and an accelerated restoration of the order of production and life. We must allow talent development to have a stage, closely integrate talents with industry, and do whatever is conducive to the achievement of talents; ensure that talent entrepreneurs are guaranteed, introduce talent development promotion regulations, form "Shandong Talent Development Group", and provide full-chain, full-factor talents Entrepreneurship support; let the value of talents be rewarded, further improve the incentive mechanism, let the talents who make contributions "win fame and fortune", adhere to the integration of production, education, research and use, promote the integration of science, education, production, education, and school to accelerate the integration of production, education and research. We should actively develop vocational education and train more high-quality craftsmen.

3   The Mode of Training Advanced Technical Talents

3.1   Internet of Things+ Platform

The Internet of Things has three characteristics: one is comprehensive perception, that is, the use of radio frequency identification, sensors, two-dimensional codes, etc. to obtain information about objects anytime and anywhere; the other is reliable transmission, which integrates various telecommunication networks and the Internet to integrate information about objects Real-time and accurate transmission; the third is intelligent processing, using cloud computing, fuzzy recognition and other intelligent computing technologies to analyze and process massive amounts of data and information, and implement intelligent control of objects. Therefore, the architecture of the Internet of Things is generally recognized as having three levels: the bottom layer is the perception layer used to perceive data, the second layer is the network layer (transport layer) for data transmission, and the uppermost layer is the application layer. It can be seen from the three-tier structure of the Internet of Things that the industry chain of the Internet of Things can be subdivided into four links: object identification, perception, processing, and information transmission. Key technologies include QR codes, radio frequency identification, sensors, smart chips, and telecom operators' Wireless transmission network, etc. The next step in the development of the Internet of Things is to continue to strengthen the integration with wearable devices, AR/VR, artificial intelligence, robots, drones, 3D printing, blockchain, etc., to achieve the Internet of Things+. Among them, wearable devices are devices that can be worn on the body, which can be worn on people, animals, and all objects. Devices that can sense, transmit and process information, which integrate multimedia, wireless communication, micro-sensing, flexible screen, and GPS positioning. The cutting-edge technologies such as systems, virtual reality, biometrics, and artificial intelligence can collect, process, feedback and share information anytime and anywhere through the combination with big data platforms, smart cloud platforms, and mobile Internet. It is a smart terminal device based on mobile Internet with high performance and low power consumption. With the help of various sensors, it interacts with the human body and objects. Generate information interaction and collect data [1].

3.2 The Guidance of Double Qualified Teachers

In August 2019, the notice of the Ministry of education and other four departments on printing and distributing the implementation plan for deepening the construction and reform of "double qualified" teachers in Vocational Education in the new era shows that this plan clearly puts forward six measures to improve the quality of "double qualified" Teachers: to build a diversified training pattern with vocational and technical normal colleges as the main body and the integration of industry and education; improve the new mechanism of teacher resource allocation of "fixed post + mobile post"; establish a two-way communication and cooperation community between school and enterprise personnel; focus on the "1+X" certificate system to carry out teacher training; create a high-level structured teaching innovation team; takes the "national craftsman's teacher" as the guide to strengthen the construction of a high-level talent team. It is also mentioned that highlighting the combination of the individual growth of "dual-qualified" teachers and the construction of the "dual-qualified" teaching team, improving teacher education and teaching ability and professional practice ability, optimizing the structure of full-time and part-time teachers, and vigorously improving the "dual-qualified" teaching team of vocational colleges The level of teacher team building, improve the secondary and higher vocational education teacher training and training system, open up the two-way flow of school and enterprise personnel, the number of "dual-professional" teachers and teaching teams is sufficient, and the dual-teacher structure has been significantly improved.

Establish a distinctively distinctive "dual-qualified" teacher qualification access and employment assessment system, smooth teacher career development channels, more complete remuneration and guarantee mechanisms, and obvious enhancement of the attractiveness of vocational education teachers.

Basically, a team of teachers with noble ethics and exquisite skills has been established, Professional and concurrent, energetic, high-quality "double-qualified" teacher team. Therefore, at the national level, it has put forward clear requirements and programmatic guidance for the construction and connotation of the dual-qualification type. Whether it is a secondary, higher vocational college or an applied undergraduate college, relying on programmatic guidance to strengthen teachers The construction of the team, first of all, teachers must have noble and excellent professional ethics and professionalism, which is the premise and the ideological guarantee for the cultivation of excellent high-tech talents; secondly, the level of students must be improved, and the students must only stay in dreams. It is impossible to create a high-quality and skilled high-tech talent. The improvement of teachers' level and technical exquisiteness are the fundamental guarantee for the achievement of student talents; once again, teachers must practice by themselves, and lead students to do projects, design products, and solve problems. Let students feel the fun of the process and design and production, and fully enjoy the endless happiness and supreme satisfaction and pride brought by the development process.

Double-qualified teachers means that teachers must not only have teacher qualifications, but also have professional qualifications, spanning vocational colleges and industry enterprises, as well as teachers of schools and employees of enterprises, in order to better promote the integration of industry, education and research. Under the background of the integration of production and education, the school-enterprise dual system and the integration of engineering and learning, from the "dual subject" of school-enterprise education to the "dual identity" of student apprentices, the key lies in the dual-qualified teachers. Some developed countries stipulate the experience of teachers in vocational colleges in terms of corporate experience and teacher education experience. For example, Germany and Singapore stipulate that teachers of professional courses in vocational colleges must have more than 5 years of corporate work experience; In order to be engaged in the profession of teachers, graduates from colleges and universities must go to higher normal colleges to learn a certain period of educational knowledge and obtain relevant certificates. One-handed theoretical teaching and one-handed practical guidance. You can not only get to the three-foot podium, but also play in various training fields. Such "double-handed" or even "all-rounder" in the field of vocational education is called "dual teacher type" teacher.

3.3 Cultivation of Higher Technical Talents

Build an Internet of things+ platform, take double qualified teachers as the guide, take Outcomes Based Education (OBE) and practical application cases as the traction, and rely on tasks to carry out heuristic, discussion, real-scene participation and other teaching methods, integrate the concept of system, soft and hard, virtual and real, and build a three-dimensional and multi-dimensional training mode of high-quality innovative talents, the cultivation of various types of competitions, school level, provincial and national innovation and entrepreneurship projects, as well as various short-term training, teacher training, practical training, factory practice, internship and other practical exercises to cultivate engineering and technical talents, and the cultivation of scientific literacy of engineering and technical talents through writing scientific and technological papers and summary research reports, strive to build an Internet of things+ platform for training senior engineering and technical talents.

At present, all secondary and higher vocational colleges and applied undergraduate colleges and universities are only discrete, immature or crossing the river by feeling the stone in the training of advanced engineering and technical talents, and do not raise these to a scientific level. In addition, some people are impatient and pursue the immediate benefits brought by "short, flat and fast" (less investment, short cycle and quick results), some methods and strategies have been deformed. College students who adhere to the "craftsman spirit" rely on their beliefs and beliefs and watch the continuous improvement and improvement of their designed products. The training paradigm of higher technical talents follows the result orientation-reverse design-continuous improvement, takes innovation, creativity and entrepreneurship as the main line, relying on the Internet of things+ high and new information technology and assisted by resources, Build innovative and entrepreneurial projects in the Internet of things+ high and new technology. Construct a six-in-one three-dimensional innovative creative entrepreneurial system of innovation methods-information technology-entrepreneurial resources-creative cases-competition practice-lean entrepreneurship, and form an innovation and entrepreneurship framework that combines industry characteristics.

To achieve the smooth implementation of the conversion between new and old kinetic energy, cultivate and bring up engineering and technical personnel with the spirit of craftsmanship, talent cultivation must be advanced, especially innovative engineering and technical personnel is the top priority. The craftsman spirit is the pursuit of excellence, the spirit of quality, the spirit of customer-oriented service. Therefore, in teaching and practice, we will take innovation and entrepreneurship as the main line, take curriculum system reform, training platform, science and technology competition and school enterprise marriage as the four carriages, and gradually establish a more reasonable and perfect practice model. Based on this model, we will create engineering and technical talents with excellent theory through rich theoretical knowledge, use electronic engineers to train and participate in various types of electronic design competitions, gradually cultivate the professional quality of engineering and technical talents, achieve the high scientific and theoretical quality of engineering and technical talents by writing scientific and technological papers, and have the practical application ability to solve specific problems in work practice through school enterprise cooperation and practical training, explore a feasible way for the cultivation of college students in engineering science and technology [2, 3].

Three Aspects. The three aspects refer to the system-oriented, soft-hard virtual reality, and the construction of a three-dimensional and multi-dimensional high-quality innovative talent training model. Schools must keep up with market demand, grasp the development level of productivity, industrial structure adjustment and the new characteristics of the talent market, so that the talent specifications can continuously adapt to the development needs of the new era. With reference to the national vocational standards, combined with the employment feedback of graduates, and build a practical and characteristic "vocational skill quality structure system" and "vocational skill quality implementation standard" with the assistance of enterprises and experts and so on. First, the capture of information system, including the conception, design, implementation and application of information system. Take information as the carrier to realize the acquisition, transmission, processing, storage and application of information. With the help of the specific application of each link from the device to the circuit in the teaching process, it can realize the grasp of the overall system of the circuit, fully integrate the source power of innovation, and realize the cultivation of engineering and technical talents through soft, hard, virtual and real. The soft aspect is to forge the overall literacy of college students and achieve the theoretical and professional literacy necessary for engineering and technical personnel, so that college students can stand tall and see far. In fact, with the help of the Internet and the Internet of things, you can receive remote training and technical guidance, and can also realize remote control and production of equipment. Although it is far away, it seems to be close at hand. Reality is to really engage in specific technical realization in the environment, comprehensively apply the learned theories and technologies to specific practice, from the production and demonstration of finished products participating in various competitions to the actual control of various equipment in the factory workshop to realize the production of various finished products, and truly become a person who understands technology and can solve the problems in the production process.

A Platform for Senior Engineering and Technical Talents. By summarizing, discussing and studying the existing practices, experiences and problems of school enterprise cooperation, we strive to form a more systematic and advanced theory of school enterprise cooperation mode, operation mechanism and guarantee mechanism. Enhance the initiative and sense of urgency of all teachers, expand cooperation ideas, take school enterprise cooperation as a strategy to improve teachers' quality, innovate school running ideas, and establish an all-round and close cooperative relationship with enterprises. Based on the four masters, we will gradually realize the gradual progress from the basic level, the promotion level to the whole skill level. This actually runs through the usual teaching practice and training process. The four focuses generally include the construction and improvement of innovation and entrepreneurship curriculum system, the construction of a number of highly skilled instructors with double qualified teachers, the construction of hardware facilities for purchasing innovation and entrepreneurship practice, so that college students can see, do and realize an all-round equipment cluster, and finally create a complete atmosphere to put college students in the environment of practice and training, always think of yourself as an engineer.

At present, students have undertaken 123 national college students' innovation and entrepreneurship training programs, 56 college students' innovation and entrepreneurship training programs in Shandong Province, and 48 college students' science and technology innovation action plan projects in Tai'an city (the number of approved college student projects accounted for 40.3% of the school). Students participate in the China Finals of the ICAN International Innovation and Entrepreneurship Competition,

Shandong University Physics Teaching Skills Competition, Normal Professional Students Practicing Skills Competition, National University Student Physics Teaching Skills Competition, National (and Shandong Province) Electronic Design Competition, Smart Car Competition, "Challenge Cup" College students' extracurricular academic science and technology works competition, Shandong University Student Science and Technology Innovation Competition, Physics Technology Innovation Competition and other discipline competitions, won a total of 14 national first prizes, 34 s prizes, 19 third prizes, and provincial first prizes. 115 items, 140 s prizes, and 188 third prizes.

Training Base. According to the requirements of professional construction and improving the quality of talent training, focusing on cultivating students' practical ability, the interaction between schools and enterprises, build a number of practical teaching bases inside and outside the school integrating many functions, such as practical teaching, vocational skill training and appraisal, vocational qualification certification and vocational quality training. It is necessary to increase investment and build a high-level school practical training base to meet the basic school practical teaching. Give full play to the role of off campus practice and training base, and hire all kinds of high-quality and capable technicians as students' practice instructors to improve students' practical ability. In order to strengthen the training of application-oriented talents, the college has 49 professional teaching and research laboratories such as the electronic engineering training center, the communication engineering comprehensive teaching experiment center, the electrical technology laboratory, the modern physics laboratory, the electronic technol ogy laboratory, and the electronic innovation laboratory, The total value of experimental equipment is nearly 40 million yuan, and 16 practical teaching bases and 9 social activity practical bases for college students have been built with enterprises and middle schools [9–12]. The college cooperated with Qingruan Innovation Technology Group Co., Ltd. to open the intelligent chip design direction under the electronic information science and technology major, and cooperated with ZTE Corporation and Beijing Huasheng Jingshi Information Technology Co., Ltd. to open the optical communication under the communication engineering major and the direction of mobile communication, and build the Ministry of Education-ZTE ICT industry-education integration innovation base.

Through the professional construction steering committee, industry and business leaders and experts are invited to participate in the formulation or revision of professional talent training programs, carefully listen to the opinions and suggestions of industry and business experts, and jointly formulate talent training plans with the company. The goal of talent training is negotiated by the school-enterprise cooperation committee; in the talent training plan and curriculum setting, there is a professional steering committee to participate; in the professional theory course teaching, the company's technical backbone is hired as part-time teachers to participate in the guidance; in skills training and practice In the link, the enterprise workshops, laboratories, R&D centers, and teaching factories are the bases; in the internship and job placement process, the cooperative enterprises are the main body. The school closely focuses on the actual production of the enterprise and the standards of the enterprise's demand for talents, and uses the professional school-enterprise cooperation committee as a platform to hire business leaders and technical backbones to participate in the curriculum reform.

4 Conclusion

The Internet of Things+ is a future form that replaces mobile phones. This future form not only completes the transfer of information between people, between people and things, and between things, but also completes the creation, transformation, and realization of remote actions and the physical world. Therefore, the new technology of the Internet of Things can not only replace the existing mobile phones, but also replace the existing models of robots. The future technology will bring an earth-shaking impact to the society and work and life. After extensive pilots and practices have formed a more mature innovation and entrepreneurship model, it can be first promoted in colleges and universities that have relevant explorations, and gradually transition to more colleges and universities to join in, and gradually expand the team of colleges and universities that practice the six integrated models., Also found problems in the active promotion, found bottlenecks restricting development, and found solutions, so that more colleges and universities can avoid detours and adapt to the promotion and application of this model more quickly. From curriculum design and development, curriculum teaching and reform, operation of training links, teaching quality evaluation and improvement of guarantee mechanism, a multi-dimensional and relatively complete professional core competence training approach provides intelligence for the training of professional talents in applied undergraduate colleges. Support and cultivate more senior technical talents with craftsman spirit for employers and the society.

References

1. Gao, Z.H., Sun, W.S.: Internet of Things-Architecture. Protocol Standards and Wireless Communication. Tsinghua University Press (2020)
2. Ma, S.Q., Meng, F.C., Ma, Y., Su, J.: Automatic integrated exhaust fan based on at89s51 single chip microcomputer. In: ICCCS 2018, pp. 118–127 (2018)
3. Ma, Y., Li, Z., Liu, Y., Liu, H., Ma, S.: Discussion on the application of industrial internet. In: Sun, X., Pan, Z., Bertino, E. (eds.) ICAIS 2019. LNCS, vol. 11634, pp. 297–308. Springer, Cham (2019). https://doi.org/10.1007/978-3-030-24271-8_27
4. Zhao, J., et al.: Research on cultivating senior technical talents based on the internet of things platform. In: Sun, X., Zhang, X., Xia, Z., Bertino, E. (eds.) ICAIS 2021. CCIS, vol. 1424, pp. 426–439. Springer, Cham (2021). https://doi.org/10.1007/978-3-030-78621-2_35
5. Meng, R., Zhou, Z., Cui, Q., Sun, X., Yuan, C.: A novel steganography scheme combining coverless information hiding and steganography. J. Inf. Hiding Privacy Protection 1(1), 43–48 (2019)
6. Fan, X.M., Xu, J.J.: The status quo of innovation and entrepreneurship education in universities in the United States, Britain and Japan. J. Jilin Med. College 6 (2019)
7. Liu, X.Y.: Analysis on the path of innovation and entrepreneurship education in colleges and universities under the background of the construction of new engineering courses– based on the enlightenment of American polytechnic institutes. J. Kaifeng Inst. Educ. 2 (2019)
8. Chen, X.L.: Research on the innovation and entrepreneurship education mode and practice in colleges and universities-taking four american colleges and universities as examples. J. Natl. Acad. Educ. Admin. 7 (2019)
9. Xia, Z., Wang, L., Tang, J., Xiong, N.N., Weng, J.: A privacy-preserving image retrieval scheme using secure local binary pattern in cloud computing. IEEE Trans. Netw. Sci. Eng. 8(1), 318–330 (2020)

10. Chen, X., Zhang, Z., Qiu, A., Xia, Z., Xiong, N.: A novel coverless steganography method based on image selection and StarGAN. IEEE Trans. Netw. Sci. Eng. (2020). https://doi.org/10.1109/TNSE.2020.3041529
11. Xia, Z., Jiang, L., Liu, D., Lu, L., Jeon, B.: BOEW: A content-based image retrieval scheme using bag-of-encrypted-words in cloud computing. IEEE Trans. Serv. Comput. (2019). https://doi.org/10.1109/TSC.2019.2927215
12. Yuan, C., Xia, Z., Sun, X., Wu, Q.M.J.: Deep residual network with adaptive learning framework for fingerprint liveness detection. IEEE Trans. Cogn. Develop. Syst. **12**(3), 461–473 (2019)

Classification of Tropical Cyclone Intensity Based on Deep Learning and YOLO V5

Lujin Li[1], Zihan Shuai[1], Jinrong Hu[1], and Yan Zhang[2(✉)]

[1] Department of Computer Science, Chengdu University
of Information Technology, Chengdu 610225, China
[2] Satellite Meteorological Center (NSMC), China Meteorological Administration (CMA),
Beijing 100086, China
zhangyan@cma.gov.cn

Abstract. Deep convolutional networks have become a common tool for image recognition and object detection. This paper proposes an algorithm based on YOLO V5 for tropical cyclone identification. The model consists of four modules, the first is the input side, using Mosaic data enhancement and other methods to increase the number of samples and improve accuracy. Secondly, Backbone: convolutional neural network that aggregates and forms image features on different fine image granularity. Then there's Neck: a series of network layers that mix and combine image features and pass them on to the prediction layer. Finally, Prediction is used to predict image features, generate boundary boxes and predict categories. Firstly, the GridSat data set and the satellite of China Meteorological Administration were used to analyze the tropical cyclone scale data, and the typhoon data set was established. Secondly, based on the Pytorch deep learning framework developed by Facebook, YOLO V5 is trained with the 1994–2013 data set, and tested with the 2014 and 2015 data. Meanwhile, various performance parameters are analyzed. Finally, the data of 2016 were used to verify the results. Experimental results show that the method proposed in this paper has good identification ability and can effectively identify tropical cyclone targets on the sea surface with fast detection speed and low missed detection rate.

Keywords: Convolutional Neural Network (CNN) · Fusion of satellite image · YOLO V5 · Image prediction · A tropical cyclone

1 Introduction

Tropical cyclone is a kind of disastrous weather which seriously affects human production and life. China is one of the countries the hardest hit by tropical cyclones in the world. They come ashore with strong winds and heavy rainfall that are often detrimental to the property safety of people in the affected areas. Tropical cyclones have an important impact on social and economic development [1], so the accurate monitoring and forecast of tropical cyclones has always been the focus of the Marine meteorological community [2]. However, because tropical cyclones usually occur in the ocean, they are difficult to

X. Sun et al. (Eds.): ICAIS 2022, CCIS 1586, pp. 280–291, 2022.
https://doi.org/10.1007/978-3-031-06767-9_23

monitor from ground-based observations. With the development of meteorological satellite remote sensing sensors, synchronous satellite remote sensing image data with high time resolution is considered as one of the most reliable observation methods, which can obtain various characteristics of tropical cyclones, such as intensity and center location [3].

In recent years, with the arrival of big data in the Internet era and the rapid development of computer hardware, machine learning and deep neural network have been widely used in speech, image recognition [4], target detection [5], machine translation, remote sensing image classification [6] and other fields. Based on this, many researchers began to think whether the successful experience of deep learning techniques in other fields could be used in the field of tropical cyclone intensity measurement and classification under the background of big data to improve the classification accuracy of traditional methods. Reduce the intensity measurement error, shorten the traditional method of time prediction, better assist disaster prevention departments timely warning, reduce casualties and economic losses.

At present, Dovrak analysis method [7] and numerical simulation analysis method [8] are the main methods to estimate tropical cyclone intensity. Dvorak analysis is an artificial method to determine tropical cyclone intensity based on empirical satellite image analysis. The Dvorak technique was used to extract the scale of tropical cyclone, and the corresponding calculation strategy was established. However, due to its subjectivity, the accuracy of estimating tropical cyclone intensity depends in many cases on the experience of the forecaster. To overcome this limitation. Many experts and scholars at home and abroad have put forward more objective methods to estimate tropical cyclone intensity. For example, Olander et al. [9] proposed an enhanced Dvorak technology. Ritchie et al. proposed a deviation-variance technique (DAV-t) based on tropical cyclone structure analysis. Dav-t quantifies pixel-based trends in brightness and temperature at the center of a tropical cyclone and uses the level of the center location to determine its intensity. The average continuous wind speed was used as the reference intensity of the tropical cyclone, and the best path data released by the Joint Typhoon Warning Center was used to verify the estimation model. The RMSE value was 12.7kT.

Numerical simulation analysis is the mainstream method of business forecasting at present. The main analytical models are MM5 and WRF. For example, Zeng Zhihua et al. [10] studied the intensity of Typhoon "Sangmei" through numerical simulation, with an average absolute error of 6.2 m/s. Wang Hui et al. improved the simulation of typhoon intensity in the mesoscale ARW-WRE model by combining the typhoon eddy dynamic initialization scheme with the large-scale approximation scheme. The RMSE of typhoon "Megi" intensity simulation was maintained at 2.2–2.5 m/s. Qian Yanzhen et al. [11] simulated the rapid change of typhoon haikui intensity by using a new generation mesoscale model wRF3.3. However, the numerical simulation analysis method is affected by the initial field, boundary conditions and other prior physical quantities, resulting in some errors in the results.

Domestic and foreign scholars use satellite cloud images to classify tropical cyclones through machine learning algorithms [12]. For example, handing et al. used a support vector machine model to classify meteorological cloud images with an accuracy of 82.4%. To solve the problem that satellite cloud images are easily disturbed by noise,

Tian Wenzhen et al. constructed a fuzzy support vector machine and optimized the hyperparameter accuracy to 88.2%. However, the features of satellite cloud images of tropical cyclones that can be extracted by machine learning algorithms are small and require a large amount of calculation [13].

This paper presents an algorithm based on YOLO V5 for tropical cyclone measurement. Firstly, the GridSat data set and the satellite of China Meteorological Administration were used to analyze the tropical cyclone scale data, and the typhoon data set was established. Secondly, based on the Pytorch deep learning framework developed by Facebook, YOLO V5 is trained with data sets from 2004 to 2013, and tested with data from 2014 and 2015. Meanwhile, various performance parameters are analyzed. Finally, the data of 2016 were used to verify the results. Experimental results show that the method proposed in this paper has good identification ability and can effectively identify tropical cyclone targets on the sea surface with fast detection speed and low missed detection rate.

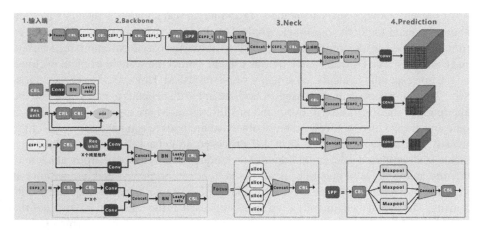

Fig. 1. YOLO v5 network structure.

2 Method

As shown in Fig. 1, the model is mainly composed of four modules. First, Mosaic data enhancement [14], adaptive anchor frame calculation, and adaptive image scaling were used to increase the number of samples and improve the accuracy. Second, Backbone: convolutional neural network that aggregates and forms image features on different fine-grained images. The third is Neck: a series of network layers that mix and combine image features and transmit image features to the prediction layer. (Usually FPN or PANET). The fourth is Prediction, which predicts image features, generates boundary boxes and predicts categories. The GIOU_Loss function is mainly used.

2.1   The Input

Mosaic data enhancement uses 4 images, randomly zooming, randomly clipping and randomly arranging, as shown in Fig. 2. Its main advantages are as follows: (1) Rich data set: random use of 4 images, random scaling, and then random distribution for stitching, greatly enrich the detection data set, especially random scaling increases a lot of small targets, so that the robustness of the network is better. (2) Reduce GPU usage. Therefore, when Mosaic enhanced training, the data of four images can be directly calculated, making the mini-batch size does not need to be very large, and one GPU can achieve a good effect.

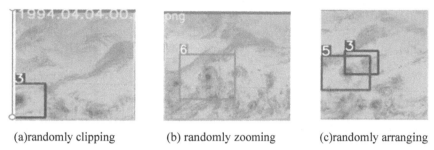

(a)randomly clipping   (b) randomly zooming   (c)randomly arranging

Fig. 2. Mosaic data enhancement: three images use randomly zooming, randomly clipping and randomly arranging.

2.2   YOLO V5 Backbone Network

Focus is the interlaced sampling splicing structure of YOLO V5. The Focus layer is used to make four copies of the input, then cut the four images into four slices through the slicing operation, then connect the four slices in depth using concat, then through the convolution layer with 32 convolution cores, and finally through batch normalization and Leaky_rclu to input the results to the next convolution layer.

BottleneckCSP is the first BottleneckCSP structure of YOLO V5: BottleneckCSP is divided into two parts, Bottleneck and The CSP. The Bottleneck is the classic residual structure: the 1×1 convolution layer (conv + batch normalization + Leaky_relu), then the 3×3 convolution layer, and finally the residual structure is added to the initial input.

SPP is the Spatial pooling layer, which is output after 1×1 convolution layer, and then down sampling is carried out through three parallel maxpools of different kernel_size. Note that for different branches, in addition, since stride = 1, Therefore, each pooling result can be added to its initial features after splicing, and finally restored to the original image with 512 convolution kernels. PANetPAN is intended for instance segmentation. The feature extractor of this network adopts a new FPN structure with enhanced bottom-up path, which improves the propagation of low-level features. Each stage of the third path takes the feature maps of the previous stage as input and processes them with a 3×3 convolution layer. The outputs are added via horizontal connections to the same phase feature diagrams of the top-down pathway that provide information for the next phase.

2.3 Loss Function

YOLO V5 uses BECLogits Loss function to calculate the Loss of Objectness Score, class Probability Score uses cross entropy Loss function, and Bounding Box uses GIOU Loss. GIoU Loss is used to calculate the Loss of bounding box. GIOU directly sets IoU to regression Loss. GIoU derived from IoU means that the minimum closure area of the two boxes is calculated first. Divide the absolute value of the ratio of C to AB by the absolute value of C to obtain the specific gravity of the region in the closure region that does not belong to the two boxes. Finally, calculate the difference between IoU and specific gravity to obtain the value of GIoU. GIoU = IoU = 1 when the two boxes approach to overlap infinitely.

$$IoU = \frac{|A \cap B|}{|A \cup B|} \tag{1}$$

$$GIoU = IoU - \frac{|C/(A \cup B)|}{|C|} \tag{2}$$

3   Experiment and Result Analysis

3.1 Experimental Dataset

GridSat Data

GridSat data are ISCCP B1 data [15], which are gridded on an isometric grid of 0.07° latitude (about 8 km) with a time resolution of 3 h. GridSat has spatial scales from 70°S T to 700°N and provides long time series satellite images since 1980. Gridsat-b1 contains data from three satellite channels: infrared window (IRWIN) channel (nearly 11 μm), visible light channel (nearly 0.6 μm), and infrared water vapor channel (IRWVP, nearly 6.7 μm). However, only GridSat's IRWIN channel can be considered of climate Data record (CDR) quality, where CDR is defined as "a measured time series of sufficient length, consistency, and continuity to determine climate variability and change." Therefore, in this study, only IRWIN channel images (IR) were used.

Satellite Analysis of Tropical Cyclone Scale Data

The scale data of tropical cyclones retrieved by satellite include all the tropical cyclones captured by satellite in the northwest Pacific Ocean, covering the space area north of the equator and 180° west, including the South China Sea. The satellite analyzes a tropical cyclone-scale data set including 6-h intervals of latitude, longitude, minimum pressure near the center of a tropical cyclone, and maximum sustained wind speed.

Based on the timing and location of the GridSat data satellite analysis of the tropical cyclone scale data, we can produce some tropical cyclone data with the dimensions of 0°−60°N and 100°−180°E as the location center. For GridSat IRWIN data, the image size is 519 × 386 pixels. According to the international Typhoon classification standard, the data set is divided into 6 categories according to the wind speed of typhoon center: tropical depression, tropical storm, severe tropical storm, typhoon, strong typhoon and super typhoon, as shown in the table. The number of tropical storm, strong tropical storm, typhoon, strong typhoon and super typhoon was 2774, 2317, 1956, 1327, 537 respectively (Table 1).

Table 1. Typhoon classification standard.

Typhoon classification	The wind speed value		
	kt	M/s	Km/h
Tropical storm	$\geq33-<48$	$\geq17-<25$	$\geq62-<89$
Severe tropical storm	$\geq48-<64$	$\geq25-<33$	$\geq89-<118$
Typhoon	$\geq64-<85$	$\geq33-<42$	$\geq118-<150$
Severe typhoon	$\geq85-<106$	$\geq42-<51$	$\geq150-<182$
Super typhoon	≥106	≥51	≥182

3.2 Experimental Setup

The algorithm in this article will be compared with Demon's algorithm, SIFT FLow and Elastix algorithm. Among them, Elastix is a software suitable for both rigid and non-rigid image registration. It contains a series of algorithms for solving medical registration problems, and is often used as a comparison experiment for the registration effects of different registration algorithms.

In the algorithm experiment of this paper, the network uses the ADAM optimization function, the 0learning rate of the feature extraction network is set to 0.03, and the learning rate of the generator and discriminator network in the GAN network is set to 0.001.

The main parameter settings of the experimental comparison algorithm in this paper are as follows: In the SIFT Flow algorithm, the.

regularization coefficient η is set to 0.005, α is set to 2, and the number of iterations is set to 200; in the Demons algorithm, the histogram level coefficient is set to 1024, and the number of iterations is set to 50; In Elastix algorithm, the transformation type is set to "BSPLINE", and the number of iterations is set to 500.

3.3 Algorithm Evaluation Indicators

The performance of the prediction model was evaluated, and the selection accuracy, recall rate, mAP and recognition accuracy were evaluated to measure the prediction accuracy of the model.

Precision. Precision is the proportion of the correct class divided by all the positive classes found, the fraction that the classifier thinks is a positive class and is a positive class to the fraction that the classifier thinks is a positive class.

$$\text{Precision} = \frac{TP}{TP + FP} \tag{3}$$

Recall. The recall rate is the proportion of positive classes found correctly/of all positive classes that should have been found correctly, the fraction of all positive classes that the classifier considers to be positive and is positive.

$$\text{Recall} = \frac{TP}{TP + FN} \tag{4}$$

mAP. mAP@0.5 & mAP@0.5:0.95 is the area enclosed after Precision and Recall are used as two axes in mAP, m represents average, the number after @ represents the threshold value for determining IOU as positive and negative samples, and @0.5:0.95 represents the mean value after the threshold value is set to 0.5:0.05:0.95.

4 Experimental Results

4.1 Comparison and Analysis of Transfer Learning Results

Generally speaking, transfer learning is to use existing knowledge to learn new knowledge, the core is to find the similarity between existing knowledge and new knowledge. In transfer learning, the existing knowledge is called source domain, and the new knowledge to be learned is called target domain. Source domain and target domain are different but related to some extent. We need to reduce the distribution difference between source domain and target domain to carry out knowledge transfer, so as to achieve data calibration (Table 2).

Table 2. Comparison of migration and non-migration effects of the same YOLO v5s and YOLO v5x.

Model	Migration	Epoch	Precision	Recall	mAP@0.5	mAP@0.5:0.95
Yolov5s	Yes	250	0.4465	0.583	0.4699	0.3077
Yolov5s	No	250	0.4142	**0.7488**	0.4821	0.3223
Yolov5x	Yes	250	0.4755	0.5456	0.4626	0.2989
Yolov5x	No	250	**0.4971**	0.6335	**0.5145**	**0.3451**

The whole network structure of the source model was migrated, and the parameters were randomly initialized and adjusted adaptively according to the typhoon data set. The basic setup for training is 250 iterations with 16 batches. The effect of the 250th iteration was selected as a comparison. The best model in 500 iterations was selected for testing.

The migration model source uses a small tutorial data set consisting of images from COCO Train2017. Eighty classes were used. In migration training, the first six categories were replaced with typhoon data sets. The other group used a blank model that had not been trained at all. After the exact same training, the untrained model performed better than the migrated model.

Comparison and Analysis Based on Network Layer Depth

Table 3. Comparison of different parameters of four models.

Model	Layers	Parameters	Gradients	GFLOPS
Yolov5s	283	7276605	7276605	17.1
Yolov5m	391	21375645	21375645	51.4
Yolov5l	449	47056765	47056765	115.6
Yolov5x	607	87775965	87775965	219.0

The experiment used four models from YOLO, which respectively contained 283, 391, 449, 607 layers. Among them, YOLOv5s is the network with the smallest depth and width of feature map, and the other three can be considered to be deepened and widened on its basis. YOLOv5s, YOLOv5m, YOLOv5l and YOLOv5x increase successively according to the number of residual structures contained in them. Feature extraction and fusion capabilities of the network are constantly strengthened, and detection accuracy is improved, but the corresponding time costs are also increasing, as shown in Table 3. S has 283 layers, 12 residual components and 1001 convolution kernels. M has 391 layers, 24 residual components and 1488 convolution kernels. L has 449 layers, 36 residual components and 1,984 convolution kernels. X has 607 layers, 48 residual components and 2480 convolution kernels (Table 4).

In the model without migration, the best model was selected after 500 times of training. The test showed that the accuracy and accuracy increased with the increase of model depth. The maximum model had the best effect, with the recognition rate of 99.2% and the accuracy rate of 70.6%, higher than that of the minimum model 64.2%. Increasing the number of samples should further increase the effectiveness of the experiment.

Related parameters in the table are described as follows:

Box: YOLO V5 uses GIOU Loss as the Loss of bounding Box, and Box is presumed to be the mean value of GIOU Loss function. The smaller the value is, the more accurate the detected boxes are.

Val Box: Verification set bounding Box loss.

Table 4. Comparison of migration and non-migration effects of the same model.

Model	Epoch	Precision	Recall	mAP@0.5	mAP@0.5:0.95	Recognition rate (%)	Accuracy of grade prediction (%)
Yolov5s	250	0.4142	0.7488	0.4821	0.3223	97.6%	64.2%
Yolov5m	250	0.4224	0.7106	0.4822	0.3248	98.4%	66.6%
Yolov5l	250	0.4458	0.662	0.4941	0.335	97.6%	**72.2%**
Yolov5x	250	**0.4971**	**0.7335**	**0.5145**	**0.3451**	**99.2%**	70.6%

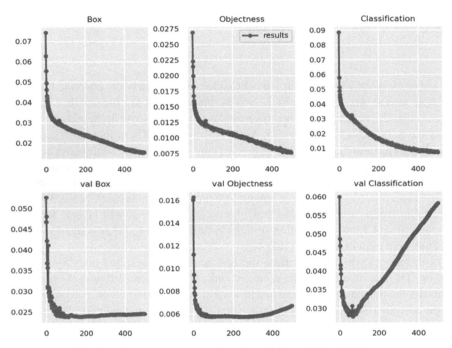

Fig. 3. Yolo V5X ran the loss function of the EPOCH 500 times.

Objectness: it is presumed to be the mean value of Loss for target detection. The smaller the value is, the more accurate the target detection is.

Val Objectness: Verifies the mean value of loss detected by the set target.

Classification: it is presumed to be the average value of loss Classification. The smaller the value is, the more accurate the Classification is.

Val Classification: Average value of verification set Classification loss.

5   Analysis and Discussion

5.1   In a Continuous Sequence, Tropical Cyclones in the Middle Cannot Be Identified

(a)2016.8.1.6   (b) 2016.8.1.12   (c)2016.8.1.18

Fig. 4. A continuous time series of tropical cyclones from 6 o'clock to 18 o'clock on August 1, 2016 identified by YOLO V5X.

Figure 4 shows three images from 6 o'clock to 18 o'clock on August 1, 2016, sorted by time. The existence of tropical cyclones was successfully identified at 6 o'clock and 18 o'clock, but could not be identified at 12 o'clock, possibly because the features were not obvious. Time sequence information, such as LSTM, can be added to increase recognition accuracy.

5.2   Some Tropical Cyclones Identify Two Possibilities

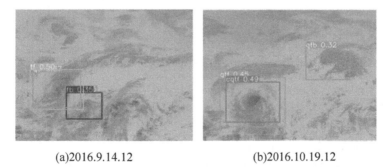

(a)2016.9.14.12   (b)2016.10.19.12

Fig. 5. Yolo V5X identify instances. (a) is 12 o'clock on September 14, 2016, and (b) is 12 o'clock on October 19, 2016. Both identified two possibilities in tropical cyclones.

Figure 5 shows the identification images at 12:00 on September 14, 2016, 12:00 on October 19, 2016, in which tropical cyclones were identified with multiple possibilities. The reason may be due to the self-created data set, the demarcations of marked tropical cyclones had errors, and the characteristics of tropical cyclones with adjacent grades also had similarities. So, it's easy for models to identify tropical cyclones as more likely.

6 Conclusion

In this paper, the model architecture of YoloV5 is used to apply the parameters of deep convolutional neural network to the typhoon cloud map data set to assist in the classification of typhoon intensity. It solves the classification problem of small sample typhoon data in meteorological field and provides an auxiliary decision-making method for typhoon prediction.

(1) In the YOLO model, the migration model was used to verify whether the classification accuracy of typhoon cloud images could be improved. It was found that the non-migration model was significantly better than the migration model after 250 epochs, although the accuracy was improved in the early stage.
(2) Under YOLO model, the recognition effect will increase gradually with the increase of model depth. Due to the size of typhoon and self-created data set, there were errors in the definition of accuracy, which led to the low mAP. However, in the final test, the accuracy rate reached 72.2%.

In the later research, the focus will be on how to add more training parameters when using convolutional neural network, instead of being confined to IR images of typhoons, to add humidity, wind speed and other information, and to consider adding attention mechanism and other methods to improve accuracy and recognition rate. Despite the use of typhoon for 23 years (1994–2016), the number of training samples is still insufficient compared with other deep learning. In the next work, we will further expand the existing work: 1) Research on the optical flow method based on end-to-end deep learning features, and further expand the algorithm of this paper; 2) Research on the multimode optical flow method based on deep learning features the registration of state-deformed images improves the applicability of this algorithm.

References

1. Zhai, A., Jiang, H.: Hurricane economic loss on maximum wind speed and storm size. Environ. Res. Lett. **9**(6), 64019–64027 (2014)
2. Huo, Z.H., Liu, Y.Z., Li, X.L., Qu, A.X.: The preliminary application of tropical cyclone targeted singular vectors in the GRAPES global ensemble forecasts. Acta Meteor. Sin. **78**(1), 48–59 (2019)
3. Dvorak, V.F.: Tropical Cyclone Intensity Analysis Using Satellite Data. NOAA Technical Report NESDIS, pp. 1–47 (1984)
4. Zhou, T., Huo, B.Q., Lu, H.L., Ren, H.L.: Research on residual neural network and its application on medical image processing. Ejournal **53**(2), 129–156 (2017)
5. Jayanthi, N., Manohari, D., Sikkandar, M.Y., Aboamer, M.A., Waly, M.I.: Multi-model detection of lung cancer using unsupervised diffusion classification algorithm. Intell. Autom. Soft Comput. **31**(2), 1317–1329 (2022)
6. Asokan, A., Anitha, J., Patrut, B., Danciulescu, D., Hemanth, D.J.: Deep feature extraction and feature fusion for bi-temporal satellite image classification. Comput. Mater. Continua **66**(1), 373–388 (2021)
7. Dvorak, V.F.: Tropical cyclone intensity analysis and forecasting from satellite imagery. Mon. Wea. Rev **103**, 420–430 (1975)

8. Wang, H.: A numerical study on then structure and intensity changes of Typhon Megi (2010) Nanjing University of Information Science & Technology (2013)
9. Olander, T.L., Velden, C.S.: The advanced Dvorak technique: continued development of an objective scheme to estimate tropical cyclone intensity using geostationary infrared satellite imagery. Wea. Forecasting **22**, 287–298 (2007)
10. Zeng, Z.H., Chen, L.S., Wang, Y.Q., Gao, Z.Q.: A numerical simulation study of super TyphoonSaomei intensity and structure changes. Acta Meteorol. Sin. **67**(5), 750–763 (2006)
11. Qian, Y.Z., Zhang, S.J., Huang, Y.W., Guo, J.M.: Numerical study on sharp enhancement of severe Typhoon Haikui (1211) offshore. J. Trop. Meteorol. **30**(06), 1069–1079 (2014)
12. Zhang, Z., Feng, J., Yan, J., Wang, X., Shu, X.: Ground-based cloud recognition based on dense_sift features. Journal of New Media **1**(1), 1–9 (2019)
13. Zheng, Z.S., Hu, C.Y., Huang, D.M.: Research on transfer learning methods for classification of typhoon cloud image. Rem. Sens. Technol. Appl. **35**(1), 202–210 (2020)
14. Knapp,K.R.: Globally gridded satellite observations for climate studies. Bull. Amer. Meteorol. Soc. **92**(7), 893–907 (2011)
15. Knapp, K.R.: Scientific data stewardship of international satellite cloud climatology project bl global geostationary observations. J. Appl. Remote Sens. **2**(1), 142–154 (2008)

STKE: Temporal Knowledge Graph Embedding in the Spherical Coordinate System

Shibo Wang[1], Ruinan Liu[1], Linshan Shen[1(✉)], and Asad Masood Khattak[2]

[1] College of Computer Science and Technology, Harbin Engineering University, Harbin 150001, China
shenlinshan@hrbeu.edu.cn
[2] College of Technological Innovation, Zayed University, Abu Dhabi 144534, UAE

Abstract. Knowledge graph embedding (KGE) aims to learn the representation of entities and predicates in low-dimensional vector spaces which can complete the missing parts of the Knowledge Graphs (KGs). Nevertheless, temporal knowledge graphs (TKGs) that include time information are more consistent with real-world application scenarios. Meanwhile, the facts with time constraints make the results of reasoning over time more accurate. Because of these, we propose a novel temporal knowledge graph embedding (TKGE) model, namely **S**pherical **T**emporal **K**nowledge Graph **E**mbedding (STKE), which embeds facts into a spherical coordinate system. We treat each fact as a rotation from the subject to the object. The entities and predicates in STKE are divided into three parts--the radial part, the azimuth part, and the polar part. The radial part aims to resize the modulus between two entities. The azimuth part is mainly used to distinguish entities with the same module length and the polar part aims to represent the transformation of the time embedding with the change of polar angle. We evaluate the proposed model via the link prediction task on four typical temporal datasets. Experiments demonstrate that STKE achieves a significant surpass compared with the state-of-the-art static knowledge graph embedding (SKGE) model and TKGE model. In addition, we analyze the representation ability of different facts in the spherical coordinate system and confirm that our model can better represent time-constrained facts.

Keywords: Temporal knowledge graph embedding · The spherical coordinate system · The radial part · The Azimuth part · The polar part

1 Introduction

The Knowledge Graphs is defined as a large-scale knowledge base consisting of entities and predicates, which describes the relations between entities in the real world. KGs are usually collections of factual triples that represent human knowledge in a structured way. As a kind of semantic network, knowledge graphs are widely used in language representation learning [1], question answering [2], semantic information retrieval [3], recommendation systems [4], etc.

In recent years, several sizable KGs have been constructed, including Dbpedia [5], YAGO [6], Nell [7], and Freebase [8]. However, there are still many missing facts that contribute to the incomplete structure and content of KGs. Many implicit predicates between entities have not been fully explored. Link prediction which is to complete missing links between entities based on known links has been proposed. For instance, one can use knowledge graph embedding models to perform an object query like (Kobe Bryant, born, ?). Most facts of the real-world knowledge have a specific period of validity, the inclusion of time information can capture the diversity of distribution of entities and predicates, e.g., (Kobe Bryant, born, ?, 1978–08-23).

Currently, compared with Static Knowledge Graphs (SKGs), fast-growing data often exhibit complex temporal dynamics, which require modeling by assigning temporal properties to entities. SKGs can't reflect information that changes dynamically [9]. TKGE models encode time information in their embeddings and get better performance than traditional KGE models in link prediction. Representative TKGs including GDELT [10], WIKIDATA [11], YAGO, and ICEWS [12], each store evolving knowledge with a time-stamp. The above TKGs store facts in two formats, (s, p, o, t) and $(s, p, o, [t_b, t_e])$, where t_b is the beginning time and t_e is the end time. Previous SKGE models do not capture temporally dynamic embedding facts, leading these models to get an ineffective performance on link prediction tasks.

To tackle this problem, TKGE models embed temporal information into triples including TTransE [13], HyTE [14], Know-Evolve [15], DE-SimplE [16], TA-DistMult [17]. Most of the existing models do not provide a comprehensive representation of the predicate but are only an extension of the previous model like TransE [18] and Dist-Mult [19]. Previous TKGE models usually treat time, entities, and predicates as different vectors in the same space, but in this case, there is no way to distinguish them well.

In this paper, we propose a novel approach for TKGE, namely STKE, which represents the temporal knowledge graph in a spherical coordinate system. We show the limitation of the existing TKGE models and the advantage of our proposed model on learning various predicate patterns over time. This work presents the following contributions:

(1) We propose a novel TKGE model called STKE, which is a translation distance model, and we embed the time-constrained facts into the spherical coordinate system.
(2) We consider entities as a spatial vector from the origin in the sphere coordinate space and each entity contains the radial part r, the azimuth part θ, and the polar part φ. For each fact, we treat the predicate as a rotational deflation matrix from the head entity to the tail entity.
(3) We take the polar part of entities as the time component, and the time-stamp acts only on the polar part and does not affect other components.

We evaluate STKE on the link prediction task, by testing the performance on the benchmark dataset that outperforms several state-of-the-art TKGE models. By testing the performance on the four TKGE datasets, our proposed model performs better than other models on the link prediction task. The experimental results demonstrate that our proposed model specializes in encoding time information and distinguishing the embedding of time-constrained entities.

The rest of this paper is organized as follows. We introduce the notations of our work and the related work about SKGs and TKGs in Sect. 2. Section 3 presents the detail of STKE. Section 4 presents the experimental datasets, protocols, results, and analysis about our model. In Sect. 5, we conclude our work and discuss future work.

2 Related Work

In this section, we define a knowledge graph $\mathcal{G} = (\mathcal{E}, \mathcal{R}, \mathcal{T})$. Let $\mathcal{E}$ denote the set of entities, $\mathcal{R}$ denotes the set of predicates/relations, and $\mathcal{T}$ denotes the set of time-stamps. The facts in TKGs are identified as quintuples $(s, p, o, [t_b, t_e])$, where $s, o \in \mathcal{E}$ are subject and object, $p \in \mathcal{R}$ is the predicate, $t_b, t_e \in \mathcal{T}$ captures the beginning time and the end time when the fact occurs. We regard the corresponding embedding in the boldface lower-case letters $\mathbf{s}, \mathbf{p}, \mathbf{o}, \mathbf{t}$. Meanwhile, we discuss two lines of relevant research which are SKGE and TKGE. Both have a significant amount of work and get good results on link prediction, of which we provide a general summary.

Static Knowledge Graph Embedding Models. SKGE models can be classified into translational models, semantic matching models, and neural network-based models. The translation model treats the process of finding a valid triplet as a translation operation of entities through predicates and measures the plausibility of a fact in terms of the distance between two entities. The most representative classical translation model is TransE. However, TransE does not perform well on multiple predicates, such as 1–N, N–1, and N-N predicates. To expand the representation capabilities of TransE, they use various embedding methods to project entities from entity space to predicate space. TransH [20] abstracts the relational vectors into a hyperplane and maps the head entity vector and the tail entity vector onto that hyperplane. But TransE and TransH still perform translation operations in the same vector space. TransR [21] models entities and relationships in two different vector spaces, namely the entity space and the entity corresponding relationship space, respectively. Recently, RotatE [22] defines each predicate as a rotation in the complex vector space from the source entity to the target entity. RotatE can model symmetric/antisymmetric, inversion, and composition predicates comprehensively. However, translational models are still not able to model the reflexive predicates.

Semantic matching models measure the plausibility of facts using a triangular norm that matches latent semantics of entities and predicates. Embedding entities and predicates into the vector space predict the plausibility of facts to hold so that complementing the knowledge graph. The bilinear model is a typical semantic matching model. It uses predicates to perform bilinear transformations to capture various interactions between facts. Some representative examples of such models include RESCAL [23], DistMult, and ComplEx [24]. RESCAL represents each predicate as a full rank matrix, computing a bilinear product between head and tail entity embedding vectors and predicate matrix by a scoring function. Nevertheless, a large number of parameters makes the model have overfitting issues. DistMult reduces the parameters using a diagonal matrix for each predicate. Both RESCAL and DistMult cannot model asymmetric predicates because the score of the triple is essentially equal to the score of its symmetric triple. To alleviate it, ComplEx extends DistMult to the complex-valued space so that model asymmetric and inverse predicates by embedding the head and tail of the entity in the complex conjugate.

Neural network-based models have received greater attention in recent years. ConvE [25] and ConvKB [26] define the score function using the convolutional neural network. R-GCN [27] proposed a graph convolutional neural network for modeling data with highly multi-relational. R-GCN introduces a transformation matrix for a specific relationship that depends on the type and direction of the edges. However, R-GCN introduces too much parameter matrix, resulting in an explosion of models that cannot be trained. CompGCN [28] embedded entity-relation composition operations into SKG, including Subtraction, Multiplication, Circular-correlation operators. However, several of the above models ignore the embedding of temporal information which cannot capture the real-time changes of facts.

Temporal Knowledge Graph Embedding Models. More recent incorporating information as facts with time constraints on static knowledge graph models can improve the performances. TTransE uses the constraints of temporal information to model the transformation of the predicate which embeds time information into the score function of TransE. TA-DistMult utilizes the score function of DistMult, adding a recurrent neural network to learn time-aware representations of predicates. Meanwhile, TA-DistMult treats time information and predicate as time-encoding sequences. HyTE extends on TransH to embed time directly into the space of entities and relationships by associating each timestamp with the corresponding hyperplane. Since real-world entities maintain predicates over time, time should be embedded into the entity. TeRo [29] defines the temporal evolution of entity embedding as a rotation from the initial time to the current time in the complex vector space. DE SimplE aims to model various relation patterns by embedding time information into diachronic entities. However, it can only represent the fact like (s, p, o, t). RE-NET [30] uses an RNN-based encoder combined with R-GCN to jointly model sequences of facts.

3 Proposed Model

In this section, we detail the proposed model STKE and its three parts--the radial part, the azimuth part, and the polar part. We treat the time-stamp as rotation and scaling of entities in spherical space. Then we propose the score function and the loss function.

3.1 STKE

Most of the existing TKGE models, which were extended from TransE and DistMult, incorporate time information in the embedding space but have limitations on learning transitive predicates or asymmetric predicates as discussed in Sect. 2. On the other hand, previous models have embedded quadruple with temporal information into the model separately, such as (Michael Jordan, Player of, NBA, 1984–09-12) and (Michael Jordan, Player of, NBA, 2003–04-16). It breaks the fact completeness constraint although it is convenient to calculate the score of facts. Therefore, we fuse the two facts into a quintuple as a training sample and embed it into the model (Michael Jordan, Player of, NBA, 1984–09-12, 2003–04-16). In addition to this, temporal information is seen as a constraint on the predicate.

To tackle the limitations of these existing KGE and TKGE models on representation and learning, we propose a new TKGE model, STKE, which maps the facts to the spherical coordinate system. STKE models entities at different levels of the hierarchy and the same level of the hierarchy by modulus and angular parts respectively.

Figure 1 illustrates the way that the facts are embedded under the spherical coordinate system. The blue line indicates the subject **s** and the orange line indicates the object **o**. We regard the polar part φ which represents the transformation of the time embedding with the change of polar angle.

Figure 2 depicts the center profile in a spherical coordinate system without the polar part, i.e., no temporal influence. The azimuth part is represented by θ which represents the transformation of the time embedding with the change of polar angle.

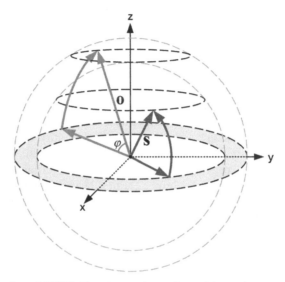

Fig. 1. The illustration of STKE. The picture shows the entities and corresponding time-stamp in a spherical coordinate system.

We embed the quintuples into the spherical coordinate and divide the entities and predicates into three parts--the radial part, the polar angle part, and the azimuth angle part. The subscript r represents the component in the radial part, θ and φ denote the azimuth angle part embedding and the polar angle part. We think of entities and predicates as three parts of a three-part concatenate operation $\mathbf{s} = (\mathbf{s}_r; \mathbf{s}_\theta; \mathbf{s}_\varphi)$, $\mathbf{p} = (\mathbf{p}_r; \mathbf{p}_\theta; \mathbf{p}_\varphi)$, and $\mathbf{o} = (\mathbf{o}_r; \mathbf{o}_\theta; \mathbf{o}_\varphi)$. It is worth noting that our polar angle is different from the polar angle in the regular spherical coordinate system. We consider the polar angle as the angle from the plane where the azimuth angle is located to the radius, not the angle between the normal vector and the radius. For the temporal embedding, we regard the time information as a change in the polar angle of the entities and predicates. In the azimuth part, we transform the normal azimuth angle into its residual angle, which makes it easier for us to understand.

In the radial part, we define predicates as a scaling of the modal length between subject and object. The most commonly used methods for modeling the head entity to tail entity transformation are the translational distance model TransE and the semantic matching model (bilinear) DistMult. It is not advisable to continue expanding the number of parameters due to the introduction of relational embedding, although it reduces the number of parameters of the previous model. Therefore, in this paper, we need to choose the model that utilizes a smaller number of parameters for modeling. As a result, the predicate is considered as a rotation of head entity to tail entity. There are various approaches to modeling relational patterns on the knowledge graph, however, these approaches mainly focus on modeling relational paths explicitly. Rotation models allow implicit learning of relational patterns, which not only have higher scalability but also provide meaningful embedding of entities and predicates.

The formula of the radial part is defined as follows:

$$\mathbf{s}_r \circ \mathbf{p}_r = \mathbf{o}_r \tag{1}$$

where $\mathbf{s}_r$, $\mathbf{p}_r$, and $\mathbf{o}_r \in \mathbb{R}^n$ and $\circ$ represents the Hermitian product. The corresponding score function of the radial part is defined as:

$$d_r(\delta_r) = \|\mathbf{s}_r \circ \mathbf{p}_r - \mathbf{o}_r\|_2 \tag{2}$$

In the azimuth angle part, we think of the predicates as the phase change between two entities in the spherical coordinate space. We convert the matrix of the corresponding part into an angle and calculate it as an angle change. The specific azimuth angle part equation is shown below.

$$(s_\theta + \mathbf{p}_\theta)\mathrm{mod}2\pi = \mathbf{o}_\theta \tag{3}$$

where s_θ, $\mathbf{p}_\theta$ and $\mathbf{o}_\theta \in (0, 2\pi]^n$. The corresponding score function of the azimuth angle part is defined as follows:

$$d_\theta(\delta_\theta) = \|\sin((\mathbf{s}_\theta + \mathbf{p}_\theta - \mathbf{o}_\theta)/2)\|_1 \tag{4}$$

Similarly, in the polar angle part, we also use the same angle processing method. We add the time information and embed it to the subject and object using the angle processing method. We assume the entities without time-stamp are time-independent, the polar angle part is just a time-generated change. The formula is obtained as:

$$\left(\mathbf{s}_\varphi + \mathbf{p}_\varphi\right)\mathrm{mod}2\pi = \mathbf{o}_\varphi \tag{5}$$

where $\mathbf{s}_\varphi$, $\mathbf{p}_\varphi$ and $\mathbf{o}_\varphi \in (0, 2\pi]^n$, $\mathbf{s}_\varphi = \mathbf{t}_b$, $\mathbf{o}_\varphi = \mathbf{t}_e$. The corresponding score function of the polar angle part is defined as follow:

$$d_\varphi\left(\delta_\varphi\right) = \|\sin\left(\left(s_\varphi + p_\varphi - o_\varphi\right)/2\right)\|_1 \tag{6}$$

where $\sin(\cdot)$ denotes sine function of each element.

The whole score function is combined by these three parts. To balance the scores of each part, we add a coefficient μ to each part guaranteeing the proportion of scores for different parts. The formulate as follow:

$$f_t(\delta) = \mu_1 d_r(\delta_r) + \mu_2 d_\varphi\left(\delta_\varphi\right) + \mu_3 d_\theta(\delta_\theta) \tag{7}$$

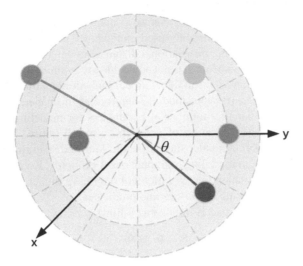

Fig. 2. The center profile in a spherical coordinate system.

3.2 Loss Function

Introducing negative sampling for optimization in the knowledge graph embedding has been shown to have a significant improvement. We use the negative sampling loss function with self-adversarial training of RotatE which samples negative facts according to the current embedding model.

$$p(\delta_j' \delta_i) = \frac{\exp \alpha f_t(\delta_j')}{\sum_i \exp \alpha f_t(\delta_i')} \tag{8}$$

is the distribution of sampling negative quintuples, where δ is a positive sample, δ' is the negative sample, $p(\delta_i')$ is the probability distribution of sampling negative samples and α is the temperature of sampling. The above probability is treated as the weight of the negative sample and the loss function is defined as follow:

$$L = -\log \sigma (\gamma - f_t(\delta))$$
$$\sum_{i=1}^{n} p(\delta_i') \log \sigma \left(f_t(\delta_i') - \gamma\right) \tag{9}$$

of which γ denotes a fixed margin, σ denotes the sigmoid function.

4 Experiments and Analysis

We present the experiments and analysis from four aspects. First, we introduce the commonly used benchmark datasets and the datasets we employ. Second, we detail the experimental settings including evaluation protocol, baselines, and Training Protocol. Third, we then show the experimental results and demonstrate the effectiveness of our model on four benchmark datasets. Finally, we study the contribution of different components of STKE.

4.1 Datasets

Common TKG benchmarks include ICEWS18, ICEWS14, ICEWS05–15, GDELT, and the subsets of YAGO3 (YAGO15k, Wikidata11k, YAGO11k, and Wikidata12k). ICEWS (Integrated Crisis Early Warning System) records political facts with timestamps. ICEWS18 extracted facts from 1/1/2018 to 10/31/2018. ICEWS14 recorded facts from 1/1/2014 to 12/31/2014. GDELT (Global Database of Events, Language, and Tone) is a record of human social behavior events extracted from the news media, including the time and the participants, and the dataset is collected from 1/1/2018 to 10/31/2018. The Wiki and YAGO contain temporal facts with a period time as $(s, p, o, [t_b, t_e])$, where t_b is the beginning time and t_e is the end time. YAGO15k and Wikidata11k only contain start time point or end time point, shaped like 'occurSince 2011' or 'occurSince 2014'. YAGO11k and Wikidata12k include time information and time annotations.

We evaluate our proposed model STKE on the task link prediction using three benchmark datasets, namely ICEWS14, ICEWS05–15, YAGO11k, and Wikidata12k. Link prediction is a widely studied task for solving incompletion of knowledge graphs. The link prediction task uses the existing facts in the knowledge graph to infer the missing facts. Link prediction corresponds to three knowledge graph complementation tasks, predicting head entities $(?, p, o)$, predicting tail entities $(s, p, ?)$ And predicting predicates $(s, ?, o)$. For the temporal knowledge graph, in addition to the prediction of entities and predicates, the prediction of temporal information is also added, i.e. $(?, p, o, t)$, $(s, ?, o, t)$, $(s, p, ?, t)$, $(s, p, o, ?)$.

Table 1. The statistics of datasets, #En and #Pe denote the number of entities and predicates. #Tr, #Va, and #Te denote the number of facts contained in the train set, validation set, and test set, respectively.

Datasets	#En	#Pe	#Tr	#Va	#Te
ICEWS14	7129	230	72826	8941	8963
ICEWS05–15	10488	251	368962	46275	46092
YAGO11k	10623	10	16408	2050	2051
Wikidata12k	12554	24	32497	4062	4062

The two event datasets, ICEWS14, and ICEWS05–15 have been widely used in the previous literature which all time annotations are time points. YAGO11k and Wikidata12k contain time information and time annotations are represented in the various forms of each fact, i.e., [1997–10-12, 2021–10-27] represents the time interval, [1997–10–12, ####-##-##] indicates the start time point and [####-##-##, 2021–10-27] means the end time point. We list the statistics of the four datasets we use in Table 1.

4.2 Experimental Settings

Evaluation Protocol: Following prior work, we evaluate our model on link prediction task over TKGs. The link prediction task aims to complete a time-wise fact with a missing entity which only filters the quintuple appearing in the dataset instead of training validation or test set. For each test quintuple $(s, p, o, [t_b, t_e])$ in the dataset, we replace either the subject s or the object o with each candidate entity to create a set of candidate quintuples. We generate candidate quintuples $(s', p, o, [t_b, t_e])$ or $(s, p, o', [t_b, t_e])$ by replacing the subject s or the object o. Then, we rank the scores of the candidate quintuples in descending order.

We choose two common evaluation metrics MRR and Hits@k. MRR(Mean Reciprocal Rank) is the means of the reciprocal ranks and Hits@k is the number of real quintuples ranked in the top k as a percentage of the total number of real quintuples. The larger the MRR value, the better the prediction performance of the model.

BaseLines: We compare our proposed method with a wide selection of SKGE and TKGE models. SKGE models include TransE, DistMult, and RotatE by ignoring the edge time stamps for all the training events. TKGE models include TTransE, HyTE, and TA-TransE.

Training Protocol: We implement our proposed model STKE in PyTorch and use Adam as the optimizer which finds the best hyperparameters according to the MRR performance on the validation set. The following settings are: the batch size b is in the range of {128, 256, 512, 1024}, the embedding dimensionality n is in the range of {250, 500, 1000}, the negative training samples size η is turned into {128, 256, 512, 1024}, margin γ among {1, 3, 6, 9, 12, 15... 28, 32} and self-adversarial sampling temperature α among {0.5, 1.0}. Regarding optimizer, the learning rate r in a range of {0.0001, 0.00005}.

4.3 Experimental Results

In this part, we show the performance of our proposed model STKE. Tables 2 and 3 summarize the link prediction results by STKE and state-of-the-art methods on three event-based datasets: ICEWS14, ICEWS05–15, and Wikidata12k. Several of the model results used for comparison are taken from previously published papers. From the experimental results, we can see:

In Table 2, On ICEWS14 and ICEWS05–15, STKE achieves better performance than baseline models in most scenarios. Compared to HyTE, STKE improved by 14.1 MRR points, 13.6 MRR points, 6.1 MRR points, and 3.6 MRR points on ICEWS14, ICEWS05–15, YAGO11k, and Wikidata12k respectively.

In Table 3, we simultaneously embed the beginning time t_b and the end time t_e into our model. STKE also surpasses ahead in most of the baseline embedding models. The overall poor performance of the model in YAGO11k compared to Wikidata12k is due to the fact that there are a large number of facts without time information in YAGO11k.

Table 2. Evaluation results on ICEWS14, ICEWS05–15 datasets. Results of DistMult and RotatE are taken from [31].

Datasets	ICEWS14				ICEWS05–15			
Metircs	MRR	Hits@1	Hits@3	Hits@10	MRR	Hits@1	Hits@3	Hits@10
TransE	.280	.094	–	.637	.294	.090	–	.663
DistMult	.439	**.323**	–	.672	**.456**	**.337**	–	.691
RotatE	.418	.291	.478	**.690**	.304	.164	.355	.595
TTransE	.255	.074	–	.601	.271	.084	–	.616
HyTE	.297	.108	.416	.655	.316	.116	.445	.681
TA-TransE	.275	.095	–	.625	.299	.096	–	.668
STKE	**.438**	.315	**.498**	**.690**	.452	.330	**.511**	**.700**

Table 3. Evaluation results on YAGO11k and Wikidata12k dataset. The best results among all models are written boldly.

Datasets	YAGO11k				Wikidata12k			
Metircs	MRR	Hits@1	Hits@1	Hits@1	MRR	Hits@1	Hits@1	Hits@1
TransE	.100	.015	.138	.244	.178	.100	.192	.339
DistMult	.158	.107	.161	.268	**.222**	.119	.238	.460
RotatE	**.167**	.103	**.167**	**.305**	.221	.116	.236	**.461**
TTransE	.108	.020	.150	.251	.172	.096	.184	.329
HyTE	.105	.015	.143	.272	.180	.098	.197	.333
TA-TransE	.161	.027	.160	.326	.178	.030	**.267**	.429
STKE	.166	**.119**	.165	.262	.216	**.120**	.230	.432

4.4 Analysis

In this section, we analyze the representation ability of the embedding model with time-constrained facts. We project the embedded time-constrained entities onto the 3D plane to visualize entity embeddings intuitively. In the whole model, we embed the whole fact under the spherical coordinate system so that we can be well presented in the 3D visualization space.

According to the introduction in Sect. 3, we process all the data as follows:

In the radial part, we use the mean value of all points to represent the modulus of entities. Since the embedding range is small, we use a logarithmic scale to better show the differences between entities. Also, due to the fact that we use a different spherical coordinate system than normal, our coordinates can be expressed as:

$$
\begin{cases}
x = r \cos \varphi \sin \theta \\
y = r \cos \varphi \cos \theta \\
z = r \sin \varphi
\end{cases}
\tag{10}
$$

Figure 3 and Fig. 4 show the visualization of entity embedding in ICEWS05–15. Figure 3 illustrates the distribution of entity 9 and entity 11 in the spherical coordinate system. Figure 4 depicts the distribution of entity 31 and entity 32 in the same situation.

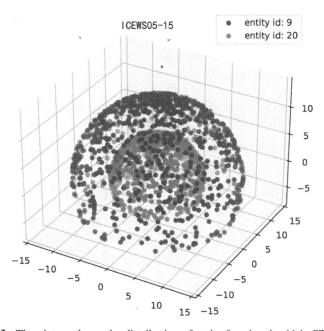

Fig. 3. The picture shows the distribution of entity 9 and entity 11 in STKE.

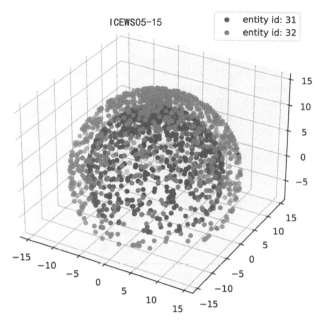

Fig. 4. The picture shows the distribution of entity 31 and entity 32 in STKE.

5 Conclusion

In this paper, we proposed STKE, a novel TKGE model which maps facts into the spherical polar coordinate system. STKE consists of two parts-the modulus part and the angular part-which can alleviate similar facts caused by temporal embeddings. Also, STKE treats temporal changes as scaling and rotation of entities embeddings in the spherical polar coordinate system. Through extensive experiments on knowledge graph link prediction tasks, we showed the effectiveness of STKE over existing state-of-art TKGE models and demonstrated its capability in distinguishing different time-constrained entities. In addition, we investigate the effect of entity embedding at different times and the performance in different time units. Further, we will extend the time constraint to more conditional constraints while maintaining high-precision predictions.

Acknowledgement. This work is supported by Basic Research Program (No. JCKY2019604B002) and Network threat depth analysis software (No. KY10800210013).

Conflicts of Interest. The authors declare that they have no conflicts of interest to report regarding the present study.

References

1. Zhou, H.J., Shen, T.T., Liu, X.L., Zhang, Y.R.: Knowledge graph: a survey of approaches and applications knowledge graph. J. Artif. Intell. **2**(2), 89–101 (2020)

2. Deng, C., Zeng, G., Cai, Z., Xiao, X.: A survey of knowledge based question answering with deep learning. J. Artif. Intell. **2**(4), 157–166 (2020)
3. Velu, A., Thangavelu, M.: Ontology based ocean knowledge representation for semantic information retrieval. Comput. Mater. Continua **70**(3), 4707–4724 (2022)
4. Li, T., Li, H., Zhong, S., Kang, Y., Zhang, Y.: Knowledge graph representation reasoning for recommendation system. J. New Media **2**(1), 21–30 (2020)
5. Aberer, K., et al. (eds.): ASWC/ISWC -2007. LNCS, vol. 4825. Springer, Heidelberg (2007). https://doi.org/10.1007/978-3-540-76298-0
6. Suchanek, F.M., Kasneci, G., Weikum, G.: Yago: a core of semantic knowledge. In: Proceedings of the 16th International Conference on World Wide Web, pp. 697–706 (2007)
7. Carlson, A., Betteridge, J., Kisiel, B.: Toward an architecture for never-ending language learning. In: Twenty-Fourth AAAI Conference on Artificial Intelligence, pp. 1306–1313 (2010)
8. Bollacker, K., Evans, C., Paritosh, P.: Freebase: a collaboratively created graph database for structuring human knowledge. In: Proceedings of the 2008 ACM SIGMOD International Conference on Management of data, pp. 1247–1250 (2008)
9. Ahn, Y., Jeong, O.: Time-aware polarisx: auto-growing knowledge graph. Comput. Mater. Continua **67**(3), 2695–2708 (2021)
10. Leetaru, K., Schrodt, P.A.: Gdelt: global data on events, location, and tone. ISA Ann. Convention **2**, 1–49 (1979)
11. Erxleben, F., Günther, M., Krötzsch, M.: Introducing Wikidata to the linked data web. In: International Semantic Web Conference, pp. 50–65. Springer (2014). https://doi.org/10.1007/978-3-319-11964-9_4
12. Lautenschlager, J., Shellman, S., Ward, M.: Icews event aggregations. Harv. Dataverse **3** (2015)
13. Jiang, T., Liu, T., Ge, T.: Encoding temporal information for time-aware link prediction. In: Proceedings of the 2016 Conference on Empirical Methods in Natural Language Processing, pp. 2350–2354 (2016)
14. Dasgupta, S.S., Ray, S.N., Talukdar, P.: Hyte: Hyperplane-based temporally aware knowledge graph embedding. In: Proceedings of the 2018 Conference on Empirical Methods in Natural Language Processing, pp. 2001–2011 (2018)
15. Trivedi, R., Dai, H., Wang, Y.: Know-evolve: deep temporal reasoning for dynamic knowledge graphs. In: International Conference on Machine Learning, pp. 3462–3471 (2017)
16. Goel, R., Kazemi, S.M., Brubaker, M.: Diachronic embedding for temporal knowledge graph completion. In: Proceedings of the AAAI Conference on Artificial Intelligence **34**, 3988–3995 (2020)
17. García-Durán, A., Dumančić, S., Niepert, M.: Learning sequence encoders for temporal knowledge graph completion. arXiv preprint arXiv:1809.03202 (2018)
18. Bordes, A., Usunier, N., Garcia-Duran, A.: Translating embeddings for modeling multi-relational data. Adv. Neural Inf. Process. Syst. **26** (2013)
19. Yang, B., Yih, W.T., He, X., Gao, J., Deng, L.: Embedding entities and relations for learning and inference in knowledge bases. arXiv preprint arXiv:1412.6575 (2014)
20. Wang, Z., Zhang, J., Feng, J.L.: Knowledge graph embedding by translating on hyperplanes. In: Proceedings of the AAAI Conference on Artificial Intelligence, pp. 1112–1119 (2014)
21. Lin, Y., Liu, Z.Y., Sun, M.S.: Learning entity and relation embeddings for knowledge graph completion. In: Twenty-ninth AAAI Conference on Artificial Intelligence, pp. 2181–2187 (2015)
22. Sun, Z., Deng, Z.H., Nie, J.Y., Tang, J.: Rotate: Knowledge graph embedding by relational rotation in complex space. arXiv preprint arXiv:1902.10197 (2019)
23. Nickel, M., Tresp, V., Kriegel, H.P.: A three-way model for collective learning on multi-relational data. In: The 28th International Conference on Machine Learning (2011)

24. Trouillon, T., Welbl, J., Riedel, S.: Complex embeddings for simple link prediction. In: International Conference on Machine Learning, pp. 2071–2080 (2016)
25. Dettmers, T., Minervini, P., Stenetorp, P.: Convolutional 2D knowledge graph embeddings. In: Thirty-second AAAI Conference on Artificial Intelligence (2018)
26. Nguyen, D.Q., Nguyen, T.D., Nguyen, D.Q., Phung, D.: A novel embedding model for knowledge base completion based on convolutional neural network. arXiv preprint arXiv:1712.02121 (2017)
27. Schlichtkrull, M., Kipf, T.N., Bloem, P., Van Den Berg, R., Titov, I., Welling, M.: Modeling relational data with graph convolutional networks. In: European Semantic Web Conference, pp. 593–607. Springer, Cham (2018). https://doi.org/10.1007/978-3-319-93417-4_38
28. Vashishth, S., Sanyal, S., Nitin, V., Talukdar, P.: Composition-based multi-relational graph convolutional networks. arXiv preprint arXiv:1911.03082 (2019)
29. Xu, C., Nayyeri, M., Alkhoury, F., Yazdi, H.S., Lehmann, J.: Tero: A time-aware knowledge graph embedding via temporal rotation. arXiv preprint arXiv:2010.01029 (2020)
30. Jin, W., Jiang, H., Qu, M., Chen, T., Zhang, C., Szekely, P., Ren, X.: Recurrent event network: global structure inference over temporal knowledge graph. In: Eighth International Conference on Learning Representations (2020)
31. Xu, C., Nayyeri, M., Alkhoury, F., Yazdi, H.S., Lehmann, J.: Temporal knowledge graph embedding model based on additive time series decomposition. arXiv preprint arXiv:1911.07893 (2019)

Improved VGG-16 Neural Network for Parameter Reduction

Zheng Jiang[1], Kaiwen Zou[1], Jiangyuan Yao[1(✉)], Deshun Li[1], and Xingcan Cao[2]

[1] Hainan University, Haikou 570228, China
yaojy@hainanu.edu.cn

[2] University of British Columbia, Vancouver, BC V6T1Z1, Canada

Abstract. With the development of Deep Learning, image recognition technology has been applied in many aspects. And convolutional neural networks have played a key role in realizing image recognition under the increasing computing power and massive data. However, if developers want to implement the training of convolutional neural networks and achieve the subsequent applications in scenarios such as personal computers, IoT devices, and embedded platforms with low Graphics Processing Units(GPUs) memory, a large number of parameters during training of convolutional neural networks is a great challenge. Therefore, this paper uses depthwise separable convolution to optimize the classic convolutional neural network model VGG-16 to solve this problem. And the VGG-16-JS model is proposed using the Inception structure dimensionality reduction and depthwise separable convolution on the VGG-16 convolutional neural network model. Finally, this paper compares the classification success rates of VGG-16 and VGG-16-JS for the application scenario of the COVID-19 mask-wearing. A series of reliable experimental data show that the improved VGG-16-JS model significantly reduces the number of parameters required for model training without a significant drop in the success rate. It solves the GPU memory requirements for training neural networks to a certain extent.

Keywords: VGG-16 · Deep learning · Convolutional neural networks

1 Introduction

Deep Learning has revolutionized many aspects of our lives, improving the usability and correctness of applications such as natural language processing(NLP) [7], speech recognition [3], image recognition [12], et al. For the field of image recognition, the commonly used implementation method is to use convolutional neural network(CNN) [15], and the training of the current convolutional neural network model is mostly limited to high-performance computing platforms with strong computing power and large GPU memory. The popularity of deep learning applications has increased the demand for high-performance computing platforms in the industry.

With the development of embedded systems, it has gradually become the main component of the Internet of Things(IoT). The wide application of IoT has also made the embedded platform solutions based on deep learning valued by scholars. IoT solutions based on convolutional neural networks have better capabilities in the fields of classification and identification [2]. AlexNet [13], VGG-13/VGG-16/VGG-19 [20], GoogLeNet [22], ResNet [9], MobileNet [10], OverFeat [25]. Most CNN contains an input layer, multiple convolutional layers, multiple subsampling layers (and some max-pooling layers), multiple layers of full connection. CNN passes the input file through these layers, and finally completes the classification and recognition task.

However, the current production capacity reduction due to the COVID-19 has reduced the supply of GPUs. At the same time, the rise of Bitcoin price and the prevalence of mining around the world have greatly increased the demand for GPUs. This led to an increase in the price of GPUs used for CNN model training and a shortage of stock at one point. The expensive Tesla series discourages individual users, but the memory capacity and computing power of its own GPU make the training of CNN models difficult. CNN is characterized by high computational load and large memory usage. Currently, the GPUs type, memory, occupancy rate used by PC and the required parameters of VGG-16 with a batch size of 64 are shown in Table 1.

Table 1. The proportion of graphics card users, graphics card memory and support for VGG-16 neural network in the fourth quarter of 2021 according to Steam statistics

Model number	Occupancy	GPU memory(GB)	Availability
NIVIDIA GeForce GTX 1060	8.19%	3/6	−
NIVIDIA GeForce GTX 1650	5.97%	4	−
NIVIDIA GeForce GTX 1050 Ti	5.75%	4	−
NIVIDIA GeForce RTX 2060	5.64%	6/12	+
NIVIDIA GeForce GTX 1050	3.14%	2/3	−
NIVIDIA GeForce GTX 1660 Ti	2.87%	6	−
NIVIDIA GeForce GTX 1660 SUPER	2.62%	6	−
NIVIDIA GeForce GTX 1070	2.50%	8	+
NIVIDIA GeForce GTX 2070 SUPER	2.12%	8	+
NIVIDIA GeForce GTX 1660	2.05%	6	−
VGG-16 with 64 batch size		7.2	

The characteristics of CNN also pose challenges to embedded systems. The core of solving this problem is to reduce the amount of parameters required for training as much as possible while ensuring that the accuracy of CNN does not drop significantly after training. Therefore, it is necessary to optimize the CNN convolutional neural network to reduce the parameters required for training.

This paper uses depthwise separable convolution [6] to optimize the VGG-16 network model, presents VGG-16-JS and successfully reduces the amount of parameters of the training model significantly without reducing the accuracy.

The rest of the paper is organized as follows. Section 2 are related works, including convolutional neural networks and depthwise separable convolutions. Section 3 presents an improved CNN model VGG-16-JS, Sect. 4 is experiments and analysis, and Sect. 5 concludes the paper.

2 Related Work

2.1 Convolutional Neural Networks

Convolutional Neural Networks were first proposed in 1988 [8]. Compared with DNN [14], CNN has a more capable visual processing system, can process 2D and 3D images, and can effectively learn and extract image features. CNNs are algorithms that are trained through gradient-based learning and are less affected by decreasing gradients.

AlexNet. AlexNet neural network was the champion network of ISLVRC 2012 competition in 2012, it improved the classification accuracy from 70%+ to 80%+. The network uses GPU equipment for network acceleration training for the first time, uses the ReLU activation [1] function for the first time, and uses dropout [24] to randomly deactivate neurons in the first two layers of the fully connected layer, which effectively reducing the phenomenon of overfitting. It also denote the operations of convolution, pooling, and full connection as C, M, D. The structure of AlexNet is to use the input of [224, 224, 3] to perform eight-layer operations in sequence, namely C1, M1, C2, M2, C3, C4, M3, D1, D2 and finally get a 1×1000 output.

VGG. The VGG neural network is divided into six versions, A-E and A-LRN, where the most used is the D configuration in the VGG neural network, that is, the VGG-16 neural network. The number 16 means that there are 13 Convolution layers and 3 FullyConnected+ReLU layers in this configuration. The network reduces parameters by stacking multiple 3×3 convolution kernels instead of one large-scale convolution kernel. The 5×5 convolution kernel is replaced by stacking two 3×3 convolution kernels, which means that two 3×3 convolution kernels have the same receptive field as a 5×5 convolution kernel. The final Soft-max function [17] converts the predictions into probability distributions. The VGG model is composed of multiple convolutional layers and pooling layers stacked, so it is easy to construct a relatively deep network structure. VGG-16 has a large amount of parameters and a high fitting ability. But at the same time, the shortcomings are also obvious. The training time of the VGG-16 model is too long, the parameter adjustment is difficult, and the required storage capacity is also large, which is not conducive to deployment. Because of the above shortcomings, the application of the VGG-16 neural network model generally adopts the transfer learning method, that is, the pre-training method [11]. Some scholars have achieved some work based on VGG-16 for dealing with covid-19 [4,5]. Some scholars have also implemented Vispnn, a VGG-inspired random pooling neural network [23]. The model of the VGG-16 neural network is shown in Fig. 1.

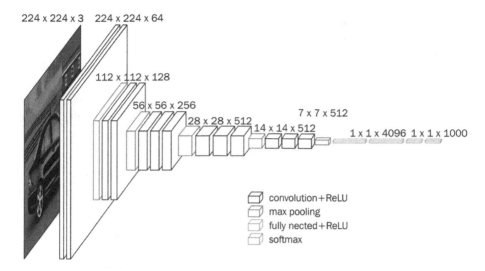

Fig. 1. VGG-16 convolutional neural network structure diagram

GoogLeNet. GoogLeNet was proposed by the Google team. The network introduced the Inception structure, through which the feature information of different scales can be fused. The network in AlexNet and VGG is a serial structure, which is a series of convolutional layers and maximum subsampling layers in series. GoogLeNet presents Inception Module [18]. The "Inception Module, native version" is a parallel structure. The feature matrix of the output of the previous layer is simultaneously input into the four branches for processing, and then the obtained four feature matrices are spliced according to the depth to obtain the output feature matrix. The two Inception structures are shown in Fig. 2.

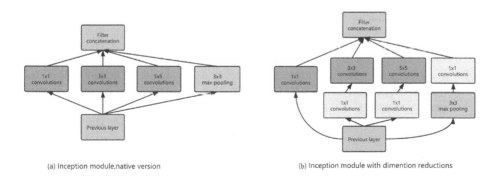

(a) Inception module,native version

(b) Inception module with dimention reductions

Fig. 2. Two types of Inception structure

The network also adds two auxiliary classifiers to optimize training on the outputs of Inception and Inception during the training of the network. Both AlexNet and VGG have only one output layer, while GoogLeNet has three output layers, two of which are auxiliary classification layers. Besides, only an average pooling layer is used in GoogLeNet instead of a fully connected layer, which greatly reduces the parameters of the model. Recently, P Sreedhar et al. have presented a classification similarity network model for image fusion using GoogLeNet [21].

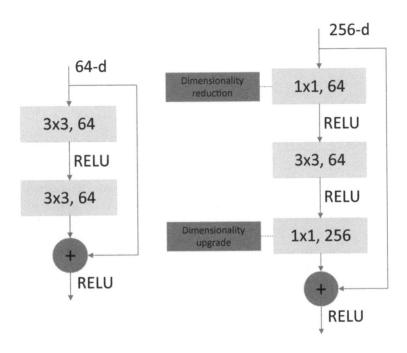

Fig. 3. Comparison of two residual structures

ResNet. The ResNet network has an ultra-deep network structure that exceeds 1000 layers and has a Residual module. ResNet discards dropout and uses Batch Normalization (BN algorithm) to speed up the training process of the model. Practices have proved that the network of various depths obtained by stacking convolutional layers and maximum subsampling layers is not the deeper the higher accuracy. As the number of network layers deepens, assuming that the error gradient of each layer is a number less than 1. In the process of backpropagation [19], each forward propagation will be multiplied by a coefficient less than 1, which will cause the gradient to disappear; Similarly, it is assumed that the error gradient of each layer is a number greater than 1. During the process of backpropagation, each forward propagation will be multiplied by a coefficient greater than 1, which will lead to the phenomenon of gradient explosion. The phenomenon of gradient disappearance and gradient explosion is generally solved by normalizing the data, weight initialization, and the BN method. For the degradation problem, the Residual method can be used to solve it. The input feature matrix in the Residual module is subjected to Converlution, ReLU, and Converlution operations with 64 3×3 convolution kernels to obtain the output, and then the original feature matrix transmitted by the shortcut with the feature matrix is used for parameter accumulation and ReLU. I. Muthumani et al. have presents a ResNet cnn with lstm based tmail text detection video framework [16]. The two Residual structures are shown in Fig. 3.

MobileNet. Traditional convolutional neural networks have high memory requirements and large computational load, which makes them unable to run on mobile devices and embedded devices. MobileNet focuses on mobile or embedded devices, and greatly reduces model parameters and computation while ensuring a small drop in accuracy. MobileNet v1 uses Depthwise Convolution(DW Convolution)and two hyper parameters α, β to reduce the amount of parameters.

Conclude. Inspired by the classical CNN model and the DW convolution proposed by the MobileNet network, we upgrade the VGG-16 combined with the Pointwise convolution(PW convolution).

2.2 Depthwise Separable Convolutions

The comparison between traditional convolution and Depthwise separable convolution which includes DW convolution and PW convolution is shown in Fig. 4. For a feature matrix with an input feature matrix of 3, four convolution kernels are used for convolution, and the depth of each convolution kernel is the same as the depth of the feature matrix. The depth of the output feature matrix is the same as the number of convolution kernels. Four convolution kernels with a depth of 3 are selected for convolution, and the depth of the output feature matrix is 4. In comparison, the depth of each convolution kernel in DW convolution is 1, which does not need to be the same as the depth of the input matrix. Each convolution kernel is only responsible for convolving with one depth layer of the input feature matrix and generating one depth layer of the output feature matrix. Therefore, the number of convolution kernels needs to be the same as the depth of the input feature matrix, which is also the same as the depth of the input feature matrix.

3   VGG-16-JS

In order to solve the problem of the huge amount of training parameters required for VGG-16 due to the introduction of deep convolutional neural networks, an improvement of the VGG-16 network was proposed, named VGG-16-JS.

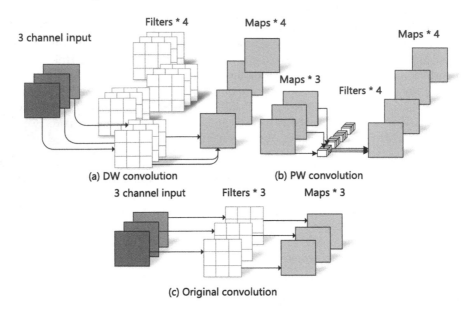

Fig. 4. Comparison diagram of traditional convolution and DW convolution process

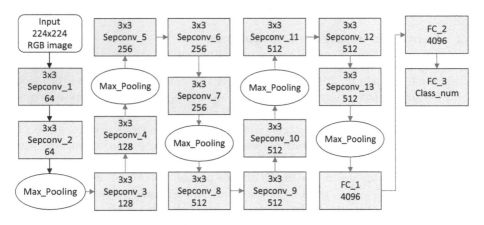

Fig. 5. VGG-16-JS convolutional neural network flowchart

VGG-16-JS combines the advantages of GooLeNet in Sect. 2.1 and MobileNet in Sect. 2.1. One is to use the 1×1 convolution kernel dimension reduction operation of the Inception structure in GoogLeNet, which reduces the dimension and then convolutes before each convolution to reduce the required parameters. The second is based on the feature of the depthwise separable convolution (SeparableConv2D), which contains the Depthwise Convolution structure and the Pointwise Convolution structure, in MobileNet. The depthwise separable convolution has the characteristics of first convolution and dimensionality reduction and then feature extraction, which can greatly reduce the parameters required for convolution.

VGG-16-JS does not involve the method of splicing multi-branch convolutions in the depth direction in the Inception structure, but only draws on the idea of using 1×1 convolution kernel convolution to reduce dimensionality to reduce training parameters. Its specific implementation is to reduce the parameters required for training by reducing the depth of the feature matrix, and finally achieve the goal of reducing the amount of calculation. The structure diagram is shown in Fig. 5.

4   Experiments and Analysis

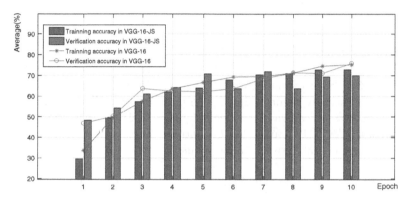

Fig. 6. The rising trend of training accuracy of VGG-16 and VGG-16-JS based on the Mask-CNN dataset (where the bar graph represents VGG-16-JS, and the line graph represents VGG-16)

We used a Windows 10 PC with Nvidia GeForce GTX1060 6 GB GPU, AMD Ryzen 5 3400G CPU, 16 GB RAM. The VGG-16-JS convolutional neural network model was built using TensorFlow2.5, Nvidia CUDA11.2, and Python3.8 as the experimental environment.

We use Mask-CNN[1] as the dataset for training and validation of VGG-16-JS and VGG-16. Mask-CNN can be used to classify images for facial mask detection. The dataset consists of nearly 12K images and is almost 328.92MB in size.

We divide the dataset into two parts: training set and validation set. The training set is used to train the convolutional neural network model, and the validation set is used to verify the accuracy of the network after training.

We take 64 as the batch size, and perform 10 epoch each time, and conduct a total of 20 experiments. The weights file is cleared after each experiment, and the average result is shown as Fig. 6.

---

[1] https://www.kaggle.com/dyiyacao/mask-cnn/data.

It can be seen that with the increase of the number of epochs, the training accuracy and verification accuracy of VGG-16 and VGG-16-JS gradually increase. After 10 epoch iterations, the average validation accuracy of VGG-16-JS reaches 73.76%, while the average validation accuracy of VGG-16 is 75.85%. The rate at which the accuracy rate of VGG-16-JS increases with the increase of epoch does not decrease significantly, and the average validation accuracy rate is 2.09% lower than that of VGG-16. This can prove that the accuracy of VGG-16-JS is not much reduced compared to VGG-16. By counting the number of parameters required for each layer of VGG-16 and VGG-16-JS, we can obtain that the total number of parameters required by the VGG-16 neural network model is 70,303,557, while the number of parameters required by VGG-16-JS is 57,261,024.

The improved VGG-16-JS requires 18.5% less parameters than VGG-16, while the classification accuracy did not decrease much.

5 Conclusion

After VGG-16-JS reduces some parameters, it can be seen that the usage of GPU memory is significantly reduced during the training process of the model. After many experiments, the average accuracy of VGG-16-JS is not significantly lower than that of the VGG-16 neural network model. This optimization of the VGG-16 convolutional neural network model is useful when the dataset is large. The reduction of parameters also facilitates the training of the VGG convolutional neural network model on personal hosts and embedded systems with relatively limited GPU devices. VGG-16-JS has the advantages of fewer training parameters and faster training speed. This not only improves performance but reduces the required hardware specifications by a notch, which can greatly reduce R&D costs.

The main innovation is that on the basis of analyzing the basic structure and operation process of VGG-16 neural network, the VGG-16 neural network is improved by VGG-16-JS using dimension reduction and depthwise separable convolution.

The improved algorithm VGG-16-JS successfully achieves the function of significantly reducing the training parameters on the premise that the accuracy is not affected and the overall structure of VGG-16 does not change much. This reduces the GPU memory threshold and training time required to train VGG-16 convolutional neural networks.

When using deep learning technology to identify and classify images, although the improved VGG-16 algorithm is used, the memory requirements for training neural network models are reduced to a certain extent, and the training time is shortened. The training time required is still not short. In future research, we will consider using distributed data analysis solutions as well as distributed training schemes to reduce training time.

Acknowledgements. This work was supported by the Hainan Provincial Natural Science Foundation of China (620RC562, 2019RC096, 620RC560), the Scientific Research Setup Fund of Hainan University (KYQD(ZR)1877), the Program of Hainan Association for Science and Technology Plans to Youth R&D Innovation (QCXM201910), and the National Natural Science Foundation of China (61802092, 62162021).

References

1. Agarap, A.F.: Deep learning using rectified linear units (relu). arXiv preprint arXiv:1803.08375 (2018)
2. Alippi, C., Disabato, S., Roveri, M.: Moving convolutional neural networks to embedded systems: the alexnet and vgg-16 case. In: 2018 17th ACM/IEEE International Conference on Information Processing in Sensor Networks (IPSN), pp. 212–223 (2018). https://doi.org/10.1109/IPSN.2018.00049
3. Amodei, D., et al.: Deep speech 2: end-to-end speech recognition in English and Mandarin. In: International Conference on Machine Learning, pp. 173–182. PMLR (2016)
4. Binsawad, M., Albahar, M., Sawad, A.: Vgg-covidnet: Bi-branched dilated convolutional neural network for chest x-ray-based covid-19 predictions. Comput. Mater. Continua, 2791–2806 (2021)
5. Buvana, M., Muthumayil, K., Kumar, S.S., Nebhen, J., Alshamrani, S.S., Ali, I.: Deep optimal vgg16 based covid-19 diagnosis model. Comput. Mate. Continua, 43–58 (2021)
6. Chollet, F.: Xception: deep learning with depthwise separable convolutions. In: Proceedings of the IEEE Conference on Computer Vision and Pattern Recognition, pp. 1251–1258 (2017)
7. Collobert, R., W.J.: A unified architecture for natural language processing: deep neural networks with multitask learning. In: Proceedings of the Twenty-Fifth International Conference on Machine Learning (ICML 2008), Helsinki, Finland, 5–9 June 2008 (2008)
8. Fukushima, K.: Neocognitron: a hierarchical neural network capable of visual pattern recognition. Neural Netw. **1**(2), 119–130 (1988)
9. He, K., Zhang, X., Ren, S., Sun, J.: Deep residual learning for image recognition. In: Proceedings of the IEEE Conference on Computer Vision and Pattern Recognition, pp. 770–778 (2016)
10. Howard, A.G., et al.: Mobilenets: efficient convolutional neural networks for mobile vision applications. arXiv preprint arXiv:1704.04861 (2017)
11. Hu, Z., Dong, Y., Wang, K., Chang, K.W., Sun, Y.: GPT-GNN: generative pre-training of graph neural networks. In: Proceedings of the 26th ACM SIGKDD International Conference on Knowledge Discovery & Data Mining, pp. 1857–1867 (2020)
12. Huang, G., Liu, Z., Maaten, L., Weinberger, K.Q.: 2017 IEEE Conference on Computer Vision and Pattern Recognition (CVPR) - Densely Connected Convolutional Networks (CVPR) (2017)
13. Krizhevsky, A., Sutskever, I., Hinton, G.E.: Imagenet classification with deep convolutional neural networks. Adv. Neural Inf. Process. Syst. **25**, 1097–1105 (2012)
14. Li, G., et al.: Understanding error propagation in deep learning neural network (DNN) accelerators and applications. In: Proceedings of the International Conference for High Performance Computing, Networking, Storage and Analysis, pp. 1–12 (2017)

15. Long, J., Shelhamer, E., Darrell, T.: Fully convolutional networks for semantic segmentation. In: Proceedings of the IEEE Conference on Computer Vision and Pattern Recognition, pp. 3431–3440 (2015)

16. Muthumani, I., Malmurugan, N., Ganesan, L.: Resnet CNN with LSTM based Tamil text detection from video frames. Intell. Autom. Soft Comput. **31**(2), 917–928 (2022)

17. Peng, H., Li, J., Song, Y., Liu, Y.: Incrementally learning the hierarchical softmax function for neural language models. In: Proceedings of the AAAI Conference on Artificial Intelligence, vol. 31, no. 1 (2017). https://ojs.aaai.org/index.php/AAAI/article/view/10994

18. Poma, X.S., Riba, E., Sappa, A.: Dense extreme inception network: towards a robust cnn model for edge detection. In: Proceedings of the IEEE/CVF Winter Conference on Applications of Computer Vision, pp. 1923–1932 (2020)

19. Rumelhart, D.E., Durbin, R., Golden, R., Chauvin, Y.: Backpropagation: the basic theory. Backpropagat. Theory Arch. Appl., 1–34 (1995)

20. Simonyan, K., Zisserman, A.: Very deep convolutional networks for large-scale image recognition. arXiv preprint arXiv:1409.1556 (2014)

21. Sreedhar, P., Satya, S., Nandhagopal, N.: Classification similarity network model for image fusion using resnet50 and googlenet. Intell. Autom. Soft Comput. **31**(3), 1331–1344 (2022)

22. Szegedy, C., et al.: Going deeper with convolutions. In: Proceedings of the IEEE Conference on Computer Vision and Pattern Recognition, pp. 1–9 (2015)

23. Wang, S.H., Khan, M.A., Zhang, Y.D.: VISPNN: VGG-inspired stochastic pooling neural network. Comput. Mater. Continua **70**(2), 3081–3097 (2022). https://doi.org/10.32604/cmc.2022.019447

24. Wu, H., Gu, X.: Towards dropout training for convolutional neural networks. Neural Netw. **71**, 1–10 (2015)

25. Zeiler, M.D., Fergus, R.: Visualizing and understanding convolutional networks. In: Fleet, D., Pajdla, T., Schiele, B., Tuytelaars, T. (eds.) ECCV 2014. LNCS, vol. 8689, pp. 818–833. Springer, Cham (2014). https://doi.org/10.1007/978-3-319-10590-1_53

Directly Recognize Who a Specific Pedestrian is with a Surveillance Camera

Xingye Li, Jin Liu$^{(\boxtimes)}$, and Zijun Yu

College of Information Engineering, Shanghai Maritime University, Shanghai, China
jinliu@shmtu.edu.cn

Abstract. In recent years, with the rapid development of large-scale network camera-based data mining and face recognition, the demand and technical feasibility of face recognition with surveillance cameras are increasing. In practical applications such as violation detection, we often have to not only find the violation but also recognize who the violator is directly from the surveillance video. However, in the monitoring scene, the occlusion of other pedestrians, unclear monitoring videos, poor monitoring angle, and excessive distance between target and camera are still pose a challenge to accurate recognition. For the sake of convenience, we refer to the above-mentioned task of recognizing a specific target from surveillance video as specific pedestrian recognition. In order to realize competitive real-time recognition in real-world scenarios, we divide the specific pedestrian recognition into three sub-problems, pedestrian tracking, face detection and face recognition. We first use the Kernelized Correlation Filters to perform pedestrian tracking, which eliminates the occlusion problem and effectively obtains the target image for face detection. Then, for the comprehensive consideration of speed and accuracy, we chose Yolov4 as the face detector based on the concept of cross-dataset evaluation. And in order to make the face detection module more convenient and effective to deploy to various scenarios, we modified Yolov4 to be anchor-free. Finally, we used ResNet-50 and Arcface loss function to extract facial features for cluster analysis of face recognition. Through the above methods, we have achieved a competitive recognition performance in the surveillance video. And through the practice in a real project, it is shown that our system can be effectively deployed in real-time specific pedestrian recognition tasks with the surveillance cameras.

Keywords: Specific pedestrian recognition · Face detection · Anchor-free

1 Introduction

With the continuous breakthrough of some related work [2, 5, 9, 18, 22, 29] on computer vision and data mining technology that can be used for large-scale network cameras, specific pedestrian recognition has become an achievable topic with a wide range of application prospects. Specific pedestrian recognition is a task aimed at recognizing who a specific pedestrian targets is in a surveillance video. It has a wide application prospect in many fields such as security, traffic and even in environmental protection.

X. Sun et al. (Eds.): ICAIS 2022, CCIS 1586, pp. 317–326, 2022.
https://doi.org/10.1007/978-3-031-06767-9_26

Different from face recognition, the target that needs to be recognized in specific pedestrian recognition tasks often does not have a clear front face, and even other factors such as video clarity, camera angle, and distance between the camera and the target are usually difficult to ensure that they are good, which also makes specific pedestrian recognition more challenging than traditional face recognition. Therefore, in order to achieve specific pedestrian recognition, we divided the task into three steps, which are also popular tasks that are widely studied in the field of computer vision: pedestrian tracking, face detection, and face recognition. In other words, specific pedestrian recognition can be considered as a comprehensive application of pedestrian tracking, face detection, and face recognition.

Although much previous work [6–8, 11, 12, 16, 17] whether in the field of pedestrian tracking, face detection or face recognition, has achieved good accuracy rates, there are still very few detectors that can be used for real-time detection. And even these detectors [13–15, 19, 20] that can detect in real time also suffer from a lack of accuracy as well as being more susceptible to the quality of the datasets, not to mention the fact that the actual surveillance videos, unlike some manually designed datasets, has more distracting factors such as low definition, unexpected occlusion in front of the camera and poor camera angles that tend to have a serious negative impact on recognition performance, especially in multi-stage combined recognition tasks.

In addition, recent work [10] has pointed out that existing state-of-the-art detectors only perform well when trained and tested on the same dataset but perform poorly in cross-dataset evaluations. This phenomenon shows that many current detectors with high performance may not have enough generalization ability. However, in actual applications, retraining the detector for each different scene will bring unacceptable overhead, and sometimes it is almost impossible to implement. Thus, there is no doubt that the detectors that can only perform well in specific scenarios but not in various scenarios have very low practicality in actual applications.

In this paper, we comprehensively compared the real-time feasibility and recognition accuracy of several mainstream detectors in the domains of pedestrian tracking, face detection, and face recognition. As a result, we selected Kernelized Correlation Filters [1], Yolov4 [15] and ResNet-50 [21] with Arcface loss function [25] for pedestrian tracking, face detection and face recognition respectively. Moreover, considering that anchor-based methods like Yolov4 always inevitably less generalized due to the problem of requiring predefined anchors for specific task, we modified the Yolov4, which is essential for face detection, to be anchor-free in order to make our whole system have better generalization ability and easier to be embedded in various tasks where specific pedestrian recognition is the ultimate goal. Then we combined these three methods and finally got one complete system, which has a certain degree of generalization performance as well as acceptable recognition accuracy and can be used for various surveillance video-based real-time application scenarios of specific pedestrian recognition. In general, the major contributions of our research can be summarized as follows:

(1) We proposed a complete system that can be used for real-time tracking and recognition of specific pedestrian targets in surveillance video. To the best of our knowledge, there is no existing complete real-time specific pedestrian recognition system that can achieve satisfactory performance in actual application scenarios.

(2) We have reduced some of the hand-designed hyper parameters in Yolov4 and made it easier to be used in various applications by modifying the anchor-based Yolov4 to anchor-free.

(3) Through further training and testing with the dataset made by the surveillance videos in an actual project, the system we proposed in this paper has initially obtained an acceptable result, which also confirmed the practicability of our system.

2 Method

In this section, we will first describe the steps our system takes to complete specific pedestrian recognition, and then introduce the specific methods and principles used to realize the functions of each step in detail.

2.1 Specific Pedestrian Recognition System

In order to realize specific pedestrian recognition for the purpose of recognizing who a specific pedestrian target is directly from surveillance video, we decomposed specific pedestrian recognition into the following steps:

(1) Track the target pedestrian and screenshot partial image of the target from the input surveillance video;

(2) Perform face detection on the image obtained in step 1 and capture the partial image of target's face according to the detection result;

(3) Repeat the above step 1 and step 2 at equal intervals, the default is 0.2 s, until the target disappears from the surveillance video;

(4) After step 3 is completed, perform face recognition on the face images obtained through the above steps to recognize the target pedestrian

The overall structure of the specific pedestrian recognition system we proposed is shown in the Fig. 1.

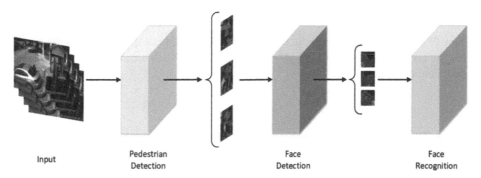

Input   Pedestrian Detection   Face Detection   Face Recognition

Fig. 1. The overall structure of the specific pedestrian recognition system.

2.2 Kernelized Correlation Filters

As the first step of specific pedestrian recognition, the pedestrian tracking module in our system aims at tracking the pedestrian target and capturing an image of the target though a set of input surveillance video sequences with the position information of the target in first frame. The tracking function of this module is mainly based on Kernelized Correlation Filters (KCF) [1].

KCF is a discriminative tracking method. It trains an object detector during tracking and uses this object detector to detect whether the predicted position of the next frame is the target. Then, updates to the object detector are implemented by using the new detection results to update the training dataset.

On the basis of [23, 24], in order to achieve high-speed object tracking, KCF uses ridge regression and the diagonalization property of the circulant matrix in the Fourier space to improve the speed of calculation.

First, based on the kernelized version of ridge regression, the solution to the optimization problem of regression is defined as follows:

$$\alpha = (K + \lambda I)^{-1} y \tag{1}$$

where α is the vector of coefficients α_i, K is the matrix with elements $K_{i,j} = k(P^i x, P^j x)$ which is circulant given a kernel (e.g. Gaussian kernel), λ is a regularization parameter ($\lambda \geq 0$) and y is the output.

Then, taking advantage of the property that the circulant matrices are all formed diagonal by the discrete Fourier transform (DFT) without regard to the generated vector x, the fast Fourier transform of α represented by $\varphi(\alpha)$ can be calculated by the following formula:

$$\varphi(\alpha) = \varphi(y) / (\varphi(k^{xx}) + \lambda) \tag{2}$$

where φ represents the discrete Foutier operator, and k^{xx} is the first row of the circulant kernel matrix K. During tracking, all the candidate patches that are cyclic shifts of base patches z are evaluated through:

$$\varphi(f(z)) = \varphi(k^{zx}) \odot \varphi(\alpha) \tag{3}$$

where $\odot$ is the element-wise product and $f(z)$ can be viewed as a spatial filtering operation over the kernel values k^{zx}. The target position is the one with the maximal value among $f(z)$ calculated by:

$$f(z) = \max\left(\varphi^{-1}(\varphi(f(z)))\right) \tag{4}$$

and the target appearance $\bar{x}^t$ and correlation filter $\varphi(\alpha^t)$ are then updated with a learning rate η as:

$$\bar{x}^t = (1 - \eta)\bar{x}^{t-1} + \eta x^t \tag{5}$$

$$\varphi(\alpha^t) = (1 - \eta)\varphi(\alpha^{t-1}) + \eta\varphi(\alpha) \tag{6}$$

Through the above methods, KCF greatly reduces the amount of calculation. Its computational complexity for the full kernel correlation is only O(nlog(n)). What's more, KCF successfully improves the speed of calculation to meet real-time requirements. It has a detection speed of more than 100 frames per second.

2.3 Yolov4-Based Face Detection Module

The purpose of the face detection module is to further extract the face image for face recognition from the target pedestrian image obtained in step 1. As the intermediate part of the system, the accuracy and real-time performance of this module is also a key concern when we design the system.

Referring to the cross-dataset evaluation method proposed in [10], we finally chose Yolov4 as the basic method to implement the face detection of this module. Details of the comparative experiments on which we based our choice of Yolov4 can be found in Sect. 4.1.

However, the Yolo series, whether it is Yolov2 [13], Yolov3 [14] or Yolov4 [15], are anchor-based object detectors. There are many hyper parameters that need to be manually set, such as scale and aspect ratio, which also makes it unable to be directly, conveniently and effectively used in various scenarios without carefully adjusting the hyper-parameters. To make matters worse, the tuning of these hyper parameters often requires extensive a priori knowledge and corresponding adjustments in different application scenarios to ensure good performance of the detector.

Therefore, in order to enable our system to be easily deployed to various application scenarios, we removed the anchor mechanism in Yolov4, and modified Yolov4 to be anchor-free by referring to the means mentioned in [3].

In anchor-based Yolov4, it predicts 3 anchor box in each grid cell, and when the center point of the ground truth in the training image falls in a cell, it selects which anchor box to use for prediction based on the IoU between each anchor box in the cell and the ground truth. So, in order to change Yolov4 to anchor-free, we just simply reduced the number of predicted boxes in each cell to only one. At the same time, based on the center sampling strategy in Fcos [3], we assigned the center position, a 3×3 area centered on the cell where the center point is located, of each object as positive samples. With such simple modification mentioned above, we successfully changed Yolov4 to anchor-free and slightly increased the mAP of Yolov4 tested on our own dataset by 0.2%.

2.4 Face Recognition Based on ResNet-50 and ArcFace

In the face recognition module, the system needs to perform feature extraction on the input face image. Then, these extracted face features are clustered with the data in the face database to recognize who the target is. Except for some special situations such as the input image itself is too blurred or the camera angle is too bad, so that there are almost no significant facial features in the image, the recognition effect of this module mainly depends on the performance of facial feature extraction. We implement the feature extraction mainly based on ResNet-50 [21] and ArcFace [25], the overall structure of it is shown in Fig. 2.

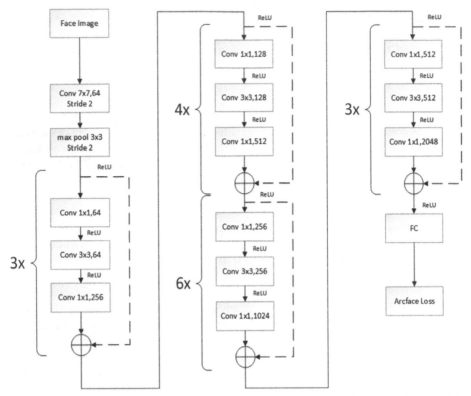

Fig. 2. The overall structure of the facial feature extraction function in face recognition module.

The formula of the Arcface loss function in Fig. 2 is as follows:

$$\mathcal{L} = -\frac{1}{N}\sum_{i=1}^{N} \log \frac{e^{r(\cos(m+\theta y_i))}}{e^{r(\cos(m+\theta y_i))} + \sum_{j=1, j\neq y_i}^{n} e^{r\cos\theta_j}} \tag{7}$$

where N is the number of samples, r is the sphere radius of the feature distribution into the high-dimensional sphere, θ_{yi} is the angle between the real sample and the predicted sample, θ_j is the angle between other samples and the predicted sample, and m is the penalty interval for increasing the inter-class distance and reducing the intra-class distance.

3 Experiment

In this section, we evaluated the accuracy and speed performance of two face detectors and two generic detectors using a cross-dataset evaluation method. The results of this experiment are also used as a basis to select the detectors to be used in the face detection module. In addition, to examine the effect of modifying Yolov4 to anchor-free on the accuracy and speed of the detection, we further evaluated anchor-based Yolov4 and anchor-free Yolov4 through cross-dataset evaluation method in Sect. 3.2. The testing environment was conducted on one Nvidia GTX 3090Ti graphic card with 24 GB memory, and an Intel(R) Xeon(R) CPU E5-2630 v4 2.20 GHz.

3.1 Face Recognition Based on ResNet-50 and ArcFace

The study in [10] shows that some current state-of-the-art pedestrian detectors have poor generalization ability, they performed worse under cross-dataset evaluations compared to generic object detectors. In practice, it is expensive to redesign the dataset for each specific application scenario, so the performance in the cross-dataset evaluation also reflects the feasibility of putting a method into practical application.

Similar to pedestrian detection, face detection is a special case of target detection, so we similarly evaluated the accuracy and speed performance of several face detectors and generic detectors in a cross-dataset evaluation.

We chose two face detectors, SSH [4] and LFFD [28], and two generic object detectors, Yolov4 and Faster R-CNN, which were on the FDDB [26] and WIDER Face [27], both of which are widely used public datasets for face detection, respectively, and then tested on the datasets come from our real project, which contains 500 images of pedestrians captured from surveillance videos. The results of the comparative experiments are shown in Table 1.

Table 1. Cross-dataset evaluation of four detectors.

Method	Training	Test time (ms/img)	mAP
Yolov4	FDDB	**7.07**	81.87
Faster R-CNN	FDDB	179.87	83.20
SSH	FDDB	30.38	**83.26**
LFFD	FDDB	7.92	79.92
Yolov4	WIDER Face (Medium)	**7.49**	82.63
Faster R-CNN	WIDER Face (Medium)	181.56	83.34
SSH	WIDER Face (Medium)	31.63	**84.58**
LFFD	WIDER Face (Medium)	8.26	81.16

Table 1 shows the FPS and average accuracy of the four models when tested across the datasets after training on two datasets respectively. As can be seen from the Table 1, Yolov4 and LFFD show excellent performance in terms of speed, processing more than 100 frames per second, that is, the test time of each image is less than 10 ms, while Faster R-CNN and SSH have a slight advantage in terms of accuracy. Considering the balance of speed and accuracy, we finally chose Yolov4, which has a significant advantage in speed and slightly better accuracy than LFFD, as the face detector of our system.

3.2   Comparison Between Anchor-Based Yolov4 and Anchor-Free Yolov4

In Sect. 2.3, we modified Yolov4 from anchor-based to anchor-free to improve the convenience and effectiveness of deploying our system to various scenarios. However, it is still unknown how this modification will affect the performance of the Yolov4 in face detection. Thus, in this section, following the cross-dataset evaluation method used in Sect. 3.1, a comparative experiment is carried out on the anchor-based Yolov4 and the anchor-free Yolov4. The experimental results are shown in Table 2.

Table 2. Comparison between anchor-based Yolov4 and anchor-free Yolov4.

Method	Training	Test time (ms/img)	mAP
Yolov4	FDDB	7.07	81.87
Anchor-free Yolov4 (ours)	FDDB	**6.90**	**82.10**
Yolov4	WIDER Face (Medium)	7.49	82.63
Anchor-free Yolov4 (ours)	WIDER Face (Medium)	**7.31**	**82.91**

As can be seen from the Table 2, due to the removal of the anchor reduces the amount of hyper parameters, the accuracy and detection speed of the Yolov4 in cross-dataset evaluation has been slightly improved.

4   Conclusion

In this paper, we evaluated and selected several mainstream methods that perform well and can be used for real-time tasks in the three domains of pedestrian tracking, face detection, and face recognition, respectively. Based on the results of the comprehensive evaluation, we proposed a system that can be used for real-time tracking and recognition of specific pedestrian targets in surveillance video. The system has a certain degree of generalization capability and can be embedded in various application scenarios where specific pedestrian recognition is the goal of the task. At present, our system has actually been implemented in a project to recognize pedestrians who discard garbage in violation of the rules in the community through surveillance video, and initially achieved an acceptable result.

Acknowledgements. This work was supported by the National Natural Science Foundation of China (No. 61872231), the National Key Research and Development Program of China (No. 2021YFC2801000), and the Major Research plan of the National Social Science Foundation of China (No. 20&ZD130).

References

1. Henriques, J.F., Caseiro, R., Martins, P., Batista, J.: High-speed tracking with kernelized correlation filters. IEEE Trans. Pattern Anal. Mach. Intell. **37**(3), 583–596 (2015)

2. Liu, J., Gu, C., Wang, J., Youn, G., Kim, J.-U.: Multi-scale multi-class conditional generative adversarial network for handwritten character generation. J. Supercomput. **75**(4), 1922–1940 (2017). https://doi.org/10.1007/s11227-017-2218-0

3. Tian, Z., Shen, C., Chen, H., He, T.: Fcos: fully convolutional one-stage object detection. In: Proceedings of the European Conference on Computer Vision (ECCV), pp. 9627–9636 (2019)

4. Najibi, M., Samangouei, P., Chellappa, R., Davis, L.S.: Ssh: single stage headless face detector. In: Proceedings of IEEE International Conference on Computer Vision (ICCV), pp. 4875–4884 (2017)

5. Jiang, X., Yu, F.R., Song, T., Leung, V.C.: Resource allocation of video streaming over vehicular networks: a survey, some research issues and challenges. IEEE Trans. Intell. Transp. Syst. (2021). https://doi.org/10.1109/TITS.2021.3065209

6. Cai, Z., Fan, Q., Feris, R.S., Vasconcelos, N.: A unified multi-scale deep convolutional neural network for fast object detection. In: Leibe, B., Matas, J., Sebe, N., Welling, M. (eds.) ECCV 2016. LNCS, vol. 9908, pp. 354–370. Springer, Cham (2016). https://doi.org/10.1007/978-3-319-46493-0_22

7. Huang, L., Zhao, X., Huang, K.: Bridging the gap between detection and tracking: a unified approach. In: Proceedings of the IEEE International Conference on Computer Vision (ICCV), pp. 3999–4009 (2019)

8. Zhou, C., Yuan, J.: Bi-box regression for pedestrian detection and occlusion estimation. In: Ferrari, V., Hebert, M., Sminchisescu, C., Weiss, Y. (eds.) ECCV 2018. LNCS, vol. 11205, pp. 138–154. Springer, Cham (2018). https://doi.org/10.1007/978-3-030-01246-5_9

9. Yang, Y.D., Wang, X.F., Zhao, Q., Sui, T.T.: Two-level attentions and grouping attention convolutional network for fine-grained image classification. Appl. Sci 9(9), 1939 (2019)

10. Hasan, I., Liao, S., Li, J., Akram, S.U., Shao, L.: Generalizable pedestrian detection: the elephant in the room. In: Proceedings of the IEEE Conference on Computer Vision and Pattern Recognition (CVPR), pp. 11328–11337 (2021)

11. Chu, X., Zheng, A., Zhang, X., Sun, J.: Detection in crowded scenes: one proposal, multiple predictions. In: Proceedings of the IEEE Conference on Computer Vision and Pattern Recognition (CVPR), pp.12214–12223 (2020)

12. Wang, J., Song, L., Li, Z., Sun, H., Sun, J., Zheng, N.: End-to-end object detection with fully convolutional network. In: Proceedings of the IEEE Conference on Computer Vision and Pattern Recognition (CVPR), pp.15849–15858 (2021)

13. Redmon, J., Farhadi, A.: Yolo9000: better, faster, stronger. In: Proceedings of the IEEE Conference on Computer Vision and Pattern Recognition (CVPR), pp.7263–7271 (2017)

14. Redmon, J., Farhadi, A.: Yolov3: an incremental improvement. arXiv:1804.02767 (2018)

15. Bochkovskiy, A., Wang, C.Y., Liao, H.Y.M.: Yolov4: optimal speed and accuracy of object detection. arXiv:2004.10934 (2020)

16. Zhu, Y., Cai, H., Zhang, S., Wang, C., Xiong, Y.: Tinaface: strong but simple baseline for face detection. arXiv:2011.13183 (2020)

17. Carion, N., Massa, F., Synnaeve, G., Usunier, N., Kirillov, A., Zagoruyko, S.: End-to-end object detection with transformers. In: Vedaldi, A., Bischof, H., Brox, T., Frahm, J.-M. (eds.) ECCV 2020. LNCS, vol. 12346, pp. 213–229. Springer, Cham (2020). https://doi.org/10.1007/978-3-030-58452-8_13

18. Yang, Y., Xu, C., Dong, F., Wang, X.: A new multi-scale convolutional model based on multiple attention for image classification. Appl. Sci **10**(1), 101 (2020)

19. Girshick, R.: Fast R-CNN. In: Proceedings of the IEEE International Conference on Computer Vision (ICCV), pp. 1440–1448 (2015)

20. Ren, S., He, K., Girshick, R., Sun, J.: Faster R-CNN: towards real-time object detection with region proposal networks. In: Advances in Neural Information Processing Systems, vol. 28, pp. 91–99 (2015)

21. He, K., Zhang, X., Ren, S., Sun, J.: Deep residual learning for image recognition. In Proceedings of the IEEE Conference on Computer Vision and Pattern Recognition (CVPR), pp. 770–778 (2016)

22. Liu, J., Lin, L., Cai, Z., Wang, J., Kim, H.J.: Deep web data extraction based on visual information processing. J. Ambient Intell. Humanized Comput., 1–11 (2017)

23. Henriques, J.F., Caseiro, R., Martins, P., Batista, J.: Exploiting the circulant structure of tracking-by-detection with kernels. In: Fitzgibbon, A., Lazebnik, S., Perona, P., Sato, Y., Schmid, C. (eds.) ECCV 2012. LNCS, vol. 7575, pp. 702–715. Springer, Heidelberg (2012). https://doi.org/10.1007/978-3-642-33765-9_50

24. Bolme, D.S., Beveridge, J.R., Draper, B.A., Lui, Y.M.: Visual object tracking using adaptive correlation filters. In: Proceedings of the IEEE Conference on Computer Vision and Pattern Recognition (CVPR), pp. 2544–2550 (2010)

25. Deng, J., Guo, J., Xue, N., Zafeiriou, S.: ArcFace: additive angular margin loss for deep face recognition. In: Proceedings of the IEEE Conference on Computer Vision and Pattern Recognition (CVPR), pp. 4690–4699 (2019)

26. Jain, V., Learned-Miller, E.: FDDB: a benchmark for face detection in unconstrained settings. Technical report, University of Massachusetts, Amherst (2010)

27. Yang, S., Luo, P., Loy, C.C., Tang, X.: Wider face: a face detection benchmark. In: Proceedings of IEEE Conference on Computer Vision and Pattern Recognition (CVPR), pp. 5525–5533 (2016)

28. He, Y., Xu, D., Wu, L., Jian, M., Xiang, S., Pan, C.: Lffd: A light and fast face detector for edge devices. arXiv:1904.10633 (2019)

29. Chang, S., Liu, J.: Multi-lane capsule network for classifying images with complex background. IEEE Access **8**, 79876–79886 (2020)

Minimizing Immune Costs in Social Networks Through Reinforcement Learning

Haichao Nie[1], Pei Li[1(✉)], Ying Zhou[2], Xiaoliang Wang[1], and Chixin Xiao[3]

[1] School of Computer Science and Engineering, Hunan University of Science and Technology,
Xiangtan 411100, China
8992077@qq.com
[2] College of Science, Northeast Forestry University, Harbin 150000, China
[3] University of Wollongong, Wollongong, Australia

Abstract. This work explores the use of social relationships to control spread of information. Spread of information through various forms in social networks. Here, the authors analyze the social relationship between individuals to model of the spread of information. In other words, the authors try to capture the interaction pattern of human beings using the social contact information and investigate its impact on the spread of information. Particularly, the authors investigate the problem of minimizing the control cost of infected persons by controlling a small fraction of the population. Current spread of information research mainly focuses on formulating immunization strategies before spread of information, while ignoring the key factor of immunization cost. To address the issue of the minimizing influence in the process of dynamic spread of information. In this paper, the authors use the Independent Cascade (IC) model for simulating the random spread of real information. Combining the Reinforcement Learning (RL) method to obtain the optimal immune strategy of each state in the process of spreading. Finally, based on experiments and evaluations on 4 real-world datasets, the simulation results validate the superiority of our strategy over existing ones. As far as we know, this is the first attempt to use the RL method to solve the problem of minimizing immune costs.

Keywords: Spread of information · Immune cost · Independent Cascade · Reinforcement Learning

1 Introduction

In this paper, we propose to use communication records to guide the use of immune nodes in social networks to minimize the cost of immunity. Most of the information can be transmitted from one person to another through social networks [1–5]. Therefore, the spread of information may pose great risks to human life and social development. If not properly controlled, it may cause some economic loss. In recent years, the popularity and development of social networks have brought great convenience to spread of information [6]. However, the convenience of information released in social networks and the lack of supervision and filtering into information content cause a large amount of misinformation to spread on social networks and polluted the social networks environment [7]. To stop information on spreading, number of interventions are available with distinct benefits or drawbacks. They either directly impact the transmission of information so that the misinformation cannot easily spread through the social networks or immunize segments of a population.

Considering the time that interventions is applied, strategies for controlling information can be classified into two categories: 1) Preventive information controlled that takes place before spread of information in social networks; and 2) reactive immune controlled that stops a piece of information from spreading out after the information outbreak is detected in social networks. Reactive strategies focus on individuals who are already affected and their close friends to protect susceptible people from being infected. Preventive strategies, on the other hand, identify nodes at high significance of immune, so that the information can be prevented from spreading out or even happening in social networks. In this paper, we have designed an immune cost strategy, which is a preventive strategy. In particular. We try to immunize a small number of highly influential people so that we can prevent them from spreading to others. These immunization policies are widely used to prevent the spread of information. However, the current immunization strategy ignores the key factor of immune node cost. As a result, the predefined immunization strategy may be very effective in controlling the large-scale spread of information. But leading to a high economic cost. Moreover, due to the rapid spread of information, the group immunization can't achieve good control effect in many cases. In the light of the problems with, we aim to select individuals of immune nodes in advance based on information extracted from people's daily life data stream, so that cost of controlled will be minimized if the population is exposed to an information later.

In this paper, we try to minimize the spread of information, rather than maximizing the spreading of a piece of information. In particular. This is the first attempt to use the Reinforcement Learning (RL) method [8] to solve the problem of minimizing immune costs. Our approach is evaluated over real world data set. The results demonstrate that the proposed the RL method outperforms other strategies in control spread of information.

Our contributions can be summarized as follows:

- We explore social relationships to determine the pattern of spread of information in social networks.
- We attempt to minimize the cost of controlling spread by immunizing a small fraction of the population. The problem is expressed in a mathematical formula. And we propose a RL method that provides preventive information control strategies.
- A comparative simulation study was conducted on four real datasets to evaluate the performance of our preventive spread of information control strategy, and the results showed that the proposed strategy is superior to existing ones.

The paper is organized as follows. Sect. 2 presents the most related work. Sect. 3 discusses the preliminary knowledge to be used in this work. The problem of minimize immune costs and its solution are detailed in Sect. 4. The proposed strategy is evaluated in Sect. 5. We conclude our work in Sect. 6.

2 Related Work

To minimize the impact of information, researchers have considered to block critical nodes to prevent the false message from spreading out. Such an idea has been applied in number of contexts. Our work is built on prior research on spread of information. In this section, we review the most related work along these directions.

The work of [9] has proposed a random uniform immunization policy for individuals, an approach that requires immunization of almost all nodes in the networks to suppress information diffusion. Cohen et al. [10] have provided an acquaintance immunization strategy that is more effective than random immunization, and it also solves the defect that the global information of the networks needs to be known in the target immunization. A new graph partitioning strategy has been proposed by Chen et al. [11]. Compared with the target strategy, it needs to reduce the immune dose by 5% to 50% and achieves the same degree of network immune effect. An immunization method has been introduced by Gallows et al. [12], which randomly selects a node and requires neighbors with more links than his own or above a given threshold and immunizes them. This strategy retains the advantage of being purely local, without the need for understand the global network's structure or identification of the highest degree nodes. Ellina et al. [13] to achieve the goal of minimizing spread within a limited time, vaccinations for susceptible populations, treatment of infected persons, and control strategies aimed at reducing indirect transmission are proposed. Zhong et al. [14] have established a quantitative simulation model of network spread of information mechanism. The Strategies for spread of information is studied from the perspective of system dynamics and proposed a model for evaluating spread of information strategies in a dynamic environment. Liu et al. [15] have designed an optimal filter to achieve the goal of maximizing information propagation and minimizing control consumption and developed an optimal controller using state estimation methods. A control strategy based on optimal filtering is established, combined with the principle of separation, to form a complete solution for optimal control of spread of information networks under random disturbances. A new model of spread of information based on immunity has been provided by [16]. The model also considers factors such as information tolerance, social reinforcement and memory enhancement. Based on the hormone transmission mechanism, a model of information diffusion (EIID) based on endocrine immunity is proposed.

Although the immunization strategies proposed in previous literature reduce the scope of spread of information, they consider simpler situations, such as immunization strategies are determined before spread of information and the strategies cannot be changed during the process of real spread of information. However, in real social networks, immunization strategies for spread of information are not static, and they also depend on the current situation of spread of information. For example, when information is propagated to a node, the predefined strategy may not be the best control strategy. If the previous control strategy is followed, it is likely that the goal of controlling the information with minimal immunization cost will not be achieved.

In addition, the immunization strategies in the above literature do not consider the immunization cost as an important factor. Therefore, combining the advantages and disadvantages of the above-mentioned articles, this paper proposes the use of RL to minimize the cost of immunization. This approach allows the optimal immunization strategy to be changed in time during the spread of information process to achieve the goal of information control.

3 Related Work

3.1 The Network Model

We investigate the spread of information in social networks constructed over social relationships records. Define the network model as G (V, E, W), where V denotes the node set, E denotes the edge set, and W represents the edge weight set. A node $v \in V$ represents an individual, while an edge e_{ij} between nodes i and j indicate that there exist relationships between the two nodes. Attached to the edge e_{ij} is the weight w_{ij}, which is used to quantify the relationship between i and j. If the relationship is done through planes, then w_{ij} can include information such as the number of the plane flights and the times of flight. If the relationship is made through journals, then w_{ij} can be the number of readers of the journals.

3.2 Propagation Model

We employ an Independent Cascade (IC) model [17] to study the spread of information in social networks. In this model, the spread of process takes place at discrete time intervals. Nodes in the model are either active or inactive. The spread starts with an initial active node. Assume node i become active at step t. Then i will attempt to activate each of its inactive neighbors, j, with a activate probability h_{ij}, which indicates the tendency of j to be activated by i. If i succeeds, j becomes active at step $t + 1$. In this paper, the activation probability h_{ij} is the weight w_{ij} after processing. If j has multiple active neighbors at step t, their activation contacts with j would be sequenced in a random order. The nodes are independent and do not affect each other. When all nodes have been activated once, the IC process is terminated. In this work, we aim is to use IC to simulate the spread of process of real information.

3.3 Reinforcement Learning Networks

Reinforcement Learning process describes an agent-environment interaction process where agent performs action a_t according to environment's state s_t, meanwhile environment transits to next new state s_{t+1} and returns an immediate reward r_t due to agent's taken action. Among them, s_t is current situation of spread of information. a_t is the next node of spread of state s_{t+1} is the next state after spread of information through node a_t. Thus, an agent-environment interaction sequence can be represented as:

$$s_0, a_0, r_0, s_1, a_1, r_1, \cdots \tag{1}$$

The agent's action policy $\pi(a_t|s_t)$ is a strategy function that maps from a state to a probability distribution of possible actions and $\pi(a_t|s_t)$ is used to determine whether the current node is immunized. If the node is immunized, re-select the node from the list of propagating nodes. Instead, the information is propagated to the next node. Repeat until the propagation is completed. The objective of a Reinforcement Learning agent is to maximize the cumulative future rewards which includes rewards from current time step until end of the interaction by executing the optimal policy.

Two networks are used to build Reinforcement Learning (RL) method [18]. One is policy networks, the other is value networks. Policy networks that can learn stochastic policies, which is more effective in high-dimensional or continuous action space and better convergence properties. Value networks that evaluate these policies, which can reduce the variance of policy evaluation and avoid converging to a local rather than global policy optimum. The policy networks combine the complementary strengths of both parties to enhance the accuracy of factual predictions. In terms of value scores, the policy network is updated to obtain a more accurate probability. At the beginning, both policies and values are chosen randomly. Similarly, the value network is adjusted by the real rewards of policy selection.

The reinforcement learning approach combines deep convolutional neural networks and policy-valued networks. Them, deep convolutional neural networks, trained solely by Reinforcement Learning. Reinforcement Learning method uses a deep neural network $(p, v) = f_\theta(s)$ with parameters θ. This neural network $f_\theta(s)$ takes the spread of information states s as an input and outputs a vector of move probabilities p with components $p_a = \Pr(a|s)$ for each action a and a scalar value v estimating the expected outcome z of the spread from node s, $v \approx \mathrm{E}[a|s]$. Reinforcement Learning method learns these move probabilities and value estimates entirely from self-spread. These are all used to guide the search for minimization of its impact in the future. Specifically, the parameters θ is adjusted by gradient descent on a loss function L that sums over mean-squared error and cross-entropy losses

$$L = (z - v)^2 - \pi^T \log p + l\|\theta\|^2 \qquad (2)$$

where l is a parameter controlling the level of L_2 weight regularization. The vector π represents a probability distribution over moves. The updated parameters are used in subsequent process of self-spread.

In the Reinforcement Learning method, the neural network consists of a "body" followed by both policy and value "heads". The body consists of a rectified batch-normalized convolutional layer followed by 19 residual blocks. Each such block consists of two rectified batch-normalized convolutional layers with a skip connection. Each convolution applies 256 filters of kernel size 3×3 with stride 1. Padding is "same". The activation functions of policy and value networks are softmax and tanh, respectively. Learning rate γ is set to 0.01. L_2 weight regularization is 0.0001. Adam is used for optimization. During neural network training, each episode executes 500 times. The min-batch size is 80% of the results. Learn 2 times per episode. The maximum number of steps per episode is set to 800. The cumulative future rewards for Reinforcement Learning are Cost. If the propagation ends, immediate reward r_t is 0, the others are -1.

4   Immune Cost Algorithm

4.1   Problem Define

Different from target selection in viral marketing, which attempts to maximize the number of nodes that can be affected by the target set, we try to minimize the immune costs over G by immunizing a small number of nodes. Assume K is an active set, $K \subset N$. N is the total number of nodes in G. Given a networks G (V, E, W) and the transition matrix T, we aim to immune a set A of K nodes, $A \subset V$, so that the value of Cost will be minimized if spread ends. Assume that spread appears at some nodes with a probability q, where q is a float less than 1. Then our goal is to find A of K nodes for vaccination, so that Cost is minimized. Then the problem can be mathematically described as:

$$minCost = \sum_{i=0}^{N} M_i + m_i c \qquad (3)$$

where $Cost$ is the cost of controlling spread, M is the total number of people infected after the spread of information ends, m is the number of immune nodes, and c is the standard of immunity.

4.2 Propagation Model

To solve (3), we design a model framework. The model framework mainly includes three parts: data pre-processing, simulation the random propagation of real information, and strategy planning to minimize the cost of immunization.

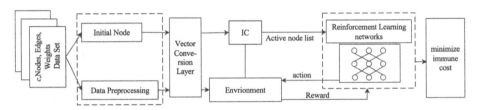

Fig. 1. A strategy framework for minimizing the cost of immunization

The flow of the framework is as follows. Firstly, the pre-processed nodes, edges, weight dataset and c are transformed into N × N adjacency matrix after the data transformation layer. Secondly, in the process of information random propagation, IC is used to simulate the form of real information random propagation. Take the initial node as input and output the next list of spread of information nodes. Finally, in the planning process of minimizing immune cost, the vector transformation layer is used to connect the process of spreading information authentically and the reinforcement learning networks, and the vectors are coded uniformly, so that the Reinforcement Learning can use

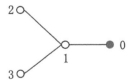

Fig. 2. Node 0 is the starting point of the initial spread. The weight of each side is the propagation probability. The direction of spread is from right to left.

the real spread of information process to calculate the immediate reward and optimize the immune strategy. The final output is the minimum of the immune cost.

We use an example to introduce the working process of the framework. It is assumed that every node can be activated. The input matrix of the framework is 4×4 matrix, $c = 0.05$. Node and edge data are transformed into

$$\begin{bmatrix} 0 & 1 & 0 & 0 \\ 0 & 0 & 1 & 1 \\ 0 & 0 & 0 & 0 \\ 0 & 0 & 0 & 0 \end{bmatrix}$$

The input of IC is initial spread node 0, and the output is the active node list containing only node 1. The output of IC is used as the input of Reinforcement Learning network. Thus, the output of Reinforcement Learning policy network is

$$\begin{bmatrix} 0 & 0.1 & 0 & 0 \\ 0 & 0 & 0 & 0 \\ 0 & 0 & 0 & 0 \\ 0 & 0 & 0 & 0 \end{bmatrix}$$

Represents propagation from node 0. Node 1 is not immune, and the probability of spreading to node 1 is 0.13. The output of value network is 0.25. Next, one active node is randomly selected from the active node list as the propagation node. At time, node 1 acts as the propagation node, and the list of active nodes is empty. Taking node 1 as the input, the IC outputs the list of active nodes including nodes 2 and 3. At time, the propagation state changes to

$$\begin{bmatrix} 0 & 0 & 0 & 0 \\ 0 & 0 & 1 & 1 \\ 0 & 0 & 0 & 0 \\ 0 & 0 & 0 & 0 \end{bmatrix}$$

After 20 times of training, the output of Reinforcement Learning policy network is

$$\begin{bmatrix} 0 & 0 & 0 & 0 \\ 0 & 0 & 0 & 0 \\ 0 & 0 & 0 & 0 \\ 0 & 0 & 0 & 0 \end{bmatrix}$$

The output of value network is 0.89. Training results show that nodes 2, 3 are immune. Therefore, immune node 1 can obtain the minimum immune generation value under the condition of $c = 0.05$.

4.3 Case Analysis

This section introduces the advantages of our algorithm through a simple example. The node of initial spread of information is node 0. Traditionally, there are two strategies for each node. Case 1, nodes are not immune. Case 2, immunize nodes.

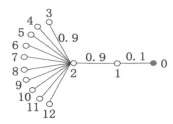

Fig. 3. Node 0 is the starting point of the initial spread. The weight of each side is the propagation probability. The direction of spread is from right to left.

- If case 1, then the probability of information infecting nodes.

  a. At node 1.

$$1 * 0.1 = 0.1 \tag{4}$$

  b. At node 2.

$$0.1 * 0.1 + 0.9 * 0.1 = 0.19 \tag{5}$$

  c. At node 3 to 12.

In the event of random spread of information, nodes $3, \cdots, 12$ are independent of each other. Each event may or may not happen. Probability of propagation 0.9 is the probability of event φ occurring. The event obeys the binomial distribution $\varphi \sim B(10, 0.9)$. The probability that the event happens exactly k times is $C_{10}^k p^k (1 - 0.9)^{10-k}$, there is

$$E\varphi = 0 * C_{10}^0 (0.9)^0 (1 - 0.9)^{10} + 1 * C_{10}^1 (0.9)^1 (1 - 0.9)^{10-1} + \cdots$$

$$+ k * C_{10}^k (0.9)^k (1 - 0.9)^{10-k} + \cdots 10 * C_{10}^{10} (0.9)^{10} (1 - 0.9)^0$$

$$= 10 * 0.9 = 9 \tag{6}$$

Probability of infecting nodes $3, \cdots, 12$.

$$0.1 * 0.9 * 9 = 0.81 \tag{7}$$

- If case 2, then the cost of node immunity.

  d. Immune node 1.

$$Cost\_1 = 0 + 1 * c = c \tag{8}$$

  e. Immune node 2.

$$Cost\_2 = 1 + 1 * c = 1 + c \tag{9}$$

The advantages of this algorithm are as follows. If the information is not propagated to node 1 with probability 0.9, then no immune control is applied to node 1. The cost of immunization is

$$Cost\_3 = 0 \tag{10}$$

If the information is propagated to node 1, the immunity cost of node 2 is

$$Cost\_4 = 0.1 * (1 + c) = 0.1 + 0.1 * c \tag{11}$$

Discuss the size of $Cost\_1$ and $Cost\_4$.

$$s.t. \begin{cases} c > 0.1 + 0.1 * c \\ c > 0 \end{cases} \tag{12}$$

That is, if $0 < c < \frac{1}{9}$, then, $Cost\_1 < Cost\_4$, immune node 1. If $c = \frac{1}{9}$, then, $Cost\_1 = Cost\_4$, immune node 2. If $c > \frac{1}{9}$, then, $Cost\_1 > Cost\_4$, the immune cost is the same.

Since the information has 0.9 probability of not propagating downward, it is possible to discuss whether the nodes are immune when the information propagation downward occurs. This is the advantage of the proposed algorithm. However, the paper [19] believes that node 1 is structural hole spanner, and the optimal control strategy is to immunity node 1.

Next, briefly describe the difference between the algorithm in this paper and the previous algorithms in mathematical form. Set the initial spread of information graph to G_0. With the continuous spread of information. Immunity action a_0, and it becomes $G_1, \cdots$, and immunity action a_∞, and it becomes G_∞, which means that the spread ends after all nodes attempt to activate once. In the past, algorithms were predefined control strategies before immunization. The immunization strategy is one-time $Cost = M_\infty + m_0 c$. However, the algorithm in this paper considers that in the process of spread of information, different node states have different optimal control strategies, and its immunization strategies are diverse $Cost = M'_\infty + \sum_{i=0}^{\infty} m_i c$.

In conclusion, the immunization strategy in this article is better than the one-time immunization strategy.

5   Simulation Study

5.1   Simulation Configure

This paper is based on the research of nodes. Given the performance of the compute, we implement the proposed Reinforcement Learning method over 4 real-world data sets from Pajek datasets (http://vlado.fmf.uni-lj.si/pub/networks/data/). Statistics of the

Table 1. Datasets.

Networks	No. of nodes	No. of edges	Mean. of weights
Dining	26	100	0.15
Karate	34	76	0.29
Graph drawing Contests	47	264	0.58
GlossGT	72	114	0.53

datasets is shown in Table 1. Normalization processing is a statistical probability distribution to normalize the weight between 0 and 1. In this simulation, we let $w = w_i/\max(w_i)$. Here, w_i represents the weight of edges.

In our simulations, the initial infected person is only one person and is randomly selected in each experiment. We report our experimental results by an average of 50 runs. Meanwhile, the transition probability is 0.05 in IC.

5.2 Simulation Results

To verify the strength of the proposed strategy, we implement two other approaches for performance comparison. One is HIS (The theory of structural holes) strategy [19]. The other is degree centrality.

HIS strategy in the sense that individuals would benefit from filling the "holes" (called as structural hole spanners) between people or groups that is otherwise disconnected. HIS strategy is to divide the network into communities, and "holes" are the key nodes to link communities. HIS method is to immunize "holes" to control spread of information. That study provides evidence for the theory of structural holes, 1% of Twitter users who span structural holes control 25% of the information diffusion on Twitter.

Degree center method is based on the order of node degree, from large too small to select nodes for immunity. Degree-1 is the largest node to be selected for immunization. Degree-2 is to select the largest two nodes for immunization. Increasing in turn. It is argued by the previous work [20] that degree centrality yields promising results in predicting the risk of infection, compared to other centrality metrics.

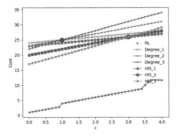

Fig. 4. Dining results.

Figure 4 reports the minimize immune Cost vs. the immune standard c, and the experimental results of Dining data set. From the results, we observe that the minimize immune costs increase as the number of immune standard c increases. Degree-1, Degree-2 and Degree-3 intersect at coordinates (1, 25). HIS-1, HIS-2 and HIS-3 intersect at coordinates (3, 26). Before the intersection, the larger the K, the smaller the Cost. After the crossing point, the greater the K, the greater the Cost. The results demonstrate that compared to the other two strategies, the proposed method has the least immune cost.

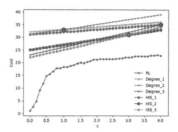

Fig. 5. Karate results.

Figure 5 reports the minimize immune Cost vs. the immune standard c, and the experimental results of Karate data set. From the results, we observe that the minimize immune costs increase as the number of immune standard c increases. Degree-1and Degree-2 intersect w at coordinates (1, 33). Degree-3 and HIS-1 intersect at coordinates (4, 35). HIS-2 and HIS-3 intersect at coordinates (3, 33). Before the intersection, the larger the K, the smaller the Cost. After the crossing point, the greater the K, the greater the Cost. The results demonstrate that compared to the other two strategies, the proposed method has the least immune cost.

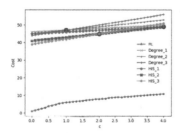

Fig. 6. Graph Drawing Contests results.

Figure 6 reports the minimize immune Cost vs. the immune standard c, and the experimental results of Graph Drawing Contests data set. From the results, we observe that the minimize immune costs increase as the number of immune standard c increases. Degree-1, Degree-2 and Degree-3 intersect at coordinates (1, 47). HIS-1 and HIS-2 intersect at coordinates (4, 49). HIS-2 and HIS-3 intersect at coordinates (4, 45). Before the intersection, the larger the K, the smaller the Cost. After the crossing point, the greater the K, the greater the Cost. The results demonstrate that compared to the other two strategies, the proposed method has the least immune cost.

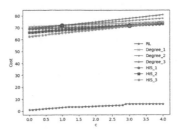

Fig. 7. GlossGT results.

Figure 7 reports the minimize immune Cost vs. the immune standard c, and the experimental results of GlossGT data set. From the results, we observe that the minimize immune costs increase as the number of immune standard c increases. Degree-1, Degree-2 and Degree-3 intersect at coordinates (1, 72). HIS-1 and HIS-2 intersect at coordinates (2, 72). HIS-2 and HIS-3 intersect at coordinates (4, 74). Before the intersection, the larger the K, the smaller the Cost. After the crossing point, the greater the K, the greater the Cost. The results demonstrate that compared to the other two strategies, the proposed method has the least immune cost.

6   Conclusion

In this paper, we design a spread of information control strategy to set up defenses against information breakout ahead of time. The social communications are explored to extract social information such that we can determine the pattern of information transmissions among individuals. We attempt to minimize the control cost of infected individuals by immune a small fraction of the population. This minimization problem can be solved and thus we propose an influence minimization algorithm. Simulations and comparisons are conducted to evaluate the performance of the proposed spread of information control strategy over 4 real-life datasets. The results indicate that the proposed strategy is superior to existing ones. Due to equipment reasons, the experimental data is too small. The next step will be to try to study it with a larger data set.

Acknowledgments. This work was supported by the Hunan Provincial Natural Science Foundation of China (No. 2021JJ30283).

References

1. Yang, Y., Liu, H., Zhou, J.: Epidemic spreading-information dissemination coupling mechanism in heterogeneous areas. Comput. Mater. Continua **67**(3), 3311–3327 (2021)
2. Chen, L., Hong, L., Liu, J.: Analysis and prediction of new media information dissemination of police microblog. J. New Media **2**(2), 91–98 (2020)

3. Majeed, F., Yousaf, N., Shafiq, M., Basheikh, M.A., Khan, W.Z.: Personalized information retrieval from friendship strength of social media comments. Intell. Autom. Soft Comput. **32**(1), 15–30 (2022)
4. Amin, S., Uddin, M.I., Zeb, M.A., Alarood, A.A., Mahmoud, M.: Detecting information on the spread of dengue on twitter using artificial neural networks. Comput. Mater. Continua **67**(1), 1317–1332 (2021)
5. Wang, P., Wang, Z., Ma, Q.: Research on the association of mobile social network users privacy information based on big data analysis. J. Inf. Hiding Privacy Prot. **1**(1), 35–42 (2019)
6. Bakshy, E., Rosenn, C.I., Marlow, L.: Adamic: the role of social networks in information diffusion. In: 20th World Wide Web, pp. 519–528. Association for Computing Machinery (2012)
7. Han, S.Y.: Daejeon: rumor blocking through online link deletion on social networks. Comput. Rev. **60**(11), 408–409 (2019)
8. Cohen, J.E.: Infectious diseases of humans: dynamics and control. JAMA, J. Am. Med. Assoc. **268**(23), 33–81 (1992)
9. Pastor-Satorras, R., Vespignani, A.: Immunization of complex networks. Phys. Rev. E Stat. Nonlin. Soft Matter Phys. **65**(3 Pt 2A), 036–104 (2002)
10. Cohen, R., Havlin, S., Ben-Avraham, D.: Efficient immunization strategies for computer networks and populations. Phys. Rev. Lett. **91**(24), 247–901 (2003)
11. Chen, Y., Paul, G., Havlin, S.: Finding a better immunization strategy. Phys. Rev. Lett. **101**(5), 58–701 (2008)
12. Gallos, L.K., Liljeros, F., Argyrakis, P.: Improving immunization strategies. Phys. Rev. E **75**(4), 45104 (2007)
13. Grigorieva, E., Khailov, E., Korobeinikov, A.: Optimal control for an epidemic in populations of varying size. In: Conference Publications 2015(special), pp. 549–561 (2015)
14. Zhong, Z.: System dynamics simulation of information diffusion strategies for typhoon disasters. J. Coastal Res. **83**(sp1), 741–753 (2018)
15. Liu, F., Zhang, Z., Buss, M.: Optimal filtering and control of networks information epidemics. Automatisierungstechnik **69**(2), 122–130 (2021)
16. Liu, Y., Qi, J., Ding, Y.: An endocrine-immune system inspired controllable information diffusion model in social networks. Neurocomputing **301**(2), 25–35 (2018)
17. Kempe, D., Kleinberg, J., Tardos, É.: Maximizing the spread of influence through a social network. In: Proceedings of the Ninth ACM SIGKDD International Conference on Knowledge Discovery and Data Mining, pp. 137–146 (2003)
18. Zhang, L., Li, D., Xi, Y., Jia, S.: Reinforcement learning with actor-critic for knowledge graph reasoning. Sci. China Inf. Sci. **63**(6), 1–3 (2020). https://doi.org/10.1007/s11432-018-9820-3
19. Lou, T., Tang, J.: Mining structural hole spanners through information diffusion in social networks. In: 21st World Wide Web, pp. 825–836. Association for Computing Machinery (2013)
20. Han, B., Hui, P., Kumar, V.A., Marathe, M.V., Shao, J., Srinivasan, A.: Mobile data offloading through opportunistic communications and social participation. IEEE Trans. Mob. Comput. **11**(5), 821–834 (2012)

End-to-End Speech Synthesis Method for Lhasa-Tibetan Multi-speaker

Xiaona Xu[1] , Wanyue Ma[1] , Zhengjia Dan[1] , Huilin Ma[1(✉)] , Tianyi Liu[2] , and Yue Zhao[1]

[1] Minzu University of China, Beijing 100081, China
ma.huilin@163.com
[2] Department of Computer Science and Engineering, Santa Clara University, 500 El Camino Real, Santa Clara, CA 95053, USA

Abstract. Tibetan text-to-speech generally focuses on a single speaker or a single dialect, and there is a lack of research on Tibetan multi-speaker speech synthesis. This paper explores the speech synthesis methods based on an end-to-end model for Lhasa-Tibetan multi-speaker. We propose to convert Tibetan characters into Latin letters to improve the effect of model learning. We compare the end-to-end model using the speaker ID embedded into the spectrogram feature prediction network against using some WaveNet vocoders trained on specific speaker data. Referring to the results of objective and subjective experiments, our method has better speech quality than the model using some WaveNet vocoders trained on specific speaker data.

Keywords: End-to-end speech synthesis · Multi-speaker · Lhasa-Tibetan dialect

1 Introduction

Speech synthesis technology converts text into speech, which generates a corresponding speech waveform for a given target text. There are various speech synthesis applications in man-machine interaction, assistive technology, media and entertainment. With the development of speech synthesis technology, multi-speaker speech synthesis has attracted more research interest of researchers on synthesizing different speakers' speech in a unified speech synthesis model [1–3].

As one of the Chinese minority languages, Tibetan is mainly divided into three major dialects: Ü-Tsang, Kham and Amdo. Although the characters of all dialects are the same, due to their different pronunciations, people in different regions have difficulties with communication. In addition, because of the lack of technical standards and language resources in Tibetan, its research is still in the developing stage.

For the research of Tibetan speech synthesis technology, there are generally three methods: statistical parameter modeling, speech synthesis unit selection, waveform splicing, and deep learning. However, the Tibetan speech corpus is still in the stage of construction and development. At the same time, traditional speech synthesis methods usually require researchers to have more linguistic knowledge, which is not conducive to

X. Sun et al. (Eds.): ICAIS 2022, CCIS 1586, pp. 340–350, 2022.
https://doi.org/10.1007/978-3-031-06767-9_28

the study of Tibetan speech synthesis [4–7]. Therefore, the effect of speech synthesis based on deep learning is better than that based on statistical parameters and waveform splicing.

Some works have shown that the end-to-end speech synthesis has better performance than traditional methods. The work of [8] showed that the end-to-end method takes a shorter time than the statistical parameter method. The works of [9–12] found that the performance of the TTS (text-to-speech) system has been further improved through using end-to-end neural network frameworks. Tacotron2, an advanced TTS system, consists of an encoder-decoder architecture and a neural WaveNet vocoder [13, 14]. Since the synthesized voice by the Tacotron series is the closest to natural speech, it is widely used and researched.

For the research on Tibetan speech synthesis, the work of [5] proposed a speech synthesis method which is a breakthrough in traditional recurrent neural network and convolutional neural network, using the Seq2Seq model and Griffin-lim as a vocoder for Tibetan speech synthesis, and obtained a clearer and more natural synthesized speech. Based on the Seq2Seq model, the work of [12] proposed to use WaveNet as a vocoder to conduct experiments. The experimental results show that the synthesized speech by WaveNet has better clarity and naturalness.

Combining the advantages of Tacotron2 and WaveNet, this paper proposes an end-to-end speech synthesis method for Tibetan multi-speaker. The main method is to insert the speaker ID in the Tibetan text, and Tibetan characters are transcribed by the corresponding Latin alphabets. The preprocessed text will be input to a sequence-to-sequence feature prediction network, which outputs a predicted Mel spectrogram. And then WaveNet is trained by the target speaker's speech data and the Mel spectrogram.

The contributions of this paper are as follows: (1) Proposing an end-to-end speech synthesis method for Lhasa-Tibetan multi-speaker. All modules are merged into one system. Our method can be used to synthesize different speaker voices. (2) Transliterating Tibetan characters into Latin letters using the Wiley transliteration. This process will effectively enhance the learning effect of the model under the limited Tibetan speech data. (3) The speaker ID is embedded in the model to synthesize speech for the specific speaker.

2 Method

2.1 Text Preprocessing

Although Tibetan has a very long history, the orthography of written language is still unchanged. The work of [15] has detailed the structure of Tibetan sentences: Tibetan letters are composed of 30 consonants and 4 vowels, and each sentence consists of a sequence of single syllables. The writing order is from left to right. Figure 1 is an example of a Tibetan sentence.

Each syllable in Tibetan has a root character, which is the central consonant of the syllable. A vowel tag can be above or below the root character to indicate different syllables. Sometimes there is a superscript character at the top of the root character, one or two subscript characters at the bottom, and a prescript character in front, indicating that the initials of the syllable are compound consonants. Sometimes there are one or

འཇར་ཚོན་གྱི་ཆུལ་གྱིས་ཁྱེད་ཀྱི་བར་སྣང་ལ་སྤྲོས་ཆོག་པར་ཞུ།

Fig. 1. A Tibetan sentence.

two postscripts after the root character, which means that the syllable ends with one or two consonants. The structure of Tibetan syllables is shown in Fig. 2.

Speech synthesis units affect the effect of synthesis. A Tibetan syllable can have 20,450 spelling schemes. The work of [16] explored the problem of selecting Tibetan synthesis unit and proposed a Tibetan speech synthesis method that combines components, combination components, characters, words, and phonemes. If Tibetan monosyllables are used as the primitives of speech synthesis, a large amount of corpus needs to be built, which is not easy to implement. The Tibetan speech synthesis system in [17] uses Tibetan consonants and vowels as the primitives of speech synthesis, but this often requires researchers to have a lot of knowledge of Tibetan linguistics. The works of [18, 19] used phonemes as speech synthesis units, but it is necessary to build a phoneme dictionary, which increases the workload of front-end analysis. In this paper, 26 Latin letters are used as speech synthesis primitives and Tibetan text can be transcribed in Latin letters by the Willy transliteration scheme. This approach will effectively reduce the required training data, the workload of text processing, and improve the synthesis efficiency.

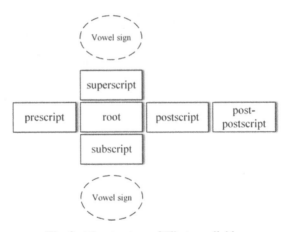

Fig. 2. The structure of Tibetan syllables.

Figure 3 shows the converted Tibetan sentences obtained by using the Willy transliteration scheme.

ja' tshon gyi tshul gyis khyed kyi bar snang la spros chog par zhu

Fig. 3. Example of Willie Transliteration.

2.2 Spectrogram Feature Prediction Network

The Tacotron2 model was designed and developed by Google in 2017. Since its synthesis quality is close to the human voice, it is used by many researchers in the speech synthesis field. An end-to-end speech synthesis system based on the Tacotron2 model is designed in this paper. The first part of the model is the spectrogram feature prediction network with an attention mechanism, which is mainly composed of encoder, attention mechanism and decoder. We use the Tibetan text transcribed by the Latin alphabet and inserted by speaker IDs as the input sequence of the spectrogram feature prediction network. After encoding and decoding operations, the second part of the model is WaveNet vocoder, which is used to synthesize the target speaker's speech waveform.

The encoder consists of a character embedding layer, a 3-layer convolutional neural network, and a Long Short Term Memory Network (LSTM). The decoder is composed of Pre-Net, LSTM, linear projection and Post-net. The new sequence is obtained by the input sequence through the encoder, and then the Mel spectrogram is obtained through the attention mechanism and the decoder. The encoder and decoder implement the conversion from text to context vector, and the WaveNet vocoder converts the context vector into waveform samples. Figure 4 below shows the model of end-to-end speech synthesis for Lhasa-Tibetan multi-speaker [20, 21].

Feature Extraction of Mel Spectrogram. In order to simulate the human ear auditory system and obtain a better speech synthesis effect, the spectrogram feature prediction network will output the Mel spectrograms. Mel spectrogram is the addition of Mel filter function to the general speech spectrogram, so that the frequency of the sound is within the range of human hearing.

Attention Mechanism. Usually, a very long sequence passes through the encoder to get a fixed-length context vector, but that may cause that the encoder cannot represent the entire information of the sequence. At the same time, because the vector is continuously generated on the timeline, the subsequent vectors may cover the previous sequence. So more information will be lost in the subsequent decoding process, which is not conducive to the model learning. Therefore, the attention mechanism needs to be added to the system [22].

The attention mechanism aims to select some key information in a sequence to improve the efficiency of the neural network. It gives different weights for different information data. Attention mechanism makes it possible to focus on the encoding results related to the current in each step during decoding, thereby reducing the difficulty of learning the output representation of the encoder [23, 24]. Its working principle is shown in Fig. 5.

In the sequence-to-sequence model with the attention mechanism, the input n-frame sequence is encoded by the encoder into a context vector c, where a_n is the input n-th frame, and h_n is the output of the encoder. The formula (1) is as follows:

$$c = \text{encoder}(a_1, a_2, a_3 \ldots a_n)$$
$$= h_1, h_2, h_3 \ldots h_n \tag{1}$$

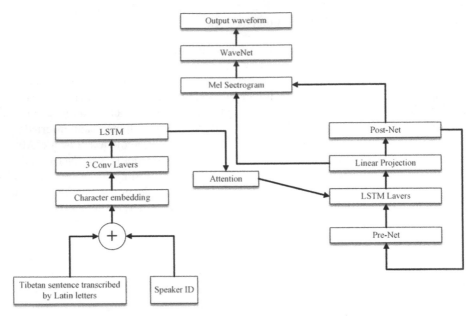

Fig. 4. The model of end-to-end speech synthesis for Lhasa-Tibetan multi-speaker.

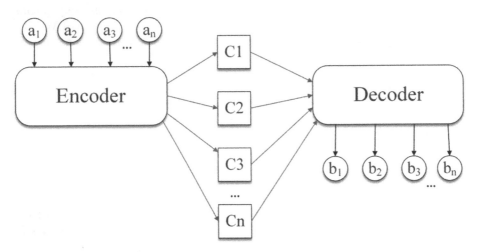

Fig. 5. Sequence-to-sequence model diagram with an attention mechanism.

The attention mechanism connecting the encoder and the decoder will combine each different c to select key information for decoding, so that the model will be more accurate. The output of the encoder is calculated by the formula (2), where h_j is the eigenvector output by the encoder and the a_{ij} is the weight.

$$c_i = \sum_{j=1}^{T_i} a_{ij}h_j \tag{2}$$

a_{ij} is calculated by the formula (3), and e_{ij} represents the matching degree between the j-th input of the encoder and the i-th character of the decoder, and the e_{ij} formula (4) is as follows.

$$a_{ij} = \frac{\exp(e_{ij})}{\sum_{k=1}^{T_x} \exp(e_{ik})} \tag{3}$$

$$e_{ij} = a(s_{i-1}, h_j) \tag{4}$$

2.3 Vocoder

Google's end-to-end model Tacotron [25] first converts voice or text data into frequency spectrum and then uses a vocoder to obtain synthesized speech. The vocoder in Tacotron is the Griffin-lim algorithm for the time-domain waveform. The Griffin-lim algorithm reconstructs speech when only the amplitude spectrum is known but the phase spectrum is unknown. It can estimate the discarded phase information and use a short-time inverse fourier transform to convert the linear spectrogram into the time domain waveform. It is a simple and efficient vocoder. However, because the waveform generated by the Griffin-lim vocoder is too smooth, the synthesized speech quality is poor, and it sounds unnatural.

This work uses the WaveNet model as a vocoder to cover the limitation of the Griffin-lim algorithm. WaveNet is mainly composed of stacked dilated causal convolutions, and it uses causal convolution to increase the receptive field of convolution. WaveNet synthesizes speech by fitting the distribution of audio waveforms by the autoregressive method, which means after inputting predicted sampling points, these convolutional layers and functions of gating activation are passed, and WaveNet will predict the next sampling point according to the input sampling points, then finally synthesize speech by predicting the value of the waveform at each time step [8].

WaveNet usually used the traditional acoustic and linguistic features as the input of the model for speech synthesis. To improve the model's efficiency and reduce the loss of details, in this paper, we choose the Mel spectrogram as the input of WaveNet for training. Mel spectrogram emphasizes the details of low frequency, which is very vital for the accuracy of speech. And it is easier to train with the square error loss [26]. Therefore, in this work, we will train WaveNet vocoder for multi-speaker's speech synthesis.

3 Experiments Settings

The spectrogram feature prediction network is trained on a Tibetan speech data of 4 speakers. The speech data are about 9.97 h with 7419 text sentences. Speech data files are converted to a 16 kHz sampling rate, with 16 bit quantization.

The training data is shown in Table 1. For the training process, the batch size is 8, and after 50,000 iterations, the learning rate is reduced from 10^{-3} to 10^{-4}.

WaveNet vocoder is trained based on the data of multi-speaker. Each spectrogram frame is precisely aligned with the waveform sample.

Table 1. Details of experimental data.

Speaker	Number of text sentences	Time of the speech data (Hours)
Speaker-A	1827	3.175
Speaker-B	1932	2.43
Speaker-C	1818	2.89
Speaker-D	1842	1.475

4 Experimental Results

This paper adopts two experimental methods for the model evaluation: subjective and objective experiments. In the subjective experiment, we randomly selected 20 listeners. After listening to the synthesized speech, they will score it according to the scoring criteria in Table 2. Finally, the scores of all listeners are calculated as the average opinion score (MOS) of the synthesized speech. The higher the MOS, means the better the speech synthesis effect. In the objective experiment, the root mean square error (RMSE) of the time domain sequence is calculated to measure the difference between the synthesized speech and the reference speech. Among them, the smaller the RMSE, the closer the synthesized speech is to the reference and the better the speech synthesis effect.

4.1 Subjective Experiment

In the subjective experiment, we randomly selected 20 listeners. After listening to the synthesized speech, the original speech was used as a reference, and the synthesized speech was scored according to the scoring criteria in Table 2. In order to evaluate the effect of the model's synthesis speech, we compared the speech of using the speaker ID embedded into the spectrogram feature prediction network with using WaveNet vocoders trained on specific speaker data without embedding speaker ID in Tibetan text. Finally, the scores of all listeners are calculated as the average opinion score (MOS) of the synthesized speech. Table 3 shows the results.

From the experiment results, it can be seen that the synthesized speech effect obtained by our model is good. By the way, the synthesis quality of speaker-A is the highest, because the data is larger.

Table 2. Subjective evaluation criteria.

Score	Sound quality
5	Very good
4	Good
3	Not bad
2	Bad
1	Very bad

Table 3. Subjective evaluation results.

Speaker	MOS of using the speaker ID embedded into the spectrogram feature prediction network	MOS of using WaveNet vocoders trained on specific speaker data without embedding speaker ID in Tibetan text
Speaker-A	4.16	3.68
Speaker-B	4.03	3.55
Speaker-C	4.12	3.24
Speaker-D	3.88	3.16

4.2 Objective Experiment

The objective experiment mainly calculates the root mean square error (RMSE) of the time-domain sequence. The RMSE formula is shown in formula (5), where $L_{1,t}$ and $L_{2,t}$ respectively represent the time series values of the reference speech and synthesized speech at a time t.

$$RMSE = \sqrt{\frac{\sum_{t=1}^{n}(L_{1,t} - L_{2,t})^2}{n}} \tag{5}$$

We randomly select 10 text sentences, using the end-to-end speech synthesis method for Lhasa-Tibetan multi-speaker, and calculate the average RMSE to evaluate the closeness of the synthesized speech and the reference speech. In order to evaluate the performance of the model, we compared it with the model using WaveNet vocoders trained on specific speaker data without embedding speaker ID in Tibetan text. These models are used to synthesize the same 10 text sentences and calculate the average value of RMSE. The results are shown in Table 4.

It can be seen from the Table 4 that the RMSE value of the speaker ID embedded into the spectrogram feature prediction network (0.183, 0.211, 0.220, 0.254) is less than the RMSE value of using WaveNet vocoder trained by speaker-A (0.235), speaker-B (0.240), speaker-C (0.277) and speaker-D (0.293). The speech synthesis quality obtained by speaker-A is relatively better, because the data is larger.

Table 4. Comparative evaluation results.

Speaker	RMSE value of using the speaker ID embedded into the spectrogram feature prediction network	RMSE value of using WaveNet vocoders trained on specific speaker data without embedding speaker ID in Tibetan text
A	0.183	0.235
B	0.211	0.240
C	0.220	0.277
D	0.254	0.293

Figure 6 is the Mel spectrogram of target speech and predicted spectrogram of speaker-A obtained by our method. Figure 7 is for speaker-B. It can be seen that both are very similar.

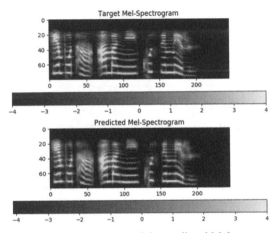

Fig. 6. The target speech Mel spectrogram and the predicted Mel spectrogram of Speaker-A.

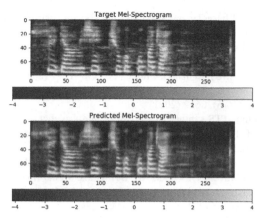

Fig. 7. The target speech Mel spectrogram and the predicted Mel spectrogram of Speaker-B.

5 Summary

This paper constructs an end-to-end speech synthesis method for Lhasa-Tibetan multi-speaker, including a spectrogram feature prediction network embedded speaker ID and a WaveNet vocoder which converted the Mel spectrograms to time-domain waveform. In the text processing, the Wiley transliteration scheme was used to convert Tibetan characters into Latin letters, which effectively reduced the scale of training data. Referring to the results of objective and subjective experiments, our method has better speech quality than the model using some WaveNet vocoders trained on specific speaker data.

References

1. Fan, Y., Qian, Y., et al.: Multi-speaker modeling and speaker adaptation for DNN-based TTS synthesis. In: 2015 IEEE International Conference on Acoustics, Speech and Signal Processing (ICASSP), South Brisbane, QLD, Australia, pp. 4475–4479 (2015)
2. Cooper, E., et al.: Zero-shot multi-speaker text-to-speech with state-of-the-art neural speaker embeddings. In: 2020 IEEE International Conference on Acoustics, Speech and Signal Processing (ICASSP), Barcelona, Spain, pp. 6184–6188 (2020)
3. Jia, Y., Zhang, Y., Weiss, R.J., et al.: Transfer learning from speaker verification to multispeaker text-to-speech synthesis. Adv. Neural. Inf. Process. Syst. **31**, 4485–4495 (2018)
4. Huang, C.: Frontiers of Tibetan studies in 2019. J. Tibet Nationalities Univ. (Philos. Soc. Sci. Ed.) **41**(5), 47–52 (2020)
5. Du, G.: Research on Tibetan speech synthesis technology based on neural network. M.S. dissertation, Qinghai Normal University (2019)
6. Luo, L.: Research and implementation of sequence-to-sequence Tibetan Lhasa speech synthesis. M.S. dissertation, Northwest University for Nationalities (2019)
7. Liu, F.: Research on key technologies of Tibetan speech synthesis system. J. Tibet Univ. (Nat. Sci. Ed.) **31**(2), 87–91 (2016)
8. Ling, Z., Wu, H.: Study on speech synthetic vocoder based on WaveNet. Artif. Intell. **1**, 83–91 (2018)
9. Luo, L., Li, G., et al.: End-to-end speech synthesis for Tibetan Lhasa dialect. J. Phys: Conf. Ser. **1187**(5), 052061 (2019)

10. Zhao, Y., Hu, P., et al.: Lhasa-Tibetan speech synthesis using end-to-end model. IEEE Access **7**, 140305–140311 (2019)
11. Li, G., Luo, L., et al.: End-to-end Tibetan speech synthesis based on phones and semi-syllables. In: 2019 Asia-Pacific Signal and Information Processing Association Annual Summit and Conference (APSIPA ASC), Lanzhou, China, pp. 1294–1297 (2019)
12. Ding, Y., Cai, R., Gong, B.: Tibetan speech synthesis based on an improved neural network. MATEC Web Conf. **336**(5), 0612 (2021)
13. Shen, J., et al.: Natural TTS synthesis by conditioning wavenet on mel spectrogram predictions. In: 2018 IEEE International Conference on Acoustics, Speech and Signal Processing (ICASSP), Calgary, AB, Canada, pp. 4779–4783 (2018)
14. Tobing, P., Wu, Y., et al.: An evaluation of voice conversion with neural network spectral mapping models and WaveNet vocoder. APSIPA Trans. Signal Inf. Process. **9**, E26 (2020)
15. Gongbao, C.: Research on Tibetan speech synthesis technology. M.S. dissertation, Qinghai University for Nationalities (2014)
16. Cairang, Z., Li, Y., Cai, Z.: Selection of Tibetan speech synthesis unit. J. Softw. **26**(6), 1409–1420 (2015)
17. Gongbao, C.: Research on Tibetan speech synthesis based on consonants and vowels. Inf. Comput. (Theoret. Ed.) **1**, 52–53 (2014)
18. Yang, H., Oura, K., Wang, H., Gan, Z., Tokuda, K.: Using speaker adaptive training to realize Mandarin-Tibetan cross-lingual speech synthesis. Multimedia Tools Appl. **74**(22), 9927–9942 (2014). https://doi.org/10.1007/s11042-014-2117-9
19. Li, M., Zhang, G., et al.: The phoneme automatic segmentation algorithms study of Tibetan lhasa words continuous speech stream. Advanced Materials Research, pp. 2051–2054 (2013)
20. Soonil, K.: 1D-CNN: speech emotion recognition system using a stacked network with dilated CNN features. J. Big Data **67**(3), 4039–4059 (2021)
21. Kalphana, I., Kesavamurthy, T.: Convolutional neural network auto encoder channel estimation algorithm in mimo-ofdm system. Comput. Syst. Sci. Eng. **41**(1), 171–185 (2022)
22. Prabhu, K., et al.: Facial expression recognition using enhanced convolution neural network with attention mechanism. Comput. Syst. Sci. Eng. **41**(1), 415–426 (2022)
23. Almars, A.M.: Attention-based Bi-LSTM model for Arabic depression classification. Comput. Mater. Continua **71**(2), 3091–3106 (2022)
24. Sun, J., Li, Y., Shen, Y., et al.: Joint self-attention based neural networks for semantic relation extraction. J. Inf. Hiding Privacy Prot. **1**(2), 69–75 (2019)
25. Skerry-Ryan, R., Battenberg, E., et al.: Towards end-to-end prosody transfer for expressive speech synthesis with tacotron. In: International Conference on Machine Learning (ICML), Stockholm, Sweden, pp. 4693–4702 (2018)
26. Tamamori, A., Hayashi, T., et al.: Speaker-dependent wavenet vocoder. In: Interspeech 2017, Stockholm, Sweden, pp. 1118–1122 (2017)

Prediction Model of Optimized Grey Neural Network Based on Mind Evolutionary Algorithm

Zhen Luo[1], Xiuwen Yan[1], Juan Wang[1], Wenjin Cheng[1], and Qian Yu[2(✉)]

[1] 48th Research Institute of CETC, Changsha 410111, China
[2] Department of Vehicle Engineering, Hunan Automotive Engineering Vocational College, Zhuzhou 412000, China
yuqian_hn@163.com

Abstract. In order to improve the prediction mode accuracy of grey neural network, a prediction model of optimized grey neural network based on mind evolutionary algorithm (MEA) is proposed. Firstly, using MEA with extremely strong global search ability to train and optimize the grey parameters of grey neural network. Secondly, calculate the weights and thresholds of grey neural network using the optimized grey parameters. After comparative study of the prediction mode of MEA optimized grey neural network(MEA-GNNM), genetic algorithm optimized grey neural network (GA-GNNM) and not optimized grey neural network (GNNM) on the prediction for silicon epitaxial layer thickness, the results show that MEA-GNNM has higher prediction accuracy than other two models.

Keywords: Grey neural network · Mind evolutionary algorithm · Genetic algorithm

1 Introduction

Grey System Theory is a system science theory put forward by Chinese scholar Professor Deng Julong in 1982. The gray model is a model built in the gray system. It can predict the development and change of the eigenvalues of the uncertain system [1–5]. It has the advantages of flexible and convenient modeling, small amount of data, and no requirement for data to have better distribution rules [6]. Artificial neural networks have shown great advantages in the prediction of various time series due to their good non-linear quality and self-adaptation and self-learning capabilities [7]. Therefore, some scholars combined the gray model and the neural network to establish the gray neural network model, which makes full use of the complementarity of the characteristics of the two models, and makes up for the shortcomings of using the gray model or neural network alone. However, reference [8] shows that although the gray neural network greatly improves the prediction accuracy of using a single model, it is more sensitive to the initial weight and threshold of the neural network. If the initial values of these parameters are set unreasonably, it is easy to cause the gray neural network to converge

X. Sun et al. (Eds.): ICAIS 2022, CCIS 1586, pp. 351–361, 2022.
https://doi.org/10.1007/978-3-031-06767-9_29

slowly and fall into local optima. For this reason, this paper proposes to combine the mind evolutionary algorithm [9] and gray neural network to establish MEA-GNNM, and use the mind evolutionary algorithm to optimize the gray parameters of the gray neural network, so that the optimized initial weights and thresholds can be calculated, the convergence speed of the gray neural network can be improved and the possibility of falling into the local optimum can be reduced. In order to verify the effectiveness of MEA-GNNM, MEA-GNNM and GA-GNNM [10] and GNNM [11] are used to predict silicon epitaxial layer thickness at the same time, and the prediction performance of the three models is compared. Experimental results show that MEA-GNNM has higher prediction accuracy than GA-GNNM and GNNM.

2 Mind Evolutionary Algorithm

The mind evolutionary algorithm [12] was proposed by Sun Chengyi and other researchers in 1998, and its ideas originated from imitating the evolutionary process of human thinking. This algorithm inherits the "group" and "evolution" ideas of genetic algorithm, and proposes new operators: "convergence" and "alienation". These two operations avoid the double defects of crossover and mutation in genetic algorithm, and overcome the problems of long calculation time and unknowable calculation results of genetic algorithm [13]. Zhang Yishuai used the mind evolutionary algorithm to optimize the BP neural network, and carried out a short-term natural gas prediction analysis for a county in Yinchuan [14]; Zhao Ruiyong established a prediction model based on MEA optimized BP neural network, and predicted the temperature of microwave heating lignite [15]; Wu Wei applied the mind evolutionary algorithm in the medical field and established a MEA-BP prediction model to predict the incidence of hemorrhagic fever with renal syndrome [16]. The system structure diagram of the mind evolutionary algorithm is shown in Fig. 1.

The mind evolutionary algorithm mainly includes the following steps [17]:

1) Group generation: randomly generate individuals in the solution space, all individuals form a group, and calculate the score of each individual according to the fitness function.
2) Subgroup generation: According to the individual scores, the first M individuals with the highest scores are regarded as the winning individuals, and the total N individuals from M + 1 to M + N are regarded as temporary individuals. Then using the selected winning individuals and temporary individuals as the center to generate M winning subgroups and N temporary subgroups, the number of individuals in each subgroup is K/(M + N).
3) Convergence operation: The process in which individuals within each subgroup compete to become the winner is called convergence. If a subgroup no longer produces new individuals in the process of convergence, it means that the subgroup has matured, that is, the process of convergence of the subgroup is over.
4) Alienation operation: In the entire solution space, mature subgroups compete to become the winner, and constantly explore new points in the solution space. This process is called alienation. In the process of alienation, if the score of a temporary

subgroup is higher than the score of a winning subgroup, the temporary subgroup will replace the winning subgroup. If the score of a temporary subgroup is lower than the score of any winning subgroup, the temporary subgroup is discarded and the individuals in it are released. Finally, the global optimal individual and its score in this iteration process can be obtained.

5) Iterative operation: After the alienation operation, the released individuals will be replenished by new temporary subgroups, and the process (3) and (4) are repeated until the score of the best individual no longer increases or the iteration ends, and finally the best individual is output.

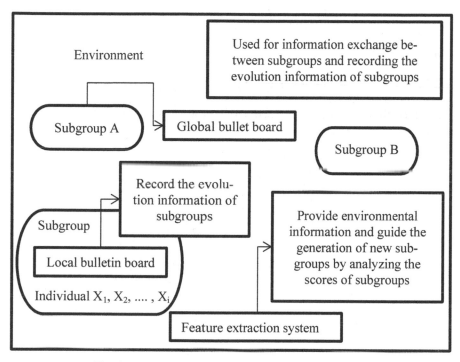

Fig. 1. System structure of mind evolutionary algorithm.

3 MEA Optimized Grey Neural Network

3.1 Grey Neural Network

Suppose that the original series of eigenvalues of the uncertain system $x_t^{(0)}(t = 0, 1, 2, \cdots N - 1)$ is accumulated, and the new series $x_t^{(1)}$ shows an exponential growth law, so a continuous function or differential equation can be used to fit and predict. For the convenience of expression, the original sequence $x_t^{(0)}$ is denoted as x(t), the sequence after an accumulation $x_t^{(1)}$ is denoted as y(t), the prediction result is recorded as z(t).

The differential equation of the gray neural network model with n parameters is expressed as:

$$\frac{dy_1}{dt} + ay_1 = b_1 y_2 + b_2 y_3 + \cdots + b_{n-1} y_n \tag{1}$$

where $y_2, \cdots, y_n$ are the system input parameters; y_1 is the system output parameter; $a, b_1, b_2, \cdots, b_{n-1}$ are the coefficients of the differential equation.

The time response of formula (1) is

$$
z(t) = \left(y_1(0) - \frac{b_1}{a} y_2(t) - \frac{b_2}{a} y_3(t) - \ldots - \frac{b_{n-1}}{a} y_n(t) \right) e^{-at}
$$
$$
+ \frac{b_1}{a} y_2(t) + \frac{b_2}{a} y_3(t) + \cdots + \frac{b_{n-1}}{a} y_n(t) \tag{2}
$$

Make

$$
d = \frac{b_1}{a} y_2(t) + \frac{b_2}{a} y_3(t) + \ldots + \frac{b_{n-1}}{a} y_n(t)
$$

then formula (2) can be transformed into the following formula

$$
\begin{aligned}
z(t) &= \left((y_1(0) - d) \cdot \frac{e^{-at}}{1 + e^{-at}} + d \cdot \frac{1}{1 + e^{-at}} \right) \cdot (1 + e^{-at}) \\
&= \left((y_1(0) - d) \left(1 - \frac{1}{1 + e^{-at}} \right) + d \cdot \frac{1}{1 + e^{-at}} \right) \cdot (1 + e^{-at}) \\
&= \left((y_1(0) - d) - y_1(0) \cdot \frac{1}{1 + e^{-at}} + 2d \cdot \frac{1}{1 + e^{-at}} \right) \cdot (1 + e^{-at})
\end{aligned} \tag{3}
$$

Mapping formula (3) to an extended BP neural network can get a gray neural network with n input parameters and one output parameter. The topology of the gray neural network is shown in Fig. 2.

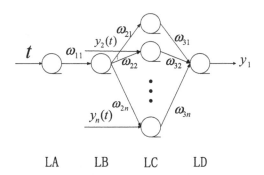

LA   LB   LC   LD

Fig. 2. Topology of grey neural network

In Fig. 2, t is the serial number of the input parameter; $y_2(t), \cdots, y_n(t)$ are the gray neural network input parameter;

$\omega_{21}, \omega_{22}, \cdots, \omega_{2n}, \omega_{31}, \omega_{32}, \cdots, \omega_{3n}$ are the gray neural network weight; y_1 is the predicted value of the gray neural network; LA, LB, LC, and LD respectively represent the four layers of the gray neural network.

The initial weight of the gray neural network can be calculated by the following formula:

$$\omega_{11} = a,$$

$$\omega_{21} = -y_1(0), \omega_{22} = \frac{2b_1}{a}, \omega_{23} = \frac{2b_2}{a}, ..., \omega_{2n} = \frac{2b_{n-1}}{a},$$

$$\omega_{31} = \omega_{32} = ... = \omega_{3n} = 1 + e^{-at} \tag{4}$$

The threshold of the LD layer of the gray neural network is

$$\theta = (1 + e^{-at})(d - y_1(0)) \tag{5}$$

Suppose the output of the LA layer of the gray neural network is h, and the output of the LB layer is s, and the output of the LC layer are $c_1, c_2, \cdots, c_n$, and the output of the LD layer is d. Then the calculation formula of $h, s, c_1, c_2, \cdots, c_n, d$ are as follows:

$$h = \omega_{11}t \tag{6}$$

$$s = \frac{1}{1 + e^{-\omega_{11}t}} \tag{7}$$

$$c1 = s\omega_{21}, c2 = y_2(t)s\omega_{22}, c3 = y_3(t)s\omega_{23}, ..., cn = y_n(t)s\omega_{2n} \tag{8}$$

$$d = \omega_{31}c_1 + \omega_{32}c_2 + ... + \omega_{3n}c_n - \theta_{y1} \tag{9}$$

The gray neural network uses the gradient descent method to modify the weights and thresholds of the network, so that the actual output value of the gray neural network prediction model is constantly approaching the expected output value. The correction process is as follows:

(1) Calculate the error between the predicted output value and the expected output value of the gray neural network.

The error of the LD layer is

$$\delta = d - y_1(t) \tag{10}$$

The error of the LC layer is

$$\delta_1 = \delta(1 + e^{-\omega_{11}t}), \delta_2 = \delta(1 + e^{-\omega_{11}t}), ..., \delta_n = \delta(1 + e^{-\omega_{11}t}) \tag{11}$$

The error of the LB layer is

$$\delta_{n+1} = \frac{1}{1 + e^{-\omega_{11}t}}\left(1 - \frac{1}{1 + e^{-\omega_{11}t}}\right)(\omega_{21}\delta_1 + \omega_{22}\delta_2 + ... + \omega_{2n}\delta_n) \tag{12}$$

(2) Adjust the weights and thresholds of the network according to the error between the predicted output value and the expected output value of the gray neural network. Suppose the learning rate of the gray neural network is μ, then the weight and threshold adjustment formula is

$$\omega_{21} = -y_1(0), \omega_{22} = \omega_{22} - \mu\delta_2 s, ..., \omega_{2n} = \omega_{2n} - \mu\delta_n s \tag{13}$$

$$\omega_{11} = \omega_{11} + ht\delta_{n+1} \tag{14}$$

$$\theta = (1 + e^{-\omega_{11}t})\left(\frac{\omega_{22}}{2}y_2(t) + \frac{\omega_{23}}{2}y_3(t) + ... + \frac{\omega_{2n}}{2}y_n(t) - y_1(0)\right) \tag{15}$$

3.2 MEA Optimization Grey Neural Network Algorithm

This paper uses the MEA algorithm to train and optimize the gray parameters of the gray neural network, and then uses the optimized parameters to calculate the initial weight and threshold of the network, and then uses the initialized gray neural network to train and predict. The specific process is as follows:

1) The samples are divided into training samples and test samples. The training samples are used to train the network, and the test samples are used to test the prediction accuracy of the network.
2) Use MEA algorithm to get optimized grey neural network parameters $a, b_1, b_2, \cdots, b_{n-1}$.
3) According to formula (4) and (5), the initial weights and thresholds of the optimized grey neural network.
   $\omega_{11}, \omega_{21}, \omega_{22}, \cdots, \omega_{2n}, \omega_{31}, \omega_{32}, \cdots, \omega_{3n}, \theta$ are calculated.
4) Determine the maximum number of iterations, the maximum allowable error δ_{max}, and the gray neural network learning rate.
5) For each input sequence $(t, y(t)), t = 1, 2, 3 \cdots, N$, calculate the output of the four layers of gray neural network LA, LB, LC, and LD from formulas (6), (7), (8), (9).
6) Calculate the grey neural network prediction error by formulas (10), (11), (12).
7) Adjust the weights and thresholds of the gray neural network according to formulas (13), (14), (15).
8) If $\delta < \delta_{max}$ or the number of training times reaches the maximum number of iterations, the training ends, otherwise, return to step (5).
9) Input test samples, calculate the prediction accuracy of the grey neural network after training.

4   Design and Analysis of Experimental Results

4.1   Experimental Design

In order to verify the effectiveness of the prediction model proposed in this paper, three prediction models of MEA-GNNM, GA-GNNM and GNNM were used to predict the silicon epitaxial layer thickness. There are many factors influencing the silicon epitaxial layer thickness. This paper selects the five factors of pressure, concentration of silicon source, temperature, crystal orientation and time of deposition to predict the silicon epitaxial layer thickness. The data in this paper has been normalized. In the paper, 30 data are randomly selected as training samples to train the network, and the other 6 data are used as prediction samples to test the network.

The gray neural network structure is determined to be 1-1-6-1 based on the sample, and the parameters of the mind evolutionary algorithm are set as: population size is 100, the number of winning subgroups is 5, the number of temporary subgroups is 5, and the number of iterations is 20.

The evaluation system of the experiment uses absolute error err, average absolute error MAE and relative error perr, namely

$$err = \left| x_i - \hat{x}_i \right| \tag{16}$$

$$MAE = \frac{1}{N_p} \sum_{i=1}^{N_p} \left| x_i - \hat{x}_i \right| \tag{17}$$

$$perr = \frac{\sum_{i=1}^{N_p} (x_i - \hat{x}_i)^2}{\sum_{i=1}^{N_p} x_i^2} \tag{18}$$

where x_i and $\hat{x}_i$ are the actual value and the predicted value of the silicon epitaxial layer thickness respectively; N_p is the number of predicted samples.

4.2 Analysis of Experimental Results

In order to make the experimental results more objective, each experiment was repeated 1000 times in the paper, and then the average absolute error MAE and relative error perr were taken as statistical averages. Figure 3 shows the prediction results of three prediction models in an experiment. Table 1 shows the actual silicon epitaxial layer thickness in the 6 test samples and the statistical average of 1,000 predictions by the three models. Table 2 shows the statistical average of the average absolute error MAE and the relative error perr obtained by the three prediction models for the silicon epitaxial layer thickness after 1000 prediction experiments.

It can be seen from Fig. 3 that the three prediction models can predict the silicon epitaxial layer thickness, but the overall prediction effect of MEA-GNNM is the best, and the overall prediction effect of GA-GNNM is better than that of GNNM.

It can be seen from Table 1 that the predicted values of the three prediction models for the silicon epitaxial layer thickness can approximate the actual thickness. It can be seen from Table 2 that the prediction error of MEA-GNNM proposed in this paper is the smallest, and the prediction error of GA-GNNM is smaller than that of GNNM. In summary, it can be seen that the MEA-GNNM proposed in this paper is an effective prediction model.

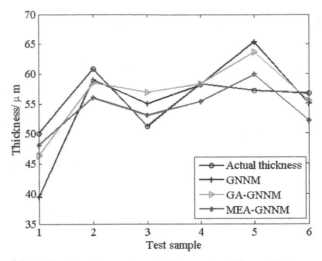

(a) Predicted and true value of silicon epitaxial layer thickness

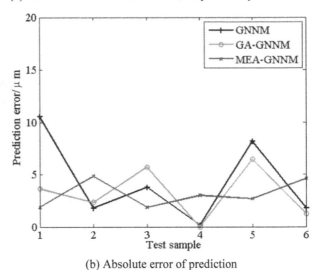

(b) Absolute error of prediction

Fig. 3. Predicted results.

There is still a certain error in the prediction of the silicon epitaxial layer thickness in the whole system, which is mainly related to the following factors:

1) In the calibration of the prediction model, although the mathematical model created by applying the mind evolution gray neural network has high accuracy, there is still a certain nonlinear error. The number of training samples can be increased, thereby reducing the nonlinear error, and finally further improving the prediction accuracy of the thickness.

Table 1. The prediction results of silicon epitaxial layer thickness

Test sample	Actual thickness/μm	GNNM	GA-GNNM	MEA-GNNM
		Predicted value/μm	Predicted value/μm	Predicted value/μm
1	50.01	39.45	46.35	48.13
2	60.82	59.01	58.48	55.98
3	51.14	54.92	56.86	53.01
4	58.29	58.14	58.29	55.29
5	57.17	65.33	63.61	59.86
6	56.70	54.92	55.42	52.10

Table 2. The prediction error of silicon epitaxial layer thickness

Predictive model	GNNM	GA-GNNM	MEA-GNNM
MAE/μm	4.38	3.23	3.15
Perr/%	1.07	0.50	0.36

2) GNN needs to determine many parameters, and there is no effective method for parameter selection. For example, if the selected learning rate parameter is too large, it will easily lead to unstable learning; if the selected learning rate parameter is too small, the training time will be prolonged. Many of these parameters can only be given a rough range based on experience, and there is a lack of simple and effective methods to determine parameters, resulting in insufficient stability of the algorithm.

5   Conclusion

Aiming at the problem that the gray neural network is sensitive to the initial values of network weights and thresholds, this paper proposes a prediction model based on the mind evolutionary algorithm to optimize the gray neural network: first use the mind evolutionary algorithm to obtain the optimized gray parameters of the gray neural network, then calculate the initial value of the network weight and threshold according to the gray parameters, and then establish the gray neural network model according to the optimized initial value.

In order to verify the effectiveness of the prediction model proposed in this paper, the three prediction models of GNNM, GA-GNNM and MEA-GNNM are used to predict silicon epitaxial layer thickness at the same time, and the prediction errors of the three models are compared. The results show that the prediction error of the proposed model MEA-GNNM is smaller than the other two prediction models, so MEA-GNNM is an effective prediction model.

Acknowledgement. The author(s) thank colleagues who have provided the process data.

Funding Statement. The author(s) disclosed receipt of the following financial support for the research, authorship, and/or publication of this article: this work was supported by the Scientific Research Project of Hunan Provincial Department of Education (18C1462), the Major Science and Technology Project of Hunan Province (2020GK1030), the Industry Fund Project of CETC (20201105).

Conflicts of Interest. The author(s) declared no potential conflicts of interest with respect to the research, authorship, and/or publication of this article.

References

1. Kanthavel, R., Dhaya, R.: Prediction model using reinforcement deep learning technique for osteoarthritis disease diagnosis. Comput. Syst. Sci. Eng. **42**(01), 257–269 (2022)
2. Aldossary, M.: A review of energy-related cost issues and prediction models in cloud computing environments. Comput. Syst. Sci. Eng. **36**(02), 353–368 (2021)
3. Grace, R.K., Manimegalai, R.: Design of neural network based wind speed prediction model using gwo. Comput. Syst. Sci. Eng. **40**(02), 593–606 (2022)
4. Humayun, M., Alsayat, A.: Prediction model for coronavirus pandemic using deep learning. Comput. Syst. Sci. Eng. **40**(03), 947–961 (2022)
5. Duhayyim, M.A., Alsolai, H., Al-Wesabi, F.N.: Optimized stacked autoencoder for iot enabled financial crisis prediction model. Comput. Mater. Continua **71**(01), 1079–1094 (2022)
6. Li, S.C., Lu, J.Y., Cheng, L.: Research on temperature of electromagnetic rail launcher based on gray model. J. Natl. Univ. Defense Technol. **42**(05), 90–97 (2020)
7. Tian, N.M., Lan, H.X., Wu, Y.M.: Performance comparison of bp artificial neural network and cart decision tree model in landslide susceptibility prediction. J. Geo-Inf. Sci. **22**(12), 2304–2316 (2020)
8. Zhang, J., Chen, L., Lai, Z.L.: Tunnel deformation prediction based on grey neural network with improved genetic algorithm. Sci. Surv. Mapp. **46**(02), 55–61 (2021)
9. Yu, D.L., Li, Y.M., Ding, B.: Failure diagnosis method for electric submersible plunger pump based on mind evolutionary algorithm and back propagation neural network. Inf. Control **46**(06), 698–705 (2017)
10. Zhang, K., Liu, B.P., Huang, D.: Elite genetic improved nonlinear gray neural network operator and military expenditure multi-objective combination forecasting application. Syst. Eng. Electron. **40**(05), 1070–1078 (2018)
11. Zhang, P., Chang, Y.: Software fault prediction based on grey neural network. In: Proceedings of the ICNC, pp. 466–469. IEEE (2012)
12. Sun, C.Y., Sun, Y., Wei, L.J.: Mind-evolution-based machine learning: framework and the implementation of optimization. In: Proceedings of the INES, pp. 355–359. IEEE (1998)
13. Li, G., Li, W.H.: Facial feature tracking based on mind evolutionary algorithm. J. Jilin Univ. (Eng. Technol. Ed.) **45**(02), 606–612 (2015)
14. Zhang, Y.S., Lai, H.G., Li, Y.: Short-term gas load forecasting based on MEA optimized BP neural network. Autom. Instrum. **31**(05), 15–19 (2016)
15. Zhao, R.Y., Zhou, X.Z.: Research on temperature prediction of microwave heating lignite based on bp neural network optimized by mind evolutionary algorithm. Transducer Microsyst. Technol. **35**(10), 43–48 (2016)

16. Wu, W., Guo, J.Q., An, S.Y.: Application of mind evolutionary algorithm optimized neural network model to predict the incidence of hemorrhagic fever with renal syndrome. Chin. J. Health Stat. **33**(01), 27–30 (2016)
17. Liu, J.: On application of mind evolutionary algorithm in bp neural network fitting nonlinear function. J. Mianyang Normal Univ. **34**(02), 79–83 (2015)

An End-to-End Multi-dialect Tibetan Speech Synthesis Method

Xiaona Xu[1] ⓘ, Yana Lang[1] ⓘ, Yue Zhao[1(✉)] ⓘ, Ning Li[1] ⓘ, and Tianyi Liu[2] ⓘ

[1] Minzu University of China, Beijing 100081, China
zhaoyueso@muc.edu.cn
[2] Department of Computer Science and Engineering, Santa Clara University, 500 El Camino Real, Santa Clara, CA 95053, USA

Abstract. The end-to-end speech synthesis model, Tacotron2, which is based on neural network theory, drives advancements in speech synthesis technology. This paper proposed an end-to-end multi-dialect Tibetan speech synthesis technique based on the Tacotron2 model. First the Wiley transliteration scheme is used to convert Tibetan characters into corresponding Latin letters, which reduces the size of the training corpus, reduces the workload of front-end text processing and improves the efficiency of speech synthesis. Then an end-to-end multi-dialect shared speech synthesis model is established for Amdo pastoral dialect, Dege-Kham dialect and Yushu-Kham dialect, which maps the Latin transliteration vector of Tibetan character to Mel spectrograms. In the end, the dialect ID is appended to the text to help the model learn the characteristics of three dialects during training. The results of experiments show that the effect of synthesized speech is improved with dialect ID.

Keywords: Tibetan speech synthesis · End-to-end model · Multi-dialect

1 Introduction

Speech synthesis is a key technology for human-computer interaction, and it has slowly penetrated all aspects of our lives, such as in automatic speech navigation systems and automatic reading in reading software. Speech synthesis, or text-to-speech (TTS) technology, is a process of converting target text into smooth and intelligent speech. Since the neural network was proposed, the speech synthesis technology has taken a big step forward.

Tibetan language has a long history and is an important part of Chinese language and culture. In China, Tibetan language is mainly spoken in the Tibet Autonomous Region and five regions of local autonomous prefectures including Qinghai, Sichuan, Gansu and Yunnan. Nowadays, Tibetan language has developed into a state that different regions use the same script yet with different dialects. Tibetan language is divided into three main dialect systems: Ü-Tsang dialect, Kham dialect and Amdo dialect [1].

Previous studies on Tibetan speech synthesis mostly focused on the synthesis techniques for a single dialect, such as Lhasa-Ü-Tsang dialect or Amdo dialect [2–5]. Some

X. Sun et al. (Eds.): ICAIS 2022, CCIS 1586, pp. 362–373, 2022.
https://doi.org/10.1007/978-3-031-06767-9_30

works also studied the technology of Chinese-Tibetan bilingual cross-language speech synthesis, but most of them used corpus-based speech splicing synthesis and parameter synthesis. The work of [6] used the method of speech splicing and synthesis to realize the cross-language conversion from Lhasa-Ü-Tsang dialect to Chinese. The work of [7] focused on designing Chinese-Tibetan bilingual cross-language synthesis system using the method of statistical parameters speech synthesis. The work of [8] designed a Chinese-Tibetan bilingual cross-language speech conversion method based on the waveform splicing synthesis method and the STRAIGHT algorithm. In these works, speech splicing technology relies on a large-scale corpus, which consumes much time and workload, and the parameter synthesis rule is not effective. They all rely on the professional knowledge of linguistic experts and need to spend a lot of time analyzing phonemes, intonations, rhythms, etc. And in the process of speech synthesis, the work done in blocks may lead to poor connection in the later stage.

Since deep learning and neural network technology were proposed, the field of speech synthesis has implemented an end-to-end speech synthesis method [9, 10]. The work of [11] compared the Tacotron-based end-to-end method with the HMM-based parametric speech synthesis method, and the results showed that the effect of the end-to-end synthesis is better. The single-language end-to-end speech synthesis technology based on Tacotron2 has achieved better results [12–15]. In the research on multilingual speech synthesis, Wu et al. [16] realized a deep neural network(DNN)-based Mandarin and Tibetan speech synthesis. Recent works [17, 18] proposed the phonetic conversion method from Amdo dialect to Lhasa-Ü-Tsang dialect based on DNN. A recent work [19] studied Tibetan phonetic conversion technology under the condition of parallel and non-parallel corpus. The work of [20] applied the sequence-to-sequence model to realize Lhasa-Ü-Tsang speech synthesis and the synthesized speech was more fluent and natural compared with the traditional HMM and DNN-HMM speech synthesis technology. Since the end-to-end TTS model can produce higher quality speech compared with the classic method, the extension of the end-to-end TTS framework is also used for multilingual modeling [21, 22]. Zhang et al. achieved a high-quality cross-language synthesis of sufficient data scenarios [23]. However, there are still few researches in the field of Tibetan multi-dialect speech synthesis.

Cai et al. used a shared phoneme set to investigate bilingual multispeaker TTS and cross-lingual synthesis between of Chinese and English [24]. The language attributes were distinguished by the use of digital markers in front of the language and text. As Tibetan has the characteristics of the same script and different dialects in different regions, based on the neural network end-to-end model, this paper designed an experiment to embed dialect ID in front of text for different Tibetan dialects to implement the synthesis of three dialects: Amdo pastoral dialect, Dege-Kham dialect and Yushu-Kham dialect. The difference between our work and the work of [24] is that the training process in [24] needs to provide a representation of the same input phonemes and add language ID before the same input phonemes to determine the type of synthesized language in the sentences containing both Chinese and English. However, because Tibetan has the same script and different dialects, it only needs to add dialect ID before the script text and the model can learn the unique characteristics of the dialects.

Our contributions can be summarized as follows: (1) We use Willy transliteration to convert Tibetan characters into Latin letters, which reduces the size of the training corpus, so that the workload of front-end text processing is reduced and the efficiency of speech synthesis is improved. (2) An end-to-end multi-dialect speech synthesis model is established, which integrates all the modules into one model, reducing model connection time and mistakes. It realizes the speech synthesis for Amdo pastoral dialect, Dege-Kham dialect and Yushu-Kham dialect using one speech synthesis system. (3) The dialect ID is embedded in front of the text to assist the model in learning the characteristics of three dialects in a targeted manner, allowing the model to synthesize speech more effectively.

The rest of this paper is organized as follows: Sect. 2 introduces the model of end-to-end multi-dialect speech synthesis. The experiments are presented in detail and the results are discussed as well in Sect. 3. Finally, we describe our conclusions in Sect. 4.

2   Model Structure

Our model consists of two parts: the cyclic sequence-to-sequence feature prediction network and the WaveNet vocoder, showed in Fig. 1. First, the cyclic sequence-to-sequence feature prediction network is an end-to-end feature prediction network. It gets rid of the dependence on front-end text and speech signal processing such as phoneme analysis and prosody analysis. Then, the end-to-end mode changes the previous mode of independent processing of each module, which reduces the time spent on module connection and the errors caused by module connection. In our work, the corresponding <text, audio> pair with dialect ID are input to train the model. During speech synthesis, the cyclic feature prediction network will map the features of the text into the Mel frequency spectrogram. Then send the spectrogram to the WaveNet vocoder, and the vocoder will synthesize the speech waveform based on the spectrogram [25].

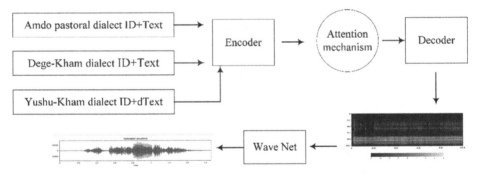

Fig. 1. End-to-end multi-dialect Tibetan speech synthesis model.

In our work, the classic framework of the Tacotron2 model is used, and a low-level acoustic representation, the Mel spectrogram is used to connect the feature prediction network and the vocoder. Comparing with the linear graph, the Mel spectrum is a more compact expression. The acoustical signal is one-dimensional, so only the time domain information can be seen intuitively, but the frequency domain information cannot be seen. To solve this problem, a short-time Fourier transform analysis method is used in the model: firstly, a long speech signal is framed and windowed; secondly, Fourier transform is performed on each frame; and then the result of each frame is stacked along another dimension to obtain a spectrogram. In order to obtain acoustical feature of a suitable size, it will generally pass through the Mel filter bank and be turned into a Mel spectrum due to the spectrogram being large. Then the frequency spectrum is converted into a waveform through the vocoder WaveNet.

2.1 Tibetan Script

Tibetan script is an ancient alphabetic script, which has evolved into its present form after years of development. They consist of 30 consonants and 4 vowels. Like Chinese language, it is written and spelled according to syllables from left to right. The syllables are separated by a "''", and each Tibetan sentence is ended with a "I". Figure 2 below shows an example of a Tibetan sentence.

Fig. 2. Tibetan sentence.

Each syllable in Tibetan has a root, which is the basis of spelling. The root will be accompanied by a label, which includes the vowel symbol and the upper and lower characters. Generally, a Tibetan character includes root, vowel, subscript and superscript, prescript and postscript, illustrated in Fig. 3 below.

	Vowel		
	Superscript		
Prescript	Root	Postscript	Post-postscript
	Subscript		
	Vowel		

Fig. 3. Tibetan phonological structure.

The Tibetan spelling order is shown in Fig. 4:

	5		
	2		
1	3	6	7
	4		
	5		

Fig. 4. Tibetan spelling order.

When there is no additional mark, the letter before the two-letter syllable is the root. In three-letter syllables, usually, the middle letter is the root. If the last two letters are གས༌ ངས༌ བས༌ མས, the first letter is the root. In the four-letter syllables, the second letter is the root. In general, the root has its vowel. When you need to change the vowel, add a vowel symbol above or below the root to mark it.

2.2 Encoder

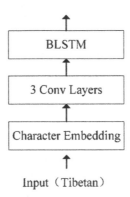

Fig. 5. Encoder model.

The function of the encoder is to convert the Tibetan character sequence into an intermediate representation and extract the features of the input sentence. In our work, the Tibetan text with dialect ID is converted into an intermediate representation. As shown in Fig. 5 above, the encoder includes a convolutional layer and a BLSTM layer. Its input is multiple Tibetan sentences, and the basic unit of each sentence is a character, and each character will be encoded as a 512-dimensional vector. Then the vector will be sent to the three-layer convolutional layer, and the convolutional layer will perform large-span modeling of the input sequence vector context. After convolution, it undergoes normalization and excitation function. Finally, a bidirectional LSTM layer is connected to generate intermediate features. The BLSTM layer contains 512 units, with 256 units forward and reverse [26]. The output of the encoder will be passed as the input to the attention mechanism, and the attention mechanism will focus on the position information of the input sequence.

2.3 Decoder

The decoder shown in Fig. 6 maps the intermediate features extracted by the encoder to the feature Mel spectrogram. The decoder is an autoregressive recurrent neural network. It outputs the intermediate features by the encoder as a spectrogram, which can only predict one frame at a time. The spectrum frame predicted in the previous section is first passed into a two-layer fully connected Pre-Net composed of 256 hidden ReLU units per layer. The output of Pre-Net and the attention context vector are spliced together

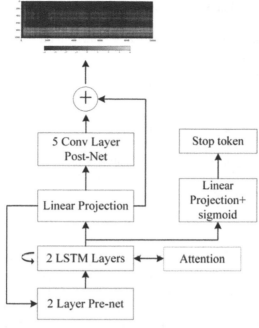

Fig. 6. Decoder model.

and passed to an LSTM layer. The output of the LTSM layer is spliced together with the attention context vector again and then undergoes a linear transformation to predict the target spectrum frame. Finally, the target spectrum frame undergoes a 5-layer convolution "Post-Net" to predict a residual error to be superimposed on the spectrum frame before convolution to improve the target spectrum image. While predicting the spectrum frame, the output of the decoder LSTM is spliced with the attention context vector. It will be projected into a scalar and passed to the sigmoid activation function to predict whether the output sequence has been completed or the prediction spectrum generation needs to continue, and if not, it will stop.

2.4 Attention Mechanism

Attention mechanism originally refers to a brain signal processing mechanism of our humans. We use it to select key information to improve the efficiency and accuracy of information processing. It is used in the Tacotron2 model so that the model can pay attention to the key information of the input sequence. The attention mechanism allows the model to have different attention to different parts of the sequence by reasonably assigning the weight of each element in the sequence. The focus of the model will be on parts that are more relevant to the core content. It can also pay attention to the possible associations between the input sequence and the output sequence. In speech synthesis, it refers to the correlation between the input text sequence and the output speech sequence. The hybrid attention mechanism used in this work combines the content-based attention mechanism and the location-based attention mechanism to connect the encoder and the decoder [27].

The attention mechanism is essentially a weighted summation of the element values in the output sequence of the encoder so that the element values have different proportions. The attention mechanism in step i is

$$e_{i,j} = score(s_i, c\alpha_{i-1}, h_j) = v_a^T \tanh(W_{s_i} + Vh_j + Uf_{i,j} + b) \qquad (1)$$

where v_a, W, U and b are the parameters to be trained, s_i is the current hidden state of the decoder, h_j is the current hidden state of the encoder, $Uf_{i,j}$ is the location feature obtained by convoluting of the previous attention weight α_{i-1}, $f_i = F * c\alpha_{i-1}$. The hybrid attention mechanism in Tacotron2 can simultaneously attend to the content and position of input elements, improving the accuracy of speech synthesis.

2.5   WaveNet Vocoder

WaveNet vocoder is a deep neural network that can generate original audio waveforms, and it is a complete probabilistic autoregressive model. It predicts the probability distribution of the current audio sample based on the samples that have been generated before. The previous Tacotron model is a typical end-to-end model, from the encoder to the vocoder all in one. Tacotron model uses the Griffin-Lim algorithm when generating audio, which directly converts the acoustic parameters in the speech synthesis system into speech waveforms. This vocoder not only requires training, nor does it need to predict the phase spectrum. Instead, the phase information is estimated through the relationship between frames to reconstruct the speech waveform. It is simple and convenient, but the audio synthesized directly using the Griffin-Lim algorithm is too smooth. The synthesized speech is of poor quality and cannot capture the characteristics of multiple dialects [28].

In our work, the modified WaveNet vocoder is used to inversely transform the Mel spectrum characteristics into time-domain waveform samples. Since the acoustical signal is a one-dimensional vector in time, in order to deal with the long-span dependence on time in the speech synthesis process, WaveNet uses causal convolution to ensure that the model does not violate the time sequence of the data when modeling the data. The prediction P that the model can output at time t does not depend on data at a future time. In the training phase, since the time steps of the real data are known, the conditional probability predictions of all time steps can be performed in parallel. The speed of causal convolution prediction will be very fast, but it requires many layers. The synthesis model needs to look back at the speech signal for at least a few seconds in order to generate a coherent sentence, as it has to consider word-to-character, word-to-word and sentence-to-sentence coherence. However, with 16k sampling rate, there are 16, 000 samples per second of the speech signal. With the original method, a few seconds of speech signal would make the model too complex to train. To solve the above problem, WaveNet introduces the extended convolution. In this way, the perceptual field is increased without a significant burden on the calculation. WaveNet performs well when synthesising speech through the combination of causal and extended convolution.

3 Experiments and Results

3.1 Experimental Data

The training data consists of Amdo pastoral dialect, Dege-Kham dialect and Yushu-Kham dialect, as shown in Table 1. It consists of 7.63 h of training data and 1.1 h of test data. The speech data files are converted to a 16 kHz sampling rate and 16-bit quantization accuracy.

Table 1. Data sets.

	Dialect	Number of text sentences	Duration (hour)
Training data	Amdo pastoral	2671	2.68
	Dege-Kham	2226	1.74
	Yushu-Kham	2448	3.21
Test data	Amdo pastoral	337	0.4
	Dege-Kham	300	0.36
	Yushu-Kham	322	0.34

3.2 Comparative Experiments

Experiment 1: Add dialect ID in front of the text of Amdo pastoral dialect, Dege-Kham dialect and Yushu-Kham dialect. Train the model, and the model will learn the differences and distinguish the dialects by themselves. When synthesizing, add a dialect ID before the text of the input synthesized speech to synthesize the target dialect.

Experiment 2: Train all <audio, text> pairs without id, and directly synthesize the speech corresponding to the text without ID control during synthesis. Compare the results of the two experiments.

We train a shared feature prediction network on the datasets of Amdo pastoral dialect, Dege-Kham dialect and Yushu-Kham dialect dialect. On a single GPU, we used the teacher-forcing method to train the feature prediction network, the input of the decoder was the correct output, not the predicted output, with a batch size of 8. Then, the predicted outputs from the shared feature prediction network are aligned with the real speech. We train waveform networks for dialects by using the aligned predicted outputs.

3.3 Results

In order to evaluate the performance of the model and the ability of the model to learn dialects, our work evaluates the experimental results from both objective and subjective dimensions. Objectively, the root mean square error (RMSE) of the time-domain sequence is calculated to compare the speech synthesized by the model with the real speech. The smaller the RMSE, the closer the synthesized speech is to the real speech, and the better the speech synthesis quality. The formula of RMSE is shown in Eq. 2, where $I_{1,t}$ and $I_{2,t}$ respectively represent the value of the time series of reference speech and synthesized speech at time t.

$$RMSE = \sqrt{\frac{\sum_{t=1}^{n}\left(I_{1,t} - I_{2,t}\right)^2}{n}} \tag{2}$$

In this experiment, 5 sentences were randomly selected from the test data set for Amdo pastoral dialect, Dege-Kham dialect and Yushu-Kham dialect. Step 1: use the end-to-end Tibetan speech synthesis model trained with ID to synthesize the corresponding dialect. Then the synthesized Tibetan dialect voice is compared with the real voice, and the RMSE value is calculated. Step 2: use the model without ID training to synthesize the Tibetan language of the same text. Then compare the synthesized Tibetan dialect speech with the real speech. Using the above objective evaluation method, we calculate the average RMSE value of the two methods respectively. It is used to analyze the performance of the model. The experimental result is shown in Table 2.

Table 2. Dialects RMSE values.

	Amdo pastoral	Dege-Kham	Yushu-Kham
With dialect ID	0.17	0.18	0.17
Without dialect ID	0.19	0.20	0.24

Table 3. Grading standards.

Voice quality	Score
Very good	5.0
Good	4.0
Moderate	3.0
Bad	2.0
Very bad	1.0

As shown in the table, for the Amdo pastoral dialect, the RMSE value of the speech synthesis model with ID was 0.17, and the RMSE value of the speech synthesized by the speech synthesis model without ID was 0.19. For the Dege-Kham dialect, the RMSE value of the speech synthesis model with ID for the Tibetan dialect was 0.18, and the RMSE value of the speech synthesized by the speech synthesis model without ID was 0.20. For the Yushu-Kham dialect, the RMSE value of the speech synthesis model with ID was 0.17, and the RMSE value of the speech synthesis model without ID was 0.24.

Therefore, we can see that the quality of the synthesized speech combined with ID training has better performance.

Figure 7 shows the predicted spectrum and the target spectrum for multiple dialects, which are very similar.

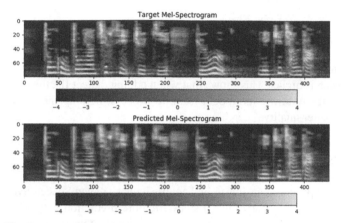

Fig. 7. Comparison of predicted spectrogram and target spectrogram.

In subjective experiments, an analogy scoring method is used. Based on the scoring criteria in Table 3, 10 reviewers compared the synthesized dialect speech in Experiment 1 with the real speech in the test set and gave MOS scores. The multi-dialect MOS scores of Experiment 1 are shown in Table 4.

Table 4. Experiment 1 Multi-dialect MOS scores.

Dialect	MOS
Amdo pastoral	4.15
Dege-Kham	3.98
Yushu-Kham	4.19

The reviewer scored the comparison between the synthesized speech based on Experiment 2 and the real speech. Since Tibetan has the same text and different pronunciations in different Tibetan areas, it is not possible to specify the type of synthetic dialect without marking. So when synthesizing, give the same test text as Experiment 1. Compared with the Amdo pastoral dialect, Dege-Kham dialect and Yushu-Kham dialect in the test set respectively, and gave MOS scores. Table 5 shows the multi-dialect MOS scores of Experiment 2.

Table 5. Experiment 2 Multi-dialect MOS scores.

Dialect	MOS
Amdo pastoral	3.80
Dege-Kham	3.92
Yushu-Kham	3.74

Comparing Table 4 and Table 5, the results show that the MOS value of ID training synthetic speech is higher. This shows that when adding dialect ID, the model will learn to distinguish them during the model training process, helping the model synthesize dialects with better quality.

4 Conclusions

In this paper, we proposed an end-to-end Multi-dialect Tibetan Speech Synthesis model based on Tacotron2. It incorporates a shared feature prediction network, which maps the character vector to the Mel spectrogram, and a WaveNet vocoder, which synthesizes multi-dialect Tibetan speech. In the experiment, firstly, Willy transcription scheme is used to convert Tibetan characters into Latin letters, which decreases the size of the training corpus, reduces the workload of front-end text processing, and enhances the modeling efficiency. Secondly, the dialect ID is added to the front of the text, which helps the model distinguish the phonetic features of Amdo pastoral dialect, Dege-Kham dialect and Yushu-Kham dialect during the training process. The experimental results show that after training with dialect ID, synthesized speech of Amdo pastoral dialect, Dege-Kham dialect and Yushu-Kham dialect shows higher performance.

Funding Statement. This work was supported by two projects. Y Zhao received the grant with no. 61976236 and no. 2020MDJC06.

Conflicts of Interest. The authors declare that they have no conflicts of interest.

References

1. Sun, Y., et al.: Tibetan question generation based on sequence to sequence model. Comput. Mater. Continua **68**(3), 3203–3213 (2021)
2. Zhang, J.: Research on Tibetan Lhasa speech synthesis based on hmm. Northwest University for Nationalities, M.S (2014)
3. Cairang, Z.: Research on Tibetan speech synthesis technology based on mixed primitives. Shaanxi Normal University, Ph.D (2016)
4. Du, G.: Research on Tibetan speech synthesis technology based on neural network. Qinghai Normal University, M.S (2019)
5. Xu, S., et al.: Acoustic modeling for Lhasa Tibetan speech synthesis based on daem algorithm, In: 5th International Conference, New York, NY, USA, pp. 188–192 (2016)

6. Jia, H.: Research on prosody control method in Chinese-Tibetan bilingual cross-language speech conversion. Northwest Normal University, M.S (2016)
7. Wang, H.: Research on Chinese-Tibetan bilingual cross-lingual statistical parameter speech synthesis. Northwest Normal University, M.S (2015)
8. Wang, Z.: Research on Chinese-Tibetan bilingual cross-language speech conversion method. Northwest Normal University, M.S (2015)
9. Ilyas, Q.M., et al.: An enhanced deep learning model for automatic face mask detection. Intell. Autom. Soft Comput. **31**(1), 241–254 (2022)
10. Shen, J., Pang, R., et al.: Natural TTS synthesis by conditioning WaveNet on mel spectrogram pre-dictions. In: 2018 IEEE International Conference on Acoustics, Speech and Signal Processing (ICASSP), Calgary, AB, Canada, pp. 4779–4783 (2018)
11. Xie, X.: Research on the speech synthesis technology of Tibetan dialect in Lhasa-Ü-Tsang. Tibet University, M.S (2021)
12. Wu, J.: Development and application of dialect speech synthesis system based on Tacotron2. Xidian University, M.S (2020)
13. Xie, Y.: Research on end-to-end speech synthesis technology based on a small number of data sets. Beijing Forestry University, M.S (2020)
14. Zhao, Y., Hu, P., et al.: Lhasa-Tibetan speech synthesis using end-to-end model. IEEE Access **7**, 140305–140311 (2019)
15. Liu, Z.: Research based on end-to-end Mongolian speech synthesis method. Inner Mongolia University, M.S (2019)
16. Wu, P., Yang, H., et al.: Using deep neural network to realize Chinese-Tibetan bilingual speech synthesis. In: Proceedings of the 14th National Conference on Human-Machine Speech Communication (NCMMSC 2017), p. 5. China (2017)
17. Ruan, W.: Research on cross-language speech conversion from Chinese to Tibetan based on DNN. Northwest Normal University, M.S (2018)
18. Xing, X.: Research on the phonetic conversion of Amdo dialect to Lhasa-Ü-Tsang dialect based on deep learning. Northwest Normal University, M.S (2020)
19. Zhao, G.: Research on Tibetan Voice Conversion Based on Deep Learning. Northwest Normal University, M.S (2020)
20. Luo, L.: Research and Realization of Tibetan Lhasa Speech Synthesis from Sequence to Sequence. Northwest University for Nationalities, M.S (2019)
21. Xu, X., Yang, L., et al.: End-to-end speech synthesis for tibetan multidialect. Complexity **2021**, 1–8 (2021)
22. Zhou, X., Tian, X., et al.: End-to-end code-switching tts with cross-lingual language model. In: ICASSP 2020–2020 IEEE International Conference on Acoustics, Speech and Signal Processing, Barcelona, Spain (2020)
23. Zhang, Y., et al.: Learning to speak fluently in a foreign language: multilingual speech synthesis and cross-language voice cloning. In: Proceedings of Interspeech 2019, pp. 2080–2084 (2019)
24. Cai, Z., Yang, Y., Li. M.: Cross-lingual multispeaker text-to-speech under limited-data scenario. arXiv:2005.10441 (2020)
25. Wang, H., et al.: CTSF: an end-to-end efficient neural network for Chinese text with skeleton feature. Journal on Big Data **3**(3), 119–126 (2021)
26. Almars, A.M.: Attention-based bi-lstm model for arabic depression classification. Comput. Mater. Continua **71**(2), 3091–3106 (2022)
27. Sun, J., Li, Y., Shen, Y., et al.: Joint self-attention based neural networks for semantic relation extraction. J. Inf. Hiding Privacy Protection **1**(2), 69–75 (2019)
28. Tamamori, A., Hayashi, T., Kobayashi, K., Takeda, K., Toda, T.: Speaker-dependent wavenet vocoder. In: Interspeech 2017, Stockholm, Sweden, pp. 1118–1122 (2017)

A Hybrid Automatic Text Summarization Model for Judgment Documents

Jianquan Ouyang[1]([✉]) [iD], Wenpeng Huang[1] [iD], and Tianming Liu[2]

[1] Key Laboratory of Intelligent Computing Information Processing, Ministry of Education, School of Computer Science and School of Cyberspace Science, Xiangtan University, Xiangtan, China
oyjq@xtu.edu.cn

[2] Department of Computer Science, The University of Georgia, GA Athens, USA

Abstract. Judgment documents are the final carrier of judicial trial activities, and they are an indispensable component for assisting sentencing decision-making and standardizing the scale of judgment. At present, the number of public judgment documents in China has reached 120 million, and it does not stop there, which brings a significant challenge for users to obtain useful information. To solve this problem, this paper proposes a hybrid automatic text summarization model for judgment documents. The method is divided into two stages. The first stage is, through extracting abstract technology, to extract key sentences from the original text to form a set of them. In the second stage, the set of key sentences extracted in the previous stage will be copied or rewritten to generate the final summary using the sequence generation model. The ROUGE indexes of this method in the automatic summarization experiment of judgment documents are 59.79, 37.71, and 52.67, which are 5.26, 7.25, and 10.41 higher than the benchmark model UniLM, respectively. The method proposed in this paper can effectively be applied in the automatic summarization service of judgment documents and solve the problem of information overload thereof and, finally, provide a new way for users to gain smooth access to judgment documents and information.

Keywords: Judgment documents · Abstractive summarization · Extractive summarization · Information overload

1 Introduction

In the judicial field, the judgment documents are the final carrier of judicial trial activities. The judgment documents of existing cases are an important basis for aiding sentencing decisions and regulating the scale of judgment. These documents as original unstructured texts, however, are hampering effective access for people to useful information therefrom, and this is an unhappy situation that has become all the more exacerbated with the sharp increase in publicly available judgment documents in the country. Therefore, automatic analysis and processing of the content of judgment documents are of great importance to improve the efficiency and quality of judgment. The automatic summarization aims directly at the content of the judgment documents, summarizing the judgment process and the logic of the decisions involved, both of which are at the core of every case. And in this way, readers are assured of quick access not only to the important information in various cases but to the logic of judgment arguments. Due to the length of the judgment document, it is easy to have sentence redundancy and poor cohesion by directly extracting key sentences from it to form an abstract.

To effectively summarize the content of judicial documents automatically, this paper based on related research proposes a hybrid automatic text summarization model for judicial documents - a two-stage automatic text summarization model based on the ALBERT-UniLM model, which includes key sentence extraction and text sequence generation. Several key sentences are extracted from the judgment documents to obtain extracted text summaries, which are used as the input corpus for the next stage of the abstractive model. Then we use natural language processing technology to compress further and refine the extracted key sentences to generate texts that are more concise and readily comprehensible so as to replace the extracted key sentences. In the first stage of key sentence extraction, an improved Dilate Residual Gate Convolutional Neural Network (DRGCNN) will be applied to the multi-classification of sentence functions of the judgment documents for the extraction of key sentences to operate according to our goal. In the second stage of text sequence generation, a hierarchical decomposition of relative position-coding is proposed to solve the problem that the maximum input of ALBERT is limited to 512 characters. And finally, an attention mechanism and a copy mechanism are introduced to solve the issues of generating word duplicates and the inability to generate unregistered words outside the word list.

2 Related Work

As an important research task in natural language processing, the study of automatic text summarization techniques first originated in the 1950s. Automatic text summarization techniques can be divided into single-document summarization techniques and multi-document summarization techniques according to the number of documents processed. According to the method of document formation, it can also be divided into extractive summarization and abstractive summarization.

The extractive summarization extracts key sentences from the original document and recombines them to form a summary. It is necessary that the extracted key sentences express the central ideas of the original document. This technique of extracting key sentences was first used based on statistical analysis [4, 8, 10]. In 2016, Federico et al. [2] used the TextRank algorithm to construct a sentence graph model on the basis of the relationships between sentences, and then scored and ranked these sentences to obtain summaries. In 2019, Yang Liu [13] used a form of multi-utterance splicing to make the BERT model better characterize the text location information by changing the location embedding of the BERT pre-trained language model, solving the problem of length limitation of this model, and achieving good results in extractive text automatic summarization techniques. In the same year, Xu et al. [21] proposed a neural model for single-document summarization based on joint extraction and syntactic compression, consisting of a sentence extraction model and a compression model for better access to article content. Zhang et al. [22] designed a new CNN network structure to improve the detection accuracy of spatial-domain steganography, allowing the neural network to obtain more information. In 2021, Liu et al. [12] proposed an unsupervised extractive text summarization method. It starts with a sentence graph automatically constructed from each document and then selects the meaningful sentences as summary sentences based on the similarity and relative distance between them. In the same year, some better studies provided new ideas for accomplishing the task of text summarization [9, 16]. The extractive summarization can ensure the coherence of the extractive sentences and the fidelity of the abstract sentences to the original text. Still, the generated abstracts are less readable, continuous, and cohesive due to the lack of understanding of the chapter structure and the lack of consideration of keywords and phrases in context.

The abstractive summarization, based on the understanding of original documents through computer, uses the deep learning model to absorb a large amount of text data, which will be encoded and decoded to regenerate abstract content by the methods of paraphrases and replacements. In 2014, Kyunghyun et al. [3] proposed a sequence-to-sequence model framework consisting of an encoder-decoder. In 2018, Tooba et al. [19] improved the Seq2Seq model by using a local attention mechanism instead of a global attention mechanism and achieved good results in solving the problem of generating repetitive words. In 2019, Jacob et al. [5] proposed a fine-tuning based on ALBERT for abstractive summaries. It uses a bi-directional Transformer model to obtain feature presentations of text, which, through this simple model structure, is nonetheless more effective. In 2020, Xiao et al. [20] proposed an enhanced sequence-to-sequence model. It enhances the correlation between the encoder and decoder through a padding generation mechanism and a noise-aware generation method, making the generated summary more faithful to the source document. In 2021 Armen et al. [1] proposed a pre-fine-tuning model. By adding the pre-tuning stage between the pre-trained language model and the fine-tuning, the model can better learn the representations of different characters, which has achieved good results in the abstractive text auto-summarization task. In addition, E. Heidary, M. Y. Saeed, etc., also provide some excellent solutions for text summarization tasks [7, 17]. Although the abstractive summary technique can generate a more fluent summary, the generated sentences are not logical and are prone to information loss when dealing with long texts.

This paper proposes a two-stage automatic text summarization model based on the ALBERT-UniLM model that embraces both models' advantages. It employs the ALBERT pre-trained language model as the text vector representer for both the extractive summarization phase and the abstractive summarization phase to address the semantic representation of long text with long-range context dependency. This model combines extractive and abstractive methods to obtain key sentences from the text and obtain summaries from the obtained key sentences, making the generated summary content specific with better readability, accuracy, and logic.

3   Method

The two-stage automatic text summarization model based on the ALBERT-UniLM model proposed in this paper combines the ALBERT pre-trained language model with the UniLM model. The first stage is to perform extractive summarization. The second stage uses the key sentence ensemble obtained from the extractive stage as input to perform an abstractive summary. The structure is shown in Fig. 1.

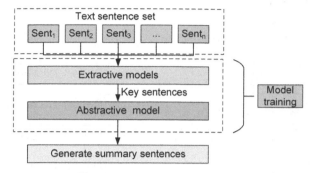

Fig. 1. Model structure diagram.

The process of extractive summary of judgment documents can be formally described as this: a single judgment document D is a collection of n sentences, expressed as $D = \{sent_1, sent_2, sent_3, \ldots, sent_n\}$. A sentence is a collection of words. Then the i-th sentence can be represented as $sent_i = \{w_{i1}, w_{i2}, \ldots, w_{in}\}$, where w_{ij} denotes the j-th word in the current sentence $sent_i$. The extractive summary of the judgment document can be regarded as a digest consisting of k key sentences extracted from the original text of the Judgment document, denoted as $D = \{sent_1, sent_2, sent_3, \ldots, sent_k | k < n\}$. The process of generating a summary of the judgment document can be formally described in the following way. The text sequence x in the generative stage is denoted as $X = x_1, x_2, \ldots, x_n\}$, where n is the length of the sequence. The output digest $Y = \{y_1, y_2, \ldots, y_m\}$, $m < n$. Then the generative phase can be modeled as a conditional probability model as $P(y_1, \ldots, y_m | x_1, \ldots, x_n)$.

3.1 Extractive Model

This paper uses the ALBERT pre-trained language model to obtain text vectors, a lightweight pre-trained language model based on the BERT model. The model structure is shown in Fig. 2.

In the encoding stage, in addition to token embedding, segment embedding and position embedding are also required for input. The three embedding techniques are spliced as the input of the ALBERT model, and the sentence vector $X = (x_1, x_2, \ldots, x_n) = ALBERT(sent_1, sent_2, sent_3, \ldots, sent_n)$ is obtained through the pre-training layer of the ALBERT model; $sent_i$ is denoted as the i-th sentence in the original text, and x_i corresponds to the vector of $sent_i$ encoded by ALBERT. In the classification layer of the model, this paper, based on the literature [11], proposes the Dilate Residual Gate Convolutional Neural Network (DRGCNN). In DRGCNN, the convolutional structure of the convolutional neural network is improved to enhance the ability of the model to learn long-range contextual semantic information. A gating mechanism is introduced to

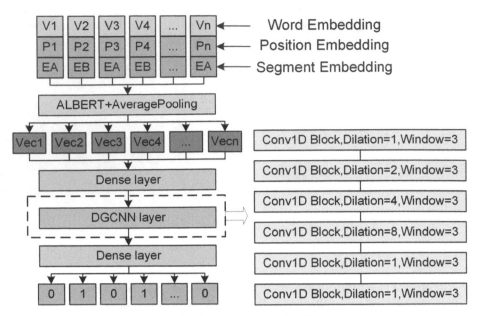

Fig. 2. Extractive model structure.

control the flow of information, and a residual mechanism to solve the gradient disappearance problem and increase the multi-channel transmission of information. Finally, a stacked multilayer DRGCNN network is used to do summary key sentence extraction.

To further solve the long-term dependence of the sequence and enlarge the receptive field of convolution, the primitive input sequence X for the convolution can be expressed as $X = [x_1, x_2, \ldots, x_n]$. Unlike image convolution operations, text often appears as a one-dimensional convolution. The convolution kernel is W. The feature map C_i of an arbitrary convolution operation is shown in Eq. (1).

$$c_i = \sum\nolimits_{k=0}^{n} w_c x_{i \pm k} \tag{1}$$

where Wc represents the one-dimensional convolution kernel, also called the weight coefficient, which is a learnable parameter. k represents the distance from the input identifier i, and the resulting feature map can represent the degree of relevance between the input X_i and the context.

Compared with the convolutional network, the convolutional width is expanded by adding the Dilated coefficient α. Then the network depth is increased by stacking the Dilated convolutional neural network layers, thus effectively solving the long-distance dependence problem of text sequences and extracting globally valid information. When $\alpha = 1$, the Dilated convolution operation is equivalent to the full convolution operation. Only when $\alpha > 1$, the Dilated convolution can learn the contextual information at a longer distance, as shown in Eq. (2).

$$c_i = \sum\nolimits_{k=0}^{n} w_c x_{i \pm k\alpha} \tag{2}$$

the convolutional neural network with the introduction of the gating mechanism is shown in Eq. (3).

$$Y = conv_1(X) \otimes \sigma(conv_2(X)) \tag{3}$$

where $conv_1$ and $conv_2$ are the two convolution operations, and the weights are not shared, and σ is the Sigmod function. Activating one of the convolutions and then calculating the outer product between the two can alleviate the problem of the disappearance of the gradient of the neural network. The residual structure is introduced based on the gated convolutional network, as shown in Eq. (4).

$$Y = X \otimes (1 - conv_2(X)) + conv_1(X)\sigma(conv_2(X)) \tag{4}$$

Then through the fully connected layer, sentences are classified into key and non-key ones, and the cross entropy is selected as the loss function during training. Through the extraction model a set of key sentences is obtained, which will be used as the input of the generative model.

3.2 Abstractive Model

The abstractive stage of judgment documents aims to allow the machine to generate a smooth and readable abstract based on the understanding of the input text. A sequence-to-sequence generation model is adopted at this stage, and Generate a new text sequence from the summary sequence obtained in the extractive phase. The Unilm pre-trained language model is also adopted [6], which can be seen as an extension of BERT but is more suitable for text generation. Finally, the encoded vector is used as the input of the generative neural model mentioned in this paper, through which the summary sentences are generated. The overall structure of the abstractive automatic summary model is shown in Fig. 3, which is divided into the data preprocessing layer, Unilm encoding layer, and summary generation layer.

The text is encoded by the Unilm pre-trained language model in the data preprocessing layer. The input to the model consists of word embedding, positional embedding, and segment embedding. The word embedding and segment embedding are done in the same way as the extractive model, during the positional embedding, a hierarchical decomposition of the location encoding. we first using the BERT trained location encoding vector as $p_1, p_2, \ldots, p_n$, and constructing a new set of location encoding $q_1, q_2, \ldots, q_m$ (where $m > n$) by Eq. (5).

$$q_{(i-1) \times n+j} = \varphi u_i + (i - \varphi)u_j \tag{5}$$

where $q_{(i-1) \times n+j}$ is the position code; φ is the hyperparameter with a value of 0.4. u is a vector, which represents the basis vector of the q vector, transformed by the trained position p vector through $u_p = \frac{p_{pos} - \varphi p_1}{1 - \varphi}$; pos represents the position of the words in sentences, and the value range is $[0, n]$. Given that $q_1 = p_1, q_2 = p_2, \ldots, q_n = p_n$, it can be calculated that $u_p = \frac{p_{pos} - \varphi p_1}{1 - \varphi}, i = 1, 2, \ldots, n$. And then the word embedding, positional embedding and segment embedding are all spliced as the input of the Unilm model; the sentence vector $X = (x_1, x_2, \ldots, x_n) = Unilm(sent_1, sent_2, \ldots, sent_n)$ is obtained upon

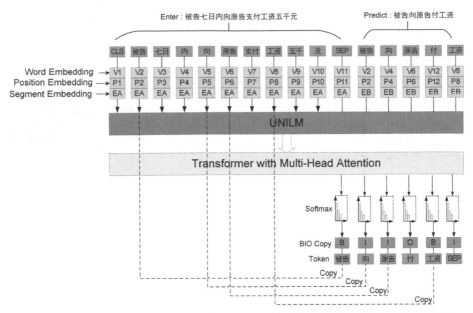

Fig. 3. Abstractive model structure. The data processed by the model are Chinese data. The input and output are written in Chinese characters.

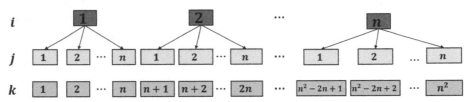

Fig. 4. Hierarchical breakdown structure diagram. It represents the corresponding relationship between position k and position i, j.

the Unilm model pre-training layer. Figure 4 shows the position k after the hierarchical decomposition transformation in relation to the position before the transformation.

The purpose of the summary generation layer is to generate the encoded text by using a sequence-to-sequence generation algorithm in order to obtain a summary. After encoding in the Unilm layer, the Transformer layer of the multi-attention mechanism is then to learn document-level features. This sequence-to-sequence generative model is limited by the vocabulary size during the generation process and is prone to out-of-vocabulary (OOV). The copying mechanism is introduced in the decoding process of the model, and it includes the operation of both copying and generating where the former is responsible for copying some key information from the input text to the output sequence and the latter for generating new words that are not in the word list. The summary generation layer is described in detail as follows.

For a multilayer Transformer's backbone network, a text sequence $X = x_1, x_2, \ldots, x_n$ of input length n is given. Then the output H_0 of the Transformer layer of the first layer is shown in Eq. (6).

$$H0 = Transformer0(x) \tag{6}$$

Transformer after L layer can be expressed as Eq. (7), and the final result is shown in Eq. (8).

$$H^l = Transformer_1\left(H^{l-1}\right) \tag{7}$$

$$H^l = \left[h_1^L, h_2^L, \ldots, h_n^L\right] \tag{8}$$

where $l \in [1, L]$ and h_i^L represents the contextual information of x_1 input. In each Transformer module, a multi-headed attention mechanism is added to amalgamate the output modules and mark the parts of the output sequence that need attention. For the l-th Transformer layer, the output of a self-attention head A_l is computed via:

$$Q = H^{l-1}W_1^Q, K = H^{l-1}W_1^K \tag{9}$$

$$M_{ij} - \begin{cases} 0, \text{ Allow joining} \\ 1, \text{ Prevent joining} \end{cases} \tag{10}$$

$$A_l = Softmax\left(\frac{QK^T}{d_k} + M\right)\left(H^{l-1}V_l\right) \tag{11}$$

where the $H_{l-1} \in R^{n \times d_n}$ is the linear projection of the previous layers, Queries, Values, and Keys; and the projection parameters are $W_1^Q, V_l \in R^{d_n \times dk}d$. The Mask matrix M controls whether joins are allowed between Tokens, and different Mask matrices M are to control attention to different contexts.

The Transformer layer already completes the model generating operation and then introduces a copy mechanism to solve the problems caused by the generation process. Suppose at decoding time t, and the relevance weight is calculated based on the last layer H_t of Transformer and the output O_j of Decoder, as shown in Eq. (12). Meanwhile, calculation of the attention weight of the j-th word is carried out as shown in Eq. (13).

$$U_t^j = h_t w_e o_j \tag{12}$$

$$\partial_t^j = \frac{expu_t^j}{\sum_{K=1}^N expu_t^k} \tag{13}$$

the attention distribution can be interpreted as the degree of attention received of the i-th word when searching the context. Averaging the information weight of the attention distribution through Eq. (14) brings the context representation vector $h_t^{'}$:

$$h_t^{'} = \sum_i^N \partial_t^j h_t \tag{14}$$

where $h_t^{'}$ is the context vector, which means that the desired information is obtained according to the distribution of attention. h_t is the output of the last layer of Transformer at time t. ∂_t^j is the attention distribution of the j-th word. The context vector is connected with the output O_j of the Decoder, and the vocabulary distribution $P_t^{vocab}(w)$ is generated through two linear layers. The calculation process is as Eq. (15):

$$P_t^{vocab}(w) = \text{softmax}\left(V'\left(V\left[O_j, h_t^{'}\right] + b\right) + b'\right) \qquad (15)$$

where the gating $g_t \in [0, 1]$ will be copied to determine that the current output option is to copy the original text to generate the current text. The calculation process formula of g_t is Eq. (16).

$$g_t = Sigmoid\left(w_g \cdot \left[h_i, o_j\right] + b_g\right) \qquad (16)$$

where the $P_t^{vocab}(w)$ represents the probability that the current word w is generated in a given vocabulary, so the final probability of choosing copy or generation is shown in the Eq. (17).

$$P_t(w) = (1 - g_t)P_t^{vocab}(w) + g_t \sum_{i:w_i=w} \partial_t^i \qquad (17)$$

where $\sum_{i:w_i=w} \partial_t^i$ represents the probability of choosing to copy from the source document according to the attention distribution. If w is a word out of the vocabulary, then $P_t^{vocab}(w) = 0$, if w does not appear in the source document, then $P_t^{vocab}(w) = 0$. The final loss function of the probability distribution of the extended lexicon is the Eq. (18):

$$Loss = \frac{1}{T} \sum_{t=0}^{T} -\log(P_t(w)) \qquad (18)$$

The generation probability $P_t(w)$ is calculated according to the vocabulary distribution and the attention distribution. Finally, the text summary is automatically generated according to the generation probability and the vocabulary distribution.

4 Experiments

4.1 Datasets

The experimental data comes from the judicial summary track of the China Law Research Cup CAIL2020 Judicial Artificial Intelligence Challenge. These data and the court judgment documents that are provided and marked by the Beijing Judicial Big Data Institute contain about 10,000 judgment documents and corresponding judicial abstracts where the judgment documents involved are all first-instance civil judgments.

4.2   Implementation Details

The parameters of the hybrid automatic text summarization model based on the ALBERT-UniLM model mainly contain the parameters of ALBERT and UniLM models. The ALBERT model uses a factorization of the text word embedding parameters to reduce the matrix word embedding parameters from $(V \times H)$ to $O(V \times E + E \times H)$ by dividing the subarray. The parameters of the two matrices are used for model learning. The model's parameter vector can be significantly reduced by sharing the parameters without debilitating the learning effect of the model. The ALBERT model in this paper adopts the Chinese pre-training model ALBERT-Base released by Google and sets the maximum sequence length as 128, Train_batch_size as 16, and Learning_rate as $5e-5$.

The UniLM model sets the hidden vector dimension to 768, Learning_rate to $1e-4$, Num_warmup_steps to 500, Num_training_steps to 10000, Epochs to 55. Batch_size to 16, Beam_search to decode Beam_size is set to 5.

4.3   Experimental Results and Analysis

In order to verify the superiority of the two-stage automatic text summarization model based on the ALBERT-UniLM model in handling the text summarization task, seven models were selected in the experimental part of this paper to generate metrics for comparison. The chosen benchmark models include three extractive summarization models and four abstractive summarization models. The selected models are described as follows:

LEAD-3: This model is an extractive summarization, which selects the first three sentences of the body of the judgment document as text summary.

TextRank [14]: This model is inspired by the graph algorithm model, which generates summaries by evaluating the importance amongst text sentences and then ranking and reorganizing them.

Seq2Seq + Attention [15]: This model combines a sequence-to-sequence framework with an attention mechanism and is currently the standard structural model for studying summary generation tasks.

Pointer-Generator [18]: This model is based on the Seq2Seq model, which selects summary words through a pointer network and adds an overriding mechanism to solve the problem of wrong output information and unregistered words.

NeuSum [23]: This model integrates the selection strategy into the scoring model and solves the previous problem of the separation of sentences scoring and sentences selection in extractive text summaries.

BERT + LSTM: This model uses the Seq2Seq infrastructure, replaces Encoder with bidirectional Transformer encoding, and Decoder with LSTM.

UniLM: This model adopts Seq2Seq infrastructure, replaces Encoder with bidirectional Transformer encoding module and Decoder with UniLM.

ALDRGCNN: This model is the extractive model proposed in this article.

UniLMPG: This model is the abstractive model proposed in this article.

HATSM: This model is a hybrid text automatic summarization model based on the ALBERT-UniLM model proposed in this article.

The specific comparative experimental results are shown in Table.1.

Table 1. Comparison of experimental results.

Method		Rouge		
		N = 1	N = 2	N = 3
Extractive summarization	LEAD-3	24.97	14.26	20.64
	NeuSum	45.24	15.47	38.42
	TextRank	26.37	15.38	20.48
Abstractive summarization	Seq2Seq + Attention	47.59	21.64	37.14
	Pointer-Generator	52.36	32.14	44.24
	UniLM (Baseline)	54.53	30.46	42.26
Paper model	ALDRGCNN	49.78	20.76	37.67
	UniLMPG	56.14	31.87	45.61
	HATSM	**59.79**	**37.71**	**52.67**

From this table, we can draw the following conclusions:

1) The extractive summarization model ALDRGCNN proposed in this paper is better than NeuSum. This is due to the fact that DRGCNN can learn the contextual semantic information in the judgment document by stacking on the neural network for the classification of key sentences.
2) Compared with the UniLM model and other models, the ALBERT-UniLM model proposed in this paper achieves the best results in all three ROUGE evaluation indexes. It shows that the model for text summary generation through two stages can effectively combine the advantages of the ALBERT model and UniLM model, and the hierarchical decomposition relative position-coding endows the model with better word and phrase characterization ability, which results in more fluent generated summaries.

5   Conclusion

In this paper, we propose a hybrid automatic text summarization model based on the ALBERT-UniLM model for judgment documents. The experimental results show that, compared with the other methods mentioned in this paper, ours achieves the highest ROUGE score on the judicial summary dataset and obtains smoother and more complete text summaries, which verifies the effectiveness of the summarization model proposed in this paper. Since the second stage of the two-stage model is based on the first stage, the effect of the extracted digest directly affects that of the abstractive model, which, admittedly, counts as certain limitation on the part of our proposed method. Integration of the two stages into one model will be undertaken in the future.

Acknowledgements. This research has been supported by Key Projects of the Ministry of Science and Technology of the People Republic of China (No. 2020YFC0832401) and the National College Student Innovation and Entrepreneurship Training Program (No. 202110530001).

References

1. Aghajanyan, A., Gupta, A., Shrivastava, A., Chen, X., Zettlemoyer, L., Gupta, S.: Muppet: Massive multi-task representations with pre-finetuning. In: Proceedings of the 2021 Conference on Empirical Methods in Natural Language Processing, EMNLP 2021, Virtual Event/Punta Cana, Dominican Republic, pp. 5799–5811. Association for Computational Linguistics (2021)
2. Barrios, F., López, F., Argerich, L., Wachenchauzer, R.: Variations of the similarity function of textrank for automated summarization. CoRR abs/1602.03606 (2016)
3. Cho, K., et al.: Learning phrase representations using RNN encoder-decoder for statistical machine translation. In: Moschitti, A., Pang, B., Daelemans, W. (eds.) Proceedings of the 2014 Conference on Empirical Methods in Natural Language Processing, EMNLP 2014, 25–29 October 2014, Doha, Qatar, A meeting of SIGDAT, a Special Interest Group of the ACL, pp. 1724–1734. ACL (2014)
4. Conroy, J.M., O'Leary, D.P.: Text summarization via hidden markov models. In: Proceedings of the 24th Annual International ACM SIGIR Conference on Research and Development in Information Retrieval, pp. 406–407. ACM (2001)
5. Devlin, J., Chang, M., Lee, K., Toutanova, K.: BERT: pre-training of deep bidirectional transformers for language understanding. In: Proceedings of the 2019 Conference of the North American Chapter of the Association for Computational Linguistics: Human Language Technologies, NAACL-HLT 2019, vol. 1, pp. 4171–4186. Association for Computational Linguistics (2019)
6. Dong, L., et al.: Unified language model pre-training for natural language understanding and generation. In: Advances in Neural Information Processing Systems 32: Annual Conference on Neural Information Processing Systems 2019, NeurIPS2019, BC, Canada, pp. 13042–13054 (2019)
7. Heidary, E., et al.: Automatic text summarization using genetic algorithm and repetitive patterns. Comput. Mater. Continua **67**(1), 1085–1101 (2021)
8. Edmundson, H.P.: New methods in automatic extracting. J. ACM **16**(2), 264–285 (1969)
9. Guo, W., Jia, R., Zhang, Y.: Semantic link network based knowledge graph representation and construction. J. Artif. Intell. **3**(2), 73 (2021)
10. Kupiec, J., Pedersen, J.O., Chen, F.: A trainable document summarizer. In: SIGIR'95, Proceedings of the 18th Annual International ACM SIGIR Conference on Research and Development in Information Retrieval. Seattle, Washington, USA, 9–13 July 1995 (Special Issue of the SIGIR Forum), pp. 68–73. ACM (1995)
11. Li, Y., Zhang, X., Chen, D.: CSRNet: dilated convolutional neural networks for understanding the highly congested scenes. In: 2018 IEEE Conference on Computer Vision and Pattern Recognition, CVPR 2018, Salt Lake City, UT, USA, 18–22 June 2018, pp. 1091–1100. Computer Vision Foundation/IEEE Computer Society (2018)
12. Liu, J., Hughes, D.J.D., Yang, Y.: Unsupervised extractive text summarization with distance-augmented sentence graphs. In: SIGIR '21: The 44th International ACM SIGIR Conference on Research and Development in Information Retrieval, Virtual Event, Canada, pp. 2313–2317. ACM (2021)
13. Liu, Y.: Fine-tune BERT for extractive summarization. CoRR abs/1903.10318 (2019)
14. Mihalcea, R., Tarau, P.: TextRank: bringing order into text. In: Proceedings of the 2004 Conference on Empirical Methods in Natural Language Processing, EMNLP2004, A meeting of SIGDAT, a Special Interest Group of the ACL, held in conjunction with ACL 2004, 25–26 July 2004, Barcelona, Spain, pp. 404–411. ACL (2004)
15. Paulus, R., Xiong, C., Socher, R.: A deep reinforced model for abstractive summarization. CoRR abs/1705.04304 (2017)

16. Qu, J., Liu, J., Yu, C.: Adaptive multi-scale hypernet with bi-direction residual attention module for scene text detection. J. Inf. Hiding Privacy Protect. **3**(2), 83 (2021)
17. Saeed, M.Y., et al.: An abstractive summarization technique with variable length keywords as per document diversity. Comput. Mater. Continua **66**(3), 2409–2423 (2021)
18. See, A., Liu, P.J., Manning, C.D.: Get to the point: Summarization with pointer-generator networks. In: Proceedings of the 55th Annual Meeting of the Association for Computational Linguistics, ACL 2017, Vancouver, Canada, pp. 1073–1083. Association for Computational Linguistics (2017)
19. Siddiqui, T., Shamsi, J.A.: Generating abstractive summaries using sequence to sequence attention model. In: 2018 International Conference on Frontiers of In-formation Technology, FIT 2018, Islamabad, Pakistan, December 17–19 2018, pp.212–217. IEEE Computer Society (2018)
20. Xiao, D., et al.: ERNIE-GEN: an enhanced multi-flow pre-training and fine-tuning framework for natural language generation. In: Proceedings of the Twenty-Ninth International Joint Conference on Artificial Intelligence, IJCAI 2020, pp. 3997–4003. ijcai. Org (2020)
21. Xu, J., Durrett, G.: Neural extractive text summarization with syntactic com-pression. In: Proceedings of the 2019 Conference on Empirical Methods in Natural Language Processing and the 9th International Joint Conference on Natural Language Processing, EMNLP-IJCNLP2019, Hong Kong, China, pp. 3290–3301. Association for Computational Linguistics (2019)
22. Xu, J., Durrett, G.: Neural extractive text summarization with syntactic compression. In: Proceedings of the 2019 Conference on Empirical Methods in Natural Language Processing and the 9th International Joint Conference on Natural Language Processing, EMNLP-IJCNLP 2019, Hong Kong, China, 3–7 November 2019, pp. 3290–3301. Association for Computational Linguistics (2019)
23. Zhou, Q., Yang, N., Wei, F., Huang, S., Zhou, M., Zhao, T.: Neural document summarization by jointly learning to score and select sentences. In: Proceedings of the 56th Annual Meeting of the Association for Computational Linguistics, ACL 2018, Melbourne, Australia, vol. 1, pp. 654–663. Association for Computational Linguistics (2018)

Quantum Fuzzy Principal Component Analysis

Cheng Wang[1,2], Shibin Zhang[1,2]([✉]), and Jinyue Xia[3]

[1] School of Cybersecurity, Chengdu University of Information Technology, Chengdu 610225, China
cuitzsb@cuit.edu.cn
[2] Advanced Cryptography and System Security Key Laboratory of Sichuan Province, Chengdu 610255, China
[3] International Business Machines Corporation (IBM), Armonk, NY 14201, USA

Abstract. At present, principal component analysis is widely used in the dimensionality reduction processing of high-dimensional data. On the premise of ensuring that the information loss in the construction process is as little as possible, several irrelevant new variables far less than the number of original variables are generated by constructing a series of linear combinations of original variables, which constitute a low-dimensional space. The information contained in it can better restore the information of original variables in high-dimensional space. In other words, it finds the best low rank approximation by calculating the eigenvalues and eigenvectors of the original matrix. However, classical principal component analysis is very sensitive to outliers and missing values. If there are outliers or missing data in the data matrix, the effect of the algorithm is often poor. With the increase of matrix data, the operation cost also increases exponentially, resulting in large time complexity. Aiming at the problems of classical principal component analysis, we proposed a quantum fuzzy principal component analysis algorithm in this paper. By introducing fuzzy sets to fuzzify the covariance matrix, the influence of outliers or missing values is reduced. At the same time, in order to reduce the complexity of the algorithm, we use the parallelism of quantum computing to accelerate our algorithm. The results show that compared with the classical principal component analysis, the algorithm is more effective and the algorithm efficiency is better.

Keywords: Principal component analysis · Fuzzy sets · Quantum computing · Quantum fuzzy principal component analysis

1 Introduction

There are practical problems in machine learning, such as data clustering and face recognition, which usually involve a large high-dimensional data. Due to the high dimension and many attributes of data, it often leads to "dimension disaster". This requires a method to simplify the data and reduce the dimension of high-dimensional data. Most of the information represented by the original variables is reconstructed by using a group of new variables with few dimensions and no correlation. In this way, the analysis of new variables can get the same effect as the analysis of original variables. Principal component analysis just provides an idea to solve the "dimension disaster". Principal component analysis was first proposed by Hotelling at 1933. Its main purpose is to improve the efficiency of algorithm analysis and processing. A given original variable is transformed into another set of irrelevant new variables by linear transformation. Each new principal component is a linear combination of original variables, and each principal component is not related to each other. At present, the research on principal component analysis has been applied to pattern recognition [1], medical field [2] and fault detection [3].

However, the advent of the big data era has triggered a series of new challenges. The complexity of big data will inevitably lead to the uncertainty of big data. Various uncertainties in big data bring great challenges to the accuracy, efficiency and robustness of big data calculation and analysis methods. Moreover, when dealing with massive data, if there are some problems in the data, such as outliers, missing data and weak linear correlation between variables, it will lead to the analysis results with low reliability. Therefore, it is necessary to propose some effective methods to reduce the influence of extreme values. Fuzzy theory provides a mathematical tool that other theories are not competent to solve this kind of problems, makes fuzzy sets participate in decision-making, and reduces the impact of outliers and missing data.

At the same time, when processing massive data, the efficiency of classical machine learning is not high, and quantum computing has special parallelism. Therefore, quantum computing can be used to solve the operation efficiency of classical machine learning. And there are more and more researches on quantum machine learning [4–6]. At present, the research on quantum machine learning is mainly to design quantum algorithms that can solve machine learning problems faster than classical methods. With the emergence of quantum random access memory, algorithms such as quantum support vector machine [7], quantum generator [8], quantum principal component analysis [9] and quantum generative adversarial network [10] have been proposed one after another, after that, a large number of quantum machine learning algorithms have emerged to deal with various problems in real life. For example, the problem in the process of data classification [11–14], the data fitting problem in linear system and regression [15, 16] and cluster analysis [17]. A large number of quantum experiments [18] show that quantum machine learning algorithm has obvious efficiency advantages over classical machine learning algorithm.

In view of the shortcomings of the above classical principal component analysis algorithm, this paper proposes a quantum Fuzzy Principal component analysis model. By introducing the theory of fuzzy mathematics, the data matrix is fuzzed by fuzzy set. After adding the fuzzy membership function, a new fuzzy covariance matrix is constructed, so that the fuzzy set can participate in the decision-making of the algorithm, this reduces the impact of outliers or missing values. At the same time, using the parallelism of quantum algorithm, the principal component analysis method is accelerated to reduce its time complexity. The results show that compared with the classical principal component analysis, the algorithm is more effective and the algorithm efficiency is better.

The subsequent section of this paper are as follows. Section 2 briefly describes the classical principal component analysis. Section 3 mainly introduces our quantum Fuzzy Principal component analysis algorithm. In Sect. 4, the runtime and effectiveness of the algorithm are analyzed. Conclusions are drawn in the last section.

2 Principal Component Analysis

The central task of principal component analysis is to decompose the covariance matrix or correlation matrix. Its central idea is that sample set X contains n p-dimensional samples, with. We hope to find a low dimensional subspace $\mathbb{R}^d (d < p)$ of $\mathbb{R}^p$, and $y_2, \cdots , y_n \in \mathbb{R}^d$. is the projection of $x_1, x_2, \cdots , x_n \in \mathbb{R}^p x_1, x_2, \cdots , x_n \in \mathbb{R}^p$ on subspace $\mathbb{R}^d$, so as to minimize the information loss when $y_1, y_2, \cdots , y_n$ is used to describe $x_1, x_2, \cdots , x_n$. That is to find less d comprehensive variables from the initial p variables, which can reflect the initial data as much as possible and are independent of each other.

The initial data matrix X is:

$$X = \begin{bmatrix} x_{11} & x_{12} & \cdots & x_{1p} \\ x_{21} & x_{22} & \cdots & x_{2p} \\ \vdots & \vdots & \vdots & \vdots \\ x_{n1} & x_{n1} & \cdots & x_{np} \end{bmatrix} = [x_1, x_2, ..., x_p] \tag{1}$$

Among them,

$$x_i = (x_{1i}, x_{2i}, \cdots , x_{ni})^T, i = 1, 2, \cdots , p \tag{2}$$

Obtain the covariance matrix of data matrix X:

$$C_{ij} = \frac{1}{n-1} \sum_{k=1}^{n} \left(x_i^k - \overline{x_i} \right) \left(x_j^k - \overline{x_j} \right), (i, j = 1, 2, \cdots , p) \tag{3}$$

where are respectively,

$$\overline{x_i} = \frac{1}{p} \sum_{j=1}^{p} x_{ij}, j = 1, 2, \cdots , n, \overline{x_j} = \frac{1}{n} \sum_{i=1}^{n} x_{ij}, j = 1, 2, \cdots , p \tag{4}$$

Since the covariance matrix is a non-negative definite matrix, there is an orthogonal matrix U, which satisfies the following formula:

$$UCU^T = \Lambda = \begin{bmatrix} \lambda_1 & & & \\ & \lambda_2 & & \\ & & \ddots & \\ & & & \lambda_p \end{bmatrix} \tag{5}$$

where $\lambda_1 \geq \lambda_2 \geq \cdots \geq \lambda_p \geq 0$ and $U^T = (U_1, U_2, \cdots , U_p)$. U_j is the j-th column in U^T. Let $X = \left(X^{(1)}, X^{(2)}, \cdots , X^{(p)} \right)^T$, new principal components $Y^{(j)} = U_j^T X$ can be obtained, and it can be proved that there is no correlation between $Y^{(1)}, Y^{(2)}, \cdots , Y^{(p)}$. The first d principal components are selected to replace the initial p variables for analysis, so as to reduce the dimension of the original data.

3 Quantum Fuzzy Principal Component Analysis

The quantum Fuzzy Principal Component Analysis we proposed is an improved method based on quantum principal component analysis. By introducing fuzzy theory, it makes up for the shortcomings of quantum principal component analysis in dealing with uncertain information.

3.1 Constructing Fuzzy Covariance Matrix

First, as shown in Table 1, a finite sample set can be expressed as $X_\omega(\omega = 1, 2, \cdots, n) \in \mathbb{R}^p$, where n is the number of samples and p is the number of initial variables. Each attribute corresponds to a fuzzy membership, where the fuzzy membership function is expressed as $\mu_A(\omega)(\omega = 1, 2, \cdots, n)$.

Table 1. Initial data.

Sample number	Attribute			
ω	X_1	X_2	$\cdots$	X_p
1	X_{11}	X_{12}	$\cdots$	X_{1p}
2	X_{21}	X_{22}	$\cdots$	X_{2p}
$\vdots$	$\vdots$	$\vdots$	$\ddots$	$\vdots$
n	X_{n1}	X_{n2}	$\cdots$	X_{np}
Fuzzy membership (A)	$\mu_A(1)$	$\mu_A(2)$	$\cdots$	$\mu_A(n)$

Secondly, calculate the mean value of each sample X_ω. And the mean is $\overline{x_i} = (X_{i1} + X_{i2} + \cdots + X_{ip}), i = 1, 2, \cdots, n$.

Third, the fuzzy set A can be determined by the fuzzy membership function $\mu_A(\omega)$. Further, the sum of fuzzy membership degrees of all samples in the sample set $(N(A))$ and the sum of deviation squares of the sample set (S_{ij}) can be obtained:

$$N(A) = \sum_{\omega=1}^{n} \mu_A(\omega) \tag{6}$$

$$S_{ij} = \sum_{\omega=1}^{n} (x_{i\omega} - \overline{x_i})(x_{j\omega} - \overline{x_j})\mu_A(\omega) \tag{7}$$

Finally, the fuzzy covariance matrix after adding the fuzzy membership function $\mu_A(\omega)$ is:

$$FC_{ij} = \frac{S_{ij}}{N(A)} = \frac{\sum_{\omega=1}^{n} (x_{i\omega} - \overline{x_i})(x_{j\omega} - \overline{x_j})\mu_A(\omega)}{\sum_{\omega=1}^{n} \mu_A(\omega)} \tag{8}$$

$\overline{x_i}$ is the arithmetic mean of the *i-th* attribute in the data matrix X. through the above processing, because in the process of extracting the principal component, the principal component analysis adds the fuzzy membership degree to the covariance matrix to participate in the decision-making, which can make the algorithm more reliable when dealing with outliers.

3.2 Constructing Fuzzy Covariance Matrix

In order to make our algorithm more efficient, we use quantum principal component analysis to solve the fuzzy covariance matrix. Let the processed fuzzy covariance matrix be, and after standardizing its trace, we get:

$$\sigma_{ij} = \frac{FC_{ij}}{tr(FC_{ij})} = \frac{\sum_{\omega=1}^{n}(x_{i\omega} - \overline{x_{\omega}})(x_{j\omega} - \overline{x_{\omega}})\mu_A(\omega)}{tr\left(\frac{\sum_{\omega=1}^{n}(x_{i\omega}-\overline{x_{\omega}})(x_{j\omega}-\overline{x_{\omega}})\mu_A(\omega)}{\sum_{\omega=1}^{n}\mu_A(\omega)}\right)\sum_{\omega=1}^{n}\mu_A(\omega)} \tag{9}$$

For the nonnegative matrix σ with $tr(\sigma) = 1$, For matrix A, this matrix can get a spectral decomposition:

$$\sigma = \sum_{j=1}^{N}\lambda_j|\chi_j\rangle\langle\chi_j| \tag{10}$$

With $0 \le \lambda_j \le 1$ and $\sum_{j=1}^{N}\lambda_j = 1$, where λ_i and χ_i are eigenvectors and eigenvalues respectively. We just want to compute it by quantum principal component analysis. The goal of the algorithm is to determine the first r eigenvalues of σ and their corresponding eigenvectors (eigenvalues are sorted from large to small), so that it can be better estimated by a low rank matrix:

$$\rho = \sum_{j=1}^{r}\lambda_j|\chi_j\rangle\langle\chi_j| \tag{11}$$

With $r \ll N$. The approximate steps of our algorithm are as follows:

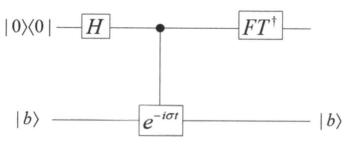

Fig. 1. Quantum algorithm structure. The process of using quantum algorithm to find principal components is briefly described.

First, as shown in Fig. 1, a random quantum state $|b\rangle$ is initialized and $|b\rangle$ is used as the input part of the algorithm.

$$|b\rangle = \sum_{j=1}^{N}\beta_j|\mu_j\rangle\langle\mu_j| \tag{12}$$

Secondly, after $|b\rangle$ passes through the first part in Fig. 1, the quantum state is converted to $|b_1\rangle$ due to the action of H gate.

$$|b_1\rangle = |t\rangle\langle t| \otimes \sum_{j=1}^{N}\beta_j|\mu_j\rangle\langle\mu_j| \tag{13}$$

$$H = \frac{1}{\sqrt{2}} \begin{bmatrix} 1 & 1 \\ 1 & -1 \end{bmatrix} \tag{14}$$

Finally, after all operations, assuming that we can effectively prepare the controlled unitary operation U, after the controlled U operation and inverse Fourier transform $(FT^\dagger)$, we get the quantum state $|b_2\rangle$. At this time, the eigenvalue and eigenvector have been entangled.

$$U = e^{-it\sigma} \tag{15}$$

$$|b_2\rangle = \sum_{j=1}^{N} \beta_j |\lambda_j\rangle\langle\lambda_j| \otimes |\mu_j\rangle\langle\mu_j| \tag{16}$$

Throughout the above process, the conversion process of quantum states is shown in Fig. 2:

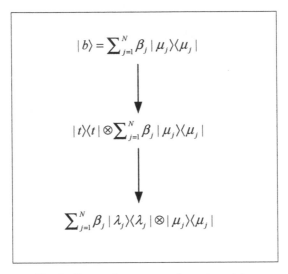

Fig. 2. Conversion process of quantum states.

3.3 Quantum Circuit Implementation

After the controlled U operation $\left(U = e^{-i\sigma t}\right)$ of quantum state $\sigma = \sum_{j=1}^{N}\lambda_j|\chi_j\rangle\langle\chi_j|$, we get:

$$U|\chi_j\rangle = e^{-i\sigma t}|\chi_j\rangle = e^{-i\beta_j t}|\chi_j\rangle \tag{17}$$

The quantum phase estimation is used to estimate the value of β_j. Therefore, the main framework of our algorithm is the quantum phase estimation algorithm. Firstly,

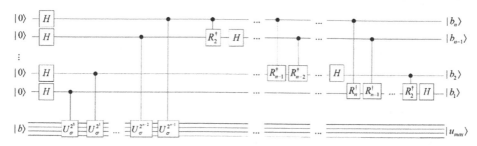

Fig. 3. Quantum circuit implementation.

the eigenvalue of the target unitary operator is extracted and placed in the probability amplitude of the quantum state, and then the phase in the probability amplitude is extracted and placed in the ground state of the quantum state (Fig. 3).

The first n qubits in Fig. 2 are initialized to $|0\rangle$ and used to obtain their maximum eigenvalues from the matrix σ and binary coding. The remaining qubits initialize a random quantum state $|b\rangle$ and encode the eigenvector corresponding to the eigenvalue. The single qubit gate H represents the Hadamard gate as shown in Eq. (14). The controlled $U_\sigma^{2^k}$ gate indicates that U_σ is applied to the target qubit 2^k times. And U_σ as shown in Eq. (15). The controlled $R_k^\dagger$ gate representation applies the matrix to the target qubit.

$$R_k^\dagger = \begin{bmatrix} 1 & 0 \\ 0 & e^{2\pi i/2^k} \end{bmatrix} \qquad (18)$$

After all the operations are completed, we can get the final quantum state $|\theta\rangle$ of our algorithm.

$$|\theta\rangle = |b_n b_{n-1}...b_2 b_1\rangle \otimes |\mu_{max}\rangle \qquad (19)$$

where $|b_n b_{n-1}...b_2 b_1\rangle$ is the n-bit estimated value of the eigenvalue, and $|\mu_{max}\rangle$ is the eigenvector corresponding to the eigenvalue.

4   Analysis

4.1   Runtime Analysis

Quantum phase estimation plays a good role in our algorithm and greatly controls the time cost. If the eigenvalue λ_j is well estimated within the error range ϵ, controlled U gates need to be performed $O(\frac{1}{\epsilon})$ times in the phase estimation. Since the runtime taken to implement the U operation and prepare the initial state $|b\rangle$ is $O(polylog(np))$, the total time cost by our algorithm is $O(\frac{polylog(np)}{\epsilon})$. Compared with the time cost $O(poly(np))$ of classical principal component analysis, our algorithm accelerates exponentially.

4.2   Effectiveness Analysis

Next, I will verify the effectiveness of QFPCA. The actual data are used for comparative analysis. Table 2 lists the track and field records of men in different countries and regions

Table 2. Men's track and field records in different countries and regions.

Country or region	800 m (min)	1500 m (min)	3000 m (min)
Argentina	18.1	3.70	14.04
Australia	1.74	3.75	13.28
Fuzzy sets	0.25	0.45	0.30

(only two countries and regions are selected in this paper), and each sample is given a fuzzy membership degree:

Through the preliminary observation of the data, it is found that the data of Argentina is abnormal at 800 m. In order to demonstrate the anti-interference ability of our algorithm, we carried out simple experiments and obtained the following records.

Firstly, for the classical principal component analysis, we carried out some simple experiments in two different cases. When there are outliers or no outliers, the corresponding eigenvalues are extracted according to the obtained covariance matrix. As shown in the Figs. 4 and 5:

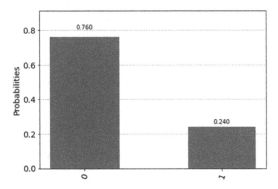

Fig. 4. Measurement results with outliers in QPCA.

According to the results of quantum experiment, the eigenvalues can be calculated. The results of eigenvalues are shown in the following Table 3.

Table 3. Eigenvalue in QPCA

Eigenvalue	No outliers	Outliers
λ_1	81.340934	55.968115
λ_2	0.0079323	37.163851

Then, for our proposed algorithm, we experiment it under normal and abnormal conditions respectively. Accordingly, we can get the experimental results, as shown in the Figs. 6 and 7. The eigenvalues are shown in Table 4.

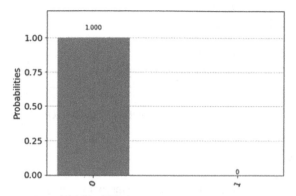

Fig. 5. Measurement results without outliers in QPCA.

Table 4. Eigenvalue in QFPCA

Eigenvalue	No outliers	Outliers
λ_1	48.808614	43.575456
λ_2	0.0056045	20.534168

Compared with QPCA, when there are outliers, the difference between the maximum eigenvalue obtained by QFPCA and the maximum eigenvalue in normal state is small. Through the above experiment, we can draw a conclusion. QFPCA performs better than QPCA when there are outliers in the data matrix.

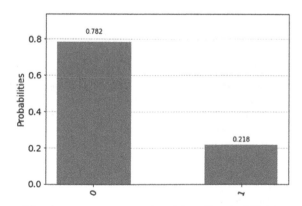

Fig. 6. Measurement results with outliers in QFPCA.

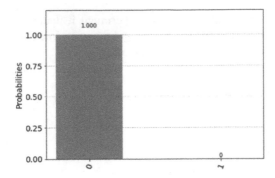

Fig. 7. Measurement results without outliers in QFPCA.

5   Conclusions

In this paper, we proposed a quantum Fuzzy Principal component analysis algorithm. By introducing the theory of fuzzy mathematics and using fuzzy sets to fuzzify the data matrix, the algorithm reduces the influence of outliers or missing values. At the same time, using the parallelism of quantum computing, the principal component analysis method is accelerated to reduce its time complexity. The analysis results show that when the data dimension is low, the algorithm has exponential speed than the classical principal component analysis algorithm. When there are outliers in the data set, the algorithm also performs better than the classical principal component analysis algorithm. This shows that our algorithm can better adapt to reality. Therefore, the algorithm makes up for the application of quantum machine learning in the field of fuzzy mathematics and provides more new ideas for the development of quantum machine learning in the future.

Acknowledgement. I sincerely thank my mentor Professor Zhang Shibin. The careful guidance from beginning to end has given me a lot of enlightenment and avoided detours. I would also like to thank our team's Professor Chang Yan, Associate Professor Yan Lili and Dr. Lin Chen for their help. Finally, I would like to thank the students who discussed the problem with me.

Funding Statement. This work is supported by the National Natural Science Foundation of China (No. 62076042), the Key Research and Development Project of Sichuan Province (No. 2021YFSY0012, No. 2020YFG0307, No. 2021YFG0332), the Science and Technology Innovation Project of Sichuan (No. 2020017), the Key Research and Development Project of Chengdu (No. 2019-YF05-02028-GX), the Innovation Team of Quantum Security Communication of Sichuan Province (No. 17TD0009), the Academic and Technical Leaders Training Funding Support Projects of Sichuan Province (No. 2016120080102643).

References

1. Wang, Q., Gao, Q.: Robust 2DPCA and its application. In: Proceedings of the IEEE Conference on Computer Vision and Pattern Recognition Workshops, pp. 79–85. IEEE, Las Vegas (2016)

2. Medeiros, L., Almeida, H., Dias, L., Perkusich, M., Fischer, R.: A gait analysis approach to track Parkinson's disease evolution using principal component analysis. In: 29th International Symposium on Computer-Based Medical Systems, pp. 48–53. IEEE, Belfast and Dublin (2016)

3. Gajjar, S., Kulahci, M., Palazoglu, A.: Real-time fault detection and diagnosis using sparse principal component analysis. J. Process. Control **67**, 112–128 (2018)

4. Ciliberto, C., et al.: Quantum machine learning: a classical perspective. Proc. Roy. Soc. A: Math. Phys. Eng. Sci. **474**(2209), 20170551 (2018)

5. Huang, H.Y., et al.: Power of data in quantum machine learning. Nat. Commun. **12**(1), 1–9 (2021)

6. Sheng, Y.B., Zhou, L.: Distributed secure quantum machine learning. Sci. Bull. **62**(14), 1025–1029 (2017)

7. Li, Z., Liu, X., Xu, N., Du, J.: Experimental realization of a quantum support vector machine. Phys. Rev. Lett. **114**(14), 140504 (2015)

8. Liu, J.G., Wang, L.: Differentiable learning of quantum circuit born machines. Phys. Rev. A **98**(6), 062324 (2018)

9. Lloyd, S., Mohseni, M., Rebentrost, P.: Quantum principal component analysis. Nat. Phys. **10**(9), 631–633 (2014)

10. Zeng, J., Wu, Y., Liu, J.G., Wang, L., Hu, J.: Learning and inference on generative adversarial quantum circuits. Phys. Rev. A **99**(5), 052306 (2019)

11. Cong, I., Duan, L.: Quantum discriminant analysis for dimensionality reduction and classification. New J. Phys. **18**(7), 073011 (2016)

12. Schuld, M., Fingerhuth, M., Petruccione, F.: Implementing a distance-based classifier with a quantum interference circuit. Europhys. Lett. **119**(6), 60002 (2017)

13. Schuld, M., Petruccione, F.: Quantum ensembles of quantum classifiers. Sci. Rep. **8**(1), 1–12 (2018)

14. Kerenidis, I., Landman, J., Luongo, A., Prakash, A.: q-means: a quantum algorithm for unsupervised machine learning. arXiv:1812.03584 (2018)

15. Wiebe, N., Braun, D., Lloyd, S.: Quantum algorithm for data fitting. Phys. Rev. Lett. **109**(5), 050505 (2012)

16. Wang, G.: Quantum algorithm for linear regression. Phys. Rev. A **96**(1), 012335 (2017)

17. Aïmeur, E., Brassard, G., Gambs, S.: Quantum speed-up for unsupervised learning. Mach. Learn. **90**(2), 261–287 (2013)

18. Shao, C., Li, Y., Li, H.: Quantum algorithm design: techniques and applications. J. Syst. Sci. Complexity **32**(1), 375–452 (2019)

A Handwritten Number Recognition Scheme Based on Improved Convolutional Neural Network Algorithm

Changlin Li, Chenglei Pan$^{(\boxtimes)}$, Fang Chen, Jie Li, Siyuan Fu, and Wanyi Zeng

Beijing Electronic Science and Technology Institute, Beijing 100070,
People's Republic of China
chengleip123@163.com

Abstract. In this paper, the existing handwritten numeral recognition scheme is improved, the identification accuracy is low, because of the K - Nearest Neighbor algorithm results visualization result is not stable, the problem of insufficient, put forward the use of Euclidean Distance, choosing appropriate parameters, visual output solution was improved, the K - Nearest Neighbor algorithm accuracy increased to a higher level, And the results of the algorithm are more stable. In addition, because the Convolutional Neural Network algorithm convergence is low, the problem such as low accuracy, long operation time, used to increase convolution pool, the optimized result output, increase the dropout layer method to solve, in the end, the Convolutional Neural Network algorithm convergence and accuracy are increased, reducing the amount of calculation and calculation algorithm of time. At the end of the paper, the practical application of handwritten number recognition, namely a handwritten number recognition system based on machine learning, is given. This method is not only suitable for MNIST data sets, but also any handwritten digital image. An improved image brightness judgment scheme is proposed, which makes the handwritten digital image not affected by light and darkness, and greatly enhances the function of the handwritten digital recognition scheme.

Keywords: K-nearest neighbor · Handwritten digit recognition · MNIST data sets · Convolutional neural networks

1 Introduction

The research of handwritten numerals recognition is how to use electronic computers to automatically recognize handwritten Arabic numerals. The information processed by character recognition can be divided into two categories: one is text information, which mainly deals with text, written or printed text information. At present, the print version and online versions have been mature [1, 2]. The second is data information, mainly composed of various numbers and statistical data in Arabic, such as postal code, statistical reports, etc. The core technology of processing this kind of information is handwritten number recognition. Besides, machine learning has gradually come into people's view

© The Author(s), under exclusive license to Springer Nature Switzerland AG 2022
X. Sun et al. (Eds.): ICAIS 2022, CCIS 1586, pp. 398–412, 2022.
https://doi.org/10.1007/978-3-031-06767-9_33

[3]. Its application covers all fields of artificial intelligence, mainly using induction and synthesis. Machine learning has been applied to all branches of artificial intelligence, such as expert systems, automatic reasoning, natural language understanding, pattern recognition, computer vision, intelligent robots, and other fields [4–9]. Recently, Y. Xue improved the handwritten number recognition based on convolutional neural network algorithm [10], Saleem proposed a hybrid trainable system for writer identification of arabic handwriting [11], Abbas created an intelligent handwritten document recognition algorithm [12]. Therefore, handwritten number recognition based on machine learning has attracted more and more attention.

2 Related Work

The handwritten digit database used here is the MNIST data set, which consists of 60,000 training samples and 10,000 test samples, and each sample is a 28 × 28 pixel gray-scale handwritten digit picture.

The training data label is a 55000 × 10 vector. The label here uses one-hot encoding, as shown in Fig. 1. Each label corresponds to a vector of length 10, with values only 0 and 1, and only the corresponding number the bit is 1, and the rest are 0. For example, the one-hot code corresponding to the value 0 is [1, 0, 0, 0, 0, 0, 0, 0, 0, 0].

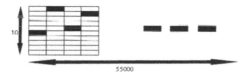

Fig. 1. Label of MNIST training samples.

KNN algorithm is a classification method, which was first proposed by Cover and Hart, and the theoretical research has been relatively mature [13]. The KNN algorithm sequentially performs the following operations on unclassified samples: First, calculate the distance between each classified sample and the current unclassified sample, and sort them in ascending order according to the distance; Then, select the first K classified samples in the sequence, and count the classification results of each; Finally, the classification result with the highest frequency among the K classified samples is the predicted classification result of the current unclassified sample. The algorithm flow is shown in Fig. 2.

CNN is one of the representative algorithms of machine learning. It can classify the input information according to the hierarchical structure [14]. The core technology of CNN includes local perception, parameter sharing, convolution, and pooling. Local perception is to obtain the characteristics of global connection in the case of local connection [15].

The main function of the convolutional layer in the CNN structure is to extract local features through the convolution kernel and the original image. The formula for convolution operation is:

$$X_{h,w}^n = w^n \otimes X_{h,w}^{n-1} + b^n \tag{1}$$

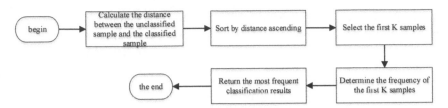

Fig. 2. Flow chart of KNN algorithm.

where $X_{(h,w)}^{n-1}$ is the input feature, $X_{h,w}^{n}$ is the output feature, h and w are the height and width of the feature respectively, w^n is the weight value, b^n is the offset value, $\otimes$ is the convolution operation.

Pooling can be effective because the characteristics of the image are invariant. As shown in Fig. 3, the image is pooling, 75% of the activation information is discarded, and the maximum value is retained.

The fully connected layer is to stitch all the feature maps of the two-dimensional image into one-dimensional vector features as the input of this layer. The output of the fully connected layer is obtained by the weighted summation of the input and the activation function, the formula is as follows [16]:

Fig. 3. Flow chart of KNN algorithm.

$$u^l = w^l x^{l-1} + b^l \tag{2}$$

$$x^l = f(u^l) \tag{3}$$

where u^l is the net activation of the fully connected layer, which is obtained by weighting and biasing the feature map x^{l-1} output by the previous layer. w^l is the weight coefficient of the fully connected layer, and b^l is the bias term of the fully connected layer.

3   Implementation and Problems of Key Algorithms

3.1   Implementation of K Nearest Neighbor Algorithm

Figure 4 shows the specific implementation steps of the KNN algorithm. For the read test images of the MNIST data set, the dimensionality expansion is first required. Here, there are 5 test pictures randomly read, 500 training pictures, and each picture is a 28 × 28 pixel gray value matrix. Because 5 test pictures need to be compared with 500 training pictures, and each picture has 784 values, the result of the comparison will be 5 × 500 × 784 data, but the size of the read test picture data is 5 × 784, the dimension expansion is required here, and the data of the test picture is expanded to 5 × 1 × 784, which is consistent with the dimension of the comparison result.

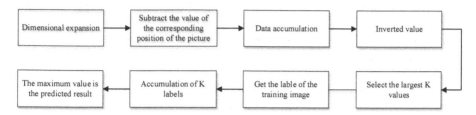

Fig. 4. Flow chart of KNN algorithm.

The 5 test pictures and 500 training pictures are compared one by one to obtain the distance between the test picture and each training picture. Here, the distance is obtained by subtracting the corresponding positions of the matrix, because each picture is composed of a matrix of gray values. The smaller the difference between the values of the corresponding positions, and the closer the distance between the two pictures is.

To get the distance of the entire picture, it is also necessary to add up the difference on each pixel. Before that, it is necessary to take the absolute value of each difference.The next step is to reverse and select the largest K values. The purpose of inverting each distance is to select the largest K values later, which were originally the smallest, to ensure that the K most similar training pictures are selected. The essence of the K nearest neighbor algorithm is to predict the test set pictures through the training set pictures. To get the most similar pictures, you also need to know which number from 0–9 these K pictures are, so next, you need to get the label of each picture. After getting the numbers of the most similar pictures, you need to decide which one is the predicted result. Here, by counting the frequency of occurrence of K numbers, the predicted result is the most frequent occurrence.

The specific operation is to add and sum these K labels. According to the characteristics of the label storage structure, the result will be a 1 × 10 matrix, where the largest value is located at the position corresponding to the number with the most occurrences, which is the predicted result. Finally, the predicted result is compared with the actual tag to get the correct rate of recognition.

$$p9[]= [1\ 1\ 1\ 0\ 7]$$
$$p10[]= [8\ 7\ 1\ 0\ 7]$$
$$ac= 60.0$$

Fig. 5. KNN algorithm running results.

Figure 5 is the running result of the KNN algorithm, p9 is the predicted result, and p10 is the actual result. The comparison can get the correct rate of recognition.

3.2 Implementation of Convolutional Neural Network Algorithm

First of all, adjust the data dimension in the same way. Convert the two-dimensional data into four-dimensional data. The first in the convolutional neural network structure is the convolutional layer and w_0 is the weight coefficient, which is obtained by truncating the normal distribution, and the variance is 0.1. [5, 5, 1, 32] indicates that the size of the convolution kernel is 5×5, and there are 32 convolution kernels in total, and the convolution operation will generate 32 feature maps b_0 is the offset, the initial average value is 0.1. Since the convolution operation will output 32 feature maps, and the addition operation needs to ensure that the dimensions of the data are consistent before and after the data, the dimension of the offset is also set to 32. The next step is to perform the convolution operation: $w_0 \otimes X + b_0$, where X is the image data after dimension expansion, $\otimes$ is the convolution operation. After the convolution operation, the result of linear change can be obtained, and then the ReLU excitation function is used for nonlinear mapping to obtain the result of the convolution.

For the pooling layer, the purpose is to reduce the amount of data. The maximum pool method is used here. For the fully connected layer, its operation is similar to that of the convolutional layer, except that the activation function + convolution operation of the convolutional layer becomes the activation function + multiplication and addition operation..

The final output layer uses the Softmax function, which is an extension of the logic function. It can compress an N-dimensional vector of any real number into another N-dimensional real vector so that the range of each element is between 0 and 1, and all the sum of the elements is 1.

Figure 6 shows the running results of the CNN algorithm. It can be seen that the final recognition accuracy rate can reach 84%.

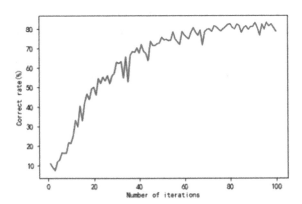

Fig. 6. CNN algorithm running results.

3.3 Differences of the Two Algorithms

By comparing the KNN algorithm and CNN algorithm for handwritten digit recognition, it can be seen that each algorithm has its unique advantages. For the KNN algorithm, its principle is relatively simple, the code is easy to implement, easy to understand, no parameter estimation and modification are required, and no training is required. For the CNN algorithm, the user does not need to care about the specific features at all. The feature extraction package is realized, and the convolution kernel is shared, which can handle high-dimensional data well.

4 Optimization and Improvement of Key Algorithms

4.1 The Improvement of K Nearest Neighbor Algorithm and Its Effect

Visualization of Results. The results of the previous KNN algorithm are only predicted results, actual results, and correct rates, which are not intuitive and convincing. If the test pictures are displayed and the predicted results and actual results are attached to the side, it can make people look more intuitive and easier to understand. To realize this function, the Matplotlib module is introduced into the code.

As shown in Fig. 7, the randomly selected MNIST test set pictures are displayed, and the prediction results and correct results are marked above the pictures. Compared with the two-line array of the previous results, it is more intuitive.

Choose Suitable Parameters. To improve the recognition rate and stability, you can start with the structural parameters of the KNN algorithm, and through a large number of calculations and comparisons, find the best parameters.

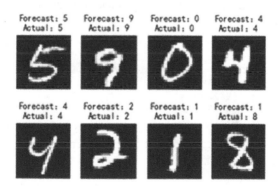

Fig. 7. Results after visualization.

The first is the selection of the K value. The value range is all positive integers. As the K value increases, the algorithm finds more similar pictures, and the amount of calculation also increases. To ensure the running speed of the program, the range of K value selected here is 1 to 20, and these 20 values are respectively substituted into the code through a loop to obtain the correct rate of the corresponding recognition. Then the

20 sets of data obtained are drawn into a line graph through the Matplotlib module, as shown in Fig. 8. It can be seen from the figure that the K value is not as large as possible, but it will increase the amount of code calculation. Here the final decision K value is 4.

In addition to the K value, the size of the training set will also have a greater impact on the performance of the algorithm. If the training set is too small, the selected K samples will differ greatly from the samples to be classified, and the recognition accuracy will be reduced. If the training set samples are too large, the amount of calculation will increase, the algorithm running time will be too long, and the performance requirements of the computer will be relatively high. To obtain a suitable training set size, the same method of finding the optimal K value is adopted, that is, a loop with the training set size as a variable is added. It can be seen from Fig. 9 that the accuracy rate is not always increasing and fluctuates, but the overall accuracy is getting higher and higher. To stabilize the accuracy rate above 90%, the training set size is set to 5000.

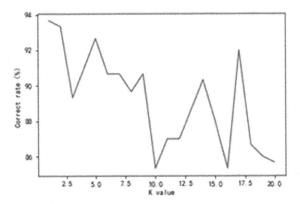

Fig. 8. The influence of K value on accuracy.

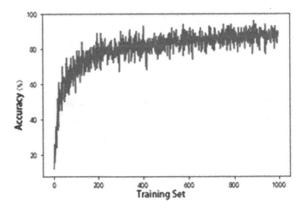

Fig. 9. Influence of training set on accuracy.

In addition to the K value and the training set, it is also optimized for the size of the test set. The previous correct rate was not high and the fluctuations were large. The reason was that the test selected too few samples, only 5 samples. After a lot of data testing, it was decided to increase the test sample to 200. By modifying the three parameters of K value, training set and test set, the effect of the algorithm has been improved, and the final accuracy rate has been improved and stabilized between 91% and 94%.

Switch to Euclidean Distance. In the previous implementation of the KNN algorithm, the distance between the test sample and the training sample was calculated by direct subtraction, and then the absolute value was taken and then accumulated, and summed. Taking into account that the Euclidean distance is squared and then the root sign is taken, the training samples with large differences can be made larger, but the original samples with small differences have little effect, and the samples with large differences can be better excluded. Here replace the direct subtraction distance with the Euclidean distance. Through the result of calculation, the correct rate of handwritten digit recognition reached 96%, which was higher than the previous 91% to 94% correct rate, which proved the feasibility of the improved scheme.

4.2   Improvement and Effect of Convolutional Neural Network Algorithm

Optimize Output Results. For the improvement of the CNN algorithm, the first is to display the changes in the recognition accuracy and the size of the loss function with the number of iterations, which can make people to see the effectiveness of neural network training.

It can be seen from Fig. 10 that the recognition accuracy and the value of the loss function change rapidly first and then slowly change with the number of iterations. But overall, the effect of training is getting better and better.

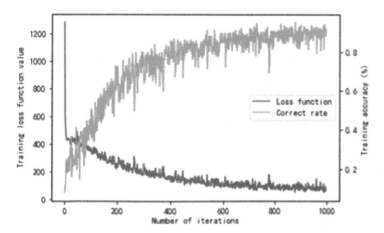

Fig. 10. The change of accuracy and loss function with the number of iterations.

For the improvement of the correct rate, the number of iterations and output is modified here. The previous program is to iterate 100 times and output the result of the recognition accuracy rate once for each training, and the number of iterations after the modification is 1000 times, and then output the recognition accuracy rate after every 50 pieces of training It can be seen from Fig. 11 that the recognition accuracy rate reaches 94%, and the efficiency is much improved.

Change the Network Structure. To further improve the accuracy of recognition and the degree of convergence of the results, a layer of convolutional pooling is added on the original basis. Adding more convolutional pooling operations can improve the accuracy of recognition to a certain extent, but at the same time, it will consume more computing time and computer resources. Based on improving the recognition accuracy rate, it is ensured that the computing time is within an acceptable range, so only one layer of convolutional pooling is added here.

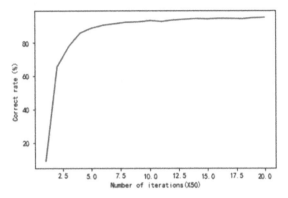

Fig. 11. The optimized output of the CNN algorithm

For the newly added layer of convolutional pooling, its code is similar to the previous layer of convolutional pooling, and the main changes are the values of some parameters. To ensure the matching of data dimensions, the output of the previous layer of the structure needs to be consistent with the input of the next layer of the structure. The newly added convolution pooling layer has a convolution kernel of 5×5. The 32 feature maps output by the first layer become input in the second layer, and 64 feature maps are output. The parameters of the fully connected layer are also To change accordingly. Previously, only one 4×4 maximum sampling pool was used, and it was modified to two 2×2 sampling pools.

As shown in Fig. 12, by comparing and highlighting the advantages of the two-layer convolutional pooling layer, it can be seen that the line of the two-layer structure is always above the one-layer structure, indicating that the convergence of the two-layer structure is better. And the accuracy of the two-layer convolutional pooling structure is higher, 96.02% and the final recognition accuracy of the one-layer structure is 94.76%.

Reduce Computing Time. For the recognition of handwritten numbers, the standard for judging the pros and cons is not only the correct rate of recognition but the time required for recognition also needs to be taken into account.

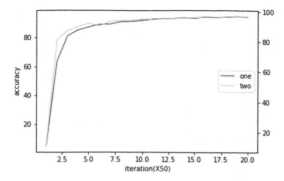

Fig. 12. Comparison of one layer and two-layer structure.

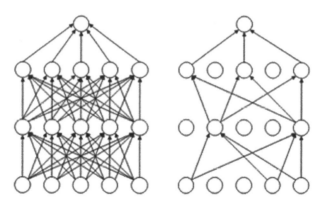

Fig. 13. Standard neural network and network with dropout.

The method adopted here is to add a Dropout layer to the fully connected layer, which prevents over-fitting of the network and also reduces the amount of calculation. As shown in Fig. 13, some neurons are discarded and the amount of calculation is reduced, thereby reducing the calculation time.

As shown in Fig. 14 it can be seen that the two curves almost overlap, indicating that whether or not the dropout layer is added has little effect on the final recognition accuracy and convergence.

As shown in Fig. 15, it can be seen that the computing time with the Dropout layer is much lower than the computing time without the Dropout layer. Adding the Dropout layer has little effect on the recognition results, but it can significantly reduce the computing time and optimize the CNN algorithm.

5   Handwritten Digit Recognition System Based on Machine Learning

5.1   Handwritten Digit Recognition Development Environment

Here is the Anaconda software, an open-source Python distribution. Its main feature is that it is open-source, the installation process is simple, and the Python language can be used with high performance.

For the built compilation platform, TensorFlow is used, which is an end-to-end open-source machine learning platform that can provide multiple levels of abstraction, can use high-level APIs to build and train models, and iterate models quickly and debug models well.

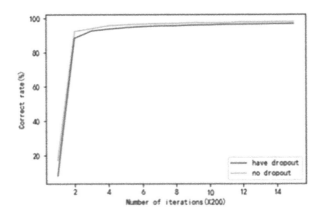

Fig. 14. Influence of dropout on accuracy.

5.2   Handwritten Digit Recognition Development Environment

The convolutional neural network is used as the core algorithm, but it takes time to train, which does not meet the requirements of practical applications. In this regard, Keras is

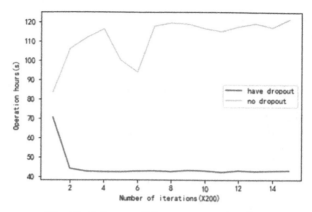

Fig. 15. Influence of dropout on running time.

used here, a deep learning framework, which can save the network structure trained by the convolutional neural network algorithm [17]. The next time the handwritten digit recognition is performed, it can be directly called without spending time training. Keras uses TensorFlow as the backend to quickly build a deep learning network and flexibly select training parameters for network training.

5.3 Handwritten Digit Recognition Development Environment

The numbers written on paper are often a series in our life, such as telephone numbers. And the pictures in the MNIST data set are all 28 × 28 pixels in size, and any picture in real life is much larger than it. Therefore, the picture of handwritten digits cannot be directly imported into the previously trained model. It needs to separate the handwritten numbers in the picture one by one, and then convert them into the same format of the MNIST data set before they can be imported into the model.

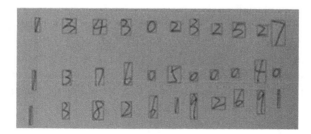

Fig. 16. Handwritten numeral segmentation results.

For image segmentation, first process the picture, first grayscale the picture, and the value of each pixel becomes 0 to 255; Then reverse the grayscale image and reverse the black and white threshold [18]. After the image preprocessing is completed, the image can be segmented. The Cv2. Findcontours() function in the OpenCV-Python interface is

410   C. Li et al.

mainly used here, which is mainly used for contour detection in image processing, and the return value is the coordinates of the upper left corner and the lower right corner of the border. As shown in Fig. 16, the numbers on the picture can be well segmented.

5.4 Handwritten Digit Recognition Development Environment

After the recognition model is built and the image preprocessing is completed, the recognition effect of the system needs to be checked. Figure 27 shows the operating results of the handwritten digit recognition system. The upper left corner of each digit is the predicted result after recognition. Although it is not guaranteed that all of them are recognized correctly, the results of the system are still satisfactory (Fig. 17).

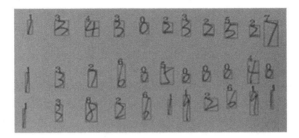

Fig. 17. Running results.

At the same time, there are some problems in the implementation process. If the handwritten digital picture is recognized in a dark environment, the effect of picture segmentation is not very good. As shown in Fig. 38 not only is a number divided into several parts but some numbers are not recognized.

It was found that it was a binarization problem in the image preprocessing process. Because the threshold of binarization is an intermediate value of 128, if a picture is dark, the gray value of most of the pixels is higher than 128, resulting in the result of binarization being all black.

To avoid this kind of problem, a function for judging the brightness and darkness of the image is added before the image binarization process. Still take the gray value of 128 as the dividing line, and then the number of dark pixels is divided by all the pixels in the image to get a ratio of dark pixels, And finally correspond to different thresholds for different ratios [19]. The result is shown in Fig. 4. After adding the function to determine the brightness of the image, the handwritten digital pictures with different brightness and darkness can be recognized (Figs. 18 and 19).

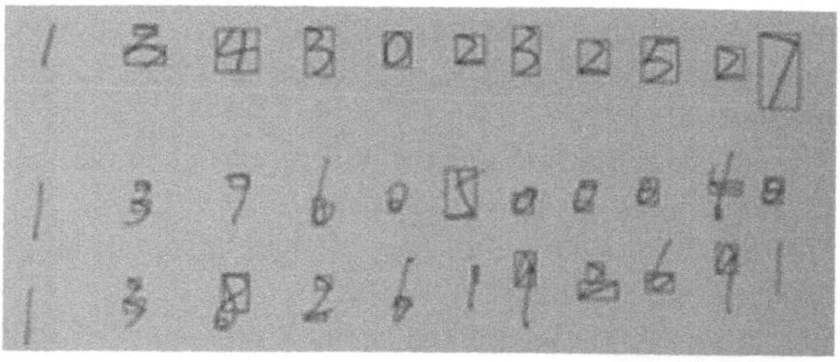

Fig. 18. The segmentation effect is affected by the light.

Fig. 19. Recognition results of different light and dark levels.

6   Concluding Remarks

This paper improves the existing handwritten digit recognition algorithm. By changing to Euclidean distance, selecting appropriate parameters, and visual output, the recognition accuracy rate in the K nearest neighbor algorithm is increased to 80% and the result is more stable and intuitive; By adding a convolutional pooling layer, optimizing the resulting output, adding a Dropout layer, etc., the convergence and recognition accuracy of the convolutional neural network algorithm is improved, and the running time is shortened; and by adding a function to judge the brightness of the picture, the picture of the handwritten digit is not affected by the light and dark.

Acknowledgment. We gratefully acknowledge anonymous reviewers who read drafts and made many helpful suggestions. This work is supported by the Higher Education Department of the Ministry of Education Industry-university Cooperative Education Project (202002186009) and the Chinese College Students' Innovation and Entrepreneurship Training program (X202110018015).

References

1. Xu, C., Lai, W., et al.: Research on character recognition of printed documents based on deep learning. Mod. Electron. Technol. **23**, 72–75 (2020)

2. Singh, H., Sharma, R.K., Singh, V.P.: Online handwriting recognition systems for Indic and non-Indic scripts: a review. Artif. Intell. Rev. **54**(2), 1525–1579 (2020). https://doi.org/10.1007/s10462-020-09886-7
3. Li, Z., Yang, Z., et al.: Research progress on the integration of complex networks and machine learning. Comput. Appl. Softw. **36**(4), 10–28 (2019)
4. Li, J., Xi, W.: The detection algorithm of the rule base of the drilling fluid design expert system. Comput. Eng. Appl. **56**(4), 256–261 (2020)
5. Tang, K., Jiang, B., et al.: Multi-dimensional attribute automatic reasoning and recognition based on decision tree. Comput. Modern. **2**, 83–87 (2017)
6. Yuan, M., Hu, C., Hu, X., et al.: An automatic reasoning problem solving algorithm based on barrel tree. Comput. Sci. **1**, 211–217 (2013)
7. Shen, X., Wang, X., Wang, Y.: Research on EEG signal recognition algorithm based on sample entropy and pattern recognition. Comput. Eng. Sci. **42**(8), 1482–1488 (2020)
8. Cao, Y., et al.: Overview of research on generative adversarial networks and computer vision applications. J. Image Graph. **23**(10), 1433–1449 (2018)
9. Zhu, X., Chen, R., Xia, H., et al.: Design of intelligent robot fruit picking recognition system. Appl. Res. Comput. **9**, 2711–2714 (2014)
10. Xue, Y., et al.: Handwritten character recognition based on improved convolutional neural network. Intell. Autom. Soft Comput. **29**(2), 497–509 (2021)
11. Saleem, S.I., Abdulazeez, A.M.: Hybrid trainable system for writer identification of Arabic handwriting. Comput. Mater. Continua **68**(3), 3353–3372 (2021)
12. Abbas, S., Alhwaiti, Y., Fatima, A., Khan, M.A., Khan, M.A., et al.: Convolutional neural network based intelligent handwritten document recognition. Comput. Mater. Continua **70**(3), 4563–4581 (2022)
13. Lu, K., Xu, H.: ML-KNN algorithm based on nearest neighbor distance weight. Appl. Res. Comput. **37**(4), 982–985 (2020)
14. Bengio, Y., Courville, A., Vincent, P.: Representation learning: a review and new perspectives. IEEE Trans. PAMI, special issue Learning Deep Architectures (2013)
15. Yan, W., Yi, S., Dabo, Z.: A novel deep convolutional neural network structure for off-line handwritten digit recognition. In: 2019 International Conference on Big Data Technologies, pp. 216–220 (2019)
16. Chang, L., Deng, X., Zhou, M., et al.: Convolutional neural network in image understanding. Acta Automatica Sinica **42**(9), 1300–1312 (2016)
17. Guo, M., Yang, M., Ma, J.: Keras-based MNIST data set recognition model. Mod. Inf. Technol. **3**(14), 18–19 (2019)
18. Hochuli, A.G., Oliveira, L.S., Britto, Jr.A.S., et al.: Handwritten digit segmentation: is it still necessary? Patt. Recogn. **78**, 1–11 (2018)
19. Liang, D., Yu, H., et al.: An improved kernel possibility c-means clustering image segmentation algorithm. Mod. Electron. Technol. **43**(5), 46–50 (2020)

D^3: A Novel Face Forgery Detector Based on Dual-Stream and Dual-Utilization Methods

Jingtian Wang, Xiaolong Li$^{(\boxtimes)}$, and Yao Zhao

Institute of Information Science, Beijing Jiaotong University, Beijing 100044, China
lixl@bjtu.edu.cn

Abstract. The rapid development of computer vision and deep learning techniques make it easy for non-professionals to create realistic fake faces. As a result, a large number of fake faces are spread on the Internet. Therefore, accurately identifying fake faces is of great significance for protecting citizens' legal rights and maintaining social stability. In this light, a novel face forgery detector named D^3 based on dual-stream and dual-utilization methods is proposed. Specifically, considering the subtle differences in the inter-frame correlation and edge details between real and fake faces, temporal stream and spatial stream are used comprehensively. In the temporal stream, Convolutional Neural Networks (CNN) and Long Short-Term Memory (LSTM) networks are introduced and trained to learn the inter-frame correlation. In the spatial stream, the Multi-Angle Filters (MAF) and CNN are introduced and trained to learn the edge details of the image. Moreover, to further improve the detection ability, the dual-utilization method is considered. That is to say, the relevant network model is used twice in each stream, the first time the initial network is trained to learn classification, and the second time the pre-trained network is used to extract features. Finally, the temporal and spatial features output by the two streams are spliced into spatio-temporal features, which are used to train a SVM-based classifier to achieve the final classification of true and fake faces. Compared with some state-of-the-art methods, the superiority of the proposed algorithm in face forgery detection is validated by related experiments.

Keywords: Digital forensics · Deepfakes · Face forgery detection

1 Introduction

Digital media information, such as images or videos, is one of the most important sources of information for people, and it is extremely susceptible to tampering. In response to various tampering techniques, a large number of digital media forensics methods have been proposed in the past. These methods have excellent detection capabilities for traditional tampering techniques. However, in recent years, some new forgery methods based on computer vision and deep learning have been proposed, which can generate realistic fake images or videos. Traditional detection methods have been unable to effectively deal with such high-quality forged information. Therefore, it has become a serious challenge to accurately judge the accuracy of various digital media information today. Among them, one that needs special attention is the authentication of forged face information.

As one of the most important biological information, due to its close relationship with personal identity, face information is widely used in various scenarios, such as face unlocking, face scan payment, etc. Therefore, faces are often forged by criminals in various ways. In Fig. 1, it shows a common technique of tampering, face swap. In this picture, the actress's face is replaced with another face. Such manipulation or forgery of real faces will seriously infringe citizens' right to portrait, privacy, reputation and even property. If the victim is a politician, face forgery may even undermine social stability and national security. Therefore, realizing the accurate recognition of forged faces is an arduous but significant task.

Fig. 1. A typical example of face-swapping.

In order to accomplish this task, a series of face forgery detection methods have been proposed in the past few years [1–4]. In [1], both with a low number of layers, two networks are proposed to detect forged videos of faces at a mesoscopic level of analysis. In [2], based on a CNN, a multi-task learning approach to simultaneously detect manipulated images and videos is proposed. Specifically, information gained by performing one task is shared with the other task and thereby enhance the performance of both tasks. Considering the unique artifact caused by the up-sampling component included in the common Generative Adversarial Networks (GAN) pipeline, a novel detection method is proposed in [3]. Considering that biological signals hidden in portrait videos can be used as an implicit descriptor of authenticity, a deep fake detector based on spatial coherence and temporal consistency of biological signals is introduced in [4]. Generally speaking, these methods have good detection capabilities for the current forged faces. However, in the face of forgery techniques with more diverse forms and more realistic visual effects, it is still very necessary and urgent to continue to study the detection technology of fake faces in depth.

In this paper, a novel face forgery detector named D^3 based on dual-stream and dual-utilization methods is proposed in this paper. Specifically, the spatial stream that mainly focuses on edge details and the time stream that focuses on inter-frame correlation are introduced and used comprehensively. In each stream, the corresponding network model is used twice for different purpose. For the first time, the initial network is trained to classify true and fake faces during the learning process. And for the second time, the pre-trained optimal network is used to extract features of true and fake faces. Finally, the features extracted from the temporal and spatial stream are spliced into spatio-temporal features, which are used to train a SVM-based classifier to achieve the final classification. The proposed algorithm has an outstanding performance on detecting face forgery, and it is experimentally validated better than some state-of-the-art works.

2   Related Works

In this section, face forgery techniques and some related detection methods based on time and space information are briefly introduced.

2.1   Face Forgery

Face forgery refers to the technique of generating fake faces by tampering with real faces. In recent years, many face forgery algorithms have been proposed. The most influential technique is face-swapping, that is, one person's face is replaced with another face. Deepfakes, which originated from a fake video made by a Reddit user named "Deepfakes" in 2017, is the most popular and representative face-swapping technique [5]. As shown in Fig. 2, one shared encoder and two different decoders are introduced and trained. Face swap is realized by encoding the input source face and decoding it with the target decoder. However, the visual effects of fake faces generated by Deepfakes are not stable. Therefore, on the basis of Deepfakes, by introducing GAN, a novel face-swapping method called Faceswap-GAN with more realistic visual effects is proposed in [6].

2.2   Face Forgery Detection

Almost all fake images or videos have some traces left in the forgery process in the temporal or spatial domain. Therefore, time and space information is often used as an important criterion to realize the classification of true and fake faces. In the past few years, a large number of time-based and space-based face forgery detection methods have been proposed.

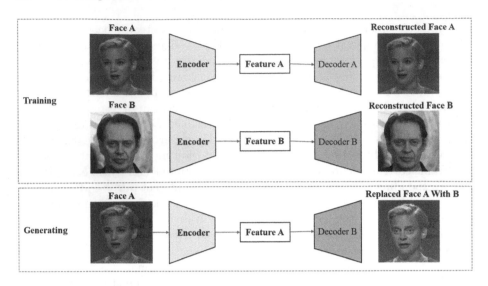

Fig. 2. Basic framework of Deepfakes.

Considering the temporal inconsistencies between frames introduced by the face-swapping process, a two-stage analysis composed of a CNN to extract features at the frame level followed by a temporally-aware Recurrent Convolutional Network (RNN) is proposed in [7]. In [8], based on the observation that errors introduced by splicing synthesized face region into the original image can be revealed when 3D head poses are estimated from the face images, a new method to expose AI generated fake face images or videos is proposed. Based on detection of eye blinking in the videos, which is a physiological signal that is not well presented in the synthesized fake videos, a new method to expose fake face videos generated with neural networks is proposed in [9]. In [10], considering the temporal artefacts left in the synthesis process, a recurrent convolutional model is proposed to identify tampered faces in videos. And in [11], a Convolutional LSTM based Residual Network is proposed to detect unnatural looking artifacts that are present between frames of deepfake videos. Realizing the existence of temporal artifacts within deepfake videos, Dynamic Prototype Network (DPNet) , an interpretable and effective solution that utilizes dynamic representations to explain deepfake temporal artifacts is proposed in [12]. In [13], based on LSTM networks that predict emotion from audio and video Low-Level Descriptors (LLDs), a novel method is proposed for detecting deepfakes of a human speaker using the emotion predicted from the speaker's face and voice. And in [14], inspired by the mechanism of how human beings detect forgery data, i.e. browsing and scrutinizing, Bita-Net, a novel model with the two-pathway architecture is proposed to detect deep forgery, concretely, the browsing pathway scans the entire video at a high frame rate to check the temporal consistency, while the scrutinizing pathway focuses on analyzing key frames of the video at a lower frame rate.

In [15], based on the observation that tampering artifact and local noise residual left in the process of face tampering, a two-stream network is proposed for face tampering detection. Specifically , one is a CNN based face classification stream to detect tampering artifacts and the other is a steganalysis feature based triplet stream. Inspired by steganalysis and natural image statistics, a novel method to identify GAN generated images using a combination of pixel co-occurrence matrices and deep learning is proposed in [16]. Then, on the basis of [16], a method for distinguishing GAN-generated from natural images is proposed in [17] by exploiting inconsistencies among spectral bands. Specifically, cross-band co-occurrence matrices and spatial co-occurrence matrices are both used as input to a CNN model, which is trained to distinguish between real and synthetic faces. In [18], based on the observations that the Deep Network Generated (DNG) images are more distinguishable from real ones in the chrominance components, especially in the residual domain, an effective and interpretable method is proposed to identify DNG images. In [19], based on the findings that mining forgery patterns with the awareness of frequency could be a cure, a novel Frequency in Face Forgery Network is proposed for face forgery detection. Specifically, in [19], two different but complementary frequency-aware clues are considered, frequency-aware decomposed image components and local frequency statistics. The forgery patterns are deeply mined via the two-stream collaborative learning framework.

3   Methods

As shown in Fig. 3, the proposed face forgery detector is mainly composed of two streams, the temporal stream focusing on the difference in the inter-frame correlation between true and false videos, and the spatial stream focusing on the difference in edge details between true and fake face images. Furthermore, in each stream, the corresponding network module is used twice for different purposes. The first process is shown by the dotted line. The initial network model is trained with a large amount of data to achieve the binary classification of true and fake faces. In this process, the differences between true and fake faces in the temporal and spatial domain are gradually learned by the relevant network until the model achieves the best classification results. The second process is shown by the solid line. The relevant pre-trained model is used as the feature extractor to extract the temporal and spatial features of the face information. Finally, the features extracted from the two streams are spliced into spatio-temporal features, which are used to train SVM to achieve the final classification of true and fake faces.

And the details of dual-stream and dual-utilization methods in the proposed algorithm are given as bellow:

3.1   Temporal Stream

The temporal stream mainly includes three parts: ResNet-50, LSTM and SD1-Net.

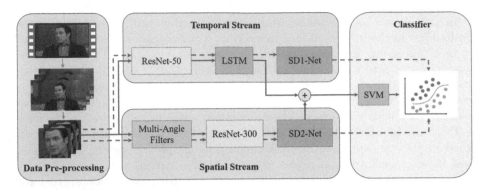

Fig. 3. Basic framework of the proposed algorithm. The dotted line represents the first use process of the algorithm, i.e., training the relevant network model to achieve binary classification. And the solid line represents the second use process of the algorithm, i.e., using the features extracted by the pre-trained model to train the SVM for final classification.

In order to learn the inter-frame correlation more conveniently, based on the excellent performance in the 2015 ImageNet Large Scale Visual Recognition Challenge, ResNet-50 [20] is adopted to first convert each frame into a 1000-dimensional feature vector. Then, these feature vectors are sent to LSTM, a RNN that is particularly suitable for processing temporal information. The LSTM is followed by a simple network of our design, SD1-Net, and the structure is shown in Fig. 4.

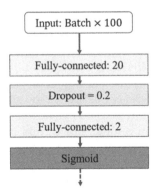

Fig. 4. Basic structure of SD1-Net.

In the first use process, ResNet-50, LSTM and SD1-Net are trained as a whole model, temporal inconsistencies between frames introduced by the face forgery is learned by the model in training process. When the optimal classification result is achieved, it has the strongest ability to discover the traces left by the fake video in the temporal domain. Then, the model are used for the second time. It should be noted that the model is used as a feature extractor this time, and the 100-dimensional feature vectors output by the LSTM are used as the final output of the temporal stream.

3.2 Spatial Stream

The spatial stream is mainly composed of three parts, including MAF, ResNet-300 and SD2-Net.

As shown in Fig. 5, MAF consists of six edge filters, including four Sobel operators and two Laplacian operators, which are used to calculate edge details in different directions and types. Sobel operator is suitable for extracting information of different edge directions and Laplace operator is sensitive to more detailed edge information. These two kinds of operators are considered together to provide more comprehensive edge information. In the actual operation of the algorithm, each filter will be convolved with the gray-scale face image, and six feature maps containing edge information are the output of MAF. However, it is not convenient to directly distinguish between true and fake faces only relying on these feature maps. Therefore, inspired by neural networks that can learn more subtle differences between true and fake information during the training process, ResNet-300 is introduced. It should be emphasized that ResNet-300 does not refer to an independent network, but refers to six parallel ResNet-50 models. Each model corresponds to a filter and is responsible for learning more detailed information from the feature map. Finally, in order to match the ResNet-300 model, SD2-Net is designed. The specific structure is shown in Fig. 6.

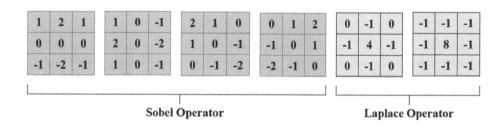

Fig. 5. Multi-Angle Filters.

The use of spatial stream is roughly the same as that of temporal stream. Simply put, the model is trained first, and then the features are extracted by the pre-trained model. The only thing to note is that in the spatial stream, the 500-dimensional features output by the second fully connected layer of SD2-Net are used as the final output.

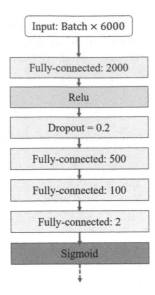

Fig. 6. Basic structure of SD2-Net.

4   Experiment

In order to verify the effectiveness and generalization of the proposed algorithm, a series of quantitative experiments are performed. The specific details are shown below.

4.1   Datasets

FaceForensics++ [21] is the most widely used face dataset in recent years, including 1000 real videos and more than 4000 fake videos made by various face forgery methods, such as Deepfakes, Face2Face, Faceswap, etc. Each video has three different resolution versions: high, medium and low. In this paper, a dataset including 1000 real videos and 1000 Deepfakes videos is adopted and referred to as DF. Notably, only medium resolution data is used. Celeb-DF [22] is a new large-scale face dataset for Deepfakes forensics, which is proposed in 2019. This dataset includes 590 real videos and 5639 corresponding high-quality Deepfakes videos generated by improved face forgery techniques.

4.2   Implementation Details

The videos in the dataset used in the experiment are all converted to frames. And in order to improve the efficiency of the algorithm and remove redundant information irrelevant to detection, the face area is cropped from each frame by MTCNNFaceDetector and saved as image with the size of 224 × 224. In addition, Pytorch 1.8 is selected as the deep learning framework. And to further improve the running speed, RTX 3090 GPU is chosen to train the relevant models. In the actual operation process, the relevant network models of temporal and spatial stream are independently trained. Specifically, the SGD optimizer is used and the learning rate is uniformly set to 0.001. The batchsize of the spatial stream is 16, while in the temporal stream, a batchsize contains 10 videos, and 10 consecutive frames of each video are selected for training. Besides, in the use of SVM, the Radial Basis Function (RBF) kernel is adopted.

4.3   Comparison Experiment

In order to verify the ability of the proposed algorithm to detect fake faces, a variety of the most advanced methods proposed in recent years are selected for comparison, including Steg.Features [23], LD-CNN [24], Bayer [25], Rahmouni [26], MesoNet [1], OC-FakeDect [27], F^3-Net [19], FWA [28], Xception [21] and SPSL (Xception) [29]. Table 1 shows the performance of each algorithm on DF dataset. Since the true and fake samples are evenly distributed, ACC (%) is selected as the evaluation indicator. It can be seen from Table 1 that the proposed algorithm achieves the best results on DF dataset, which means that it has stronger detection capability for fake faces.

Table 1. Performance comparison between the proposed and compared methods on DF dataset.

Methods	Datasets
	DF
Steg.Features [23]	73.6
LD-CNN [24]	75.0
Bayer [25]	84.6
Rahmouni [26]	85.5
MesoNet [1]	87.2
OC-FakeDect [27]	88.4
F^3-Net [19]	90.4
FWA [28]	93.0
Xception [21]	94.1
SPSL (Xception) [29]	93.5
Proposed	96.2

4.4   Ablation Experiment

In order to verify the effectiveness of dual-stream and dual-utilization methods in the proposed algorithm, an ablation experiment is carried out. Experimental results are shown in Table 2. Single-utilization refers to the direct use of the pre-trained binary-classification network model to achieve classification. The process is shown by the dotted line in Fig. 3. And dual-utilization refers to the method of training the binary-classification network model first, and then using the features extracted by the pre-trained network model to train a SVM-based classifier for classification, i.e., the process shown by the dotted line in Fig. 3 is executed first, and then the process shown by the solid line is executed. It can be seen from Table 2 that in each individual stream, the dual-utilization method is more effective than the single-utilization method. And the combined use of two streams has a better detection effect than using any one of them alone. Therefore, the dual-stream and dual-utilization methods are validated to be effective by experiments.

Table 2. Performance comparison using different components and strategies of the proposed algorithm on DF dataset. ACC (%) is adopted.

Methods	Datasets
	DF
Temporal Stream + Single-Utilization	91.3
Temporal Stream + Dual-Utilization	93.8
Spatial Stream + Single-Utilization	91.0
Spatial Stream + Dual-Utilization	94.1
Dual Stream + Dual-Utilization (Proposed)	96.2

Table 3. Cross-dataset performance comparison between the proposed and compared methods on Celeb-DF dataset. AUC (%) is adopted.

Methods	Datasets
	Celeb-DF
HeadPose [8]	54.6
MesoNet [1]	54.8
VA-MLP [30]	55.0
SMIL [31]	56.3
FWA [28]	56.9
Capsule [32]	57.5
Proposed	60.3

4.5   Cross-dataset Experiment

Finally, to test the generalization of the proposed algorithm, the cross-dataset comparison experiment is performed. Comparison methods include HeadPose [8], MesoNet [1], VA-MLP [30], SMIL [31], FWA [28] and Capsule [32]. For fairness, all methods are trained on DF dataset and tested on Celeb-DF dataset. It can be seen from Table 3 that although the generalization of the proposed algorithm is not particularly good, it still has advantages over other algorithms.

5 Conclusion

In this paper, based on dual-stream and dual-utilization methods, a novel face forgery detector named D^3 is proposed. According to dual-stream method, the differences in edge details and inter-frame correlation between real and fake faces are comprehensively considered. And through dual-utilization method, neural network which has the advantage of learning information in deeper level and SVM which is suitable for classification using high-dimensional features are utilized. The proposed method is experimentally validated to be better than some of the most advanced works [1,19,21,23–29]. Next, we intend to introduce the attention mechanism into the proposed method for better performance. In addition, improving the generalization is also in our future planning.

Acknowledgements. This work was supported by the National Key Research and Development Program of China (No. 2019QY2203).

References

1. Afchar, D., Nozick, V., Yamagishi, J., Echizen, I.: MesoNet: a compact facial video forgery detection network. In: 2018 IEEE International Workshop on Information Forensics and Security (WIFS), pp. 1–7. IEEE (2018)
2. Nguyen, H.H., Fang, F., Yamagishi, J., Echizen, I.: Multi-task learning for detecting and segmenting manipulated facial images and videos. arXiv preprint arXiv:1906.06876 (2019)
3. Zhang, X., Karaman, S., Chang, S.F.: Detecting and simulating artifacts in GAN fake images. In: 2019 IEEE International Workshop on Information Forensics and Security (WIFS), pp. 1–6. IEEE (2019)
4. Ciftci, U.A., Demir, I., Yin, L.: FakeCatcher: detection of synthetic portrait videos using biological signals. IEEE Trans. Patt. Anal. Mach. Intelli. (2020)
5. Deepfakes github (2017). https://github.com/deepfakes/faceswap
6. Faceswap-gan (2019). https://github.com/shaoanlu/faceswap-GAN
7. Güera, D., Delp, E.J.: Deepfake video detection using recurrent neural networks. In: 2018 15th IEEE International Conference on Advanced Video and Signal Based Surveillance (AVSS), pp. 1–6. IEEE (2018)
8. Yang, X., Li, Y., Lyu, S.: Exposing deep fakes using inconsistent head poses. In: ICASSP 2019–2019 IEEE International Conference on Acoustics, Speech and Signal Processing (ICASSP), pp. 8261–8265. IEEE (2019)
9. Li, Y., Chang, M.C., Lyu, S.: In Ictu Oculi: Exposing AI created fake videos by detecting eye blinking. In: 2018 IEEE International Workshop on Information Forensics and Security (WIFS), pp. 1–7. IEEE (2018)
10. Sabir, E., Cheng, J., Jaiswal, A., AbdAlmageed, W., Masi, I., Natarajan, P.: Recurrent convolutional strategies for face manipulation detection in videos. Interfaces (GUI) **3**(1), 80–87 (2019)
11. Tariq, S., Lee, S., Woo, S.S.: A convolutional LSTM based residual network for deepfake video detection. arXiv preprint arXiv:2009.07480 (2020)
12. Trinh, L., Tsang, M., Rambhatla, S., Liu, Y.: Interpretable and trustworthy deepfake detection via dynamic prototypes. In: Proceedings of the IEEE/CVF Winter Conference on Applications of Computer Vision, pp. 1973–1983 (2021)

13. Hosler, B., et al.: Do deepfakes feel emotions ? A semantic approach to detecting deepfakes via emotional inconsistencies. In: Proceedings of the IEEE/CVF Conference on Computer Vision and Pattern Recognition, pp. 1013–1022 (2021)
14. Ru, Y., Zhou, W., Liu, Y., Sun, J., Li, Q.: Bita-Net: bi-temporal attention network for facial video forgery detection. In: 2021 IEEE International Joint Conference on Biometrics (IJCB), pp. 1–8. IEEE (2021)
15. Zhou, P., Han, X., Morariu, V.I., Davis, L.S.: Two-stream neural networks for tampered face detection. In: 2017 IEEE Conference on Computer Vision and Pattern Recognition Workshops (CVPRW), pp. 1831–1839. IEEE (2017)
16. McCloskey, S., Albright, M.: Detecting GAN-generated imagery using saturation cues. In: 2019 IEEE International Conference on Image Processing (ICIP), pp. 4584–4588. IEEE (2019)
17. Barni, M., Kallas, K., Nowroozi, E., Tondi, B.: CNN detection of GAN-generated face images based on cross-band co-occurrences analysis. In: 2020 IEEE International Workshop on Information Forensics and Security (WIFS), pp. 1–6. IEEE (2020)
18. Li, H., Li, B., Tan, S., Huang, J.: Identification of deep network generated images using disparities in color components. Sign. Process. **174**, 107616 (2020)
19. Qian, Y., Yin, G., Sheng, L., Chen, Z., Shao, J.: Thinking in frequency: face forgery detection by mining frequency-aware clues. In: Vedaldi, A., Bischof, H., Brox, T., Frahm, J.-M. (eds.) ECCV 2020. LNCS, vol. 12357, pp. 86–103. Springer, Cham (2020). https://doi.org/10.1007/978-3-030-58610-2_6
20. He, K., Zhang, X., Ren, S., Sun, J.: Deep residual learning for image recognition. In: Proceedings of the IEEE Conference on Computer Vision and Pattern Recognition, pp. 770–778 (2016)
21. Rossler, A., Cozzolino, D., Verdoliva, L., Riess, C., Thies, J., Nießner, M.: Face-Forensics++: learning to detect manipulated facial images. In: Proceedings of the IEEE/CVF International Conference on Computer Vision, pp. 1–11 (2019)
22. Li, Y., Yang, X., Sun, P., Qi, H., Lyu, S.: Celeb-DF: a large-scale challenging dataset for deepfake forensics. In: Proceedings of the IEEE/CVF Conference on Computer Vision and Pattern Recognition, pp. 3207–3216 (2020)
23. Fridrich, J., Kodovsky, J.: Rich models for steganalysis of digital images. IEEE Trans. Inf. Foren. Secur. **7**(3), 868–882 (2012)
24. Cozzolino, D., Poggi, G., Verdoliva, L.: Recasting residual-based local descriptors as convolutional neural networks: an application to image forgery detection. In: Proceedings of the 5th ACM Workshop on Information Hiding and Multimedia Security, pp. 159–164 (2017)
25. Bayar, B., Stamm, M.C.: A deep learning approach to universal image manipulation detection using a new convolutional layer. In: Proceedings of the 4th ACM Workshop on Information Hiding and Multimedia Security, pp. 5–10 (2016)
26. Rahmouni, N., Nozick, V., Yamagishi, J., Echizen, I.: Distinguishing computer graphics from natural images using convolution neural networks. In: 2017 IEEE Workshop on Information Forensics and Security (WIFS), pp. 1–6. IEEE (2017)
27. Khalid, H., Woo, S.S.: OC-FakeDect: classifying deepfakes using one-class variational autoencoder. In: Proceedings of the IEEE/CVF Conference on Computer Vision and Pattern Recognition Workshops, pp. 656–657 (2020)
28. Li, Y., Lyu, S.: Exposing deepfake videos by detecting face warping artifacts. arXiv preprint arXiv:1811.00656 (2018)
29. Liu, H., et al.: Spatial-phase shallow learning: rethinking face forgery detection in frequency domain. In: Proceedings of the IEEE/CVF Conference on Computer Vision and Pattern Recognition, pp. 772–781 (2021)

30. Matern, F., Riess, C., Stamminger, M.: Exploiting visual artifacts to expose deep-fakes and face manipulations. In: 2019 IEEE Winter Applications of Computer Vision Workshops (WACVW), pp. 83–92. IEEE (2019)
31. Li, X., et al.: Sharp multiple instance learning for deepfake video detection. In: Proceedings of the 28th ACM International Conference on Multimedia, pp. 1864–1872 (2020)
32. Nguyen, H.H., Yamagishi, J., Echizen, I.: Capsule-forensics: using capsule networks to detect forged images and videos. In: ICASSP 2019–2019 IEEE International Conference on Acoustics, Speech and Signal Processing (ICASSP), pp. 2307–2311. IEEE (2019)

Surface Defect Detection of Medium and Thick Plates Based on MASK-RCNN

Jian Liu[1]($\boxtimes$), Tao Liu[1], Yu Rong[1], Rui Cao[2], and Lixin Tian[2]

[1] University of Science and Technology Beijing, Beijing 100083, China
17865597058@163.com
[2] Dawning Information Industry Co. Ltd., Tianjin 300384, China

Abstract. Intelligent surface defect detection of steel plate is an important technical means to ensure the quality of steel products and realize intelligent production. The existing steel plate surface detection methods are generally manual, with low efficiency and accuracy. With the continuous development of acquisition equipment, the pictures collected by industrial cameras can provide more feature information. In addition, the deep learning method can make full use of the image feature information from the image, and effectively solve the problems of time-consuming and low accuracy of the traditional methods. Therefore, a method of using mask RCNN network to detect steel plate surface defects is proposed in this paper. Aiming at the common surface defects of steel plate, such as cracks, iron oxide skin pressing, overburning and pitting, the training set and verification set are established and input into the neural network. The results of the test set show that the average accuracy of the model reaches 0.63, and the average intersection union ratio is greater than 80%. It has good model migration ability and broad application prospects.

Keywords: Medium thickness plate · Mask RCNN · Object detection · Data enhancement

1 Introduction

1.1 A Subsection Sample

The production technology of steel plate is an important symbol of the development level of iron and steel industry. It has extremely important applications in automobile industry, aerospace, chemical equipment and other important industrial categories. Medium plate is mainly used in construction engineering, machinery manufacturing, container manufacturing, shipbuilding, bridge construction and so on. With the increasing demand of some users of medium and heavy plate, mainly in high-precision and cutting-edge industries, for the surface quality of steel plate. The surface quality of steel plate has gradually attracted people's attention [1].

Surface defects not only make it difficult for medium and heavy plates to meet the production requirements of users, but also cause serious production accidents such as

X. Sun et al. (Eds.): ICAIS 2022, CCIS 1586, pp. 426–436, 2022.
https://doi.org/10.1007/978-3-031-06767-9_35

belt breaking, stacking and parking, serious wear of rolls, and incalculable impact on production enterprises [2].

Based on the above situation, major production enterprises attach great importance to the surface defect detection of medium and heavy plates. The traditional detection method is mainly visual inspection, and there is no stable and efficient detection method in the production process. The conventional method is to use manual sampling inspection after the plate is cooled, but this method has some disadvantages: a. It requires experienced steel rolling workers, and is easily affected by objective factors. There is no objective evaluation standard and the speed is slow; b. The test data cannot be saved in time, and the test methods cannot be saved to guide later production; c. When manually detecting the back, it is necessary to turn over the steel plate. Turning over the bulky medium and thick plate is not only costly, but also easy to cause damage to it; d. The internal temperature of the plate after surface cooling is still very high, so it is difficult to ensure the safety of the inspectors.

In recent years, With the development of CCD [3] technology, industrial cameras are widely used in the field of surface detection, enabling enterprises and researchers to obtain a large number of pictures and materials of production sites, Thanks to this, a series of achievements have been made in the surface detection technology of medium and heavy plates. Massive surface defect data can also be stored in the database for future viewing [4].

In order to further improve the detection efficiency and reduce the interference of objective conditions. Automated surface inspection has also made great progress. With the rapid development of computer and machine vision technology, the steel plate surface detection technology based on vision has become mature. Machine learning methods such as BP neural network, SVM classifier and decision tree also participate in the research of image classification. However, there are great differences between traditional machine learning algorithms, and the effect is good for specific problems, but the accuracy of changing application scenarios often varies greatly, algorithm migration ability is weak.

In recent years, in-depth learning has made breakthrough achievements in various fields. Especially thanks to the improvement of GPU computing power, by designing large-scale neural network structure, massive data input and reverse gradient parameter update, the complex feature extraction process is omitted. In the field of metal surface detection, deep learning algorithm is gradually introduced to solve some target detection problems [5].

The field of target detection algorithms includes two technical development routes. One is the candidate region based target detector represented by fast RCNN and faster RCNN, also known as two-stage method. This kind of detector is divided into two stages: first, region proposals are generated from the image, and then the final object frame is generated from region proposals. The second is the single detector represented by yolov3/yolov4/yolov5, also known as one-stage target detection algorithm [6]. The one-stage target detection algorithm does not need the region proposal stage, and directly generates the category probability and position coordinate value of the object. After one stage, the final detection result can be obtained directly, so it has a faster detection speed [7]. In comparison, the two-stage method has higher detection accuracy, but the detection time will also increase. The one-stage method is often used in occasions with high real-time requirements.

2   Algorithmic Principles

Based on fast RCNN, Mask RCNN uses ROIAlign instead of ROIPooling, and adds a full convolution network to generate a mask branch. Mask RCNN generates two prediction branches, including a class branch and a mask branch, which improves the accuracy of target detection [8].

2.1   BACKBON

When the number of network layers increases to a certain extent, the error rate increases. The reason is that too many layers make it more difficult for the gradient to decline. ResNet network solves this problem. Feature pyramid network (FPN) is a well-designed multi-scale detection method [9], FPN structure includes three parts: bottom-up, top-down and horizontal connection. As a general architecture, FPN can be used in combination with various network structures, such as VGG, ResNet [10], etc. the structure of ResNet + FPN is adopted in this paper, The network structure is shown in the Fig. 1 below.

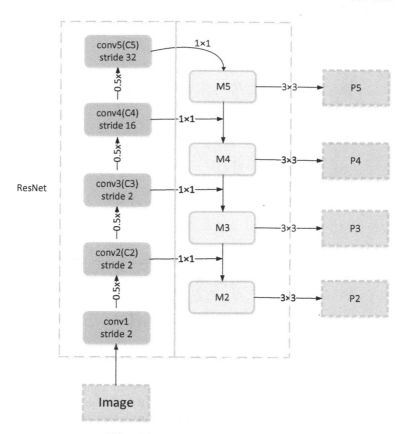

Fig. 1. ResNet + FPN example diagram.

2.2 RPN Network

RPN, namely target recommendation network, is used to generate possible target regions [13]. Its essence is to slide on the feature map through windows with different proportions, and then generate candidate regions. It slides on the feature map to construct category independent candidate regions using 3×3 convolution networks. The candidate region is classified by classifier to determine whether it is the target region [14]. RPN network has four main functions: a. Category prediction and box regression; b. Generate anchor boxes; c. Border filtering; d. Loss calculation (Fig. 2).

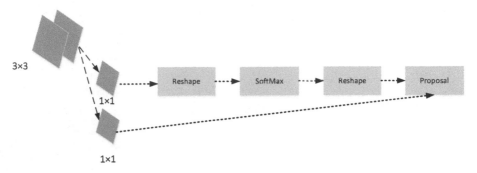

Fig. 2. RPN example diagram.

2.3 ROI

According to the candidate frame generated by RPN, the key is how to select the appropriate feature map according to the size of the candidate frame, select by the following criteria:

$$k = \left\lfloor k_0 + \log_2(\sqrt{wh}/224) \right\rfloor \tag{1}$$

Mask RCNN proposes the roialign method to replace ROI pooling, which can retain the approximate spatial position. ROI pooling involves two quantization and rounding processes, which will lead to the loss of some pixel areas. Roialign adopts bilinear interpolation. When the RoI area is mapped to the size of the feature map, floating-point numbers are retained. For each pooling area, the coordinate positions of some sampling points (still floating-point numbers) are calculated. The eigenvalues of the sampling points are obtained by bilinear interpolation [15]. Finally, the results of roialign are obtained by pooling these sampling points (Fig. 3).

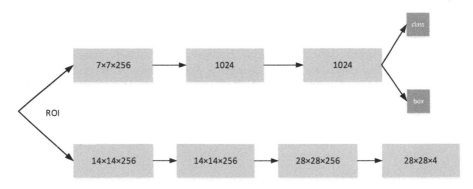

Fig. 3. Predict branch.

In the network structure of mask rcnn, some network structures of fast r-cnn are used, and only one additional mask prediction branch is added. Mask predicts that the branch will get size m × m × 2K output, the mask size is m × m. Each mask contains two prediction channels of the object or background [16], and K is the number of predicted object categories.

2.4 Loss

The loss form of mask r-cnn is:

$$L = L_{cls} + L_{reg} + L_{mask} \tag{2}$$

L_{mask} is the cross entropy loss of a binary classification, During network training, when the IoU of RoI and ground truth is greater than 0.5, they are marked as positive samples, and only positive samples are calculated. At the same time, only the mask of the corresponding category of ground truth is calculated, and other mask predictions do not calculate loss. That is, the mask prediction of each category in Mask RCNN is independent, and there is no competition between different categories of masks. Therefore, mask prediction and classification prediction are decoupled.

3 Methodology

3.1 Image Acquisition

The experimental data in this paper are the surface defect images of steel plate collected in the production line of a domestic medium and heavy plate factory, including scratches, warping, cracks, overburning, pitting, iron oxide skin pressing and other defects. According to the number and common degree of steel plate surface defect images, 120 images of crack, overburning, pitting and iron oxide skin pressing are selected as training data. The training set and verification set are divided according to the ratio of 7:3 for training. In addition, before training the surface defect samples, the coco data set is used to pre train the network weight to avoid over fitting in the training process to the greatest extent.

3.2 Image Overlays

Image annotation plays an important role in computer vision. The goal of image Overlays is task specific tags related to tasks. This may include text-based labels (classes), labels drawn on images (i.e. borders), or even pixel level labels. The tasks requiring image annotation mainly include object detection, line/edge detection, image classification, pose prediction, key point recognition and so on. For polygonal objects, you can use polygonal annotation boxes. According to different annotation objects, you can use 2-D or 3-D annotation boxes. The plane box is fast and simple to label, can provide approximate object information, and can quickly verify the accuracy of the algorithm.

In this experiment, labelme labeling software is used for labeling, and the English name of surface defects is used for classification, Due to the memory limitation of the graphics card, and in order to reduce the amount of calculation and shorten the calculation time, the rectangular frame is used to select the target area. All annotation information, including coordinates, class aliases and so on, will be saved to the corresponding JSON file with the same name. Themarking is shown in the Fig. 4.

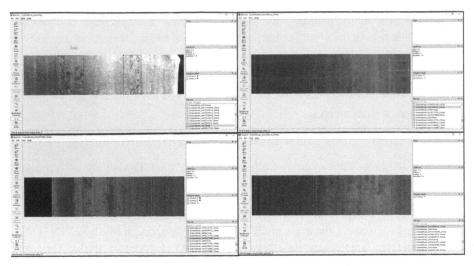

Fig. 4. Labelme program.

3.3 Data Enhancement

The main function of image enhancement algorithm is to carry out a series of processing on the image collected by imaging equipment to enhance the overall effect or local details of the image, so as to improve the contrast between the whole and part, suppress unnecessary detail information, improve the quality of the image and make it conform to the visual characteristics of human eyes [17].

In addition to simply expanding the sample size of picture data, generalized data enhancement also includes enhancing sample quality, such as alleviating the negative impact on system performance caused by inter class sample data imbalance, inter class sample overlap and difficult to distinguish boundary samples [11].

For a long time, the most widely used amplification method is to process the image at the overall level. After collecting the image data or pictures of specific surface defects, build the image database, and perform physical geometric operations such as rotation, scaling and mirroring on the pictures in the image library. Some common specific operation methods include the following. a. Rotation method: rotate the original image at a certain angle after selecting a certain step, and then insert the rotated image with the nearest neighborhood method to ensure the integrity of the image. However, this method may not be accurate enough; b. Scaling method: perform bilinear interpolation on the sampleimage to enlarge or reduce the coordinate value in the same scale; c. Mirror image method: flip the image horizontally or vertically, and the target area will change accordingly; d. Translation method: the training data samples are translated with the same step size. This method helps to increase the generalization ability of cnn.

Data enhancement can also be carried out at the pixel level, which can not only increase the data capacity, but also increase the contrast of the target area and highlight the characteristics of the target. Specific applications include a. Noise interference method: by adding salt and pepper noise or Gaussian noise to the image; b. Gaussian blur: by using Gaussian functions with different variances to blur the image data, the accuracy of the image detection system can be effectively improved [12]; c. Image jitter: by changing the contrast of the sample images in the training set to varying degrees, that is, by increasing or decreasing the proportion of some colors in a certain color space, or changing the order of color channels to achieve sample amplification.

Starting from the demand of increasing the number of samples and improving the adaptability of the model, in order to further improve the accuracy of model classification and increase the number of samples, a variety of data amplification methods are adopted, including image mirror transformation, vertical flip, color difference transformation and other data enhancement methods. The following figure is a data enhancement picture (Figs. 5 and 6).

Fig. 5. Linear interpolation transformation.

Fig. 6. Mirror transform.

After data enhancement, the number of samples is shown in the following table (Table 1):

Table 1. Sample statistics for training.

	Over burning	Crack	Iron oxide press in	Pitting
Training set	94	84	138	62
Validation set	16	22	32	28

3.4 Experimental Environment

The system environment of this experiment is: the operating system is centos-7.9, and the Linux kernel version is 3.10.0–1160.41.1.el7.x86_ 64, gcc version 4.8.5. The py-Mask-RCNN network algorithm is configured, the deep learning framework built by tensorflow 1.13.1-gpu is adopted, the python 3.6-bit main programming language is selected, the NVIDIA Tesla k40m computing platform is adopted in computer hardware, and cuda-10.2 is used to accelerate the algorithm. The training and testing of the algorithm in this paper are completed in the environment of GPU.

3.5 Parameter Setting

According to the above specific experimental methods, the model is trained, in which 140 pictures are randomly selected from 200 pictures as the training set and the remaining 60 as the verification set. The parameter setting is fine tuned with the experimental process, and the number of iterations is 3000, in which the learning rate is set as the weight attenuation rate of 0.001 and 0.0001.

3.6 Evaluating Indicator

Mean average precision (map) is used as an index to evaluate the accuracy of the training model. Map is an algorithm performance index used to predict target location and category. It refers to the average value of average precision (AP) of multiple categories. A higher map value indicates that the model is better. In image segmentation, each class can draw a curve according to the accuracy P (precision) and recall R (recall), and the average accuracy AP is the area under the curve. The calculation formula of multiple indicators is as follows:

$$P = \frac{T_p}{T_p + F_p} \tag{3}$$

$$R = \frac{T_P}{T_P + F_N} \tag{4}$$

$$A_p = \int_0^1 P(R)dR. \tag{5}$$

$$m_{AP} = \frac{\sum_1^k A_p}{k} \tag{6}$$

where Tp represents the number of correctly predicted positive samples. Fp represents the number of samples in which negative samples are predicted tobe positive samples. FY represents the number of samples in which positive samples are predicted to be negative samples, and K represents the number of categories; P refers to the accuracy, which refers to the proportion of correctly detected samples in all actually detected samples; R refers to the recall rate, which refers to the proportion of correctly detected samples to the number of samples to be detected.

4 Results

A total of 20 pictures were used in the test set, and the relevant evaluation indexes were calculated by comparing the truth mask. In the experiment, it is considered that the recognition result is correct when the IOU of truth mask and detection mask is ≥ 0.5 and the confidence is greater than 0.7.

Some representative test results are shown in the Fig. 7–8. At the same time, through statistics, the recognition accuracy and recall rate of surface defects on the test set are shown in Table.

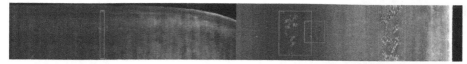

Fig. 7. Cracks and iron oxide indentation test results.

Fig. 8. Fever and pitting test results.

Table 2. Statistics of various defect detection results.

	Over burning	Crack	Pitting	Iron oxide press in
Accuracy rate	1	0.929	1	0.71
Recall Rate	0.875	0.75	0.5	0.636

After calculation. In this experiment, the map value in the test set is 0.63. The average recognition time is 0.75 s. Average identification cross merge ratio $\geq 80\%$ (Table 2).

By analyzing the experimental results, the following conclusions can be obtained:

(1) The average intersection and merging ratio of surface defects detected by the model is greater than 80%, which can better detect the location of defects. For small-scale targets such as pockmarks, distributed surface defects have low detection accuracy.
(2) From the detection results, it can be seen that Mask RCNN algorithm has a certain effect on the detection of surface defects. It is proved that for the surface detection of medium and thick plates, the algorithm can be well transplanted to the scene of surface defect detection.

5   Conclusion

Based on the traditional target detection algorithm Mask RCNN network, this paper first enhances the data of the surface defect pictures taken by the medium and heavy plate surface detector, then labels them with labelme, extracts the features in combination with ResNet-101, inputs them into the network for training and detection, and achieves certain results.

At present, we only carry out some simple data processing. In the future work, we will explore more effective feature fusion methods, make more full use of the information mined in the image, optimize the algorithm structure and speed up the network training speed.

References

1. Liang, Y., Zhan, K.: Surface defect detection of medium and heavy plates based on binarized normed gradients. Surf. Technol. **48**(10), 336–341 (2019)
2. Tsai, D., Chiang, I., Tsai, Y.: A shift-tolerant dissimilarity measure for surface defect detection. IEEE Trans. Industr. Inf. **8**(1), 128–137 (2012)
3. Yamaguchi, K.: Analog signal processing circuit for ccd camera, and analog signal processing method. U.S. Patent Application 11/553,514 (2007)
4. Kushwaha, A., Aslam, M.: Roughness enhanced surface defects and photoconductivity of acid etched ZnO nanowires. In: International Conference on Emerging Electronics, pp. 1–4 (2012)
5. Jian, C., Gao, Y.: Ao: Automatic surface defect detection for mobile phone screen glass based on machine vision. Appl. Soft Comput. **52**, 348–358 (2017)
6. Redmon, J., Farhadi, A.: YOLOv3: an incremental improvement. arXiv:1804.02767v1 (2018)
7. Redmon, J., Farhadi, A.: YOLO9000: better, faster, stronger. In: IEEE Conference on Computer Vision and Pattern Recognition (CVPR), pp.7263–7271 (2017)
8. He, K., Gkioxari, G., Dollár, P., Girshick, R.: Mask R-CNN. In: IEEE International Conference on Computer Vision (ICCV), pp.2980–2988 (2017)
9. Jiang, H., Learned-Miller, E.: Face detection with the faster R-CNN. In: 12th IEEE International Conference on Automatic Face & Gesture Recognition (FG 2017), pp. 650–657 (2017)
10. Szegedy, C., Ioffe, Vanhoucke, Alemi: Inception-v4, Inception-ResNet and the Impact of Residual Connections on Learning. arXiv:1602.07261 (2016)
11. Loshin, D.: Data enhancement. The Practitioner's Guide to Data Quality Improvement, pp. 313–325 (2011)
12. Zhang, Z., Weng, Y.: RIDE: region-induced data enhancement method for dynamic calibration of optical see-through head-mounted displays. In: IEEE Virtual Reality, pp. 245–246 (2017)
13. Ju, X.: An overview of face manipulation detection. J. Cyber Secur. **2**(4), 197–207 (2020)
14. Wang, X., Wang, Q.: Application of dynamic programming algorithm based on model predictive control in hybrid electric vehicle control strategy. J. Internet Things **2**(2), 81–87 (2020)
15. Abu-Alhaija, M., Turab, N.M.: Automated learning of ecg streaming data through machine learning internet of things. Intell. Autom. Soft Comput. **32**(1), 45–53 (2022)
16. Devi, S.K., Subalalitha, C.N.: Deep learning based audio assistive system for visually impaired people. Comput. Mater. Continua **71**(1), 1205–1219 (2022)
17. Palanisamy, P.N., Malmurugan, N.: FPGA implementation of deep learning model for video analytics. Comput. Mater. Continua **71**(1), 791–808 (2022)

Video-Based Pedestrian Re-identification with Non-local Attention Module

Ji Zhang[1], Li Cheng[1], Zihao Xin[1], Fuhua Chen[2], and Hongyuan Wang[1(✉)]

[1] Changzhou University, Changzhou 213164, Jiangsu, China
hywang@cczu.edu.cn
[2] West Liberty University, University Drive, West Liberty 26074, USA

Abstract. This paper studies a video-based person re-identification (Re-ID) model with non-local attention module. Firstly, on the basis of the residual module embedded in the 3D convolutional neural network, an non-local attention module is added. This module can associate the long-distance information among video frames, and establish connections between pixels at a certain distance, and enrich the pedestrian feature representations from local and global aspects; Then, many experiments on two public video-based datasets Mars and DukeMTMC-VideoREID proves that our proposed method is competitive with some recent video-based Re-ID methods.

Keywords: Video-based person re-identification · 3D convolutional neural network · Non-local attention mechanism

1 Introduction

Pedestrian re-recognition (Re-ID) aims to retrieve specific pedestrians under non-overlapping cameras in different environments [1–3]. Specifically, given a probe image or video of a target pedestrian, the task of pedestrian Re-ID is to identify the pedestrian from a multi-camera network gallery or video library in the non-overlapping view-field. However, pedestrian images or videos are susceptible to pedestrian wearing, background, light and shade, camera positions and other various factors [4, 5], which resulted in the tremendous differences between pedestrian appearances and effect the precision of recognition.

Pedestrian Re-ID is of great practical significance and has attracted more and more attention from researchers, and a lot of related works have been proposed [6]. Pedestrian Re-ID includes image-based and video-based pedestrian Re-ID [7]. Although many image-based pedestrian Re-ID methods have been widely studied, videos are the first-hand information captured by surveillance cameras in the actual scene. Therefore, we study the pedestrian Re-ID based on video in this paper. Traditional pedestrian Re-ID methods attempt to use manual features to detect pedestrians including texture space features (such as LBP [8], Gabor [9]), local features (such as SIFT [10], HOG [11], SURF [12]), special features (such as SDALF [13], LOMO [14]). Wang [15] proposed a spatio-temporal descriptors based method, which integrated HOG3D [16] features and

X. Sun et al. (Eds.): ICAIS 2022, CCIS 1586, pp. 437–447, 2022.
https://doi.org/10.1007/978-3-031-06767-9_36

gait energy maps, and designed a flow energy profile to detect gait cycle, and extracted motion features using local minimum or maximum frames to identify, select and match reliable spatio-temporal features. You [17] proposed a push-up distance learning model by improving LMNN [18] algorithm, which reduced intra-class distance and increases inter-class distance, and integrated color and HOG3D [16] features while extracting features, in order to obtain good feature expression. Compared with manual designed feature extraction, deep learning based ones includes: Zhang [19] proposed an effective "relational aware global attention" (RGA) module, which can capture global structure information for better attentional learning. Specifically, for each feature position, in order to grasp the global structure information and local appearance information compactly, the shallow convolution model is used to learn attention through stacking relation, that is, its paired correlation with all feature positions and feature itself. Lin [20] introduced an attribute-based neural network, which integrated local pedestrian attribute features to improve the convolutional neural network, and combined pedestrian identity loss and attribute classification loss function to construct a new loss function to measure the video-based pedestrian Re-ID network model.

In this paper, 3D convolutional neural network and the residual module (3D-RESNet50) [21] is used to build the basic framework, and the non-local attention module is embedded in this framework. Video-level features are proposed and embedded into multiple feature level representations. This framework can effectively improve the accuracy of pedestrian Re-ID, and experiments on two video datasets (DukemtMC-VideoREID [22] and Mars [9]) verify the effectiveness of our method.

The main contributions of this paper are as follows:

(1) Non-local attention module (NLAM) is used in this paper, which considers different frames and different spatial-temporal positions when extracting features, and establishes pixel-wised connections at a certain distance between frames to extract more effective local and global spatio-temporal information.
(2) Experimental results on two video datasets (dukemtMC-VideoREID [22] and Mars [9]) are shown that the proposed method can significantly improve the accuracy of video pedestrian Re-ID.

2   Related Work

2.1   Attentional Mechanism

Attentional mechanism [23] is started from human visual attention mechanism, which is similar to observation of the external mechanism of human. Namely, when observe external things, features from some important parts are more inclined to observe than other ones, and then the features from different parts are integrated, thus the overall appearances can be observed. The recursive model uses time steps to correspond the outputs and positions of each time for calculation. This sequential operator can eliminate parallel running during training, but can introduce memory limitations if the video clip is too long. Therefore, it is necessary to introduce attention mechanism, which can process the dependency of video clips without considering the distances between network input and output clips [25]. In this paper, attention mechanism is used to plot global and local dependencies between inputs and outputs.

Generally speaking, attention mechanism can be divided into two kinds: soft attention and strong attention. The former focuses on the attention areas [26] or channels [27], and the latter focuses on the attention points. Liu [28] proposes a multi-directional attention network to jointly utilize global and local content of images. Li [29] considers both spatial and temporal attention to enhance representational ability. For spatial attention, they use a penalty term to promote multiple attention to different salient regions. Meanwhile, temporal attention is used to assign weights to different salient regions in each frame of the video trajectory. For sequence matching, attention is usually used to solve problems of intra-sequence corruption or misalignment between sequences. Attention pooling network is adopted to align sequences considering the interaction between sequence pairs in [30]. Both inter-sequence and intra-sequence attention are considered. Specifically, they handle feature-pair alignment by inter-sequence attention, which in turn performs feature refinement within a sequence in [31]. In view of the existing methods of single attentional mechanism (such as head, shoulders, legs, etc.), Chen [32] notes that this module scheme can't use multi-scale space clues, and will be spread by many significant parts. A multi-granularity and multi-attention network is proposed in [32], and two multi-attention modules, which can discover multiple differentiated regions of video frames automatically, extract multi-granularity information with multi-scale features.

3 Video-Based Person Re-identification with Non-local Attention Module

The overall framework flow chart with non-local attention module (NLAM) proposed in this paper is shown in Fig. 1. Firstly, uniform sampling and random erasure are performed on the input pedestrian videos, and the newly combined videos are fed into the 3D-RESNet50 network model, which added NLAM, and feature extraction is performed. When NLAM extracts features from feature locations, the network can pay attention to the spatial and temporal information connection of video clips, extract video-level features, and embed video features into multiple feature-level representations. Then, the global time feature pooling layer is used to further refine the temporal feature based on the extracted spatio-temporal features. Finally, cross entropy loss of label smoothing regularization is used for recognize pedestrians.

3.1 Non-local Mean Module (NLMM)

Non-local mean algorithm [33] is used to evaluate and compare the performance in image denoising. Given a discrete noisey image, the pixel is estimated as the weighted average of all pixels in the image, as shown in Formula 1:

$$y_i = \frac{1}{C(\mathbf{x})} \sum_{\forall j} f(\mathbf{x}_i, \mathbf{x}_j) g(\mathbf{x}_j) \tag{1}$$

where x is the input, $C(\mathbf{x})$ is the normalized function, and i is one of the positions of the output feature graph. Generally, this position can be space, time or spatio-temporal

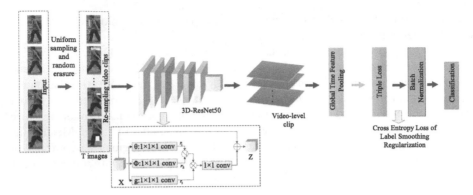

Fig. 1. Flowchart of overall framework.

mixture. f depends on the correlation between i and j. g computes the input signal representation of j position. Since j traverses all positions of the input, i.e., signals at all positions participate in a weighted sum, it is a non-local operation.

In contrast, the recurrent neural network generally calculates the signal of the previous position in current position and time dimension, while the convolutional neural network is the signal of the region covered by the convolution kernel. Non-local operations are also different from full joins, because the latter uses directly learned weights rather than those based on relationships between pair-wise information. In addition, different from non-local operations, full joins require fixed-size inputs and lose position correspondence (e.g., information between x_i and x_j at position i). Non-local operations can combine convolution neural networks and recurrent neural networks directly. When it is added in prior layers of deep networks (all full-connection layers are added in last layers), we can extract non-local and local information simultaneously, and a richer model hierarchy can be built.

3.2 Self-attention Module (SAM)

As a partial feature learning module, attention module can be used to enhance the discrimination ability of features of deep layers, and divided into three steps [34]:

1. Calculate the similarity f between the comparison query and the key-value pair, as shown in Formula (2):

$$f(Q, K_i), i = 1, 2, ..., m \tag{2}$$

where, Q is the query vector, K is the key-value pair.

2. Normalize the similarity f with Softmax, as shown in Formula (3):

$$\alpha_i = \frac{e^{f(Q,K_i)}}{\sum_{j=1}^{m} e^{f(Q,K_i)}}, i = 1, 2, ..., m \tag{3}$$

where, α_i is the normalization weight.

3. Calculate the attention vector, which equals the weighted sums of all the values in the key-value pairs

$$\sum_{i=1}^{m} \alpha_i K_i \qquad (4)$$

By paying attention to all positions and embedding them into the space, the self-attention module calculates the weighted value to get the response of a certain position. The selection of the similarity function f is a big deal for the performance of the model. Commonly used similarity functions include: Gaussian function, embedded Gaussian function, dot production, and so on. In this paper, we use embedded Gaussian function as follow:

$$f(x_i, x_j) = e^{\theta(x_i)^T \phi(x_j)} \qquad (5)$$

where, $\theta(x_i) = W_\theta x_i$ and $\phi(x_j) = W_\phi x_j$ are two embeddings, which are used to map the original space to the linear vector space. The normalization factor is $\sum_{\forall j} f(x_i, x_j)$.

The embedded Gaussian function is used to calculate the similarity to realize the attention operation of non-local operation. The self-attention model and non-local operation are combined to improve the model performance of the network, and the segmental self-attention network is applied to video pedestrian re-recognition.

3.3 Non-local Attention Module (NLAM)

In this section, the non-local operations in Formula (1) are embedded into NLAM. Then, NLAM is added to 3D-RESNet50 and defined as that in Formula (6):

$$z_i = W_z \frac{1}{\sum_{\forall j} e^{\theta(x_i)^T \phi(x_j)}} \sum_{\forall j} e^{\theta(x_i)^T \phi(x_j)} g(x_j) + x_i \qquad (6)$$

where W_z is a weight and "$+x_i$" is a residual connection. The advantage of the latter is that the new non-local attention modules can be arbitrarily embedded into the pre-trained network model without any destruction of its original representation.

Firstly, with three embedded weights W_θ, W_ϕ, W_g in embedded Gaussian function, input X, sized $T \times H \times W \times 1024$ (where T, H, W are the channel, the height and the width of the image, respectively), can be reduced to three outputs (sized $T \times H \times W \times 512$) defined as r_1, r_2 and r_3. The details of NLAM is shown in Fig. 2. Where "$\otimes$" denotes matrix multiplication, and "$\oplus$" denotes element-wise sum. The softmax operation is performed on each row. The boxes denoted as θ, ϕ, g are $1 \times 1 \times 1$ convolutions. Here, we show the embedded Gaussian version, with a bottleneck of 512 channels.

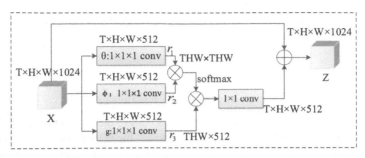

Fig. 2. Structure of non-local attention module.

4 Experiments and Results

In this paper, a large number of experiments are conducted on two public datasets, MARS [9] and DukeMTMC-VideoREID [22], to verify the effectiveness of our model. The statistics information of two datasets are shown in Table 1.

Table 1. The statistics of video-based person ReID datasets.

Dataset	#ID (human)	#Seq	#Train (human)	#Test (human)	#Cam	#Label
Mars	1261	20478	625	636	6	DPM
DukeMTMC-VideoREID	1812	4832	702	702	8	/

4.1 Datasets

Mars [9] is the largest video pedestrian re-recognition data set so far. The Mars dataset consists of 1,261 pedestrians with different identities, each of whom appears in at least two cameras. The video segments of Mars are generated by DPM detectors and GMMCP trackers automatically, which make Mars more realistic and certainly more challenging than previous video datasets. Mars contains 625 identities for training, 636 identities for testing.

DukeMTMC [22] is a large data set for multi-camera tracking. The data set is captured in outdoor scenes with noisy background, illumination change, pedestrian posture and perspective changes, and occlusion. To improve the experimental effect, a subset of DukeMTMC for video-based Re-ID, DukemTMC-VideoreID, is used in this paper. Because of manually annotation in this dataset, each identity has only one video clip in each camera. DukemTMC-VideoreID contains 2,196 training videos and 2,636 testing ones, where, 702 identities for training, 702 identities for testing, and 408 identities for interference.

In this paper, three common indicators for pedestrian Re-ID, rank-K, mAP and mINP, are used to evaluate the performance of models. Rank-k represents the probability of correct matching in the top-K lists, which reflects the retrieval accuracy; Mean value of Average Precision (mAP) reflects recall rate; MINP is a new model evaluation standard [35], which mainly aimed at measuring pedestrian Re-ID algorithm, include evaluating the ability to retrieve or identify the most difficult correct matches.

4.2 Experimental Parameter Settings

In this paper, 3D-RESNet50 is adopted as the backbone network of feature extraction. The output of the first and second full connection layers are 1024 and N dimensions, respectively, where N represents the number of categories in the training set. For the video datasets used in this paper, Mars and DukeMTMC-VideoREID, N is set to 625 and 702, respectively. In this paper, a first-order optimization algorithm that can replace the traditional stochastic gradient descent process is used in training stage: adaptive moment estimator [36] optimizer, which can update the neural network weights iteratively based on the training data. Set the batch size to 32, and resize the input image to 256128 × 1. During the training of 3D-RESNet50, each batch contained 32 video clips and 480 images. The learning rate is initially set at 0.01 and reduced by 10 times every 20 epochs until the learning rate reached 0.0001. For uniform sampling and random erasure training, $T = 15$ frames are extracted from each video clip as the input of each training cycle. In the testing stage, each input image finally extracted features of 2048 dimensions and the similarity between images is measured by Euclidean distance.

Our experiments are based on Ubuntu 16.04, Cuda10 and Cudnn7.6 environments and Python 3.7, Pytorch 1.3.1 and TorchVision 0.4.2 deep learning frameworks. The hardware configuration is 4 GTX 2080Ti GPUs (11 GB).

4.3 Experimental Evaluation

Experiments with Non-local Attention Module (NLAM). The baseline method used in this paper is that in [37]. Experimental results on baseline method, embedding NLAM into baseline method (Baseline + NLAM) are shown in Tables 2 and 3, respectively. With the addition of NLAM, Baseline + NLAM method improves Rank-1 from 93.6% to 95.0%, improves mAP from 86.1% to 87.7%, and improves mINP from 89.1% to 91.2% on DukeMTMC-VideoReID dataset. And on Mars dataset, our method improves Rank-1 from 86.1% to 87.7%, improves mAP from 80.5% to 82.6%, and improves mINP from 59.8% to 62.8%. This indicates that with the addition of NLAM, the network can associate the long-distance information between video frames and establish the connection between pixels at a certain distance between video frames.

Comparative Experiments with Our and Other Methods. In addition to the above comparative experiments, our method proposed in this paper is also compared with some advanced methods, including ETAP-Net (supervised) [35], STAN [31], ADFD-TA [37], STMP [39], 3DCNN + NLA [21], KHAN [40], STA [41], GLTR [42] and VRSTC [43]. As shown in Table 4, Rank-1 and mAP of our method exceeds or competitives with all other methods on two datasets, except Rank-1 compared with VRSTC. It is proved that, our method, which effectively uses local and global time and space information to distinguish similar pedestrians and further improves the accuracy of pedestrian

Table 2. Comparison of NLAM on DukeMTMC-VideoREID.

Methods	Rank-1 (%)	Rank-5 (%)	Rank-10 (%)	Rank-20 (%)	mAP (%)	mINP (%)
Baseline	93.6	98.9	99.6	99.7	92.8	89.1
Baseline + NLAM	**95.0**	**99.0**	**99.7**	**99.9**	**94.9**	**91.2**

Table 3. Comparison of NLAM on Mars.

Methods	Rank-1 (%)	Rank-5 (%)	Rank-10 (%)	Rank-20 (%)	mAP (%)	mINP (%)
Baseline	86.1	85.1	97.1	98.0	80.5	59.8
Baseline + NLAM	**87.7**	**95.8**	**97.2**	**97.9**	**82.6**	**62.8**

identification in network, is superior to the current advanced methods in comprehensive performance.

Table 4. Comparison of some methods on mars and DukeMTMC-VideoREID.

Methods	Mars		DukeMTMC-VreID	
	Rank-1 (%)	mAP (%)	Rank-1 (%)	mAP (%)
ETAP-Net (CVPR18) [35]	80.8	67.4	83.6	78.3
STAN (CVPR18) [31]	82.3	65.8	–	–
ADFD-TA (CVPR19) [37]	82.6	71.2	–	–
STMP (AAAI19) [39]	84.4	72.7	–	–
3DCNN + NLA (ACCV19) [21]	84.3	77.0	–	–
KHAN (CVPR19) [40]	85.7	77.8	–	–
STA (AAAI19) [41]	86.3	80.8	94.2	**94.9**
GLTR (ICCV19) [42]	87	78.6	94.3	93.7
VRSTC (CVPR19) [43]	**88.5**	82.3	**95.0**	93.5
NLAM (ours)	87.7	**82.6**	**95.0**	**94.9**

5 Summary

In this paper, a new model for video pedestrian Re-ID is proposed with NLAM. In our model, NLAM is added in 3D-RESNet50 network to make full use of global and local spatio-temporal information. Many evaluation experiments are conducted on large video datasets, Mars and DukeMTMC-VideoREID, and experimental results show that the proposed method can effectively extract global and local information. The accuracy and efficiency of our method are superior to many other method.

References

1. Jiang, T.: A review of person re-identification. J. New Media **2**(2), 45–60 (2020)
2. Dai, Y., Luo, Z.: Review of unsupervised person re-identification. J. New Media **3**(4), 129–136 (2021)
3. Zhang, D., Ge, Y., Dong, Z., et al.: Deep high-resolution representation learning for cross-resolution person re-identification. IEEE Trans. Image Process. **30**, 8913–8925 (2021)
4. Zeng, M., Tian, C., Wu, Z.: Person re-identification with hierarchical deep learning feature and efficient XQDAmetric. In: Proceedings of the 26th ACM International Conference on Multimedia, pp. 1838–1846. ACM, New York (2018)
5. Luo, Z.: Review of GAN-based person re-identification. J. New Media **3**(1), 11–17 (2021)
6. Leng, Q., Ye, M., Tian, Q.: A survey of open-world person re-identification. IEEE Trans. Circuits Syst. Video Technol. **30**(4), 1092–1108 (2019)
7. Zhang, Y., Wang, H., Zhang, J., et al.: One-shot video-based person re-identification based on neighborhood center iteration strategy. J. Softw. (2021). https://doi.org/10.13328/j.cnki.jos.006108
8. Ojala, T., Pietikainen, M., Maenpaa, T.: Multiresolution gray-scale and rotation invariant texture classification with local binary patterns. IEEE Trans. Pattern Anal. Mach. Intell. **24**(7), 971–987 (2002)
9. Zheng, L., et al.: Mars: a video benchmark for large-scale person re-identification. In: Leibe, B., Matas, J., Sebe, N., Welling, M. (eds.) ECCV 2016. LNCS, vol. 9910, pp. 868–884. Springer, Cham (2016). https://doi.org/10.1007/978-3-319-46466-4_52
10. Lowe, D.: Distinctive image features from scale-invariant keypoints. Int. J. Comput. Vis. **60**(2), 91–110 (2004)
11. Dalal, N., Triggs, B.: Histograms of oriented gradients for human detection. In: 2005 IEEE Computer Society Conference on Computer Vision and Pattern Recognition, pp. 886–893. IEEE, Los Alamitos (2005)
12. Karanam, S., Li, Y., Radke, R.: Person re-identification with discriminatively trained viewpoint invariant dictionaries. In: Proceedings of the IEEE International Conference on Computer Vision, pp.4516–4524. IEEE, Piscataway (2015)
13. Bay, H., Tuytelaars, T., Van Gool, L.: Surf: speeded up robust features. In: Leonardis, A., Bischof, H., Pinz, A. (eds.) ECCV 2006. LNCS, vol. 3951, pp. 404–417. Springer, Heidelberg (2006). https://doi.org/10.1007/11744023_32
14. Liao, S., Hu, Y., Zhu, X., et al.: Person re-identification by local maximal occurrence representation and metric learning. In: Proceedings of the IEEE Conference on Computer Vision and Pattern Recognition, pp. 2197–2206. IEEE, Piscataway (2015)
15. Wang, T., Gong, S., Zhu, X., Wang, S.: Person re-identification by video ranking. In: Fleet, D., Pajdla, T., Schiele, B., Tuytelaars, T. (eds.) ECCV 2014. LNCS, vol. 8692, pp. 688–703. Springer, Cham (2014). https://doi.org/10.1007/978-3-319-10593-2_45
16. Klaser, A., Marszałek, M., Schmid, C.: A spatio-temporal descriptor based on 3D-gradients. In: BMVC 2008–19th British Machine Vision Conference, pp. 1–10. Springer; British Machine Vision Association, Berlin (2008)
17. You, J., Wu, A., Li, X., et al.: Top-push video-based person re-identification. In: Proceedings of the IEEE Conference on Computer Vision and Pattern Recognition, pp.1345–1353. IEEE, Piscataway (2016)

18. Weinberger, K., Saul, L.: Distance metric learning for large margin nearest neighbor classification. J. Mach. Learn. Res. **10**(2), 1–8 (2009)
19. Zhang, Z., Lan, C., Zeng, W., et al.: Relation-aware global attention for person re-identification. In: Proceedings of the IEEE/CVF Conference on Computer Vision and Pattern Recognition, pp. 3189–3195. IEEE, Piscataway (2020)
20. Lin, Y., Zheng, L., Zheng, Z., et al.: Improving person re-identification by attribute and identity learning. Pattern Recogn. **95**, 151–161 (2019)
21. Liao, X., He, L., Yang, Z., Zhang, C.: Video-based person re-identification via 3D convolutional networks and non-local attention. In: Jawahar, C.V., Li, H., Mori, G., Schindler, K. (eds.) ACCV 2018. LNCS, vol. 11366, pp. 620–634. Springer, Cham (2019). https://doi.org/10.1007/978-3-030-20876-9_39
22. Ristani, E., Solera, F., Zou, R., Cucchiara, R., Tomasi, C.: Performance measures and a data set for multi-target, multi-camera tracking. In: Hua, G., Jégou, H. (eds.) ECCV 2016. LNCS, vol. 9914, pp. 17–35. Springer, Cham (2016). https://doi.org/10.1007/978-3-319-48881-3_2
23. Mnih, V., Heess, N., Graves, A., et al.: Recurrent Models of visual attention. arXiv:1406.6247 (2014)
24. Li, Y., Wang, X.: Person re-identification based on joint loss and multiple attention mechanism. Intell. Autom. Soft Comput. **30**(2), 563–573 (2021)
25. Kim, Y., Denton, C., Hoang, L., et al.: Structured attention networks. arXiv:1702.00887 (2017)
26. Jaderberg, M., Simonyan, K., Zisserman, A., et al.: Spatial transformer networks. arXiv:1506.02025 (2015)
27. Hu, J., Shen, L., Sun, G.: Squeeze-and-excitation networks. In: Proceedings of the IEEE Conference on Computer Vision and Pattern Recognition, pp. 7132–7141. IEEE, Piscataway (2018)
28. Liu, X., Zhao, H., Tian, M., et al.: Hydraplus-net: attentive deep features for pedestrian analysis. In: Proceedings of the IEEE International Conference on Computer Vision, pp. 350–359. IEEE, Piscataway (2017)
29. Li, S., Bak, S., Carr, P., et al.: Diversity regularized spatiotemporal attention for video-based person re-identification. In: Proceeding of the IEEE Conference on Computer Vision and Pattern Recognition, pp. 369–378. CVPR, Salt Lake City (2018)
30. Xu, S., Cheng, Y., Gu, K., et al.: Jointly attentive spatial-temporal pooling networks for video-based person re-identification. In: Proceedings of the IEEE International Conference on Computer Vision, pp. 4733–4742. IEEE, Piscataway (2017)
31. Si, J., Zhang, H., Li, C., et al.: Dual attention matching network for context-aware feature sequence basedperson re-identification. In: Proceedings of the IEEE Conference on Computer Vision and Pattern Recognition, pp. 5363–5372. IEEE, Piscataway (2018)
32. Chen, L., Zhang, H., Xiao, J., et al.:Sca-CNN: spatial and channel-wise attention in convolutional networks for image captioning. In: Proceedings of the IEEE Conference on Computer Vision and Pattern Recognition, pp. 5659–5667. IEEE, Piscataway (2017)
33. Buades, A., Coll, B., Morel, J.: A non-local algorithm for image denoising. In: 2005 IEEE Computer Society Conference on Computer Vision and Pattern Recognition, pp. 60–65. IEEE, Piscataway (2005)
34. Vaswani, A., Shazeer, N., Parmar, N., et al.: Attention is all you need. arXiv:1706.03762 (2017)
35. Wu, Y., Lin, Y., Dong, X., et al.: Exploit the unknown gradually: one-shot video-based person re-identification by stepwise learning. In: Proceedings of the IEEE Conference on Computer Vision and Pattern Recognition, pp. 5177–5186. IEEE, Piscataway (2018)
36. Kingma, D., Ba, J.: Adam: a method for stochastic optimization. Comput. Sci. (2014)
37. Chen, Li., Wang, H., Zhang, Y., et al.: Video-based person re-identification method by jointing evenly sampling erasing-random and global temporal feature pooling. J. Comput. Appl. **41**(01), 164–169 (2021). (in Chinese)

38. Zhao,Y., Shen, X., Jin, Z., et al.: Attribute-driven feature disentangling and temporal aggregation for video person re-identification. In: Proceedings of the IEEE/CVF Conference on Computer vision and pattern recognition, pp. 4913–4922. IEEE, Piscataway (2019)
39. Liu, Y., Yuan, Z., Zhou, W., et al.: Spatial and temporal mutual promotion for video-based person re-identification. In: Proceedings of the AAAI Conference on Artificial Intelligence, Menlo Park, pp. 8786–8793. AAAI, CA (2019)
40. Su, X., Qu, X., Zou, Z., et al.: K-reciprocal harmonious attention network for video-based person re-identification. IEEE Access **7**, 22457–22470 (2019)
41. Fu, Y., Wang, X., Wei, Y., et al.: STA: spatial-temporal attention for large-scale video-based person re-identification. In: Proceedings of the AAAI Conference on Artificial Intelligence,Menlo Park, CA, pp. 8287–8294 (2019)
42. Li, J., Wang, J., Tian, Q., et al.: Global-local temporal representations for video person re-identification. In: Proceedings of the IEEE/CVF International Conference on Computer Vision, pp. 3958–3967. IEEE, Piscataway (2019)
43. Hou, R., Ma, B., Chang, H., et al.: VRSTC: occlusion-free video person re-identification. In: Proceedings of the IEEE/CVF Conference on Computer Vision and Pattern Recognition, pp. 7183–7192. IEEE, Piscataway (2019)

Long-Tailed Classification Based on Dual Branch Learning Network

Xinyi Qiu[✉], Jun Li, Yifei Wei, and Mei Song

School of Electronic Engineering, Beijing University of Posts
and Telecommunications, Beijing 100876, China
qiuxy@bupt.edu.cn

Abstract. The phenomenon of long-tailed data distribution widely exists in every corner of life. And in fact, the fundamental solution to long-tailed distribution problem is actually the combination of imbalanced classification and few-shot learning. At present, the mainstream methods under the framework of deep learning are re-sampling, re-weighting and other strategies like transfer learning. This paper proves that when dealing with long-tailed data, the conventional deep learning methods turn to show a low accuracy of few-shot samples and many-shot samples. Therefore, this paper proposes a long-tailed recognition model based on Dual Branch Learning Network (DBLN). While the imbalanced learning branch is using class-balanced loss function to modify model preference for head data, DBLN leads in a data augmentation learning branch based on improved rebalanced Mixup algorithm. These two branches update the weights by sharing dynamic parameters. DBLN model shows an excellent performance in improving the tendency of the deep learning algorithm to prefer the head classes and the recognition ability of the tail data. The experiments on two benchmark datasets (imbalanced CIFAR-10/100 dataset and rail fastener dataset which contains 5,000 rail pictures about 4 types of fasteners) show that the proposed improved dual branch long-tailed recognition model is superior to other advanced methods.

Keywords: Long-tailed recognition · Imbalanced learning · Anomaly detection

1 Introduction

There is a large gap between the ideal image environment and the application scene in the real world. The image datasets in visual research are generally balanced, that is, the number of instances in each category in the training set is roughly the same. Although, the large-scale visual datasets in practical application are usually unbalanced. A few categories contain magnanimous samples, while the great majority classes have only a small number of samples. The number of samples in each category follows the long-tailed distribution. The concept of long tail [1] was first proposed by Chris Anderson in October 2004 to describe the business and economic models of websites such as Amazon and Netflix.

The phenomenon of long-tailed distribution widely exists in various industries. A few classes occupy most of the data, which are called head classes. However, sometimes

X. Sun et al. (Eds.): ICAIS 2022, CCIS 1586, pp. 448–457, 2022.
https://doi.org/10.1007/978-3-031-06767-9_37

the tail data is more valuable to users [2]. For instance, abnormal network traffic will cause greater harm to users' privacy and security, and violations with low occurrence rate may cause economic and security harm to production and manufacturing.

In real life, rail fasteners dataset is proved to follow the long-tailed distribution as in Fig. 1. Although the frequency of abnormal rail fasteners is low, the cost of fastener breakdown is high. So the application scenario of this paper is based on the detection of rail fastener conditions. As a high-precision feature extraction method, deep learning can continuously learn when it occurs to a large number of rail data [3]. Compared with other machine learning methods, deep learning can accurately identify some fastener abnormalities, such as fastener looseness and fastener covered by foreign objects.

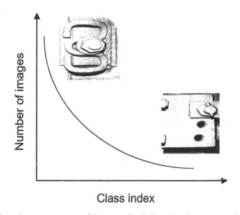

Fig. 1. The phenomenon of long-tailed distributions on rail fasteners.

As an important means of intelligent innovation industry, deep learning has achieved remarkable performance in various industries [4, 5]. When traditional machine learning cannot solve the long-tailed problem perfectly and efficiently, deep learning appears in the field of vision of researchers. Actually, the learning of long-tailed datasets is a combination of imbalanced classification problem and few-shot learning problem. To solve the long-tailed classification problem, there are many studies to improve the recognition accuracy of tail data. At present, there are three mainstream methods under the framework of deep learning: re-sampling, re-weighting and transfer learning.

Re-sampling methods are mainly different from the traditional learning strategies that each picture has the same probability to be selected. The sampling frequency of different classes in dataset is inversely weighted according to the number of samples. The most used strategy in recent research is class-balanced sampling, and SMOTE [6] is a classic algorithm in the early stage. SMOTE is similar to the Mixup strategy studied in this paper, which is to make data difference in input space. Recent research on decoupled feature learning and classifier learning is also based on re-sampling strategy, which can bring better long-tailed learning results [7]. Imbalanced learning of decoupling representation and classifier is divided into two stages: normal sampling in feature extraction stage and balanced sampling in classifier learning stage.

Re-weighting strategies focus on assigning different weights to different classes (or even different samples) to solve the problem of long-tailed distribution, which is mainly reflected in re-weighting the loss function according to different categories. At present, there are many variants of such methods, and the simplest is to treat the reciprocal of the number of samples as the weight value to loss function [8]. In 2019, Cui [9] quantified the number of effective samples by considering data overlap, weighted according to the number of "effective" samples. In 2019, Cao [10] first used innovative LDAM loss function training net-work through a two-step training method, and then combined with the traditional re-sampling weights to optimize the tail class. In addition, equalization loss [11] was proposed to deal with such problem between positive samples in object detection task.

The basic idea of the long-tailed classification methods based on transfer learning is to model the most class samples and few class samples respectively, and transfer the learned information or representation or knowledge of the most class samples to few classes. In 2019, Liu [12] proposed that, by combining the dynamic meta vector of memory feature and direct visual feature, the tail class can use the relevant head information through similarity, so as to improve the recognition ability of the model to the tail class. Some researchers believe that this method attends to the trivialities and neglect the essentials, and the road of follow-up research methods will be narrower and more difficult. This is also the reason why the very simple and uncomplicated decoupling method mentioned above is proposed. Recently, transfer learning is not favored by mainstream re-searchers due to the overly complex network model [13, 14].

This work brings the following contributions. Aiming at the characteristics and difficulties of long-tailed distributed image recognition, a Dual Branch Learning Network is proposed in this paper. The algorithm introduces a data augmentation learning branch based on Mixup strategy on the basis of imbalanced learning branch with class-balanced loss function. The new data of minibatch is obtained by linear interpolation of the input image and interpolation inclined to tail classes of samples' one-hot label, as to optimize the feature learning and classification boundary. On the other hand, imbalanced learning branch improves the preference of the network for the head class by re-weighted loss function. And the data augmentation learning branch improves the Mixup algorithm to make it more inclined to identify the tail data. The DBLN is verified on the open dataset CIFAR-10/100 [15] and the rail fastener dataset, and better experimental results are obtained.

2   Overall Framework

2.1   Long-Tail Recognition Model

This paper proposes a long-tailed recognition residual neural network model based on dual branch learning. The DBLN structure is shown in Fig. 2 as follows.

DBLN mainly includes two parts: imbalanced learning branch and data augmentation learning branch. Each branch is divided into three stages: data input, feature extraction and problem formulation. DBLN uses ResNet18 as the backbone of feature extraction stage. The final total loss is calculated by the hyperparameter α as Eq. (1) shows, and the

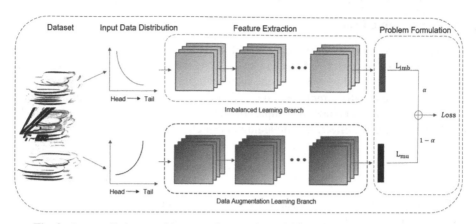

Fig. 2. Long-tailed recognition neural network model based on dual branch learning.

two branches share the weights in the feature extraction stage. The network parameters are learned by back propagation according to the total loss.

In DBLN, the imbalanced learning branch uses the re-weighting technology to influence the preference of the network for the head class and divide a reasonable decision boundary for different categories. When the number of class samples is large, the classification interval of model learning is smaller. In this paper, the reciprocal of the number of effective samples proposed by Cui is used as the re-weighing loss function of the class balance term, the theory quantifies the number of effective samples by considering data overlap. Focal loss [16] is used as the general classification loss function to cope with long-tailed problem.

Data augmentation learning branch introduces a regularizer into the network by improved Mixup algorithm. Different from the data linear interpolation of Mixup algorithm, the improved Mixup algorithm proposed shifts the data interpolation to the direction of few-shot class in the data input stage, and assigns a larger share of few-shot labels to the mixed samples.

Because the improved Mixup algorithm can change the recognition ability of neural network to few shot classes from the perspective of data distribution, it can treat the rail fastener state classification in this paper more pertinently. The class balanced focal loss function only affects the branch in the final loss calculation process. And the focal loss is not that fit to the dataset in this paper because of its long-tailed level is not that extreme. Therefore, when the two branches are weighted and added, the weights is distributed as shown in the Eq. (2). With the increase of training epoch, the weights assign to the data augmentation branch increases linearly. The dynamic weighting process of two-branch Loss value of DBLN is shown in Eq. (1), and L_{mu} represent the loss brought by imbalanced learning branch and the data augmentation branch based on Mixup method, respectively. The parameter α changes with the training epochs. T/T_{max} represents the proportion of the current epoch in the whole training process.

$$Loss = \alpha L_{imb} + (1 - \alpha)L_{mu} \qquad (1)$$

$$\alpha = 1 - T/T_{max} \qquad (2)$$

2.2 Re-weighting Branch

In this paper, the imbalanced learning branch uses re-weighting strategy to revise the preference of the network for the head class. The concept of effective sample number proposed by Cui is used to re-weight the data representation. The number of effective samples is defined as the sample volume, which can be calculated by a simple formula Eq. (3). Where n_i is the number of samples belong to class i, super parameter $\beta \in [0, 1)$. And E_{n_i} represents the effective sample number of class i.

$$E_{n_i} = \frac{1 - \beta_i^{n_i}}{1 - \beta_i} \qquad (3)$$

Equation (4) shows class-balanced loss function calculated by the algorithm proposed by Cui. In order to simplify the process, the β_i in Eq. (3) is considered as $\beta_i = (N_i - 1)/N_i = (N - 1)/N = \beta$. N means the expected total volume for all data image.

$$CB(p, y) = \frac{1}{E_n} L(p, y) = \frac{1 - \beta}{1 - \beta^{n_y}} L(p, y) \qquad (4)$$

In this paper, Focal loss is selected as the general classification loss function $L(p, y)$. Then the number of effective samples became the category weight parameter widely used in Focal loss. Therefore, the re-weighted loss function used in the imbalanced learning branch is as Eq. (5). C is the total number of all categories, and γ is the parameter to describe whether the sample can be classify easily.

$$L_{imb}(p, y) = -\frac{1 - \beta}{1 - \beta^{n_y}} \sum_{i=1}^{C} \left(1 - p_i^t\right)^{\gamma} \log\left(p_i^t\right) \qquad (5)$$

2.3 Data Augmentation Learning Branch

Mixup method is an algorithm for class mixing augmentation of images used in computer vision. It can mix images between different classes, so as to expand the training dataset. The Mixup algorithm is orthogonal to any network architecture used for classification. Therefore, the Mixup method can be used for the corresponding dataset in any network where the classification task is to be performed.

The improved Mixup strategy define the quantity ratio μ of the selected class i and class j as in Eq. (6), which symbolizes the degree of imbalance between two classes. n as the number of one specific class. And parameter λ obeys beta distribution as $\lambda \sim Beta(\alpha, \alpha)$.

$$\mu = \begin{cases} n_i/n_j & n_i > n_j \\ n_j/n_i & otherwise \end{cases} \qquad (6)$$

The algorithm proposed divides the samples into countless batches, of which x_i is one batch of samples and y_i is the label corresponding to the sample x_i. And (x_j, y_j) is another pair of samples. As in Eq. (7), the so-called new sample x^{im} and its corresponding label y^{im} are obtained by mixing (x_i, y_i) and (x_j, y_j).

$$\begin{cases} x^{im} = \lambda x_i + (1 - \lambda)x_j \\ y^{im} = \lambda_y y_i + (1 - \lambda_y)y_j \end{cases} \tag{7}$$

When μ reaches a certain value, data augmentation branch will interfere the label of the mixed sample, force it to shift to the minority, and then change the decision plane to improve the minority detection accuracy. In the data input stage, the class interpolation is shifted to the direction of few-shot samples. Based on the rebalanced Mixup method, the extent of deviation to few-shot is reasonable by shifting λ_y as Eq. (8). In this paper, the super parameter k is set to 4.

$$\lambda_y = \begin{cases} \lambda^2 & \mu > k \\ \lambda & otherwise \end{cases} \tag{8}$$

3 Experiment

3.1 Datasets

This paper compares DBLN model with the most advanced methods to combat the class imbalance on the following datasets: (1) manually created imbalanced CIFAR-10/100 datasets, (2) real railway track images.

(1) CIFAR-10 is a computer vision dataset for pervasive object recognition collected by Hinton's students Alex krizhevsky and Ilya sutskever. It contains 60,000 RGB color pictures sized by 32 * 32, with a total of 10 various classes. It includes 50,000 pictures for training set and 10,000 images for test set.

CIFAR-100 has 100 classes, which are subdivided into 20 super classes and 5 subclasses corresponding to each major class. The categories are completely mutually exclusive and there is no overlap between different categories. The number of training samples and test samples is the same as that of CIFAR-10.

In this experiment, the datasets are artificially manufactured into imbalanced datasets with a long-tailed degree of 100, that is, the proportion of the number of samples between the first class of the head and the last class of the tail is 100. Taking CIFAR-10 as an example, the number of sample categories follows the form of exponential decline as shown in Fig. 3.

(2) The PNG format image with the size of 16 bit 250 * 250 of railway track picture stores the depth map information of rail, so the picture information is not affected by external factors such as lighting. As shown in Fig. 4 below, it is divided into four categories: normal fastener (Fig. 4a), inclined fastener (Fig. 4b) and blocked fastener (Fig. 4c). 4,800 fastener images are selected as training set, including 3500 images of normal fasteners, 1250 images of blocked fasteners, 100 images of missing fasteners and 50 images of inclined fasteners. Another 2,000 fastener images are selected as the test set, 500 in each of the four categories.

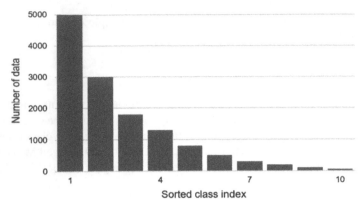

Fig. 3. Data distribution in the imbalanced CIFAR-10.

Fig. 4. Samples of different rail fastener states.

3.2 Baseline Methods

On CIFAR-10/100 dataset, the proposed algorithm is compared with seven methods, and ResNet-18 is used as the baseline. The core idea of Mixup is to virtually create mixed samples to train the neural model through the combination of feature and label pairs. Remix [17] puts forward the concept of mixing factor in linear interpolation based on Mixup. The manifold Mixup algorithm is influenced by Mixup, which is different from the plug and play idea of other algorithms. Manifold Mixup [18] extends the mixing of input data to the mixing of output of intermediate hidden layer. BBN [19] simply achieves a very high accuracy by sharing parameters with two branches. One branch uses the original data, the other branch uses the re-sampling algorithm for training.

For the railway dataset, Shot Multi-Box Detector (SSD) combined Supported Vector Machine (SVM) [20] is used as the baseline. SSD, as a one stage detector, adopts a target detection algorithm based on regression. The core idea of this algorithm is to train the network model through the relationship between the anchor, the ground bounding boxes and the prediction bounding boxes, and then classify it with SVM. The basic idea of Histogram of Oriented Gradient (HOG) with SVM [21] is that for an image, the appearance or shape of the local position can be described by the distribution of local gradient or edge direction, so as to locate and classify. This paper also tested the Mixup algorithm mentioned above on rail fastener images.

3.3   Implementation Details

This paper uses Ubuntu16 system, runs in python 3.8 environment. This paper runs 800 epochs in network training, and the network parameters in final epoch are used in test and subsequent application. The GPU is NVIDIA GTX1080Ti and the deep learning network acceleration library is CUDA 10.2.

3.4   Results on Imbalanced CIFAR

Table 1 shows the Top-1 accuracy results of different algorithms on the long-tailed CIFAR-10/100 dataset, where † denotes the results from the original paper. These comparison algorithms include many current mainstream methods to improve the ability of long-tailed recognition, including data re-sampling methods, a variety of cost sensitive learning methods to improve the loss function, and head-to-tail knowledge transfer methods.

Table 1 indicates that the model proposed in this paper has an absolute advantage over other algorithms, which shows that the hierarchical learning idea of rough classification and then detailed classification is effective in the long-tailed recognition task. Compared with the LDAM method using only imbalanced learning branch, the introduction of small sample learning branch can bring obvious performance improvement. Manifold Mixup and the BBN method which separates feature learning from classifier learning show close results to the model in this paper, while the simple ResNet-18 has the worst results. Table 1 shows that the model in this paper obtains the suboptimal solution and the BBN obtains the optimal solution on the CIFAR-100-LT dataset.

Table 1. Top-1 accuracy on imbalanced CIFAR-10/100 using ResNet-18.

	CIFAR-10	CIFAR-100
Baseline	68.01	33.51
Mixup	70.43	39.83
Manifold mixup	74.09	42.48
Remix†	75.36	41.94
Remix	73.14	40.38
LDAM	73.35	39.60
BBN	76.03	43.21
DBLN	**77.79**	42.79

3.5   Results on Rail Fastener Dataset

When the model proposed in this paper is applied to the comparison between the rail fastener dataset and baseline, as shown in Table 2, in two different verification criteria, the model proposed by us has a higher accuracy in the other three categories except Hidden category. Among the Hidden classes, SSD + SVM performs the best, with an advantage of about 3% over DBLN scheme. The reason is that there is little difference in the actual appearance between hidden and normal fasteners, and the main difference is whether there are shelters, such as cables, screws, etc. Therefore, in DBLN model, some samples are labeled hidden but are classified as Normal.

Table 2. Top-1 accuracy of different type of fasteners on rail dataset.

	Normal	Hidden	Slop
SSD + SVM	96.2	**73.8**	51.3
HOG + SVM	89.6	57.1	43.9
Mixup	92.2	60.7	53.4
DBLN	**98.3**	70.5	**56.6**

4 Conclusion

Firstly, this paper demonstrates the universality of the proposed long-tailed classification model DBLN and its advantages over other algorithms on the public dataset CIFAR-10/100-LT. Then the model is applied to the real railway track picture with larger data size, which is better than the current railway anomaly recognition methods in terms of recognition time and recognition accuracy. DBLN shows great performance except hidden samples. The results of DBLN proposed in this paper for the specific long-tail problemed prove that the re-sampling strategy and data augmentation methods adopted by the two channels are effective solutions to the long-tailed datasets.

Acknowledgement. This work was supported by the National Natural Science Foundation of China (61871046).

References

1. Jamal, M.A., Brown, M.: Rethinking class-balanced methods for long-tailed visual recognition from a domain adaptation perspective. In: Conference on Computer Vision and Pattern Recognition, pp. 7607–7616. IEEE (2020)
2. Thai, N.H., Nghia, N.T.: Long-tail effect on ECG classification. In: 2017 International Conference on System Science and Engineering, pp. 34–38. IEEE (2017)
3. Zhao, X.X.: Railway fastener detection based on convolution neural network, China (2016)
4. Qu, Z., Sun, H., Zheng, M.: An efficient quantum image steganography protocol based on improved EMD algorithm. Quant. Inf. Process. **20**(2), 1–29 (2021). https://doi.org/10.1007/s11128-021-02991-8

5. Wei, Y., Yu, F.R., Song, M., Han, Z.: Joint optimization of caching, computing, and radio resources for fog-enabled iot using natural actor-critic deep reinforcement learning. IEEE Internet Things J. **6**(2), 2061–2073 (2019)

6. Nitesh, V., Chawla, K.W.: Bowyer: SMOTE: synthetic minority oversampling technique. J. Artif. Intell. Res. **16**, 321–357 (2002)

7. Sun, W., Mu, S.: Long-tailed recognition of peach leaf diseases images based on decoupling representation and classifier. In: 4th International Conference on Big Data and Artificial Intelligence, pp. 209–213. IEEE (2021)

8. Huang, C., Li, Y.: Deep imbalanced learning for face recognition and attribute prediction. Pattern Anal. Mach. Intell. **42**(11), 2781–2794 (2020)

9. Cui, Y., Jia, M.: Class-balanced loss based on effective number of samples. In: 2019 Conference on Computer Vision and Pattern Recognition, pp. 9260–9269. IEEE (2019)

10. Kang, H., Vu, T.: Learning imbalanced datasets with maximum margin loss. In: IEEE International Conference on Image Processing, pp. 1269–1273. IEEE (2021)

11. Tan, J.: Equalization loss for long-tailed object recognition. In: Conference on Computer Vision and Pattern Recognition, pp. 11659–11668. IEEE, Seattle (2020)

12. Hu, X., Jiang, Y.: Learning to segment the tail. In: Conference on Computer Vision and Pattern Recognition, pp. 14042–14051. IEEE (2020)

13. Liu, J., Sun, Y.: Deep representation learning on long-tailed data: a learnable embedding augmentation perspective. In: Conference on Computer Vision and Pattern Recognition, pp. 2967–2976. IEEE (2020)

14. Liu, Z., Miao, Z.: Large-scale long-tailed recognition in an open world. In: 2019 Conference on Computer Vision and Pattern Recognition, pp. 2532–2541. IEEE (2019)

15. Ayi, M., El-Sharkawy, M.: RMNv2: reduced mobilenet V2 for CIFAR10. In: 10th Annual Computing and Communication Workshop and Conference, pp. 287–0292. IEEE (2020)

16. Doi, K., Iwasaki, A.: The effect of focal loss in semantic segmentation of high resolution aerial image. In: 2018 International Geoscience and Remote Sensing Symposium, pp. 6919–6922. IEEE, Valencia (2018)

17. Mangla, P., Singh, M.: Charting the right manifold: manifold mixup for few-shot learning. In: 2020 Winter Conference on Applications of Computer Vision, pp. 2207–2216. IEEE (2020)

18. Chou, H.-P., Chang, S.-C., Pan, J.-Y., Wei, W., Juan, D.-C.: Remix: rebalanced mixup. In: Bartoli, A., Fusiello, A. (eds.) ECCV 2020. LNCS, vol. 12540, pp. 95–110. Springer, Cham (2020). https://doi.org/10.1007/978-3-030-65414-6_9

19. Zhou, B., Cui, Q.: BBN: bilateral-branch network with cumulative learning for long-tailed visual recognition. In: Proceedings of the IEEE/CVF Conference on Computer Vision and Pattern Recognition, pp. 9716–9725. IEEE (2020)

20. Liu, W., Anguelov, D.: SSD: single shot multibox detector. In: European Conference on Computer Vision, pp. 21–37. AMS (2016)

21. Nguyen, N., Bui, D.: A novel hardware architecture for human detection using HOG-SVM co-optimization. In: 2019 IEEE Asia Pacific Conference on Circuits and Systems, pp. 33–36. IEEE (2019)

Hamming Code Aided Joint Iterative Detection and Decoding Receiver of Polar Coded SCMA System

Yongqiang Zhang[1], Jian Liu[1(✉)], Rui Cao[2], and Lixin Tian[2]

[1] School of Computer and Communication Engineering, University of Science and Technology Beijing, Beijing 100083, China
liujian@ustb.edu.cn
[2] Dawning Information Industry Co., Ltd, Tianjin 300384, China

Abstract. With the continuous development of the 5th generation wireless systems(5G). Sparse Code Multiple Access (SCMA) technology has become more and more important in the enhanced mobile broadband communication (eMBB) scenario due to its lower error rate, higher throughput and stronger high-speed mobile communication capabilities. The polar coded SCMA (PC-SCMA) system that combines the polar coding with the SCMA system will further improve the performance and reduce the bit error rate (BER) of the SCMA system. However, under low signal-to-noise ratio (SNR) conditions, the joint iterative detection and decoding algorithm(JIDD) of PC-SCMA system has the problem of decoding divergence. Under high SNR conditions, fixed number of iterations leads to waste of computing resources and high system delay. To solve this problem, we proposed the hamming code aided joint detection and decoding algorithm (H-JIDD) in which the extended hamming code is added as an early stopping condition to lock the correct codes. Simulation results show that our proposed H-JIDD algorithm improves the performance of PC-SCMA system.

Keywords: Polar code · Sparse code multiple access · Decoding divergence · Extended hamming code

1 Introduction

With the rapid development of mobile Internet services and Internet of things (IoT) business applications, indicators such as the number of user connections, transmission rates, system capacity, and system delays have put forward higher requirements for the 5th generation wireless systems (5G) [1, 2]. Among the communication technologies for 5G, the new non-orthogonal multiple access technology (NOMA) represented by superimposed transmission has obvious advantages in enhancing spectrum efficiency, improving user connection capabilities, and reducing air interface transmission delay, which has received widespread attention [3–6]. The sparse code multiple access (SCMA) technology proposed by Huawei can realize modulation and spread spectrum operations

© The Author(s), under exclusive license to Springer Nature Switzerland AG 2022
X. Sun et al. (Eds.): ICAIS 2022, CCIS 1586, pp. 458–470, 2022.
https://doi.org/10.1007/978-3-031-06767-9_38

at the same time. The transmitted bits are directly mapped into codewords in a multi-dimensional sparse codebook at the transmitter, which can be decoded at the receiver using low-complexity message passing multi-user detection algorithm. This technology has superior performance and has been extensively studied [7–10].

As a widely used and researched channel coding scheme, polar coding is based on the polarization operation of the communication channel, and the channel capacity is differentiated through the capacity chain rule to improve the performance of the channel coding scheme [11]. Reference [12] proposed the convolutional polar code while designing the corresponding decoding algorithm. In the reference [13], through the design of the ring buffer strategy, the code word truncation, repetition and puncturing methods are combined to achieve the mixed rate matching and improved polar code performance. Reference [14] obtained the global bounds of the Bhattacharyya parameters by studying the coding scheme of the polar code and improve the efficiency of coding through the repeated use of the uniquely designed merging operation. Reference [15] realized coupled polar codes by sharing a few information bits between the code blocks of cascaded polar codes. Reference [16] talked about the transformation of the polarization process of polar codes into polynomial order calculation, and proposed a method to reduce the polynomial order of arbitrary multi-element of channel polarization. The combination of polar code and SCMA system can further improve the performance. In the polar coded SCMA(PC-SCMA) system, the design of the decoding and detection algorithm has always been a hot issue that has been concerned by the majority of researchers [17].

The decoding and detection algorithm of the PC-SCMA system can be divided into independent detection and joint detection. In the independent detection, the mainly detection algorithm of SCMA is the message passing algorithm (MPA) [18], and the polar code decoding scheme mainly has soft input hard output (SIHO) algorithm [19] and soft input soft output (SISO) algorithm [20]. In the SIHO algorithm, the idea of the successive cancellation (SC) decoding algorithm is to detect the received codewords one by one and decode them in recursive order. The continuous cancellation list (SCL) decoding algorithm is improved on the basis of SC decoding algorithm [21], after each level of path search, only one path in the SC decoding algorithm is changed to enter the next level of path search instead of retaining as many paths as possible to enter the next level of search, the retaining width of the path is set according to system error code performance, hardware storage capacity, etc. The SISO algorithm mainly includes the belief propagation (BP) algorithm [22] and soft cancellation (SCAN) algorithm. Since the decoding process of the polar code can be represented by a factor graph, the belief propagation idea can be used to transfer the likelihood value between the nodes of the factor graph. The BP algorithm is a belief propagation algorithm based on soft information transfer and soft decision in the factor graph. It calculates the likelihood ratio information of the node based on the information passed over and theoretically it will converge to a certain state after several iterations [23]. The information transmission of the SCAN algorithm adopts a continuous elimination rule similar to the SC decoding algorithm, but the SCAN algorithm does not make a hard decision. The bit information of the upper level is output as the soft information of the next level and the likelihood information is calculated. Reference [19] shows that the joint detection and decoding algorithm combining BP algorithm and MPA algorithm can make full use of the internal information of the PC-SCMA system to improve system performance. Reference [16] designed a joint iterative detection and decoding (JIDD) algorithm combining the SCAN algorithm and MPA algorithm. Unlike the reference [19] that requires the internal iteration of the BP algorithm and the MPA algorithm, the JIDD algorithm only uses the external iterative combined MPA and SCAN can achieve a higher bit error rate (BER) performance, which improves the performance of the PC-SCMA system and reduces the decoding complexity at the receiver. Reference [24] proposed a serial joint iterative detection and decoding scheme (S-JIDD). The S-JIDD algorithm merges the update of intermediate variables into the update of resource nodes during the iteration process. It can effectively optimize the convergence speed and save a lot of storage space in the process.

However, the JIDD algorithm of the PC-SCMA system still has problems. The receiver has decoding divergence in the iterative decoding process at low SNR conditions [25]. At the same time, under the condition of high SNR, the determination of the number of iterations leads to the waste of computing resources and high system delay. In order to overcome this problem and further improve the BER performance, we designed the extended hamming code aided joint decoding and detection (H-JIDD) algorithm. In the joint iteration process, the extended hamming code was added as a condition for early stop. Before the decoding divergence occurs, the decoding iteration process is terminated and the correct codewords are locked. The simulation results show that the H-JIDD algorithm we proposed can effectively improve the BER performance of the PC-SCMA system, while reducing the complexity of the joint detection and decoding algorithm, achieving a good balance between BER and complexity. The rest of the paper is organized as follows. Section 2 introduces the system model, Section 3 presents the hamming code aided joint iterative detection and decoding algorithm, Section 4 introduces the simulation results and discussion, and Section 5 makes the conclusion.

2 System Model

The uplink of PC-SCMA can be represented in Fig. 1. The information bit of K users can be written as $\mathbf{I} = \{i_1, i_2, ..., i_K\}$, and the information bits of each user k can be expressed as $i_k = \{i_{k,1}, i_{k,2}, ..., i_{k,i\_N}\}$, where $1 \leq k \leq K$, i_N represents the length of the information bits. The information bits of each user are firstly polar encoded, which can be expressed as $\mathbf{P} = \{p_1, p_2, ..., p_K\}$, where the information bits of user k after polar encoding can be expressed as $p_k = \{p_{k,1}, p_{k,2}, ..., p_{k,p\_N}\}$, where p_N represents the code length of the polar encoding. Afterwards, the polar coded information $\mathbf{P}$ passes through the interleaver, which can be expressed as $\mathbf{\Lambda} = \{a_1, a_2, ..., a_K\}$. The output $a_k = \{a_{k,1}, a_{k,2}, ..., a_{k,Q}\}$ of the interleaver is mapped to the K-dimensional complex codeword $x_k = \{x_{k,1}, x_{k,2}, ..., x_{k,M}\}$ by the SCMA encoder, where $Q = \log_2 M$. K users share B orthogonal time-frequency resources, where $K > B$, and transmit data to the base station. The load of the PC-SCMA system can be expressed as the ratio K/M, where M is the dimension of the SCMA codeword. The factor matrix containing 6 user

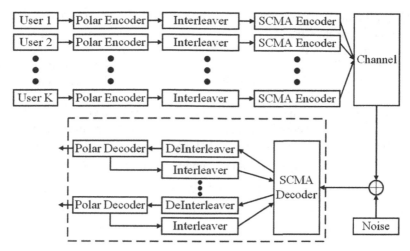

Fig. 1. PC-SCMA system model for H-JIDD receiver.

nodes and 4 resource nodes can be expressed as

$$R = \begin{bmatrix} 0\ 1\ 1\ 0\ 1\ 0 \\ 1\ 0\ 1\ 0\ 0\ 1 \\ 0\ 1\ 0\ 1\ 0\ 1 \\ 1\ 0\ 0\ 1\ 1\ 0 \end{bmatrix} \tag{1}$$

For an uplink SCMA system, the signals transmitted by each user on the sub-carrier frequency domain resources are superimposed on the receiver with signals of other users, other signal sources and noise after channel attenuation, and the l-th received signal can be expressed as

$$y^l = \sum_{k=1}^{K} H_k^l x_k^l + z^l \tag{2}$$

where $H_k^l = diag(h_{1,k}^l, h_{1,k}^l, ..., h_{B,k}^l)$ represents the channel gain matrix of the l-th transmission signal between the base station and the k-th user, where $1 \le l \le L = (p\_N/Q)$ and $y^l = [y_1^l, y_2^l, ..., y_M^l]^T$. $h_{b,k}^l$ represents the channel gain between the frequency domain resource b and the user k. $x_k^l = [x_{k,1}^l, x_{k,2}^l, ..., x_{k,M}^l]^T$ represents the l-th codeword of user k. $z^l = [z_1^l, z_2^l, ..., z_M^l]^T$ represents additive white Gaussian noise that obeys a normal distribution.

The joint detection and decoding algorithm mainly includes three steps: function node update, prior message update, and variable node update. The JIDD algorithm makes the combination of the factor graph of the SCAN algorithm and the factor graph of the MPA algorithm. Firstly, the information of function node is updated according to the signal received. Then the information is passed to the connected variable node. In the priori information updating progress of the factor graph, the external information calculated from the function node of the SCMA detector is passed to the decoder node of polar code, and then the information output by the polar code decoder is passed to the MPA detector as the input external information of MPA to calculate the priori information about the codeword of the variable node. In the process of updating variable nodes, variable nodes update information and pass the updated information to adjacent function nodes.

For the convenience of description, we firstly make the following symbol definition. The information from function node f_j to variable node v_i and the information from v_i to f_j are represented as $I_{f_j \to v_i}(X_l^i)$ and $I_{v_i \to f_j}(X_l^i)$, respectively. Set $p \in \{S_i^v\}$ represents the set of function nodes connected to variable node v_i, and set $p \in \{S_j^f\}$ represents the set of variable nodes connected to function nodes f_j. $p \in \{S_i^v \setminus j\}$ and $p \in \{S_j^f \setminus i\}$ respectively represent the set $p \in \{S_i^v\}$ that excludes the function node f_j and the set $p \in \{S_j^f\}$ that excludes the variable node v_i. The prior probability of the l-th codeword of the i-th user of SCMA is $P(X_l^i)$.

Function node update: when the receiver receives the channel information, the function node of the SCMA user detector updates its information and passes it to the adjacent variable node. The external information corresponding to the symbol can be expressed as

$$
\begin{aligned}
P_e^S(X_l^i) &= \prod_{p \in \{S_i^v\}} I_{f_j \to v_i}(X_l^i) \\
&= \prod_{p \in \{S_i^v\}} \sum_{X_l^p, p \in \{S_j^f \setminus i\}} \{\frac{1}{\pi N_0} \exp(-\frac{1}{N_0} ||y_{l,j} - X_l^i h_{l,j}^i - \sum_{p \in \{S_j^f \setminus i\}} X_l^p h_{l,j}^p ||^2)) \\
&\quad \cdot \prod_{p \in \{S_j^f \setminus i\}} I_{vp \to fj}(X_l^p) \}
\end{aligned}
\tag{3}
$$

where $1 \leq l \leq L$. After calculating the external information corresponding to the symbol, the external bit information of the SCMA detector can be calculated through the mapping relationship, which can be expressed as

$$
P_{e,\text{SCMA}}^B(b_{(l-1)Q+m}^i = bit) = \sum_{X_l^{i,bit} \in \{X_l^i | q_m^i = bit\}} P_e^S(X_l^{i,bit}), \, bit \in \{0, 1\}
\tag{4}
$$

where $1 \leq m \leq Q$. $\{X_l^i | q_m^i = bit\}$, $bit \in \{0, 1\}$ represents a set of SCMA codewords that satisfies the relational expression, which can be expressed as

$$
\{f_i : (q_1^i, ..., q_{m-1}^i, bit, q_{m+1}^i, ..., q_Q^i) \to X_l^i\}, \, bit \in \{0, 1\}
\tag{5}
$$

Then the log-likelihood ratio information output by the SCMA user detector is calculated, and the likelihood ratio information is de-interleaved as the prior information of the polar decoder, which can be expressed as

$$
L_{a,\text{polar}}^B(c^i) = \prod^{-1} L_{e,\text{SCMA}}^B(b^i) = \log \frac{P_{e,\text{SCMA}}^B(b_{(l-1)Q+m}^i = 0)}{P_{e,\text{SCMA}}^B(b_{(l-1)Q+m}^i = 1)}
\tag{6}
$$

The update process of a priori information: when the log-likelihood ratio information of the SCMA user detector output is de-interleaved to obtain the prior information of the decoder, the polar decoder will calculate and output the likelihood ratio information as external information, and this information will continue to be transformed as prior information of the SCMA detector. The calculation method and the order of information transfer in factor graphs can be found in reference [26]. When the left information reaches the left side of the factor graph and the right information reaches the right side of the factor graph, one decoding iteration is completed, and the external information output by the decoder passes through the interleaver again as a priori information of the SCMA detector, and it can be expressed as

$$L_{a,\text{SCMA}}^{B}(c_{(l-1)Q+m}^{i}) = \prod L_{e,\text{polar}}^{B}(c_{(l-1)Q+m}^{i}) \tag{7}$$

Since the soft information output of the polar code is unstable, a damping coefficient is added here [12]. After obtaining the prior log-likelihood ratio information of the SCMA detector, it is converted into probability domain information and remapped to SCMA symbol information, and it can be written as

$$P(X_l^i) = \prod_{m=1}^{Q} P_{a,\text{SCMA}}^{B}(c_{(l-1)Q+m}^{i} = q_m^i)$$

$$= \prod_{m=1}^{Q} \left(\frac{[L_{p,\text{SCMA}}^{B}(o_{(l-1)Q+m}^{i})]^{1-q_m^i}}{1 + L_{p,\text{SCMA}}^{B}(c_{(l-1)Q+m}^{i})} \right), q_m^i \in \{0, 1\} \tag{8}$$

Information update of variable nodes: when the variable node receives the priori information of the symbol, the variable node will update their information and update to the adjacent function node. The information transfer from the variable node to the function node can be expressed as

$$I_{vi \to fj}(X_l^i) = P(X_l^i) \prod_{p \in \{S_i^v \setminus j\}}^{Q} I_{fp \to vi}(X_l^p) \tag{9}$$

Therefore, the information transmission within the MPA user detector is completed. After the function node of the MPA is updated, the internal information of the MPA is transferred to the polar decoder again, and the next iteration is started.

3   Hamming Code Aided Joint Iterative Detection and Decoding Algorithm

3.1   Scheme Description

In each iteration of JIDD receiver, JIDD algorithm exchanges the messages between the SCMA detector and polar decoder. It only requires external iterations rather than internal iterations to complete the system decoding. Compared with the separate decoding scheme, JIDD scheme gets better performance with lower complexity. However, under the conditions of low SNR, the problem of decoding divergence may occur during the iterative decoding process. In each joint iteration, some codewords will be the correct. However, as the number of iterations increases, these parts of codewords will be different from the correct codewords. In this way, even if the iteration reaches the maximum number of iterations, they will eventually converge to the error codewords. Under the condition of high SNR, a fixed number of iterations will lead to a higher system delay and waste computing resources. In order to solve this problem, we designed the extended hamming code aided joint iterative detection and decoding receiver for polar coded SCMA system, which uses the extended hamming code as the condition for early stop in the joint iteration process. The system model of H-JIDD PC-SCMA system is shown in Fig. 2.

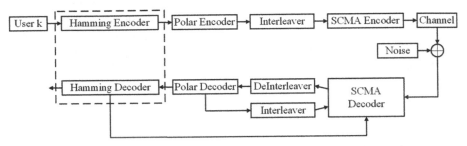

Fig. 2. System model of H-JIDD PC-SCMA system, for a single user k.

Firstly, we encode the information bits with the extended hamming code at the transmitter, and extract the check digits of the extended hamming code. Then the information bits go into the polar encoder, interleaver and SCMA encoder. The check digit of the extended hamming code and the encoded information stream are transmitted as data packets to the receiver through the channel. At the receiver, the information stream is decoded to the original data through the H-JIDD algorithm. After the information bits are decoded in each iteration, the extended hamming code checks the decoded data. If the check passes, the iterative detection of the H-JIDD receiver is terminated early. And if not, the next iteration of the detection is continued. The algorithm of H-JIDD is summarized in Algorithm 1.

Algorithm 1. Hamming code aided joint iterative detection and decoding algorithm.

---

input: *Signal received by each FN*

output: *Information code word for each VN*

Initialize:

$$I_{vi \to fj}(X_l^i) = \frac{1}{M}, i = 1, ..., I, j \in S_i^v, l = 1, ... N / Q;$$

$$R_{n,t}^i = 0, t \in \Lambda; R_{n,t}^i = \infty, t \in \Lambda^c;$$

for $iter = 0:$ $N\_iternum$ do

FN Nodes Update Process ::

  for $l = 1 : n / Q$ do

    for $i = 1 : I$ do

      $(3), (4), (5)$

    end for

  end for

Priori Information Update Process :

  for $l = 1 : I$ do

    $L_0^i = L_{e,SCMA}^B(c^i)$

    $(L_n^i, R_0^i) = SSCAN(L_0^i, R_n^i)$

  end for

  for $l = 1 : n / Q$ do

    for $i = 1 : I$ do

      $$P(X_l^i) = \prod_{m=1}^{Q} P_{a,SCMA}^B(c_{(l-1)Q+m}^i = q_m^i), \quad q_m^i \in \{0,1\}$$

      VN Nodes Update Process: $I_{vi \to fj}(X_l^i) = P(X_l^i) \prod\limits_{p \in \{S_i^v \setminus j\}}^{Q} I_{fp \to vi}(X_l^p)$

    end for

  end for

  if decoded data passes hamming code check

    output decoded data as the result of the algorithm

    break

  else

    continue

end for

3.2 Complexity Analysis

The complexity of H-JIDD of PC-SCMA system is mainly reflected in the iterative calculation process and the number of iterations. According to reference [20], the complexity θ^{JIDD} of the JIDD algorithm can be expressed as

$$\theta^{JIDD} = \theta^{JIDD}_{ADD} + \theta^{JIDD}_{MUL} + \theta^{JIDD}_{MAX} \tag{10}$$

where the adder operations θ^{JIDD}_{ADD}, multiplier operations θ^{JIDD}_{MUL} and maximum operations θ^{JIDD}_{MAX} required by the JIDD algorithm can be expressed as

$$\theta^{JIDD}_{ADD} = B \times It_{JIDD} \times ru \times M^{ru} \times (2ru - 1) + p\_N \times \log(p\_N) \times It_{JIDD} \tag{11}$$

$$\theta^{JIDD}_{MUL} = B \times It_{JIDD} \times ru^2 \times M^{ru} + p\_N \times \log(p\_N) \times It_{JIDD} \tag{12}$$

$$\theta^{JIDD}_{MAX} = B \times It_{JIDD} \times ru \times 2M \tag{13}$$

where ru represents the number of users occupied by each resource node, and It_{JIDD} represents the number of iterations required in the decoding process of the JIDD algorithm. Similarly, we can get the complexity of the H-JIDD algorithm, which can be expressed as

$$\theta^{H-JIDD} = \theta^{H-JIDD}_{ADD} + \theta^{H-JIDD}_{MUL} + \theta^{H-JIDD}_{MAX} \tag{14}$$

where the adder operations θ^{H-JIDD}_{ADD}, multiplier operations θ^{H-JIDD}_{MUL} and maximum operations θ^{H-JIDD}_{MAX} required by the H-JIDD algorithm can be expressed as

$$\theta^{H-JIDD}_{ADD} = B \times It_{H-JIDD} \times ru \times M^{ru} \times (2ru - 1) + p\_N \times \log(p\_N) \times It_{H-JIDD} \tag{15}$$

$$\theta^{H-JIDD}_{MUL} = B \times It_{H-JIDD} \times ru^2 \times M^{ru} + p\_N \times \log(p\_N) \times It_{H-JIDD} \tag{16}$$

$$\theta^{H-JIDD}_{MAX} = B \times It_{H-JIDD} \times ru \times 2M \tag{17}$$

where It_{H-JIDD} is the number of iterations required in the decoding process of the H-JIDD algorithm. Since H-JIDD uses the extended hamming code to check the information output during the iteration process as an early stop condition, the number of iterations It_{H-JIDD} required for H-JIDD decoding satisfies $It_{H-JIDD} \leq It_{JIDD}$ under any SNR conditions. Therefore, the complexity of H-JIDD scheme is lower than that of the traditional JIDD scheme, and it can be expressed as $\theta^{H-JIDD} \leq \theta^{JIDD}$. The simulation analysis of complexity will be discussed in Sect. 4.

4 Results and Discussion

In this section, we evaluate the BER performance of the PC-SCMA system and computational complexity under the H-JIDD receiver through simulation. All simulations are performed under the AWGN channel. The constellation size and system load of SCMA are $M = 4$, $K/M = 150\%$, respectively. The factor matrix R has been defined before, and the MPA detection algorithm is used for decoding. For polar coding, we use Bhattacharyya parameter binding to select the bit channel for transmitting information bits, and the decoding algorithm uses SCAN. At the same time, we add a random interleaver in the simulation.

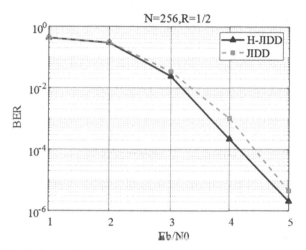

Fig. 3. Ber performance of H-JIDD with p_N = 256, R − 1/2.

Figure 3 shows the BER performance of the PC-SCMA system when the code length of the polar code is 256 and the code rate is 1/2. Here we compare the H-JIDD algorithm with JIDD algorithm. It is obvious from the Fig. 3 that when the SNR is low, there is no obvious difference between the JIDD and H-JIDD receiver. When the Eb/N0 is greater than 2dB, H-JIDD receiver reaches a lower BER than JIDD, which indicates that the H-JIDD algorithm controls the problem of decoding divergence in the conditions of low SNR. H-JIDD algorithm improves the performance of the PC-SCMA system.

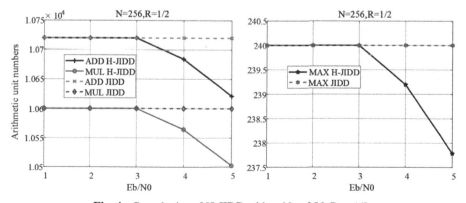

Fig. 4. Complexity of H-JIDD with p_N = 256, R = 1/2.

In Fig. 4, we compare the computational complexity of the receiver between the JIDD algorithm and H-JIDD algorithm when polar code length is 256 and code rate is 1/2. The computational complexity of the receiver is measured by the average number of adders, multipliers and comparators used by the receiver during a decoding process. It can be seen that when Eb/N0 is greater than 2dB, the number of adders, multipliers, and comparators used by the H-JIDD receiver are significantly reduced than those used by the JIDD algorithm. As the SNR continues to increase, the number of adders, multipliers and comparators used by the H-JIDD algorithm will be smaller than those used by the JIDD algorithm on average when transmitting data of the same size. This can reduce the delay of the PC-SCMA system and improve the transmission efficiency of the system.

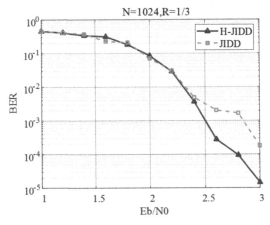

Fig. 5. Ber performance of H-JIDD with p_N = 1024, R = 1/3.

Figure 5 shows the BER performance of the PC-SCMA system when polar code length is 1024 and code rate is 1/3. When the SNR is low, the BER performance of the receiver H-JIDD algorithm and the JIDD algorithm both produce smaller fluctuations. But when the Eb/N0 is greater than 2.4dB, the receiver using H-JIDD will get a lower BER than JIDD.

In Fig. 6, we compare the computational complexity of the receiver of the JIDD algorithm and H-JIDD algorithm when polar code length is 1024 and code rate is 1/3. It can be seen that for a single decoding process, the H-JIDD receiver uses fewer adders, multipliers and comparators than the JIDD receiver when Eb/N0 is greater than 2.2 dB. As the SNR increases, the number of adders, multipliers and comparators used by the H-JIDD receiver will be significantly reduced.

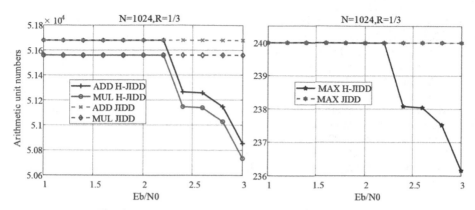

Fig. 6. Complexity of H-JIDD with p_N = 1024, R = 1/3.

5 Conclusion

In this paper, we optimized the joint iterative detection and decoding receiver of PC-SCMA to overcome the decoding divergence problem under low SNR. Specifically, we added an extended hamming code as the conditions for the early stop of the iterative detection and decoding algorithm. It could be seen from the simulation results that the H-JIDD algorithm further reduced the BER of PC-SCMA system. At the same time, compared with the JIDD algorithm, the H-JIDD algorithm improved the computational complexity of PC-SCMA system and reduced the system delay. Furthermore, the H-JIDD algorithm also saved computing resources which made a contribution to green communication.

References

1. Boccardi, F., Heath, R.W., Lozano, A., Marzetta, T.L., Popovski, P.: Five disruptive technology directions for 5G. IEEE Commun. Mag. **52**, 74–80 (2014)
2. Osseiran, A.: Scenarios for 5G mobile and wireless communications: the vision of the METIS project. IEEE Commun. Mag. **52**, 26–35 (2014)
3. Islam, S.M.R., Avazov, N., Dobre, O.A., Kwak, K.: Power-domain non-orthogonal multiple access (NOMA) in 5G systems: potentials and challenges. IEEE Commun. Surv. Tutor. **19**(2), 721–742 (2017)
4. Ding, Z., Lei, X., Karagiannidis, G.K., Schober, R., Yuan, J., Bhargava, V.K.: A survey on non-orthogonal multiple access for 5G networks: research challenges and future trends. IEEE J. Sel. Areas Commun. **35**(10), 2181–2195 (2017)
5. Sharma, M.K., Kumar, A.: Papr reduction in noma by using hybrid algorithms. Comput. Mater. Continua **69**(1), 1391–1406 (2021)
6. Abd-Elnaby, M.: Capacity and fairness maximization-based resource allocation for downlink NOMA networks. Comput. Mater. Continua **69**(1), 521–537 (2021)
7. Nikopour, H., Baligh, H.: Sparse code multiple access. In: IEEE 24th Annual International Symposium on Personal, Indoor, and Mobile Radio Communications (PIMRC), pp. 332–336 (2013)

8. Hoshyar, R., Wathan, F.P., Tafazolli, R.: CTH06-4: Novel low-density signature structure for synchronous DS-CDMA systems. In: IEEE Globecom, pp. 1–5 (2006)

9. Ji, X., Du, J., Jia, G., Fang, W.: Uplink SCMA codebook reuse transmission and reception scheme. Intell. Autom. Soft Comput. **27**(1), 221–231 (2021)

10. Ji, X., Du, J., Jia, G., Fang, W.: Low complexity decoding algorithm for uplink SCMA based on aerial spherical decoding. Intell. Autom. Soft Comput. **27**(3), 737–746 (2021)

11. Mohammed, N.A., Mansoor, A.M., Ahmad, R.B., Razalli, S.: Deployment of polar codes for mission-critical machine-type communication over wireless networks. Comput. Mater. Continua **71**(1), 573–592 (2022)

12. Saber, H., Ge, Y., Zhang, R., Shi, W., Tong, W.: Convolutional polar codes: LLR-based successive cancellation decoder and list decoding performance. In: 2018 IEEE International Symposium on Information Theory (ISIT), pp. 1480–1484 (2018)

13. Xi, F., Ye, C., Olesen, R.L.: A polar code hybrid rate matching scheme. In: 2018 European Conference on Networks and Communications (EuCNC), pp. 6–10 (2018)

14. Hanif, M., Ardakani, M.: Polar codes: bounds on bhattacharyya parameters and their applications. IEEE Trans. Commun. **66**, 5927–5937 (2018)

15. Wu, X., Yang, L., Xie, Y., Yuan, J.: Partially information coupled polar codes. IEEE Access **6**, 63689–63702 (2018)

16. Goldin, D., Burshtein, D.: On the finite length scaling of q-ary polar codes. IEEE Trans. Inf. Theory **64**, 7153–7170 (2018)

17. Pan, Z., Li, E., Zhang, L., Lei, J., Tang, C.: Design and optimization of joint iterative detection and decoding receiver for uplink polar coded SCMA system. IEEE Access **6**, 52014–52026 (2018)

18. Du, Y., Dong, B., Wang, X., Dang, G., Gao, P.: Multiuser detection scheme for SCMA systems based on serial strategy. J. Electron. Inf. Technol. **38**(8), 1888–1893 (2016)

19. Jing, S., Yang, C., Yang, J., Yóu, X., Zhang, C.: Joint detection and decoding of polar-coded SCMA systems. In: 2017 9th International Conference on Wireless Communications and Signal Processing, pp. 1–6 (2017)

20. Arikan, E.: A performance comparison of polar codes and Reed-Muller codes. IEEE Commun. Lett. **12**(6), 447–449 (2008)

21. Liu, J., Shi, Y., Liu, L., Sheng, M., Li, J.: Modeling SCMA in D2D underlaid cellular network. In: 2015 IEEE/CIC International Conference on Communications in China (ICCC), pp. 1–6 (2015)

22. Wu, Y., Zhang, S., Chen, Y.: Iterative multiuser receiver in sparse code multiple access systems. In: 2015 IEEE International Conference on Communications (ICC), pp. 2918–2923 (2015)

23. Balatsoukas-Stimming, A., Parizi, M.B., Burg, A.: LLR-based successive cancellation list decoding of polar codes. IEEE Trans. Sig. Process. **63**, 5165–5179 (2015)

24. Zhang, Y., Ge, W., Zhang, P., Gao, M.: The optimization scheme for joint iterative detection and decoding of polar coded SCMA system. Opt. Fiber Technol. **58**, 102283 (2020)

25. Sun, S., Cho, S., Zhang, Z.: Error patterns in belief propagation decoding of polar codes and their mitigation methods. In: 50th Asilomar Conference on Signals, Systems and Computers, pp. 1199–1203 (2016)

26. Fayyaz, U.U., Barry, J.R.: Polar codes for partial response channels. In: 2013 IEEE International Conference on Communications (ICC), pp. 4337–4341 (2013)

Recognition of Pedestrians' Crossing Intentions with a Conv-Transformer Network

Biao Yang[1,2] , Guocheng Yan[3] , Fujun Wang[4], Changchun Yang[2], and Xiaofeng Liu[1(✉)]

[1] College of IoT Engineering, Hohai University, Changzhou 213100, China
xfliu@hhu.edu.cn
[2] School of Microelectronics and Control Engineering,
Changzhou University, Changzhou 213100, China
[3] School of Computer Science and Artificial Intelligence,
Changzhou University, Changzhou 213100, China
[4] Graduate School of Environment and Information Sciences, YOKOHAMA National
University, Yokohama 240-8501, Japan

Abstract. Recognizing pedestrians' crossing intentions is critical for self-driving cars to avoid vehicle-pedestrian collisions. However, it is challenging to recognize pedestrians' crossing intentions based on their appearance or actions under severe conditions, including occlusions, dim illumination, and pedestrians standing far away. In this work, a Conv-transformer network is proposed to recognize pedestrians' crossing intentions. Pedestrians' appearance is modeled by a Resnet network, which will output a feature sequence describing pedestrians at different time steps. A Transformer network is then introduced to model the feature sequence to output the recognition result, which is crossing or not crossing. Evaluations on benchmarking databases, including JAAD and PIE, are performed. Results show that the proposed method can recognize pedestrians' crossing intentions precisely.

Keywords: Crossing intention · Resnet · Transformer · Vehicle-pedestrian collision

1 Introduction

The booming self-driving cars need to understand other road users' behaviors for better performance. One critical issue is recognizing pedestrians' crossing intentions, which is essential to avoid vehicle-pedestrian collisions. As shown in Fig. 1, the self-driving car needs to know whether the pedestrian wants to cross the street. Then, it can make subsequent decisions about continuing going or stopping to give way. Unlike human drivers who can recognize pedestrians' crossing intentions through verbal or non-verbal communications, it is challenging for a self-driving car to make a trade-off between safety and efficiency without the ability to recognize pedestrians' crossing intentions.

Due to its close relationship with pedestrians' safety, recognizing their crossing intentions is widely studied in the intelligent transportation system. Early researches

X. Sun et al. (Eds.): ICAIS 2022, CCIS 1586, pp. 471–479, 2022.
https://doi.org/10.1007/978-3-031-06767-9_39

Fig. 1. Illustration of recognizing pedestrians' crossing intentions.

concentrate on modeling the correlation between pedestrians' crossing intentions with their genders, ages, traffic flows, waiting times, and eye contact [1–3]. They also studied pedestrians' different performances on a signal-controlled road or road without signal control [4, 5]. To guarantee pedestrians' safeties, some researchers study how to recognize pedestrians' crossing intentions from captured traffic scene videos [6] or the simulation system, such as IFSTTR [7]. The studies mentioned above have provided solid theoretical guidance to recognize pedestrians' crossing intentions. However, most of them are not used in practice.

In order to develop a system that can recognize pedestrians' crossing intentions in practical, recent studies tried to achieve such goals from traffic scene videos containing pedestrians' crossing events. With the development of machine learning algorithms [8–10], pedestrians' appearance [11], actions [12], postures [13, 14] are widely used to model the correlation between their features and crossing decisions. Besides, the traffic context is also helpful to improve the recognition performance [15]. However, most of the former works ignore the spatiotemporal correlations in pedestrian crossing events, thus suffering from low recognition precision.

To better capture the spatiotemporal correlations that exist in pedestrian crossing events, a Conv-Transformer network is proposed in this work. The Resnet18 network is firstly used to extract crossing-related spatial features from pedestrians' appearances at each time step. A feature sequence is obtained by extracting spatial features at all time steps. Then, a Transformer network is introduced to model the temporal correlation from the feature sequence. After a good training, the Conv-Transformer network can predict whether the pedestrian will cross the street by feeding the network with the pedestrian's video clips. We perform evaluations on two benchmarking databases, named JAAD [16] and PIE [17]. Comparisons with other state-of-the-art methods reveal the effects of the proposed Conv-Transformer network in recognizing pedestrians' crossing intentions.

2   The Proposed Method

This work is devoted to helping the self-driving car better understand the scene by recognizing pedestrians' crossing intentions. The pipeline of the proposed method is illustrated in Fig. 2. Firstly, the YOLOv3 detector [18] is used to detect pedestrians in all frames. Then, the pedestrian sequence is fed into the Resnet18 network to extract spatial features, implying pedestrians' decisions to cross the street. After a feature sequence is output by the Resnet18 network, an improved Transformer network is introduced to process the sequential data to extract temporal features. By capturing the spatiotemporal features that exist in pedestrians' crossing events, the Conv-Transformer network can predict a recognition result about whether the pedestrian will cross or not. With this prediction, the self-driving car can better plan its future path to make a trade-off between safety and efficiency.

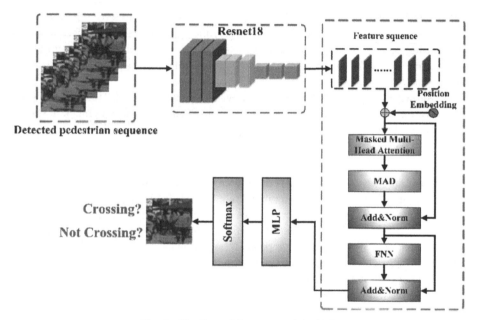

Fig. 2. Pipeline of the proposed method.

2.1   Spatial Features Extraction

In this section, we mainly discuss how to extract spatial features that imply pedestrians' crossing intentions. Given a detected pedestrian, we design a convolutional neural network (CNN) to perform automatic feature engineering in a data-driven manner. Specifically, we test different CNN backbones, including VGG, Resnet, Densenet, and Inception. A detailed comparison will be given in the next section. Finally, we use the Resnet18, which contains skip-connection to avoid gradient vanishing. Details to extract spatial features are presented as follows:

Firstly, we resize the detected pedestrian into a 168×168 patch X. Then, we feed the patch X into the Resnet18 network, which will output a 128-dimensional feature map. A global averaging pooling layer is used to convert the high-dimensional feature map into a 128-dimensional vector. The whole process can be defined as follows:

$$V_s = F_{Global}(F_{Res}(X)) \tag{1}$$

where F_{Global} and F_{Res} represent the global averaging pooling layer and the Resnet18 network, respectively.

By feeding each pedestrian patch in the video clip into the Resnet18 network, we can obtain a sequence feature, which will be fed into the improved Transformer network to model temporal correlations between different time steps.

2.2 Temporal Features Extraction

In this section, we mainly discuss how to extract temporal features from preliminarily obtained feature sequences. We abandon the commonly used LSTM or GRU networks because they cannot model global temporal correlations very well. Instead, an improved Transformer network is used to model temporal correlations in pedestrians' crossing video.

As shown in Fig. 2, the Transformer network repeatedly stacks four Transformer blocks. Before feeding the sequence feature $\{V_{Si}\}$ into the Transformer block, it should be firstly combined with position embedding, which is defined as follows:

$$\hat{V}_{Si} = PE_{(t,d)} + V_{Si} \tag{2}$$

where position embedding PE(t,d) is used to capture the sequential properties of input sequence features [19]. Then, the combined features are fed into the masked multi-head attention module to explore the correlations between different feature sequences. The attention module's output is fed into the multi-attention dropping (MAD), add&norm, FNN, and add&norm sequentially to process the extracted features. MAD is proposed in Reference [20], and we introduce such an operation to handle the over-fitting. Details of the Transformer network can be found in Reference [19].

Finally, the output of the Transformer network is fed into a three-layer multi-layer perceptron (MLP) to convert the high-dimensional vector into a 2-dimensional vector, followed by a softmax activation to generate the prediction result, which refers to crossing or not crossing.

2.3 Loss Function

The used loss function is introduced in this section. The crossing intention recognition issue is a classification problem. Therefore, a binary cross-entropy loss can be used to optimize the proposed network in an end-to-end manner. Considering some pedestrians' intentions are hard to recognize, we introduce the focal loss to replace the traditional binary cross-entropy loss. The focal loss is defined as follows:

$$L = \begin{cases} -\alpha (1 - p_k)^{\gamma} \log(p_k), & Y_k = 1 \\ -(1 - \alpha) p_k{}^{\gamma} \log(1 - p_k), & Y_k = 0 \end{cases} \tag{3}$$

where Y_k denotes the ground truth of the kth sample, and p_k represents the prediction probability given by the Conv-Transformer network. The hyper-parameter α is used to control the ratio between positive and negative samples. α is set to 0.5 empirically. Another hyper-parameter, β, is used to handle the hard samples, and β is set to 2 according to the Reference [21].

3   Experimental Evaluations

3.1   Databases

JAAD: This database is widely used to study the actions of traffic participants. It contains 346 high-resolution video clips, and each clip is about 5–15 s. Each clip shows different traffic scenes in urban environments. The database consists of pedestrians who are walking along the street, waiting on the roadside, and in the process of crossing the streets. Considering the purpose of the proposed work, we select 158 crossing samples and 78 not crossing samples from JAAD.

PIE: This database has a more extensive scale compared with JAAD. It comprises 1,842 high-resolution video clips that contain pedestrians walking or standing along different roads. All data is captured at daylight with high visibility. Therefore, this database is suitable for analyzing pedestrians' actions or intentions. In the evaluation part, we select 516 crossing samples and 852 not crossing samples from PIE.

3.2   Evaluation Metric

For both databases, a five-fold cross-validation strategy is used to evaluate and compare different methods. Accuracy is used as the evaluation metric, which is defined as follows:

$$Acc = (TP + TN)/(P + N) \qquad (4)$$

where P and N denote total numbers of crossing and not crossing samples, respectively. TP and TN denote correctly recognized numbers of crossing and not crossing samples, respectively.

3.3   Experimental Details

The proposed network is built with the Pytorch framework and is trained with an Intel I9 CPU and two NVIDIA GTX-3080 GPUs. The network is optimized with the Adam method with a learning rate, beta1, and beta2 of 0.001, 0.9, 0.999, respectively. The learning rate is reduced to half for every 100 epochs until the total 300 epochs.

3.4 Quantitative Evaluations

In this section, we mainly conduct different quantitative evaluations to verify the effects of the proposed method. We provide a detailed comparison between the used Resnet18 and other widely used backbones for the extraction of spatial features, including VGG, Densenet, and Inception. We use the same data setting and optimization strategy to guarantee fair comparisons. The Transformer head is used for all methods. Table 1 presents the comparison results on JAAD and PIE in terms of accuracy. As shown in the table, VGG and Inception achieve similar performance on both databases. Densenet achieves better performance due to the dense connections which can extract multi-scale features. Resnet18 achieves the best performance due to the used skip connections.

Table 1. xxx

Backbones	JAAD	PIE
VGG	0.831	0.829
Inception	0.833	0.830
Densenet	0.841	0.838
Resenet18	**0.852**	**0.846**

For the extraction of temporal features, we compare the introduced Transformer network with commonly GRU and LSTM. Notably, the Resnet18 is used as the backbone for all methods. Unlike the Transformer network that models temporal correlations with attention mechanism, GRU and LSTM process the sequential features recursively. Table 2 reports the comparison results of different methods on JAAD and PIE in terms of accuracy. As demonstrated in the table, GRU and LSTM have similar recognition performances. Our performance is superior to them due to the global processing of all sequential features, while GRU and LSTM always concentrate on later steps.

Table 2. Comparison results of Transformer, LSTM, and GRU on JAAD and PIE in the term of accuracy.

Backbones	JAAD	PIE
GRU	0.821	0.891
LSTM	0.822	0.871
Transformer	**0.852**	**0.846**

We also compare the proposed method with several mainstream methods, including the AlexNet-based method [22], double-channel CNN (DCCNN)-based method [12], skeleton-based method [23], and GNN (graph neural network)-based method [24]. The comparison results are given in Table 3. Compared with these strong competitors, our method still achieves the best performance.

Table 3. Comparison with mainstream methods on JAAD and PIE in the term of accuracy.

Methods	JAAD	PIE
AlexNet-based	0.725	0.744
DCCNN-based	0.742	0.782
Skeleton-based	0.814	0.808
GNN-based	0.828	0.841
Ours	**0.852**	**0.846**

Fig. 3. Illustrations of crossing and not crossing samples with prediction probabilities.

3.5 Qualitative Evaluations

In this section, we provide the qualitative evaluations of the proposed method. Specifically, we illustrate several crossing and not crossing samples and the probabilities predicted by the Conv-Transformer network. As shown in Fig. 3, four crossing and four not crossing samples with prediction probabilities are demonstrated. For neatness, the red fonts represent the not crossing probabilities, while the white fonts represent the crossing probabilities. We observe that pedestrians always do not try to cross the street if they are calling a phone. On the contrary, they have made crossing decisions when they have eye contact with drivers (except for the first not crossing sample). It is obvious that the proposed method can successfully recognize pedestrians' crossing intentions.

4   Conclusion and Discussion

In this work, a Conv-Transformer network is proposed to recognize pedestrians' crossing intentions by capturing the spatiotemporal relations in their crossing events. Unlike former works that recognize crossing intentions based on pedestrians' skeletons, the Conv-Transformer network can be optimized in an end-to-end manner. The Resnet18 network is used to extract spatial features, and an improved Transformer network is subsequently used to extract temporal features. Finally, the Transformer network can output the recognition result about whether the pedestrian will cross the street. Compared with other mainstream methods, the proposed method achieves better performance on JAAD and PIE databases.

Acknowledgement. We would like to give our sincere gratitude to Prof. Chen Yang, who provides the computing platform.

Funding Statement. This work was supported in part by National key R&D program of China 2018AAA0100800, the Key Research and Development Program of Jiangsu under grants BK20192004B and BE2018004, the National Postdoctoral Program under grant 2021M701042, the Postdoctoral Program in Jiangsu Province under grant 2021K187B, the Changzhou Applied basic Research project under grant CJ20200083, the Postgraduate Research & Practice Innovation Program of Jiangsu Province (KYCX21_2831), Guangdong Forestry Science and Technology Innovation Project under grant 2020KJCX005, the Changzhou Sci&Tech Program with Grant No. CJ20210052, International Cooperation and Exchanges of Changzhou under grant CZ20200035, and by the State Key Laboratory of Integrated Management of Pest Insects and Rodents(Grant No. IPM1914).

Conflicts of Interest. The authors declare that they have no conflicts of interest to report regarding the present study.

References

1. Herrero-Fernández, D., Macía-Guerrero, P., Silvano-Chaparro, L.: Risky behavior in young adult pedestrians: Personality determinants, correlates with risk perception, and gender differences. Transp. Res. F: Traffic Psychol. Behav. **36**, 14–24 (2016)
2. Chen, W., Zhuang, X., Cui, Z.: Drivers' recognition of pedestrian road-crossing intentions: performance and process. Transp. Res. F: Traffic Psychol. Behav. **64**, 552–564 (2019)
3. Tapiro, H., Oron-Gilad, T., Parmet, Y.: Towards understanding the influence of environmental distractors on pedestrian behavior. Procedia Manuf. **3**, 2690–2697 (2015)
4. Li, B.: A bilevel model for multivariate risk analysis of pedestrians' crossing behavior at signalized intersections. Transp. Res. Part B: Methodol. **65**, 18–30 (2014)
5. Zegeer, C.V., Richard Stewart, J., Huang, H., Lagerwey, P.: Safety effects of marked versus unmarked crosswalks at uncontrolled locations: analysis of pedestrian crashes in 30 cities. Transp. Res. Rec. **1773**(1), 56–68 (2001)
6. Meir, A., Parmet, Y., Oron-Gilad, T.: Towards understanding child-pedestrians' hazard perception abilities in a mixed reality dynamic environment. Transp. Res. F: Traffic Psychol. Behav. **20**, 90–107 (2013)

7. Dommes, A., Cavallo, V., Dubuisson, J.B.: Crossing a two-way street: comparison of young and old pedestrians. J. Saf. Res. **50**, 27–34 (2014)
8. Zhang, X.R., Zhang, W.F., Sun, W., et al.: A robust 3-D medical watermarking based on wavelet transform for data protection. Comput. Syst. Sci. Eng. **41**(3), 1043–1056 (2022)
9. Zhang, X., Sun, X., Sun, W., et al.: Deformation expression of soft tissue based on bp neural network. Intell. Autom. Soft Comput. **32**(2), 1041–1053 (2022)
10. Zhang, X.R., Sun, X., Sun, X.M., et al.: Robust reversible audio watermarking scheme for telemedicine and privacy protection. Comput. Mater. Continua **71**(2), 3035–3050 (2022)
11. Ushasukhanya, S., Karthikeyan, M.: Automatic human detection using reinforced faster-rcnn for electricity conservation system. Intell. Autom. Soft Comput. **32**(2), 1261–1275 (2022)
12. Kataoka, H., Satoh, Y., Aoki, Y.: Temporal and fine-grained pedestrian action recognition on driving recorder database. Sensors **18**(2), 627–641 (2018)
13. Fang, Z., López, A.: Intention recognition of pedestrians and cyclists by 2D pose estimation. IEEE Trans. Intell. Transp. Syst. **1**, 1–11 (2019)
14. Mínguez, R.Q., Alonso, I.P., Fernández-Llorca, D.: Pedestrian path, pose, and intention prediction through gaussian process dynamical models and pedestrian activity recognition. IEEE Trans. Intell. Transp. Syst. **20**(5), 1803–1814 (2018)
15. Yang, B., Zhan, W., Wang, P.: Crossing or not? Context-based recognition of pedestrian crossing intention in the urban environment. IEEE Trans. Intell. Transp. Syst. (2021). https://doi.org/10.1109/TITS.2021.3053031
16. Rasouli, A., Kotseruba, I., Tsotsos, J.K.: Agreeing to cross: how drivers and pedestrians communicate. In: 2017 IEEE Intelligent Vehicles Symposium (IV), pp. 264–269. IEEE (2017)
17. Rasouli, A., Kotseruba, I., Kunic, T., Tsotsos, J.K.: Pie: a large-scale dataset and models for pedestrian intention estimation and trajectory prediction. In: Proceedings of the IEEE/CVF International Conference on Computer Vision, pp. 6262–6271 (2019)
18. Wang, Y., Jia, K., Liu, P.: Impolite pedestrian detection by using enhanced yolov3-tiny. J. Artif. Intell. **2**(3), 113 (2020)
19. Ahmed, K., Keskar, N.S., Socher, R.: Weighted transformer network for machine translation. J. Artif. Intell. **2**(3), 113–124 (2020)
20. Xue, F., Wang, Q., Guo, G.: Transfer: learning relation-aware facial expression representations with transformers. In: Proceedings of the IEEE/CVF International Conference on Computer Vision, pp. 3601–3610 (2021)
21. Kingma, D.P., Welling, M.: Stochastic gradient VB and the variational auto-encoder. In: Second International Conference on Learning Representations, vol. 19, p. 121 (2014)
22. Rasouli, A., Kotseruba, I., Tsotsos, J.: Are they going to cross? A benchmark dataset and baseline for pedestrian crosswalk. In: Proceedings of the IEEE International Conference on Computer Vision Workshops, pp. 206–213 (2017)
23. Fang, Z., López, A.M.: Is the pedestrian going to cross? Answering by 2D pose estimation. In: 2018 IEEE Intelligent Vehicles Symposium (IV), pp. 1271–1276. IEEE (2018)
24. Cadena, P.R.G., Yang, M., Qian, Y., Wang, C.: Pedestrian graph: pedestrian crossing prediction based on 2D pose estimation and graph convolutional networks. In: 2019 IEEE Intelligent Transportation Systems Conference (ITSC), pp. 2000–2005. IEEE (2019)

Violent Target Detection Based on Improved YOLO Network

Zhi Zhang, Deyu Yuan, Xin Li$^{(\boxtimes)}$, and Shaofan Su

Department of Police Information Engineering and Cyber Security, People's Public Security University of China, Beijing 100038, China
lixin@ppsuc.edu.cn

Abstract. With the progress of the times, the Internet has deeply influenced everyone. The content of online information types is complex, with a large number of violence-related contents containing undesirable elements such as gore and violence, which make the online ecological environment seriously polluted and constantly pose a threat to the worlds online ecological security. Deep learning has been performing well in computer vision, and deep learning-based target detection algorithms have great potential for identifying violent elements. Target detection is an important theoretical basis for using high-level vision such as images and events. The aim of this paper is to investigate the application of deep learning techniques to the detection of violence-involved elements. By evaluating the neural network structure and spatial model, the application of the latest YOLOv5 algorithm is able to identify violence-involved elements more accurately and determine the class of elements, counting the mAP value of each class label. This is important for discovering and processing information about riot-related organisations and riot-related networks, grasping the dynamics of riot-related organisations, analysing and tracking the movements of riot-related organisations, and targeting them for combat.

Keywords: Convolutional neural networks · Violent · Network security · Deep learning · Target detection

1 Introduction

In the new era of the online environment, the online world is also full of all kinds of violence-related content. Violence-related information on the Internet means that non-governmental organisations or certain individuals have deliberately disrupted the Internet, which in turn has had a certain sensational effect on the political and economic security of local governments and the long-term stability of society. Most of them use pictures or texts on the Internet to promote ideas that contain bloody violence, rowdy crowds, violent activities, slogans of a violent nature, etc., which have an impact on the stability of the entire world. Finding ways to prevent the uncontrolled spread of violent content on the Internet is now an important issue in the field of cyberspace security.

In response to this situation, anti-violence organizations and various government agencies are particularly keen to be able to intelligently monitor and detect the volume

© The Author(s), under exclusive license to Springer Nature Switzerland AG 2022
X. Sun et al. (Eds.): ICAIS 2022, CCIS 1586, pp. 480–492, 2022.
https://doi.org/10.1007/978-3-031-06767-9_40

of images on the Internet, so as to capture the presence of information involving violent sexual elements in them. This allows for the fast, accurate and timely processing of violent content in public information, in order to improve the professional means of anti-violence organizations and government agencies to carry out security and stability maintenance and emergency response.

The principle of target detection is to understand the image at a high level of information, by evaluating the neural network structure and the spatial model, so as to abstract the characteristics of the violent elements contained in the images high level information domain. The latest target detection algorithms are used to analyse, identify and signify the violence-related elements and to rationalise the use of human and material resources of anti-violence organisations and various government agencies [1]. The system will become a powerful and intelligent weapon in the field of anti-violence for governments and organisations. It is important to detect and deal with violent organisations, to grasp information about violent networks, to track the dynamics of violent organisations, to anticipate their movements and finally to target them.

In recent years, deep learning has performed well in computer vision [2], and the YOLO family of algorithms is constantly being updated and iterated, which has given riot-related feature detection great scope for development. This paper uses literature research and ablation experiments to fully understand the current background and development status of riot-related feature detection after reviewing the relevant literature on the application of deep learning techniques to riot-related feature detection. Through the evaluation of the neural network structure and spatial model, it is found that the latest YOLOv5 algorithm performs better in this scenario, and after training a specific dataset, it is possible to build a model and thus implement a multi-labelled riot-related feature detection system. The model is improved by comparing it with the previous YOLO family of algorithms, using evaluation metrics such as mAP, and continuously processing the data and revising the training model to finalise the implementation of the system.

The contents of this paper can be summarized as follows:

1) Constructing a dataset of riot-related images. A dataset containing 15 categories of violence-related feature elements was constructed by means of web crawlers and manual supplementation.
2) Improving the latest target detection algorithm. Improving the mAP value of the improved YOLOv5 under this dataset by fusing an efficient attention mechanism and an improved loss function approach to make it better for riot control applications.
3) Build a model thus enabling a multi-labelled system for the detection of riot-related features. Images and videos that can contain features of violence-related elements can be analysed, identified and labelled, serving to save labour costs.

The following five sections are organized to describe the full text. Section 2 describes related national and international work in the area of target detection. Section 3 describes the network models and improvement strategies we use in feature detection. The experimental setup, description of the dataset, and ablation experiments and results are placed in Sect. 4. Finally, the whole Sect. 5 concludes.

2   Related Work

In recent years, research and development in various fields has been rapid due to the ability to use deep learning techniques [3]. Many universities and research companies are starting to publish results in this field in spurts. MIT and Google are leading the industry abroad, while notable Chinese ones include universities and technology companies such as Qingbei, the Institute of Chinese Academy of Sciences, Baidu and Alibaba. Different detection models learned by deep learning will produce different results for riot-related features. The existing steps for feature information detection generally have three steps, anchor frame recommendation, feature information representation and target classification [4]. The target anchor frame is first recommended by some algorithm, after which the feature vector of the anchor frame is represented by the model and finally classified according to a pre-defined category.

Neural network algorithms first started around 1980, when they were used as basic classifiers, and in October 2012, Hinton and his team, a leading academic in the industry, took first place in the ImageNet, a highly valuable image recognition competition, for deep learning models, using the well-known AlexNet [5]. The criterion for the competition at that time was the error rate, and the algorithm was 10% lower than the second place on this criterion. In the same year, buzzwords such as neural networks and machine learning kept appearing in the New York Times and entered the public eye. This was followed by the classic target detection algorithm RCNN, presented at CVPR 2014 by Ross Girshick et al. They used convolution for feature extraction and divided object detection into two steps - target classification as well as localization, implemented using both SVM and anchor frame regression, respectively. Later, improvements have been made on this basis and the well-known Fast RCNN and Faster RCNN [6] algorithms have been proposed. However, the RCNN algorithm has obvious shortcomings; its candidate anchor frames are generated using a selective search algorithm, so it always generates redundant anchor frames, and the redundant computation reduces the convolution efficiency; secondly, the backbone network of AlexNet is followed, which makes the images in the input layer must be adjusted to a fixed size, and the robustness is not high.

There has been no better solution until 2015 when Kai-Ming He and his team, based on the original structure, proposed the SPP-Net algorithm [7]. After that, a series of tedious pre-processing operations such as scale scaling and pruning of candidate regions in the input layer of the previous algorithm were replaced. The pyramid pooling structure also optimized the previous image quality problems due to scaling and cropping, reduced the workload of anchor frame selection in the preprocessing part, and improved the overall efficiency.

The Two-stage scenario described above has the two steps of anchor frame generation and possible region classification. Candidate anchor frames and anchor frame category differentiation were being performed until 2015, opening the door to One-stage with the advent of YOLO. instead of extracting candidate frames, YOLO directly divides the image into multiple grids and later localizes them according to the grid where the target center is located. YOLOv2 builds on the network architecture of YOLOv1, in which the batch normalization layer is adopted, and also borrows the idea of residual structure and improves it as well. Later, the authors also published advanced SSD algorithms such as DSSD.

Deep learning techniques are starting to take on more possibilities and are suddenly becoming a hot topic in various research areas. A big reason for this is that with the constant updates in Fine-tune and GPU technology, the difficulty of deep learning training has been effectively reduced, which makes the detection of feature objects an important area in deep learning, and the current image feature detection models built by algorithms such as SPP-NET, Faster R-CNN, YOLO [8], and SSD are widely applied in various fields [9].

However, there are still many difficulties in target detection techniques, the effect of complex image imaging environment such as illumination and occlusion on the image quality, the scale size of the target problem such as if better make the target anchor frame to better fit the large and small targets in the actual image.

In summary, in this paper, when training the model for the riot-related target detection system, many means have been tried to optimise the model in terms of pre-processing of the image dataset, in terms of modification of parameters and hyperparameters, and in terms of ways and means of training the model, so as to enhance the target detection mAP values of the trained model.

3 Models and Methods for Detection of Riot-Related Images

This paper works on a framework for violence-related image detection [10], providing a model for machines to detect violence-related information in cyberspace, which can also be embedded in cameras for alerting government agency regulators to automatically obtain intelligence information in times of emergency [11].

Current convolutional neural networks have replaced the previous traditional feature extraction methods such as HOG [12], and we can divide the steps of the target detection network into two pieces: the backbone network and the detection part, as shown in Fig. 1. The main role of the backbone network is to extract features, which is usually a modified version formed by the commonly used classification networks (e.g., VGG-16 [13], ResNet-101 [14]), etc. after tailoring. The detection part can be divided into two types (as shown in the red boxed part of Fig. 1): a one-step detection method (One-stage) and a two-step detection method (Two-stage). One-stage detection method for detecting the localization of anchor frames is directly handled by regression [15], which has made a breakthrough in speed; two-stage detection method is to first find out the region where the object may exist and then perform characterization extraction, and then classify the candidate frames to get the target frame, which has a slight advantage in the accuracy of target detection as well as localization.

3.1 YOLOv5x

In 2015, the YOLO [16] (You Only Look Once) algorithm was first proposed, which combines the regression idea of OverFeat [17] using one step, and its significant speed advantage (inference speed up to 45 frames per second) made it quickly become a leader in the field of target detection. The dataset is automatically resized to the appropriate pixel size in the algorithm, and then the step of the input layer is continued, and after obtaining the graph by means of feature extraction, the features are divided into S × S

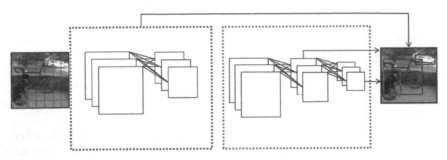

Fig. 1. Structure of the target detection network: backbone + detection in two parts.

grid regions, and then the class confidence and anchor frame coordinates within each grid are predicted by a classifier and a border regressor. The YOLO algorithm has a great advantage in speed, but it also has some problems; its localization is not accurate enough, its recall rate is low, and it is too sensitive to inter-object spacing and object size and not very robust.

YOLOv5 was released in June 2020, once released YOLOv5 was shown in the field of target detection with feature information in a better light and has been continuously maintained and updated since then, as shown in Fig. 2 for the Yolov5-5.0 network structure. The reasons for this are analyzed as follows:

(1) For better feature detection, data enhancement Mosaic is used on the input side, and the automatic anchor frame clustering calculation function and adaptive image scaling are updated to enrich the data for better results.
(2) The backbone network uses Focus, C3 structure and spatial pyramid pooling SPP [14], in which Focus acts as a slicing operation when the input layer is converted into a feature map, C3 reduces the "bottleneck", and SPP can extract features at different scales, making the networks learning effect improved. The SPP can extract features at different scales, which improves the learning of the network.
(3) GIoU is used at the output for the problems that may arise during target detection such as one target but generating multiple anchor frames, and non-extreme suppression NMS is used to solve them.

3.2 Yolov5 Fusion Attention Mechanism

Although the Yolov5 algorithm already has good detection results for publicly available datasets such as COCO, it is necessary to improve the Yolov5 algorithm to improve its detection results for specific datasets to meet the needs of anti-violence work in complex environments, which are constructed using web crawling and video screenshots in this paper. On the other hand, attention mechanisms have been widely used in various vision tasks, and their attentional information on feature maps can be effectively obtained [18]. The Convolutional Attention Module (Squeeze-and-Excitation Networks SENet) [19] learns important feature information from global information and suppresses less

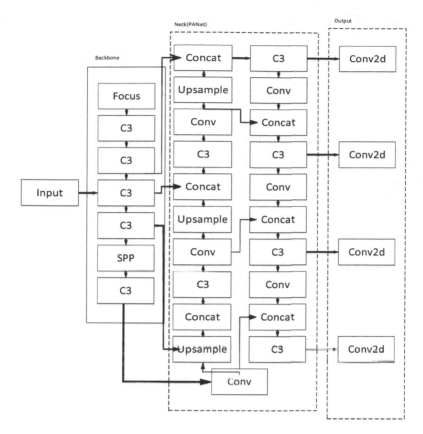

Fig. 2. Yolov5 network structure.

important information to improve the representation of the network by modeling the dependencies between channels.

Convolution in local space can make the acquisition of information insufficient, for this reason a CNN structure containing Squeeze, Excitation, Reweight is deliberately proposed as in Fig. 3 it is SENet. first global average pooling of the upper layer input features to form an S * 1 * 1 feature map (S is the number of channels), followed by 2 FC layers, after which the sigmoid activation function to obtain the weights of S * 1 * 1.

Fig. 3. SE structure diagram.

The most important function of the attention mechanism is adaptive calibration to reconstruct global information. the Backbone part of the Yolov5 network is mainly responsible for feature extraction, so the SENet is placed between the Backbone and Neck networks to optimize the output of the front and back part so that the two parts can be better connected. in this paper, the overall mAP value is improved without adding more network parameters as much as possible, which is SEYolov5.

3.3 Loss Function Using CIOU_loss

It is known that currently GIOU_Loss is the loss function of YOLOv5 in Bounding box. It combines the consideration of non-overlapping regions compared to the previous one, and also takes into account the problem that the loss of IoU will fail when there is no overlapping region block between the detection box and the real anchor box. However, the problem of the distance between the two candidate anchor boxes cannot be solved, and once the case of inclusion and width and height alignment occurs, the resulting difference set will be 0, which directly degrades to IoU. Therefore, we choose the CIOU_Loss with better effect, which is given by:

$$\text{CIoU} = 1 - IOU + \frac{\rho 2(b, bgt)}{c^2} + \alpha \upsilon \tag{1}$$

$$\alpha = \frac{\upsilon}{(1 - \text{IoU}) + \upsilon} \tag{2}$$

$$\upsilon = \frac{4}{\pi^2}(\arctan\frac{w^{gt}}{h^{gt}} - arctan\frac{w}{h})^2 \tag{3}$$

A good loss regression function, when considering the exact anchor frame coverage area and the distance between the centroids of the two anchor frames, should also count for the aspect ratio consideration. Based on GIOU_Loss, CIOU_Loss adds conditions for calculating the Euclidean distance and adds the aspect ratio factor to be considered, making the predicted anchor frames more consistent with the real frames. In this paper, CIOU_Loss is used as the loss function of the violence-related image detection network.

4   Experimental Procedure and Results

After training on a specific dataset, a model for the detection of violence-involved elements in violent scenarios was constructed on the basis of the latest target detection algorithms. This section will describe how the model design was carried out in its entirety after modelling YOLOv5 using the pytorch framework and applying it to real scenarios.

4.1   Experimental Preparation

Experimental Hardware Environment. The training of the model requires great arithmetic support, so we prefer to use GPU servers for training. The specific parameters used in this case are shown in Table 1.

Table 1. Computer experimental environment.

Configuration item	Configuration content
Operating system	Windows 10 64-bit
GPU	NVIDIA GeForce RTX 2080 Ti
CPU	Intel(R) Xeon(R) Silver 4210R CPU
Development environment (computer)	Pytorch:1.7.0 OpenCV-Python:4.5.1

Experimental Data. In order to validate the effectiveness of the detection algorithm, this paper builds a customised dataset of violence-related images, a detection model containing a feature pyramid, for multi-category detection of violence-related feature information. Most of the custom dataset is derived from crawling the web for violence-related images by searching for keyword terms, while the other part is manually supplemented by manual interception of violence-related videos from the CCTV public. After the pre-processing and labelling of the particular dataset is completed, it is divided into a training representation extraction part and a test performance part. The former dataset is then used for representation extraction, and finally the test part is used for performance statistics of the model.

Afterwards, by analysing the dataset and referring to the literature [20] and the classification and definitions of riot-related features in public search engines, fifteen more typical features were identified as riot-related target detection tags, namely bloody violence, explosive flames, rowdy crowds, smoke, controlled knives, guns, artillery, bombs, heavy weaponry, slogans, etc. For each category we collected no less than 100 tags, after which we categorised the riot-related images, randomly dividing each category into 8:2, and finally aggregating the images together.

4.2 Experimental Results and Comparative Analysis

Evaluation Indicators. As with other multi-category classification tasks, we use three evaluation metrics to macroscopically assess the effectiveness of the model, namely Precision, Recall, mAP.

$$P = \frac{TP}{TP + FP} \tag{4}$$

$$R = \frac{TP}{TP + FN} \tag{5}$$

$$AP = \sum_{i=1}^{n-1}(r_{i+1} - r_i)P_{inter}(r_i + 1) \tag{6}$$

$$mAP = \frac{\sum_{i=1}^{k} AP_i}{k} \tag{7}$$

where TP refers to correctly identified samples, FP denotes incorrectly identified samples, and FN is the correct samples that were not identified. In the Precision-Recall curve, the average of the Precision corresponding to each Recall is calculated to be the AP, and finally the average AP of all categories is the mAP. in other words, the AP is the area obtained by integrating below the P-R curve, and the mAP is the average of the AP of each category.

Yolov5 Ablation and Comparison Experiments. To verify the effectiveness of the improvement strategies proposed in this paper on a specific dataset, the following ablation experiments are conducted to determine the actual effect of each improvement strategy acting on the model, adding SENet to the initial Yolov5 in turn, using CIOU_loss. experiments use the same configuration parameters and the same dataset. The results of the experiments are shown in Table 2.

Table 2. Yolov5 ablation experiments.

SENet	CIOU_loss	Precision	Recall	mAP
-	-	0.282	0.749	0.572
√	-	0.302	0.767	0.594
-	√	0.263	0.762	0.578
√	√	0.408	0.722	0.599

The first row of Table 2 shows the effect exhibited by the original Yolov5 on the dataset with mAP of 0.572. After introducing the attention mechanism SENet, using CIOU_loss respectively, the mAP values improve, verifying that the algorithm has enhanced feature detection capabilities.

To analyze the impact of SENet and CIOU_loss on the model feature enhancement, some of the detection results were visualized and analyzed. As can be seen in Fig. 4, compared to before the introduction of SENet and CIOU_loss, the detection effect is significantly improved after the improvement, and the mAP value is more significantly improved for the same data set.

Figure 5 shows the effect of the SEYolov5 model in the detection of violence-related images, and it can be seen that the model can still achieve more satisfactory results in real scenarios.

Figure 6 shows the visualization results of SEYolov5 with the fused attention mechanism SENet and CIOU_loss.

In this paper, after several training sessions, it is found that the model converges at 800 epochs, so the epoch value is chosen to be 8 00. Compared with the traditional Yolov5 algorithm, the accuracy of the network is significantly improved by incorporating the attention mechanism and the improved loss function. The effect of the attention mechanism is more pronounced while the effect of the loss function is slightly weaker, which is related to the functions of the two modules, the attention mechanism plays an important extractive power in the network feature extraction, while the loss function

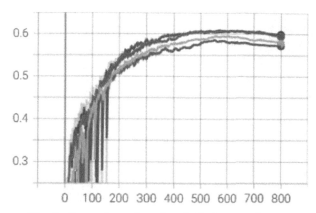

Fig. 4. Comparison of results of ablation experiments.

Fig. 5. SEYolov5 model effect.

improves the regression of the prediction frame therefore there is only a small improvement. From the evaluation results it can be seen that the neural network learns feature information from the training set data iteratively throughout the process and after testing work on the model it can be seen that our proposed SEYolov5 achieves an overall mAP of 0.599 or more with a self-built specific dataset, good performance metrics that meet the needs of daily work.

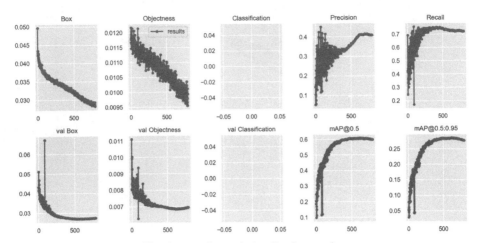

Fig. 6. Experimental visualization results.

5   Conclusion

This section summarises the current state of violence-related content on the Internet, existing problems and future prospects in this direction, and the significance of applied research.

5.1   Online Violence-Related Content Remains a Concern and a Solution

According to surveys, nearly 90 per cent of violent organisations have used social media channels to organise violent activities and have also published apps to spread violent doctrines. Violent organisations have been strongly condemned by countries around the world. However, due to their complex social background and historical factors, the threat posed by violent organisations to the world continues unabated. In order to effectively curb the spread of violence-related content on the Internet and remove the threats that exist in information networks, it is necessary to pay attention to cyber security.

5.2   Existing Problems and Future Prospects

This paper consumes a lot of time in data interception and image crawling as well as pre-processing. Because most of the data crawled on the Internet has low relevance and the violence-related features have low pixel count and inaccurate elements, the tags need to be screened and verified manually. In addition some of the tags such as gory scenes are vague and need to be judged based on experience, there are some subjective factors, and there are differences in the way the images are recognised by the machine, which also becomes a reason for the accuracy of the detection of violence-related features information. It is therefore advisable to further understand the principles of machine recognition in subsequent labelling work to minimise human factors and empirical misjudgements.

Even though the overall mAP reached a high level, not every category of target detection reached a high level. After that, we can continue to process the dataset, review the noisy labels, and perform research and analysis based on the results of target detection to correct the labeling criteria and improve the correct rate. In addition to the tags themselves, the complex application environment also brings a lot of noise, which affects the accuracy of target detection.

Further improvements can be made to the algorithm as a whole. Using pytorch it is possible to build better models, for example with a dataset with many smaller targets it is possible to consider whether a detection layer could be added, as well as using better loss functions or NMS algorithms to improve recognition accuracy. It is also possible to find more accurate riot-related images to build a better quality dataset. Or use dynamic tuning, for example, to find the best parameters to extract more accurate features and better models with continuous training.

5.3 Application Implications

This paper uses internet crawled data and manually intercepted images, which can effectively identify images with violence-related features that promote violentism in complex data in cyberspace, with an overall mAP of 0.599 or above. The algorithm also possesses strong practical significance in helping information screening and assisting anti-violence agencies in batch retrieval of massive image data in cyberspace.

The main research in this paper focuses on the design of a deep learning based violence-related feature detection system, focusing on summarising and studying the current recognition algorithm with the best feature detection effect, and designing a realistic detection in violence scenarios on this basis. As the technology is updated and iterated, more excellent algorithms and structures are bound to emerge, which can continuously enrich the technical research on violence-related feature detection.

Acknowledgement. This work was supported by the National Natural Science Foundation of China [Grants No.62071056], Open Research Fund of the Public Security Behavioral Science Laboratory, Peoples Public Security University of China [Grants 2020SYS03] and the Fundamental Research Funds for the Central Universities, Peoples Public Security University of China (2021JKF215).

References

1. AL-Marghilani, A.A.: Target detection algorithm in crime recognition using artificial intelligence. Comput. Mater. Continua **71**(1), 809–824 (2022)
2. Rajakumari, R., Kalaivani, L.: Breast cancer detection and classification using deep CNN techniques. Intell. Autom. Soft Comput. **32**(2), 1089–1107 (2022)
3. Ilyas, Q.M., Ahmad, M.: An enhanced deep learning model for automatic face mask detection. Intell. Autom. Soft Comput. **31**(1), 241–254 (2022)
4. Zhao, L., Zhao, M.: Feature-enhanced refinedet: fast detection of small objects. J. Inf. Hiding Privacy Protect. **3**(1), 1–8 (2021)
5. Lu, H.T., Zhang, Q.C.: A review of research on the application of deep convolutional neural networks in computer vision. Data Acquisition Process. **31**(1), 1–17 (2016)

6. Wang, L., Zhang, H.H.: Application of faster R-CNN models for vehicle detection. Comput. Appl. **38**(3), 666–670 (2018)

7. Purkait, P., Zhao, C., Zach, C.: SPP-net: deep absolute pose regression with synthetic views. In: British Machine Vision Conference (BMVC 2018), British (2017)

8. Zhou, X.Y., Wang, K., Li, L.Y.: A review of deep learning based target detection algorithms. Electron. Meas. Technol. **40**(11), 89–93 (2017)

9. Tang, C., Ling, Y.S., Zheng, K.D., Yang, X., Zheng, C., et al.: Deep learning based multi-window SSD target detection method. Infrared Laser Eng. **47**(1), 302–310 (2018)

10. Ju, X.: An overview of face manipulation detection. J. Cyber Secur. **2**(4), 197–207 (2020)

11. Narejo, S., Pandey, B., Vargas, D.E., Rodriguez, C., Anjum, M.R.: Weapon detection using yolo v3 for smart surveillance system. Math. Probl. Eng. (2021). https://doi.org/10.1155/2021/9975700

12. Dalal, N., Triggs, B.: Histograms of oriented gradients for human detection. In: IEEE Computer Society Conference on Computer Vision and Pattern Recognition, IEEE (2005)

13. Simonyan, K., Zisserman, A.: Very deep convolutional networks for large-scale image recognition. Comput. Sci. (2014)

14. He, K., Zhang, X., Ren, S., Sun, J.: Deep residual learning for image recognition. IEEE (2016)

15. Zhang, H.: Fast and efficient small target detection network algorithm research. Master thesis. Nanchang University, China (2020)

16. Redmon, J., Divvala, S., Girshick R., Farhadi, A.: You only look once: unified real-time object detection. IEEE Comput. Vis. Pattern Recogn. (2016)

17. Sermanet, P., Eigen, D., Zhang, X. et al.: OverFeat: integrated recognition, localization and detection using convolutional networks. arXiv:1312.6229 (2013)

18. Zhang, C.J., Zhu, L., Yu, L.: Review of attention mechanism in convolutional neural networks. Comput. Eng. Appl. (2021)

19. Jie, H, Li, S, Gang, S., et al.: Squeeze-and-excitation networks. IEEE Trans. Pattern Anal. Mach. Intell. 99 (2017)

20. Yan, L., Zhou, X., He, X.H., et al.: An integrated classification-based approach for automatic annotation of riot images. J. Terahertz Sci. Electron. Inf. **18**(2), 140–146 (2020)

Analysis and Architecture Design of a Large-Scale Event-Centric Knowledge Graph System for Dispute Resolution

Yang Zhou[1,2] , Jun Shi[1(✉)], Zhipeng Li[1], Yong Liao[1,3], Zheng Ma[1], Xuejie Ye[1],
Yangzhao Yang[1], and Xun Shao[4]

[1] Shenzhen CyberAray Network Technology Co. Ltd., Shenzhen 518038, China
jshi@nscslab.net
[2] China Academy of Electronics and Information Technology, Beijing 100041, China
[3] School of Cyber Science and Technology, University of Science and Technology of China,
Hefei 230026, China
[4] School of Regional Innovation and Social Design Engineering,
Kitami Institute of Technology, Kitami 090-8570, Japan

Abstract. Exploiting natural language processing and machine learning techniques, knowledge graph (KG) can transform disorganized raw data into structured knowledge. Recently, KG has been applied in various fields, such as intelligent search, question answering systems and so on. Most of them are usually entity KGs, which can be denoted by triples including head entities, tail entities and relations between them. This kind of KGs generally focus on named entities, e.g. people, organizations, places. With the development of the Internet and social media, large amounts of news spread rapidly and widely. Both academia and industry have particularly concerned of how to accurately mine the information and acquire the details of related events from lots of news. Besides that, events of disputes or conflicts may bring threats to social security. As a result, deeply analyzing and mining information of conflicts and disputes can effectively improve the ability of social governance. In this context, we introduce an event-centric knowledge graph to assist solving the problem. In this paper, we first discuss the architecture of our proposed event-centric knowledge graph for dispute resolution, which is suitable for large-scale data processing. Then we introduce the methods and modules to construct the proposed architecture. For each module, we discuss the details of our building methods. To this end, we capture a complete view of the proposed system.

Keywords: Event-centric knowledge graph · Natural language processing · Graph database · Dispute resolution

1 Introduction

Instantly knowledge graph (KG) is a promising technique to provide the intelligence of searching and recommendation [1, 2]. Google firstly raised the implementation scheme of

© The Author(s), under exclusive license to Springer Nature Switzerland AG 2022
X. Sun et al. (Eds.): ICAIS 2022, CCIS 1586, pp. 493–503, 2022.
https://doi.org/10.1007/978-3-031-06767-9_41

KG in 2012 [3]. After that, more and more knowledge graph applications were proposed, such as Freebase [4], DBpedia [5], Knowledge Vault [6] and so on [7, 8]. Most of these applications center on entities and particularly attract interests of researchers. In general, this kind of KG is more suitable for describing named entities rather than events. Developing with social network, a little incident usually spreads quickly and may create quite a stir on the Internet. Therefore, it is a promising trend for researchers to appropriately use KG analyzing and investigating events [9–11].

KG has an inherent advantage of analyzing and reasoning [12]. Many efforts have been spent applying KG in the public security field. A mixed storage method based on graph database was designed to construct public safety knowledge graph system [13]. The concrete application scenes were introduced, including teasing out people's relationships, discovering particular groups and so on. Knowledge graph has been also applied in building family tree and intelligent searching [14]. A police knowledge graph was proposed to aid the implementation of smart policing [15].

Dispute resolution is a realistic problem for governments all around the world, especially China, due to the large amount of population and limited resources. Compared with traditional dispute resolution methods, online dispute resolution (ODR) [16] brings a modern form of communication by means of the Internet. Many places in China have also developed dispute and conflict management applications, which mainly focus on providing platforms for collecting dispute information. However, how to reveal relations and sources of dispute events by in-depth analysis is still an open problem. Therefore, it is a key issue to intelligently analyze dispute and conflict events.

In this paper, we propose detailed construction methods which are able to automatically build knowledge graph system. Taking the advantage of KG, it is inherently easy to resolve disputes and conflicts. The key idea is that we introduce the architecture of our proposed event-centric KG system, which is designed to effectively process large amount of raw data. Another important aspect is that we analyze methods to automatically classify raw data into different dispute classes in order to improve efficiency. Besides that, we construct corresponding knowledge graph prototype system covering its full lifecycle.

The rest of paper is organized as follows. Section 2 introduces the architecture of our large-scale event-centric knowledge graph system for dispute resolution. Section 3 describes the model of data preprocessing. We present the concrete building methods of proposed system in Sect. 4. In Sect. 5, we conclude the paper.

2 System Architecture Design

We construct an event-centric KG prototype system for dispute resolution, which manipulates huge amounts of raw data. Our system is divided into 4 layers, as illustrated in Fig. 1.

Data Layer: In this layer, we collect huge amounts of data from different sources, such as forums, Weibo, URL pages, and so on. Considering the convenience of our research, we use web crawler and collect data from open source. Large amounts of disorganized raw data can be obtained after crawling.

Procession Layer: In general, large amounts of disorganized data bring difficulties in efficient construction. Therefore, we add procession layer after data layer to preprocess raw data. We introduce dichotomy method to distinguish between data belonging to disputes and the others. Multiple classifiers are later utilized to classify dispute data into different categories.

Construction Layer: Given the classified dataset, we construct our event-centric KG system by different modules covering its full lifecycle. Graph database is applied to deal with large-scale KG and improve the efficiency of the system. By implementing these steps, we can finally acquire the structured knowledge of dispute events.

Application Layer: On the basis of our KG system, a variety of algorithms can be applied and developed, such as case-based reasoning, event evolution analysis and deduction and so on. It is feasible to use these algorithms to solve realistic problems, including dispute event reasoning, dispute event sourcing, dispute event prediction, dispute event disposal and so on.

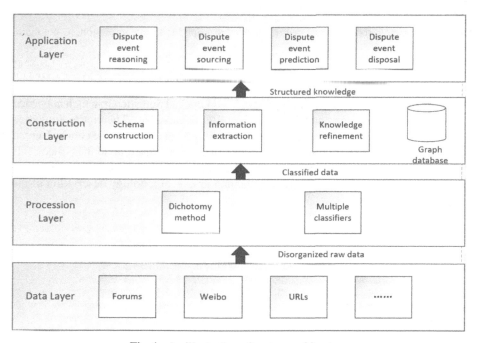

Fig. 1. An illustration of system architecture.

Figure 2 shows an example of our proposed event-centric KG prototype system. In this figure, the yellow circle represents main categories of events. All events belong to a particular category are colored in blue. Green circles denote the subsequences of events which are blue. Each event has multiple attributes which are pointed by arrows and shown in orange. Relations are labeled upon corresponding arrows.

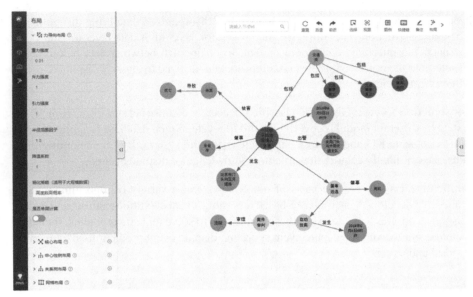

Fig. 2. Example of proposed event-centric knowledge graph for dispute resolution. (Color figure online)

We collect a report of hit-and-run traffic accident on website as shown in Fig. 3. In this case, Yu Jinping drove a car after drinking and knocked Song down, which happened on June 5, 2019. The driver had fled the scene after the accident. The victim Song died instantly identified by the traffic detachment of Beijing Municipal Public Security Bureau Mentougou Branch. On the following day, the driver gave himself up to the police. This criminal case was finally brought to trial. This event can be represented by our proposed system as Fig. 2 shown. To this end, we obtain a graphical topology description of the traffic accident event.

余金平酒驾撞死人并逃逸

2019年6月5日，余金平酒后驾车行驶至北京市门头沟区河堤路时，车辆撞到被害人宋某致其死亡，撞人后余金平驾车逃逸。经北京市公安局门头沟分局交通支队认定，事故造成宋某当场死亡。2019年6月6日，余金平到公安机关自动投案。法院最终审理此次案件。

Fig. 3. A report of a traffic accident.

3   Data Preprocessing

There are lots of noise data in the raw dataset crawled from Internet. At the same time, different dispute events usually have different semantic structures, which brings difficulties to extract information from overall data in a specific method. Therefore, we preprocess the dataset before constructing the KG to improve the efficiency of our system. Events belong to different categories are analyzed separately and independently afterward.

Specifically, we introduce a dispute incidents' classification model to achieve the goal of automatic processing. Firstly, we use BERT [17] and ERNIE [18] to extract features from raw data which consist of disputes and other noise data. And then training the model with labeled data. After this step, we use a similar method to achieve the goal of classifying multiple categories. The differences between these two steps are mainly located at the labeled data for training. Data with two kinds of labels are used in the first dichotomy method, i.e., belong or do not belong to disputes. Data labeled as specific event categories could be used to train the multiple classifier model and classify dispute data into various categories. The details of the categories of dispute incidents are shown as Table 1.

Table 1. Categories of dispute incidents.

No.	Category	Keywords
1	Medical accident	Medical accident, medical disturbance
2	Finance and securities	Security, stock, fraud, cheat
3	Private lending	Borrow money, lend money, IOU
4	Neighborhood dispute	Next door, neighbor, upstairs, downstairs
5	Labor	Salary, wage, earnings, arrears of wages
6	Forest and land	Forest, land, mountain
7	Land expropriation	Resettle, remove, demolition
8	Homestead	Homestead, house site
9	Marriage and family	Domestic violence, divorce, derailment, mistress
10	Economic contract	Refund, price
11	Traffic	Traffic, car accident
12	Others	/

4 Methods of Building KG

Many methods have been proposed to build KG, which are generally classified into two categories, i.e., "top-down" and "down-top". In this paper, we construct our KG system by means of "top-down". We construct schema first, which shows the mainly semantic structure of the KG. Under schema's guidance, we extract information and obtain N-tuples of events. At last, we refine the KG to achieve reliability and scalability. To improve the performance of KG system, graph database is introduced to store KG. Graph database [19] is a storage method which directly uses graph structure to represent and store data, including nodes, relations and attributes. It can reflect the internal structure of KG, which makes querying and storing KG efficiently.

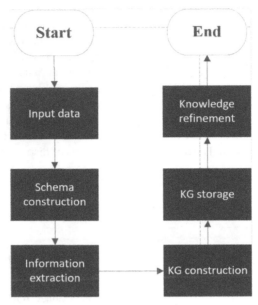

Fig. 4. The flow chart of constructing KG.

Figure 4 shows the flow chart of proposed building method, which works in pipeline. By this means, we create an event-centric KG system focusing on various dispute and conflict events.

4.1 Ontology Building Module

A domain ontology specifically defines the conceptualization, consisting the formal description of concepts, and the relations between concepts [20]. Ontology is the semantic structure of a KG and a pattern constraint on the data making up the KG [21]. Designing and building ontology play an important and fundamental role in constructing KGs. After this step, we could get a clear structure of the KG.

Generally, building ontology is based on domain knowledge, term dictionary and experts' experience in a particular field. Combining with the application scenarios of KGs, we could finally obtain the entity categories, relationships between entities, and the attributes of entities.

Many efforts have been spent building ontology of KGs. The building methods are generally based on experts' experience in field. Processing tools can also be used to automatically extract information from structured and unstructured texts. In this paper, we combine these two methods and use Protégé to build a complete ontology architecture considering the complexity of dispute resolution. Protégé [22] is one of the most popular ontology editors and frameworks for building intelligent systems developed by Stanford university. It is easy to create the ontology of dispute incidents from the top-down by using this tool.

4.2 Event Extraction Module

Methods of extracting event information or features are divided into two categories, the pipeline and the joint way [23]. The pipeline manner usually extracts features one after another, firstly recognize triggers then arguments. The joint way takes the same inputs as the pipeline but outputs triggers and arguments together. Compared to the pipeline method, the joint manner requires more computing resources. To this end, we propose to extract event information from dispute data in pipeline.

Firstly, we extract triggers by way of combining BERT, Bi-LSTM [24] and Conditional Random Fields (CRF) [25, 26]. BERT is first introduced by Google in 2018 and is regarded as a milestone in the NLP field. As an alternative to Word2Vec [27], BERT utilizes Transformer [28] to capture bidirectional relationships in statements more thoroughly. Mask Language Model (MLM) [29] and Next Sentence Prediction (NSP) are used to train multitask. By introducing BERT, we can obtain the vector representations of both words and sentences while preserving the semantic information of words in sentences. In order to avoid loss of context information, we use Bi-LSTM to extract and concatenate features from forward and backward of the inputs. And the task of sequence labeling is completed by training with CRF model. The architecture is shown in Fig. 5. BIESO (B-beginning, I-inside, E-end, S-single word entity and O outside) pattern is used to recognize triggers. As the example in Fig. 5, we recognize "shenli" in Chinese as the trigger of input sentence.

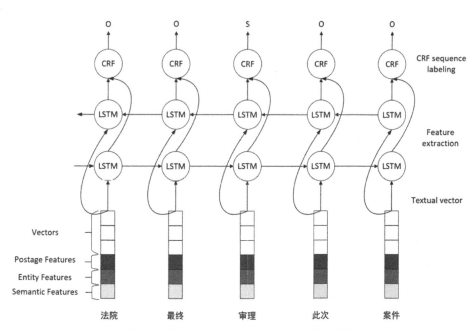

Fig. 5. BERT+Bi-LSTM+CRF model [25, 26].

We define event arguments including subject, object, occurrence time and sites of events. In simple terms, a trigger is usually described by verb. Conversely, arguments can be denoted with noun. Extracting both triggers and arguments makes completely describing events reasonable.

After having the trigger of an event, we continually combine BERT and Conditional-Layer-Norm model [30] to extract arguments. This method was proposed in the iFLY-TEKA.I.2020 event extraction challenge, which was proved to be the best scheme [31, 32]. In this method, sentences to be analyzed and the location of trigger in the text are set to be the inputs. Features are represented by the relative distance between the word and trigger. The relative distance of trigger is 0. The input of Conditional-Layer-Norm model is the output of BERT. The whole process in detail is shown in Fig. 6.

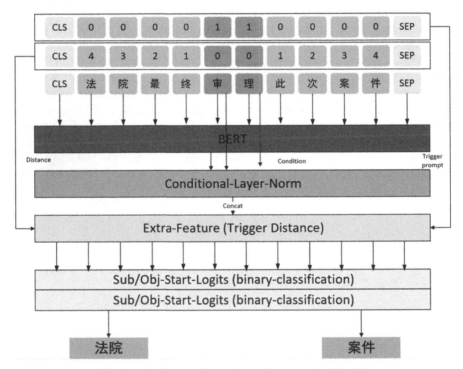

Fig. 6. BERT+Conditional-Layer-Norm model [30, 32].

4.3   Knowledge Graph Refinement Module

Given triggers and arguments of events, we can construct an event-centric KG. But there are inevitably errors or missing items. To verify the correctness and ensure the quality of KG data, we set the KG refinement module after the event extraction module. The methods of KG refinement can be divided by different dimensions, such as the completion or correction of KG data, whether consulting the expert experience, to refine entities or relations or others [33]. Considering the convenience and efficiency of implementation, we combine the knowledge crowdsourcing method [34, 35] and algorithms based on matching rules. In this case, we firstly recognize errors by means of human intelligence. Then filter these errors through whole data in KG using matching rules. For the case of incompletion, we choose crowdsourcing as the primary one considering the accuracy of KG.

5 Conclusions

In this paper, we propose an architecture of a large-scale event-centric KG for dispute resolution covering its full life cycle. By this means, our proposed KG system could be applied in many fields related to dispute events, such as reasoning, sourcing, prediction and disposal. The implementing methods are discussed in detail. Taking advantage of AI and human intelligence, our method can significantly reduce the labor and improve the efficiency of the system. Besides that, our system also has good practical prospect and is obviously referential to engineering.

Funding Statement. Our research was supported by the National Key R&D Program of China under Grant 2021YFC3300500.

Conflicts of Interest. The authors declare that there are no conflicts of interest regarding the publication of this paper.

References

1. Tao, L., Hao, L., Sheng, Z., Yan, K.: Knowledge graph representation reasoning for recommendation system. J. New Media **2**(1), 21–30 (2020)
2. Zhou, H.J., Shen, T.T., Liu, X.L., Zhang, Y.R., P.G.: Knowledge graph: a survey of approaches and applications knowledge graph. J. Artif. Intell. **2**(2), 89–101 (2020)
3. Singhal, A.: Introducing the knowledge graph: things, not strings. Off. Google Blog **5**, 16 (2012)
4. Bollacker, K., Cook, R., Tufts, P.: Freebase: a shared database of structured general human knowledge. In: AAAI, vol. 7, pp. 1962–1963 (2007)
5. Bizer, C., et al.: DBpedia-a crystallization point for the web of data. J. Web Semant. **7**(3), 154–165 (2009)
6. Dong, X., et al.: Knowledge vault: a web-scale approach to probabilistic knowledge fusion. In: Proceedings of the 20th ACM SIGKDD International Conference on Knowledge Discovery and Data Mining, pp. 601–610 (2014)
7. Yoo, S., Jeong, O.: Ep-bot: empathetic chatbot using auto-growing knowledge graph. Comput. Mater. Contin. **67**(3), 2807–2817 (2021)
8. Xu, C., Xu, J.: Provenance method of electronic archives based on knowledge graph in big data environment. J. Inf. Hiding Priv. Prot. **3**(2), 91–99 (2021)
9. Yi, W., Zhe, S., Yifan, Y., Ying, C.: Domain-specific event graph construction methods: a review. Data Anal. Knowl. Discov. **4**(10), 1–13 (2020)
10. Gottschalk, S., Demidova, E.: EventKG: a multilingual event-centric temporal knowledge graph. In: Gangemi, A., et al. (eds.) ESWC 2018. LNCS, vol. 10843, pp. 272–287. Springer, Cham (2018). https://doi.org/10.1007/978-3-319-93417-4_18

11. Cheng, D., Yang, F., Wang, X., Zhang, Y., Zhang, L.: Knowledge graph-based event embedding framework for financial quantitative investments. In: Proceedings of the 43rd International ACM SIGIR Conference on Research and Development in Information Retrieval, pp. 2221–2230 (2020)
12. Zhang, D., Jia, Q., Yang, S., Han, X., Xu, C.: Traditional Chinese medicine automated diagnosis based on knowledge graph reasoning. Comput. Mater. Contin. **71**(1), 159–170 (2022)
13. Rui, Q., Zhenhua, Z.: Application of knowledge map in public safety. Comput. Knowl. Technol. **14**(35), 196–199 (2018)
14. Peng, Z., Yuntao, H., Shimao, M.: Research on construction and application of knowledge graph in public security field. In: Proceedings of the 8th China Conference on Command and Control, Beijing, China, pp. 378–384 (2020)
15. Liyu, S., Jiajun, Q.: Applying police knowledge graph to aid the implementation of smart policing. Digit. Commun. World **7**, 23–24 (2018)
16. Mania, K.: Online dispute resolution: the future of justice. Int. Comp. Jurisprud. **1**(1), 76–86 (2015)
17. Devlin, J., Chang, M.W., Lee, K., Toutanova, K.: Bert: pre-training of deep bidirectional transformers for language understanding. arXiv:1810.04805 (2018)
18. Zhang, Z., Han, X., Liu, Z., Jiang, X., Sun, M., Liu, Q.: Ernie: enhanced language representation with informative entities. arXiv:1905.07129 (2019)
19. Miller, J.J.: Graph database applications and concepts with Neo4j. In: Proceedings of the Southern Association for Information Systems Conference, Atlanta, GA, USA, vol. 2324, no. 36 (2013)
20. Jiang, X., Tan, A.H.: Crctol: a semantic-based domain ontology learning system. J. Am. Soc. Inform. Sci. Technol. **61**(1), 150–168 (2010)
21. Dou, J., Qin, J., Jin, Z., Li, Z.: Knowledge graph based on domain ontology and natural language processing technology for Chinese intangible cultural heritage. J. Vis. Lang. Comput. **48**, 19–28 (2018)
22. Protégé, A.: A free, open-source ontology editor and framework for building intelligent systems (2013). https://protege.stanford.edu/
23. Xiang, W., Bang, W.: A survey of event extraction from text. IEEE Access **7**, 173111–173137 (2019)
24. Huang, Z., Wei X., Kai Y.: Bidirectional LSTM-CRF models for sequence tagging. arXiv:1508.01991 (2015)
25. Zhang, L.: Research on Chinese-Oriented Text Event Extraction. People's Public Security University of China, Beijing (2019)
26. Liu, W., Wang, X., Zhang, Y., Liu, Z.: Automatic-annotation method for emergency text corpus based on bert. Intell. Comput. Appl. **11**(6), 14–19 (2021)
27. Goldberg, Y., Levy, O.: Word2vec explained: deriving Mikolov et al.'s negative sampling word-embedding method. arXiv:1402.3722 (2014)
28. Vaswani, A., et al.: Attention is all you need. In: Advances in Neural Information Processing Systems, pp. 5998–6008 (2017)
29. Wu, X., Zhang, T., Zang, L., Han, J., Hu, S.: "Mask and infill": applying masked language model to sentiment transfer. arXiv:1908.08039 (2019)
30. Su, J.: Conditional text generation based on conditional layer normalization (2021). https://kexue.fm/archives/7124
31. 2021 iFLYTEK A.I. challenge (2021). http://challenge.xfyun.cn/topic/info?type=hotspot
32. WuhuRestaurant: Xf-event-extraction (2020). https://github.com/WuHuRestaurant/xfeventextraction2020Top1
33. Paulheim, H.: Knowledge graph refinement: a survey of approaches and evaluation methods. Semant. Web **8**(3), 489–508 (2017)

34. Cao, M., Zhang, J., Xu, S., Ying, Z.: Knowledge graphs meet crowdsourcing: a brief survey. In: Cloud Computing: 10th EAI International Conference, CloudComp 2020, Qufu, China, December 11–12, 2020, Proceedings, vol. 10, pp. 3–17. Springer, Heidelberg (2021). https://doi.org/10.1007/978-3-030-69992-5_1
35. Acosta, M., Zaveri, A., Simperl, E., Kontokostas, D., Auer, S., Lehmann, J.: Crowdsourcing linked data quality assessment. In: Alani, H., et al. (eds.) ISWC 2013. LNCS, vol. 8219, pp. 260–276. Springer, Heidelberg (2013). https://doi.org/10.1007/978-3-642-41338-4_17

Quantum Fuzzy Least Squares Algorithm for Uncertain Environment

Shipeng Yu[1,2], Yan Chang[1,2(✉)], Shibin Zhang[1,2], and Qirun Wang[3]

[1] School of Cybersecurity, Chengdu University of Information Technology, Chengdu 610225, China
cyttkl@cuit.edu.cn
[2] Advanced Cryptography and System Security Key Laboratory of Sichuan Province, Chengdu 610255, China
[3] School of Engineering and Technology, University of Hertfordshire, Hertford, UK

Abstract. With the development of information technology, modern society has entered the era of big data. Big data means a huge amount of data, as well as the complexity and uncertainty of data. In order to find valuable data efficiently and accurately from the big data environment, researchers use machine learning algorithms to establish relevant data models to predict and classify new data. In the process of establishing the linear system model, the commonly used method is the least square method, which can easily obtain the optimal parameters of the linear system and make the established linear model more accurate. In order to deal with the fuzziness of the data itself and reduce the influence of abnormal data on the linear model, researchers put forward the fuzzy linear model. When the amount of data is increasing, the time required for traditional computers to process data and establish models is increasing. In order to reduce the time of establishing the model, a quantum fuzzy least square method is proposed on the basis of predecessors. The algorithm uses the advantages of quantum computing in data processing to improve the efficiency of fuzzy linear model establishment and reduce the model establishment time. Relevant research and analysis prove the efficiency of the algorithm.

Keywords: Machine learning · Least square method · Linear model · Quantum computing

1 Introduction

With the development of information technology, people's lives have become digital. Modern society will produce a large amount of data every day. The world has entered the era of big data. These huge data are like a treasure, but they are full of uncertainty. We need to extract accurate and valuable data efficiently. Machine learning can help us realize this idea. Machine learning uses computers to quickly process data and establish relevant models to predict and classify new data.

In order to make the output value of the model closest to the actual measured value, the least square method is often used in machine learning to achieve this purpose. The least square method was first used to calculate planetary orbits, and then gradually used in other fields. It finds the best model parameters by minimizing the square sum of the error between the model output value and the actual measured value. The linear function established by the least square method can well represent the relationship between data.

In machine learning, in order to improve the accuracy of the model, it is often necessary to use a large amount of data to train the model. Although this method can make the model more accurate, it also means that the efficiency of model training will be reduced. The speed of modern computer processing data is limited. When the data is increasing, the time of processing these data will increase accordingly. The development of quantum technology has attracted the attention of researchers. Many people put forward the application research [1, 2] related to quantum technology. Compared with traditional computers, quantum computers have the advantage of high computational efficiency. They can often achieve exponential acceleration of data processing.

In 2009, harrow, Hassidim and Lloyd [3] proposed a new quantum algorithm, which can solve linear equations on quantum computers (next called HHL algorithm). The proposal of HHL algorithm makes researchers see the dawn of realizing quantum machine learning algorithm. With the help of HHL algorithm, researchers have proposed quantum support vector machine algorithm [4], quantum principal component analysis algorithm [5, 6], quantum Bayesian algorithm [7] and so on [8–10].

In 2012, Wiebe [11] proposed the quantum least square method for data fitting for the first time. The algorithm can efficiently determine the parameters of the general linear function and obtain a quantum state containing parameters. Researchers have proved that quantum machine learning algorithm accelerates data processing and improves the efficiency of model establishment compared with ordinary machine learning algorithm.

In the process of building machine learning algorithm model, each data point is considered to be determined and its contribution to the model is the same. However, in practical application, the data itself is fuzzy, and its influence on the process of model establishment is different. Shen [12] proposed fuzzy point data based on fuzzy set theory and used it to establish linear function. She gives each data point a fuzzy membership degree to represent the importance of each data point to the whole. Using the least square method, she established a linear model based on fuzzy point data, which is more accurate than the ordinary linear model and reduces the impact of abnormal data points on the model.

According to Shen's idea of fuzzy point data, this paper proposes a quantum fuzzy least square method. The algorithm realizes the quantization of the linear model of fuzzy point data, which makes the process of establishing the linear model faster and more efficient, and the established model is more accurate.

2 Related Work

This section mainly introduces the related technologies used in this paper, including least square method, quantum least square method and fuzzy linear model. They are the essential theoretical basis to complete the algorithm in this paper.

2.1 Least Square Method

When building a linear model, we usually use the least square method for data fitting. For a data set of N points $\{X_{ij}, Y_i\}$, the purpose of fitting is to find a linear function that can well represent the relationship between these discrete data points and establish a related linear model.

Assuming that the fitting function is expressed as,

$$f(x_i) = \sum_{j=1}^{M} x_{ij}\lambda_j \tag{1}$$

We need to substitute each data point in the data set into the function to calculate the fitting parameters. In order to optimize the linear model obtained, we use the least square method to calculate the fitting parameters.

The formula is expressed as,

$$E = |f(x_i) - y_i|^2 \tag{2}$$

where $f(x_i)$ is the output value of the linear model at x_i, and y_i is the actual measured value of the corresponding dependent variable. When x_i is multi-dimensional data, we use a matrix to express the formula. It as follows.

$$E = |X\lambda - Y|^2 \tag{3}$$

where Y is the column vector containing all y_i, X is a matrix containing all x_{ij}, and λ is a column vector containing all λ_j. When $E = 0$, the parameters obtained are optimal. If $X^T X$ is reversible, then the least squares estimate of the parameters can be obtained, that is,

$$\lambda = \left(X^T X\right)^{-1} X^T Y \tag{4}$$

2.2 Quantum Least Squares Method

The quantum least square method is to use a quantum computer to realize the formula $\lambda = \left(X^T X\right)^{-1} X^T Y$ to obtain a quantum state $|\lambda\rangle$ similar to λ.

The first step of the algorithm is to encode the Y value into the quantum probability amplitude as input. For non-Hermitian matrix X, define an isometry super operator as follows.

$$I(X) = \begin{pmatrix} 0 & X \\ X^T & 0 \end{pmatrix} \tag{5}$$

$I(X)$ is the Hermitian matrix containing all the information of X. There is a new isometric super operator as follows.

$$A = \begin{pmatrix} X^T X & 0 \\ 0 & XX^T \end{pmatrix} = I(X^T)^2 \tag{6}$$

Then the quantum least squares estimate of the fitting parameters is,

$$|\lambda\rangle = A^{-1} I\left(X^T\right) |Y\rangle \tag{7}$$

2.3 Fuzzy Least Squares Method

We will first introduce a matrix operation that is not commonly used. It's Hadamard. For two matrices of the same order, their Hadamard product is the product of the elements at the same position of the matrix.

Set $A, B \in \mathbb{C}^{m \times n}$, and $A = \{a_{ij}\}, B = \{b_{ij}\}$.

$$A \circ B = \begin{bmatrix} a_{11}b_{11} & \cdots & a_{1n}b_{1n} \\ \vdots & \ddots & \vdots \\ a_{m1}b_{m1} & \cdots & a_{mn}b_{mn} \end{bmatrix} \tag{8}$$

When fitting data points, the appearance of abnormal data points will have a bad influence on data fitting. In order to reduce the influence of abnormal data points and make the fitting accuracy more accurate, it is necessary to introduce fuzzy membership μ_i into the training data.

The degree of membership indicates the importance or confidence of the corresponding data point to the whole. Normal data points will be assigned a higher degree of membership, and abnormal data points will be assigned a lower degree of membership.

Suppose that x is an M-dimensional independent variable, y is a one-dimensional dependent variable, and (x_i, y_i) are training samples. According to the importance of each training data to the whole, we give its fuzzy membership degree $\mu_i (0 \leq \mu_i \leq 1)$. Then $((x_i, y_i), \mu_i)$ can be called the fuzzy point, $\{(x_i, y_i), \mu_i : i = 1, 2, \cdots, n\}$ is the fuzzy point set.

Assume that there are training data points $\{x_i, y_i\}(x_i = \{x_{i1}, \cdots, x_{im}\})$ and their corresponding fuzzy membership. Our fitting function as follows.

$$\mu \circ Y = (\mu, \cdots, \mu)_m \circ (X\lambda) \tag{9}$$

In the above formula, $\mu = (\mu_1, \mu_2, \cdots, \mu_n)^T$, $Y = (y_1, y_2, \cdots, y_n)^T$, $\lambda = (\lambda_1, \lambda_2, \cdots, \lambda_m)^T$ and X is an $N \times M$ matrix.

In the formula, "$\circ$" represents the product of the corresponding elements between the matrices, namely the Hadamard product.

Calculate the minimum weighted residual sum of squares as follows.

$$E = |\mu \circ Y - (\mu, \cdots, \mu)_m \circ (X\lambda)|^2 \tag{10}$$

The least square estimate of λ is,

$$\lambda = \left[((\mu, \cdots, \mu)_m \circ X)^T ((\mu, \cdots, \mu)_m \circ X) \right]^{-1} ((\mu, \cdots, \mu)_m \circ X)^T (\mu \circ Y) \tag{11}$$

We use a diagonal matrix to represent μ', which is expressed as follows.

$$\mu' = \begin{bmatrix} \mu_1 & \cdots & 0 \\ \vdots & \ddots & \vdots \\ 0 & \cdots & \mu_n \end{bmatrix} = diag(\mu_1, \mu_2, \cdots, \mu_n) \tag{12}$$

Equation 11 can be expressed as follows.

$$\lambda = \left[(\mu'X)^T (\mu'X) \right]^{-1} (\mu'X)^T (\mu'Y) \tag{13}$$

3 Quantum Fuzzy Least Squares Algorithm

In general, the data matrices generated in practical applications are not all Hermitian matrices, so we need to process the relevant data matrix to make it a Hermitian matrix in order to perform Hamiltonian simulation [13] on it and apply it to a quantum computer. For non-Hermitian matrix X, the processing method in HHL is expressed as follows.

$$C = \begin{pmatrix} 0 & X \\ X^T & 0 \end{pmatrix} \tag{14}$$

In Wiebe's article, it is further described as using the isometric super operator I to represent the Hermite operator, and its expression is shown in Eq. (5). In addition, Eq. (6) is introduced to represent the corresponding operator. By introducing these two super operators, the data matrix can be transformed accordingly.

We first need to prepare the input quantum states of the algorithm. The input quantum state is expressed as follows.

$$|\mu'Y\rangle = \sum_{p=M+1}^{M+N} \mu_i y_i |p\rangle / |\mu'Y| \tag{15}$$

It is a normalized quantum state. We use amplitude encoding to store the data $\mu'Y$ on the amplitude value of the input quantum state.

In order to apply unitary operators in quantum circuits, this paper introduces the isometric super-operators I and A. And the corresponding expression are represented as,

$$I\left((\mu'X)^T\right) = \begin{pmatrix} 0 & (\mu'X)^T \\ \mu'X & 0 \end{pmatrix} \tag{16}$$

$$A = \begin{pmatrix} (\mu'X)^T(\mu'X) & 0 \\ 0 & \mu'X(\mu'X)^T \end{pmatrix} = I((\mu'X)^T)^2 \tag{17}$$

Firstly, $I\left((\mu'X)^T\right)$ needs to be applied to the quantum state $|\mu'Y\rangle$. This requires quantum simulation, because $I\left((\mu'X)^T\right)$ is not a unitary operator, but a Hermitian operator. We use quantum simulation to convert $I\left((\mu'X)^T\right)$ into a unitary operator as follows,

$$exp(-iI\left((\mu'X)^T\right)t_0/T) \tag{18}$$

We assume that α_i is the eigenvalue of $I\left((\mu'X)^T\right)$, and v_i is the corresponding eigenvector.

Then We can get quantum states $|\mu'Y\rangle = \sum_{i=1}^N \beta_i |v_i\rangle$. Perform phase estimation [14, 15] to get the quantum state $\sum_{i=1}^N \beta_i |v_i\rangle |\tilde{\alpha}_i\rangle$, where $\tilde{\alpha}_i$ is the estimated value of α_i. Note that in this step, we need to multiply each eigenvalue instead of dividing by each eigenvalue.

Add a qubit $|0\rangle$ and perform a controlled flip to make it change from $|0\rangle$ to $\sqrt{1 - C^2\tilde{\alpha}_i^2}|0\rangle + C\tilde{\alpha}_i|1\rangle$, where $C \in O(max|\alpha_i|)^{-1}$. And then All quantum states become as follows,

$$\sum_{i=1}^{N} \left(\sqrt{1 - C^2\tilde{\alpha}_i^2}|0\rangle + C\tilde{\alpha}_i|1\rangle \right) \beta_i|v_i\rangle|\tilde{\alpha}_i\rangle \tag{19}$$

Then perform the inverse phase estimation and measure the auxiliary qubit. If the measurement result is $|1\rangle$, we get a quantum state similar to $I((\mu'X)^T)|\mu'Y\rangle$.

We use the quantum state obtained in the previous step as the input of the HHL algorithm, and convert $A = I((\mu'X)^T)^2$ to unitary operation. We finish the algorithm by using the HHL algorithm, and the final result is $|\lambda\rangle = A^{-1}I((\mu'X)^T)|\mu'Y\rangle$.

Liu and Zhang [16] provides a new idea to calculate the parameter fitting problem of linear equations. They regard $(X^TX)^{-1}X^T$ as a whole X^+, which is the Moore–Penrose pseudo-inverse of X. Their algorithm is not the same as the Wiebe's algorithm, but more like the HHL algorithm. Their algorithm reduces the time complexity of solving the parameters, so it shows better performance. Drawing on his ideas, we further improved the algorithm of this article.

Note that the isometric super operator $A = I(X^T)^2$, so $A^{-1} = I(X^T)^{-2}$. In this article, it should be expressed as,

$$A^{-1} = I((\mu'X)^T)^{-2} \tag{20}$$

$$A^{-1}I\left((\mu'X)^T\right) = I((\mu'X)^T)^{-2}I\left((\mu'X)^T\right) = I((\mu'X)^T)^{-1} \tag{21}$$

The first step is still to prepare the input quantum state of the algorithm $|\mu'Y\rangle = \sum_{p=M+1}^{M+N} \mu_iy_i|p\rangle/|\mu'Y|$, which satisfies the normalization.

The second step is to perform phase estimation, transform the Hermitian matrix $I((\mu'X)^T)^{-1}$ into a unitary operator $exp(iI((\mu'X)^T)t_0/T)$, and we get quantum states $|\mu'Y\rangle = \sum_{i=1}^{N} \beta_i|v_i\rangle$. We assume that α_i is the eigenvalue of $I\left((\mu'X)^T\right)$, and v_i is the corresponding eigenvector. After this step, the eigenvalue of $I((\mu'X)^T)^{-1}$ is stored in the clock register. In the entire quantum system, all quantum states are in $\sum_{i=1}^{N} \beta_i|v_i\rangle|\tilde{\alpha}_i\rangle$.

Add an auxiliary qubit, which stores a quantum state $|0\rangle$. We use the clock register as the control bit to flip the auxiliary qubit. The quantum state obtained after the inversion is expressed as,

$$\sqrt{1 - \frac{C^2}{\tilde{\alpha}_i^2}}|0\rangle + \frac{C}{\tilde{\alpha}_i}|1\rangle \tag{22}$$

At this time, all quantum states in the three quantum registers are expressed as follows,

$$\sum_{i=1}^{N} \left(\sqrt{1 - \frac{C^2}{\tilde{\alpha}_i^2}}|0\rangle + \frac{C}{\tilde{\alpha}_i}|1\rangle \right) \beta_i|v_i\rangle|\tilde{\alpha}_i\rangle \tag{23}$$

The next step is to use the inverse phase estimation to cancel the calculation and restore the eigenvalues $\tilde{\alpha}_i$ stored in the clock register to $|0\rangle$. The purpose of this step is to resolve the entanglement between the quantum state in the clock register and the input quantum state.

The last step is to measure the auxiliary register. If the measured result is $|1\rangle$, then the quantum state retained in the input register is the result we want.

In addition, we note that the input of our quantum algorithm is the result of multiplying μ' and Y. If we consider the time complexity of the input data calculation process, we can use quantum algorithms to further reduce the time complexity of the input data calculation process.

Then the expression of our entire algorithm should be expressed as follows.

$$|\lambda\rangle = I((\mu'X)^T)^{-1}\mu'|Y\rangle \tag{24}$$

Firstly, we should prepare the input quantum state $|Y\rangle$, and it's y in the dataset. Then convert the Hermitian matrix μ' into a unitary operator, which acts on the input quantum state. According to the previous method, we perform phase estimation, controlled flipping, and inverse phase estimation. Finally, the auxiliary qubits are measured, and the resulting quantum state $\mu'|Y\rangle$ is obtained. Then the quantum state $\mu'|Y\rangle$ obtained in the previous step is used as the input quantum state, and the HHL algorithm is performed to obtain the final result. The quantum circuit diagram can be represented as Fig. 1.

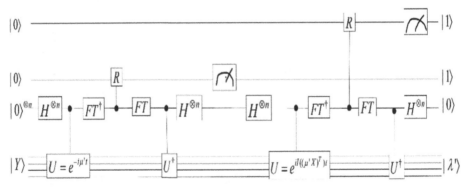

Fig. 1. Quantum circuit diagram mainly includes phase estimation, controlled flip, inverse phase estimation and measurement auxiliary qubits.

The whole quantum circuit diagram can be divided into two parts. The first part is to apply μ' to the input quantum state. Firstly, the n qubits are passed through n quantum H gates to obtain an equilibrium state as follows.

$$|\varphi\rangle = \frac{1}{2^{n/2}} \sum_{z=0}^{n/2-1} |z\rangle \tag{25}$$

The input quantum state stores the eigenvalue of μ' on the equilibrium quantum state $|\varphi\rangle$ through a related unitary operation, and then performs the inverse Fourier transform. We take the n-bit quantum state as the control bit and flip the $|0\rangle$ state in the auxiliary register. After the flip is completed, the Fourier transform and inverse unitary operation are performed. Finally, H gate are used to change n qubits into $|0\rangle$ state. The last step of this part is the measurement of auxiliary qubit. If the measurement result is quantum state $|0\rangle$, we can perform the second part of the quantum circuit.

The second part of the quantum circuit diagram is similar to the first part, except that the unitary operation in the second part is different from the first part. The unitary operation in the first part is obtained according to μ', while the unitary operation in the second part is obtained according to $I((\mu'X)^T)^{-1}$. In the first part, the state $|0\rangle$ of N qubits is finally restored to the original quantum state, we can continue to use them in the second part. In the whole quantum circuit diagram, their final state and initial state are the same and do not change. The last part of the second part is the measurement of auxiliary qubits. When the measured result is $|1\rangle$, the quantum state in the input qubit register is the result we want to get.

4 Analysis of Algorithms

In the previous section, we only introduced the general process of the algorithm, and did not analyze the complexity and accuracy of the algorithm. Next, we will analyze the algorithm to prove the superiority of the algorithm.

4.1 Time Complexity Analysis

As mentioned earlier, we are targeting fuzzy data, that is, a data set with fuzzy membership. In this data set, except for the data obtained from actual observations, each data is assigned a fuzzy membership degree. This means that we first need to process the data and multiply the fuzzy membership with the observed data. In this step, μ' is an $N \times N$ diagonal matrix, X is an $N \times M$ matrix, and Y is an N column vector. Because μ' is a diagonal matrix, the rest of the elements are all 0 except for the elements on the diagonal. When we calculate $\mu'X$ and $\mu'Y$, we only need to calculate that the elements in the diagonal matrix are not 0, which can effectively reduce the time complexity of processing data. Therefore, in the data preprocessing stage, the algorithm complexity is expressed as follows.

$$O(NM) \tag{26}$$

In the quantum algorithm, in order to improve the probability of success, we should use amplitude amplification to effectively reduce the number of repetitions of the algorithm. The complexity of quantum algorithm should be the time of simulation multiplied by the number of repetitions. The Hamiltonian simulation time is expressed as follows.

$$O(log(N)s^3\kappa/\epsilon) \tag{27}$$

In the above formula, κ is the condition number of $\mu'X$, s represents the sparsity of the matrix and is the maximum value of non-zero elements in any row and column, and ϵ is the maximum allowed distance between the result obtained by the quantum algorithm and the exact solution.

When we input $|\mu'Y\rangle$ as the quantum state of the quantum algorithm, we use amplitude amplification to reduce the number of repetitions. At this time, the complexity of the quantum algorithm is expressed as follows.

$$O(log(N)s^3\kappa^2/\epsilon) \tag{28}$$

If only $|Y\rangle$ is used as the input of the quantum algorithm, amplitude amplification does not bring benefits. Because the algorithm first needs to obtain $\mu'|Y\rangle$. The complexity of the quantum algorithm is expressed as follows.

$$O(log(N)s^3\kappa^4/\epsilon) \tag{29}$$

Although the complexity of quantum algorithm is improved, the time of data preprocessing is eliminated.

4.2 Accuracy Analysis

Most of the existing quantum algorithms are based on HHL algorithm, and this paper is no exception. Therefore, the correctness analysis of this paper is closely related to the results of HHL algorithm. In HHL algorithm, the quantum state obtained by the algorithm is similar to the desired result. The result obtained by our algorithm is also a quantum state similar to λ. Compared with the quantum least square fitting algorithm, this algorithm introduces fuzzy point data, which can effectively reduce the impact of abnormal data on the model and improve the accuracy of the model.

5 Concluding Remarks

This paper presents a quantum fuzzy least squares algorithm, which is very helpful to establish the relevant fuzzy linear model.

By introducing fuzzy membership degree into traditional data, fuzzy linear model is more accurate than traditional linear model. Using the acceleration of quantum computing, the algorithm in this paper can make the fuzzy linear model more efficient in the process of processing data and establishing the model.

With the continuous development of quantum computing technology, more quantum algorithms will appear. We hope that the least square method can have more applications in quantum algorithms.

Acknowledgement. In the research process of this article, many people provided help. Thanks to Associate Professor Yan Lili and Dr. Lin Chen for their help in the research of this article. Thanks to everyone in the laboratory, we had a fruitful discussion together.

Funding Statement. This work is supported by the National Natural Science Foundation of China (No. 62076042), the Key Research and Development Project of Sichuan Province (No. 2021YFSY0012, No. 2020YFG0307, No. 2021YFG0332), the Science and Technology Innovation Project of Sichuan (No. 2020017), the Key Research and Development Project of Chengdu (No. 2019-YF05-02028-GX), the Innovation Team of Quantum Security Communication of Sichuan Province (No. 17TD0009), the Academic and Technical Leaders Training Funding Support Projects of Sichuan Province (No. 2016120080102643).

References

1. Yan, L.L., Chang, Y., Zhang, S.B., et al.: A quantum multi-proxy weak blind signature scheme based on entanglement swapping. Int. J. Theor. Phys. **56**(2), 634–642 (2017)
2. Chang, Y., Zhang, S.B., Yan, L.L., et al.: Device-independent quantum key distribution protocol based on hyper-entanglement. Comput. Mater. Contin. **65**(1), 879–896 (2020)
3. Harrow, A.W., Hassidim, A., Lloyd, S.: Quantum algorithm for linear systems of equations. Phys. Rev. Lett. **103**(15), 150502 (2009)
4. Rebentrost, P., Mohseni, M., Lloyd, S.: Quantum support vector machine for big data classification. Phys. Rev. Lett. **113**(13), 130503 (2014)
5. Lloyd, S., Mohseni, M., Rebentrost, P.: Quantum principal component analysis. Nat. Phys. **10**(9), 631–633 (2014)
6. Lin, J., Bao, W.S., Zhang, S., et al.: An improved quantum principal component analysis algorithm based on the quantum singular threshold method. Phys. Lett. A **383**(24), 2862–2868 (2019)
7. Low, G.H., Yoder, T.J., Chuang, I.L.: Quantum inference on Bayesian networks. Phys. Rev. A **89**(6), 1–11 (2014)
8. Zhang, Z., Fitzsimons, J.K., Fitzsimons, J.F.: Quantum-assisted Gaussian process regression. Phys. Rev. A **99**(5), 052331 (2019)
9. Tang, E.: A quantum-inspired classical algorithm for recommendation systems. In: Proceedings of the 51st Annual ACM SIGACT Symposium on Theory of Computing, pp. 217–228. Association for Computing Machinery, Phoenix (2019)
10. Dong, D., Chen, C., Li, H., Tarn, T.J.: Quantum reinforcement learning. IEEE Trans. Syst. Man Cybern. Part B (Cybern.) **38**(5), 1207–1220 (2008)
11. Wiebe, N., Braun, D., Lloyd, S.: Quantum algorithm for data fitting. Phys. Rev. Lett. **109**(5), 1–5 (2012)
12. Shen, J.: Linear regression analysis based on fuzzy point data. J. Nat. Sci. Heilongjiang Univ. **24**(3), 361–364 (2007)
13. Berry, D.W., Ahokas, G., Cleve, R., Sanders, B.C.: Efficient quantum algorithms for simulating sparse Hamiltonians. Commun. Math. Phys. **270**(2), 359–371 (2007)
14. Cleve, R., Ekert, A., Macchiavello, C., Mosca, M.: Quantum algorithms revisited. Proc. R. Soc. London. Ser. A: Math. Phys. Eng. Sci. **454**(1969), 339–354 (1998)
15. Luis, A., Peřina, J.: Optimum phase-shift estimation and the quantum description of the phase difference. Phys. Rev. A **54**(5), 4564 (1996)
16. Liu, Y., Zhang, S.: Fast quantum algorithms for least squares regression and statistic leverage scores. Theoret. Comput. Sci. **657**, 38–47 (2017)

Research on Instruction Pipeline Optimization Oriented to RISC-V Vector Instruction Set

Zhen Zhang[1] and Xin Yu[2(✉)]

[1] Beijing Key Laboratory of Information Service Engineering, Beijing Union University, Beijing 100101, China
[2] College of Urban Rail Transit and Logistics, Beijing Union University, Beijing 100101, China
18810536705@163.com

Abstract. Traditional general-purpose processors are scalar processors, and only one data result is obtained when an instruction is executed. But nowadays, there are a lot of data parallel computing operations in deep learning algorithms. At this time, it is particularly important to improve the parallelism of data so as to improve the performance of operations. SIMD technology can significantly improve parallelism. As an open source simplified instruction set architecture, RISC-V has released a stable SIMD instruction set version. On these foundations, this article will explore the optimization of data parallelism on the XT-910 chip based on the RISC-V architecture of PingtouGe Semiconductor, and conduct instruction pipeline optimization research to fit its pipeline architecture, reduce latency, and improve instruction throughput. The experimental results show that after using the instruction pipeline optimization method, the performance of the memory copy algorithm on the RISC-V platform under different data scales is improved by 1.52 times compared with that before the optimization.

Keywords: Deep learning algorithm · SIMD technology · RISC-V · Data parallelism · Instruction pipeline optimization

1 Introduction

Nowadays, the chip industry is a strategic industry at the national science and technology level, and it is the driving force for the development of the information industry, while the development of my country's SOC chip industry is lagging. In today's chip field, where demand from all walks of life is increasing day by day, ARM processors occupies a high market in the embedded field, and Intel x86 architecture processors have a monopoly in the PC and server fields. Due to commercial reasons and intellectual property protection, traditional instruction set architectures such as ARM and X86 architectures require high licensing fees. The RISC-V [1] architecture instruction set is an open source instruction set architecture designed and released by the University of California, Berkeley in 2014 [2]. Academic institutions or commercial organizations can use it freely, which also allows the RISC-V instruction set architecture to build microprocessors in almost all fields by combining or extending the instruction set, which can meet the needs of various

X. Sun et al. (Eds.): ICAIS 2022, CCIS 1586, pp. 514–523, 2022.
https://doi.org/10.1007/978-3-031-06767-9_43

applications from microcontrollers to supercomputers [3]. The competitive landscape of processor architecture dominated by ARM and Intel x86 will be greatly changed due to the emergence of RISC-V.

One of the most important design aspects of the processor is the pipeline design. The depth of the pipeline seriously affects the processing speed of the processor and the tension of each processing module. At present, the hardware scheduling capability of high-performance processors has been very strong, and the main frequency has been very high. Therefore, hardware designers hope that the instruction set can be structured and simplified in order to design processors with higher frequencies and lower power consumption. The early classic pipeline is a five-stage pipeline, which are fetching, decoding, executing, fetching, and writing back. The length of the pipeline not only affects the throughput rate, but also affects the area overhead. The development of pipeline stages in recent years is shown in Fig. 1.

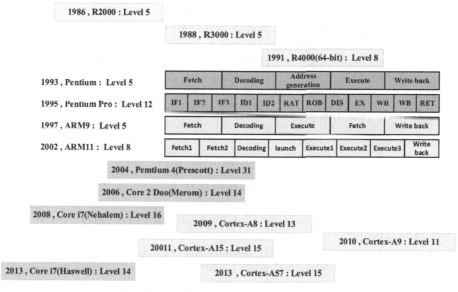

Fig. 1. The development of pipeline stages.

Modern high-performance processors tend to have a deeper level of pipeline than the earliest processors. The more stages of the pipeline, the finer the pipeline is cut, the smaller the hardware logic contained in each stage of the pipeline, and the better the throughput performance, which is the positive meaning of the deepening of the pipeline [4]. However, due to the deepening of the pipeline depth, more registers will be consumed and more area overhead will be brought. On the other hand, pipeline hazards and pipeline bubbles are more likely to occur. For branch prediction failures, only the method of flushing the pipeline can be used to solve the problem, which greatly wastes processor performance.

Therefore, for the RISC-V processor architecture with fixed pipeline depth, this article will adopt the method of instruction pipeline optimization to minimize the occurrence of pipeline cavitation and pipeline risk. Based on the above background, this article analyzes the XT-910 architecture pipeline stages, and uses the RISC-V instruction set to optimize the three instruction sequences of addressing, decoding and execution of the instruction pipeline in the algorithm process, and finally realizes the RISC Research on the optimization of instruction pipeline under - V architecture, and verify the optimization effect, and found that its algorithm performance has been improved by 1.5 times.

The rest of this article is organized as follows. The second section summarizes the RISC-V architecture and related work content. The third section introduces the specific method of instruction pipeline optimization and the optimization steps. The fourth section introduces the experimental platform and analyzes the optimized performance in detail. Finally, the conclusion of this article is drawn.

2   Background and Related Work

RISC-V is now the most popular choice for academic researchers and hardware company engineers. The most important reason is its open source spirit. These open source licenses have encouraged many researchers to devote themselves to developing a mature ecosystem for RISC-V. Therefore, more and more people are willing to join the community. Undeniably, it is compatible with X86, ARM, MIPS [5–7], PowerPC, SPARC [8–12] openRISC [13–15] As well as other ISAs under the popular GPU and DSP, RISC-V is still in its infancy. We have seen many RISC-V efforts have made progress, some of which are highlighted below:

ETH Zurich and the University of Bologna provide three flavors of the core of the RISC-V PULP platform [16]-RI5CY (32-bit, 4-stage pipeline), zero-risk (32-bit, 2-stage pipeline) and Ariane (64-bit, 6-stage pipeline) [17]. In addition, IIT-Madras has been committed to developing a series of Shakti RISC-V processors, from 3-stage pipelined ordered cores to unordered multi-threaded cores with target operating frequencies of 1.5–2.5 GHz [18, 19].

The RISC-V programming model assumes a model composed of three types of registers, each type of register has its own independent memory. The kernel program runs in the register memory, so it provides the functions of allocating, releasing and copying the device memory, as well as the function of transferring data between the register memory and the chip memory. However, there are also memories with different transmission speeds. Reasonable use of registers to increase instruction throughput and reduce time delay is the key to improving transmission efficiency.

After the pipeline processor splits the instructions into different stages, if the hardware used in each stage is independent of each other, then registers can be added after each stage of the corresponding hardware circuit, thereby enabling the pipeline processor. The whole process is: filling the assembly line—filling the assembly line—emptying the assembly line. In the pipeline filling stage, all hardware is in working condition, theoretically the performance is 5 times that of non-pipeline.

But the actual application benefits are not so big. The hardware used in each stage is not actually independent of each other; the added registers will also increase the delay; the cycle division of each stage is also difficult to be consistent, which will cause more pipeline hazards, such as an instruction that needs to use the previous instruction The result of the calculation, but the result has not been written back. This situation is called a data hazard. In order to solve this type of hazard, the processor will use empty instructions to wait, which will increase the delay and produce pipeline cavitation.

However, logically, the parallel processing of processors on RISC-V is through vector computing technology, which also increases the parallelism of computing by extending the register bit width; but the difference is that vector registers are variable-length registers. It is not embedded in the opcode like SIMD. Therefore, the RISC-V vector processor is pipelined, that is, the instruction pipeline optimization processing can also achieve the effect of pipeline parallelization. But from the hardware point of view, in fact, not all processors are capable of pipeline execution. As far as possible, instruction pipeline optimization should be used to reduce pipeline cavitation as much as possible. The 32 vector registers form the vector pipeline. The vector pipeline is suitable for execution and needs to meet the following two conditions: 1. 32 vector registers are free 2. All current instruction parameters are ready, and there is no memory access violation.

The experiment platform of this article uses XT-910—RISC-V architecture processor. Before 2020, the sifiveu74 core [20] is the world's highest performance RISC-V application processor, which can reach 5.1 CoreMark/MHz like the ARM Cortex-A55 core [21]. The XT-910 is a 12 nm 64-bit RISC-V processor with 16 cores and a frequency

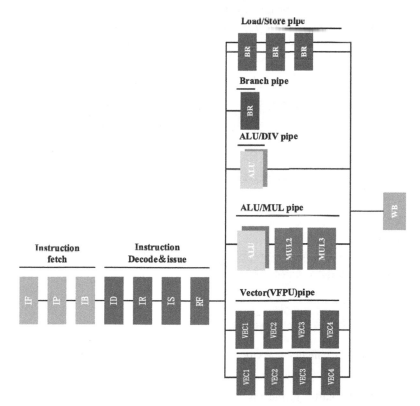

Fig. 2. 12-stage pipeline in XT-910 core.

of 2.5 GHz. XT-910 supports 9–12 deep pipeline architecture, out-of-order execution, and XT-910 implements RV64GCV, which means that it supports basic 64-bit RISC-V ISA (RV64G) and supports compact 16-bit wide instructions (C) And standard 32-bit wide instructions. It has the characteristic of RISC-V vector expansion. It also includes more than 50 non-standard instructions to speed up various tasks. The tool chain has also been optimized to a large extent to improve efficiency and performance. XT-910 processor achieves 7.1 CoreMark/MHz, which is 40% faster than u74.The pipeline of theXT-910core is shown in Fig. 2. The "frontend" of the pipeline consists of 7 stages.

3   Instruction Pipeline Optimization Method

The way to improve data parallelism in algorithm optimization methods is vector computing technology. Like the traditional SIMD technology, it also expands the register bit width to increase the parallelism of the calculation; but the difference is that the vector register is a variable-length register, not embedded in the opcode like SIMD. The representative of vector technology is RISC-V V extended instruction set and ARM's SVE architecture.

The V extension of the RISC-V vector instruction set uses the Single Instruction Multiple Data (SIMD) ISA set. The most critical part of the V extension is its configurable vector unit, which allows the programmer to set the number of vector elements and the supported element width, as shown in Fig. 3. Although the V extension specification is still in progress. V extended version 0.7 [22] is sufficient to build prototypes for performance exploration research experiments.

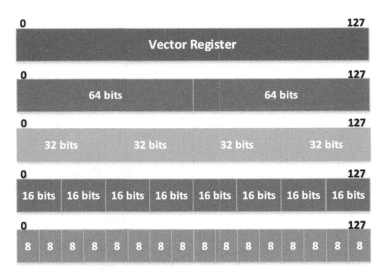

Fig. 3. Configurable vector register length of RISC-V V extension.

In the RISC-V platform, the instruction pipeline optimization method is used to improve data parallelism. Instruction pipeline optimization in the optimization of the memory copy algorithm, under the premise that the register conditions are free, by dividing the work steps, optimizing the instruction sequence, so that the hardware is in a fully loaded state, so as to improve the computational efficiency and achieve the effect of the instruction pipeline. That is, when the memory access address of the memory access instruction in the loop is not calculated, the calculation instruction is placed after the first memory access instruction, so that the address phase of the second instruction is delayed by one clock cycle or a no-operation instruction is inserted after the jump instruction. Wait for the jump address to be calculated, and then take the address, in order to achieve the effect of pipeline processing data. The RISC-V architecture, like the traditional SIMD technology, also increases the parallelism of calculations by extending the register bit width; but the difference is that the vector register is a variable-length register, not embedded in the opcode like SIMD. Therefore, this paper refers to the more popular algorithm optimization methods [23–27]. To analyze the implementation of instruction pipeline optimization, and to achieve consistency in software and hardware co-optimization.

The reason why instruction pipeline optimization can improve performance is that its essence is to take advantage of parallelism in time. It allows instructions that should be executed sequentially to be parallelized in time to a certain extent to avoid excessive pipeline cavitation. The optimization of instruction pipeline on the RISC-V platform will make the hardware and software more decoupled, and it will be more friendly to its programmers. It is a technical model of software and hardware collaboration. The instruction pipeline optimization methods of different architectures are also different. For details, please see Table 1.

Table 1. Algorithm example.

Algorithm 1 Memory copy algorithm after optimization of instruction pipeline of different architectures	
ARM Neon_memory copy	RISC-V_memory copy
loop_start:	
subs x2,x2,#96	
ldp q3,q4,[x1,#0]	Loop_start:
stp q3,q4,[x0,#0]	vsetvli t0, a2, e8, m4
ldp q3,x4,[x1,#32]	vlb.v v0, (a1)
stp q3,x4,[x0,#32]	add a1, a1, t0
ldp q3,x4,[x1,#64]	sub a2, a2, t0
stp q3,x4,[x0,#64]	vsb.v v0, (a3)
add x1,x1,#96	add a3, a3, t0
add x0,x0,#96	bnez a2, Loop_start
bgt loop_start	

Algorithm 1 is a typical application memory copy based on the ARM Neon instruction and the RISC-V V instruction. For the code part of ARM, LDP and STP are respectively designated as 128-bit wide load and store operations, and each cycle operates 96 bytes. As for the RICS-V code, the above-mentioned loop control is completely realized by the vsetvli instruction and the sub instruction. The software does not need to display how much data is calculated in each loop, but only needs to give the total data amount. Even if the length of the vector register in the hardware is changed from 128 to 256, the above code does not require any modification, which is more in line with its pipeline architecture. This is to fit the instruction pipeline optimization of the RISC-V architecture.

From the above comparison, it can be seen that since each architecture instruction set limits the data operation bit width, each time the hardware expands the degree of parallelism, it means the instruction expansion and the code rewriting, which will add more extra labor to the developer. Also very unfriendly. However, with the continuous expansion of processor application fields, the demand for data hardware parallelism is also increasing, and the upgrade of hardware architecture parallelism seems to be an inevitable trend. Looking at the development of the Intel SIMD instruction set, from 64 bits in MMX to 128 bits in the SSE series, 256 bits in AVX and AVX2, and 512 bits in the latest AVX-512, the bit width of registers has been expanded in just 20 years. 8 times. This is no small task for software adaptation.

Therefore, optimizing the instruction flow of the RISC-V instruction set, which has the advantages of variable length and convenient software maintenance, is in line with the research progress. However, since the operand itself does not specify the operand type, it needs to be specifically set by the vsetvli instruction. When frequent data type switching occurs, it will inevitably bring more instructions. In addition, in addition to the operation data type, the vector length (VL) is also set non-display through the vsetvli instruction. In a superscalar out-of-order processor, if the vector length is frequently changed, it may bring potential performance loss. In addition, the development time of the RISC-V V instruction set is relatively short. Compared with the SIMD instruction set developed for many years, such as ARM Neon, it is still lacking in the richness of instruction functions. Therefore, when encountering some specific scenarios, More instructions need to be used to implement the corresponding functions, which further reduces the overall performance. At this time, the above-mentioned instruction pipeline optimization is required to improve instruction flexibility and performance.

4   Performance Evaluation

The instruction pipeline optimization in this article is implemented on the XT-910 processor of the RISC-V architecture, which supports the basic 64-bit RISC-V ISA (RV64G), and supports the compact 16-bit wide instructions (C) and the standard 32-bit wide instruction. It has the characteristic of RISC-V vector expansion. It also includes more than 50 non-standard instructions to speed up various tasks. The specific configuration is shown in Table 2.

Regarding the performance of instruction pipeline optimization, it can be obtained from the performance analysis graph below. After the instruction pipeline optimization, the performance of the algorithm has been significantly improved. Not only does it allow instructions to operate in every clock cycle, but also through instructions reduce the redundancy of memory access operations and greatly improve the performance of the algorithm.

Table 2. XT-910core configurations.

Feature	Configuration
Core number per cluster	1, 2, 4
L1 data cache	32 KB,64 KB
L1 instruction cache	32 KB,64 KB
L2 cache size	256 KB–8 MB
Vector extension	Yes/no

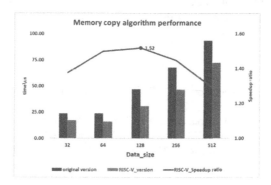

Fig. 4. Memory copy algorithm performance.

It can be seen from Fig. 4 that when the data size exceeds 128 bit, the efficiency is reduced after optimization occurs. The reason is that the register is 128-bit, and can only process 128-bit data at the same time. When the register size is exceeded, the algorithm will fall into problems such as waiting for memory access and re-addressing.

But when the data size is less than 128 bits, the algorithm optimization effect under the RISC-V platform is more obvious. The reason is that the RISC-V architecture has a 128-bit register bit number. Under the 128-bit specification, the register can be fully loaded without clock waiting and resource waste.

The optimal acceleration effect of 128-bit scale is higher than that of other scales. The highest speedup ratio reaches 1.52 times, and the speedup is the best on this platform.

The optimization results show the importance and necessity of instruction pipeline optimization on RISC-V; at the same time, the test results of the optimization method also show that parallel optimization based on RISC-V is a complex process that requires comprehensive consideration of instructions, registers, and parallelism. The impact of algorithm complexity on computing efficiency.

5   Citations

This article optimizes the performance of the algorithm from the optimization of the instruction pipeline of the RISC-V vector instruction set. The optimized algorithm not only has a significant improvement in performance, but the introduced optimization methods and ideas are also very versatile and can be applied to parallel optimization of other algorithms on RISC-V. The optimized algorithm not only has a significant improvement in performance, but also has better real-time performance and code simplicity, which improves its engineering application value. The only shortcoming is that this article has not fully explored the performance potential under the RISC-V architecture. Although the RISC-V vector technology has some imperfections, it solves the binary incompatibility problem caused by the SIMD technology. The same code can run on any vector bit-width processor based on the RISC-V architecture, which means that the software maintenance cost is greatly reduced, which is of great significance to the construction of its ecology. And as a means to improve the performance of the processor, fully combining the hardware architecture features and instruction set features for in-depth optimization is the focus of the next step of this article.

References

1. Waterman, A., Lee, Y., Patterson, D.A., et al.: The RISC-V instruction set manual, volume I: base user–level ISA. EECS Dep. **7**(9), 475 (2011)
2. Waterman, A., Lee, Y., Patterson, D.A., et al.: The RISC-V instruction set manual, volume I: User-level ISA. CS Division, EECE Department, University of California, Berkeley (2014)
3. Waterman, A.S.: Design of the RISC-V instruction set architecture. UC Berkeley (2016)
4. Hennessy, J.L., Patterson, D.A.: Computer Architecture: A Quantitative Approach. Elsevier, Amsterdam (2011)
5. Gross, T.R., Jouppi, N.P., Hennessy, J.L., Przybylski, S., Rowen, C.: A retrospective on "MIPS: a microprocessor architecture." IEEE Comput. Soc. **36**(4), 73–76 (2016)
6. Hennessy, J., Jouppi, N., Baskett, F., Gill, J.: MIPS: a VLSI processor architecture. In: VLSI Systems and Computations, pp. 337–346. Springer, Heidelberg (1981). https://doi.org/10.1007/978-3-642-68402-9_37
7. Hennessy, J., et al.: MIPS: a microprocessor architecture. ACM SIGMICRO Newsl. **13**(4), 17–22 (1982)
8. Feehrer, J., et al.: The Oracle Sparc T5 16-Core processor scales to eight sockets. IEEE Micro **33**(2), 48–57 (2013)
9. Kongetira, P., Aingaran, K., Olukotun, K.: Niagara: a 32-way multithreaded sparc processor. IEEE Micro **25**(2), 21–29 (2005)
10. Konstadinidis, G., et al.: Architecture and physical implementation of a third generation 65 nm, 16 Core, 32 thread chip-multithreading SPARC processor. IEEE J. Solid-State Circuits **44**(1), 7–17 (2009)
11. Leon, A.S., Tam, K.W., Shin, J.L., Weisner, D., Schumacher, F.: A power-efficient high-throughput 32-thread SPARC processor. IEEE J. Solid-State Circuits **42**(1), 7–16 (2007)
12. Tremblay, M., Chaudhry, S.: A third-generation 65nm 16-Core 32-thread plus 32-scout-thread CMT SPARC® processor. In: 2008 IEEE International Solid-State Circuits Conference - Digest of Technical Papers. San Francisco, pp. 82–83. IEEE, CA (February 2008)
13. Gautschi, M., et al.: SIR10us: a tightly coupled elliptic-curve cryptography co-processor for the OpenRISC. I: 2014 IEEE 25th International Conference on Application-Specific Systems, Architectures and Processors, pp. 25–29. IEEE, Zurich (June 2014)
14. Lopez-Parrado, A., Valderrama-Cuervo, J.-C.: OpenRISC-based System-on-Chip for digital signal processing. In: 2014 XIX Symposium on Image, Signal Processing and Artificial Vision, pp. 1–5. IEEE, Armenia (September 2014). http://ieeexplore.ieee.org/document/7010123/

15. Mehdizadeh, N., Shokrolah-Shirazi, M., Miremadi, S.G.: Analyzing fault effects in the 32-bit OpenRISC 1200 microprocessor. In: 2008 Third International Conference on Availability, Reliability and Security, pp. 648–652. IEEE (March 2008)
16. Pulp platform. https://pulp-platform.org/
17. Zaruba, F., Benini, L.: The cost of application-class processing: energy and performance analysis of a Linux-ready 1.7 GHZ 64bit RISC-V core in 22nm fdsoi technology (April 2019)
18. Shakti processor program. https://shakti.org.in/
19. Gala, N., Menon, A., Bodduna, R., Madhusudan, G.S., Kamakoti, V.: SHAKTI processors: an open-source hardware initiative. In: 29th International Conference on VLSI Design and 15th International Conference on Embedded Systems, VLSID 2016, Kolkata, India, January 4–8, 2016, pp. 7–8 (2016)
20. The sifive u74 standard core. https://www.sifive.com/cores/u74
21. Arm cpu cortex-a55. https://www.arm.com/products/silicon-ip-cpu/cortex-a/cortex-a55?utm source=google&utmmedium=cpc&utmcampaign=2019brandmk30cpussearchbol&utmsou rce=google&utmmedium=cpc&gclid=EAIaIQobChMI6ujPg3V4wIVWB-tBh3migfFEAA YASAAEgL9MvDBwE
22. 2018. riscv-v-spec. https://github.com/riscv/riscv-v-spec
23. Dubey, R., Agrawal, J.: An improved genetic algorithm for automated convolutional neural network design. Intell. Autom. Soft Comput. **32**(2), 747–763 (2022)
24. Sharma, M., Pathik, B.: Crow search algorithm with improved objective function for test case generation and optimization. Intell. Autom. Soft Comput. **32**(2), 1125–1140 (2022)
25. Cheng, C., Lin, D.: Image reconstruction based on compressed sensing measurement matrix optimization method. J. Internet Things **2**(1), 47–34 (2020)
26. Almotiri, S.H., Al Ghamdi, M.A.: Network quality assessment in heterogeneous wireless settings: an optimization approach. Comput. Mater. Contin. **71**(1), 439–455 (2022)
27. Lu, J., Fei, G.: Non-linear localization algorithm based on newton iterations. J. Internet Things **2**(4), 129–134 (2020)

The Nexus Between Air Pollution and Life Insurance Demand in China: Evidence from Deep Machine Learning

Ruiyun Wanyan[1], Liang Yang[1(✉)], Ming Pu[1,3], Tongpu Zhao[1], and Ling Zeng[2]

[1] Southwestern University of Finance and Economics, Chengdu 611130, China
yangliang@swufe.edu.cn
[2] Sichuan University, Chengdu 611130, China
[3] The Ohio State University, Columbus 43210, USA

Abstract. It is a certain fact that air pollution will damage the human body mechanism. While being aware of air pollution, one will surely become bad tempered in considering of the negative impact on his health, which leads to the increase of his risk aversion coefficient. The change of the risk aversion coefficient is a key factor of the insurance demand. With this assumption, we analyze the nexus between the air pollution and life insurance demand based on the monthly data of 36 cities in China from 2012 to 2018, using deep leaning methods. We find that the air pollution index has a significantly positive impact on the demand of life insurance, health insurance and personal insurance. While having a direct impact on the life insurance demand, its impact on the property insurance is not significant. In addition, the life insurance also receives impacts from the economic development level, social insurance cost and educational level etc.

Keywords: Air pollution · Insurance demand · Empirical study · Deep machine learning

1 Introduction

Air pollution not only has a negative impact on people's health, also hinders the economic development (Mele and Magazzino 2020). In recent years, because of the imperative demand on economic development, local governments tolerate the pollution from those high pollution enterprises, which usually generate a higher economic profit. As a result, the air pollution is getting more severe. In fact, air pollution has drawn attention from the society for a long time. Environmental Monitoring of China was established in 1981 to supervise the air quality in the country. Later, according to "Environmental protection law of the people's Republic of China" and "Law of the People's Republic of China on the Prevention and Control of Atmospheric Pollution", the government issued the Ambient Air Quality Standard. China begins to publish the weekly report on air qualities in some big cities and the monthly urban air pollution index (Air Pollution Index, API), which is one of most important air pollution indices. We can find that the air quality is getting worse through a brief analysis on these indices.

© The Author(s), under exclusive license to Springer Nature Switzerland AG 2022
X. Sun et al. (Eds.): ICAIS 2022, CCIS 1586, pp. 524–539, 2022.
https://doi.org/10.1007/978-3-031-06767-9_44

With the increase of our residents' living standard, people have a higher demand on the life qualities and have put more attention on the severe impact of air pollution on the environment. The analysis on the impact of air pollution on people's lifestyle and strategy has attracted wide attention from the academia for a long time. According to Bullinger (1990), air pollution not only endangers people's health, but also cause negative impact on their psychic and mental condition. Based on the analysis on stock and security investment, Levy and Yagil (2011) find that the air pollution can insert significant impact on the investor's mood, which in turn affect their investment strategy, and thus the economic decisions. The research of Chen and Chen (2020) reveals that the air pollution will increase people's risk aversion, which will stimulate their demand for commercial medical insurance.

The purpose of our research is to investigate if there exists some nexus between air pollution and the demand of life insurance, given the impact of the former on people's economic decision. We try to use empirical methods as well as machine learning to verify the existence of such correlation. The remaining parts of this paper is organized as: Sect. 2 reviews the related literatures, Sect. 3 sets up the model and carry out related analysis, Sect. 4 is the empirical analysis, followed by the conclusion.

2 Literature Review

2.1 The Influencing Factors of Life Insurance Demand

The literature on the influencing factors of life insurance demand originates from Yaari (1965). The main finding is that one can enhance his expected utility function via purchasing life insurance under the fair actuarial price so that his post-retirement life can be better arranged. Hakansson (1969) and Fischer (1973) extend Yaari's model and conclude that heritage motivation, mortality and labor income are all positively related to the life insurance demand. According to Lewis (1989), the household demand for life insurance and the optimal amount can be derived by solving the utility maximization problem for the beneficiary. These literatures focused on theoretical analysis. Later, many researchers investigate the problem using empirical methods to analyze the topic of life insurance consumption. Using the idea of Lewis (1989), Browne and Kim (1993) demonstrate that the national income, dependence ratio and social security cost have a positive impact on life insurance consumption while those of the religion, inflation rate and political policy are negative. Outreville (1996) finds that personal disposable income and the development of financial industry will promote the life insurance expense while the inflation anticipation and monopolistic market structure will restrain such expense. Beck and Webb (2003) find that only national income, inflation rate and financial development have significant influence on the regional disparities. Li et al. (2007) analyze the life insurance consumption in OECD countries and find that the income level, dependence ratio and educational level are positively related to the dependent variable. Koo and Lim (2021) reveal that the time heterogeneity plays an important role in the life insurance decision.

The above researches usually assume that the influencing factors such as wealth, age and geographic location remains stable and adopt the economic man hypothesis. However, with the development of the insurance and the broadening of the research horizon, scholars find that the influencing factors on life insurance demand are not limited to the economic factor or simple institutional ones. The recent research in behavioral economics suggests that mood swings may alter the risk aversion and thus affect some important economic decisions. Chui and Kwok (2008) confirm the significant impact of the cultural factors on life insurance demand. Schmidt (2012) and Outreville (2014) point out that the research framework in behavioral economics can explain some odd event and referred it as "behavioral insurance". This progress indicates that, to study the influencing factors of life insurance demand, the scholars has extended their consideration from objective variables to more subject ones such as culture and awareness.

2.2   The Influence of Air Pollution on Insurance Purchase Decision

Based on the findings of current literature, the air pollution exerts an impact on economic decision through an indirect path. The air pollution directly harms people's health and leads to a bad mood among the victim, which may increase the risk aversion of those people. When they are more risk averse, they tend to avoid the potential risks, which is reflected by their economic decisions. As to the life purchase decision model, this path is realized as follows.

In the first step, the air pollution will cause negative mood among people in a remarkable way, which was confirmed by a large volume of literature in psychology. Evans et al. (1987) find that one becomes more risk averse after experiencing life-and-death matters. Evans and Jacobs (1981) also confirm that air pollution may bring about bad temper or irresponsible behaviors of the people. Evans et al. (1988) show that the air pollution will cause the bad health condition and depression to the people. Similar conclusions are also confirmed by Hall et al. (2010) via comparing the air quality in 1989 and 2008 in California.

Secondly, with negativities being generated, one will become more risk averse. Constans and Mathews (1993) and Slovic and Peters (2006) find out that the negative mood increases the risk aversion and this increased risk averse attitude will change the subjective anticipation of the risk severity in the future time. Pennings and Garcia (2009) also find that air pollution and adverse environment will increase the risk aversion and thus influence the economic decisions. This point of view has been supported by many scholars who believe that the air pollution may cause discomforts, which will decrease one's favor toward the outside environment and leads to the increase of risk aversion.

Finally, enhanced risk aversion will increase people's demand for insurance. In fact, risk aversion is the presumption for insurance because only risk averse individuals may purchase insurance. Since the concept of risk aversion coefficient was proposed by Pratt (1964) and Arrow (1965), it has been wide adopted in the research in finance and economics. From the perspective of insurance, risk aversion is demonstrated to be positively related to insurance demand in different countries or regions. Petrolia et al. (2013) find that highly risk averse families tend to purchase more insurance using the household data, therefore the risk aversion and demand for insurance are positively correlated. Outreville (2014) believes that one's attitude towards risk receives a wide impact from age, gender, occupation and many other factors. No matter which factor cause the increase in risk aversion, it will further increase the demand for insurance.

The fact that air pollution will influence the economic decision has been verified in many other fields. For example, by comparing the disparity in stock market returns of different locations, Levy and Yagil (2011) confirm that the air pollution will lower the stock market return by causing the bad mood to the investors. Lepori (2016) confirms the negative correlation between the air pollution and stock market return. Given the impact of air pollution on economic decisions, one may naturally ask if the air pollution will cause the risk aversion of the people, and thus increase the demand for life insurance. The research on such topic is relatively rare and our research aims to fill this gap.

This paper is based on the panel data on API and life insurance demand of 84 months in 36 cities in China. To exclude the influence of other factor, we have selected the GDP, savings level, income level, social security cost, education level, dependence ratio and urbanization level as the control variables.

3 Model Assumption and Variable Selection

3.1 Dependent Variable

Many variables which can measure the demand for life insurance, the variables most-widely used is insurance penetration and insurance density. The life insurance penetration is the ratio of total life insurance premium over the GDP. The life insurance density is defined as the ratio of total life insurance premium over the total population size. In considering that our research aims to study the influence of air pollution on the life insurance demand, which is a decision made by individuals, so we adopt the life insurance density to measure the demand. This is consistent with much previous research (Browne and Ki 1993; Outreville 1996 and 2014). Because the life insurance includes life insurance, casualty insurance and health insurance, our model analyze the impact of air pollution on these products separately.

3.2 Independent Variables

This article uses Air Pollution Index (API) as the measurement of the air quality for different cities. API is a multi-dimensional numerical value, which focus on the possible impacts of the polluted air inhaled on the human body. It mainly focuses the concentration of harmful substance such as nitrogen dioxide, sulfur dioxide and carbon monoxide, etc. The air quality is divided into six grades, from 1 to 6, and the larger number means the more severe pollution, which causes a greater harm to the human health. From June 1997, China began to issue weekly report of the air quality of 47 key cities. Since the indices on early version of API are not comprehensive, the Chinese government switch from API to AQI, where the concentration of PM2.5 and O_3 are put under supervision. Based on the related previous research, we propose the following Hypothesis, referring to Levy and Yagil (2011) and Lepori (2016):

H: Air pollution is positively related to the life insurance demand.

Table 1. Variable descriptions and data sources.

		Descriptions of indicators	Data sources	Expected trends
Explained variables	Life insurance density	The ratio of the monthly life insurance premium income to the local population, yuan/person; life	Local Insurance Regulatory Commission's website	NA
	Accident insurance density	The ratio of accident insurance premium income to the local population in the current month, yuan/person; accident	Same as above	NA
	Health insurance density	The ratio of health insurance premium income to the local population in the current month, yuan/person; health	Same as above	NA
	Personal insurance density	The ratio of personal insurance premium income to the local population in the current month, yuan/person; personal	Same as above	NA
Explained variable for comparison	Property insurance density	The ratio of property insurance premium income to the local population in the current month, yuan/person; property	Same as above	NA

(continued)

Table 1. (*continued*)

		Descriptions of indicators	Data sources	Expected trends
Explanatory variable	Air pollution index	Mainly measures the concentration of harmful substances in the air such as nitrogen dioxide, sulfur dioxide, carbon monoxide, etc. The larger the air pollution index, the more serious the air pollution, and the more unfavorable to the health of residents. API		+
Control variables	Per capita GDP	GDP per capita, ten thousand yuan/person, gdp	Local statistical yearbook	+
	Per capita savings	Yuan/person, deposit	Same as above	+
	Per capita social security expenditure	Yuan/person, social	Same as above	+
	Per capita disposable income	Yuan/person, income	Same as above	+
	Education level	Population in regular higher education institutions per 10,000 people, education	Population and Employment Statistics Yearbook	
	Urbanization rate	%, urban	Local statistical yearbook	+

Notes: The data have been calculated by the author. Personal insurance premiums refer to the sum of the premiums of life insurance, accident insurance and health insurance.

3.3 Control Variables

A large volume of literature reveals that the life insurance demand is affected by the variables of four categories, namely the economic factors, the demographic factors, the institutional factors and other factors (Outreville 2014; Millo and Carmeci 2015). Since China is a traditional centralized country and there is no sharp difference between the regulations, so our model does not include institutional variables. Taking the representativeness and availability of the data, we choose per capita GDP, per capita savings deposit balance and per capita disposable income as economic factors (Browne and Kim 1993). We also choose education level and urbanization from demographic factors and social security cost form other factors (Dewar 1998; Szpiro and Outreville 1986). Also, the improvement of social security system will stimulate the life insurance demand. Previous literatures shown that the impact of the social security system on the life insurance demand may be ambiguous: on one hand, a better social security system may refrain the life insurance demand because of the substitution effects. On the other hand, the spread of the social security system may increase the residents' risk awareness and thus increase the life insurance demand.

4 Empirical Results

4.1 Description of Variables and Data Sources

The data in this paper are monthly data from Jan. 2012 to Dec. 2018, focusing on 4 municipalities, capital cities of 27 provinces and autonomous regions and 5 municipalities with independent planning status (Dalian, Qingdao, Ningbo, Xiamen and Shenzhen). The 36 cities were chosen because the API index of these cities is relatively standardized. Related data sources and indicators are shown in the following table:

To ensure the stability of the data of each variable, logarithmic operations were performed on the data other than the level of urbanization. Simple statistical description of the data before processing is shown in the Table 2.

4.2 Model Setting and Testing

According to the analysis in the third part of this paper, the basic model sets as follows:

$$INS_{it} = \alpha + \beta API_{it} + \eta_1 gdp_{it} + \eta_2 deposit_{it} + \eta_3 social_{it} + \eta_4 income_i + \eta_5 education_{it} + \eta_6 urban_{it} + \lambda D_{month} + \varepsilon_{it} \tag{1}$$

In the above formula, INS_{it} refers to the insurance demand index, specifically including four categories, namely the per capita life insurance demand, the per capita accidental injury insurance demand, the per capita health insurance demand and the per capita personal insurance demand in the t month of the i-th city, in which the life insurance demand is the sum of the first three. α is a constant term. API_{it} represents the air quality index of the i-th city in month t, β is its coefficient. gdp_{it} is the per capita GDP level of the i-th city in month t. $deposit_{it}$ represents the per capita savings level of the i-th city in month t. $social_{it}$ is the per capita social security expenditure level of the i-th city in month t. $income_{it}$ is the per capita disposable income level of the i-th city in month t.

Table 2. A simple statistical description of each variable.

	Mean	S.E.	MED	S.D.	Kurtosis	Skewness	Area	Min.	Max.	Obs.
Life	89.055	1.4888	69.617	81.638	25.338	3.9142	996.44	0.1195	996.56	3007
Accident	4.2344	0.1046	2.7781	5.7533	23.864	4.6386	45.012	0.0135	45.025	3024
Health	9.9680	0.1853	7.0117	10.162	16.294	3.3454	96.868	0.0009	96.869	3009
Personal	102.35	1.7010	80.182	93.537	24.155	3.8643	1105.1	0.0135	1105.1	3024
Property	49.811	1.0355	35.666	56.940	38.860	5.2459	702.90	1.7180	704.62	3024
API	72.151	0.3950	69.869	21.722	8.5233	1.6581	229.03	23.806	252.84	3024
gdp	6.3890	0.1031	5.0195	5.6670	18.902	3.9413	43.730	1.2949	45.025	3024
Deposit	46014	658.78	36574	36227	18.220	3.6283	297306	1281.7	298588	3024
Social	774.74	8.3901	642.768	454.92	0.8135	1.0582	2587.2	19.121	2606.3	2940
Income	21185	133.91	20029	7363.8	0.0153	0.6921	44603	22.370	44626	3024
Education	575.89	4.8373	497.03	266.01	0.5808	0.5671	1201.4	69.032	1270.4	3024
Urban	0.5930	0.0033	0.6093	0.1833	0.5053	0.2169	0.7913	0.2087	1.0000	3024

Notes: In order to simplify the variables, although logarithmic operations have been performed on the above variables, the expressions of the variables still follow the description in Table 1. Unless otherwise specified, the same below. The data of urbanization level are missing in some cities, so the number of observations is inconsistent with other variables.

$education_{it}$ represents the education level of the i-th city in month t. $urban_{it}$ represents the i-th city's urbanization level in month t. η_i are their coefficient. D_{month} is the monthly variable matrix and λ is its coefficient.ε_{it} is the residual term. After testing, time fixed effect model is used to estimate the model (1).

4.3 Empirical Results

This paper uses R to analyze the model (1) and take the demand of different insurance types as the explained variables. The regression results obtained are shown in Table 3.

It can be seen from Table 3 that the relationship between the urban air pollution index and the demand for personal insurance is significantly positive, that is, the higher the air pollution index, the corresponding demand for personal insurance will rise, which is consistent with the basic assumptions of this paper. This conclusion is also reflected in the life insurance model and health insurance model. Moreover, the addition of the air pollution index will increase the $\widehat{R}^2$ of the model. To our surprise, the relationship between air pollution and accident insurance demand is not significant. Among the control variables, the relationship between per capita GDP, per capita savings deposit balance, per capita social security expenditure, education level and personal insurance demand is significantly positive, while per capita disposable expenditure and urbanization level are only significant in the accident insurance model. But it is not significant in other models. The reason that per capita disposable expenditure is not significant in other models may be related to multicollinearity.

Further, to analyze the specific path of air pollution's impact on personal insurance demand, this paper introduces the cross-term of API and income, API and education

Table 3. Empirical results of influencing factors of personal insurance demand.

	Life1	Life2	Casualty1	Casualty2	Health1	Health2	Personal1	Personal2
API		0.165***		− 0.176		0.018*		0.145***
		(5.308)		(−1.228)		(2.464)		(5.088)
gdp	0.003**	0.002*	0.023***	0.023***	0.014**	0.014**	0.004**	0.004**
	(2.665)	(2.502)	(5.549)	(5.735)	(2.946)	(2.930)	(3.187)	(3.033)
Deposit	0.556***	0.565***	0.520***	0.510***	0.569***	0.570***	0.549***	0.557***
	(12.79)	(13.05)	(11.03)	(10.87)	(10.68)	(10.69)	(13.76)	(14.01)
Social	0.228***	0.233***	0.089*	0.084*	0.112**	0.112**	0.216***	0.220***
	(8.311)	(8.521)	(2.993)	(2.833)	(3.316)	(3.329)	(8.562)	(8.763)
Income	0.024	0.013	0.227***	0.216***	0.017	0.018	0.015	0.006
	(0.668)	(0.374)	(5.899)	(5.626)	(0.399)	(0.424)	(0.457)	(0.174)
Education	0.453***	0.455***	0.097	0.095	0.162*	0.162*	0.418***	0.420***
	(7.236)	(7.305)	(1.431)	(1.403)	(2.105)	(2.107)	(7.272)	(7.337)
Urban	0.070	0.123	0.503*	0.447*	0.210	0.216	0.090	0.136
	(0.346)	(0.606)	(2.286)	(2.039)	(0.843)	(0.864)	(0.481)	(0.731)
N	2868	2868	2868	2868	2868	2868	2868	2868
$\hat{R}^2$	0.44416	0.44934	0.41020	0.41557	0.29388	0.29383	0.47752	0.48197
F-stat	386.434	338.439	335.836	294.444	200.144	171.535	442.742	386.533
P-value	0.00000	0.00000	0.00000	0.00000	0.00000	0.00000	0.00000	0.00000

Notes: 1. In the above table, the corresponding T statistics are in parentheses below the variables. 2. The first row in the table indicates different explained variables respectively, life1 and life2 indicate that the explained variables are life insurance densities, casualty1 and casualty2 indicates that the explained variable is accident insurance density, health1 and health2 indicate that health insurance density is the explained variable and personal1 and personal2 indicate that the explained variable is personal insurance density. 3. '***', '**', '*' and '♥' significant at 99.9%, 99%, 95%, and 90% confidence levels respectively. The same below.

and API and Urban into the model. First, we use life insurance density as the explained variable to conduct regression on the model. The results are shown in Table 4.

It can be seen from Table 4 that among the three cross-terms of the introduced model, only the cross-term between API and income is weakly significant at the 90% confidence level for life insurance model. For health insurance model, only the cross-term between API and urban Faintly significant at the 90% confidence level. When the explained variables are replaced with other variables, the conclusions are basically same.

Meanwhile, this paper also verifies the relationship between air pollution and property insurance. Using property insurance density as the explained variable for regression analysis and the results obtained are shown in Table 5.

It can be seen from Table 5 that no matter whether API or APIorder is used as the explanatory variable, the results are not significant. This shows that at present, air pollution will not have a significant impact on the demand for property insurance. In terms

Table 4. Empirical results on the path of air pollution's impact on the demand for life insurance and health insurance.

	life1	life2	life3	life4	health1	health2	health3	health4
API	0.165***	0.078	1.084▾	1.149	0.003▾	-0.214	-0.437	-0.143
	(5.308)	(0.746)	(1.750)	(1.555)	(1.793)	(-1.638)	(-0.520)	(-0.161)
API*urban		0.141		0.085		0.370▾		0.354▾
		(0.872)		(0.514)		(1.826)		(1.688)
API*income			0.127▾	0.112▾			0.046	0.022
			(1.787)	(1.709)			(0.538)	(0.249)
API*education				0.025				-0.045
				(0.395)				(-0.599)
controls	yes	yes	yes	yes	yes	yes	yes	yes
N	2868	2868	2868	2868	2940	2940	2940	2940
$\hat{R}^2$	0.44934	0.44933	0.44979	0.44955	0.29051	0.29124	0.29051	0.29113
F-stat	338.439	296.204	296.763	237.314	173.004	151.939	151.399	121.520
P-value	0.00000	0.00000	0.00000	0.00000	0.00000	0.00000	0.00000	0.00000

Table 5. Verification results of the relationship between air pollution and property insurance demand.

	1	2	3
API		0.003	
		(0.104)	
APIorder			−0.038
			(−1.478)
Controls	Yes	Yes	Yes
N	2868	2868	2868
$\hat{R}^2$	0.5436	0.54341	0.54375
F-stat	868.242	694.353	695.322
P-value	0.00000	0.00000	0.00000

of control variables, economic development level, per capita income level, education level and urbanization level are significant factors affecting property insurance demand.

4.4 Further Demonstration Based on Deep Learning Method

The final nonlinear method is the artificial neural network. They are the currently preferred approach for complex machine learning problems. Their flexibility draws from the ability to entwine many telescoping layers of nonlinear predictor Interactions. Also, their complexity ranks neural networks among the least transparent, least interpretable and most highly parameterized machine learning tools (Gu et al. 2020).

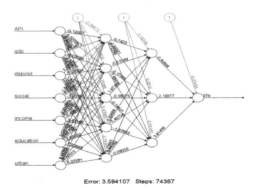

Error: 3.594107 Steps: 74367

Fig. 1. Neural network structure and parameter estimation results of model 1.

Figure 1 shows the neural network structure and parameter estimation results of the per capita model. The specific neural network structure used in this paper is a four-layer deep neural network and the number of neurons in each layer is 9, 5, 3 and 1 respectively. The parameter weight of each neuron is shown in Fig. 1.

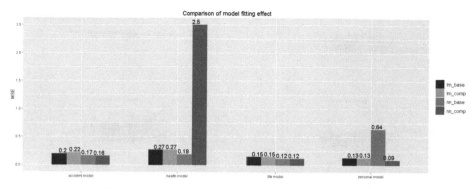

Fig. 2. Comparison of fitting effects of various models.

It can be seen from Fig. 2 that after adding the explanatory variable API, whether it is a traditional lm model or a neural network model, except for individual models, the fitting effect of the remaining models is significantly improved. At the same time, from the fitting effect of the lm model and the neural network model, except for a few models, the neural network model is better than the lm model in most cases.

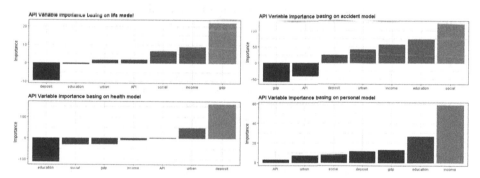

Fig. 3. API variable importance generalization weights.

It can be seen from Fig. 3 that API has positive effects on three models except accident insurance model in variable importance ranking based on connection weights. Among them, in the ranking of relative variable importance, API is more important to life insurance and health insurance.

Figure 4 shows the importance of API variables under different models. API's generalized weights indicators for life insurance and health insurance are relatively large and the results are basically consistent with the conclusions in Fig. 3. At the same time, the value of accident insurance is relatively small and concentrated, indicating that the impact of API on this insurance is very limited.

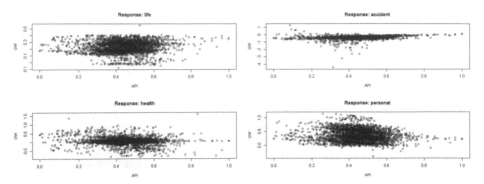

Fig. 4. Importance of API variables in different models.

5 Explanation of Results

Through the empirical analysis and deep learning results in the third part of this paper, it can be found that air pollution can have a significant impact on the demand for personal insurance. Also, there is a significant correlation between other control variables and the demand for personal insurance. The detailed analysis is as follows.

First, there is a significant positive correlation between air pollution index and personal insurance demand, which is consistent with the basic assumption of this paper. Table 3 shows that the relationship between air pollution index and personal insurance, health insurance and life insurance is significantly positive, that is, air pollution will increase people's risk aversion, thus increasing people's demand for life insurance, health insurance and other personal insurance products. By comparing Table 3 and Fig. 3, it can be found that this conclusion is robust. Meanwhile, according to the results of Table 4, at present, the impact of air pollution on the demand for personal insurance is mainly reflected by per capita disposable income, that is, regions with higher per capita disposable income pay more attention to the harmful effects of air pollution on people's health, thus increasing people's demand for personal insurance products. In addition, the air pollution index has no significant impact on the demand for accident insurance and property insurance. The possible reason is that there is no direct correlation between accident insurance, property insurance and people's health. Therefore, there is no direct correlation between people's level of risk aversion and the purchase of such insurance products.

Second, the economic level and the demand for personal insurance are significantly positively correlated. First of all, the impact of per capita GDP on the demand for personal insurance is significantly positive. This conclusion is consistent with the research results of many scholars (Browne and Kim 1993; Beck and Webb 2003; Outreville 1996; Zhuo 2001, etc.). It is also in line with the basic principles of the market mechanism. Only when the economic level rises, the demand will rise accordingly. Secondly, the relationship between the level of household savings and the demand for personal insurance is significantly positive. It shows that the increase in the savings level of Chinese residents at present has stimulated the demand for personal insurance products to a certain extent. Also, the savings of personal insurance products have not been fully utilized.

Finally, the relationship between per capita income level and personal insurance demand is not significant. The most likely reason is that the variables selected in this paper have multicollinearity. From the results in Table 3, it can be found that when the per capita disposable income and the intersection of API and per capita disposable income are introduced at the same time, this variable becomes significant, which shows that the per capita disposable income can still significantly affect the demand for personal insurance.

Third, the relationship between per capita social security expenditure and personal insurance demand is significantly positive, which is also in line with the basic expectations of this paper. This conclusion is consistent with the views of scholars such as Zhuo (2001) and Yin et al. (2008) indicating that at the present stage, the development of China's commercial insurance depends to a certain extent on the progress of social insurance. Because the development of social insurance has driven people's insurance awareness to a certain extent, when the awareness of insurance increases, people's awareness of commercial insurance also rises, which also increases the demand for personal insurance. On the other hand, there is a complementary relationship between personal insurance and social insurance, because the risk protection provided by social insurance cannot fully meet people's demand for risk protection, which requires commercial insurance to play its unique compensation protection function.

Fourth, the relationship between education level and personal insurance demand is significantly positive, but the relationship between the level of urbanization and personal insurance demand is not significant. The relationship between education level and personal insurance demand verifies the correctness of the research conclusions of Dewar (1998) and Szpiro and Outreville (1986). The relationship between the level of urbanization and the demand for personal insurance is not significant, indicating that the current urbanization process in China cannot affect the demand for personal insurance products of Chinese residents, but it will affect people's demand for property insurance.

6 Conclusion and Discussion

Theoretical research results show that air pollution does not directly affect economic decisions, but will eventually affect people's economic decisions. First of all, air pollution will directly cause people's physical condition to deteriorate, thereby producing negative emotions. Secondly, people's negative emotions will further affect their attitude towards risk, making people be more risk-averse. Finally, when people are averse to risks, they tend to avoid the occurrence of risks. This is reflected in the economic decision-making field that people pay more attention to the prevention of risks. In the insurance field, it is manifested that air pollution will eventually affect people's insurance demand. However, no scholar has analyzed the relationship between this two at present and this paper attempts to fill this gap. This paper takes 36 cities in China as the analysis object, selects monthly data from 2012 to 2018, analyzes the relationship between air pollution index and insurance demand using empirical research methods, and then uses machine learning methods to verify the empirical conclusion. The results found that when economic, social, and demographic variables are used as control variables, the relationship between the air pollution index and the demand for personal insurance, health insurance and life insurance is significantly positive. However, the relationship between air pollution, accident insurance and property insurance is not significant. This shows that, at present, the changes in people's attitudes towards risk brought about by air pollution can only affect the field of personal insurance but cannot drive changes in people's overall risk attitudes.

At the same time, this article finds that economic variables are the most direct cause of all insurance demand. The development of social security is also directly related to people's understanding of insurance, and changes in population structure affect people's attitudes towards insurance products as well. In this context, promoting the development of China's insurance market can start from many aspects such as economic development, social progress and demographic structure.

References

Outreville, J.F.: Life insurance markets in developing countries. J. Risk Insur. **63**(2), 263–278 (1996)

Bullinger, M.: Environmental Stress: Effects of Air Pollution on Mood, Neuropsychological Function and Physical State. Springer, Netherlands (1990)

Chen, F., Chen, Z.: Air pollution and avoidance behavior: a perspective from the demand for medical insurance. J. Clean. Prod. **259**, 120970 (2020)

Chui, A.C.W., Kwok, C.C.Y.: National culture and life insurance consumption. J. Int. Bus. Stud. **39**(1), 88–101 (2008)

Constans, J., Mathews, A.: Mood and the subjective risk of future events. Cogn. Emot. **7**, 545–560 (1993)

Dewar, D.M.: Do those with more formal education have better health insurance opportunities? Econ. Educ. Rev. **17**(3), 267–277 (1998)

Evans, G.W., Colome, S.D., Shearer, D.F.: Psychological reactions to air pollution. Environ. Res. **45**(1), 1–15 (1988)

Evans, G.W., Jacobs, S.V., Dooley, D., Catalano, R.: The interaction of stressful life events and chronic strains on community mental health. Am. J. Community Psychol. **15**(1), 23–34 (1987)

Evans, G.W., Jacobs, S.V.: Air pollution and human behavior. J. Soc. Issues **57**(1), 95–125 (1981)

Fischer, S.: A life cycle model of life insurance purchases. Int. Econ. Rev. **14**(1), 132–152 (1973)

Gu, S., Kelly, B., Xiu, D.: Empirical asset pricing via machine learning. Rev. Financ. Stud. **33**(5), 2223–2273 (2020)

Hall, J.V., Brajer, V., Lurmann, F.W.: Air pollution, health and economic benefits–lessons from 20 years of analysis. Ecol. Econ. **69**(12), 2590–2597 (2010)

Hall, J.V., Brajer, F.W.V.: Lurmann: air pollution, health and economic benefits-lessons from 20 years of analysis. Ecol. Econ. **69**(12), 2590–2597 (2010)

Koo, J.E., Lim, B.H.: Consumption and life insurance decisions under hyperbolic discounting and taxation. Econ. Model. **94**, 288–295 (2021)

Lepori, G.M.: Air pollution and stock returns: evidence from a natural experiment. J. Empir. Financ. **35**, 25–42 (2016)

Levy, A., Tamir, B.J.: Yagil: air pollution and stock returns in the US. J. Econ. Psychol. **32**(3), 374–383 (2011)

Lewis, F.D.: Dependents and the demand for life. Am. Econ. Rev. **79**(3), 452–467 (1989)

Li, D.H., Donghui, F.L., Moshirian, P.M.F., Nguyen, T.N.P.: The demand for life insurance in OECD countries. J. Risk Insur. **74**(3), 637–652 (2007)

Magazzino, C., Mele, M., Sarkodie, S.A.: The nexus between COVID-19 deaths, air pollution and economic growth in New York State: evidence from deep machine learning. J. Environ. Manag. **286**, 112241 (2021)

Mark, J., Browne, K.: Kim: an international analysis of life insurance demand. J. Risk Insur. **60**(4), 616–634 (1993)

Mele, M., Magazzino, C.: A machine learning analysis of the relationship among iron and steel industries, air pollution, and economic growth in China. J. Clean. Prod. **277**, 123293 (2020)

Outreville, J.: Francois: risk aversion, risk behavior, and demand for insurance: a survey. J. Insur. Issues **37**(2), 158–186 (2014)

Pennings, J.M.E., Garcia, P.: The informational content of the shape of utility functions: financial strategic behavior. MDE: Manag. Decis. Econ. **30**(2), 83–90 (2009)

Peters, S.: Ellen: risk perception and affect. Curr. Dir. Psychol. Sci. **15**(6), 322–325 (2006)

Petrolia, D.R.A., Landry, C.E.B., Coble, K.H.A.: Risk preferences, risk perceptions, and flood insurance. Land Econ. **89**(2), 227–245 (2013)

Szpiro, G.G.: Relative risk aversion around the world. Econ. Lett. **6**(1), 19–21 (1986)

Thorsten, B., Ian, W.: Economic, demographic, and institutional determinants of life insurance consumption across countries. World Bank Econ. Rev. **1**, 51–88 (2003)

Yaari, M.E.: Uncertain lifetime, life insurance, and the theory of the consumer. Rev. Econ. Stud. **32**(2), 137–150 (1965)

Yin, C., Zhao, G., Zhou, W.: Empirical analysis and prediction of life insurance premium income in China. Insur. Stud. **1**, 48–52 (2008)

Zhuo, Z.: Empirical analysis of life insurance demand in China. Insur. Stud. **5**, 10–12 (2001)

Image Steganalysis Based on CNN and Transfer Learning for Small-Sample Condition

Ru Zhang, Sheng Zou, Zhen Yang[✉], Fan Liu, and Jianyi Liu

School of Cyber Space Security, Beijing University of Posts and Telecommunications, Beijing 100876, China
yangzhenyz@bupt.edu.cn

Abstract. Image steganography has drawn severe multimedia security threat because it can transmit secret message. Existing steganalysis methods depend on known stegnography algorithm or existing big stego datasets to detect stego image existence. However, real world stego image sample is hard to collect and their stegnography algorithm are mainly unknown, which becomes two obstacles for image steganalysis. In this paper, we propose a transfer learning based image steganalysis model for small-sample condition. Parameter sharing method is used in our model to achieve transfer learning between different stegnography algorithms. The features are that the same series of steganography algorithms have similar data prior distribution. The similarities among different steganography algorithms is searched to realize transfer learning among different algorithms and optimize detection training. It makes algorithm can train quickly without losing the accuracy in small number of dataset. Comparing the detection accuracy and learning efficiency of the detection algorithm before and after, the performance of our model (on a small training set) is better than small sample training. At the same time, we analyzes the relationship and correlation between steganography algorithms. Our model optimizes the existing research results from a posteriori perspective.

Keywords: Image steganalysis · Convolutional neural network · Transfer learning · Small sample learning

1 Introduction

Information hiding refers to hiding some secret text information or image information in a multimedia carrier, and transmitting information that will not attract the attention of the observer [1]. Various information hiding algorithms have been proposed, including spatial domain algorithms [2] and frequency domain algorithms. Embedding based steganography cannot avoid the statistical bias problem, so coverless steganography methods [3] are proposed to achieve generative steganography [4]. This technology is vulnerable to malicious use, for example, malicious code is embedded in the carrier for network attack or used by criminals; Passing on secret plans, planning terrorist attacks

X. Sun et al. (Eds.): ICAIS 2022, CCIS 1586, pp. 540–551, 2022.
https://doi.org/10.1007/978-3-031-06767-9_45

and other criminal acts. For instance, "911" incident is analyzed to use videos and pictures on the Internet to embedd secret information to pass on criminal plans to terrorists. Therefore, image steganalysis technology develops rapidly.

The traditional steganalysis algorithm is an independent feature extraction and classification module, and the classification results will not optimize the extraction of steganalysis features. The key of the algorithm is the feature extraction module, and the quality of the extracted steganographic features directly determines the quality of the algorithm. With the development of steganography, the workload, complexity and difficulty of steganalysis will be greatly improved. People began to look for new tools to apply in this field. Deep learning is on the rise, Convolutional Neural Network (CNN), Generative Adversarial Network (GAN), Recurrent Neural Network (RNN) and other deep model research have made great achievements. This has attracted the attention of experts in the field of information hiding, who hope to use deep learning technology to break through the current bottleneck. The convolutional neural network can automatically extract the steganographic features, liberate the labor and reduce the manpower and energy; Secondly, the existence of pooling layer in deep learning algorithm greatly reduces the dimension of features used in classification, which reduces the complexity of classification calculation. Due to the specificity of the neural network to solve the problem, different tasks require different datasets, but in most cases, people can only get a small number of samples of a single type for training. In the field of steganalysis, transfer learning can be used to solve the problems of low embedding rate convolutional neural network steganalysis algorithm training difficulties, inability to converge, and low accuracy. But when faced with a new type of information hiding algorithm, it is difficult for us to obtain a dataset of the same size as the known algorithm's, and using a small dataset to train an empty model will inevitably cause problems such as poor generalization and overfitting.

In response to the above problems, this article proposes image steganalysis based on CNN and transfer learning for small-sample condition. We adopt the parameter-sharing pre-training model transfer learning method, and use the commonality between spatial adaptive steganalysis algorithms to perform transfer learning. For the detection of unknown steganography algorithms, the training efficiency and detection accuracy are improved. This method finds similarities among different algorithms, successfully realizes transfer learning among different algorithms, optimizes detection training and reducing the amount of data required for training.

2   Related Works

We introduce traditional and deep learning-based steganalysis algorithms in the section.

2.1   Steganalysis Technology Based on Traditional Methods

Traditional spatial steganalysis methods include feature extraction and classification training. For example: SPAM [5], SRM [6], PSRM [7], TLBP [8], etc. Later, adaptive steganalysis algorithms appear. It estimates the probability of image pixel modification and assigns different noise residual weights.

In addition to the spatial domain, early steganalysis in the JPEG domain (compressed domain) used the method of constructing features in the embedded domain, generally using carrier DCT coefficients to calculate the noise residual of the image, then statistical modeling to extract the features, and finally classification. Representative algorithms include PEV [9], JRM [10], etc. Algorithms such as DCTR [11], PHARM [12], SCA [13] use the characteristics of decompressed signal amplification and block changes, combined with phase information to design noise residual characteristics.

2.2 Steganalysis Technology Based on Deep Learning

With the research of Deep Learning [14] technology and the development of GPU (Graphic Processing Units [15]) computing in recent years, many neural network learning models have emerged, and their overall network structure mimics the human brain.

Convolutional neural network [16] is most suitable for steganalysis tasks. It is the same as the traditional steganalysis process. The convolutional layer extracts residuals and features. The final collection operation and fully connected layer classification of the convolutional neural network are very similar to the final classifier in the traditional method, which is used to output the final classification result.

In 2014, Tan et al. [17] first proposed a four-layer neural network (three convolutional layers and a fully connected layer). They let everyone see that the use of deep learning neural networks for steganalysis has great potential [18]. In 2015, Qian et al. [19] proposed Qian-Net. Through experiments, it is found that the correct rate of Qian-Net is 3% to 5% lower than SRM (on the BOSSbase dataset). The proposal of Qian-Net laid the foundation for the following research. In 2016, Xu et al. [20] made changes on Qian-Net and proposed Xu-Net. Through the detection of S-UNIWARD and HILL on the BOSSbase dataset, very good results have been achieved.

In 2017, Ye [21] et al. proposed a major result: Ye-Net. Ye-Net uses the TLU [22] activation function. In the experiment, Ye-Net is significantly better than the traditional detection model in the detection ability of WOW, S-UNIWARD and HILL algorithms.

In 2018, Yedroud [23] et al. further modified Xu-Net, combining the advantages of Ye-Net. Their model's effect is slightly better than that of Xu-Net and Ye-Net.

In 2020, Zhang et al. [24] proposed the Zhu-Net network. Two separable convolutional blocks [25, 26] are used to replace the traditional convolutional layer. Before the fully connected layer, spatial pyramid pooling [27] is used for processing, and features are mapped to a fixed length to realize the processing of images of different sizes.

In 2018, Boroumand et al. [28] proposed a model SR-Net that can be used to detect airspace and JPEG domain. The SR-Net model has achieved good results in both the spatial domain and the JPEG domain.

3   Method

We design our method based on transfer learning of parameter sharing, as shown in Fig. 1.

3.1 Problem Description

Just like Ye et al.'s previous research [29, 30], this problem can also be called the mismatch problem, which belongs to the mismatch between the training dataset and the test dataset. We hope to optimize this problem through the transferring of deep learning. Ye et al. have more research on using transfer learning to solve the carrier mismatch problem based on traditional machine learning and traditional steganalysis methods, and propose a new model to use transfer learning to solve problems such as difficulty in training and poor training effects when the embedding rate is low. It is not optimized to solve the mismatch between the training set and the test set. Qian et al. also used transfer learning to explore transfer learning of deep steganalysis, and solved the problem of poor performance when the embedding rate is low.

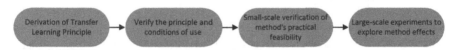

Fig. 1. Work flow chart of ideas in this paper.

We hope to use the transfer learning method to quickly train and detect the unknown algorithm (the unknown algorithm assumed in this article).

The steganalysis method of transfer learning mini-batch training set based on parameter sharing selects two analysis models: Zhu-Net and Ye-Net, to verify the effectiveness of the method, select Zhu-Net and Ye-Net as the initial network for verification, Detect a variety of adaptive information hiding algorithms for spatial image content commonly used in the paper, and select an algorithm with higher detection accuracy, WOW algorithm as a known algorithm, as the pre-training original task training set, and other adaptive information hiding The algorithm assumes an unknown target domain algorithm, and each steganography algorithm detects three different embedding rates.

Through years of application, it has been discovered that even though convolutional neural networks have unique advantages in the field of machine vision and have achieved very great achievements, training requires a large number of high-quality training samples. For steganalysis tasks, when applied in practice, many unknown information hiding algorithms are bound to be encountered. The amount of data embedded in these algorithms will be small and it is difficult to train. However, the network after pre-training on a large dataset of known related task algorithms has shown good performance, that is, it has learned some useful steganographic features, and some of these features are likely to be these related steganographics. The algorithms have in common, so the use of transfer learning to initialize the detection network can help the training of unknown hidden algorithms.

3.2 Transfer Learning in Steganalysis

The transfer learning method based on parameter sharing should pay attention to the similar prior distribution of the two data domains before and after transferring. Therefore, to explore the effectiveness of the transfer learning method for parameter sharing in this paper, it is necessary to determine whether the prior distribution of the hypothetical known information hiding algorithm is similar to that of the unknown information hiding algorithm embedded in the dataset data. In order to better understand and rationally utilize the similarity of prior distributions, we need to observe and measure them in different ways. We can see the similarity of the distribution directly, or we can use digitized measures to see the difference and similarity of the initial prior distribution of data under different embedding algorithms. Common mathematical quantities used to measure the difference between distributions are Euclidean distance, KL divergence, JS divergence, cosine similarity, Earth mover's distance, and so on.

We want to use quantitative numerical indicators to calculate the differences in the data distribution between samples of different embedding algorithms to determine whether the initial distribution is similar. In this paper, we select the Earth mover's distance, Wasserstein distance, as a quantitative numerical indicator to measure this gap. Here, we measure the distance between the embedded image and the carrier image using different image information hiding algorithms and the distribution distance between the unknown algorithm and the known algorithm to prove the similarity of the prior distribution of the algorithm. The measurements were spread out at three embedding rates: 0.4 bpp, 0.2 bpp, and 0.1 bpp. The measurement results are as follows:

Table 1. Prior distribution difference table between different embedding algorithms.

S-UNIWARD	0.4bpp	0.2bpp	0.1bpp
WOW	0.00836	0.00640	0.00354
Carrier	0.01667	0.00672	0.00372
HUGO	0.4bpp	0.2 bpp	0.1 bpp
WOW	0.00904	0.00949	0.00306
Carrier	0.01464	0.00979	0.00317
HILL	0.4 bpp	0.2 bpp	0.1 bpp
WOW	0.01911	0.00659	0.00375
Carrier	0.02215	0.00837	0.00378

From Table 1, we can see clearly that under all embedding rates, assume that the distance between unknown algorithms & hypothetical known algorithms and carriers is very small, that is, the distance between distributions is no more than 0.008, and the prior distribution is very similar.

Moreover, as shown in Table 2, the distribution gap between the unknown algorithm and the hypothetical known algorithm is smaller, which improves the possibility of transfer learning to improve the learning ability of the unknown algorithm. Similarly, using the earth mover's distance, we compare the statistical differences between the source task Y and the target task Y', as shown below (the output Y under random discrimination is selected for comparison).

In summary, we can see that there is a similarity between source task X and target task X', source task Y and target task Y', which conforms to our previous inferences and better meets the preconditions of parameter-sharing transfer learning.

Table 2. The statistical gap between Y and Y' in Zhu-Net.

S-UNIWARD	0.4bpp	0.2bpp	0.1bpp
WOW	0.0795	0.0930	0.0717
Random	0.2868	0.1693	0.0718
Hugo	0.4bpp	0.2 bpp	0.1 bpp
WOW	0.0535	0.0388	0.0263
Random	0.3128	0.2235	0.1173
HILL	0.4 bpp	0.2 bpp	0.1 bpp
WOW	0.0636	0.0748	0.0610
Random	0.3027	0.1875	0.0825

3.3 Training Strategy

Based on all the previous descriptions, we can conclude that some spatial image content adaptive information hiding algorithms have similar steganographic behavior, that is, they may produce similar steganographic features. In other words, parameter sharing is essentially sharing the steganography for the model. Therefore, in subsequent model fine-tuning, we only transfer and share the parameters of the network's convolution layer structure. The specific strategies are as follows:

Source Domain Learning: Learn in a hypothetical training set of known embedding algorithms, first training a batch of detection models for known embedding algorithms.

Parameter Transferring: We assume that the results of model pre-training are shown in Formula 1, where H is the model, (c, f) is the combination of model parameters, (c', f') is the combination of model parameters after training, C is the randomly initialized convolution layer parameters, F is the randomly initialized full connection parameter, C' is the convolution layer parameter after training, F' is the model training parameter, and X is the pre-training sample. Y is the corresponding classification result. Based on the analysis in Sect. 3.2, the source domain sample X is similar to the target domain sample X', and the target domain Y is similar to Y', so parameter transferring can be used.

After completing the pre-training, we use the Pytorch deep learning framework to reload the model and share the pre-training parameters, but the parameters do not involve the full connection layer. The full connection layer is rebuilt and randomly initialized, and the new full connection layer is added to the convolution layer of the shared parameter model. The process is parameter sharing, which aims to share the shared steganographic features that may exist between the related embedding algorithms to help learning on the target task, as shown in Formula 2. The specific transfer sharing method is shown in Fig. 2.

$$H\big((c', f), X'\big) = \big(c'', f''\big), Y' \tag{1}$$

$$H\big((c', f), X'\big) \tag{2}$$

Target Task Fine-Tuning: After using the pre-training parameters to initialize the model, we start to fine-tune the detection model on the target task dataset. The premise of determining that the target task can be used for fine-tuning is that the data prior distribution and result distribution of the target task are similar to those of the training task, and the specific value is determined by Wasserstein distance.

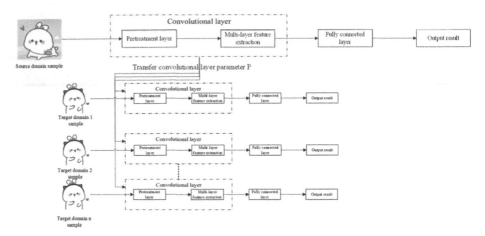

Fig. 2. Schematic diagram of transfer learning method.

4   Experiments

4.1   Datasets

In this paper, a single standard dataset BOSSBase (v1.01) is used to test the relevant performance indicators of all test networks. The dataset BOSSBase contains 10000 grayscale images from seven different cameras, all of which are 512×512 pixels in size and never compressed. Due to our GPU computing power and time constraints, we use matlab to resample the original image into 256×256 pixels for our experiments.

4.2   Experiments Settings

According to the previous work, we choose four common spatial image content adaptive information hiding algorithms: WOW, SUNIWARD, HUGO and HILL. According to the detection situation in other papers, we choose the WOW algorithm as the known information hiding algorithm, and the other three algorithms as the unknown steganography algorithm. Ye net and Zhu net are selected as steganalysis algorithms. In the experiment, the two steganalysis algorithms are pretrained on the hypothetical known steganography datasets, and then fine tuned on different target task datasets.

As for the embedding algorithm used, we use Matlab with a random embedding key to implement it, using the most common content adaptive steganography methods, namely WOW, SUNIWARD, HUGO and HILL algorithms. The embedding rates are respectively: 0.4 bpp, 0.2 bpp, and 0.1 bpp.

It should be noted that when fine-tuning training is carried out on the target task dataset, we adjust the initial value of the learning rate to 0.001.

Finally, we will compare the learning situation and accuracy of the detection algorithm in 4000 training samples without transfer learning and the learning situation and accuracy of the detection algorithm in 2000 training samples with transfer learning to verify whether transfer learning is useful.

4.3 Results

The experiment is carried out in the way of gradual exploration. As the attempt is relatively large, we first choose the single detection algorithm, and under the assumption that there is a pretraining of the known detection algorithm, we carry out the parameter sharing transfer learning of the same size training dataset fine-tuning for some hypothetical unknown algorithms.

The selected detection algorithm is Zhu-Net, the known algorithm is WOW, the unknown algorithm is S-UNIWARD and HUGO, the training dataset size is 4000, and the comparison index is accuracy and learning. The experimental results are shown in Table 3.

From the comparison of accuracy rates, it can be seen that the detection accuracy of Zhu-Net under transfer learning is higher than that of the same size training dataset.

Table 3. Comparison of Zhu-Net using transfer learning with 4000 training samples.

Fine-tuned training set of 4000 sample pairs		
Detecting S-UNIWARD with Zhu-Net	No transfer learning	transfer learning
0.4bpp	78.68%	82.72%
0.2bpp	66.93%	68.29%
0.1bpp	57.18%	59.28%
Detecting HUGO with Zhu-Net	No transfer learning	transfer learning
0.4bpp	81.28%	83.4%
0.2bpp	72.35%	74.43%
0.1bpp	61.68%	65.11%

Without using transfer learning at least 2% higher. This gives us confidence in reducing the training set and performing more experiments later.

From the comparison of Fig. 3, we can see that in the same round, the decrease in the loss of the detection model that use transfer learning is greater than that of the detection model that does not use transfer learning.

With this foundation, let's start the formal experiment. We use 4000 training samples of known information hiding algorithms to initialize the detection model, use half of the training samples of unknown hiding algorithm (2000 samples) to fine-tune the training, and use the training dataset contains 4000 samples of unknown algorithm to train the contrast group. The comparison indexes are learning situation and test dataset accuracy.

Table 4 and Table 5 respectively show the accuracy of the two detection algorithms Zhu-Net and Ye-Net after using transfer learning when the scale of the unknown algorithm training set is halved. After using transfer learning, the detection accuracy of the

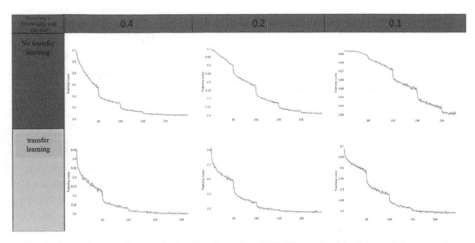

Fig. 3. Learning efficiency of Zhu-Net detecting S-UNIWARD with 4000 training samples.

two detection algorithms can reach the accuracy of large-scale training samples without transfer learning. Although the accuracy of some groups did not improve significantly, they all reached the same level. If in reality, only a small training set can achieve the same performance as a large training set, it can help solve many problems. It also reduces the cost of training and makes better use of the known knowledge. Based on the above data, in terms of accuracy, transfer learning based on parameter sharing can indeed play a good role in assisting the training of related location algorithm.

In addition to the accuracy, we also compared the learning efficiency of the detection model before and after transfer learning.

Figure 4 shows the comparison of the learning efficiency of Zhu-Net in detecting S-UNIWARD, as the diagram is too complicated, others were not shown, and the two detection algorithms with transfer learning both have achieved similar results. After the picture is enlarged, we can make a horizontal and vertical comparison. At the same

Table 4. Comparison of Zhu-Net's learning accuracy rate that use 2000 training samples.

Train dataset containing 2000 samples		
Zhu-Net detecting S-UNIWARD	No transfer（4000 samples）	transfer（2000 samples）
0.4bpp	78.68%	82.33%
0.2 bpp	66.93%	68.23%
0.1 bpp	57.18%	58.88%
Zhu-Net detecting HUGO	No transfer（4000 samples）	transfer（2000 samples）
0.4 bpp	81.28%	82.58%
0.2 bpp	72.35%	72.39%
0.1 bpp	61.68%	64.17%
Zhu-Net detecting HILL	No transfer（4000 samples）	transfer（2000 samples）
0.4 bpp	80.27%	81.14%
0.2 bpp	68.75%	68.8%
0.1 bpp	58.25%	58.34%

iterations, the loss of the detection model of transfer learning decreases more than that of the detection model without transfer learning.

Table 5. Comparison chart of Ye-Net's learning accuracy rate that use 2000 training samples.

	Train dataset containing 2000 samples	
Ye-Net detecting S-UNIWARD	No transfer（4000 samples）	transfer（2000 samples）
0.4	74.24%	77.05%
0.2	61.3%	63.42%
0.1	54.91%	55.12%
Ye-Net detecting HUGO	No transfer（4000 samples）	transfer（2000 samples）
0.4	77.33%	77.35%
0.2	68.1%	68.14%
0.1	61.11%	61.12%
Ye-Net detecting HILL	No transfer（4000 samples）	transfer（2000 samples）
0.4	74.7%	75.98%
0.2	64.02%	64.05%
0.1	57.15%	57.16%

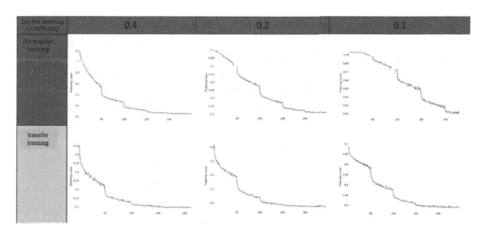

Fig. 4. Comparison of the learning efficiency of Zhu-Net detecting S-UNIWARD with 2000 training samples.

5 Conclusion

In this paper, we propose an optimization of convolutional neural network based steganalysis method. We explores the difference of data distribution between different related information hiding algorithms, introduces the transfer learning of parameter sharing, shares the steganographic features between related information hiding algorithms, reduces the sample size of unknown information hiding algorithm, improves the accuracy of detection algorithm, and improves the learning efficiency of detection algorithm training. We analyzes and proves the proposed method from two aspects, namely accuracy and learning efficiency, and proves that the transfer learning method based on parameter sharing can optimize the training and learning of unknown information hiding algorithm. The experiment results show that the spatial image content adaptive information hiding algorithm is similar in data distribution, because of some common steganographic features. Our method can optimize the learning efficiency of the detection model and the subsequent detection efficiency, It can reduce the sample size of the detection model when learning the same source unknown steganography algorithm, and improve the learning efficiency and detection accuracy.

Acknowledgement. The authors are deeply indebted to anonymous reviewers for their constructive suggestions and helpful comments. The work is supported by the National Key Research and Development Program of China (No. 2019YFB1406504), the National Natural Science Foundation of China (No. U1836108, No. U1936216, No. 62002197, No. 62001038) and the Fundamental Research Funds for the Central Universities (No. 2021RC30).

References

1. Wang, J., Cheng, M., Wu, P., Chen, B.: A survey on digital image steganography. J. Inf. Hiding Priv. Prot. **1**(2), 87–93 (2019)
2. Alhomoud, A.M.: Image steganography in spatial domain: current status, techniques, and trends. Intell. Autom. Soft Comput. **27**(1), 69–88 (2021)
3. Luo, Y., Qin, J., Xiang, X., Tan, Y.: Coverless image steganography based on multi-object recognition. IEEE Trans. Circuits Syst. Video Technol. **31**, 2779–2791 (2021)
4. Yang, Z., Guo, X., Chen, Z., Huang, Y., Zhang, Y.: RNN-stega: linguistic steganography based on recurrent neural networks. IEEE Trans. Inf. Forensics Secur. **14**(5), 1280–1295 (2018)
5. Pevny, T., Bas, P., Fridrich, J.: Steganalysis by subtractive pixel adjacency matrix. IEEE Trans. Inf. Forensics Secur. **5**(2), 215–224 (2010)
6. Fridrich, J., Kodovsky, J.: Rich models for steganalysis of digital images. IEEE Trans. Inf. Forensics Secur. **7**, 868–882 (2012)
7. Holub, V., Fridrich, J.: Random projections of residuals for digital image steganalysis. IEEE Trans. Inf. Forensics Secur. **8**(12), 1996–2006 (2013)
8. Li, B., Li, Z., Zhou, S.: New steganalytic features for spatial image steganography based on derivative filters and threshold LBP operator. IEEE Trans. Inf. Forensics Secur. **13**(5), 1242–1257 (2018)
9. Pevny, T., Fridrich, J.: Merging Markov and DCT features for multi-class JPEG steganalysis. In: Steganography, and Watermarking of Multimedia Contents IX, vol. 6505, 28–40. International Society for Optics and Photonics (2007)
10. Kodovsky, J., Fridrich, J.: Steganalysis of JPEG images using rich models. In: Media Watermarking, Security, and Forensics 2012, p. 83030. International Society for Optics and Photonics (2012)
11. Holub, V., Fridrich, J.: Low-complexity features for JPEG steganalysis using undecimated DCT. IEEE Trans. Inf. Forensics Secur. **10**(2), 219–228 (2015)
12. Holub, V., Fridrich, J.: Phase-aware projection model for steganalysis of JPEG. In: Media Watermarking, Security, and Forensics 2015, p. 94090. International Society for Optics and Photonics (2015)
13. Denemark, T.D., Boroumand, M., Fridrich, J.: Steganalysis features for content-adaptive JPEG steganography. IEEE Trans. Inf. Forensics Secur. **11**(8), 1736–1746 (2016)

14. Nielsen, M.A.: Neural Networks and Deep Learning. Determination Press, San Francisco (2015)
15. Soto, R.T.: Programación paralela sobre arquitecturas heterogéneas. Universidad Nacional de Colombia, Bogotá (2016)
16. Sahiner, B., Chan, H.P., Petrick, N.: Classification of mass and normal breast tissue: a convolution neural network classifier with spatial domain and texture images. IEEE Trans. Med. Imaging **15**(5), 598–610 (2002)
17. Tan, S., Li, B.: Stacked convolutional auto-encoders for steganalysis of digital images. In: Signal and Information Processing Association Annual Summit and Conference (APSIPA), pp. 1–4 (2014)
18. Reinel, T.S., Raul, R.P., Gustavo, I.: Deep learning applied to steganalysis of digital images: a systematic review. IEEE Access 7, 68970–68990 (2019)
19. Qian, Y., Dong, J., Wang, W., et al.: Deep learning for steganalysis via convolutional neural networks. In: Media Watermarking, Security, and Forensics 2015, p. 94090J. International Society for Optics and Photonics (2015)
20. Xu, G., Wu, H.Z., Shi, Y.: Structural design of convolutional neural networks for steganalysis. IEEE Signal Process. Lett. **23**(5), 708–712 (2016)
21. Ye, J., Ni, J., Yi, Y.: Deep learning hierarchical representations for image steganalysis. IEEE Trans. Inf. Forensics Secur. **12**, 2545–2557 (2017)
22. Morishita, I.: Analysis of an adaptive threshold logic unit. IEEE Trans. Comput. **19**(12), 1181–1192 (1970)
23. Yedroudj, M., Comby, F., Chaumont, M.: Yedroudj-net: an efficient CNN for spatial steganalysis. In: 2018 IEEE International Conference on Acoustics, Speech and Signal Processing (ICASSP), pp. 2092–2096 (2018)
24. Zhang, R., Zhu, F., Liu, J., Liu, G.: Depth-wise separable convolutions and multi-level pooling for an efficient spatial CNN-based steganalysis. IEEE Trans. Inf. Forensics Secur. **15**, 1138–1150 (2019)
25. Szegedy, C., et al.: Going deeper with convolutions. In: Proceedings of the IEEE Conference on Computer Vision and Pattern Recognition, pp. 1–9 (2015)
26. Chollet, F.: Xception: deep learning with depthwise separable convolutions. In: Proceedings of the IEEE Conference on Computer Vision and Pattern Recognition, pp. 1251–1258 (2017)
27. He, K., Zhang, X., Ren, S.: Spatial pyramid pooling in deep convolutional networks for visual recognition. IEEE Trans. Pattern Anal. Mach. Intell. **37**, 1904–1916 (2015)
28. Boroumand, M., Chen, M., Fridrich, J.: Deep residual network for steganalysis of digital images. IEEE Trans. Inf. Forensics Secur. **14**(5), 1181–1193 (2018)
29. Ye, D.: Steganalysis based on transfer learning. Chin. J. Netw. Inf. Secur. **3**(1), 23 (2017)
30. Dengpan, Y., Shunzhi, J., Shiyu, L., ChangRui, L.: Faster and transferable deep learning steganalysis on GPU. J. Real-Time Image Proc. **16**(3), 623–633 (2019). https://doi.org/10.1007/s11554-019-00870-1

Find the Unseen Actions: Abnormal Action Recognition

Jianyang Zhai[1]([✉]), Siqi Wang[1], En Zhu[1], Xinwang Liu[1], and Wei Chen[2]

[1] National University of Defense Technology, Changsha, China
zhaijianyang@nudt.edu.cn
[2] School of Computer Science, University of Birmingham, Birmingham, England

Abstract. Deep neural networks are gaining increasing traction in action recognition. Existing literature are based on a basic assumption that the test sample belongs to a certain category in the training set. However, this assumption is severely limited in real world where unseen (socalled "abnormal") events may occur. Most existing methods usually fail to identify abnormal actions, which are usually classified as a normal category. To address these issues, we propose abnormal action recognition that effectively detect unpredictable abnormal actions. Specifically, we treat multiple categories of the training set as normal categories, and the test set contains normal and abnormal categories (not belonging to any of the categories in the training set). We study abnormal action recognition from three aspects: 1) The softmax distribution of the classifier; 2) Mahalanobis distance-based confidence score; 3) Classification feature. Finally, we analyze the experiment in detail and discuss the idea of improving the recognition of abnormal actions. Our codes and results can be verified at https://github.com/zhaijianyang/abnormal-action-recognition.

Keywords: Abnormal action recognition · Anomaly detection · Video analysis · Deep neural networks

1 Introduction

In recent years, computer science and artificial intelligence have developed rapidly and have made substantial progress in medical [26,29], industrial [1, 33,37] and other fields. At the same time, video analysis technology [19,42] has rapidly emerged and received widespread attention. One of the core aspects of video analysis is action recognition [7,38,41]. The accuracy and speed of action recognition directly affect the results of the subsequent work of the video analysis system. At present, the action recognition model [3,39] based on deep neural network has been able to achieve high accuracy. However, the existing action recognition algorithms assume that the test sample belongs to a certain category in the training set. When the classifier is applied to actual tasks, the classifier usually fails if the test sample is abnormal. What's more frightening is that the classifier usually gives a high degree of confidence to abnormal sample [25,27], which will seriously affect the results of video analysis. Therefore, the recognition of abnormal actions is a necessary and valuable research.

The Out-Of Distribution (OOD) detection of images has made great progress [12,31,36], and they usually detect whether the images are out of distribution samples. However, compared with images, videos are time-sequential and have richer semantic features. Video is greatly affected by the environment, lighting and surrounding objects. It is very challenging to study abnormal action recognition algorithms suitable for videos.

Different from general video abnormal detection [4,24,28], they usually detect whether each frame of the video is abnormal, and do not determine whether an action clip is abnormal. In fact, an action requires several consecutive frames to be determined. For example, opening a door and closing a door are two completely different but very similar actions. The type of action cannot be determined from a certain frame, let alone whether the action is abnormal. Therefore, our purpose is to detect whether the action is abnormal through a video clip.

In this paper, we propose abnormal action recognition and study abnormal action recognition from three aspects. First of all, from the perspective of the softmax distribution of classification, an intuitive idea is that correctly classified samples will get a larger softmax score compared to misclassified samples and abnormal samples [11]. The softmax score distribution of the statistical testing data can be used to detect abnormal actions. Secondly, different network layers can extract different feature maps, which record different levels of information. We detect abnormal samples by fusing different feature maps. Third, One-Class Support Vector Machine (OCSVM) [30] is a classic algorithm for abnormal detection. We extract the features of action clips to train the OCSVM model, and then to detect its effect on abnormal action recognition.

The main contributions of this paper can be summarized as follows:

- Aiming at the shortcoming that action classification cannot recognize abnormal data, we propose abnormal action recognition. Due to the diverse and uncertain of abnormal actions, we only model normal actions.
- We study abnormal actions recognition from three aspects. We propose to recognize abnormal actions without changing the classification accuracy. Extensive experiments proves the feasibility of the research on abnormal action recognition.
- We discuss some ideas for improvement and future work. This is a meaningful research direction, and we hope that more researchers will study abnormal action recognition.

2   Problem Description and Evaluation

In this paper, we mainly focus on the recognition of abnormal actions. Assuming that there are k classes in the training set, we think these k classes are normal classes, and other unseen classses are abnormal classes. For example, if we regard walking and running as normal actions, then playing ball, dancing, etc. are all abnormal actions. Our goal is to model normal actions, and when there are unseen actions, the model can recognize them as abnormal actions.

For all actions in the open world, we define two classes, normal actions and abnormal actions. The detector outputs a score for both the normal and abnormal action. Unseen abnormal actions are diverse, and there may be class imbalance, so we use AUROC (Area Under the Receiver Operating Characteristic Curve) as the evaluation metric [6]. The AUROC evaluation metric takes into account the trade-off of positive examples and negative examples, and is relatively stable in the case of class imbalance.

3   Method Introduction

In this part, we study abnormal actions recognition from three aspects. The method is introduced below.

3.1   Softmax Distribution

Softmax Prediction Probability. Hendrycks and Gimpel [11] first proposed a deep model-based Out-Of Distribution detection method, and conducted a large number of experiments on image classification, emotion classification, text classification, speech recognition tasks. Here, we study the impact of softmax prediction probability on abnormal action recognition.

One of the basic points of the literature [11] is that compared to misclassified actions and abnormal actions, actions that are classified correctly will get a higher softmax probability. We first train an action recognition classifier $f = (f_1, \ldots, f_C)$, where C is the number of classes. Then, for each sample x, we use the **maximum softmax score**, i.e., $S(x) = \max_i S_i(x)$ as its anomaly score. Specifically,

$$S_i(x) = \frac{\exp f_i(x)}{\sum_{j=1}^{C} \exp f_j(x)}. \tag{1}$$

Out-of-DIstribution Detector for Neural Networks. ODIN [21] proposed the use of temperature scaling and input preprocessing to improve the performance of OOD detection. In this subsection, we explore its performance in abnormal action recognition.

The temperature scaling can be used to distill the knowledge in the neural network [13] and calibrate the confidence in classification tasks [10]. Through experiments, it is found that temperature scaling can be used to separate the softmax scores of normal and abnormal action, making abnormal action recognition effective. For each input x, we calculate its softmax score, $S(x; T) = \max_i S_i(x; T)$. Specifically,

$$S_i(x; T) = \frac{\exp\left(f_i(x)/T\right)}{\sum_{j=1}^{C} \exp\left(f_j(x)/T\right)}, \tag{2}$$

where $T \in \mathbb{R}^+$ is the temperature scaling parameter.

ODIN [21] found that perturbations have different effects on in-distribution and out-of-distribution samples. In particular, perturbation has a greater impact on in-distribution samples, making it easier to separate normal and abnormal samples.

$$\tilde{x} = x - \varepsilon \, \text{sign} \left(-\nabla_x \log S(x; T) \right), \tag{3}$$

where the parameter ε is the perturbation magnitude. As we shall see later, the perturbation is also applicable to video action clips. It can separate the softmax scores of normal actions and abnormal actions. We also discuss the influence of the temperature scaling parameter T on the recognition of abnormal actions.

For each action clip x, we first calculate the preprocessed action clip x according to the Eq. (2). Next, we feed the preprocessed action clip $\tilde{x}$ into the neural network, calculate its calibrated softmax score $S(\tilde{x}; T)$ and compare the score to the threshold δ. An action clip is classified as normal if the softmax score is greater than the threshold and vice versa. Mathematically, the action abnormal detector can be described as

$$g(x; \delta, T, \varepsilon) = \begin{cases} 1 & \text{if } \max_i p(\tilde{x}; T) \leq \delta, \\ 0 & \text{if } \max_i p(\tilde{x}; T) > \delta. \end{cases} \tag{4}$$

3.2   Mahalanobis Distance-Based Confidence Score

Lee et al. [18] proposed the use of Mahalanobis distance-based confidence score for images OOD detection. Their method based on softmax classifier and generative classifier under GDA (Gaussian discriminant analysis) is equivalent. Here, we only consider the effect of this method in the recognition of abnormal actions.

Calculate Anomaly Score. Suppose we have pre-trained a action classifier, and then we compute the features of all training samples $\{(x_1, y_1), \ldots, (x_N, y_N)\}$ and calculate the mean and covariance for each class:

$$\widehat{\mu}_c = \frac{1}{N_c} \sum_{i:y_i=c} f(x_i), \quad \widehat{\Sigma} = \frac{1}{N} \sum_c \sum_{i:y_i=c} (f(x_i) - \widehat{\mu}_c)(f(x_i) - \widehat{\mu}_c)^\top, \tag{5}$$

where N_c is the number of training samples with label c, and $f(\cdot)$ denotes the output of the penultimate layer of classifier. We compute the Mahalanobis distance of the test sample x to the Gaussian distribution for each class and then we calculate abnormal score $M(x)$, i.e.,

$$M(x) = \max_c - (f(x) - \widehat{\mu}_c)^\top \widehat{\Sigma}^{-1} (f(x) - \widehat{\mu}_c). \tag{6}$$

Algorithm 1: Calculating the Mahalanobis distance-based abnormal score.

Data: Test sample $\boldsymbol{x}$, parameters of Gaussian distributions $\left\{ \widehat{\mu}_{\ell,c}, \widehat{\boldsymbol{\Sigma}}_\ell : \forall \ell, c \right\}$,
      noise ε, and weights α_ℓ.

Result: Abnormal score for test sample $\sum_\ell \alpha_\ell M_\ell$.

Initialize score vectors: $\mathbf{M}(\mathbf{x}) = [M_\ell : \forall \ell]$;

for *each layer* $\ell \in 1, \ldots, L$ **do**

    Find the closest class: $\widehat{c} = \arg\min_c (f_\ell(\mathbf{x}) - \widehat{\mu}_{\ell,c})^\top \widehat{\boldsymbol{\Sigma}}_\ell^{-1} (f_\ell(\mathbf{x}) - \widehat{\mu}_{\ell,c})$;

    Add pertubation to test sample:

    $\widehat{\mathbf{x}} = \mathbf{x} - \varepsilon \, \text{sign} \left(\nabla_{\mathbf{x}} (f_\ell(\mathbf{x}) - \widehat{\mu}_{\ell,\widehat{c}})^\top \widehat{\boldsymbol{\Sigma}}_\ell^{-1} (f_\ell(\mathbf{x}) - \widehat{\mu}_{\ell,\widehat{c}}) \right)$;

    Calculating abnormal score:

    $M_\ell = \max_c - (f_\ell(\widehat{\mathbf{x}}) - \widehat{\mu}_{\ell,c})^\top \widehat{\boldsymbol{\Sigma}}_\ell^{-1} (f_\ell(\widehat{\mathbf{x}}) - \widehat{\mu}_{\ell,c})$.

end

Input Pre-processing. By adding small controlled noise, normal and abnormal samples can be better separated. Specifically, we add the small perturbation to each test sample $\boldsymbol{x}$, and then get the pre-processed input sample $\widehat{\boldsymbol{x}}$:

$$\widehat{\boldsymbol{x}} = \boldsymbol{x} + \varepsilon \, \text{sign} \left(\nabla_{\boldsymbol{x}} M(\boldsymbol{x}) \right) = \boldsymbol{x} - \varepsilon \, \text{sign} \left(\nabla_{\boldsymbol{x}} (f(\boldsymbol{x}) - \widehat{\mu}_{\widehat{c}})^\top \widehat{\boldsymbol{\Sigma}}^{-1} (f(\boldsymbol{x}) - \widehat{\mu}_{\widehat{c}}) \right), \quad (7)$$

where $\widehat{c}$ is the index of the closest class and ε is a magnitude of noise. There are many prior works [9,20,21] that use similar input preprocessing, the difference is that the perturbation is added here to increase the proposed metric (6).

Feature Ensemble. First, for all training samples, we extract the ℓ−th hidden features of pre-trained classifier, denoted by $f_\ell(\boldsymbol{x})$, and calculate the mean and covariance for each class, i.e., $\widehat{\mu}_{\ell,c}$ and $\widehat{\Sigma}_\ell$. Then, for each test sample $\boldsymbol{x}$, we utilize Eq. (6) to calculate the abnormal score for the ℓ−th layer. The feature ensemble method is described in Algorithm 1. First, we calculate abnormal scores for all layers, and then integrate them: $\sum_\ell \alpha_\ell M_\ell(\mathbf{x})$, where $M_\ell(\cdot)$ and α_ℓ is the abnormal score at the ℓ−th layer and its weight, respectively. Specifically, referring to the method in [23], we train a logistic regression detector to find the weights of each layer.

3.3 Classification Feature

OCSVM [30] is a classic method for abnormal detection and a strong baseline. This method models the training data and maps the training data to a compact space, which meets the needs of abnormal action recognition, because our training data only has normal samples. In our experiments, we model the classification features. In our experiment, we first fit the model with the classification features of the training data, and then evaluate the effect of abnormal action recognition on the test set.

4 Experiment

In this section, We introduce the datasets, the experimental setup and analyzed the experimental results in detail.

4.1 Datasets

HMDB-51. HMDB-51 [17] is one of the most commonly used datasets in the field of action recognition. HMDB-51 comes from a wide range of sources, some from movies, and some from websites, such as Google Video and youtube. The dataset contains 6849 clips with a total of 51 action classes, and each class contains at least 101 clips. The actions classes can be grouped in five types: body movements for human interaction, body movements with object interaction, feneral body movements, general facial actions smile, facial actions with object manipulation.

UCF-101. UCF-101 [34] is an action recognition data set of realistic action videos, collected from YouTube. UCF-101 has a total of 13320 clips divided into 101 categories, which is diverse in action and is one of the challenging action recognition datasets. Video scenes have a high degree of complexity, such as cluttered backgrounds, poor lighting conditions, and diverse object appearances and object sizes. The action categories can be divided into five types: 1) Sports, 2) Playing Musical Instruments, 3) Human-Human Interaction, 4) Body-Motion Only, 5) Human-Object Interaction.

4.2 Setups

Datasets. In the official settings, HMDB51 and UCF101 both have three training and test splits. We experiment on the split 1. We divide the data set into normal and abnormal classes. For fairness, we use five divisions to conduct experiments, and finally take the average of the test results. Specifically, for a data set with C classes, we divide the training set into five segments according to the order of classification labels. Each time we select one segment as the abnormal class and discard it, and train the classifier with the other classes as the normal class, and the test set remains unchanged.

Training and Testing. We conduct experiments on abnormal action recognition tasks. Our code is based on mmaction2 [5], which implements the existing popular action recognition algorithm. Unless otherwise stated, our classification model uses I3D [3] by default. Specifically, we fine-tune the model from Kinetics [16] pre-trained weights. The training parameters are: 25 training epochs, initial learning rate 0.0005 (decays by 0.1 at epoch 15&20), weight decay 1e−4, batch size 16, and dropout 0.5. During the test, they [3,5] used multiple crops to improve the test accuracy, but we use the same data processing as during the validation.

4.3 Results

Our abnormal action recognition tasks are all performed on a pre-trained classification model. The obvious advantage is that no additional detectors are required to be trained. In Table 1, we report the classification accuracy of the pre-trained model.

Table 1. Classification accuracy of pre-trained models on UCF-101 and HMDB-51. All values are percentages.

Datasets	Splits1	Splits2	Splits3	Splits4	Splits5	Mean
UCF-101	95.60	95.58	94.91	94.40	94.47	94.99
HMDB-51	72.11	72.76	71.38	70.33	81.08	73.53

Main Results. We report the performance of the four methods on UCF-101 and HMDB-51 in Table 2. We use T = 1000 for ODIN and Mahalanobis. Since the hyperparameter ε has different effects on performance, we choose the one that maximizes the average AUROC. Specifically, we use $\varepsilon = 0.000001$ for ODIN and $\varepsilon = 0.0005$ for Mahalanobis on HMDB-51. We use $\varepsilon = 0.00005$ for ODIN and $\varepsilon = 0.0001$ for Mahalanobis on UCF-101.

Table 2. Abnormal action recognition performance. All values are percentages.

Datasets	Method	Splits1	Splits2	Splits3	Splits4	Splits5	Mean
UCF-101	Softmax	85.32	89.25	90.78	91.45	92.80	89.92
	Odin	87.39	90.34	92.75	92.95	92.25	**91.14**
	Mahalanobis	89.66	87.96	90.35	90.41	90.09	89.69
	Oc-svm	87.67	89.10	90.81	91.79	91.65	90.20
HMDB-51	Softmax	68.50	71.74	82.14	79.76	79.17	76.26
	Odin	69.86	70.56	84.09	81.60	76.79	**76.58**
	Mahalanobis	65.77	61.38	80.03	77.14	66.24	70.11
	Oc-svm	67.62	66.18	80.39	79.02	71.03	72.85

Architecture Analysis. In this section, we study the influence of network architecture on the recognition of abnormal actions. Due to the limited experimental conditions, we only compare the effects of TSM [22] and I3D on the HMDB-51 dataset. As shown in Fig. 1, the classification accuracy of the two classifiers is similar, but I3D has stronger abnormal action recognition performance than TSM. This is a phenomenon worth studying. In future work, we may study the influence of more architectures on the recognition of abnormal actions.

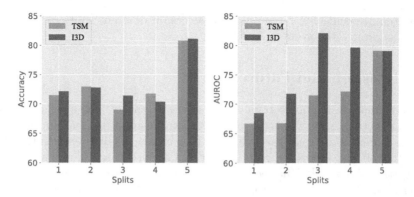

Fig. 1. Performance comparison between TSM and I3D architecture.

Hyperparameter Analysis. A larger temperature scaling parameter T can make the softmax scores of abnormal and normal samples more separable [21]. In this subsection, we study the influence of the parameter ε on the HMDB-51 dataset and we use $T = 1000$ for ODIN. Table 3 and Table 4 shows that small perturbation have little impact on the performance of ODIN, and for the Mahalanobis algorithm, it can improve the performance of abnormal action

Table 3. The effect of ε on the performance of ODIN. All values are percentages except ε.

ε	0	0.0014	0.0001	0.00001	0.000001
Split1	69.85	70.51	70.24	69.93	69.86
Split2	70.55	64.88	69.97	70.52	70.56
Split3	84.10	79.30	82.68	83.97	84.09
Split4	81.58	80.45	82.33	81.72	81.60
Split5	76.80	73.79	76.13	76.75	76.79
Mean	76.58	73.79	76.27	76.58	76.58

Table 4. The effect of ε on the performance of Mahalanobis. All values are percentages except ε.

ε	0	0.01	0.005	0.002	0.0014	0.001	0.0005	0.0001
Split1	65.25	56.09	59.50	62.85	64.08	65.03	65.77	65.71
Split2	59.07	59.03	58.27	58.62	59.92	60.82	61.38	59.61
Split3	79.90	70.87	73.48	76.93	78.66	79.80	80.03	79.55
Split4	76.05	66.32	70.58	75.37	76.33	76.99	77.14	76.74
Split5	65.78	60.29	59.74	63.04	63.60	65.10	66.24	63.08
Mean	69.21	62.52	64.31	67.36	68.52	69.55	70.11	68.94

recognition. Specifically, ε has different effects on different split, we choose the ε that maximizes the average AUROC.

5 Discussion and Future Work

We study abnormal action recognition from three aspects. The first is to identify abnormal actions from the softmax score distribution of normal and abnormal samples, which is a strong baseline. How to increase the difference in the distribution of softmax scores between normal and abnormal samples is still a problem worthy of research. The second is to use feature maps to identify abnormal actions. The Mahalanobis [18] method achieves high performance in the OOD detection of images, but the performance in videos is not ideal. Maybe we should study a method suitable for video feature maps. The third is to use classification features to identify abnormal actions. Supervised learning can produce semantic representations, but only to the extent that these representations are sufficient to distinguish categories within the domain. The network is not encouraged to learn additional features beyond the minimum necessary for classification. How to make the network learn task-independent, higher semantic features is the key to improving the recognition of abnormal actions.

In addition, compared with images, videos are time-sequential and rich in motion information. Optical flow [15] has rich information of motion dynamics. Many video tasks, such as action recognition [8,32,35] and video anomaly detection [2,14,28,40], make full use of optical flow information, and task performance has also been improved. In future work, we will also consider fusing optical flow to improve the performance of abnormal action recognition.

6 Conclusion

In this paper, we propose abnormal actions recognition, and study the recognition of abnormal actions from three directions: softmax score distribution, feature maps and classification features. This is a new problem that has not been studied, and our research can be used as a baseline. We discussed some ideas about future work and encourage more researchers to study abnormal action recognition.

Acknowledgements. The work is supported by NUDT Research Project under Grant No. ZK20-10.

References

1. Alghassab, M.A.: Defect detection in printed circuit boards with pre-trained feature extraction methodology with convolution neural networks. CMC-Comput. Mater. Contin. **70**(1), 637–652 (2022)

2. Cai, R., Zhang, H., Liu, W., Gao, S., Hao, Z.: Appearance-motion memory consistency network for video anomaly detection. In: Proceedings of the AAAI Conference on Artificial Intelligence, vol. 35, pp. 938–946 (2021)
3. Carreira, J., Zisserman, A.: Quo vadis, action recognition? A new model and the kinetics dataset. In: Proceedings of the IEEE Conference on Computer Vision and Pattern Recognition, pp. 6299–6308 (2017)
4. Chang, Y., Tu, Z., Xie, W., Yuan, J.: Clustering driven deep autoencoder for video anomaly detection. In: Vedaldi, A., Bischof, H., Brox, T., Frahm, J.-M. (eds.) ECCV 2020, Part XV. LNCS, vol. 12360, pp. 329–345. Springer, Cham (2020). https://doi.org/10.1007/978-3-030-58555-6_20
5. Contributors, M.: Openmmlab's next generation video understanding toolbox and benchmark (2020). https://github.com/open-mmlab/mmaction2
6. Davis, J., Goadrich, M.: The relationship between precision-recall and roc curves. In: Proceedings of the 23rd International Conference on Machine Learning, pp. 233–240 (2006)
7. Feichtenhofer, C., Fan, H., Malik, J., He, K.: Slowfast networks for video recognition. In: Proceedings of the IEEE/CVF International Conference on Computer Vision, pp. 6202–6211 (2019)
8. Feichtenhofer, C., Pinz, A., Zisserman, A.: Convolutional two-stream network fusion for video action recognition. In: Proceedings of the IEEE Conference on Computer Vision and Pattern Recognition, pp. 1933–1941 (2016)
9. Goodfellow, I.J., Shlens, J., Szegedy, C.: Explaining and harnessing adversarial examples. arXiv preprint arXiv:1412.6572 (2014)
10. Guo, C., Pleiss, G., Sun, Y., Weinberger, K.Q.: On calibration of modern neural networks. In: International Conference on Machine Learning, pp. 1321–1330. PMLR (2017)
11. Hendrycks, D., Gimpel, K.: A baseline for detecting misclassified and out-of-distribution examples in neural networks. arXiv preprint arXiv:1610.02136 (2016)
12. Hendrycks, D., Mazeika, M., Dietterich, T.: Deep anomaly detection with outlier exposure. arXiv preprint arXiv:1812.04606 (2018)
13. Hinton, G., Vinyals, O., Dean, J.: Distilling the knowledge in a neural network. arXiv preprint arXiv:1503.02531 (2015)
14. Hu, J., Zhu, E., Wang, S., Wang, S., Liu, X., Yin, J.: Two-stage unsupervised video anomaly detection using low-rank based unsupervised one-class learning with ridge regression. In: 2019 International Joint Conference on Neural Networks (IJCNN), pp. 1–8. IEEE (2019)
15. Ilg, E., Mayer, N., Saikia, T., Keuper, M., Dosovitskiy, A., Brox, T.: Flownet 2.0: Evolution of optical flow estimation with deep networks. In: Proceedings of the IEEE Conference on Computer Vision and Pattern Recognition, pp. 2462–2470 (2017)
16. Kay, W., et al.: The kinetics human action video dataset. arXiv preprint arXiv:1705.06950 (2017)
17. Kuehne, H., Jhuang, H., Garrote, E., Poggio, T., Serre, T.: HMDB: a large video database for human motion recognition. In: 2011 International Conference on Computer Vision, pp. 2556–2563. IEEE (2011)
18. Lee, K., Lee, K., Lee, H., Shin, J.: A simple unified framework for detecting out-of-distribution samples and adversarial attacks. arXiv preprint arXiv:1807.03888 (2018)
19. Li, J., Liu, X., Zong, Z., Zhao, W., Zhang, M., Song, J.: Graph attention based proposal 3G convnets for action detection. In: Proceedings of the AAAI Conference on Artificial Intelligence, vol. 34, pp. 4626–4633 (2020)

20. Liang, S., Li, Y., Srikant, R.: Principled detection of out-of-distribution examples in neural networks. arXiv preprint arXiv:1706.02690, pp. 655–662 (2017)
21. Liang, S., Li, Y., Srikant, R.: Enhancing the reliability of out-of-distribution image detection in neural networks. arXiv preprint arXiv:1706.02690 (2017)
22. Lin, J., Gan, C., Han, S.: TSM: temporal shift module for efficient video understanding. In: Proceedings of the IEEE/CVF International Conference on Computer Vision, pp. 7083–7093 (2019)
23. Ma, X., et al.: Characterizing adversarial subspaces using local intrinsic dimensionality. arXiv preprint arXiv:1801.02613 (2018)
24. Markovitz, A., Sharir, G., Friedman, I., Zelnik-Manor, L., Avidan, S.: Graph embedded pose clustering for anomaly detection. In: Proceedings of the IEEE/CVF Conference on Computer Vision and Pattern Recognition, pp. 10539–10547 (2020)
25. Moosavi-Dezfooli, S.M., Fawzi, A., Fawzi, O., Frossard, P.: Universal adversarial perturbations. In: Proceedings of the IEEE Conference on Computer Vision and Pattern Recognition, pp. 1765–1773 (2017)
26. Mushtaq, I., Umer, M., Imran, M., Nasir, I.M., Muhammad, G., Shorfuzzaman, M.: Customer prioritization for medical supply chain during covid-19 pandemic. Comput. Mater. Contin. **70**, 59–72 (2021)
27. Nguyen, A., Yosinski, J., Clune, J.: Deep neural networks are easily fooled: high confidence predictions for unrecognizable images. In: Proceedings of the IEEE Conference on Computer Vision and Pattern Recognition, pp. 427–436 (2015)
28. Nguyen, T.N., Meunier, J.: Anomaly detection in video sequence with appearance-motion correspondence. In: Proceedings of the IEEE/CVF International Conference on Computer Vision, pp. 1273–1283 (2019)
29. Rajakumari, R., Kalaivani, L.: Breast cancer detection and classification using deep CNN techniques. Intell. Autom. Soft Comput. **32**(2), 1089–1107 (2022)
30. Schölkopf, B., Williamson, R.C., Smola, A.J., Shawe-Taylor, J., Platt, J.C., et al.: Support vector method for novelty detection. In: NIPS, vol. 12, pp. 582–588. Citeseer (1999)
31. Sehwag, V., Chiang, M., Mittal, P.: SSD: a unified framework for self-supervised outlier detection. arXiv preprint arXiv:2103.12051 (2021)
32. Sevilla-Lara, L., Liao, Y., Güney, F., Jampani, V., Geiger, A., Black, M.J.: On the integration of optical flow and action recognition. In: Brox, T., Bruhn, A., Fritz, M. (eds.) GCPR 2018. LNCS, vol. 11269, pp. 281–297. Springer, Cham (2019). https://doi.org/10.1007/978-3-030-12939-2_20
33. Shin, H.K., Lee, S.W., Hong, G.P., Sael, L., Lee, S.H., Kim, H.Y.: Defect-detection model for underground parking lots using image object-detection method. Comput. Mater. Contin. **66**(3), 2493–2507 (2020)
34. Soomro, K., Zamir, A.R., Shah, M.: UCF101: a dataset of 101 human actions classes from videos in the wild. arXiv preprint arXiv:1212.0402 (2012)
35. Sun, S., Kuang, Z., Sheng, L., Ouyang, W., Zhang, W.: Optical flow guided feature: a fast and robust motion representation for video action recognition. In: Proceedings of the IEEE Conference on Computer Vision and Pattern Recognition, pp. 1390–1399 (2018)
36. Tack, J., Mo, S., Jeong, J., Shin, J.: CSI: novelty detection via contrastive learning on distributionally shifted instances. arXiv preprint arXiv:2007.08176 (2020)
37. Wang, B., Li, M., Jiang, J.: An enhanced nonlocal self-similarity technique for fabric defect detection. J. Inf. Hiding Priv. Prot. **1**(3), 135 (2019)
38. Wang, J., Lin, Y., Ma, A.J., Yuen, P.C.: Self-supervised temporal discriminative learning for video representation learning. arXiv preprint arXiv:2008.02129 (2020)

39. Yang, C., Xu, Y., Shi, J., Dai, B., Zhou, B.: Temporal pyramid network for action recognition. In: Proceedings of the IEEE/CVF Conference on Computer Vision and Pattern Recognition, pp. 591–600 (2020)
40. Yu, G., et al.: Cloze test helps: effective video anomaly detection via learning to complete video events. In: Proceedings of the 28th ACM International Conference on Multimedia, pp. 583–591 (2020)
41. Yun, S., Oh, S.J., Heo, B., Han, D., Kim, J.: Videomix: rethinking data augmentation for video classification. arXiv preprint arXiv:2012.03457 (2020)
42. Zeng, R., et al.: Graph convolutional networks for temporal action localization. In: Proceedings of the IEEE/CVF International Conference on Computer Vision, pp. 7094–7103 (2019)

CGFMD: CNN and GRU Based Framework for Malicious Domain Name Detection

Wuping Ke[1], Desheng Zheng[1(✉)], Cong Zhang[2], Biying Deng[1], Hui Yao[3], and Lulu Tian[4]

[1] Southwest Petroleum University, Chengdu 610500, China
zheng_de_sheng@163.com
[2] AECC Sichuan Gas Turbine Establishment, Mianyang 621000, China
[3] Civil Aviation Administration of China, Chengdu 610041, China
[4] Brunel University London, Middlesex UB8 3PH, UK

Abstract. With the rapid development of Internet technology, the Internet has penetrated into all aspects of people's life. Botnet and malware are important issues facing network security. These malicious services often use Domain Generation Algorithm (DGA) to avoid security detection. DGA detection is one of the key technologies of malicious C & C communication detection. The identification of malicious domain names generated by DGA has always been an important topic to maintain network security. At present, there are some problems in the identification of malicious domain names, such as single identification method, low accuracy and low identification efficiency. We propose a malicious domain name detection model CGFMD based on CNN-GRU. It combines word vector mapping with convolution neural network to automatically extract the potential features of malicious domain names. At the same time, GRU network is added to the model to solve the long-term dependence problem. The experimental results show that CGFMD algorithm has higher detection accuracy and lower false positive rate than traditional methods. It saves cumbersome manual feature extraction, and can recognize DGA domain names efficiently.

Keywords: Malicious domain name identification · Convolution neural network · GRU · Cyberspace security

1 Introduction

With the continuous innovation and development of more and more powerful internet, modern artificial intelligence and other modern technologies, people's daily life more depends on the internet, and internet applications penetrate into all aspects of people's lives. However, as the internet brings convenience to people's daily life, there are many dangers exist in the use of the internet. Botnets and malware are important issues facing network security. No matter individuals or enterprises, they are always facing the problem of network security in the process of using the network and participating in network activities. In our personal use of the network, there are data leaks such as account leakage, password leakage and personal information leakage, which has become a great

X. Sun et al. (Eds.): ICAIS 2022, CCIS 1586, pp. 564–574, 2022.
https://doi.org/10.1007/978-3-031-06767-9_47

trouble to our daily work and life. There have been a large number of network security problems, whether out of interest or destruction. For example, the recent source code leakage of software suppliers of central banks and securities institutions in dozens of countries around the world, a serious data leakage accident in the Bank of the Cayman Islands, the internet of things chip manufacturer Advantech was blackmailed for 82.82 million yuan, and the Manchester United system was threatened by hacker attacks and ransom of millions of British pounds. These network security problems have caused huge losses.

These attacks are often implemented using botnets. In everyone's daily life, we use our own mobile phone or home computer to participate in the network. We read comments, like and forward them on social media. Friends we meet in the game world, and even favorite objects matched by dating app, may not be human behind them. Mass account production and huge speech dissemination are all caused by botnets. The erosion of botnets does not care whether the object is poor or rich, good or bad. As long as someone participates in the system of Internet communication, they may be infringed. Botnet is a new type of attack, which evolved from the traditional evil cause code form. It spreads the virus through some special means and embeds the malicious program into the attacker's host, and the criminals become the controllers in the infected host network [1]. A control & command server is set up in the Botnet, which is a key server. Criminals use this server to control the infected hosts in the botnet and send instructions to these infected hosts, so as to control them to achieve the purpose of attackers. Therefore, the central machine in the botnet is the core used by criminals. If the server used to control the infected host can be killed, the botnet will be killed [2]. In order to prevent the C & C server from being killed by security personnel, a botnet based on domain generation algorithm method appears. The main function of the DGA algorithm here is to automatically generate fake domain names, and there are a large number of domain names generated. Attackers only need to register a few of them. Once the controlled host accesses a registered domain name, the attacker server can communicate with it. Therefore, the detection of malicious domain names is very important.

2 Related Works

2.1 Malicious Domain Name Detection

In terms of detecting DGA domain names, there are mainly the following methods: analyze all network traffic of possible risk clients, find out abnormal DNS requests, find out suspicious domain names and limit them [3]. This method is time-consuming and laborious, and the efficiency is particularly low. Reverse engineering is used to explain the virus program and domain name generation algorithm [4], which cannot distinguish the unknown DGA domain name. Collision with the DGA domain name library organizes the connection with the C & C server by setting a blacklist [5]. The blacklist method is very fragile for protection. Most DGA algorithms are random, and the number of random domain names generated is very large and variable. It is difficult to include all suspicious domain names in the blacklist. With the development of artificial intelligence, machine learning and deep learning are applied to detect DGA domain names and show a very good detection effect [6]. At present, there are also some researches using CNN model for classification, S. Lee uses the CNN model to classify and detect small moths [7]. Zheng et al. designed an efficient barcode image recognition algorithm [8].

With the development of hardware, various fields of machine learning and deep learning have developed rapidly in recent years. The commonly used algorithms for DGA domain name recognition include support vector machine (SVM) [9], convolutional neural network (CNN) [10], bidirectional cyclic neural network (BRNN) [11], etc. In addition, there are FANCI system [12] and featureless method hidden Markov model (HMM) [13]. In addition, adversarial sample attack and defense is a research hotspot in recent years [14–16]. Attackers generate adversarial samples through small modifications to make the prediction of deep neural network wrong. The generated adversarial samples can reveal the vulnerability of neural networks, and repair these fragile neural networks to improve the security and robustness of the model. Therefore, adding countermeasure sample training to the model can increase the robustness of the model.

2.2 Gate Recurrent Unit

Gate Recurrent Unit(GRU) is a kind of recurrent neural network (RNN). The most common cyclic neural networks are long short term memory network (LSTM [17–19]) and GRU network. Like LSTM, they are also proposed to solve the problem of back propagation and gradient disappearance in long-term memory. In fact, GRU and LSTM have similar effects in solving gradient disappearance in many scenarios. We choose GRU in model training in this paper. Because its role and effect are similar to LSTM, but it has fewer parameters to be trained, so the model training speed will be greatly improved.

LSTM and GRU have the same effect in most cases, and they are easier to train, which greatly improves the efficiency of model training. Therefore, we prefer to use GRU in most experiments. The input and output structure of GRU is the same as that of general recurrent neural network. Compared with LSTM model, GRU model has fewer parameters to be trained. There are only two gate functions: reset gate and update gate, while LSTM model has three gate functions: input, forgetting and output.

2.3 Natural Language Processing

From the analysis of the characteristics of CNN, CNN is very effective in computer vision. In natural language processing (NLP), the best aspect of CNN is the processing of text classification. Yu, P. et al. did a study on obtaining detailed answers in machine reading comprehension [20]. If the convolution neural network is used to process text sentences like image processing, in multiple convolution and pooling, the features of the arrangement relationship between the front and back of the sentence cannot be retained, and basically only the features of the words in a sentence can be extracted. Therefore, pure CNN is not suitable for sequential text classification tasks. In the application of convolutional neural network in natural language, its principle is actually similar to the operation of images. Each sentence or string to be processed can actually be regarded as an image with channel 1. In the process of text processing, each word can be mapped into a feature vector by word vector mapping. This feature vector contains the characteristics of the word. All words in a text are segmented and embedded, and if the length is not enough, a complement operation is performed. Then, stitching all word vectors together is similar to the pixel set of an image. After such processing, the text can be convoluted like an image.

3   Method

This section will briefly introduce the framework for malicious domain name detection and then introduce each component in detail (Fig. 1).

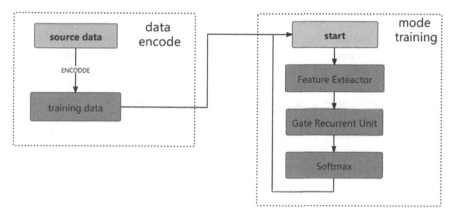

Fig. 1. The architecture of the CGFMD, including data encode and mode training.

3.1   Data Encode

Because this model automatically extracts features, and because all domain names are original domain names, they are separated into two files. We need to preprocess the data before the experiment, so that the current domain name information can be better used by the deep learning model. Therefore, the first step of preprocessing is to use pandas to read two files and add labels respectively, then merge the two files and sort them randomly, and finally convert the data type to int8 and save it as a data.csv file. Due to the uneven length of domain names, the second step is to set the length of all domain names to 75, fill in the front of domain names less than 75 characters with "!" and save them as file named data_pad.csv. In the third step of preprocessing, all characters in the domain name file are separated by commas and saved as file named data_split.csv. In the last step of preprocessing, the obtained file converts characters into numbers according to the corresponding relationship and saves them as file named data_encode.csv. If the semantics of embedded domain names are correctly learned by encoding vectors as real values, similar characters appear in the same clusters close to each other in high-dimensional geometric space [21].

3.2 Word Vector Mapping

In the convolutional neural network, our input is the domain name data preprocessed. In the word embedding layer, we can simply understand it as transforming a feature into a vector, such as one hot coding, which is the easiest to understand. However, in practical application, the dimension will be very high after transforming the feature into one hot coding. Therefore, we will convert the sparse feature of one hot into dense feature, which is usually transformed into our commonly used embedding. Deep learning framework provides an embedded layer for neural networks that can process text data. It has a limitation on input, that is, all inputs must be integer encoded. In the data preprocessing phase, the domain name data has been mapped to integer form. The dimension of character embedding is considered as one of the super parameters of deep learning algorithm. The embedded layer is defined as the first hidden layer of the network. In the embedded layer: turn the characters of the domain name into dense vectors. Each time the input data in the input layer is a domain name, there are as many input nodes as there are word characters. Each domain name is a string with a length of 75. Enter a domain name, for example: "!...... Com" is "36, 36, 36... 12, 24, 22" after preprocessing. Input "36, 36, 36... 12, 24, 22" into this embedded layer. According to the dictionary length one hot code, form a matrix with the shape of [75, 41] as shown in the figure, multiply it by the initialization weight matrix with the shape of [41, 128], and finally output the output matrix with the shape of [75, 128]. Through this process, one-dimensional domain name data can be mapped to multi-dimensional vector space. This operation is convenient for convolution network to extract domain name feature information. The process of word embedding layer is shown in Fig. 2.

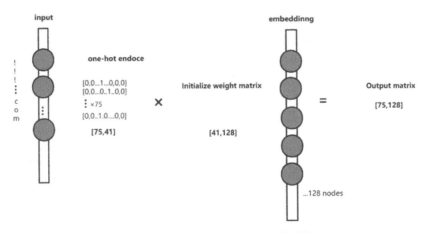

Fig. 2. The architecture of word embedding.

3.3 Algorithm Introduction

One dimensional convolution is generally used to process text, mainly used to process information input in natural language processing, so the input is usually a long text, which is the list of words. In the word embedding layer [22], the domain name has been mapped to the word list with the shape of [75, 128]. The features are automatically extracted by setting an appropriate step size for one-dimensional convolution layer. In this process, the hidden features of domain names can be extracted instead of the traditional manual extraction, which is time-consuming and labor-consuming. In the process of convolution, 128 groups [23] of convolution check word vectors with width of 3 are used for convolution operation. Then, the important features in each group of convolution results are extracted through the maximum pool layer and spliced to form a simple feature vector. Finally, the probability of two classes is classified by softmax function. In the training process, the important features of the previous time are added to the current time learning process through GRU structure to strengthen which important signals. The architecture of training mode is shown in Fig. 3.

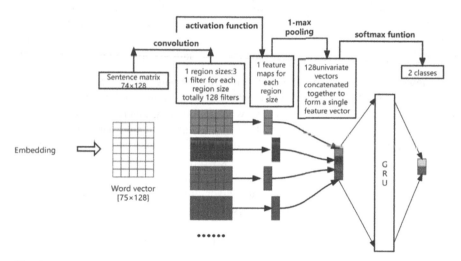

Fig. 3. The architecture of training mode, including embedding, convolutional and GRU.

4 Experiment

4.1 Experimental Environment

The operating system used in the experiment is Ubuntu 18.04, the CPU is Intel Xeon(R)CPU E5-2609 v4 @ 1.70 GHz, the GPU is NVIDIA 1080Ti with 8 GB of memory.

4.2 Experimental Setup

Dataset. The experiment in this paper uses the DGA domain name published by 360net-lab as the black sample, and the white sample uses Alexa top 1 million, which is the domain name with the largest number of visits in the world, as the white sample.

Table 1. The statistics of datasets.

	Training set	Validation set	Test set
DGA domain	800000	100000	100000
Real domain	800000	100000	100000
Total	1600000	200000	200000

The above black-and-white samples are used as the data set for model training. The data set contains a total of 2 million pieces of data. It is open data and is widely used in experiments related to human DGA domain name recognition. Because deep learning requires a large number of samples, a total of 1.6 million pieces of data are selected for the experiment. This paper randomly divides the data set, and randomly divides the 1.6 million pieces of domain name data into 80% as the training set for training the model, 10% as the test set for testing the model, and the last 10% for verification in the process of model training, that is, the verification set. The data set division is shown in Table 1.

Parameters. One dimensional convolution is generally used to process text, mainly used to process information input in natural language processing, so the input is generally a long text, that is, a list of words. In the word embedding layer, the domain name has been mapped to the word list of [75, 128]. the features are automatically extracted by setting an appropriate step size for one-dimensional convolution layer. In the process of convolution, 128 groups of convolution check word vectors with width of 3 are used for convolution operation. Then, the important features in each group of convolution results are extracted through the maximum pool layer and spliced to form a simple feature vector. Finally, the probability of two classes is classified by softmax function, and the sum of probability is one.

In the training process, the important features of the previous time are added to the current time learning process through GRU structure to strengthen which important signals. Several important parameters need to be set: The first one is Filters: number of filters is set to 128; The second one is kernel size: the size of the convolution kernel. The convolution kernel itself should be two-dimensional. Only one dimension needs to be specified here, because the length of the second dimension is consistent with the length of the word vector. The convolution kernel can only go from top to bottom, not from left to right, that is, it can only follow the order of words in the text and the order of columns. The convolution kernel size is set to 3; The third one is Strips: the step size of each convolution, set to 1 for each step; The fourth one is Padding: prevent the outermost data from being fully learned; Finally, set the activation function "Relu".

The specific and detailed structural parameters of CGFMD model network are shown in Table 2:

In the process of model training, there are many optimization algorithms that can be used to find the global optimal value of the loss function. Common optimization algorithms include gradient descent method, random gradient descent method [24], momentum optimization algorithm [25], RMSPROP optimization algorithm [26], Adam optimization algorithm, etc. The traditional random gradient descent method (SGD) is not

Table 2. CGFMD model network

Layer Type	Architecture
Embedding	128 units
Relu convolutional	128 filters (3 × 3),1
Max pooling	2 × 2
GRU	64 filters (3 × 3),1
Tanh fully connect	256 units
Sigmoid fully connect	1 units

used to update the parameters. Adam optimization algorithm is an extension of random gradient descent method. Recently, it is widely used in deep learning experiments in natural language processing and computer vision. Adam algorithm is different from the traditional random gradient descent algorithm. The random gradient descent maintains a single learning rate (i.e. alpha) to update all weights, and the learning rate will not change during the training process. Adam designs independent adaptive learning rates for different parameters by calculating the first-order moment estimation and second-order moment estimation of the gradient. In the process of CGFMD model training, the parameters are updated by the adaptive learning rate obtained by Adam optimization algorithm.

4.3 Baselines

In order to verify the effectiveness of the model, we choose the traditional machine learning algorithm and deep learning model as the baseline method. Naive Bayes (NB) is a traditional machine learning method. It uses the knowledge of probability and statistics to classify the sample data set. Because of its solid mathematical foundation, the misjudgment rate of Bayesian classification algorithm is very low. Multilayer perceptron (MLP) is a feedforward artificial neural network model, which maps multiple input data sets to a single output data set. We use the above two methods as experimental baseline.

4.4 Experimental Results

The evaluation indicators of this article are as follows:

- TP: Positive examples of correctly classified
- FN: Positive cases that are misclassified
- TN: Negative cases that are correctly classified
- FP: Negative cases that are misclassified

$$Acc = \frac{TP + TN}{TP + FN + TN + FP} \qquad (1)$$

$$Pr\,ecision = \frac{TP}{TP + FP} \tag{2}$$

$$Recall = \frac{TP}{TP + FN} \tag{3}$$

$$F1 = \frac{precision \cdot recall}{precision + recall} \tag{4}$$

The cost function we use is cross entropy function:

$$J(\theta) = -\frac{1}{m}\left[\sum_{i=1}^{n}\left(y^{(i)}\log h_\theta\left(x^{(i)}\right) + \left(1 - y^{(i)}\right)\log\left(1 - h_\theta\left(x^{(i)}\right)\right)\right)\right] \tag{5}$$

The confusion matrix of CGFMD model is obtained through experiments, as shown in the Table 3:

Table 3. The confusion matrix of CGFMD.

	0	1
0	190987	3229
1	2722	159164

Table 4. The performance comparison for malicious domain name detection.

	Precision	Recall	F1
NB	0.740	0.713	0.701
MLP	0.951	0.950	0.950
CGFMD	**0.980**	**0.980**	**0.981**

In this paper, the training model is built based on Naive Bayesian model, multilayer perceptron model and cyclic neural network model. The public malicious domain name and normal domain name data are selected as the training data set. After a certain number of iterative training, the accuracy of the model is tested on the test set, and the performance of each model is different. Among them, the accuracy of the model based on 2-g feature extraction and naive Bayes is 74%. Based on 2-g feature extraction and multi-layer perceptron, the accuracy of the model is 95%, as shown in the Table 4. GRU and CNN based recurrent neural network model (CGFMD) has the best effect, the accuracy of the model reaches 98%, and has relatively accurate malicious domain name recognition ability.

5 Conclusion

With the research and innovation of machine learning and deep learning algorithms by scholars from all walks of life in natural science, the models of deep learning and machine learning have been very powerful in conventional application. The research and development of deep learning has become an important trend to study various fields and solve practical problems. The application of deep learning is more and more widely. It has achieved amazing performance in many fields and attracted the attention of more and more scientific researchers. It also provides a new idea for the related research of network security.

In this paper, we propose a malicious domain name detection model CGFMD based on CNN-GRU. It combines word vector mapping with convolution neural network to automatically extract the potential features of malicious domain names. At the same time, GRU network is added to the model to solve the long-term dependence problem. We select 360 and Alexa domain name data to test the algorithm. After testing, the accuracy of the detection algorithm is as high as 0.980, which proves that the algorithm is effective and feasible. The experimental results show that CGFMD algorithm has higher detection accuracy and lower false positive rate than traditional methods. It saves cumbersome manual feature extraction, and can recognize DGA domain names efficiently. In the next work, we will add countermeasure samples to the model to improve the robustness of the model.

References

1. Zhu, J.W., Han, X.H., Zhou, Y.: Research and development of botnets. J. Softw. **19**(3), 702–715 (2008)
2. Jiang, J., Zhu, J.W., Duan, Y.X.: Research on botnet mechanisms and defenses. J. Softw. **23**(1), 82–96 (2012)
3. Yu, B., Smith, L., Threefoot, M.: Semi-supervised time series modeling for real-time flux domain detection on passive dns traffic. In: Proceedings of the International Workshop on Machine Learning and Data Mining in Pattern Recognition, pp. 258–271 (2014)
4. Geffner, J.: End-to-end analysis of a domain generating algorithm malware family. In: Black Hat, USA, pp. 57–67 (2013)
5. Sato, K., Lshibashi, K., Toyono, T.: Extending black domain name list by using cooccurrence relation between DNS queries. IEICE Trans. Commun. **95**(3), 794–802 (2012)
6. Szegedy, C., Zaremba, W., Sutskever, I., Bruna, J.: Intriguing properties of neural networks. In: Proceedings of the International Conference on Learning Representations, pp. 461–472 (2014)
7. Lee, S.: A study on classification and detection of small moths using CNN model. Comput. Mater. Continua **71**(1), 1987–1998 (2022)
8. Zheng, D., Ran, Z., Liu, Z., Li, L., Tian, L.: An efficient bar code image recognition algorithm for sorting system. Mater. Continua **64**(3), 1885–1895 (2020)
9. Cortes, C., Vapnik, V.: Support-vector networks. Mach. Learn. **20**(3), 273–297 (1995)
10. Krizhevsky, A., Sutskever, I., Hinton, G.E.: ImageNet classification with deep convolutional neural networks. In: Advances in Neural Information Processing Systems, pp. 1097–1105 (2012)
11. Schuster, M., Paliwal, K.K.: Bidirectional recurent neural networks. IEEE Trans. Signal Process. **45**(11), 2673–2681 (1997)

12. Schuppen, S., Teubert, D., Herrmann, P.: (FANCI): feature-based automated NXDomain classification and intelligence. In: USENIX, pp. 1165–1181 (2018)
13. Antonakakis, M., Perdisci, R., Nadji, Y.: From throw-away traffic to bots: detecting the rise of DGA-based malware. In: USENIX, pp. 491–506 (2012)
14. Papernot, N., Mcdaniel, P., Jha, S.: The limitations of deep learning in adversarial settings. In: IEEE European Symposium on Security & Privacy, pp. 521–527 (2016)
15. Radford, A., Metz, L., Chintala, S.: Unsupervised representation learning with deep convolutional generative adversarial networks. Comput. Sci. 1(4), 89–96 (2015)
16. Moosavi-Dezfooli, S., Fawzi, A., Frossard, P.: DeepFool: a simple and accurate method to fool deep neural networks. In: Computer Vision and Pattern Recognition, Las Vegas, LV, USA, pp. 2574–2582 (2016)
17. Hochreiter, S., Schmidhuber, J.: Long short-term memory. Neural Comput. 9(8), 1735–1780 (1997)
18. Cheng, S.M., Cheng, T.Y., Liang, Y.L.: DGA domain name detection method based on bilstm neural network. Network Security Technology & Application, pp. 15–17 (2019)
19. Ran, Z., Zheng, D., Lai, Y., Tian, L.: Applying stack bidirectional LSTM model to intrusion detection. Comput. Mater. Continua 65(1), 309–320 (2020)
20. Yu, P., Xiaoyu, L.: Verification mechanism to obtain an elaborate answer span in machine reading comprehension. Neurocomputing 466, 80–91 (2021)
21. Wang, Q., Zhang, Y., Li, P.: Cross-domain sentiment classification based on word2vec. Appl. Res. Comput. 35(10), 2924–2927 (2018)
22. Mikolov, T., Sutskeverllya, C.: Kai: Distributed representations of words and phrases and their compositionality. J. Softw. 19(3), 702–715 (2008)
23. Liu, Y., Zhao, K.J., Ge, L.S.: A fast DGA domain name classification algorithm based on deep learning. J. Shandong Univ. 54(7), 106–112 (2019)
24. Orr, G.B., Müller, K.-R. (eds.): Neural Networks: Tricks of the Trade. LNCS, vol. 1524. Springer, Heidelberg (1998). https://doi.org/10.1007/3-540-49430-8
25. Sutskever, I., Martens, J., Dahl, G.: On the importance of initialization and momentum in-deep leaming. In: International Conference on Machine Learning, pp. 1139–1147 (2013)
26. Tieleman, T., Hinton, G.: Lecture 6.5-rmsprop: divide the gradient by a running average of itsrecent magnitude. Neural Netw. Mach. Learn. 4(2), 26–31 (2012)

Quintuple Implication Principle on Intuitionistic Fuzzy Sets

Shui-Ling Zeng$^{(\boxtimes)}$ and Li-Xiang Lei

College of Information Science and Engineering, Jishou University, Jishou 416000, China
106940773@qq.com

Abstract. Intuitionistic fuzzy inference Quintuple Implication Principle methods are discussed. Using the properties of the intuitionistic triangular module generated by the left continuous triangular module, the equivalent relationship between the residual intuitionistic implication operator associated with the intuitionistic triangular module and the correlation operator of the residual implication operator is given, and the fuzzy inference model of the Quintuple Implication Principle is proposed, The expression and decomposition formula of the solution of quintuple I algorithm for intuitionistic fuzzy reasoning are given and their reducibility is discussed. It is proved that the quintuple I algorithm has good reducibility in theory. Finally, the α-quintuple I algorithm based on IFMP problem is given, and the numerical examples of quintuple I algorithm and α- quintuple I algorithm are given.

Keywords: Quintuple implication principle · Intuitionistic fuzzy reasoning · α-quintuple implication algorithm · Residual intuitionistic implication

1 Introduction

Fuzzy reasoning, as the theoretical core of fuzzy control technology [1], has been widely used in uncertain reasoning, intelligent control, image processing, decision-making, and many other fields [2]. The most basic reasoning problems of fuzzy reasoning are called the fuzzy modus pones (FMP)for approximate reasoning with fuzzy propositions [3]. If given the major premise: If x is A, then y is B, and the minor premise: x is A^*, then FMP can be expressed in Table 1.

Table 1. Rules of FMP.

Suppose	$A(x) \rightarrow B(y)$
And given	$A^*(x)$
Calculate	$B^*(y)$

Here $A(x)$, $A^*(x)$ is a fuzzy set on the domain X, $B(y)$, $B^*(y)$ is a fuzzy set on the domain Y. This problem is usually called FMP (Fuzzy Modus Ponens) problem. The

X. Sun et al. (Eds.): ICAIS 2022, CCIS 1586, pp. 575–589, 2022.
https://doi.org/10.1007/978-3-031-06767-9_48

CRI (Compositional Rule of Fuzzy Inference) algorithm was proposed by Professor Zadeh [4], the founder of the fuzzy theory, however, the CRI algorithm lacks logic in the reasoning process. Therefore, in view of this problem, Professor Wang replaced the conjunction operation with the residual implication operator, and proposed the full implication triple I algorithm [5]. after the full implication reverse triple I algorithm is proposed [6]. No matter in the reasoning process of the CRI algorithm or triple I algorithm, the approximation degree of A and A^* (or B and B^*) is not taken into account, so that the calculation results are meaningless in some cases. In reference [7], a fuzzy reasoning quintuple implication principle is proposed, which effectively overcomes the above shortcomings. Once proposed, the quintuple implication principle has attracted the attention of many scholars. Reference [8] studied the robustness and approximation of the quintuple implication principle of fuzzy reasoning. Some scholars combined fuzzy reasoning with interval analysis, proposed the quintuple implication principle of interval-valued fuzzy reasoning and studied its properties, and achieved a series of results [9–11]. Reference [12] combined fuzzy reasoning with interval-valued analysis and proposed the quintuple implication principle of fuzzy reasoning based on interval-valued, which further enriched the theoretical research of the quintuple implication principle.

To describe the uncertainty of things, Atanassov proposed the concept of intuitionistic fuzzy sets [13]. Intuitionistic fuzzy sets introduce true and false membership degrees, which can explain the uncertainty of things or phenomena more widely. Intuitionistic fuzzy sets, interval-valued fuzzy sets and interval-valued intuitionistic fuzzy sets, as further extensions of fuzzy sets, can better deal with uncertain information. They have been widely used in clustering analysis, image processing and target detection [14–17]. Reference [18] conducted in-depth research on the theory of intuitionistic fuzzy reasoning; And proposed the residual intuitionistic implication operator, thus establishing an internal connection between intuitionistic fuzzy sets and fuzzy reasoning. reference [19] and reference [20] studied the triple I algorithm of residual intuitionistic fuzzy reasoning. Intuitionistic fuzzy implication operator and residual implication operator induced by left continuous tricorne have diversity [21], which further extends fuzzy reasoning on intuitionistic fuzzy sets [22–26].

At present, few studies are combining intuitionistic fuzzy sets with other reasoning methods. In this paper, the intuitionistic fuzzy sets are combined with the quintuple implication principle of interval-valued intuitionistic fuzzy reasoning proposed in reference [27] and the triple I algorithm of residual intuitionistic fuzzy reasoning proposed in reference [28] to study the quintuple implication principle of intuitionistic fuzzy reasoning. Of course, the FMP problem of fuzzy sets is also extended to intuitionistic fuzzy sets, which is called IFMP (Intuitionistic Fuzzy Modus Ponens) problem. The expression and decomposition form of the solution of the quintuple implication principle of intuitionistic fuzzy reasoning is further discussed. Then we discuss the reducibility of the residual intuitionistic fuzzy reasoning quintuple-I algorithm, and propose the quintuple-I algorithm for the IFMP problem. Finally, we give an example analysis of the quintuple-I algorithm and the α-quintuple I algorithm.

2 Preliminary Knowledge

This section recalls some basic concepts and results, which we shall need in the subsequent sections.

Definition 2.1 [29]. $\otimes$ is a triangular module on L, $L \in [0, 1]$, $\forall a, b, c \in L$ satisfied:

(1) $a \otimes b = b \otimes a$,   (commutativity)
(2) $(a \otimes b) \otimes c = a \otimes (b \otimes c)$,   (associativity)
(3) $a \otimes b \leq a \otimes c$, and $b \leq c$,   (monotonicity)
(4) $a \otimes 1 = a$.   (boundary condition)
(5) The t-conorm $\oplus$ is called the dual t-conorm of the norm $\otimes$ if $a \oplus b = 1 - (1 - a) \oplus (1 - b)$, $\forall a, b \in L$ and analogously, the t-norm $\otimes$ is called the dual t-norm of t-conorm $\oplus$ if $a \otimes b = 1 - (1 - a) \oplus (1 - b)$, $\forall a, b \in L$.

Definition 2.2 [29]. A t-norm $\otimes$ is a left-continuous t-norm if $\forall a, b \in L$, $\otimes$ satisfies $(\underset{i \in I}{\vee} a_i) \otimes b = \underset{i \in I}{\vee}(a_i \otimes b)$.

A t-conorm $\oplus$ is a right-continuous t-conorm if $\forall a, b \in L$, $\oplus$ satisfies $(\underset{i \in I}{\wedge} a_i) \oplus b = \underset{i \in I}{\wedge}(a_i \oplus b)$.

Proposition 2.1 [29]. A t-norm $\otimes$ is left-continuous, iff the dual t-conorm $\oplus$ of the t-norm is right-continuous.

Proposition 2.2 [19, 29]. If $\otimes$ is a left-continuous t-norm then there exists a binary operation $\rightarrow$ (the $\otimes$-residuum) on L such that $(\otimes, \rightarrow)$ satisfy the residual principle, $a \otimes b \leq c$, $a \leq b \rightarrow c$ where $\rightarrow$ is given by $a \rightarrow b = \vee\{x \in L | x \otimes a \leq b\}$, and is called residual implication derived from $\otimes$.

Proposition 2.3 [19]. If $\oplus$ is a right-continuous t-conorm then there exists a binary operation $\ominus$ (the $\mathbb{O}$-residuum) on L such that $(\oplus, \ominus)$ forms a coadjoint pair, $c < a \oplus b$, iff $c \ominus b \leq a$ and $\ominus$ given by $a \rightarrow b = \vee\{x \in L | x \otimes a \leq b\}$, and is called residual implication derived from $\otimes$, $a \ominus b = \wedge\{x \in L | a \leq x \oplus b\}$, and

$$B^*(y) = \sup_{x \in X}\{A^*(x) \otimes (A(x) \rightarrow B(y))\}, y \in Y. \tag{1}$$

the $\oplus$-residuum $\ominus$ is called fuzzy difference operator derived from $\oplus$.

Proposition 2.4 [19]. $\rightarrow$, $\oplus$, $\ominus$ are called associated operators of $\otimes$, if $(\otimes, \rightarrow)$ is a adjoint pair, $(\oplus, \ominus)$ is a co-adjoint pair and $\oplus$ is the dual t-conorm of the norm $\otimes$, $\forall a, b \in L$, $\ominus$ satisfies

$$a \ominus b = 1 - (1 - b) \rightarrow (1 - a), L \in [0, 1]. \tag{2}$$

Definition 2.3 [13]. An intuitionistic fuzzy set on the nonempty universe of discourse X is given by $A = \{x \in X \,|\, (x, A_t(x), A_f(x))\}$, where

$$A_t(x) : X \rightarrow [0,\ 1],\ x \rightarrow A_t(x);$$
$$A_f(x) : X \rightarrow [0,\ 1],\ x \rightarrow A_f(x);$$
$$A_t(x) + A_f(x) \in [0,\ 1].$$

$A_t(x)$ and $A_f(x)$ denote a membership function and a non-membership function of x to A.

As a generalization of fuzzy sets, intuitionistic fuzzy sets extend the character value from $[0,\ 1]$ to the triangle domain $L^* = \{(u,\ v) \in [0,\ 1]^2 \,|\, u + v \leq 1\}$. If $A_t(x) + A_f(x) = 1$, $\forall a,\ b \in L$. then intuitionistic fuzzy sets degenerate into fuzzy sets. The set of all intuitionistic fuzzy sets in X is denoted as $IFSs(X)$, a partial order on L^* can be defined as follows:

$$\forall \alpha,\ \beta \in IFS,\ \alpha = (a_1,\ a_2),\ \beta = (b_1,\ b_2),\ \alpha \leq \beta \text{ if and only if } a_1 \leq b_1,\ a_2 \geq b_2.$$

Obviously, $\alpha \wedge \beta = (a_1 \wedge b_1,\ a_2 \vee b_2)$, $\alpha \vee \beta = (a_1 \vee b_1,\ a_2 \wedge b_2)$, $0^* = (0,\ 1)$ and $1^* = (1,\ 0)$ are the smallest element and the greatest element of L^*, respectively. It's easy to verify the fact that $(IFS,\ \leq)$ is a complete lattice.

Definition 2.4 [19]. $\otimes_{L^*}$ is called an intuitionistic t-norm derived from t-norm $\otimes$ if

$$\alpha \otimes_{L^*} \beta = (a_1 \otimes b_1,\ a_2 \oplus b_2) \tag{3}$$

And, $\oplus_{L^*}$ is called an intuitionistic t-conorm derived from t-conorm $\oplus$ if

$$\alpha \oplus_{L^*} \beta = (a_1 \oplus b_1,\ a_2 \otimes b_2) \tag{4}$$

Proposition 2.5 [19]. $(L^*,\ \otimes_{L^*},\ 1^*)$ is a commutative monoid and $\otimes_{L^*}$ is isotone, $(L^*,\ \oplus_{L^*},\ 0^*)$ is a commutative monoid and $\oplus_{L^*}$ is isotone.

Proposition 2.6 [19] Let $\otimes$ be a left-continuous t-norm, then

1) $\otimes_{L^*}$ derived from $\otimes$ is a left-continuous intuitionistic t-norm on L^*, i.e., $(\underset{i \in I}{\vee} \alpha_i) \otimes_{L^*}$
    $\gamma = \underset{i \in I}{\vee} (\alpha_i \otimes_{L^*} \gamma)$;
2) $\oplus_{L^*}$ derived from $\otimes$ is a right-continuous intuitionistic t-norm on L^*, i.e., $(\underset{i \in I}{\wedge} \alpha_i) \oplus_{L^*}$
    $\gamma = \underset{i \in I}{\wedge} (\alpha_i \oplus_{L^*} \gamma)$.

Theorem 2.1 [19]. Let $\otimes_{L^*}$ be an intuitionistic t-norm derived from a left-continuous t-norm $\otimes$, then there exists a binary operation $\rightarrow_{L^*}$ on L^* such that $\gamma \otimes_{L^*} \alpha \leq \beta \Leftrightarrow \gamma \leq \alpha \rightarrow_* \beta$ and $\rightarrow_{L^*}$ is given by $\alpha \rightarrow_* \beta = \vee\{\eta \in L^* \,|\, \eta \otimes_* \alpha \leq \beta\}$.

Theorem 2.2 [20]. Let $\alpha,\ \beta \in L^*$, $\alpha = (a_1,\ a_2)$, $\beta = (b_1,\ b_2)$, $\alpha \leq \beta$, $L^* \in [0,\ 1]$, $\rightarrow_{L^*}$ is a residual intuitionistic implication derived from a left-continuous t-norm $\otimes$, then

$$\alpha \rightarrow_{L^*} \beta = ((a_1 \rightarrow b_1) \wedge (1 - (b_2 \ominus a_2)),\ b_2 \ominus a_2) \tag{5}$$

Theorem 2.3 [20]. Let α, $\beta \in L^*$, $\alpha = (a_1, a_2)$, $\beta = (b_1, b_2)$, $\alpha \leq \beta$, $L^* \in [0, 1]$, $\ominus_{L^*}$ is a residual intuitionistic fuzzy difference operator derived from a left-continuous t-norm $\otimes$, then

$$\alpha \ominus_{L^*} \beta = (a_1 \ominus b_1, (b_2 \to a_2) \wedge (1 - a_1 \ominus b_1)) \tag{6}$$

From Theorem 2.2 and Theorem 2.3, $\forall \alpha$, $\beta \in L^*$, then

$$\alpha \to_{L^*} \beta = ((a_1 \to b_1) \wedge ((1 - a_2) \to (1 - b_2)), 1 - (1 - a_2) \to (1 - b_2)) \tag{7}$$

3   The Quintuple I Algorithm Based on Intuitionistic Fuzzy Sets

Recalling the basic problems on intuitionistic fuzzy reasoning, i.e., Intuitionistic Fuzzy Modus Ponens (IFMP) is the most basic problems in intuitionistic fuzzy reasoning, and its form is shown in Table 2.

Table 2. Rules of IFMP.

Suppose	$A(x) \to_{L^*} B(y)$
And given	$A^*(x)$
Calculate	$B^*(y)$

On the basic fuzzy inference rules of the triple-I method about IFMP, the IFMP problem of intuitionistic fuzzy inference quintuple-I method is considered in Table 3.

Table 3. Rules of quintuple-I method.

Suppose	$A(x) \to_{L^*} B(y)$
Given	$A^*(x) \to_{L^*} A(x),$
And given	$A^*(x)$
Calculate	$B^*(y)$

Here $A(x)$, $A^*(x)$ is an intuitionistic fuzzy set on the domain X, $B(y)$, $B^*(y)$ is an intuitionistic fuzzy set on the domain Y. respectively, and $\to_{L^*}$ is the residual intuitionistic fuzzy implication on L^*. we denote $A(x) = (A_t(x), A_f(x))$, $B(y) = (B_t(y), B_f(y))$, $A^*(x) = (A_t^*(x), A_f^*(x))$, $B^*(y) = (B_t^*(y), B_f^*(y))$, $A_{-f}(x) = 1 - A_f^*(x)$, $B_{-f}(x) = 1 - B_f(x)$, $A_{-f}^*(x) = 1 - A_f^*(x)$, $B_{-f}^*(y) = 1 - B_f^*(y)$. Clearly, A_t, A_f, A_t^*, A_f^* is a fuzzy set on the domain X, B_t, B_f, B_t^*, B_f^* is a fuzzy set on the domain Y.

Definition 3.1 [28]. The IFMP problem expression of intuitionistic fuzzy reasoning is decomposed into the following two FMP problems, and the decomposition expression of the triple I method are shown in Table 4 and Table 5.

Table 4. *IFMP* $- B_t^*(y)$ method.

Suppose	$A_t(x) \to_* B_t(y)$
And given	$A_t^*(x)$
Calculate	$B_t^*(y)$

Table 5. *IFMP* $- B_{-f}^*(y)$ method.

Suppose	$A_{-f}(x) \to_* B_{-f}(y)$
And given	$A_{-f}^*(x)$
Calculate	$B_{-f}^*(y)$

B^* is called the *QIP* solution of *IFMP*, if $B^*(y)$ is the smallest element on *IFSs*(Y) satisfying for all $x \in X$ and $y \in Y$:

$$(A(x) \to_{L^*} B(y)) \to_{L^*} \left(\left(A^*(x) \to_{L^*} A(x) \right) \to_{L^*} \left(A^*(x) \to_{L^*} B^*(y) \right) \right) = 1^* \qquad (8)$$

Theorem 3.1 If $\to_{L^*}$ is the residual implication induced by a left-continuous t-norm $\otimes$, then the *QIP* solutions of *IFMP* are given by the following formulas:

$$B^*(y) = \bigvee_{x \in X} \left\{ A^*(x) \otimes_{L^*} \left(\left(A^*(x) \to_{L^*} A(x) \right) \otimes_{L^*} \left(A(x) \to_{L^*} B(y) \right) \right) \right\}, \ y \in Y \qquad (9)$$

Proof: From formula (9), it follows that

$$A^*(x) \otimes_{L^*} \left(\left(A^*(x) \to_{L^*} A(x) \right) \to_{L^*} \left(A(x) \to_{L^*} B(y) \right) \right) \leq B^*(y), \ y \in Y \qquad (10)$$

Since $(\otimes_{L^*}, \to_{L^*})$ is an intuitionistic adjoint pair, then

$$(A(x) \to_{L^*} B(y)) \leq \left(\left(A^*(x) \to_{L^*} A(x) \right) \to_{L^*} \left(A^*(x) \to_{L^*} B^*(y) \right) \right), \ y \in Y. \qquad (11)$$

$$\forall x \in X, \ (A(x) \to_{L^*} B(y)) \to_{L^*} \left(\left(A^*(x) \to_{L^*} A(x) \right) \to_{L^*} \left(A^*(x) \to_{L^*} B^*(y) \right) \right) = 1^*, \ y \in Y.$$

If there exists $C(y) \in IFSs(Y)$ satisfying

$$(A(x) \to_{L^*} B(y)) \to_{L^*} \left(\left(A^*(x) \to_{L^*} A(x) \right) \to_{L^*} \left(A^*(x) \to_{L^*} C(y) \right) \right) = 1^*, \ y \in Y,$$

Then

$$(A(x) \to_{L^*} B(y)) \leq \left(\left(A^*(x) \to_{L^*} A(x) \right) \to_{L^*} \left(A^*(x) \to_{L^*} C(y) \right) \right), \ y \in Y,$$

$$A^*(x) \otimes_{L^*} \left((A(x) \to_{L^*} B(y)) \otimes_{L^*} \left(A^*(x) \to_{L^*} A(x) \right) \right) \leq C(y), \ \forall x \in X, \forall y \in Y.$$

From formula (9), we have $B^*(y) \leq C(y)$. for all $y \in Y$. Hence, $B^*(y)$ given by the formula (9) is the QIP solution of IFMP.

Remark 3.1. For the QIP solution of IFMP given by formula (9), if $A^*(x) \to_{L*} A(x) = (1, 0)$ then.

$$B^*(y) = \bigvee_{x \in X} \{A^*(x) \otimes_{L*} ((A(x) \to_{L*} B(y)))\}, \forall y \in Y. \tag{12}$$

Corollary 3.1. Suppose that $\to_{L*}$ in IFMP is a residual intuitionistic implication derived from a left-continuous t-norm $\otimes$, then QIP solutions $B^*(y) = (B_t^*(y), B_f^*(y))$ of IFMP can be expressed as follows, respectively:

$$B_t^*(y) = \bigvee_{x \in X} \left\{ \begin{array}{l} A_t^*(x) \otimes (((A_t^*(x) \to A_t(x)) \wedge (A_{-f}^*(x) \to A_{-f}(x))) \otimes \\ ((A_t(x) \to B_t(y)) \wedge (A_{-f}(x) \to B_{-f}(y)))) \end{array} \right\} \tag{13}$$

$$B_f^*(y) = \bigwedge_{x \in X} \left\{ A_f^*(x) \oplus ((1 - A_{-f}^*(x) \to A_{-f}(x)) \oplus (1 - A_{-f}(x) \to B_{-f}(y))) \right\} \tag{14}$$

where $\to$, $\oplus$ are associated operators of $\otimes$.

From formula (12) and combined with Definition 3.1, the IFMP problem of intuitionistic fuzzy reasoning quintuple-I method can be decomposed into two expressions are shown in Table 6 and Table 7.

Table 6. $FMP - QIP - B_t^*(y)$ model.

Suppose	$A_t(x) \to B_t(y)$
Given	$A_t^*(x) \to A_t(x),$
And given	$A_t^*(x),$
Calculate	$B_t^*(y)$

Table 7. $FMP - QIP - B_{-f}^*(y)$ model.

Suppose	$A_{-f}(x) \to B_{-f}(y),$
Given	$A_{-f}^*(x) \to A_{-f}(x),$
And given	$A_{-f}^*(x)$
Calculate	$B_{-f}^*(y)$

Hence, approximate Solution of $B^*(y)$ in IFMP is

$$\tilde{B}^*(y) = (B_t^*(y) \wedge B_{-f}^*(y), 1 - B_{-f}^*(y)).$$

Then, the expression of $B_t^*(y)$ as follows:

$$B_t^*(y) = \bigvee_{x \in X} \{A_t^*(x) \otimes ((A_t^*(x) \to A_t(x)) \otimes (A_t(x) \to B_t(y)))\}, \forall x \in X, y \in Y.$$

And, the expression of $B^*_{-f}(y)$ as follows:

$$B^*_{-f}(y) = \bigvee_{x \in X} \left\{ A^*_{-f}(x) \otimes \left(\left(A^*_{-f}(x) \to A_{-f}(x) \right) \otimes \left(A_{-f}(x) \to B_{-f}(y) \right) \right) \right\}, \forall x \in X, y \in Y.$$

From the expressions of $B^*_t(y)$ and $B^*_{-f}(y)$, the approximate $\tilde{B}^*(y)$ solution of IFMP have the following forms, respectively:

$$\tilde{B}^*(y) = (B^*_t(y) \wedge B^*_{-f}(y), 1 - B^*_{-f}(y)) \tag{15}$$

The expressions of $FMP - QIP - B^*_t(y)$:

$$B^*_t(y) = \bigvee_{x \in X} \left\{ A^*_t(x) \otimes \left((A^*_t(x) \to A_t(x)) \otimes (A_t(x) \to B_t(y)) \right) \right\}, \forall x \in X, y \in Y. \tag{16}$$

The expressions of $FMP - QIP - B^*_{-f}(y)$

$$B^*_{-f}(y) = \bigvee_{x \in X} \left\{ A^*_{-f}(x) \otimes \left(\left(A^*_{-f}(x) \to A_{-f}(x) \right) \otimes \left(A_{-f}(x) \to B_{-f}(y) \right) \right) \right\},$$

$$\forall x \in X, y \in Y. \tag{17}$$

Theorem 3.2. If $B^*_t(y)$ and $B^*_{-f}(y)$ are the QIP solutions of FMP problem, $FMP - QIP - B^*_t(y)$ model and $FMP - QIP - B^*_{-f}(y)$ model are obtained by formula (13) and formula (14), then the solution $\tilde{B}^*(y)$ given by formula (15) is the approximate solution of the QIP solution of IFMP.

Proof: Obviously $\tilde{B}^*(y) \in IF(y)$, we only need to prove $\tilde{B}^*(y) \leq B^*(y)$, from Theorem 3.2 and formula (7) we have

$$B^*(y) = \bigvee_{x \in X} (A^*(x) \otimes_{L^*} ((A^*(x) \to_{L^*} A(x)) \otimes_{L^*} (A(x) \to_{L^*} B(y))))$$

$$= \bigvee_{x \in X} \left\{ \left(A^*_t(x), A^*_f(x) \right) \otimes_{L^*} \left(\begin{array}{c} \left((A^*_t(x) \to A_t(x)) \wedge \left(A^*_{-f}(x) \to A_{-f}(x) \right) \right) \otimes \\ ((A_t(x) \to B_t(y)) \wedge \left(A_{-f}(x) \to B_{-f}(y) \right)), \\ \left(\left(1 - A^*_{-f}(x) \to A_{-f}(x) \right) \oplus \left(1 - A_{-f}(x) \to B_{-f}(y) \right) \right) \end{array} \right) \right\}$$

$$= \bigvee_{x \in X} \left\{ \begin{array}{c} A^*_t(x) \otimes \left(\begin{array}{c} \left((A^*_t(x) \to A_t(x)) \wedge \left(A^*_{-f}(x) \to A_{-f}(x) \right) \right) \otimes \\ ((A_t(x) \to B_t(y)) \wedge \left(A_{-f}(x) \to B_{-f}(y) \right)) \end{array} \right), \\ A^*_f(x) \oplus \left(\left(\left(1 - A^*_{-f}(x) \to A_{-f}(x) \right) \oplus \left(1 - A_{-f}(x) \to B_{-f}(y) \right) \right) \right) \end{array} \right\}$$

$$\leq \left(\bigvee_{x \in X} A^*_t(x) \otimes \left((A^*_t(x) \to A_t(x)) \otimes (A_t(x) \to B_t(y)) \right) \right)$$

$$\wedge \left(\bigvee_{x \in X} A^*_t(x) \otimes \left(\left(A^*_{-f}(x) \to A_{-f}(x) \right) \otimes \left(A_{-f}(x) \to B_{-f}(y) \right) \right) \right),$$

$$\left(\bigwedge_{x \in X} A^*_f(x) \oplus \left(\left(1 - A^*_{-f}(x) \to A_{-f}(x) \right) \oplus \left(1 - A_{-f}(x) \to B_{-f}(y) \right) \right) \right)$$

$$\leq \left(\begin{array}{c} B^*_t(y) \wedge \left(\bigvee_{x \in X} A^*_{-f}(x) \otimes \left(\left(A^*_{-f}(x) \to A_{-f}(x) \right) \otimes \left(A_{-f}(x) \to B_{-f}(y) \right) \right) \right), \\ 1 - \bigvee_{x \in X} A^*_{-f}(x) \otimes \left(\left(A^*_{-f}(x) \to A_{-f}(x) \right) \otimes \left(A_{-f}(x) \to B_{-f}(y) \right) \right) \end{array} \right)$$

$$= \left(B^*_t(y) \wedge B^*_{-f}(y), 1 - B^*_{-f}(y) \right)$$

$$= \tilde{B}^*(y)$$

Theorem 3.3. If QIP-IFMP degenerates into QIP-FMP, then A, B, A^* degraded to fuzzy sets, therefore the solutions of formula (9) and formula (15) satisfies fuzzy set.

Proof: If A, B, A^* degraded to fuzzy sets, and $A_t = 1 - A_f = A_{-f}$, $B_t = 1 - B_f = B_{-f}$, $B_f = B_{-f}$ at the same times, $A_t^* = 1 - A_f^* = A_{-f}^*$, from Theorem 3.2 and formula (7) we have

$$B^*(y) = \bigvee_{x \in X} (A^*(x) \otimes_{L^*} ((A^*(x) \to_{L^*} A(x)) \otimes_{L^*} (A(x) \to_{L^*} B(y))))$$

$$= \bigvee_{x \in X} \left\{ \left(A_t^*(x), A_f^*(x)\right) \otimes_{L^*} \left(\begin{array}{l} \left(\left(A_t^*(x) \to A_t(x)\right) \wedge \left(A_{-f}(x) \to A_{-f}^*(x)\right) \right) \otimes \\ \left((A_t(x) \to B_t(y)) \wedge \left(A_{-f}(x) \to B_{-f}(y)\right)\right), \\ \left(\left(1 - A_{-f}^*(x) \to A_{-f}(x)\right) \oplus \left(1 - A_{-f}(x) \to B_{-f}(y)\right)\right) \end{array} \right) \right\}$$

$$= \bigvee_{x \in X} \left\{ \begin{array}{l} A_t^*(x) \otimes \left(\left(\left(A_t^*(x) \to A_t(x)\right)\right) \otimes \left((A_t(x) \to B_t(y))\right)\right), \\ A_f^*(x) \oplus \left(\left(\left(1 - A_f^*(x) \to A_f(x)\right) \oplus \left(1 - A_f(x) \to B_f(y)\right)\right)\right) \end{array} \right\}$$

$$= \bigvee_{x \in X} \left\{ \begin{array}{l} A_t^*(x) \otimes \left((A_t^*(x) \to A_t(x)) \otimes (A_t(x) \to B_t(y))\right), \\ 1 - A_{-f}^*(x) \otimes \left(\left(A_f^*(x) \to A_f(x)\right) \otimes \left(A_f(x) \to B_f(y)\right)\right) \end{array} \right\}$$

$$= \left(\begin{array}{l} \bigvee_{x \in X} \left\{A_t^*(x) \otimes \left((A_t^*(x) \to A_t(x)) \otimes (A_t(x) \to B_t(y))\right)\right\}, \\ \bigwedge_{x \in X} \left\{1 - A_{-f}^*(x) \otimes \left(\left(A_f^*(x) \to A_f(x)\right) \otimes \left(A_f(x) \to B_f(y)\right)\right)\right\} \end{array} \right)$$

$$= \left(\begin{array}{l} \bigvee_{x \in X} \left\{A_t^*(x) \otimes \left((A_t^*(x) \to A_t(x)) \otimes (A_t(x) \to B_t(y))\right)\right\}, \\ 1 - \bigvee_{x \in X} \left\{A_{-f}^*(x) \otimes \left(\left(A_f^*(x) \to A_f(x)\right) \otimes \left(A_f(x) \to B_f(y)\right)\right)\right\} \end{array} \right)$$

$$= \left(B_t^*(y), 1 - B_t^*(y)\right)$$

Therefore, B^* is also a fuzzy set, which can be obtained from formula (7), then

$$B_{-f}^*(y) = \bigvee_{x \in X} \left\{A_{-f}^*(x) \otimes \left(\left(A_{-f}^*(x) \to A_{-f}(x)\right) \otimes \left(A_{-f}(x) \to B_{-f}(y)\right)\right)\right\}$$

$$= \bigvee_{x \in X} \left\{A_t^*(x) \otimes \left((A_t^*(x) \to A_t(x)) \otimes (A_t(x) \to B_t(y))\right)\right\} = B_t^*(y)$$

From formula (15), we have $\tilde{B}^*(y) = (B_t^*(y), 1 - B_t^*(y)) = (B_t^*(y), B_f^*(y))$, so the Theorem 3.3 proved.

Theorem 3.4. The QIP method for IFMP is recoverable, that is $A^* = A$, from formula (7), we have $B^* = B$, and the solutions of formula (15) satisfies $\tilde{B}^* = B$, and there exists $x_0 \in X$ satisfying $A(x_0) = 1^*$.

Proof: If $A^* = A$ and there exists $x_0 \in X$ satisfying $A(x_0) = 1^*$, then

$$B(y) \geq B^*(y)$$
$$= \bigvee_{x \in X} \left\{A^*(x) \otimes_{L^*} ((A^*(x) \to_{L^*} A(x)) \otimes_{L^*} (A(x) \to_{L^*} B(y)))\right\}$$
$$\geq A^*(x_0) \otimes_{L^*} (A^*(x_0) \to_{L^*} A(x_0)) \otimes_{L^*} (A(x_0) \to_{L^*} B(y)))$$
$$= 1^* \otimes_{L^*} (1^* \to_{L^*} 1) \otimes_{L^*} (1^* \to_{L^*} B(y))$$
$$= B(y)$$

That is, $B^*(y) = B(y)$. Hence, the QIP method for IFMP is recoverable.

Example 1. If $X = \{x_1, x_2, x_3\}$, $Y = \{y_1, y_2, y_3\}$, X, $Y \in [0, 1]$, and the $(\otimes_{L*}, \rightarrow_{L*})$ is the intuitionistic

adjoint pair derived from left-continuous t-norms $\otimes_G$, suppose that

$$A(x) = \{(x_1, 0.5, 0.3), (x_2, 0.7, 0.2), (x_3, 0.9, 0.1)\}$$
$$B(y) = \{(y_1, 0.6, 0.2), (y_2, 0.8, 0.1), (y_3, 0.6, 0.3)\}$$
$$A^*(x) = \{(x_1, 0.4, 0.2), (x_2, 0.6, 0.1), (x_3, 0.7, 0.2)\}$$

calculate the solutions of $IFMP - B^*(y) - QIP$.

$\forall a, b \in [0, 1]$, $\rightarrow$, $\oplus$, $\ominus$ are called associated operators of $\otimes$, $(\otimes, \rightarrow)$ is a adjoint pair, $(\oplus, \ominus)$ is a co-adjoint pair and $\oplus$ is the dual t-conorm of the norm $\otimes$, we have

$$a \otimes_G b = a \wedge b, \quad a \rightarrow_G b = \begin{cases} 1, & a \le b; \\ b, & a > b. \end{cases}, \quad a \oplus_G b = a \vee b,$$

$$b \ominus_G a = \begin{cases} 0, & b \le a; \\ b, & b > a. \end{cases}$$

From formula (15), we have

$$B_t^*(y_1) = \bigvee_{x \in X} \left\{ \begin{array}{l} A_t^*(x) \otimes (((A_t^*(x) \rightarrow A_t(x)) \wedge (A_{-f}(x) \rightarrow A_{-f}^*(x))) \\ \otimes ((A_t(x) \rightarrow B_t(y_1)) \wedge (A_{-f}(x) \rightarrow B_{-f}(y_1)))) \end{array} \right\}$$

If $(\otimes_{L*}, \rightarrow_{L*})$ is an adjoint pair, $(\oplus_{L*}, \ominus_{L*})$ is a co-adjoint pair derived from left-continuous t-norms $\otimes_G$ then, we have the same result

$$B_t^*(y_1)\Big|_{x=x_1} = \left\{ \begin{array}{l} A_t^*(x_1) \otimes (((A_t^*(x_1) \rightarrow A_t(x_1)) \wedge (A_{-f}(x_1) \rightarrow A_{-f}^*(x_1))) \otimes \\ ((A_t(x_1) \rightarrow B_t(y_1)) \wedge (A_{-f}(x_1) \rightarrow B_{-f}(y_1)))) \end{array} \right\}$$

$$B_t^*(y_1)\Big|_{x=x_1} = 0.4$$

$$B_t^*(y_1)\Big|_{x=x_2} = \left\{ \begin{array}{l} A_t^*(x_2) \otimes (((A_t^*(x_2) \rightarrow A_t(x_2)) \wedge (A_{-f}(x_2) \rightarrow A_{-f}^*(x_2))) \otimes \\ ((A_t(x_2) \rightarrow B_t(y_1)) \wedge (A_{-f}(x_2) \rightarrow B_{-f}(y_1)))) \end{array} \right\}$$

$$B_t^*(y_1)\Big|_{x=x_2} = 0.6$$

$$B_t^*(y_1)\Big|_{x=x_3} = \left\{ \begin{array}{l} A_t^*(x_3) \otimes (((A_t^*(x_3) \rightarrow A_t(x_3)) \wedge (A_{-f}(x_3) \rightarrow A_{-f}^*(x_3))) \otimes \\ ((A_t(x_3) \rightarrow B_t(y_1)) \wedge (A_{-f}(x_3) \rightarrow B_{-f}(y_1)))) \end{array} \right\}$$

$$B_t^*(y_1)\Big|_{x=x_3} = 0.6$$

And $B_f^*(y_1) = \bigwedge_{x \in X} \left\{ A_f^*(x) \oplus ((1 - A_{-f}^*(x) \rightarrow A_{-f}(x)) \oplus (1 - A_{-f}(x) \rightarrow B_{-f}(y_1))) \right\}$, we have the result

$$B_f^*(y_1)\Big|_{x=x_1} = A_f^*(x_1) \oplus ((1 - A_{-f}^*(x_1) \rightarrow A_{-f}(x_1)) \oplus (1 - A_{-f}(x_1) \rightarrow B_{-f}(y_1)))$$

$$B_f^*(y_1)\Big|_{x=x_1} = 0.3$$

$$B_f^*(y_1)\Big|_{x=x_2} = A_f^*(x_2) \oplus ((1 - A_{-f}^*(x_2) \to A_{-f}(x_2)) \oplus (1 - A_{-f}(x_2) \to B_{-f}(y_1)))$$

$$B_f^*(y_1)\Big|_{x=x_2} = 0.2$$

$$B_f^*(y_1)\Big|_{x=x_3} = A_f^*(x_3) \oplus ((1 - A_{-f}^*(x_3) \to A_{-f}(x_3)) \oplus (1 - A_{-f}(x_3) \to B_{-f}(y_1)))$$

$$B_f^*(y_1)\Big|_{x=x_3} = 0.2$$

Similarly,

$$B_t^*(y_1) = B_t^*(y_1)\Big|_{x=x_1} \vee B_t^*(y_1)\Big|_{x=x_2} \vee B_t^*(y_1)\Big|_{x=x_3}$$
$$= 0.4 \vee 0.6 \vee 0.6 = 0.6.$$

$$B_t^*(y_2) = B_t^*(y_2)\Big|_{x=x_1} \vee B_t^*(y_2)\Big|_{x=x_2} \vee B_t^*(y_2)\Big|_{x=x_3}$$
$$= 0.4 \vee 0.6 \vee 0.7 = 0.7.$$

$$B_t^*(y_3) = B_t^*(y_3)\Big|_{x=x_1} \vee B_t^*(y_3)\Big|_{x=x_2} \vee B_t^*(y_3)\Big|_{x=x_3}$$
$$= 0.4 \vee 0.6 \vee 0.6 = 0.6.$$

$$B_f^*(y_1) = B_f^*(y_1)\Big|_{x=x_1} \wedge B_f^*(y_1)\Big|_{x=x_2} \wedge B_f^*(y_1)\Big|_{x=x_3}$$
$$= 0.3 \wedge 0.2 \wedge 0.2$$
$$= 0.2.$$

$$B_f^*(y_2) = B_f^*(y_2)\Big|_{x=x_1} \wedge B_f^*(y_2)\Big|_{x=x_2} \wedge B_f^*(y_2)\Big|_{x=x_3}$$
$$= 0.3 \wedge 0.2 \wedge 0.2 = 0.2.$$

$$B_f^*(y_3) = B_f^*(y_3)\Big|_{x=x_1} \wedge B_f^*(y_3)\Big|_{x=x_2} \wedge B_f^*(y_3)\Big|_{x=x_3}$$
$$= 0.3 \wedge 0.3 \wedge 0.3 = 0.3.$$

Therefore, we have the result

$$B^*(y) = \{(y_1, 0.6, 0.2), (y_2, 0.7, 0.2), (y_3, 0.6, 0.3)\}. \tag{18}$$

4 The α-Quintuple I Algorithm Based on Based on Intuitionistic Fuzzy Sets

Based on the Quintuple I algorithm to solve FMP problem and IFMP problem, we can view the α-Quintuple I algorithm in IFMP Problem as reasoning problem, so we propose the following solving principle.

The α-Quintuple I algorithm model in IFMP:

$\alpha - QIP - IFMP$: B^* is called the α-QIP solution of IFMP if B^* is the smallest element on $IFSs(Y)$ satisfying

$$(A(x) \to_{L^*} B(y)) \to_{L^*} ((A^*(x) \to_{L^*} A(x)) \to_{L^*} (A^*(x) \to_{L^*} B^*(y))) \geq \alpha \quad (19)$$

where $\alpha \in L^*$.

Theorem 4.1. If $\to_{L*}$ is a residual intuitionistic implication derived from a left-continuous t-norm $\otimes$, and $(\otimes_{L*}, \to_{L^*})$ is an intuitionistic adjoint pair, the QIP solutions of IFMP have the following forms:

$$B^*(y) = \bigvee_{x \in X} \{A^*(x) \otimes_{L*} ((A^*(x) \to_{L^*} A(x)) \to_{L^*} (A(x) \to_{L^*} B(y))) \otimes_{L*} \alpha\}, \alpha \in L^*, y \in Y \quad (20)$$

Proof: From formula (4.2), for all $x \in X$, then

$$A^*(x) \otimes_{L*} ((A^*(x) \to_{L^*} A(x)) \to_{L^*} (A(x) \to_{L^*} B(y))) \otimes_{L*} \alpha \leq B^*(y), \ y \in Y,$$

Since $(\otimes_{L*}, \to_{L^*})$ is an adjoint pair on intuitionistic sets, then

$$((A(x) \to_{L^*} B(y)) \to_{L*} (A^*(x) \to_{L^*} A(x))) \otimes_{L*} \alpha \leq A^*(x) \to_{L^*} B^*(y), \ y \in Y$$

And, we have

$$(A(x) \to_{L^*} B(y)) \to_{L^*} ((A^*(x) \to_{L^*} A(x)) \to_{L^*} (A^*(x) \to_{L^*} B^*(y))) \geq \alpha.$$

If there exists $C(y) \in IFSs(Y)$ satisfying

$$(A(x) \to_{L^*} B(y)) \to_{L^*} ((A^*(x) \to_{L^*} A(x)) \to_{L^*} (A^*(x) \to_{L^*} C(y))) \geq \alpha, x \in X, y \in Y.$$

Since $(\otimes_{L*}, \to_{L^*})$ is an intuitionistic adjoint pair on IFMP, then

$$(A(x) \to_{L^*} B(y)) \otimes_{L^*} \alpha \leq (A^*(x) \to_{L^*} A(x)) \to_{L^*} (A^*(x) \to_{L^*} C(y)), x \in X, y \in Y$$
$$\Leftrightarrow A^*(x) \otimes_{L*} ((A(x) \to_{L^*} B(y)) \otimes_{L*} (A^*(x) \to_{L^*} A(x))) \otimes_{L*} \alpha \leq C(y), x \in X, y \in Y$$

Therefore, we have $B^*(y) \leq C(y)$ for all $y \in Y$. Hence, $B^*(y)$ given by the formula (4.2) is the QIP solution of IFMP.

Corollary 2. Suppose that $\to_{L*}$ is a residual intuitionistic implication derived from a left-continuous t-norm $\otimes$, and $(\otimes_{L*}, \to_{L^*})$ is an intuitionistic adjoint pair, $\alpha = (a, b) \in L^*$, then

$$B^*(y) = \begin{pmatrix} \bigvee_{x \in X} \left\{ \begin{array}{l} A_t^*(x) \otimes (((A_t^*(x) \to A_t(x)) \wedge (A_{-f}(x) \to A_{-f}^*(x))) \otimes \\ ((A_t(x) \to B_t(y)) \wedge (A_{-f}(x) \to B_{-f}(y)))) \otimes a \end{array} \right\}, \\ \bigwedge_{x \in X} \left\{ A_f^*(x) \oplus ((1 - A_{-f}^*(x) \to A_{-f}(x)) \oplus (1 - A_{-f}(x) \to B_{-f}(y))) \oplus b \right\} \end{pmatrix}, y \in Y$$

where $(\otimes, \to)$ is an adjoint pair, $(\otimes_{L*}, \to_{L^*})$ derived from a left-continuous t-norm $\otimes$.

Example 2. If $X = \{x_1, x_2, x_3\}$, $Y = \{y_1, y_2, y_3\}$, X, $Y \in [0, 1]$, and the $(\otimes_{L*}, \rightarrow_{L*})$ is the intuitionistic adjoint pair derived from left-continuous t-norms $\otimes_G$, suppose that

$$\alpha_1 = (0.6, 0.2), \quad \alpha_2 = (0.5, 0.3)$$

$$A(x) = \{(x_1, 0.5, 0.3), (x_2, 0.7, 0.2), (x_3, 0.9, 0.1)\}$$
$$B(y) = \{(y_1, 0.6, 0.2), (y_2, 0.8, 0.1), (y_3, 0.6, 0.3)\}$$
$$A^*(x) = \{(x_1, 0.4, 0.2), (x_2, 0.6, 0.1), (x_3, 0.7, 0.2)\}$$

calculate the solutions of $\alpha - QIP - IFMP - B^*(y)$.

From Corollary 2, we have

$$B^*(y) = \left(\bigvee_{x \in X} \left\{ \begin{array}{l} A_t^*(x) \otimes_G (((A_t^*(x) \rightarrow_G A_t(x)) \wedge (A_{-f}(x) \rightarrow_G A_{-f}^*(x))) \otimes_G \\ ((A_t(x) \rightarrow_G B_t(y)) \wedge (A_{-f}(x) \rightarrow_G B_{-f}(y)))) \otimes_G a \end{array} \right\}, \right.$$
$$\left. \bigwedge_{x \in X} \left\{ A_f^*(x) \oplus_G ((1 - A_{-f}^*(x) \rightarrow_G A_{-f}(x)) \oplus_G (1 - A_{-f}(x) \rightarrow_G B_{-f}(y))) \oplus_G b \right\} \right)$$

$$B_t^*(y_1) = \bigvee_{x \in X} \left\{ \begin{array}{l} A_t^*(x) \otimes (((A_t^*(x) \rightarrow A_t(x)) \wedge (A_{-f}(x) \rightarrow A_{-f}^*(x))) \\ \otimes ((A_t(x) \rightarrow B_t(y_1)) \wedge (A_{-f}(x) \rightarrow B_{-f}(y_1)))) \end{array} \right\}$$

If $(\otimes_G, \rightarrow_G)$ is an adjoint pair, $(\oplus_G, \ominus_G)$ is a co adjoint pair derived from left-continuous t-norms $\otimes$, then, we have the same result.
(1) $\alpha_1 - QIP - IFMP - B_1^*(y)$:

$$B_t^*(y_1) = B_t^*(y_1)\big|_{x=x_1} \vee B_t^*(y_1)\big|_{x=x_2} \vee B_t^*(y_1)\big|_{x=x_3}$$
$$= 0.4 \vee 0.6 \vee 0.6 = 0.6.$$

$$B_t^*(y_2) = B_t^*(y_2)\big|_{x=x_1} \vee B_t^*(y_2)\big|_{x=x_2} \vee B_t^*(y_2)\big|_{x=x_3}$$
$$= 0.4 \vee 0.6 \vee 0.6 = 0.6.$$

$$B_t^*(y_3) = B_t^*(y_3)\big|_{x=x_1} \vee B_t^*(y_3)\big|_{x=x_2} \vee B_t^*(y_3)\big|_{x=x_3}$$
$$= 0.4 \vee 0.6 \vee 0.6 = 0.6.$$

$$B_f^*(y_1) = B_f^*(y_1)\big|_{x=x_1} \wedge B_f^*(y_1)\big|_{x=x_2} \wedge B_f^*(y_1)\big|_{x=x_3}$$
$$= 0.3 \wedge 0.2 \wedge 0.2 = 0.2.$$

$$B_f^*(y_2) = B_f^*(y_2)\big|_{x=x_1} \wedge B_f^*(y_2)\big|_{x=x_2} \wedge B_f^*(y_2)\big|_{x=x_3}$$
$$= 0.3 \wedge 0.2 \wedge 0.2 = 0.2.$$

$$B_f^*(y_3) = B_f^*(y_3)\big|_{x=x_1} \wedge B_f^*(y_3)\big|_{x=x_2} \wedge B_f^*(y_3)\big|_{x=x_3}$$

$$= 0.3 \wedge 0.3 \wedge 0.3 = 0.3.$$

Therefore,

$$B_1^*(y) = \{(y_1, 0.6, 0.2), (y_2, 0.6, 0.2), (y_3, 0.6, 0.3)\}. \tag{21}$$

(2) $\alpha_2 - QIP - IFMP - B_2^*(y)$:
Similarly,

$$B_2^*(y) = \{(y_1, 0.5, 0.3), (y_2, 0.5, 0.3), (y_3, 0.5, 0.3)\}. \tag{22}$$

Acknowledgement. We are grateful to the peoples for the support and encouragement.

Funding Statement. This work was supported by the National Natural Science Foundation of China (no. 61966014), in part by the Innovation Project Foundation of Jishou University, China, under Grant JGY202119 and Grant JGY202117, in part by the Natural Science Foundation of Jishou University, China, under Grant Jdx19033 and Grant Jdy21065, in part by the National college student innovation and entrepreneurship Projects of China (no. 202110531019).

References

1. Zadeh, L.A., Klir, G.J., Yuan, B.: Fuzzy sets, fuzzy logic, and fuzzy systems: selected papers. World Sci. **6**, 394–432 (1996)
2. Gaines, B.: Foundations of fuzzy reasoning. Int. J. Man Mach. Stud. **8**(6), 623–668 (1976)
3. Wang, L.: Analysis and design of hierarchical fuzzy systems. IEEE Trans. Fuzzy Syst. **7**(5), 617–624 (1999)
4. Zadeh, L.A.: Outline of a new approach to the analysis of complex systems and decision processes. IEEE Trans. Syst. Man Cybern. **1**, 28–44 (1973)
5. Guojun, W.: The full implication triple I method for fuzzy reasoning. Sci. China (Ser. E) **29**(1), 43–53 (1999)
6. Song, S., Wu, C.: Reverse triple I method of fuzzy reasoning. Sci. China Ser. F Inf. Sci. **45**(5), 344–364 (2002)
7. Zhou, B., Xu, G., Li, S.: The quintuple implication principle of fuzzy reasoning. Inf. Sci. **297**, 202–215 (2015)
8. Li, D., Qin, S.: Performance analysis of fuzzy systems based on quintuple implications method. Int. J. Approx. Reason. **96**, 20–35 (2018)
9. Luo, M., Zhao, R., Liu, B.: Interval-valued fuzzy reasoning algorithms based on Schweizer-Sklar t-norms and its application. Eng. Appl. Artif. Intell. **87**, 103313 (2020)
10. Luo, M., Wu, L., Fu, L.: Robustness analysis of the interval-valued fuzzy inference algorithms. J. Intell. Fuzzy Syst. **38**(1), 685–696 (2020)
11. Luo, M., Wang, Y., Zhao, R.: Interval-valued fuzzy reasoning method based on similarity measure. J. Log. Algebraic Methods Program. **113**, 100541 (2020)
12. Li, D., Qin, S.: The quintuple implication principle of fuzzy reasoning based on interval-valued S-implication. J. Log. Algebraic Methods Program. **100**, 185–194 (2018)
13. Atanassov, K.: Intuitionistic fuzzy sets. Fuzzy Sets Syst. **20**, 87–96 (1986)
14. Mishra, S., Prakash, M.: Digital mammogram inferencing system using intuitionistic fuzzy theory. Comput. Syst. Sci. Eng. **41**(3), 1099–1115 (2022)

15. Bhalla, K., Koundal, D., Bhatia, S., Khalid, M., Tahir, M.: Fusion of infrared and visible images using fuzzy based siamese convolutional network. Comput. Mater. Continua **70**(3), 5503–5518 (2022)
16. Alyas, T., Javed, I., Namoun, A., Tufail, A., Alshmrany, S.: Live migration of virtual machines using a mamdani fuzzy inference system. Comput. Mater. Continua **71**(2), 3019–3033 (2022)
17. Hassan, S., Khanesar, M.A., Hussein, N.K., Belhaouari, S.B., Amjad, U.: Optimization of interval type-2 fuzzy logic system using grasshopper optimization algorithm. Comput. Mater. Continua **71**(2), 3513–3531 (2022)
18. Cornelis, C., Deschrijver, G., Kerre, E.: Implication in intuitionistic fuzzy and interval-valued fuzzy set theory: construction, classification, application. Int. J. Approx. Reason. **35**(1), 55–95 (2004)
19. Zheng, M.C., Shi, Z.K., Liu, Y.: Triple I method of intuitionistic fuzzy reasoning based on residual implicator. Sci. China Inf. Sci **43**, 810–820 (2013)
20. Zheng, M., Shi, Z., Liu, Y.: Triple I method of approximate reasoning on Atanassov's intuitionistic fuzzy sets. Int. J. Approx. Reason. **55**(6), 1369–1382 (2014)
21. Deschrijver, G., Cornelis, C., Kerre, E.E.: On the representation of intuitionistic fuzzy t-norms and t-conorms. IEEE Trans. Fuzzy Syst. **12**, 45–61 (2004)
22. Ahmad, M., Jaffar, M.A., Nasim, F., Masood, T., Akram, S.: Fuzzy based hybrid focus value estimation for multi focus image fusion. Comput. Mater. Continua **71**(1), 735–752 (2022)
23. Zheng, M., Liu, Y.: Multiple-rules reasoning based on Triple I method on Atanassov's intuitionistic fuzzy sets. Int. J. Approx. Reason. **113**, 196–206 (2019)
24. Liu, Y., Zheng, Mu-Cong.: Mechanisms of mixed fuzzy reasoning for asymmetric types. In: Fan, Tai-He., Chen, Shui-Li., Wang, San-Min., Li, Yong-Ming. (eds.) Quantitative Logic and Soft Computing 2016. AISC, vol. 510, pp. 293–300. Springer, Cham (2017) https://doi.org/10.1007/978-3-319-46206-6_29
25. Jiayin, P.: Reverse triple I method of intuitionistic fuzzy reasoning based on residual implicator. Pattern Recogn. Artif. Intell. **31**, 525–536 (2018)
26. Mei, J., Xiaojing, H., Rong, W.: Robustness of intuitionistic fuzzy inference reverse triple I methods based on similarity. Acta Electron. Sin. **48**(02), 265–271 (2020)
27. Jin, J., Ye, M., Pedrycz, W.: Quintuple Implication Principle on interval-valued intuitionistic fuzzy sets. Soft. Comput. **24**(16), 12091–12109 (2020). https://doi.org/10.1007/s00500-019-04649-1
28. Zheng, M., Shi, Z., Liu, Y.: Triple I method of intuitionistic fuzzy reasoning based on residual implicator. Scientia Sinica Informationis **43**(6), 810–820 (2013)
29. Klement, E.P., Mesiar, R., Pap, E.: Triangular norms. Position paper I: basic analytical and algebraic properties. Fuzzy Sets Syst. **143**(1), 5–26 (2004)

A Module Based Full Cycle Construction Method of Domain-Specific Knowledge Graph

Zheng Ma[1], Zhiqiang Hu[1], Jun Shi[1], Zhipeng Li[1], Yang Zhou[1], Yong Liao[1], Yangzhao Yang[1], Zhenyuan Gao[1], Jie Zhang[1(✉)], and Xun Shao[2]

[1] Shenzhen CyberAray Network Technology Co., Ltd., Shenzhen 518042, China
mazheng_2008ok@163.com
[2] School of Regional Innovation and Social Design Engineering, Kitami Institute of Technology, Kitami 090-8507, Japan

Abstract. Knowledge graph (KG) is booming since Google announced the concept about it in 2012, and its underlying semantic technologies support inference and reasoning natively, provides the possibility of artificial intelligence (AI) to develop to be explainable. Meanwhile, the knowledge graph has emerged as a major area in artificial intelligence and been widely applied to various fields along with the continuous development of intelligent service applications. Knowledge graph construction involves a variety of technologies and methods, currently researchers are focus on the accuracy of specific algorithms. However, there are still many challenges in the construction of knowledge graph for lack of the full life cycle of knowledge graph construction methods. This paper proposed a module based full cycle construction of domain-specific knowledge graph, including five sub modules. We designed a standardized graph construction process, which can realize the semi-automatic knowledge graph construction with the least manual intervention. Knowledge graph designers can not only facilitate the procedures for the construction model preparation and integration, but also can increase the speed and efficiency of the knowledge graph construction. At last, a knowledge graph is constructed by our methodology as a case study, which demonstrated to verify the superiority and practicality of the proposed method.

Keywords: Knowledge graph · Knowledge graph construction · Module-based · Artificial intelligence · Full cycle · Domain-specific knowledge graph

1 Introduction

With the rapid development of Internet technology, a large quantity of data on the Web ('Big Data') has been accumulated in the last decades, which spawned the revival of artificial intelligence. However, the concept of the "black box" in machine learning do not provide human-understandable insights on how a specific decision was achieved. In 2012, Google announced the concept of knowledge graph, and the research on knowledge graph is booming since then. Knowledge graph is a knowledge base that uses a graph-structured data model or topology to integrate data, which consists of a large quantity of concepts, instances, events and their relationships which makes it can effectively manage large-scale data and provide a reference for scientific research through

© The Author(s), under exclusive license to Springer Nature Switzerland AG 2022
X. Sun et al. (Eds.): ICAIS 2022, CCIS 1586, pp. 590–603, 2022.
https://doi.org/10.1007/978-3-031-06767-9_49

various disciplines such as graph algorithm, mathematics, and information visualization. Knowledge graph and its underlying semantic technologies are the modern implementations of symbolic AI, which expose connections and relations, and support inference and reasoning natively, provides the possibility of artificial intelligence to develop to be explainable. Meanwhile, the knowledge graph has emerged as a major area in Artificial Intelligence and been widely applied to various fields along with the continuous development of intelligent service applications, like search engines, personalized recommender systems, artificial intelligence customer service, information analysis and research systems.

Knowledge graph construction involves a variety of technologies and methods, including ontology design, entity recognition, relation extraction, event extraction, etc. Current research focuses on the accuracy of specific algorithms. However, there are still many challenges in the construction of knowledge graph, lack of the full life cycle of knowledge graph construction. This paper provides an overall framework based full life cycle construction of domain-specific knowledge graph, including five sub modules, which describes the detailed construction procedure. Each of the modules is independent so that the researcher can amend and perfect any incomplete module according to his requirement without influencing the function of the others. As a result of this distributed form, designers can not only facilitate the procedures for the preparation and integration, but also can increase the speed and efficiency of the knowledge graph construction.

In summary, our contributions are 3-fold as follows.

- The knowledge graph construction process is divided into five modules, and design a standardized graph construction process, which can realize the semi-automatic knowledge graph construction with the least manual intervention. The model contains different algorithm libraries, and the user can choose based on their demand. Input variables, output variables and parameters of the module is introduced particularly to improve the reusability and applicability of the construction process.
- This method can achieve a reasonable incremental updates of knowledge graph, and ensure the reliability and efficiency of knowledge. Therefore, we can iteratively construct a knowledge graph based on the increasing of corpus and make it possible to build a large-scale knowledge graph.
- This paper depicts the algorithms and models involved in the construction of knowledge graph, assigns them to specific modules, defines the connection between various algorithms, and facilitates the management between algorithms.

The rest of the paper is organized as follows: Sect. 2 reviews the background and related work; Sect. 3 presents an overview of pipelined method of constructing knowledge graph, and then systematically describes the proposed method; Sect. 4 demonstrates an exemplary case to verify the superiority and practicality of the proposed method; Sect. 5 discusses future work and concludes the paper.

2   Background and Related Work

The knowledge graph is essentially a large-scale semantic network, rich in entities, concepts and relationships between them. The basic unit in knowledge graph is the "entity—relation—entity" triple (RDF triple), or well known "subject, predicate, object" semantic triple (SPO). Current research on knowledge graph construction focuses on the definition and extraction of SPO triples, which are ontology development, information extraction and entity resolution.

2.1   Ontology Development

An ontology is a formal explicit description of concepts in a domain of discourse concepts (classes), properties of each concept describing various features and attributes of the concept (slots), and restrictions on slots (facets). Individual instances of classes are called as entities, and the connection between classes is known as relations. An ontology together with a set of individual instances of classes, relations constitute a knowledge graph [1].

Ontology is generally developed by domain experts manually, following the steps below [1].

Step 1: Determine the domain and scope of the ontology, consider reusing existing ontologies.
Step 2: Enumerate important terms in the ontology.
Step 3: Define the classes and the class hierarchy.
Step 4: Define the properties of classes—slots.
Step 5: Define the facets of the slots.
Step 6: Create instances.
Hundreds of tools for building ontologies are developed and applied in industry and academia. The most commonly used, fully developed, and well-known ontology construction tools are Protégé-2000, Ontolingua Server, Ontosaurus, WebOnto, OntoEdit, WebODE, OILEd, DUET, etc. [2]

2.2   Information Extraction

Information extraction (IE) is a fundamental component in any knowledge graph construction pipeline, whether domain-specific or generic. The goal of information extraction is to extract knowledge from heterogeneous data sources, which are usually semi-structured and unstructured text data. The technologies mainly include named entity recognition, relation extraction and event extraction.

Named Entity Recognition. Named Entity Recognition (NER) is a technology which automatic identification of entities from text data. Given a document and a set $T = \{t_1, t_2, \ldots, t_n\}$ of n entity types (defined in an ontology, in ontology development stage), a NER system generally returns a set of extracted mentions, where each mention may be expressed in the form $(t, start - offset, end - offset)$, with $t \in T$[3]. In practice, the named entity recognition technology can be classified in supervised methods, semi-supervised methods and unsupervised methods.

Supervised methods are the current dominant technique for addressing the named entity recognition problem which based on the idea of providing labeled instances of named entities, annotated by domain experts manually; the labeled data are then used to train the select appropriate learning algorithm which is further used to recognize and classify named entities out of unannotated text data.

Supervised methods of named entity recognition was based on traditional machine learning in the early days, and later deep learning was adopted, until now the attention mechanism, graph neural network and other research models have been continuously developed over time. The traditional machine learning methods used mainly includes: Hidden Markov Model (HMM), Maximum Entropy (ME), Maximum Entropy Markov Model (MEMM), Support Vector Machine (SVM), Conditional Random Fields (CRF), etc. Among them, the CRF model is most widely used due to its advantage in interfering the internal and contextual feature information in the process of labeling a location, which is very suitable for the sequence labeling problem under named entity recognition. With the continuous development of artificial intelligence, neural networks or deep learning are widely used in named entity recognition task. Deep learning hardly requires feature engineering and domain knowledge, for its automatic feature extraction and analysis on the input, and has achieved relatively good results. In the NER task, the commonly used neural networks mainly include Convolutional Neural Network (CNN), Recurrent Neural Network (RNN) and networks based on attention mechanism. Among them, the BiLSTM-CRF architecture has become the baseline method for named entity recognition task.

Supervised methods acquire a large set of training data, which annotated by domain experts manually, making this task time consuming and labor intensive. Unlike supervised methods, semi-supervised methods are designed to significantly reduce labeling effort by introduce specific technique which using patterns or algorithm to automatic annotate text data. The most common used and influential semi-supervised NER method is "bootstrapping", which generally requires a set of seeds for initiating the learning process. Bootstrapping first generate a set of seeds, entities and relations, by annotated or collected handful. Then accumulating the patterns found around these seeds in a sufficiently large corpus. With this pattern generalization approach, starting only from a seed of 10 examples facts, it is possible to generate one million facts in large corpora (hundreds of millions of webpages) with a precision of about 88%, an impressive performance metric [3].

Clustering is the quintessential unsupervised machine learning approach [4]. The cluster-based NER system extracts named entities from clustering groups based on contextual similarity. The key idea is to use vocabulary resources (such as WordNet), lexical resources, vocabulary patterns and statistical information calculated on a large corpus to infer named entities. In specifically, unsupervised named entity recognition involves the direct methods like dictionary matching or regular expression matching.

Relation Extraction. Relation Extraction is a technology which detecting and classifying relationships between entities extracted from the text. A relation usually denotes a well-defined relationship between two or more entities in ontology development stage. At present, the mainstream approaches of relation extraction can be classified as follows: rule-based methods and statistic-based methods, while statistics-based methods include supervised approaches, semi-supervised approaches, unsupervised approaches and distant supervision approaches [5].

Rule-based approaches need to predefine rules that describe the structure of the relationship mentions, which requires a deep understanding of the domain background. The method is considered labor-intensive, as most of the required work is hands-on even with the use of certain tools. Nevertheless, the rule-based relation extraction approaches are easy to implement and fast to run, so we could do better as rule-based algorithm a baseline.

Statistics-based approaches can be simply classified into four categories: unsupervised, semi-supervised, supervised and distant supervision [5]. Unsupervised methods extract strings of words between entities in large amounts of text, and clusters and simplifies these word strings to produce relation-string [6]. However, the extracted result may not be easy to do ontology mapping and the accuracy of the method is low, since there is not a standard form of relationships in unsupervised approaches. Semi-supervised approaches in relation extraction are quite similar with the semi-supervised NER method. The most common used semi-supervised relation extraction method is also "bootstrapping", which first introduced in DIPRE [7], and then extended in Snowball [8], KnowItAll [9] and TextRunner [10]. Supervised approaches are the most widely used methods for relation extraction and have achieved relatively high performance. In the supervised paradigm, relation extraction task is treated as a classification problem, so several of classification algorithms in natural language processing can be used to address the relation extraction problem. Distant supervision automatically generates training examples and learns features through aligning free text with KBs like Freebase, a large semantic database [5]. This technique can be used to addressing the problem of lacking of annotated training data and reducing the cost of the relation extraction algorithm.

Event Extraction. Event extraction aims at detecting the existence of an event reported in text, and if existing, discovering event-related information from the text, such as the "5W1H" about an event (i.e., who, when, where, what, why and how) [11]. Event extraction task can be classified as closed-domain event extraction and open-domain event, which closed-domain event extraction uses predefined event schema to discover and extract desired events of particular type from text, while open-domain event extraction aims at detecting events from texts without predefined event schemas and clustering similar events via extracted event keywords.

Closed-domain event schema contains event types and their corresponding event structures, which commonly defined as event mention, event trigger, event argument and argument role. Event types and event structures combine together to form Event N-Triples. Open-domain event extraction contains following tasks: story segmentation, first story detection, topic detection, topic tracking and story link detection. The first two tasks focus on event detection, and the rest three tasks are for event clustering.

The methods for event extraction can be classified as pattern-based approaches, machine-learning-based approaches, deep-learning-based approaches, semi-supervised-learning-based approaches and unsupervised-learning-based approaches [11]. Pattern-based approaches are a kind of pattern matching technique, which patterns are usually manually constructed by experts with professional knowledge and well-defined with high quality, so event extraction based on pattern matching can often achieve high accuracy for domain-specific applications. Machine-learning-based approaches uses traditional machine learning algorithms, like support vector machine (SVM), maximum entropy (ME) and etc., learning classifiers from training data and applying classifiers for event extraction from new text, and can be generally divided into four subtasks: trigger detection, trigger/event type identification, argument detection and argument role identification. Deep-learning-based approaches introduce neural network structures like Graph Neural Network (GNN), Convolutional Neural Network (CNN), Recurrent Neural Network (RNN) and its variants like Long and Short Term Memory (LSTM), Gated Recurrent Unit-based RNN (GRU), to automatic extract diverse features like lexical, syntactic, semantic features and etc. To address the problem that obtaining labeled corpus is a rather cost prohibitive task for its time-consuming and labor-intensive annotation process, semi-supervised-learning-based approaches use bootstrapping and knowledge bases like Freebase, Wikipedia and WordNet to do data expansion. Unsupervised-learning-based approaches mainly focus on open-domain event extraction tasks, like detecting trigger and arguments based on cluster and word similarities.

2.3 Entity Resolution

Entity resolution is a problem to determining whether two entities refer to the same underlying entity, since the obtained entities and attributes from heterogeneous data contains a large amount of redundancy and error information. The relationship between the entities may also be flat, lack of hierarchy and logic. Therefore, entity resolution is a technique to clean and integrate the extracted knowledge, which consists of two parts: entity linking and knowledge merging.

Entity linking refers to the operation of extracting entity objects from text and linking them to the corresponding entity objects in the knowledge base [12]. It generally has two processes: entity disambiguation and coreference resolution. Entity disambiguation is the task of linking mentions of ambiguous entities to their referent entities in a knowledge base such as Wikipedia. Entity disambiguation mainly adopts the clustering method based on the similarity between entity object and reference item. The define of similarity between entities is typically used the vector space model, combining entity itself and its surrounding items to constitute the feature vectors. Coreference resolution is the task of finding all linguistic expressions (called mentions) in a given text that refer to the same real-world entity. Learning-based coreference models can be classified into three broad categories of mention-pair, entity-mention and ranking model. The cluster ranking approaches is widely used in coreference resolution problem, which aimed at combining the best of the entity-mention models and the ranking models.

Knowledge merging is a technique to expand constructed knowledge graph data, since there consists a lot of third-party semantic knowledge base products or structured data. Merging the knowledge (entities, relations, properties) from these knowledge bases to our knowledge graph is a relatively straightforward enhancing and optimizing approach.

3   Proposed Methods

This section presents the proposed module based full-life-cycle method for construction domain knowledge graph. We first describe the overall framework of the method, and then details of every step of the proposed method are provided in the following subsections.

3.1   Architecture Overview

This paper proposes a pipelined modular knowledge graph construction method, each module adopts standard-defined data input and output. The method includes five modules: ontology building module, information extraction module, knowledge mapping module, knowledge fusion module and knowledge verification module. Through the five-module pipelined data process and the iterative expansion process between the graphs, the construction and expansion of the domain-specific knowledge graph can be realized. Besides, the functions of each module are transparent, and the internal algorithm of the module can be customized and reused according to the characteristics of the specific data source. The pipelined modular construction method can facilitate the parallelization of knowledge graph construction and the accumulation of algorithms, so that the technical solution has strong applicability and optimization capabilities. An architecture overview of our method is shown in Fig. 1.

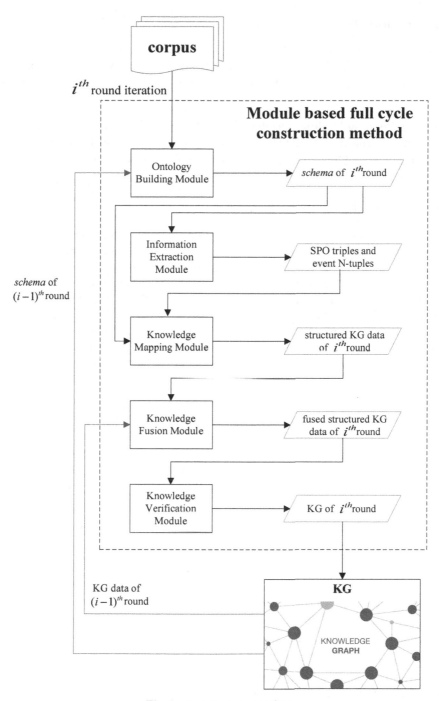

Fig. 1. Architecture overview.

3.2   Modules in Detail

This section describes the details of our proposed module-based knowledge graph construction method, specify ontology building module, information extraction module, knowledge mapping module, knowledge fusion module and knowledge verification module.

Ontology Building Module. Ontology is used to describe concepts, attributes, and axioms in a specific domain. Building an ontology is the first step in the construction of a domain knowledge graph. All data and algorithm processes in the subsequent procedure of knowledge graph construction must correspond to the concept of the ontology. The definition of ontology is mainly embodied in the definition of the SPO triples (Subject, Predicate, and Object) of the knowledge graph.

The purpose of this module is to build the ontology of the domain knowledge graph. In order to achieve the accumulation and reuse of expert experience, this module has designed an ontology library to store the ontology constructed by experts based on business requirements. At the same time, in order to realize the iterative construction of knowledge graphs in the same domain, the construction phase of the knowledge graph requires that the ontology of every iteration constructed iteratively be compatible. This module involves the research of ontology development in academia, so the research results about ontology development can be used to construct ontology.

The input of this module is the schema (ontology) of the $(i-1)^{th}$ round, follow the definition below:

$$input = \begin{cases} empty, \ i = 1 \\ schema \ of \ i-1, \ i > 1 \end{cases}$$

After the expert analysis and reference of ontology library, the output of this module is the schema of the ith round, compatible with the previous construction round to achieve iterative update of the knowledge graph. The structure of ontology building module is shown in Fig. 2.

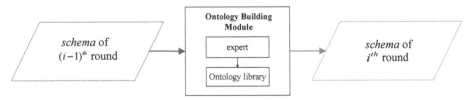

Fig. 2. The structure of ontology building module.

Information Extraction Module. Information extraction is aimed to extract the essential information that constitutes the knowledge graph from large number of texts, including knowledge graph triples (entities, objects, relationships) and event N-tuples (event trigger words, event types, event arguments, and arguments Role). Information Extraction is a key step in the construction of knowledge graphs. The current research on knowledge graph construction in academia and industry is mainly concentrated in information extraction.

This module divides information extraction methods into structured/semi-structured corpus based and unstructured corpus based. The structured/semi-structured data information extraction is mainly based on rule matching methods, according to the structure of the data. The rules and regexes are accumulated to a library of regular and can be reused in the next iteration. Unstructured data information extraction consists of rule-based methods and model-based methods. Model-based methods include various deep learning models, including entity extraction algorithms, relationship extraction algorithms and event argument/role/type extraction algorithms. Rule-based methods consist of regular rules and dependency parsing, which is a supplement to the model-based method. Part of the technology of this module involves the research of information extraction in academia like entity extraction technology, relation extraction technology and event extraction technology, which can be used in this module process.

The input of this module is the corpus and the schema of this round (i^{th} round). After interfering by the information extraction algorithm of this module, the output is the SPO triples and event N-tuples. The structure of information extraction module is shown in Fig. 3.

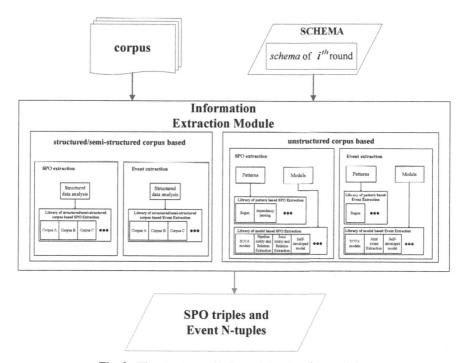

Fig. 3. The structure of information extraction module.

Knowledge Mapping Module. Knowledge mapping is used to map the result of information extraction into structured knowledge graph data according to the definition of schema. The knowledge mapping module is mainly rule-based, namely mapping the information extraction results to the structured node and edge data of the knowledge graph based on rules.

The input of this module is the output of information extraction module and the schema of this round (i^{th} round). After interfering by the mapping rules of this module, the output is the structured data of our knowledge graph. The structure of knowledge mapping module is shown in Fig. 4.

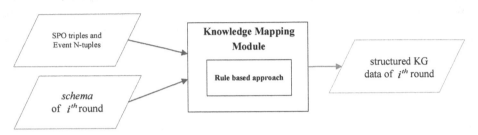

Fig. 4. The structure of knowledge mapping module.

Knowledge Fusion Module. The knowledge fusion module is used to fusion of the previous round of knowledge graph data and the current round of graph data, that is, the iteration of the knowledge graph construction. Besides, this module is a refinement of knowledge graph data based the knowledge completion and correction algorithm. This module includes a knowledge completion module and a multi-graph fusion module. The function of knowledge completion module is the attribute completion and relationship completion of the knowledge graph, and improves the quality of the knowledge graph; the function of multi-graph fusion module is the fusion of the previous round of the knowledge graph data with the current round data, which realizes the iterative expansion of the knowledge graph. Some of the technologies in this module involve the research of entity resolution in academia, like entity disambiguation, entity linking and knowledge merging with knowledge base, which can be used in this module process.

The input of this module is the knowledge graph data of this round (i^{th} round) D_i together with the data of $(i-1)^{th}$ round D_{i-1}, follow the definition below:

$$D_{i-1} = \begin{cases} empty, \ i = 1 \\ knowledge \ graph \ data \ of \ iteration \ i-1, \ i > 1 \end{cases}$$

After this module's knowledge completion and multi-graph fusion, the output is the fused structured knowledge graph data. The structure of knowledge fusion module is shown in Fig. 5.

Knowledge Verification Module. Knowledge verification is the last step of the knowledge graph construction process and a key step to ensure the quality of the graph.

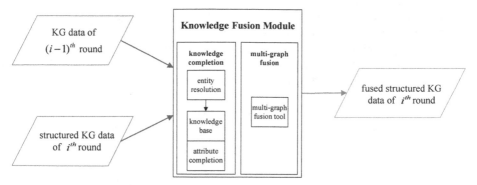

Fig. 5. The structure of knowledge fusion module.

The knowledge verification module includes algorithm verification and manual verification. The algorithm verification uses regexes and patterns to do preliminary screening of the overall graph, reducing the subsequent manual workload; manual verification uses knowledge crowdsourcing algorithms including display crowdsourcing and implicit crowdsourcing to continuously improve the quality of the graph.

The input of this module is the fused structured knowledge graph data. After the knowledge verification of this module, the output is the final high-quality knowledge graph constructed for this round, and the quality of subsequent graph iteration expansion and business requirements are guaranteed. The structure of knowledge verification module is shown in Fig. 6.

Fig. 6. The structure of knowledge verification module.

4   Case Study

This section presents experiments regarding our framework, along with their results. As for the experimental set-up, we collect 8000 lines of text data from Wikipedia and organized them into semi-structured data as our corpus.

According to the modular knowledge graph construction method described above, the knowledge graph is constructed. Through the ontology building module, we define 13 entities such as persons, organizations, schools, occupations and places, as well as 40 relations like graduated, parents, spouses, children, affiliation, etc. The entities and relationships constitute the ontology definition of the knowledge graph. After information extraction module, knowledge mapping module, knowledge fusion module and knowledge verification module, we constructed a knowledge graph with 13808 different entities and 16243 different relationships. More precisely, there are 2178 persons, 1035 organization, 8276 events, 596 schools, etc. Figure 7 shows a sample of the knowledge graph we have built, though the actual knowledge graph we have constructed is much larger. As can be seen in the figure, it contains rich information of represent different types of entities and shows the semantic relationships between different types of entities.

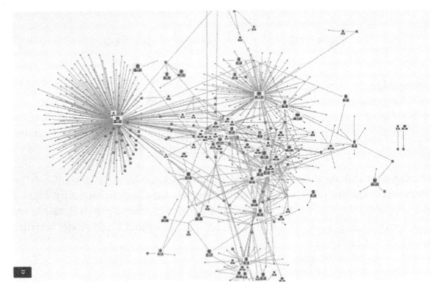

Fig. 7. Sample of the knowledge graph we constructed.

5   Conclusions

In this paper, we proposed a module based full cycle construction method of domain-specific knowledge graph and presented all technical details of each module in our proposed general framework for knowledge graph construction, including ontology building module, information extraction module, and knowledge mapping module, knowledge fusion module and knowledge verification module. We applied our method to build an experimental knowledge graph, the resulting knowledge graph contains a considerable number of RDF triples which shows the effectiveness of our method.

In the future, we plan to build a large-scale web-based knowledge graph and investigate the applications of it, including semantic reasoning, knowledge representation, recommender systems, etc. Furthermore, we will research in multi-modal knowledge graphs and improving our method to adaptation of constructing multi-modal knowledge graphs.

Acknowledgement. The authors would like to thank the staff of our Product Development Department for their help in collecting experimental data used in our case study. The authors would also like to thank the staff of our R&D Department for their assistance with the data verification of the knowledge graph constructed in our case study.

Funding Statement. The authors received no specific funding for this study.

Conflicts of Interest. The authors declare that they have no conflicts of interest to report regarding the present study.

References

1. Noy, N.F., McGuinness, D.L.: Ontology development 101: a guide to creating your first ontology (2001)
2. Xu, G., Xu, F.: A comparative study of ontology-building tools. Lib. Inf. Serv. **50**(1), 44–48 (2006)
3. Kejriwal, M.: Domain-Specific Knowledge Graph Construction. Springer, Cham (2019). https://doi.org/10.1007/978-3-030-12375-8
4. Anil, K.J., Richard, C.D.: Algorithms for Clustering Data. Prentice-Hall Inc, USA (1988)
5. Cui, M., Li, L., Wang, Z., You, M.: A survey on relation extraction. In: Li, J., Zhou, M., Qi, G., Lao, N., Ruan, T., Du, J. (eds.) CCKS 2017. CCIS, vol. 784, pp. 50–58. Springer, Singapore (2017). https://doi.org/10.1007/978-981-10-7359-3_6
6. Yan, Y., et al.: Unsupervised relation extraction by mining Wikipedia texts using information from the web. In: Proceedings of the Joint Conference of the 47th Annual Meeting of the ACL and the 4th International Joint Conference on Natural Language Processing of the AFNLP (2009)
7. Brin, S.: Extracting patterns and relations from the world wide web. In: Atzeni, P., Mendelzon, A., Mecca, G. (eds.) WebDB. LNCS, vol. 1590, pp. 172–183. Springer, Heidelberg (1999). https://doi.org/10.1007/10704656_11
8. Agichtein, E., Luis, G.: Snowball: extracting relations from large plain-text collections. In: Proceedings of the Fifth ACM conference on Digital Libraries (2000)
9. Etzioni, O., et al.: Web-scale information extraction in knowitall: (preliminary results). In: Proceedings of the 13th International Conference on World Wide Web (2004)
10. Yates, A., et al.: Textrunner: open information extraction on the web. In: Proceedings of Human Language Technologies: The Annual Conference of the North American Chapter of the Association for Computational Linguistics (NAACL-HLT) (2007)
11. Xiang, W., Bang, W.: A survey of event extraction from text. IEEE Access 7, 173111–173137 (2019)
12. Li, Y., et al.: Mining evidences for named entity disambiguation. In: Proceedings of the 19th ACM SIGKDD International Conference on Knowledge Discovery and Data Mining (2013)

A Transferable Framework for Few-Shot Human Activity Recognition

Zhang Yifei[1]([✉])[ID], Wang Haoyu[1][ID], Feng Tian[1][ID], and Tian Zijian[2][ID]

[1] Beijing University of Posts and Telecommunications, Beijing 100876, China
{zyfff,wanghaoyu2,fengtian2019}@bupt.edu.cn
[2] University of Tsukuba, Ibaraki 305-8577, Japan
2121576@s.tsukuba.ac.jp

Abstract. With the progress of sensor technology and the vigorous development of deep learning methods, using deep learning methods to complete sensor-based human activity recognition (HAR) tasks has become a research area of concern. Researchers have proposed various accurate, efficient, and low-cost methods to realize sensor-based HAR. In practical application scenarios, the frequency of the human body performing various movements often varies greatly, which causes great difficulties to the task of action recognition. However, most existing models can achieve better performance in the case of balanced category distribution and ignore the impact of data imbalance. In the field of HAR, few studies have been done on few-shot. Aiming at the low accuracy of the network in the case of imbalanced sample distribution, this paper proposed a transferable HAR framework. This framework can be superimposed on the existing deep network to improve the accuracy of recognition. Experiments of this framework on two kinds of deep networks were completed, and the accuracy is greatly improved, which verifies the portability of the model. Three different datasets were used in the experiment, including Opportunity, UniMiB-SHAR, and PAMAP2, to verify the effectiveness of the framework on different data sets. The experimental results are discussed in-depth and the contribution points of the proposed framework are analyzed.

Keywords: Deep learning · Human activity recognition · Autoencoder

1 Introduction

Over the past decade, sensor technology has made extraordinary advances in several areas, including accuracy, size, computing power, manufacturing costs, and more [1]. Therefore, various sensor-based technologies have received extensive attention. Sensor-based human activity recognition (HAR) is one of them. Sensor-based HAR, which processes, calculates, and analyzes the data collected

Supported by ICN&CAD Laboratory of School of Electronic Engineering, Beijing University of Posts and Telecommunications.

by the various types of wearable sensing devices (e.g. accelerometers, gyroscopes, or magnetic field sensors [2]), has a wide range of applications in many fields, such as healthcare [3,4], athletic competitions [5], smart cities [6]and smart home [7].

Traditionally, after processing data collected from sensing devices, hand-crafted features are extracted for classification [8]. However, the effectiveness of this features extraction method relies heavily on human expertise, which is unstable and wasteful. Moreover, these features can only be used for tasks in specific scenarios, and cannot be generalized to a large scale, resulting in poor portability. Different from this traditional hand-crafted feature extraction method, the deep learning model can automatically extract high-dimensional features, independent of domain knowledge, and has good portability, so it has been widely used in HAR [9,10]. Therefore, this research is carried out in the field of deep learning. The framework proposed in this paper is based on the depth features extracted from the deep learning model. Based on these deep learning models, the accuracy of activity recognition is improved significantly.

For common deep learning models, a large amount of labeled data with relatively uniform distribution is often required as a training set to train the model, so that the model can achieve high accuracy. When the data distribution of the training set is not uniform, the accuracy of the model is often not satisfactory. As such, the problem of few-shot detection has become a hot issue in the field of deep learning. [11] In the HAR task, the amount of data corresponding to all kinds of actions is often very uneven distribution. Therefore, designing a model that can use a large number of base class data and a small amount of new class data can achieve a better recognition effect is a very valuable research direction, which is also one of the objectives of this research. In this study, a framework based on autoencoder (AE) is designed, which can effectively improve the accuracy of human action recognition tasks on an imbalanced training set.

In addition, the portability of the framework is another research objective of this research. In other words, the depth features based on the framework proposed in this paper can be extracted from different models. And the experimental results have verified that the proposed framework has a significant improvement effect on different deep learning models.

The contributions of this paper can be summarized as follows:

1. A HAR framework based on depth features is proposed, which can markedly improve the original recognition accuracy.
2. The proposed framework can effectively solve the problem of few shot detection with a weakly supervised learning method.
3. The designed framework has good transferability and can be effective for multiple deep models (such as CNN, NAS, etc.)

2   Related Work

In the past decade, machine learning-based algorithms and deep learning-based algorithms were both utilized to complete sensor-based HAR tasks. In [12], Yin et al. employed machine learning models, such as support vector machine

(SVM) and kernel nonlinear regression (KNLR), to detect abnormal activities from data collected by sensors. Furthermore, the proposed model can reduce the false-positive rate in an unsupervised manner to improve the problem caused by data imbalance. Chen et al. [13] employed principal component analysis (CT-PCA) to eliminate the effect of orientation variations and online support vector machine (OSVM) which just needs a little bit of data to upload to improve the effectiveness. In [14], motion data from wearable sensors is the input of random forests (RF), which was utilized to classify human activities. Experiment results showed the proposed algorithm is valid. With the rise of deep learning, some studies have begun to use the deep learning-based algorithm in the field of sensor-based HAR.

With the emergence and development of deep learning, some studies began to apply the deep learning model to HAR tasks. In [15], Machine Learning and Deep Learning methods exist at the same time. Random Forest (RF) was a binary classifier to predict activity is static or moving. Next step, they used Support Vector Machine (SVM) and 1D Convolutional Neural Network (CNN) to identify individual static activity and moving activity. In [16], researchers just used CNN to recognize human activities. This study employed CNN to classify the data collected from wrist-worn accelerometers into Section A, Section B, and Section C. It proved that deep learning methods, such as CNN, are more effective and robust than conventional machine learning methods. Chen et al. [17] only employed CNN, without any classifier, to recognize human activities. By modifying convolution kernels and other parameters of CNN, the accuracy of 31688 samples from 100 subjects reached 93.8%. Tao et al. [18] employed CNN and bidirectional gated recurrent unit (BiGRU) to recognize the human activity. The study introduced an attention mechanism to strengthen the influence of key input. This year, Singh et al. [19] proposed a deep neural network architecture that also introduced a self-attention mechanism. They conducted experiments on six publicly available datasets and the experiment results showed that the proposed model works better than previous state-of-the-art methods. In [20], Alemayoh et al. designed an iOS application software installed in smartphones that can record motion data and recognize real-time activities. In the study, the time-series data of motion sensors is processed into images that are classified by CNN. Lawal et al. [21] also made use of images from data processing to classify activities. Moreover, they studied the problem of the best position for the sensor, and the experimental results show that the shin and waist are the best places in the body for placing sensors. Neither Machine Learning nor Deep Learning methods mentioned above are portable, and the improvement effect of the model is relatively simple. In this paper, we proposed a framework that can be superimposed on multiple deep networks to improve the classification. In addition, all of the above methods require labeled data as a training set. HAR tasks under weakly supervised scenarios cannot be well completed. Weakly supervised methods were considered in this study. Principal components analysis (PCA) is a simple way to reduce the dimensionality of data. Autoencoder (AE) is a nonlinear generalization of PCA, which outperformed previous methods to reduce dimensionalities, such as PCA, latent semantic analysis (LSA), and locally linear embedding [22]. The superior performance of AE makes its good performance in many fields of application. In [23], researchers utilized AE to learn the relation between received signal strength and unknown parameters of the channel. Then, they determine the location of devices in combination with the least-squares solution. There are also some applications of AE in the medical field. GFPred is a method based on a graph convolutional AE and a fully-connected AE with an attention mechanism, which can predict drug-disease associations to help to find novel uses of approved drugs [24]. In [25], convolutional denoising AE is utilized to detect freezing of gait (a condition wherein Parkinson's patients can move their feet) which can help shorten or prevent episodes. Considering the superior performance of AE and the characteristics of training with unlabeled data, in this study, we consider using AE to complete HAR tasks under data imbalance.

On the problem of class imbalance, the existing researches mainly include two types of methods: one is to change the data distribution, usually data augmentation, and the other is to improve the classification effect by modifying the classification model [26]. In [27], the study was conducted on the HAR mission, Chen and Yao try to solve the class imbalance of labeled data by over-sampling and under-sampling of feature space, which changed the distribution of data. In [28], data augmentation methods are put to use to solve this problem in image detection applications. Guan et al. [29] used integrated LSTM to mitigate the impact of data imbalance, which is the second category. In [30], they employed Xtreme Gradient Boosting, Siamese Neural Network, and Deep Neural Network to handle the class imbalance problem in a network-based intrusion detection system. In general, there are little researches on data imbalance in the HAR field. Therefore, the research content of this paper is very worthy of research.

3 Model and Methods

This framework aims to improve the accuracy of human action recognition from the original deep network in a weakly supervised way under the condition of imbalanced distribution of training datasets. In this chapter, we will introduce some basic knowledge of frameworks and then expand on the detailed description of our proposed framework. In Sect. 3.1, we will first introduce the whole process of HAR with the help of an overall framework diagram. In Sect. 3.2.1, basic knowledge of autoencoder and NAS will de introduced. In Sect. 3.2.2, there is the proposed framework.

3.1 Overall Framework

HAR based on sensor data needs to process the original data from the sensor first. When raw data is processed to a specific size, it can be used to train the network better. A classification result can be obtained by training a deep network for classification with unevenly distributed data sets. But the results are often unsatisfactory. This study puts forward a framework based on AE to improve the classification results.

After the deep training network training, the deep features of the data can be obtained. Due to the particularity of the autoencoder structure, only one kind of data can be used for training. Therefore, it is only necessary to extract the deep features of the base class data from the deep network as the input data of autoencoder training. During the test, the test dataset is first passed through the deep network to get the deep features of the test data. These depth features are then taken as the input of the autoencoder, at which time the autoencoder will output an output result, which has the dimension consistent with the dimension of the deep feature. Then the similarity between the output and the depth feature is calculated. If the similarity is greater than the set threshold, the class is judged to be a base class, otherwise, it is judged to be a new class. All processes are shown in Fig. 1.

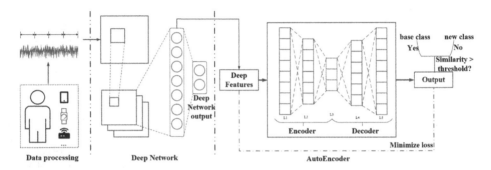

Fig. 1. Framework of sensor-based HAR. The framework takes the appropriate window and stride and processes the data collected from smartphones or wearable sensors to produce specific size matrixes. The processed data are sent into the deep network for training, and then the deep features of the base class are extracted for Autoencoder training. During the test, the deep features are obtained through the data through the deep network and then transmitted into AE to obtain the Loss value between the output and the deep features, which is used to judge whether it is the base class or a new class.

3.2   Models

Basic Models

Autoencoder. Autoencoder is a special neural network architecture whose input and output are the same format. Autoencoders are trained to capture input data in lower dimensions by unsupervised means. In the back segment of the neural network, the low-dimensional information expression is reconstructed back to the high-dimensional data expression. Among them, the network that obtains the lower dimension representation of data is called the encoder network, and the network that decodes the lower dimension information to obtain the output data with the same dimension as the input data is called the decoder network.

The input of the autoencoder can be defined as $x \in R$ where n is the dimensions of input data. According to the characteristic that the input data and the output data of the autoencoder have the same dimension, the output data can be expressed as $\hat{x} \in R^n$. If the function of encoder network is defined as $P : R^n \longrightarrow R^m$ and the function of decoder network is defined as $Q : R^m \longrightarrow R^n$, then $\hat{x} = Q \circ P(x)$. The training target of the autoencoder is to reduce the loss function between input data and output results. In this research, the P network and Q network are composed of a full connection layer and Relu activation function. The loss function is Mean Squared Error (MSE):

$$L(x, \hat{x}) = \frac{1}{n} \sum_{i=1}^{n} (x_i - \hat{x}_i)^2 \tag{1}$$

Neural Architecture Search (NAS). NAS is an intelligent method used to help solve the problems of structural optimization and parameter adjusting in deep learning research. This method does not require the manual design of network structure and does not need manual adjustment of parameters. The principle of NAS is that given a set of candidate neural network structures called search space, the optimal network structure can be found by some strategy. The advantages and disadvantages of neural network structure, that is, the performance is measured by some indexes such as accuracy and speed, which is called performance evaluation. In each iteration of the search process, "samples" are generated from the search space to obtain a neural network structure called "sub-network". The subnetwork is trained on the training sample set and its performance is evaluated on the verification set. The network structure is optimized step by step until the optimal sub-network is found. Search space, search strategy, and performance evaluation strategy are the core elements of the NAS algorithm. The search space defines the collection of searchable neural network structures, that is, the space of solutions. The search strategy defines how to find the optimal network structure in the search space. The performance evaluation policy defines how to evaluate the performance of the searched network structure. Different implementations of these elements result in different NAS algorithms.

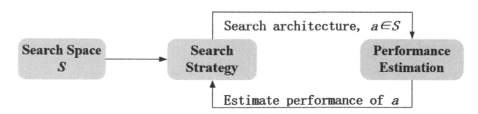

Fig. 2. Framework of Neural Architecture Search. In the predefined search space, network a is searched based on the search strategy. Then, a is evaluated based on the performance evaluation policy, and the evaluation result is returned to the search policy.

Proposed Model. The framework of human action recognition proposed in this paper is mainly based on autoencoder. Firstly, a deep network is used to extract features from the preprocessed sensor data. Deep networks, such as CNN and those networks searched by NAS, have a full connection layer at their last layer. The output of the full connection layer is the identification result of the original output of the deep network, while the input of the last full connection layer is a kind of deep feature of data. In this study, the deep features of the base class are used as the input of the autoencoder to train the autoencoder. Then, an autoencoder containing feature information of base class data is obtained. This kind of Autoencoder has good reconstruction ability for base class data, but relatively poor reconstruction ability for other types of data. Then we can use this property to determine the category of data. In the testing stage, the deep features of the test data are firstly extracted through the deep network, and then the depth features are fed into the trained Autoencoder. At this point, the similarity between the output results of Autoencoder and the deep features is observed. In this study, Pearson Correlation Coefficient and Spearman's Rank Correlation Coefficient are calculated, and the average of the two is taken as the final similarity between the input and output of Autoencoder. Pearson Correlation Coefficient and Spearman's Rank Correlation Coefficient are computed as follows:

$$S_1(x, \hat{x}) = \frac{n \sum x_i \cdot \hat{x}_i - \sum x_i \sum \hat{x}_i}{\sqrt{n \sum x_i^2 - (\sum x_i)^2} \cdot \sqrt{n \sum \hat{x}_i^2 - (\sum \hat{x}_i)^2}} \tag{2}$$

$$S_2(x, \hat{x}) = \frac{\sum (x_i - \bar{x}_i) \cdot (\hat{x}_i - \bar{\hat{x}}_i)}{\sqrt{\sum (x_i - \bar{x}_i)^2 \cdot \sum (\hat{x}_i - \bar{\hat{x}}_i)^2}} \tag{3}$$

where S_1 is Pearson Correlation Coefficient, S_2 is Spearman's Rank Correlation Coefficient. After obtaining the similarity, the base class and the new class can be distinguished by setting the threshold value to complete the HAR task.

4 Experiments Process and Results

In this section, we first introduce the basic information of the three benchmark datasets used in this study. Section 4.2 introduces the setting of hyperparameters for model training, as well as the distribution of sample data of train set and test set to simulate the situation of class imbalance in model training and objectively describe the model performance. Finally, the experiment results of the model are presented in Sect. 4.3.

4.1 Benchmark Datasets

The purpose of this study is to design a HAR framework applicable to sensor data, so the data used should be the sensor data provided by smartphones, smart bracelets, or other wearable devices. And these datasets should include multiple human activity types to verify the validity of the proposed framework. Researchers have collected several datasets for HAR, including the Opportunity

[31], UniMiB-SHAR [32], PAMAP2 [33], and Skoda [34] datasets. To prove the validity of the proposed framework, we validated it on three datasets, including opportunity, UniMiB-SHAR, and PAMAP2.

Opportunity. Data of opportunity datasets were obtained from four subjects. Every subject has employed a set of sensors, including 24 custom Bluetooth wireless accelerometers and gyroscopes, 2 Sun SPOTs and 2 InertiaCube3, the Ubisense localization system, and a custom-made magnetic field sensor. The sensor data were acquired at a frequency 30 Hz. Subjects were asked to complete 17 daily activities, such as opening and closing the fridge, turning on and off the lights, drinking, and so on. Therefore, there are 17 classes labels of activities and a Null class that contains no meaningful activity. In this study, 113-dimensional data were used, with linear interpolation to insert missing values. And the sliding window and sliding steps are 0.8 s and 0.4 s respectively.

UniMiB-SHAR. Data were collected from 30 subjects, including 24 women and 6 men. The subjects were asked to complete 17 kinds of activities such as running, bicycling, going upstairs and downstairs, standing, and so on. Placing a Samsung Galaxy Nexus I9250 smartphone in his or her pocket, the smartphone's 3-axis accelerator collected data on their movements at a frequency 50 Hz. Then, the 3s sliding window is used to segment the collected data.

PAMAP2. Data were collected from nine subjects, including eight men and one woman. One of them is left-handed, the rest are right-handed. Participants were asked to complete 12 activities, such as lying, sitting, standing, walking, and running. And casually engage in other activities such as watching TV, driving, folding laundry, and playing soccer. In total, more than ten hours of data were collected from 18 different activities. During the data collection process, three inertial measurement units (IMUs) were fixed on the chest, wrist, and ankle of the dominant hand, and a heart rate chest band was fixed on the chest. The sampling frequency is set 100 Hz. In our experiment, we downsampled the data to 33.3 Hz and sliced it using sliding windows of 5.12 s with 78% overlap between adjacent windows.

4.2 Model Training

Train Set and Test Set. Experiments in this study used all classes of the Opportunity and UniMiB-SHAR datasets, as well as 12 classes of data from the PAMAP2 dataset. First, the train set and test set were divided into a 7:3 ratio. We picked the class with the largest amount of data as the base class. The train set consists of a large number of base classes and a small number of other classes, as shown in Table 1.

Table 1. Data distribution of train set.

Dataset	Base class	New class	Imbalance rate
Opportunity	10000	100	100
UniMiB-SHAR	1588	10	158.8
PAMAP2	1687	10	168.7

To objectively reflect the performance of the model, the test set consists of an equal number of base class data and new class data.

Model Settings. The structure of CNN we use is $C(32) - C(64) - L(12) - L(2)$, where $C(n_c)$ denotes a convolutional layer with n_c feature maps, $L(n_l)$ is a fully connected layer with n_l units. The structure of the employed autoencoder is $L(256) - L(64) - L(20) - L(64) - L(256)$. The network structure searched by NAS is $C(36) - C(12) - C(12) - C(12) - C(12) - C(12) - C(12) - C(12) - C(12) - R(64) - R(64) - L(17)$, where $R(n_r)$ is a long short-term memory (LSTM) layer with n_r cells. Refer to the literature [35] for specific experimental details of the network structure searched by NAS. Our models are all implemented based on PyTorch. The computing platform used in the experiment was equipped with an Intel E5-2620 at 2.10 GHz, 9.6 GB RAM, and an 11 GB NVIDIA 1080 Ti GPU. We then employed the Adadelta optimizer and the gradient descent algorithm for all the trainable parameters. During the training and testing phase, the batch size was set to 128. The epoch and learning rate are shown in the following table.

Table 2. Data distribution of train set.

Dataset	CNN	(CNN+)AE	NAS	(NAS+)AE
Opportunity	50,0.0005	200,0.001	150,0.025	200, 0.0015
UniMiB-SHAR	50,0.0005	200,0.001	300,0.025	500, 0.0015
PAMAP2	50,0.0005	200,0.001	300,0.025	300, 0.0015

4.3   Result

Using Opportunity, UniMiB-SHAR, and PAMAP2 datasets, the human activity recognition accuracy on CNN and NAS and the human activity recognition accuracy of the proposed framework are shown in Table 3. In the three datasets, no matter which class of data is regarded as the new class of data, the framework can improve the original accuracy.

Table 3. Accuracy of CNN and NAS before and after overlay the proposed framework.

Opportunity					UniMiB-SHAR					PAMAP2				
Data	CNN	CNN+AE	NAS	NAS+AE	Data	CNN	CNN+AE	NAS	NAS+AE	Data	CNN	CNN+AE	NAS	NAS+AE
1	0.79	**0.85**	0.87	**0.96**	0	0.85	**0.97**	0.80	**0.97**	0	0.81	**0.92**	0.93	**0.98**
2	0.86	**0.98**	0.91	**0.98**	1	0.91	**1.00**	0.98	**1.00**	1	0.95	**0.96**	0.95	**0.99**
3	0.78	**0.90**	0.89	**0.96**	2	0.95	**0.99**	0.77	**0.93**	2	0.95	**0.98**	0.97	**0.98**
4	0.86	**0.96**	0.88	**0.97**	4	0.84	**0.99**	0.64	**0.67**	3	0.76	**0.84**	0.90	**0.97**
5	0.66	**0.92**	0.81	**0.94**	5	0.81	**0.99**	0.61	**0.76**	5	0.88	**0.94**	0.94	**0.97**
6	0.61	**0.82**	0.78	**0.88**	6	0.75	**0.96**	0.52	**0.57**	6	0.81	**0.96**	0.93	**0.99**
7	0.69	**0.84**	0.85	**0.94**	7	0.86	**1.00**	0.85	**0.97**	7	0.59	**0.71**	0.78	**0.99**
8	0.71	**0.91**	0.83	**0.92**	8	0.94	**0.99**	0.95	**0.98**	8	0.65	**0.81**	0.76	**0.94**
9	0.75	**0.83**	0.87	**0.94**	9	0.80	**0.93**	0.95	**1.00**	9	0.55	**0.76**	0.58	**0.91**
10	0.76	**0.88**	0.86	**0.93**	10	0.94	**1.00**	0.86	**1.00**	10	0.61	**0.66**	0.86	**0.98**
11	0.82	**0.90**	0.87	**0.94**	11	0.78	**0.94**	0.90	**1.00**	11	0.88	**0.95**	0.94	**0.99**
12	0.83	**0.94**	0.88	**0.92**	12	0.92	**0.98**	0.85	**0.99**	–	–	–	–	–
13	0.81	**0.88**	0.92	**0.96**	13	0.92	**0.99**	0.88	**0.99**	–	–	–	–	–
14	0.77	**1.00**	0.75	**0.93**	14	0.84	**0.98**	0.81	**0.98**	–	–	–	–	–
15	0.84	**0.89**	0.91	**0.97**	15	0.90	**1.00**	0.82	**1.00**	–	–	–	–	–
16	0.77	**0.82**	0.81	**0.91**	16	0.89	**1.00**	0.85	**0.92**	–	–	–	–	–
17	0.79	**0.97**	0.86	**0.95**	–	–	–	–	–	–	–	–	–	–

To reflect the average performance of the proposed framework on a dataset, we calculated the average value of each column of data in Table 3 to obtain the average accuracy of action recognition before and after CNN and NAS superimposed frames when each class of each dataset was regarded as a new class. The result is shown in Fig. 3.

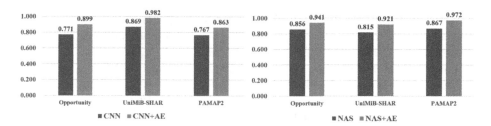

Fig. 3. The average accuracy of HAR before and after CNN and NAS superimposed the proposed framework.

As shown in Fig. 3, the average accuracy of all frames is increased by about 0.1. It follows that our proposed framework is valid for multiple datasets and multiple infrastructures. Therefore, it can also be said that the framework has good portability. We also discuss the differences in the improvement effects of the framework on various types of data, as shown in Fig. 4. It shows that the framework can improve the original accuracy of all classes on all three datasets.

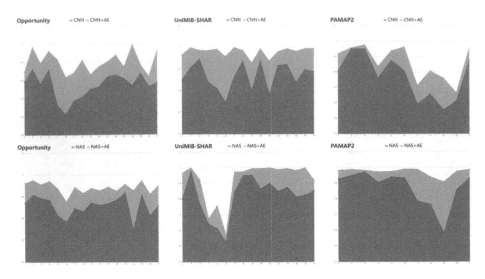

Fig. 4. The first column is the effect of the stacking framework on the Opportunity dataset. The blue part is the classification accuracy before stacking, and the green part is the improved part after stacking. The second column is the result on the UniMiB-SHAR dataset, and the third column is the result on PAMAP2. The first row of each column is the effect of the CNN superimposed frame, and the second row is the network by NAS search.

As can be seen from the figure, for some classes with low accuracy originally, such as CNN as a deep network, Class 7 and 15 on Opportunity dataset, and Class 6 and 11 on UniMiB-SHAR, the accuracy was improved more by the framework. This is because to reconstruct the input data that is more similar to the input data, the autoencoder will focus on learning the important features of the input data, and there is a big difference between the features of these data and the important features of the base data, so after stacking the framework, high accuracy will be achieved. Therefore, the framework can not only improve the original accuracy but also narrow the accuracy gap of all kinds of data, which has a certain effect on balancing the accuracy of all kinds of data.

5   Conclusion

In the field of sensor-based human motion recognition, few researches focus on data imbalance. However, in practical application scenarios, the distribution of data is often very unbalanced. Therefore, the focus of this study is how to improve the accuracy of action recognition in the case of uneven data distribution. Given AE's excellent performance in many tasks, this study proposed a weakly supervised transferable HAR framework based on AE. Experiments are carried out on both CNN and NAS networks to verify the portability of the proposed framework. To verify the effectiveness of the framework, experiments were carried out on Opportunity, UniMiB-SHAR, and PAMAP2 sensor datasets respectively. The accuracy has been effectively improved. In the future, we will continue to conduct experiments under different data imbalance rates to explore the improvement effect of this framework on data with different imbalance rates. In addition, we will continue to improve based on this framework and extend the idea of this study to the multi-classification problem.

Acknowledgment. The author acknowledges ICN&CAD Laboratory of School of Electronic Engineering, Beijing University of Posts and Telecommunications, for the experimental environment. Special thanks are due to Wang Xiaojuan, He Mingshu, and Wang Xinlei for their great help in this work. This work was supported by the National Natural Science Foundation of China (Grantno.62071056) and the action plan project of Beijing University of Posts and Telecommunications (No.2020XD-A03-2)

References

1. Liu, Y., Nie, L., Liu, L., Rosenblum, D.S.: From action to activity: sensor-based activity recognition. Neurocomputing, **181**, 108–115 (2016)
2. Bulling, A., Blanke, U., Schiele, B.: A tutorial on human activity recognition using body-worn inertial sensors. ACM Comput. Surv. (CSUR) **46**(3), 1–33 (2014)
3. Cheng, X., He, J., Zhang, X., Yao, C., Tseng, P.-H.: Geometrical kinematic modeling on human motion using method of multi-sensor fusion. Inf. Fus. **41**, 243–254 (2018)
4. Hanif, M.A., et al.: Smart devices based multisensory approach for complex human activity recognition. Comput. Mater. Continua (2022)
5. Margarito, J., Helaoui, R., Bianchi, A.M., Sartor, F., Bonomi, A.G.: User-independent recognition of sports activities from a single wrist-worn accelerometer: a template-matching-based approach. IEEE Trans. Biomed. Eng. **63**(4), 788–796 (2015)
6. Sagl, G., Resch, B., Blaschke, T.: Contextual sensing: integrating contextual information with human and technical geo-sensor information for smart cities. Sensors **15**(7), 17013–17035 (2015)
7. Tolstikov, A., Hong, X., Biswas, J., Nugent, C., Chen, L., Parente, G.: Comparison of fusion methods based on DST and DBN in human activity recognition. J. Control Theory Appl. **9**(1), 18–27 (2011)
8. Wang, Y., Cang, S., Hongnian, Yu.: A survey on wearable sensor modality centred human activity recognition in health care. Expert Syst. Appl. **137**, 167–190 (2019)
9. Wang, J., Chen, Y., Hao, S., Peng, X., Lisha, H.: Deep learning for sensor-based activity recognition: a survey. Pattern Recogn. Lett. **119**, 3–11 (2019)
10. Deotale, D., et al.: Hartiv: human activity recognition using temporal information in videos. CMC-Comput. Mater. Continua, **70**(2), 3919–3938 (2022)
11. Wang, X., Huang, T.E., Darrell, T., Gonzalez, J.E., Yu, F.: Frustratingly simple few-shot object detection. arXiv preprint arXiv:2003.06957 (2020)
12. Yin, J., Yang, Q., Pan, J.J.: Sensor-based abnormal human-activity detection. IEEE Trans. Knowl. Data Eng. **20**(8), 1082–1090 (2008)
13. Chen, Z., Zhu, Q., Soh, Y.C., Zhang, L.: Robust human activity recognition using smartphone sensors via CT-PCA and online SVM. IEEE Trans. Ind. Inform. **13**(6), 3070–3080 (2017)

14. Xu, L., Yang, W., Cao, Y., Li, Q.: Human activity recognition based on random forests. In: 2017 13th International Conference on Natural Computation, Fuzzy Systems and Knowledge Discovery (ICNC-FSKD), pp. 548–553. IEEE (2017)
15. Shuvo, M.M.H., Ahmed, N., Nouduri, K., Palaniappan, K.: A hybrid approach for human activity recognition with support vector machine and 1D convolutional neural network. In: 2020 IEEE Applied Imagery Pattern Recognition Workshop (AIPR), pp. 1–5. IEEE (2020)
16. Panwar, M., et al.: CNN based approach for activity recognition using a wrist-worn accelerometer. In: 2017 39th Annual International Conference of the IEEE Engineering in Medicine and Biology Society (EMBC), pp. 2438–2441. IEEE (2017)
17. Chen, Y., Xue, Y.: A deep learning approach to human activity recognition based on single accelerometer. In: 2015 IEEE International Conference on Systems, Man, and Cybernetics, pp. 1488–1492. IEEE (2015)
18. Tao, S., Zhao, Z., Qin, J., Ji, C., Wang, Z.: Attention-based convolutional neural network and bidirectional gated recurrent unit for human activity recognition. In: 2020 5th International Conference on Mechanical, Control and Computer Engineering (ICMCCE), pp. 1132–1138. IEEE (2020)
19. Singh, S.P., Sharma, M.K., Lay-Ekuakille, A., Gangwar, D., Gupta, S.: Deep convl-stm with self-attention for human activity decoding using wearable sensors. IEEE Sensors J. **21**(6), 8575–8582 (2020)
20. Alemayoh, T.T., Lee, J.H., Okamoto, S.: Deep learning based real-time daily human activity recognition and its implementation in a smartphone. In: 2019 16th International Conference on Ubiquitous Robots (UR), pp. 179–182. IEEE (2019)
21. Lawal, I.A., Bano, S.: Deep human activity recognition with localisation of wearable sensors. IEEE Access, **8**, 155060–155070 (2020)
22. Hinton, G.E., Salakhutdinov, R.R.: Reducing the dimensionality of data with neural networks. Science, **313**(5786), 504–507 (2006)
23. Im, C., Jung, S., Lee, C.: A deep autoencoder approach to received signal strength-based localization with unknown channel parameters. In: 2020 International Conference on Artificial Intelligence in Information and Communication (ICAIIC), pp. 152–154. IEEE (2020)
24. Xuan, P., Gao, L., Sheng, N., Zhang, T., Nakaguchi, T.: Graph convolutional autoencoder and fully-connected autoencoder with attention mechanism based method for predicting drug-disease associations. IEEE J. Biomed. Health Inform. **25**(5), 1793–1804 (2020)
25. Noor, M.H.M., Nazir, A., Wahab, M.N.A., Ling, J.O.Y.: Detection of freezing of gait using unsupervised convolutional denoising autoencoder. IEEE Access **9**, 115700–115709 (2021)
26. Buda, M., Maki, A., Mazurowski, M.A.: A systematic study of the class imbalance problem in convolutional neural networks. Neural Netw. **106**, 249–259 (2018)
27. Chen, K., Yao, L., Zhang, D., Wang, X., Chang, X., Nie, F.: A semisupervised recurrent convolutional attention model for human activity recognition. IEEE Trans. Neural Netw. Learn. Syst. **31**(5), 1747–1756 (2019)
28. Shorten, C., Khoshgoftaar, T.M.: A survey on image data augmentation for deep learning. J. Big Data, **6**(1), 1–48 (2019)
29. Guan, Yu., Plötz, T.: Ensembles of deep LSTM learners for activity recognition using wearables. Proceedings of the ACM on Interactive, Mobile, Wearable and Ubiquitous Technologies **1**(2), 1–28 (2017)
30. Bedi, P., Gupta, N., Jindal, V.: I-siamids: an improved siam-ids for handling class imbalance in network-based intrusion detection systems. Appl. Intell. **51**(2), 1133–1151 (2021)

31. Roggen, D., et al.: Collecting complex activity datasets in highly rich networked sensor environments. In: 2010 Seventh International Conference on Networked Sensing Systems (INSS), pp. 233–240. IEEE (2010)
32. Micucci, D., Mobilio, M., Napoletano, P.: Unimib shar: a dataset for human activity recognition using acceleration data from smartphones. Appl. Sci. **7**(10), 1101 (2017)
33. Reiss, A., Stricker, D.: Introducing a new benchmarked dataset for activity monitoring. In: 2012 16th International Symposium on Wearable Computers, pp. 108–109. IEEE (2012)
34. Zappi, P., Lombriser, C., Stiefmeier, T., Farella, E., Roggen, D., Benini, L., Tröster, G.: Activity recognition from on-body sensors: accuracy-power trade-off by dynamic sensor selection. In: Verdone, R. (ed.) EWSN 2008. LNCS, vol. 4913, pp. 17–33. Springer, Heidelberg (2008). https://doi.org/10.1007/978-3-540-77690-1_2
35. Wang, X., Wang, X., Lv, T., Jin, L., He, M.: Harnas: human activity recognition based on automatic neural architecture search using evolutionary algorithms. Sensors **21**(20), 6927 (2021)

Incorporating Syntactic and Semantic Information into Compound Sentence Discrimination and Relation Recognition

Wenjing Jiao[1], Tingxin Wei[2,3], Weiguang Qu[1,2(✉)], Junsheng Zhou[1], Yanhui Gu[1], and Bin Li[2]

[1] School of Computer and Electronic Information/School of Artificial Intelligence, Nanjing Normal University, Nanjing 210023, China
wgqu_nj@163.com
[2] School of Chinese Language and Literature, Nanjing Normal University, Nanjing 210097, China
[3] International College for Chinese Studies, Nanjing Normal University, Nanjing 210097, China

Abstract. Compound sentences contain at least two independent clauses which account for a large proportion in natural language, especially in Chinese. Therefore, the discrimination and relation recognition of compound sentences are essential yet crucial to text understanding. Based on the presence of connective words, compound sentences can be categorized as explicit sentences and implicit sentences. The current researches have achieved significant performance on explicit sentences, while that of implicit sentences remains unsatisfactory due to the missing of connective words. To address this issue, this paper proposes a joint model based on the enhanced sentence representation combining the syntactic information, semantic roles and local feature within the sentence to distinguish the compound sentence and recognize its semantic relation at once. First, utilize the syntactic tree of the sentence and encode it with Tree-LSTM to obtain the contextual and syntactical information of the sentences, then semantic role information encoded by Bi-LSTM is used to capture deep semantic information for sentence representation. In the discrimination module, CNN is used to obtain local semantic features, while in the relation recognition module, sentence matching is introduced to fuse the information between the two clauses. Experimental results on CAMR and CDTB corpus show that the F1 value of compound sentence discrimination reaches 95.90%, which increases by about 10.24% compared with state of the art of this task, and that of semantic relation recognition reaches 83.88%, which increases about 4.47% than state of the art.

Keywords: Joint model · Syntactic and semantic information

1 Introduction

In natural language, sentences can be categorized as single sentences and compound sentences that contain at least two coherent clauses, each of which can stand as an

X. Sun et al. (Eds.): ICAIS 2022, CCIS 1586, pp. 618–631, 2022.
https://doi.org/10.1007/978-3-031-06767-9_51

independent sentence. The basic difference between compound sentences and single sentences is that a compound sentence has two or more set of subject-predicates, while a single sentence has only one. Eg1 and eg2 below are examples of compound sentence and single sentence respectively. Eg1 is a compound sentence since it consists of the two clauses "他不但获得了冠军(*He not only won the championship*)" and "而且还打破了世界纪录(*but also broke the world record*)", each of which contains a subject and a predicate while the meaning is coherent. Eg2 is a single sentence because there is only one pair of subject-predicate.

eg1. 他不但获得了冠军, 而且还打破了世界纪录。[Compound sentence]
(*He not only won the championship, but also broke the world record.*)
eg2. 我们有能力完全杜绝这样的事情发生。[Single sentence]
(*We are able to eliminate such things completely.*)

Based on the statistics of CDAMR corpus [19], in Chinese, compound sentences account for 48% out of all the sentences in the corpus. Besides, from the perspective of linguistics, compound sentences are regarded as the minimum of discourse since they serve as the connection of utterance and discourse. Therefore, the syntactic parsing and understanding of compound sentences are crucial to text understanding, machine translation and many other downstream applications in natural language processing.

Though the clauses of compound sentences are syntactically independent, they are semantically coherent realized by either connective words or inherently semantic logic. The ones with connective words, namely explicit compound sentences, are comparatively easy in relation recognition since the connective words serve as strong clue for the relation. However, the ones without any connective words, namely implicit compound sentences are big challenge for discrimination and relation recognition as the relation between clauses are subtle without any explicit clue given. Eg3 and eg4 below are the two examples of them.

eg3. 虽然天气很好, 但是我还是不愿意出门。[Explicit]
(*Although the weather is good, I still don't want to go out.*)
eg4. 树枝不摇了, 鸟儿不叫了。[Implicit]
(*The branches don't shake, (**and**) the birds don't chirp.*)

Eg3 is an explicit compound sentence as it contains the connective words "虽然... 但是...(*although*)", while eg4 is implicit as there is no any explicit word to indicate the relation between these two clauses. In recent studies, the F1 value of compound sentence discrimination has reached over 90%, while the best performance of relation recognition is only 69.12% [17], remaining space for further improvement.

This paper proposes a neural network-based method utilizing both syntactic information and semantic role information in compound sentence discrimination and relation recognition. Since various syntactic constituents are not equal in sentence construction and meaning expression, for example, verb phrases provide more semantics of sentences than prepositional phrases and other phrases, syntactic information of compound sentences can be used in discrimination and relation recognition. Eg5 is an example for this and Fig. 1 shows the syntactic tree of eg5 obtained by Stanford Parser. As is shown, there is a prepositional phrase "在欧洲 (*in Europe*)" in arg1, and two verb phrases "开拓市场 (*open up the market*)" and "弥补损失 (*make up for the loss*)" in arg2. It's easy to conclude that there is a causal relation between the two arguments combining the verb phrases "遭遇滑铁卢 (*encounters Waterloo-suffer failure*)" and "弥补损失 (*make up for the loss*)" while the prepositional phrase "在欧洲 (*in Europe*)" rarely provides any useful information. Therefore we utilize the syntactic information of sentences to obtain the semantic relation derived from the verb phrases.

Semantic role is the underlying relation that an argument has with the predicate within a sentence, such as agent, patient, content and manner. Acquiring semantic role information of arguments is helpful for the model to learn the semantic relation between nouns and verbs. As an example, Fig. 2 shows the semantic roles of arguments in sentence eg5 where "孟山都 (*Monsanto*)" is the agent, "滑铁卢 (*Waterloo*)" is the patient, "遭遇 (*encounter*)", "开拓 (*explore*)" and "弥补 (*make up*)" are the predicates.

eg5. arg1: 孟山都在欧洲遭遇滑铁卢 arg2: 肯定会开拓市场弥补损失
(*arg1: Monsanto encounters Waterloo in Europe, arg2: (so it) will definitely explore the market to make up for the loss.*)

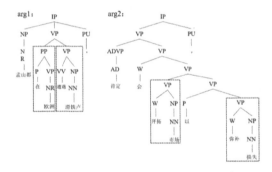

Fig. 1. Component syntax tree representation.

Fig. 2. Semantic role labeling representation.

This paper takes both the syntactic structure information and the semantic role information into consideration, and uses a neural network method to build a joint model for the discrimination and relation recognition of compound sentences. At the encoding layer, first we use Stanford Parser to obtain the syntactic trees of the input sentences, and the LTP toolkit to obtain the semantic role labels of them. Then we use GloVe and the pre-trained language model Bert to obtain the vector representation of words. Then the two arguments of compound sentences are sent to a Tree-LSTM respectively, and CNN is used to obtain local information and the sentence matching mechanism is used to fuse the relevance between sentences. Bi-LSTM is used to obtain the deep semantic information by encoding the semantic role representation. The experimental results on the corpus based on CAMR and CDTB show that our method has achieved state-of-the-art performance compared with the previous researches.

2 Related Work

For the past decades, most studies on relation recognition have been implemented on discourse. There are very few studies focusing on either the resource construction or the discrimination and relation recognition of compound sentences. The only corpus for Chinese compound sentences is CCCS [1] (Central China Normal University Corpus of Compound Sentences) which has defect that only explicit compound sentences are included. Despite this, we can use the existing discourse corpus as the compound sentence resource since compound sentences can be extracted from discourse, such as Pennsylvania Discourse Tree Bank (PDTB)[1], Rhetorical Structure Discourse Tree Bank (RST-DT)[2], Suzhou University Chinese Discourse TreeBank (CDTB) [2], Chinese Discourse Semantic Relations Corpus of Harbin Institute of Technology (HIT-CDTB)[3], and Tsinghua Chinese Tree Bank (TCT) [3].

For explicit relation recognition, the connective words can be used as an important feature. Pitler [4] used syntactic features to resolve ambiguity in the usage and marking relation of connective words so as to discriminate whether it is a connective word. Yang et al. [5] proposed a feature extraction method based on the context of connective words and its collocation, and used the Bayesian model to train and test the features. Zhang et al. [6] proposed a rule-based method for the explicit relation recognition identifying semantic types with the constructed "connective words-relation" matrix. Li et al. [7] extracted all the functional words from the TCT corpus, and trained automatic syntactic trees on the data with and without functional marker to recognize and classify relation words based on features such as syntax, lexical, and position features in the syntax tree.

Implicit relation of compound sentences is much more difficult to identify compared to explicit sentences due to the lack of connective words. Pitler et al. [8] used a naive Bayes classifier for implicit relation recognition with the sentiment polarity of words, verb categories, context, and modalities as features, these internal features bring significant improvement to the model performance. However, rule-based methods have the limitation that the performance relies on the hand-crafted features. Along with the development of deep learning method, it has been used in implicit relation recognition too. Zhang et al. [9] proposed a method based on Shallow Convolutional Neural Network (SCNN) to obtain important semantic information in both arguments. Rutherford et al. [10] proposed a model using a variant of feed-forward network that combines hidden layer representation and high-dimensional vectors to recognize implicit relation, and the results outperform that of LSTM and CNN. Qin et al. [11] combined the character-level and word-level representation in the encoding of the arguments to enhance their semantic

---

[1] http://www.seas.upenn.edu/pdtb/.

[2] http://www.isi.edu/marcu/discourse.

[3] http://ir.hit.edu.cn/hit-cdtb/index.html.

representation. Geng et al. [12] proposed a Tree-LSTM model to encode both arguments by encoding the syntactic tree recursively, which proved that a tree structured network can effectively capture the logical semantic relation and the shallow features within the discourse. Liu et al. [13] proposed to use different kinds of corpus and designed a multi-task neural network (MTNN) to synthesize different corpus-specific discourse classification tasks. Xu et al. [14] used a three-layer attention network to recognize the implicit discourse relation, in which self-attention is applied to encode the arguments, and interactive attention is used to simulate the two-way reading process to obtain the argument representation with interactive information. Jia et al. [15] proposed a Bi-LSTM-based compound sentence discrimination model by using the attention mechanism and the CNN model to exploit sentential semantic information, a Tree-LSTM-based relation recognition model, and a joint model to reduce error propagation. Sun et al. [16] proposed a multi-channel CNN based on the inner-attention mechanism to exploit the implicit semantic information within the compound sentences. Zhu et al. [17] proposed a joint model based on attention mechanism and sentence matching to capture semantic information of sentences and relation between sentences.

As we can observe, all the methods that have being used in implicit relation recognition encode the two arguments separately as input. The issue of this approach is that the sentence is splitted and the information generated by the interaction between two arguments is ignored. To address this issue, we consider both the information between the two arguments and the information provided by the complete sentence, and use both syntactic and semantic information to get better representation for the sentence discrimination and relation recognition.

3   Model

Distinguished from the traditional pipeline model, our model takes both syntactic information and semantic information in consideration to construct a joint model thus the two tasks are implemented in parallel. This method can reduce error propagation and improve task performance consequently.

The model consists of five parts, as is shown in Fig. 3: 1. Input the raw sentence, use the pre-trained language model Bert and Stanford Parser analyzer to obtain the vector representation of words and syntax tree of each argument respectively and use LTP toolkit to obtain the semantic role labels of the raw sentence; 2. Concatenate the representative vectors of the words in each argument and that of syntactic labels which are randomly initialized, and send it to Tree-LSTM to get the representation of the arguments; 3. Send the representative vectors of semantic role labels which are randomly initialized to Bi-LSTM to get the vector representation of the whole sentence; 4. In discrimination module, concatenate the outputs of Tree-LSTM from two arguments with that of Bi-LSTM, and send it to CNN to capture local features, the output of which is used to get the final prediction including explicit compound sentence, implicit compound sentence and non-compound sentence; 5. In relation recognition module, use sentence matching mechanism to capture the interaction between two arguments, and concatenate the output with that of Bi-LSTM and CNN layer from discrimination module to reduce the error propagation. The final output is used to get the relation prediction.

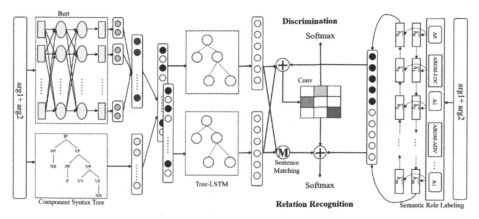

Fig. 3. The overall framework of the joint model.

3.1 Input Representation

The input of the model is a sentence $E = \{e_1, e_2, \ldots, e_n\}$, where n is the number of the words in the sentence, and $e_i = \{i^{GloVe}, i^{Bert}, i^{tag}\}$. i^{GloVe} is the GloVe embedding of the i-th word, i^{Bert} is the vector representation obtained by Bert, and i^{tag} is the tag embedding of the syntactic tree which is randomly initialized.

Next, use the LTP toolkit to get the semantic roles of the input sentences. For those sentences that have more than one layers of semantic role labelling, we only choose the first layer. We label each character with its semantic role which is the same as the one of its word. With random initialization, we get $S = \{s_1, s_2, \ldots, s_m\}$, where m is the length of the sentence, s_i is the embedding of the i-th character.

3.2 Bi-LSTM

LSTM is a kind of cyclic neural network RNN, which is suitable for processing time-serial data such as text data in this paper as it can capture long-distance dependency. This paper adopts Bi-LSTM, which input the same sequence to a forward LSTM and a backward LSTM respectively, and then concatenate the output of the forward and backward hidden layers at the last moment. The Bi-LSTM unit at each moment contains an input gate i_t, a forget gate f_t and an output gate o_t.

$$i_t = \sigma(W_{ii}s_t + W_{hi}h_{t-1} + b_{hi}) \tag{1}$$

$$f_t = \sigma(W_{if}s_t + W_{hf}h_{t-1} + b_{hf}) \tag{2}$$

$$o_t = \sigma(W_{io}s_t + W_{ho}h_{t-1} + b_{ho}) \tag{3}$$

$$g_t = tanh(W_{ig}s_t + W_{hg}h_{t-1} + b_{hg}) \tag{4}$$

$$c_t = i_t \odot g_t + f_t \odot c_{t-1} \tag{5}$$

$$h_t = o_t \odot tanh(c_t) \tag{6}$$

$$h = h_1^t \oplus h_m^t \tag{7}$$

where c_t is the state of the memory cell at the current moment, and h_{t-1} is the output of the hidden layer at the previous moment. Finally, the h with rich contextual semantic representation is obtained for subsequent modeling.

3.3 Tree-LSTM

LSTM can process sequence information and has achieved good performance in many tasks. However, the semantics of a sentence is not only a simple concatenation of its words, the syntactic information is also part of its semantics. Since LSTM cannot handle tree-structured data, such as the syntactic tree used in this paper, Tree-LSTM is introduced to encode two arguments in compound sentences as it can capture the structural information. In order to deal with tree structure efficiently and conveniently, we convert the general parse tree into a binary tree so that the unit in Tree-LSTM only need to encode the information of left children and right children at each step. Each Tree-LSTM unit contains an input gate i_j, a forget gate f_j and an output gate o_j.

$$i_j = \sigma\left(W^{(i)}e_j + U^{(i)}\left[h_j^L, h_j^R\right] + b^{(i)}\right) \tag{8}$$

$$f_j = \sigma\left(W^{(f)}e_j + U^{(f)}\left[h_j^L, h_j^R\right] + b^{(f)}\right) \tag{9}$$

$$o_j = \sigma\left(W^{(o)}e_j + U^{(o)}\left[h_j^L, h_j^R\right] + b^{(o)}\right) \tag{10}$$

$$u_j = tanh\left(W^{(u)}e_j + U^{(u)}\left[h_j^L, h_j^R\right] + b^{(u)}\right) \tag{11}$$

$$c_j = i_j \odot u_j + f_j \odot c_j^L + f_j \odot c_j^R \tag{12}$$

$$h_j = o_j \odot tanh(c_j) \tag{13}$$

where e_j is the embedding of the current node j, h_j^L and h_j^R are the output hidden vectors of the left and right children of the node, and c_j^L and c_j^R are the memory unit states of the node. The two arguments are represented as r_1 and r_2 after Tree-LSTM respectively.

$$r_i = Tree-LSTM\,(e), \ 1 \leq i \leq 2 \tag{14}$$

3.4 Compound Sentence Discrimination

In order to obtain semantic relation of the constituents within the argument, the semantic role of arguments is utilized in discrimination module. The arguments r_1 and r_2 obtained by Tree-LSTM and the semantic information h obtained in Sect. 3.2 are concatenated together to obtain r. Use r as the input for a convolutional layer, and conduct the maximum pooling operation on the convolution kernel to extract the salient features of this argument.

$$r = r_1 \oplus r_2 \oplus h \qquad (15)$$

$$c_j = f(W_c \cdot r_{j:j+h_w-1} + b_c) \qquad (16)$$

$$\hat{c} = max\{c_j\} \qquad (17)$$

where W_c represents the convolution kernel, h_w is the size of the convolution kernel, $r_{j:j+h_w-1}$ represents sliding window, b_c is the bias and f is activation functions. Finally, the maximum pooling is used to obtain the output of the convolutional layer as $\hat{c}$, and then the softmax function is used to predict the sentence category. Cross entropy is used as loss function in the discrimination module.

$$y = softmax(W\hat{c} + b) \qquad (18)$$

$$L^{judge} = \sum_{x \in D} \sum_{i \in R} y_i(x) log \hat{y}_i(x) \qquad (19)$$

where W and b are the learning parameters, D is the training dataset and R is the sentence type which includes explicit compound sentence, implicit compound sentence and non-compound sentence. $y_i(x)$ is the label of the training sample x, if the category is i, then $y_i(x)$ is 1, otherwise it is 0. $\hat{y}_i(x)$ is the probability that the sample x is predicted as type i.

3.5 Relation Recognition

For human understanding, the correlation between two clauses is critical clue to recognize the relation between them. Intuitively, the interaction of two arguments can be utilized in implicit relation recognition. For the two arguments representation r_1 and r_2 obtained by Tree-LSTM, we implement sentence matching to merge the information in them and capture the possible relevance between them. The merged pair information P is calculated as in the equation below.

$$P = (r_1 \oplus r_2) \oplus (r_1 \odot r_2) \oplus (r_1 r_2) \qquad (20)$$

where $\oplus$ means concatenation operation, $\odot$ means element-wise multiplication, and means element-wise subtraction. Semantic role information is also introduced to obtain sentential semantic representation. In order to avoid the error propagation caused by the discrimination error, the joint model combines the $\hat{c}$ obtained by the convolutional layer in the discrimination module with P to obtain the representation R of the sentence. Then softmax is used for relation classification and cross entropy is used as the loss function. R' is the type of relationship category.

$$R = P \oplus h \oplus \hat{c} \tag{21}$$

$$L^{relation} = \sum_{x \in D} \sum_{i \in R'} y_i(x) log \hat{y}_i(x) \tag{22}$$

3.6   Joint Learning

In order to update the parameters of the two tasks simultaneously, it is necessary to define a loss function for the entire model. Here we jointly tackle the discrimination and relation recognition and define the loss function of overall model as follows.

$$Loss = L^{judge} + L^{relation} \tag{23}$$

where L^{judge}, $L^{relation}$ are the loss of the discrimination and relation recognition respectively.

4   Experimentation

4.1   Data Set

Table 1. Data set statistics.

Sentence category	Relation category	Explicit	Implicit	Total
Compound sentences	And	943	1088	2031
	Causation	889	1693	2582
	Condition	855	1171	2026
	Contrast	797	980	1777
Single sentences	None			5359

The data set is from Chinese Abstract Meaning Representation (CAMR) [18] and Chinese Discourse TreeBank (CDTB) [2]. CAMR is a sentence-level semantic resource, and there are explicit and implicit compound sentences and single sentences. A total of 10925 sentences are extracted from the corpus of CAMR, including 5359 single sentences and 5566 compound sentences. To enlarge the data set, we supplement it with the corpus of CDTB containing 500 discourses, which has the annotation of discourse structures, the type of compound sentences and connective words. With this corpus, 3182 more compound sentences are extracted, and thus we have a compound sentence data set with 8748 compound sentences and 5359 single sentences. 9 relation categories of compound sentences are annotated in the data set, including causation, and, condition, contrast, temporal, or, concession, orx (exclusive choice) and progression. Since the last five categories only account for 4.23% of the data set, too less for experiment, we only implement the discrimination and relation recognition on the top four relation categories. The statistics of the data set is shown in Table 1.

4.2 Experiment Settings

The data set is divided with the proportion of 4:1 to get training set and test set. The word embedding is obtained by GloVe and the pre-training model Bert, and the embedding dimension are 100 and 768 respectively. The label dimension of syntactic tree and semantic role are both 50. In order to avoid over-fitting, the dropout strategy is used, and the value of dropout is 0.5. Adam is used to optimize the model to speed up the convergence speed. The hidden layer dimension of Tree-LSTM and Bi-LSTM are 250 and 10 respectively. The evaluation used in the experiment are precision P, recall R, and macro average F1. The main parameters are shown in Table 2.

Table 2. Experimental parameters.

Parameter	Value
Glove embedding_size	100
Bert embedding_size	768
Syntax embedding_size	50
SRL embedding_size	50
Tree-LSTM hidden_size	250
Bi-LSTM hidden_size	10
Kernel_size	4
Dropout	0.5
Learning_rate	0.001

4.3 Experimental Results and Analysis

In order to evaluate the performance of this model, we compare it with the previous work: 1. Jia's Tree-LSTM-based joint model [15], which conducted the discrimination and relation recognition at the same time, and solved the issue of error propagation caused by the discrimination in the pipeline model. 2. Zhu's joint model [17], which used attention mechanism and sentence matching to fuse inter-sentence relevance information, whereas our propose model in this paper consider both syntactic structure information and semantic role information to construct a joint model based on neural network. The results are shown in Table 3.

628 W. Jiao et al.

As is shown in the table, on the two tasks of discrimination and relation recognition, the F1 value of our model both outperforms the current best results. Zhu takes the relevance between sentences into account, consequently the F1 in the relation recognition increases by 5.28% compared with Jia's model which lacks inter-sentence relevance information. Our model introduces semantic role information on the basis of the syntactic analysis tree to obtain sentential semantic information, which brings 10.24% improvement in the discrimination task, and 4.47% improvement in the relation recognition task.

As it can be observed from the Table 3, implicit compound sentences are much more difficult no matter in discrimination or relation recognition compared with explicit ones. The discrimination performance of implicit sentences was over 10% worse than that of explicit sentences with Jia's or Zhu's model. However, with our model, the discrimination performance of explicit sentences is only about 0.3% higher than that of implicit ones. Besides, the performance of implicit relation recognition of our model also improves by 2% compared with Zhu's, which both prove the effectiveness of our model in capturing the deep interactive information of compound sentences.

Table 3. Comparison of experimental results.

Models	Category	Discrimination			Relation recognition		
		P	R	F1	P	R	F1
Jia [15]	Explicit	93.72	95.11	94.41	97.61	96.45	97.03
	Implicit	75.71	80.72	78.13	58.57	50.33	54.14
	All	85.48	85.84	85.66	74.53	73.74	74.13
Zhu [17]	Explicit	93.36	93.78	93.57	97.47	97.46	97.45
	Implicit	74.46	82.53	78.29	63.74	61.21	62.45
	All	85.26	85.53	85.40	79.43	79.38	79.41
Ours	Explicit	96.02	93.04	**94.51**	97.48	97.47	**97.48**
	Implicit	92.57	96.02	**94.26**	65.56	63.46	**64.49**
	All	95.97	95.82	**95.90**	84.84	82.94	**83.88**

[a] All means for all data sets (including explicit, implicit and single sentences).

We analyze the wrong prediction in compound sentence discrimination and relation recognition, and discovered there are three types of mistakes. 1. When there are connective words in a sentence, the model tends to predict it as a compound sentence. However, connective words can be used in single sentences too in some situation, such as "不但我的家人, 而且所有的中国人都会为我高兴 (*Not only my family, but all Chinese people will be happy for me.*)"; 2. The model does not perform well in condensed compound sentences. Since the two arguments of condensed compound sentences are in one clause with no punctuation denoted, it is a big challenge for the model and even human to distinguish it from single sentences. For example, "贪杯伤肝 (*Drink too much, the liver hurts.*)" is a causal compound sentence that looks like a single sentence. 3. Some connective words are polysemic which might mislead the prediction of the model. For example, the meaning of "就", "才" depends on the context they appear. In the sentence "沿着弯弯的小路, 就能走出大山 ((if walking) *along the winding path, you can walk out of the mountain.*)" "就" denotes a "condition" relation while in the sentence "影子跟着我, 就像一条小狗 (*The shadow followed me, just like a little dog.*)" it denotes the "and" relation which means the two arguments are coordinated.

We also compare the performance of relation recognition on each semantic category. Since it is a joint model, we view the single sentence as the non-relation category. The results of the experiment are shown in Fig. 4.

As is shown in the figure, the performance on discrimination of single sentences reaches amazingly 99%, which proves that our joint model that conducts the discrimination and relation recognition simultaneously can reduce the error propagation.

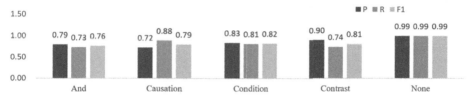

Fig. 4. Performance of each category

4.4 Model Comparison and Analysis

To explore the contribution of various information to the model, we implement ablation experiments and the results are shown in Table 4. The performance of relation recognition is only 79.41% when only Tree-LSTM is used to encode the arguments. When the semantic roles are supplemented to the encoding layer, the performance improves by 2.54% which proves the semantic roles can provide deep semantic information of the sentences. Besides, when Bi-LSTM is added to the model, the performance improves by 4.47% since it can help to learn context information while the performance improves by 4.25% when CNN is added to the model.

Table 4. Experimental comparison of different models.

Models	Category	Discrimination			Relation recognition		
		P	R	F1	P	R	F1
Tree-LSTM	Explicit	93.36	93.78	93.57	97.47	97.46	97.45
	Implicit	74.46	82.53	78.29	63.74	61.21	62.45
	All	85.26	85.53	85.40	79.43	79.38	79.41

(continued)

Table 4. (*continued*)

Models	Category	Discrimination			Relation recognition		
		P	R	F1	P	R	F1
+SRL	Explicit	94.53	94.81	**94.67**	97.73	97.43	97.58
	Implicit	84.48	83.97	84.23	64.24	61.91	63.05
	All	89.73	89.74	89.73	82.09	81.80	81.95
+SRL+ Bi-LSTM	Explicit	96.02	93.04	94.51	97.48	97.47	97.48
	Implicit	92.57	96.02	**94.26**	65.56	63.46	64.49
	All	95.97	95.82	**95.90**	84.84	82.94	**83.88**
+SRL+ Bi-LSTM +CNN	Explicit	96.57	92.00	94.23	98.40	98.31	**98.36**
	Implicit	91.11	96.26	93.61	67.15	64.09	**65.59**
	All	95.48	95.21	95.34	84.14	83.19	83.66

5   Conclusion

This paper proposes to combine syntactic and semantic information to construct a joint model for compound sentence discrimination and relation recognition. First we use syntactic tree and semantic role to enhance the representation of the sentences, encode the sentences with Tree-LSTM and Bi-LSTM, then use CNN to obtains local information, and the sentence matching mechanism to fuse the information between clauses. The experimental results show that our proposed model achieves state-of-the-art performance. In future, we will work on enlarging the corpus and explore other internal information of sentences to improve the performance of implicit relation recognition.

Acknowledgement. The authors thank the anonymous reviewers for their constructive suggestions which have resulted in improvement on the presentations. This research is supported by the National Science Foundation of China (grant 61772278, author: Qu, W.; grand number: 61472191, author: Zhou, J. http://www.nsfc.gov.cn/), the National Social Science Foundation of China (grant number: 18BYY127, author: Li B. http://www.cssn.cn) and Youth Fund for Humanities and social science of the Ministry of Education (grand number: 17YJC740084, author: Wang. L. http://www. moe.gov.cn).

References

1. Xing, F., Yao, S.: The construction and utilization of the corpus of Chinese compound sentence corpus. In: The 3rd HNC and Linguistics Research Symposium, pp. 432–439 (2005). (in Chinese)
2. Li, Y.: Research of Chinese discourse structure representation and resource construction. Doctoral thesis, Soochow University, Suzhou (2015). (in Chinese)
3. Zhou, Q.: Annotation scheme for Chinese treebank. J. Chin. Inf. Process. **31**(10), 90–93 (2004). (in Chinese)

4. Pitler, E., Nenkova, A.: Using syntax to disambiguate explicit discourse connectives in text. In: Proceedings of the ACL-IJCNLP 2009 Conference Short Papers, Suntec, Singapore, pp. 13–16. ACL (2009)

5. Yang, J., Guo, K., Shen, X., Hu, J.: Automatic identification and rule mining for relation words of Chinese compound sentences based on Bayesian model. Comput. Sci. **42**(7), 291–294 (2015). (in Chinese)

6. Zhang, M., Song, Y., Qin, B., Liu, T.: Chinese discourse relation recognition. J. Chin. Inf. Process. **27**(06), 51–57 (2013). (in Chinese)

7. Li, Y., Sun, J., Zhou, G., Feng W.: Recognition and classification of relation words in the compound sentences based on Tsinghua Chinese treebank. Acta Scientiarum Naturalium Universitatis Pekinensis **50**(01), 118–124 (2014). (in Chinese)

8. Pitler, E., Louis, A., Nenkova, A.: Automatic sense prediction for implicit discourse relations in text. In: Proceedings of the Joint Conference of 47th Annual Meeting of ACL, Suntec, Singapore, pp. 683–691. ACL (2009)

9. Zhang, B., Su, J., Xiong, D., Lu, Y., Duan, H., Yao, J.: Shallow convolutional neural network for implicit discourse relation recognition. In: Proceedings of the 2015 Conference on Empirical Methods in Natural Language Processing, Lisbon, Portugal, pp. 2230–2235. ACL (2015)

10. Rutherford, A., Demberg, V., Xue, N.: A systematic study of neural discourse models for implicit discourse relation. In: Proceedings of Conference of the European Chapter of the Association for Computational Linguistics: Volume 1, Valencia, Spain, pp. 281–291. ACL (2017)

11. Qin, T., Zhang, Z., Zhao, H.: Implicit discourse relation recognition with context-aware character-enhanced embeddings. In: Proceedings of COLING 2016, the 26th International Conference on Computational Linguistics: Technical Papers, pp. 1914–1924 (2016)

12. Geng, R., Jian, P., Zhang, Y., Huang, H.: Implicit discourse relation identification based on tree structure neural network. In: International Conference on Asian Language Processing, Singapore, pp. 334–337. IEEE (2017)

13. Liu, Y., Li, S., Zhang, X., Sui, Z.: Implicit discourse relation classification via multi-task neural networks. In: Proceedings of the Thirtieth AAAI Conference on Artificial Intelligence, Phoenix, Arizona, pp. 2750–2756. AAAI (2016)

14. Xu, S., Wang, T., Li, P., Zhu, Q.: Multi-layer attention network based Chinese implicit discourse relation recognition. J. Chin. Inf. Process. **33**(8), 12–19 (2019). (in Chinese)

15. Jia, X., Wei, T., Qu, W., Gu, Y., Zhou, J.: Automatic identification and relation recognition of complex sentence based on neural network. Comput. Eng. 1–8 (2020). (in Chinese)

16. Sun, K., Deng, D., Li, Y., Li, M., Li, Y.: Inner-attention based multi-way convolutional neural network for relation recognition in Chinese compound sentence. Journal of Chinese Information Processing **34**(06), 9–17 (2020). (in Chinese)

17. Zhu, Y.: Research and Implementation of Chinese complex sentence judgment and semantic relation recognition system. Doctoral thesis, Nanjing Normal University, Nanjing (2021). (in Chinese)

18. Qu, W., Zhou, J., Wu, X., Dai, R., Gu, M., Gu, Y.: A survey of amr research on abstract semantic representation of natural language sentences. Data Coll. Process. **32**(01), 26–36 (2017). (in Chinese)

19. Wei, T.: Construction of Chinese discourse abstract meaning representation corpus and application on zero pronoun resolution. Doctoral thesis, Nanjing Normal University, Nanjing (2021). (in Chinese)

Research on Side-Channel Attack Method Based on LSTM

Zhou Mao[1], Tong Shuai[2], Shuo Liang[2], Liguo Zhang[2(✉)], and Sizhao Li[1,2]

[1] Harbin Engineering University, Harbin 150001, China
[2] The 54th Research Institute of CETC, Shijiazhuang 050000, China
zhangliguo@hrbeu.edu.cn

Abstract. Side channel attacks recover keys or other sensitive information by using the time, power consumption, electromagnetic radiation and fault output generated when cryptographic algorithms are executed on IOT devices. It has become one of the important threats to cryptographic security devices. In recent years, deep learning technology is widely used in the field of Side Channel Attack (SCA). In this paper, a side channel attack method based on deep learning Long Short-Term Memory (LSTM) is proposed. Because of the interpretability of the internal nonlinear structure of LSTM, its system identification capability and computational complexity are superior to those of deep learning network. To test the effectiveness of the modified attack method, we evaluated it using a public ASCAD dataset. We conducted a side-channel analysis experiment for the AES-128 encryption algorithm. Experimental results show that this method achieves good attack effect and effectively alleviates the influence caused by trajectory misalignment. The interest points of the side channel power data are determined by using the correlation power analysis method, and the appropriate interest intervals are selected as feature vectors to build the neural network model. The experimental results show that compared with MLP and CNN models, LSTM network model has higher attack efficiency in side channel attack.

Keywords: Side channel attack · Long short-term memory · Deep learning

1 Introduction

In today's society, the embedded cryptographic device has a very wide range of applications, password in password set processing, the chip's operation process by certain energy consumption side channel leak, electromagnetic radiation, the information such as operation time [1], the information related to the operation of the equipment processing of data and that the attacker using these physical information through the statistical analysis method, to recover some leaked sensitive data or deduce the key, which makes the security of cryptographic devices become very important.

The traditional block cryptanalysis technique is limited by the mathematical structure of algorithm, and its attack effect is often poor. Since Paul Kocher [2] proposed timing attack and energy analysis attack in 1996, it has provided a new research direction for cryptanalysis methods. Side-channel attack has shown great potential in cracking

X. Sun et al. (Eds.): ICAIS 2022, CCIS 1586, pp. 632–644, 2022.
https://doi.org/10.1007/978-3-031-06767-9_52

cryptosystems, so side-channel attack has attracted extensive attention. In the past few years, side channel attacks (SCA) have proved to be a very effective way of attacking encryption algorithm implementations.

In recent years, deep learning technology has been introduced into the traditional side channel attack, and the effect of side channel attack based on deep learning technology exceeds the traditional side channel attack method [3]. The deep learning model is very sensitive to data and has the ability to learn and extract intrinsic features of data from original data. Therefore, the application of deep learning algorithm to side channel signal analysis of encryption hardware chip is beneficial to improve the efficiency of side channel analysis. Maghrebi et al. [4] applied deep learning technology to side-channel attack for the first time in 2016, and realized key recovery using multilayer Perceptron (MLP) and convolutional neural network (CNN) model. In 2017, Cagli et al. [5] proposed an end-to-end modeling attack method based on convolutional neural network. This method does not require preprocessing of power trajectory data or precise selection of attack points, and uses convolutional neural network to attack power trajectory with jitter protection strategy. Benadjila et al. [6] applied deep learning technology to side-channel attacks in 2019, studied its connection with classical template attacks, and solved the hyperparameter problem of multi-layer perceptron networks and convolutional neural networks. In 2021, PeiCao et al. [7] proposed cross-device side channel attack with unsupervised domain adaptation, and adopted maximum mean deviation loss (MMD) as the constraint term of classical cross entropy loss function to obtain region invariance, which proved that MMD loss could be easily calculated and embedded into standard convolutional neural network.

At present, most of the deep learning-based side channel attack technologies are studied on the parameter selection or structural optimization of the neural network model to reduce the number of power consumption trajectory required for successful attack. However, in actual attack scenarios, due to constraints of time, resources, defense policies and other conditions, it is impossible to collect a sufficient number of power trajectory, resulting in the failure of the attacker to train and test the power trajectory model. In this paper, we propose a side channel attack method based on long and short term memory network. Under high noise, we use reverse modeling to predict energy trace data. Experiments are carried out on ASCAD [6], a public dataset for deep learning side channel attack effect, which provides the electromagnetic energy trajectory of ATMega8515. Experimental results on ASCAD data set show that this method reduces the number of trajectories required for successful attack and effectively alleviates the impact of trajectory misalignment on attack results. Combined with LSTM and capability analysis in low noise, 50 energy traces can be successfully attacked, which is better than template attack [8].

The rest of this article is organized as follows. The second section introduces the related work. In the third section, a side channel attack method based on LSTM is proposed. The fourth section provides experiments and methods. The fifth section summarizes the whole paper.

2 Related Work

2.1 Advanced Encryption Standard

Advanced Encryption Standard (AES) [9] is a block cipher with the same encryption key and decryption key, which can be implemented efficiently on a variety of platforms. AES is classified into AES-128, AES-192, and AES-256 encryption algorithms based on the key length used in encryption operations. The encryption algorithm used in this paper is AES-128, and the target of the attack is the initial key of the AES-128 encryption algorithm.

a. Plaintext (P), original intelligible message or data, input of encryption algorithm, output of decryption algorithm. The length of AES128 is 128 bits.
b. Ciphertext (c), the output of the encryption algorithm, the input of the decryption algorithm, depends on the plaintext and the key. Aes-128 contains 128 bits.
c. Key (k), the data entered in the plain-text to ciphertext or ciphertext to plain-text algorithm. The length of AES128 is 128 bits.
d. Number of rounds (R), AES-128 is 10 rounds.

When THE AES algorithm runs, its energy consumption depends on the intermediate value of the algorithm. When the AES encryption algorithm is executed once, the plaintext and the key are XOR first, and then multiple rounds of encryption are performed. The first child of each round of encryption is a SubBytes, for which AES defines an S-box [10], which is a matrix of 16×16 bytes containing a permutation of the 256 numbers that can be represented by 8 bits of data.

In AES-128 encryption algorithm, the only nonlinear transformation is s-box byte replacement, after the OPERATION of S-box, the security of the whole encryption algorithm can be guaranteed to a large extent. For all 16 bytes of a set of keys [11], the attack strategy in this paper is to crack each byte one by one, and finally realize the recovery of all bytes of keys.

2.2 Energy Analysis Attack

Theoretically, decrypting encrypted data requires decrypting the key, which can only be analyzed from the plaintext input and ciphertext output of the encryption function [12]. In modern cryptography, the security of cryptography algorithm follows Kerckhoffs hypothesis and takes the key as the ultimate protection goal. Therefore, traditional cryptography analysis methods all regard cryptography algorithm as an ideal mathematical transformation. Cryptographic algorithm is a kind of mathematical transformation, the realization of which needs to rely on the processor to achieve, according to the different processor architecture, divided into software implementation and hardware implementation. When using embedded microprocessor and processor, the cryptographic algorithm can be realized by software directly. When FPGA and ASIC are used, the cryptographic algorithm is realized by internal department circuit and memory.

When any electronic device is running, it will interact with the external physical world, radiate signals and be disturbed by external signals. During the transportation of encryption and decryption, the cryptographic device will leak information to the outside world. The side channel security analysis technology is to analyze the cryptographic device and crack the key using the leaked information. Side channel attack belongs to physical attack, has nothing to do with algorithm itself, belongs to passive attack category, is not easy to be detected. For the cryptographic algorithm with strict security proof, side channel attack can still crack it. The encryption algorithm without any defense measures can be successfully cracked by side channel attack during its implementation. Figure 1 shows the side channel attack analysis model.

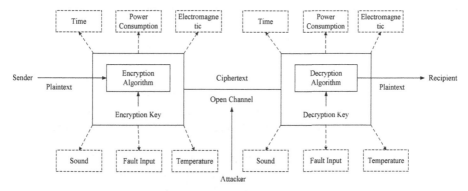

Fig. 1. Side channel attack analysis model.

Energy analysis is based on the analysis of voltage and current information during encryption and decryption of encryption chip, which is converted into energy information for analysis. Simple energy attacks (SPA) [13] in the process of calculation is based on password chip consumption characteristics of the power consumption of obtaining information related to the key, by this method the attacker can according to the energy curve characteristics and the experience itself can intuitive analysis of the instruction execution order, to instruction sequence cipher algorithm related to the data. Investigate the modular power operation of a Rivest-Shamiradleman algorithm implemented on the device. In the case of using the square multiplication algorithm, if the algorithm only performs one square operation, it indicates that the corresponding key bit is 0; if it performs one square operation and one multiplication operation, it indicates that the corresponding key bit is 1. However, simple energy attack is difficult to implement and requires a certain understanding of the cryptographic algorithm in the attacked device.

The experience gained in image recognition is not entirely suitable for the identification of energy traces in the side-channel field. This is because image features are generally quite obvious, while the effective features in side-channel data show only very small fluctuations in energy consumption with operating data values, which are completely unrecognizable to humans. That is, the signal-to-noise ratio of the side-channel data is much lower than the signal-to-noise ratio of the image. Therefore, convolutional neural networks for modeling side-channel data also require a lot of practical experience to guide. Correlation energy attacks (CPA) is presented by the Brier, etc. [14], CPA attack technology using the Pearson correlation coefficient in the statistical analysis, by an unknown but constant reference value, structure with data of hamming correlation model, using the energy consumption of sample and processing the data analyze the correlation between the hamming weight [15]. In the cryptographic chip system, the energy consumption of the cryptographic device is the energy trace, denoted as T, for encrypting (decrypting) different groups of plaintext (ciphertext) data and real keys and obtaining the cryptographic device. By guessing the key, the corresponding intermediate value is generated. According to the Hamming weight or hamming distance leakage of the intermediate value, the assumed energy consumption is calculated and denoted as D. The linear correlation coefficient between assumed energy consumption and measured energy trace is calculated according to the following formula.

$$\rho(T, D) = \frac{E(T \cdot D) - E(T)E(D)}{\sqrt{Var(T) \cdot Var(D)}} \tag{1}$$

In Formula (1), E() represents the average value, and Var() represents the variance. ρ is in the range of $[-1, 1]$. When ρ takes the maximum value of absolute value, that is, assuming that the linear correlation between energy consumption and the real measured energy trace (i.e. the correlation coefficient ρ) reaches the maximum, then the guess key corresponding to D is the correct key.

Differential energy analysis (DPA) attack is the most widely used energy analysis attack method. Compared with SPA attack methods, implementing DPA requires a large amount of energy traces, but DPA attackers do not need detailed knowledge of the attacking device and can still be implemented if the energy traces contain noise [11]. The attack sequence of DPA is to select an intermediate value of the cryptographic algorithm execution, which must be the output of a function composed of known and non-constant data and a partial key. When the device executes the cryptographic algorithm, the energy traces leaked by the side channel are collected. According to the key and plaintext data in the key hypothesis space, the corresponding intermediate value is calculated. Establish the mapping of the power consumption model, and realize the conversion from the assumed intermediate value to the assumed power consumption value. The key is recovered by statistical testing of the comparison between the hypothetical power consumption value and the actual energy trace.

2.3 Long Short-Term Memory Networks

The traditional recursive neural network (RNN) has the problem of gradient expansion or gradient disappearance during network training. In order to solve this problem, LSTM [16] is introduced. LSTM is a cyclic structure, the difference is that only the tan layer is used for calculation inside the RNN neuron, while LSTM has 4 fully connected layers for calculation. LSTM adjusts the information transfer process through gate mechanism. In Fig. 2, there are three nonlinear sum "gate" structures, namely input gate, forgetting gate and output gate. The values of the three gates are between (0,1), indicating the probability of forgetting the "hidden cell state of the previous layer". The three "gate" structures take the internal and external activation functions of the block as input, and the result of vector multiplication as output, which can be used to decide whether to activate the cell. Forgetting gate f_t controls how much information is forgotten in internal state

c_{t-1} at the moment, input gate i_t controls how much information is saved in candidate state, and output gate o_t controls how much information is to be output to external state h_t in internal state c_t at the current moment.

The inventors of the long short-term memory neural network have experimentally verified the superiority of LSTM over RNN in their paper, which is mainly reflected in the following two points [17], the three gated structures introduced by LSTM can learn long-term memory information and solve long-term dependency problems; and the activation function in LSTM is the combination of the sigmoid function and the tanh function, which keeps the gradient almost constant during backpropagation derivation, avoiding the disappearance or explosion of the gradient, and greatly accelerating the model convergence speed.

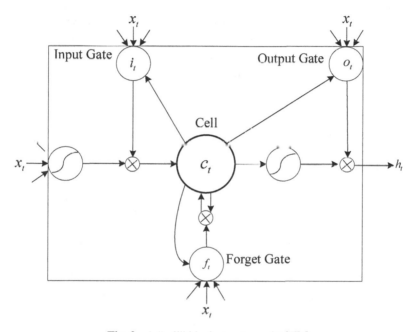

Fig. 2. A "cell" block structure of LSTM.

LSTM unit is an intermediate state, and its input includes the input x_t at the current moment and the output h_{t-1} at the previous moment. Firstly, the pre-processed input data is used as the input layer $x(t)$. The state data h_{t-1} at the previous moment is hidden, and the current input data $x(t)$ goes through an activation function sigmoid to obtain the output $f(t)$ of f_t, which has been updated at the moment. The expression is

$$f(t) = \sigma\left(W_f\left[h_{t-1}, x_t\right] + b_f\right) \tag{2}$$

where: W_f, b_f in the linear relationship, are coefficient and bias; σ is the sigmoid. In i_t, cell state is updated by $i(t)$ and $\tilde{c}_t$, where $i(t)$ calculates the current updated value through sigmoid, $\tilde{c}_t$ through tanh activation function, and f_t is updated into a new state when new data is input into LSTM unit, and the formula o_t is

$$i(t) = \sigma\left(W_i[h_{t-1}, x_t] + b_i\right) \tag{3}$$

$$\tilde{c}_t = tanh\left(W_c[h_{t-1}, x_t] + b_c\right) \tag{4}$$

where, W_i, b_i, W_c, b_c is the coefficient and bias of the linear relationship. The input information of the cell state is calculated through the input gate and the forgetting gate in turn, and then the hidden layer unit is finally obtained by updating the cell. The formula is

$$C_t = f_t C_{t-1} + i_t \tilde{c}_t \tag{5}$$

Output layer Output is calculated by the hidden layer, and these calculations are controlled by the output gate. The output of the hidden state h_t is updated, and the new h_t is divided into two modules: O_t is the hidden state h_{t-1} of the new input sequence data $x(t)$, which is the first module and calculated by sigmoid; The second module calculates the result by tanh and hidden state $C(t)$ together, namely:

$$o_t = \sigma\left(W_o[h_{t-1}, x_t] + b_o\right) \tag{6}$$

$$h_t = o_t \cdot tanh(C_t) \tag{7}$$

where, W_o, b_o is the coefficient and bias of the linear relationship.

3   LSTM - Based Side Channel Attack

To apply deep learning to side-channel attacks, three conditions need to be met [18]. a. The attacker has an encryption device that can set its own encryption program and a capture device that can collect power consumption information in the encryption process. b. On the encryption hardware, the attacker must be able to select any plaintext and key and perform any number of encryption processes. c. The attacker can collect power consumption data of at least one encryption device during the encryption process.

In the side channel attack method based on deep learning, the attacker firstly obtains enough power trace on the encryption device, determines an appropriate label for each trace to fit the relationship between the key and physical leakage, and then selects an appropriate model to train the trace [14]. Then, after the model is trained, any plaintext with any key is encrypted on the encryption device, the power consumption information in the encryption process is collected by the acquisition device, and then the obtained power trace is input into the trained model for analysis, so as to crack the key used in the encryption process.

For feedforward neural networks such as convolutional neural networks, generally only a few important features can be extracted. The LSTM network has the ability to fuse sequence information, and when the encryption device processes the encrypted data, the current work unit state is determined according to the data of all previous moments [19]. Using the LSTM network to train the time series data can use the time series in the power consumption data to convert All features are fused to extract deeper and more expressive features. Therefore, choosing an LSTM neural network to build a model on the side-channel power consumption data can get more accurate results.

3.1 Select the Data TAB

Deep learn-based side channel attack technology uses a labeled power track to train and model at a separate business. The trained model identifies which input power track belongs to. The number of categories of neural network classification depends on the number of tags, and the label of power consumption trajectory depends on the selected leakage model, so the selection of appropriate leakage model has an important impact on the performance of side channel analysis.

In the side-channel attack of block cipher algorithm, because the operation of S-box is nonlinear transformation and the power consumption is large, points on the power consumption trajectory corresponding to s-box are generally selected as analysis points [20], and different data are distinguished obviously. To attack the AES encryption algorithm by a separate line, if the plaintext is known, the s-box output of the first round is usually the attack object. As shown in Fig. 3:

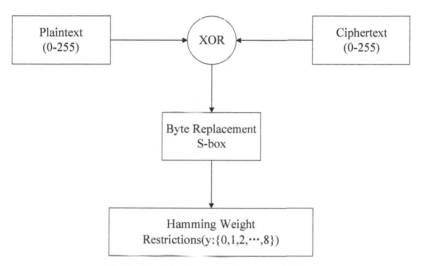

Fig. 3. Model using HW of output of S-box.

Compared with discriminating the value of single bit or the whole byte, the hamming weight of the output value of S-box is taken as the output of the model, which has low complexity and moderate number of output categories. Therefore, this paper chooses the Hamming weight of S-box as the label of power consumption trajectory for neural network modeling.

3.2 Point of Interest Choose a Choice

This paper chooses to attack the third byte of AES-128, namely K[2], because in AES, except the original key is used in the first round, the subsequent keys are all sub-keys generated by round key addition. In order to make the key cracking more efficient, this paper uses the data generated in the first round of encryption. The set label is the XOR value of the 3rd byte of the key and the 3rd byte of the plaintext in the first round of encryption, namely:

$$S_{state} = SBox[p[2] \oplus k[2]] \tag{8}$$

In the command, "$\oplus$" indicates XOR by bit. In the computer, counting starts from "0". Therefore, the third bit of the plaintext and key is denoted as P[2] and K[2] respectively. S_{state} represents the status after s-box output, that is, the label. The main reason is to target at the time of running the encryption algorithm, encryption chip first need to register call S - from within the box to perform encryption algorithm of byte replace operation, then the operation after the middle of the state is loaded into the data bus, and the capacitive load data bus is large, usually for encryption chip has great effect on energy consumption.

4   Experiment and Discussion

4.1   Prepare the Laboratory Environment

In this paper, we use the Keras deep learning open source library (Keras-2.2.4) and the TensorFlow backend (TensorFlow GPU-1.9.0), and the computer hardware configuration is Intel(R) Core(TM) I7-10510U CPU@2.30 GHz and NVIDIA GeForce GTX 1080 Ti completed all numerical calculations and model training in the experiment.

4.2   According to the Data Set

ASCAD open data set is a standard data set for deep learning-based side channel attacks to facilitate comparison of the effects of various deep learning models. The target of ASCAD is an AES algorithm implemented by software with mask protection, which is run on a target board ATMega8515 [21] with 8-bit AVR architecture. The data set contains a total of 60,000 electromagnetic energy trajectories, of which 50,000 are divided into modeling trajectories. The remaining 10,000 were used for real-time specific attacks to verify the model's effectiveness. Each original track contains 100,000 time points of sampling. For convenience, the authors separately extract 700 data points related to the third mask S-box operation in the first round of AES encryption. These data points are verified by the author to be able to resist first-order side channel attack without exposing the mask.

4.3   Attack Effect

The data set used in this paper is composed of power consumption time series data, while LSTM network has the function of long-term memory and is more effective in processing time series data than MLP and CNN network. Its powerful expression ability makes the training performance on verification set better than training set. Figure 4 and Fig. 5 show the side channel attack effect under low noise and high noise respectively.

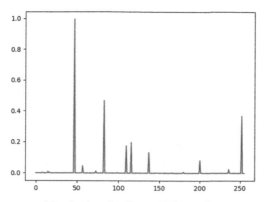

Fig. 4. Attack effect with low noise.

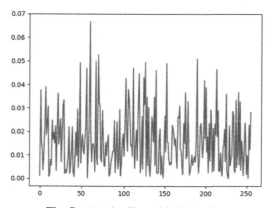

Fig. 5. Attack effect with high noise.

In order to study the performance of LSTM network in side channel attack, this paper conducts further comparative tests on other common deep learning models. MLP and CNN model structures used in reference [22] were used to comprehensively compare and analyze the side channel attack performance of all models from the aspects of model accuracy, parameter scale and side channel attack efficiency. As can be seen from Table 1, when all models are iteratively trained to the 500th EPOCHS, LSTM network has the lowest training loss and better results than other models. In addition, the parameter

Table 1. The accuracy and training time of each model when Epochs = 500.

Model	Training accuracy	Training loss	Parameter scale
MLP	0.4367	1.7016	195216
CNN	0.5523	1.2839	332736
LSTM	0.6299	1.1145	126408

scale of LSTM model is the smallest, only 126408 parameters, the model structure is the simplest, the model has lower computational complexity.

It can be seen from Table 2 that the MLP model required the least training time (11 min and 28 s), but the model was poor in generalization ability and the test accuracy was only 94.87%. CNN model has a good performance in both validation accuracy and generalization ability, and the generalization accuracy is up to 99.17%. However, the model training takes the longest time, reaching 16:28:39 s, which will waste a lot of computing resources and time and cost too much model construction. The training time of the LSTM model established in this paper is 1:31:27, which is longer than that of the MLP model, but significantly less than that of the CNN model. In terms of accuracy, the generalization ability of the LSTM model is higher than that of the MLP model and CNN model, up to 99.54%.

Table 2. Model accuracy comparison results.

Model	Training time	Verification accuracy	Test accuracy
MLP	12 m 28 s	94.87%	94.58%
CNN	16 h 28 m 39 s	99.37%	99.08%
LSTM	1 h 31 m 27 s	99.76%	99.54%

In the existing deep learning key prediction methods, each complete key attack needs to start from each byte of the key, that is, AES-128 requires 16 networks to work at the same time to obtain the complete key. In the training process of three kinds of networks, the LSTM model is more efficient than the current full key cracking model based on deep learning.

5 Conclusion

In order to study the application of deep learning in side channel attack, this paper proposes a side channel attack method based on long short-term memory network, and our method shows good results on ASCAD data set. The experimental results show that the LSTM model has the smallest parameter scale, the simplest structure and the lowest computational complexity, and has excellent performance of high precision and low loss. Therefore, in the next step, we will optimize the LSTM model to improve its robustness under display conditions. In the future, we will continue to study the performance of the deep learning model on side channel attack and find a better method for side channel attack, so as to improve the information security protection capability of encryption devices.

Acknowledgement. This work is supported by Basic Research Program (No. JCKY2019210B029).

Conflicts of Interest. The authors declare that there are no conflicts of interest regarding the publication of this study.

References

1. Zhou, Y.B., Feng, D.G.: Side-channel attacks: ten years after its publication and the im- pacts on cryptographic module security testing. Cryptology Eprint Archive Report (2005)
2. Kocher, P.C.: Timing attacks on implementations of diffie-hellman, rsa, dss, and other systems. In: Proceedings of the 16th Annual International Cryptology Conference on Advances in Cryptology. Springer (1996)
3. Wang, H.: Multi-source training deep-learning side-channel attacks. In: 2020 IEEE 50th International Symposium on Multiple-Valued Logic (ISMVL) IEEE (2020)
4. Maghrebi, H., Portigliatti, T., Prouff, E.: Breaking cryptographic implementations using deep learning techniques. In: Carlet, C., Hasan, M.A., Saraswat, V. (eds.) SPACE 2016. LNCS, vol. 10076, pp. 3–26. Springer, Cham (2016). https://doi.org/10.1007/978-3-319-49445-6_1
5. Cagli, E., Dumas, C., Prouff, E.: Convolutional neural networks with data augmentation against jitter-based countermeasures. In: International Conference on Cryptographic Hardware and Embedded Systems (2017)
6. Benadjila, R., Prouff, E., Strullu, R., Cagli, E., Dumas, C.: Deep learning for side-channel analysis and introduction to ASCAD database. J. Cryptogr. Eng. **10**(2), 163–188 (2019). https://doi.org/10.1007/s13389-019-00220-8
7. Cao, P., Zhang, C., Lu, X., Gu, D.: Cross-device profiled side-channel attack with unsupervised domain adaptation. In: IACR Transactions on Cryptographic Hardware and Embedded Systems 2021, 27–56 (2021)
8. Song, S., Chen, K., Zhang, Y.: Overview of side channel cipher analysis based on deep learning. J. Phys: Conf. Ser. **1213**(2), 22013–22022 (2019)
9. Dworkin, M., et al.: Advanced Encryption Standard (AES), Federal Inf. In: Process. Stds. (NIST FIPS), National Institute of Standards and Technology, Gaithersburg, MD (2001). https://doi.org/10.6028/NIST.FIPS.197
10. Nechvatal, J.: Report on the development of the advanced encryption standard (AES). J. Res. Natl. Inst. Stand. Technol. **106**(3), 511 (2001)
11. Wang, H., Dubrova, E.: Tandem deep learning side-channel attack against fpga implementation of AES. In: 2020 IEEE International Symposium on Smart Electronic Systems (iSES) (Formerly iNiS), pp. 147–150 (2020)
12. Kocher, P.C., Jaffe, J., Jun, B.: Differential power analysis. In: Power Analysis Attacks, pp. 119–165. Springer, Boston (2007). https://doi.org/10.1007/978-0-387-38162-6_6
13. Kocher, P., Jaffe, J., Jun, B.: Differential power analysis. In: Wiener, M. (ed.) CRYPTO 1999. LNCS, vol. 1666, pp. 388–397. Springer, Heidelberg (1999). https://doi.org/10.1007/3-540-48405-1_25
14. Brier, E., Clavier, C., Olivier, F.: Correlation power analysis with a leakage model. In: Joye, M., Quisquater, J.-J. (eds.) CHES 2004. LNCS, vol. 3156, pp. 16–29. Springer, Heidelberg (2004). https://doi.org/10.1007/978-3-540-28632-5_2
15. Pammu, A.A.: A highly efficient side channel attack with profiling through relevance-learning on physical leakage information. IEEE Trans. Dependable Secure Comput. **16**, 376–387 (2019)
16. Hochreiter, S., Schmidhuber, J.: Long short-term memory. Neural Comput. **9**, 1735–1780 (1997)
17. Serpanos, D., Yang, S., Wolf, M.: Neural network-based side channel attacks and countermeasures. In: 2020 57th ACM/IEEE Design Automation Conference (DAC), pp. 1–2 (2020)
18. Jap, D., Bhasin, S.: Practical reverse engineering of secret sboxes by side-channel analysis. In: 2020 IEEE International Symposium on Circuits and Systems (ISCAS), pp. 1–5 (2020)

19. Pedro, M., Servant, V., Guillemet, C.: Practical side-channel attack on a security device. In: 2019 31st International Conference on Microelectronics (ICM), pp. 130–133 (2019)
20. Lecun, Y., Bengio, Y., Hinton, G.: Deep learning. Nature **521**, 436 (2015)
21. Biryukov, A., De Cannière, C.: Data encryption standard (DES). In: van Tilborg, H.C.A. (ed.) Encyclopedia of Cryptography and Security. Springer, Boston (2005). https://doi.org/10.1007/0-387-23483-7_94
22. Kong, Y., Saeedi, E.: The investigation of neural networks performance in side-channel attacks. Artif. Intell. Rev. **52**(1), 607–623 (2018). https://doi.org/10.1007/s10462-018-9640-4

A Novel EEG-Based Depression Detection Framework

Yingshan Shen[✉], Muxin Xu, and Xiaomao Fan

School of Computer Science, South China Normal University, Guangzhou 510631, China
shenys@m.scnu.edu.cn

Abstract. Depression is a highly common mental illness, its clinical features are presented with low mood, loss of interest and pleasure, reduced energy, and guilt. With the people's pace of life is accelerating, more and more people suffer from depression, which seriously affects their work, study, life, and so on. Clinically, the 17-item Hamilton Depression Scale (HAMD-17) is a widely used tool for depression evaluation. However, the HAMD-17 score assessed by physical therapists is highly subjective, and time-consuming, where most of the medical providers like community hospitals would encounter a manpower shortage of such trained physical therapists. In this paper, by analyzing electroencephalogram (EEG) signals, we present a novel EEG-based depression detection framework. It uses Recursive Feature Elimination with Cross Validation (RFECV) to conduct feature selection from high-dimensional EEG-derived amplitude-index and rhythm-index features. Then, five widely used machine learning methods of Ridge Classifier (RC), Linear Discriminant Analysis (LDA), Logistic Regression (LR), Naive Bayes Classifier (NB), and k Nearest Neighbors Classifier (kNN) are employed to build automatic depression detection models. Extensive experiments results show that both RC and LDA models obtained promising performance, the F1 scores of which are up to 72.39% and 72.21%, respectively. It means that our EEG-based depression detection framework can be potentially deployed into a medical system to alleviate the manpower shortage of physical therapists for medical providers.

Keywords: Depression · EEG · Feature selection · RFECV · Machine learning

1 Introduction

Depression is a highly common mental disorder in both developed and developing countries [1]. Psychiatrists believe that depression may be a combination of biological factors, psychological factors, and social factors. However, there is no deterministic answer to it until now [2]. Clinically, depression is characterized by low mood, loss of interest and pleasure, reduced energy, guilt or low self-worth, and lack of concentration [2], which seriously affects the patients' work, study, and life as well as social activities. With the people's pace of life accelerating as well as the pressure of life increasing, the incidence of depression has increased significantly. According to World Health Organization statistics [3], more than 350 million persons worldwide suffer from depression. In China, there are over 54 million persons suffered from depression, accounting for 4.2%.

X. Sun et al. (Eds.): ICAIS 2022, CCIS 1586, pp. 645–654, 2022.
https://doi.org/10.1007/978-3-031-06767-9_53

By 2030 depression is predicted to become the second leading contributor to disease burden as measured by disability-adjusted life years [4]. Depression has become a worldwide concern of mental illness; therefore, it is essential to early diagnose depression and make interventions to prevent depression from getting worse.

Clinically, 17-item Hamilton Depression Scale (HAMD-17) [5] is a widely used tool to detect depression. This depression scale requires the joint HAMD examination by two trained physical therapists, which can avoid the subjectivity to give depression scores to some extent. However, most rural, community, and even urban hospitals lack the manpower of trained physical therapists to perform such HAMD-17 tests. Since the HAMD-17 score assessed by physical therapists is highly subjective and time-consuming, developing an automatic depression method based on physiological signals has great significance.

Electroencephalogram (EEG) [5], a technology of recording brain activity using electrophysiological metrics, is a combined postsynaptic potential formed by large numbers of neurons synchronized during brain activity, an atlas recorded by electrodes placed on the scalp surface [6]. EEG records electrical wave changes during brain activity and is a noninvasive physiological signal acquisition method. The neurological condition of a person is reflected in the electrical activity of the brain [7]. EEG waveform can distinguish depression from the healthy activity of the brain. Hence, researchers investigate the EEG waveform and spectrum to diagnose depression, which can alleviate the problem of manpower shortage of trained physical therapists in medical providers like community hospitals and provide much more objective assessment results of depression [8]. Bruder *et al.* [9] found that depressed and normal persons represented different EEG activities, which illustrated that using EEG signals can identify depression. Thibodeau *et al.* [10] described the specific relationship between EEG signals and depression. Hosseinifard *et al.* [11] integrated a variety of classical machine learning algorithms to detect depression on EEG signals, and finally achieved promising results. Bachmann *et al.* [12] used Spectral Asymmetry Index Method (SASI) and Higuchi's Fractal Dimension Method (HFD) and achieved high accuracy in both groups. Cai H *et al.* [13] collected EEG signals at Fp1, Fp2, and Fpz electrode sites and the result showed that k Nearest Neighbors Classifier (kNN) had the highest accuracy. Mahato *et al.* [14] extracted features from EEG signals and discovered the combination of alpha and theta asymmetry showed the highest classification accuracy in Support Vector Machine (SVM). Although the depression detection methods mentioned above achieved promising results, however, they are highly dependent on the quality of EEG signals and EEG devices. It is because different brand EEG devices have different sample frequencies and noise levels, which would result in the performance of the aforementioned EEG-based depression methods decreasing greatly.

In this paper, we present a novel EEG-based depression detection framework, which is based on the amplitude-index and rhythm-index features extracted by EEG devices directly instead of original EEG signals. Specifically, firstly, we recruit 92 eligible patients from Shenzhen Hospital of Traditional Chinese Medicine, collect their EEG signals, and perform HAMD-17 tests by trained physical therapists. And the amplitude-index and rhythm-index features combined with the additional two demographic statistic features of gender and age are the input of our presented depression detection framework.

Then, we standardize the amplitude-index and rhythm-index features, encode the feature of patients' gender and target variable of HAMD-17 scores into categories. Afterward, we use Recursive Feature Elimination with Cross Validation (RFECV) for feature selection to reduce the irrelevant and redundant features. Finally, five widely used machine learning methods of kNN, Ridge Classifier (RC), Linear Discriminant Analysis (LDA), Logistic Regression (LR), and Naive Bayes Classifier (NB) are utilized to build depression models. The experimental results show that the RC and LDA can achieve promising performance for depression detection.

2 Methods

In this part, we firstly introduce how to acquire the experimental data and preprocess the data. Then we recommend the principles of feature selection and RFECV. Finally, we introduce five classification methods used in this experiment. The proposed depression detection framework is shown in Fig. 1.

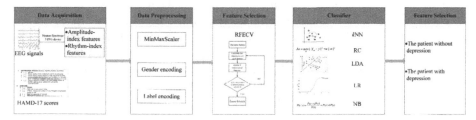

Fig. 1. The proposed depression detection framework.

2.1 Data Acquisition

92 patients from Shenzhen Hospital of Traditional Chinese Medicine are recruited to participate in this study, they suffer from mental illness for more than two weeks, but their consciousness is sober, and did not appear the symptom such as aphasia. They fully understand the purpose of this study and sign the informed consent form. Each subject is collected EEG signals by an EEG device (Neuron-Spectrum-5) as well as HAMD-17 score assessed by a physical therapist. Specifically, a physical therapist uses a 10–20 electrode placement system to place scalp electrodes on the patient's head and asks the patient to close his or her eyes keeping 30 s. Then the physician uses a Neuron-Spectrum-5 EEG device to obtain smooth EEG signals. The EEG device that the physical therapist uses has 19 channels, namely FP1-A1 FP2-A2 F3-A1 F4-A2 FZ-A2 C3- A1 C4-A2 CZ-A1 P3-A1 P4-A2 PZ-A2 O1-A1 O2- A2 F7-A1 F8-A2 T3-A1 T4-A2 T5-A1 T6-A2. And each channel has four bands: delta, theta, alpha, and beta band. The EEG device automatically extracts the rhythm-index and amplitude-index features, a total of 152 features. In addition, the physical therapists administer the HAMD-17 test to each patient, obtain their HAMD-17 scores. Two additional demographic statistic features of gender and age are also combined with the aforementioned EEG-extracted amplitude-index and rhythm-index features, a total of 154 features for subsequent processing.

2.2 Data Preprocessing

We preprocess the high-dimensional EEG-derived amplitude-index and rhythm-index features. Concretely, firstly, the channel leads in the Neuron-Spectrum-5 EEG device automatically calculate and output the features related to EEG according to the amplitude-index and rhythm-index features of the four frequency bands. Since the difference between the maximum and minimum in the same EEG feature is so large, the data need to be scaled to an appropriate range, we standardize the amplitude-index and rhythm-index features data. In this experiment, we use the MinMaxScaler method for standardization. This method is a linear transformation of the original data, converts the maximum value of each feature into a unit size, and normalizes the data into a conversion formula [0,1], which is defined to be:

$$x_i = \frac{x_i - x_{\min}}{x_{\max} - x_{\min}} \tag{1}$$

where x_{min} represents the minimum value of a feature, x_{max} represents the maximum value of a feature, and x_i represents the i_{th} data value in the feature.

Then, we encode the feature of patients' gender and target variable of HAMD-17 scores into categories. And we encode the feature of gender as male for 1 and as female for 0. According to the evaluation reference standard, it can be known that when the HAMD-17 score is higher than 17, the patient has major depression. And the HAMD-17 score below or equal to 17 indicates that the patient might have mild depression. In this experiment, we label HAMD-17 scores higher than 17 as 1 and HAMD-17 scores lower than or equal to 17 as 0.

2.3 Feature Selection

In high-dimensional datasets, there may exist many irrelevant features and redundant features [15]. The interaction between irrelevant features and redundant features leads to the instability of the classifier model, which has a negative impact on the efficiency of the model and the accuracy of the classifier. In addition, using a large number of features to design the classifier is too expensive and wastes computing resources. The goal of feature selection methods is to reduce the number of input features by picking important ones and feature selection is to select the subset from all subsets that are best for a particular task [16].

In this paper, we use RFECV [17] for feature selection. RFECV method is an improved method based on Recursive Feature Elimination (RFE). RFECV for feature selection is divided into RFE and Cross Validation (CV) [18]. Specifically, firstly, we set up 5-fold cross-validation and randomly divided all amplitude-index and rhythm-index features into five subsets. Then, we calculate the importance score for each subset of features and select the subset with the highest score, so that we know how many amplitude-index and rhythm-index features are needed to reach the highest value, and then we can figure out how many amplitude-index and rhythm-index features need to be removed. Finally, RFE with step 1 was performed for all amplitude-index and rhythm-index features. RFECV flow chart is shown in Fig. 2.

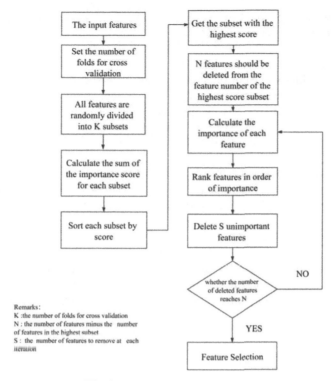

Fig. 2. The flow chart of RFECV.

2.4 Classification Algorithms

k Nearest Neighbors Classifier

kNN [19] is a widely used classification, and its implementation process is simple. The core idea of kNN algorithm is to improve the accuracy of judgment, we find the k samples closest to the sample to be tested in the feature space and determine the class of the sample to be tested according to the class of the k samples [20]. The sample to be tested belongs to the group with the largest number of samples.

In this experiment, after inputting a new sample x, the kNN calculates the distance between the labeled samples and x, and we choose the Euclidean distance to measure the distance [21]. In n-dimensional space, the Euclidean distance is calculated as:

$$d(x, y) = \sqrt{(x_1 - y_1)^2 + (x_2 - y_2)^2 + (x_3 - y_3)^2 + ... + (x_n - y_n)^2} = \sqrt{\sum_{i=1}^{n} (x_i - y_i)^2}$$

(2)

Then, each labeled sample is sorted according to the sample distance from near to far. We set k to 5, and select the 5 samples closest to x, and count the number of each group. Therefore, the group to which x belongs in the group with the largest number of samples among the 5 selected samples.

Ridge Classifier

RC [22] is a classifier variant of ridge regression. RC first converts the binary object to $\{-1,1\}$ and then treats the classification problem as a regression task. The classifier uses the least square loss to fit the classification model [23]. The loss function is as follows:

$$J\omega = \min_{\omega} ||X_\omega - y||^2 + \alpha||\omega||^2 \tag{3}$$

here α is the coefficient between the flat loss and the regular term, $\alpha \geq 0$. The greater the number of α, the more important the regular term is, which is also the penalty term. The smaller the value of α, the less powerful the regular term is.

Linear Discriminant Analysis

LDA [24] is a linear, supervised classification method, usually used for binary classification. The main idea is that we try to project the sample onto a straight line $y = \omega^T x$, so that the projection point of the same sample is as close as possible, and the projection point of the different samples is as far as possible [25]. When the new samples are classified, they are projected onto the same line, and then the category is determined according to the position of the projection point of the new samples. Figure 3 shows the idea of the LDA algorithm.

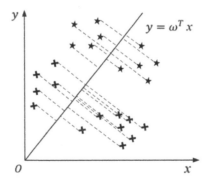

Fig. 3. Linear Discriminant Analysis.

Logistic Regression

LR [26] is a kind of generalized linear regression, which is often used to solve the problem of binary classification. Logistic regression uses the sigmoid function to make the value of the result within the interval (0,1). We can also use the sigmoid function to solve some nonlinear problems. The sigmoid' function is formulated mathematically:

$$y = \frac{1}{1 + e^{-\theta x}} \tag{4}$$

when x approaches infinity, y approaches 1, and when x approaches infinitesimal, y approaches 0.

Naive Bayes Classifier

NB [27] is one of the widely used classifier algorithms in machine learning. It is a statistical approach based on the Bayesian theorem which is used for classification by creating predictive models. Naive Bayes method is a corresponding simplification based on the Bayesian algorithm, that is, it assumes the mutual condition independence between attributes when the target value is given. In practical application scenarios, the complexity of the Bayesian method is greatly simplified. Bayes' theorem is formulated mathematically:

$$P(c|x) = \frac{P(x|c)P(c)}{P(x)} \propto P(x|c)P(c) \tag{5}$$

3 Results and Discussion

3.1 Computing Environment

The presented framework is implemented with python 3.9.7 scikit-learn 0.23.2 and pycaret 2.3.4. All experiments are trained and tested on a computer equipped with an Intel AMD Ryzen 9 5900HX with Radeon Graphics 3.30 GHz CPU and 16.0 GB memory.

3.2 Classification Performance

In this study, a tenfold cross-validation technique is used for depression model evaluation. As shown in Table 1, it can be observed that RC and LDA obtain better performance than LR, NB, and kNN. Specifically, RC achieves 70.62%, 73.49%, 69.91%, and 72.39% in terms of accuracy, recall, precision, and F1 score, respectively. As for LDA, it obtains comparable depression performance with RC, which are accuracy of 70.24%, recall of 72.50%, precision of 69.17%, and F1 score of 72.21%. Compared with LR, NB, and kNN, both RC and LDA are with linear characteristics, which can perform better on the dataset with small sample size. Regarding the precision, LR achieves the best performance, which is up to 76.00%. Compared with LR, the RC and LDA obtain better performance of accuracy, recall, and F1 score. Although the precision of RC and LDA is a little lower than that of LR, their precisions are also up to 69.91% and 69.17%. It means that RC and LDA can be potentially applied in a medical system to provide depression services. We can see that using RC and LDA as classifiers for detection gets more than 70% accuracy while using LR and NB reduces the accuracy by about 5%. kNN has the lowest accuracy, at 53%. We analyze the performance results. First, we know that both RC and LDA are linear classification methods. In this experiment, the feature samples are projected on a line, which can distinguish the different kinds of samples clearly. The results show that the RC and the LDA are suitable for the classification of this experiment and have high accuracy. Then, we learn that NB works well under the assumption that each feature distribution is independent. In this experiment, there was a strong correlation between features that did not fit the scenario. Therefore, NB is not suitable for this experiment. LR is easy to be under-fitted when the feature space is large, and the accuracy it obtained is not very high. Therefore, the accuracy obtained by using NB and LR in this experiment is not very high. Since kNN is a lazy algorithm, we need to calculate the distance between the unknown sample and all known samples. However, when the feature dimension is high, the recognition ability of the Euclidean distance is weak, and the calculated distance between samples is not accurate. In addition, kNN has a strong dependence on the selection of k value, the different selection of k value will lead to two samples being similar but belonging to different types of cases. Therefore, kNN does not obtain the unideal result in this experiment. Finally, we can conclude that because the data set used in this work is small and high-dimensional, simple linear or near-linear models perform better in dimensionless data.

Table 1. Depression detection performance.

Model	Accuracy	Recall
RC	0.7062	0.7349
LDA	0.7024	0.7250
LR	0.6738	0.5917
NB	0.6238	0.6250
kNN	0.5357	0.4417

4 Conclusion

In this paper, we present a novel framework for depression detection based on EEG signals. We first standardize high-dimensional EEG-derived amplitude-index and rhythm-index features and encode patients' gender and target variable of HAMD-17 scores into categories. Then we use the RFECV method for feature selection to eliminate unnecessary and redundant amplitude-index and rhythm-index features. After data extraction, we use five classical classification algorithms of RC, LDA, LR, NB, and kNN to build the depression models. Experimental results showed that both RC and LDA achieve promising performance in depression detection. It means that RC and LDA can be potentially applied to a medical system to provide depression detection service, which can help physical therapists facilitate timely diagnosis and alleviate the manpower shortage for medical providers.

References

1. Yary, T., Lehto, S.M., Tolmunen, T., Tuomainen, T., Kauhanen, J.: Dietary magnesium intake and the incidence of depression: a 20-year follow-up study. J. Affect. Disord. **193**, 94–98 (2016)

2. Marcus, M., Yasamy, M.T., Ommeren, M.V., Chisholm, D., Saxena, S.: Depression: a global public health concern. World Health Organization Paper on Depression, pp. 6–8 (2012)
3. Zhu, J., Wang, Z., Zeng, S., Li, X.: An improved classification model for depression detection using EEG and eye tracking data. IEEE Trans. Nano Biosci. **19**(3), 527–537 (2020)
4. Gonzalez, J., Shreck, E., Batchelder, A.: Hamilton rating scale for depression (HAM-D). Encyclopedia Behav. Med. **131**, 887–888 (2013)
5. Cheng, J., Xu, R.M., Tang, X.Y., Sheng, V.S., Cai, C.T.: An abnormal network flow feature sequence prediction approach for DDoS attacks detection in big data environment. Comput. Mater. Continua **193**, 130–136 (2016)
6. Cohen, M.X.: Where does EEG come from and what does it mean? Trends Neurosci. **40**(4), 208–218 (2017)
7. Kumar, S.D., Subha, D.: Prediction of depression from EEG signal using long short term memory (LSTM). In: Proceeding of ICOEI, pp. 1248–1253 (2019)
8. Li, D., Tang, J., Deng, Y., Yang, L.: Classification of resting state EEG data in patients with depression. In: Proceeding of HEALTHCOM, pp. 1–2 (2021)
9. Bruder, G.E., et al.: Regional brain asymmetries in major depression with or without an anxiety disorder: a quantitative electroencephalographic study. Biol. Psychiat. **41**(9), 939–948 (1997)
10. Thibodeau, R., Jorgensen, R.S., Kim, S.: Depression, anxiety, and resting frontal EEG asymmetry: a meta-analytic review. J. Abnorm. Psychol. **115**(4), 715 (2006)
11. Hosseinifard, B., Moradi, M.H., Rostami, R.: Classifying depression patients and normal subjects using machine learning techniques and nonlinear features from EEG signal. Comput. Methods Programs Biomed. **109**, 339–345 (2013)
12. Bachmann, M., Lass, J., Suhhova, A., Hinrikus, H.: Spectral asymmetry and higuchi's fractal dimension measures of depression electroencephalogram. Comput. Math. Methods Med. **2013**, 1–9 (2013)
13. Cai, H., et al.: A pervasive approach to EEG-based depression detection. Complexity **2018** (2018)
14. Mahato, S., Paul, S.: Classification of depression patients and normal subjects based on electroencephalogram (EEG) signal using alpha power and theta asymmetry. J. Med. Syst. **44**(1), 1–8 (2020)
15. Ichenihi, A., Li, W., Gao, Y., Rao, Y.: Feature selection and clustering of damage for pseudo-ductile unidirectional carbon/glass hybrid composite using acoustic emission. Appl. Acoust. **182**, 1–10 (2021)
16. Ghanem, K., Layeb, A.: Feature selection and knapsack problem resolution based on a discrete backtracking optimization algorithm. Appl. Evol. Comput. **12**(2), 1–15 (2021)
17. Hussain, A., Ugli, I., Kim, B., Kim, M., Kim, H.: Detection of different stages of copd patients using machine learning techniques. In: Proceeding of ICACT, Sydney, Australia, pp. 368–372 (2021)
18. Mustaqim, A., Adi, S., Pristyanto, Y., Astuti, Y.: The effect of recursive feature elimination with cross-validation (RFECV) feature selection algorithm toward classifier performance on credit card fraud detection. In: Proceeding of ICAICST, pp. 270–275 (2021)
19. Chethana, C.: Prediction of heart disease using different kNN classifier. In: Proceeding of ICICCS, pp. 1198–1206 (2021)
20. Li, G., Zhang, J.: Music personalized recommendation system based on improved kNN algorithm. In: Proceeding of IAEAC, Chong Qing, pp. 777–781 (2018)
21. Wahiddin, D., Roespinoedji, R., Masruriyah, A.: Color feature extraction and euclidean distance for classification of. oryza sativa nitrogen adequacy based on leaf color chart. Int. J. Psychol. Rehabil. **24**(7), 3421–3428 (2020)
22. Aljouie, A., Roshan, U.: Prediction of continuous phenotypes in mouse, fly, and rice genome wide association studies with support vector regression SNPS and ridge regression classifier. In: Proceeding of ICMLA, pp. 1246–1250 (2015)

23. Kasiviswanathanm, S., Vijayan, T.B., John, S.: Ridge regression algorithm based non- invasive anaemia screening using conjunctiva images. J. Ambient Intell. Humanized Comput. 1–11 (2020)
24. Ketsuwan, R., Padungweang, P.: A linear discriminant analysis using weighted local structure information. In: Proceeding of JCSSE, Nakhon Si Thammarat, Thailand, pp. 1–5 (2017)
25. Dess, B.W., Small, G.W.: Committee classifier based on linear discriminant analysis for the detection of radioisotopes from airborne gamma-ray spectra. J. Environ. Radioact. **217**, 1–8 (2020)
26. Zou, X., Hu, Y., Tian, Z., Shen, K.: Logistic regression model optimization and case analysis. In: Proceeding of ICCSNT, Da., pp. 1363–1367 (2019)
27. Yang, J., Huang, Y., Zhang, R., Huang, F., Meng, Q., Feng, S.: Study on PPG biometric recognition based on multifeature extraction and naive bayes classifier. Scientific Programming 1–12 (2021)

Tunnel Disease Detection Based on Spark and Deep Learning

Xia Zhao[1,2]([⊠]), Ying Zheng[1,2], Chongchong Yu[1,2], Xiangjun You[3], and Lu Zhao[4]

[1] China Light Industry Key Laboratory of Industrial Internet and Big Data, Beijing Technology and Business University, Beijing 100048, China
zhaox@btbu.edu.cn
[2] School of Artificial Intelligence, Beijing Technology and Business University, Beijing 100048, China
[3] Zhejiang HuaZhan Institute of Engineering Research and Design, Ningbo 315012, China
[4] Secregen Technology, San Mateo, CA 94402, US

Abstract. Aiming at metro shield disease detection with LiDAR scanning data, this paper proposes an approach of distributed parallel point cloud data processing and shield disease detection. The approach is based on HDFS and Spark, and converts the LiDAR point cloud data into the orthographic projection space, and generates projected image data efficiently. Based on the optimized deep neural network YOLOv5 target detection model, our approach detects four types of metro shield diseases and labels their locations and the classifications on the orthographic projection image. The experiments show that our distributed parallel process framework archives the speedup ratio of 4.96 to the approach of a single server on the LiDAR data processing. Using the optimized YOLO v5 model, with the appropriate IOU threshold, the accuracy of the water seepage and spalling detection box is higher than 90%, and that of the cracks and the cracks on joints is higher than 80%. Our approach can improve the efficiency and accuracy of metro shield disease detection significantly, and promote the intelligence of metro operation and maintenance in the rail transit industry.

Keywords: Disease detection · Spark · Deep learning · Yolov5

1 Introduction

With the rapid development of the urban metro, urban metro has become an important way of traveling for people due to its punctuality, speed, and environmental protection. The accurate and real-time disease detection in key components of metro infrastructure is essential for effective maintenance strategies and safe metro operation. Therefore, it has become a key issue in tunnel engineering that how to detect structural diseases in urban metro shield tunnels accurately, efficiently and comprehensively.

The traditional structural disease detection of urban metro shield tunnels is based on optical camera and manual inspection. Because of the large range of diseases, detecting and classifying diseases with human eyes is not only time-consuming and labor intensive, but also prone to being mistaken with a high error rate [1]. With the development of science and technology, 3D LiDAR scanner has been widely used due to its non-contact, high-efficiency, and high-precision 3D global scanning characteristics. In the metro tunnel, the scanner is installed on the track inspection trolley, which runs along the metro track. The metro shield tunnel is scanned by LiDAR, and the point cloud data is generated, which provides the data foundation for the structural tunnel diseases detection.

However, the huge amount of data generated by the LiDAR brings new challenges to data storage, analysis, and disease detection processing. For example, the point cloud data of a kilometer tunnel scanned by a LiDAR with resolution of 2 mm is about 50 GB, and the produced data by the following analysis is more than 300 GB. How to process these massive data efficiently and identify diseases automatically is an urgent issue to be solved to achieve the intelligentization of metro operation. Traditional data processing systems rely on a single server is no longer meet the requirements. Cloud computing technology with its massive and high-speed processing capability makes it competent for such work effectively [2]. It is necessary to adopt distributed parallel processing technology to improve the efficiency of data processing.

Simultaneously, how to detect the tunnel diseases based on the LiDAR data is also a challenge. There are four types structural diseases in metro shield: water seepage, cracks, spalling, and cracks in the plastering of pipe joints. Due to the multi-slits of shield assembly and various pipelines inside, it is difficult to satisfy the efficiency and accuracy requirements on tunnel diseases detection by manual and traditional image processing approaches.

In this paper, focusing on the above four types disease detection, we propose a point cloud data processing framework and the algorithm based on a distributed computing platform, to project the huge LiDAR point cloud data into cross-sectional projection graphics and orthographic projection images. We propose an approach to construct the sample data set automatically by using the annotated images of shield tunnels produced by AutoCAD manually. We optimize and train the disease detection model based on the deep neural network YOLOv5. Finally, we build up the automatic disease detection system to generate the detection result annotation images and detailed information tables. The experimental results show that our distributed parallel process framework archives the speedup ratio of 4.96 to the approach of a single server on the LiDAR data processing. Using the optimized YOLO v5 model, with the appropriate IOU threshold, the accuracy of the water seepage and spalling detection box is higher than 90%, and that of the cracks and the cracks on joints is higher than 80%. The approach and system improve the efficiency and accuracy of urban metro shield disease detection significantly, and promote the safety and intelligence of Metro operation and maintenance technology.

2   Related Work

2.1   Mass Data Processing Technology Based on Spark

Spark is a big data analysis platform proposed by AMP Lab of the University of California, Berkeley. It is characterized by memory-based calculations and propose the concept of Resilient Distributed Dataset (RDD) [3]. Spark processes a large amount of data efficiently because it can do computations in memory [4], and improves the performance of processing data greatly.

In the field of big data computing, Spark has become one of the popular computing platforms. Aydoand uses Spark to develop a high-accuracy classification application that analyzes data sets marked as spam and non-spam [5]. Semberecki completes a system for categorizing text documents based on the Spark distributed computing framework and shows how to implement natural language processing approaches and tools on the Spark platform [6]. Lee designs and achieves a distributed mobile object management system based on Kafka, Spark & Spark Streaming, HBase, and HDFS to process location information and sensor data from smart black boxes [7]. Spark has been widely used in different fields, but there is few research on urban metro disease detection.

2.2 Approaches of Metro Disease Detection

Metro disease detection approaches based on image processing technology can be divided into two categories: conventional algorithms and deep learning-based algorithms.

Conventional image processing algorithms mainly deal with relatively simple features and a small amount of data. J. Valença etc. design a crack detection algorithm that combines image processing and photogrammetry to obtain the suspected crack area on the image. They obtain the final crack image after filtering, edge connection, shape detection and other operations on the image [8]. L. Attard proposes a hybrid detection approach that combines neighborhood image difference, binary pixel comparison and optical flow approach to detect shield diseases while predicting its development trend [9]. This approach has a low detection speed and is not suitable for application in industrial scenes with a huge amount of data. Wu proposes an automatic identification algorithm for water leakage diseases that combines LiDAR scanning technology, image processing, and connects domain analysis [10]. This approach is mainly for the detection of water leakage diseases, and do not consider other types of shield diseases.

With the significant advancement of Graphic Process Unit (GPU) hardware technology, deep learning-based methods have also been applied in shield disease detection. Gong uses a multi-level loop filtering algorithm based on morphological processing and connects domain filtering to extract the suspected cracks area, and builds a convolutional neural network to classify the cracks [11]. Protopapadakis extracts 17 low-level features such as HOG, grayscale, edge, and frequency of the tunnel image, and obtains high-level features by multilayer perceptron, to detect crack tunnel diseases [12, 13]. The detection accuracy of this approach is higher, but the feature extraction consumes more time. Huang proposes a metro shield crack and leakage disease identification algorithm, which is based on the feature extraction of Full Convolution Network (FCN) for semantic segmentation, and trains the FCN model of crack and leakage respectively through multiple iterations of forward reasoning and backward learning [14]. This approach has higher accuracy, but the model is more complex, and when the object class increases, it cost more time for model training.

In order to improve the efficiency and accuracy of shield disease detection, this paper proposes an approach based on the optimized YOLOv5 model. We enhance the sample set by image processing, optimize the model based on the characteristics of the shield disease data set. We improve the selection of anchor box, loss function indicators and related model parameters, and improve the efficiency of model training, and achieve higher precision.

3 Distributed Parallel Point Cloud Data Processing Based on Spark

3.1 Space Coordinate Models of the Point Cloud Data

The point cloud data scanned by the LiDAR are stored in the LAS file, and consisted of quadruple (X, Y, Z, Ref) for each point on the shield. X, Y, Z are the coordinate values of the point in the LiDAR scanning tunnel coordinate system (STCS), and Ref is the reflectivity of the point. The origin of the STCS is the center of the tunnel at the beginning of the checked metro line. The Y-axis is toward to positive direction of the tunnel axis at the begin point. The X-axis is toward to 3 o'clock direction on the cross-section, and the Z-axis is toward to 12 o'clock direction on the cross-section.

In order to detect the disease of the shield, we project the points in the STCS to the orthographic projection coordinate system (OPCS), and generate the OPCS grayscale images of the shield tunnel. The tunnel is a tubular structure, which is split on the bottom along the line parallel with the axis of the tube. The OPCS is established on a two-dimensional plane by expanding the tube. On the start point of the axis of the tube, facing the positive direction of the tunnel. We expand the tubular surface longitudinally into a 2-dimensional plane and face the inner surface of the tube. Then the left side of the split line is on the bottom and the right side of the split line is on the top of the 2-dimensional plane. The origin of the OPCS is on the upper left corner of the 2-dimensional plane. The X-axis is on the top line of the plane, toward to the positive direction of the tunnel. The Y-axis is on the left line of the plane, toward to 6 o'clock direction.

In order to locate the diseases on the shield accurately, we project the points in STCS to the cross-sectional coordinate system (CSCS), and generate the CSCS graphics of the shield tunnel. The origin of the CSCS is the center of the tunnel on the section, the X-axis is toward to the 3 o'clock direction, and the Y axis is toward to the 12 o'clock direction.

3.2 Orthographic Projection Grayscale Images Generation

Our point cloud data processing system is implemented on the HDFS and Spark distributed parallel computing framework, which is deployed on a cluster of 6 computing nodes. The LiDAR point cloud data are stored on HDFS. Spark computing framework generates parallel computing jobs and tasks, and dispatches them to each computing node.

In each computing task, we generate a gray-scale matrix W with a resolution of L*H, L is the length and H is the width of the OPCS image, as shown in Eq. (1) and (2).

$$L = [max(X_{sn}) - min(X_{sn})] \times K \tag{1}$$

$$H = 2 \prod \times RK \tag{2}$$

where, R is the designed tunnel radius, K is the density parameter of the LiDAR scanner, which represents the number of the cloud points per meter.

The matrix W presents an image in the OPCS, and each element of W is a point projected from the measured cloud point data in the STCS. The (X_{en}, Y_{en}) of a point in OPCS image can be calculated from the correspond measured point (X_{sn}, Y_{sn}, Z_{sn}) in the OPCS, as shown in Eq. (3) and Eq. (4).

$$X_{en} = (X_{sn} - X_{min}) \times K \tag{3}$$

$$Y_{en} = \begin{cases} \left(arctan(Z_{sn}/X_{sn}) + \frac{3\pi}{2}\right) \times \theta_k, x < 0 \\ \left(arctan(Z_{sn}/X_{sn}) + \frac{\pi}{2}\right) \times \theta_k, x \geq 0 \end{cases} \tag{4}$$

where, X_{min} is the minimum value of the mileage of all measured cloud points of a segment of the tunnel, and the scale factor is $\theta_k = R \times K$.

We map the LiDAR reflectivity Ref of the point (X_{sn}, Y_{sn}, Z_{sn}) to an integer value ranging from 0 to 255, which is the gray value Pix of the point (X_{en}, Y_{en}) in the gray matrix W, calculated as Eq. (5).

$$Pix = \left(Ref - Ref_{min}\right) \times \frac{0 - 255}{Ref_{max} - Ref_{min}} \tag{5}$$

3.3 Distributed Parallel Data Processing

We implement the above data processing on the distributed parallel data processing framework. In order to generate OPCS images, the original point cloud data of the tunnel is divided into segments of 2 m by the index of mileages. The RDD parallel processing tasks are dispatched to computing nodes automatically according to the logical sequence defined by DAG, and each block of data is processed parallelly. In order to generate CSCS graphics, the section data are extracted from the point cloud data on the specified interval. Because of the independence of the section data, the data projection tasks can be scheduled and execute parallelly. We optimize and adjust the granularity of the data dynamically according to the computing power of the distributed cluster, and make trade-off between task parallelism and data processing granularity and achieve efficient and scalable capabilities. For example, we project the point cloud data into OPCS image file by the segment of 2 m, and merge them into 100 m segment data when it is needed.

4 Metro Shield Disease Detection Based on YOLOv5

4.1 The Structure of YOLOv5

The YOLO models transform the target detection issue into a regression issue, and detect quickly. Compared with YOLOv3 [15], YOLOv5 has smaller average weight file, shorter training time and inference time on the similar average detection accuracy.

As shown in Fig. 1, in the feature extraction stage, Cross-stage Partial Networks (CSP) are used as the backbone to extract the information-rich characteristics from an input image [16]. The feature map is compressed through the Focus and CSP structure, and the feature information is transferred and fused through the FPN network, and fused feature map is generated. In the prediction stage, YOLOv5 improves the prediction performance through the PAN structure, and generates multi-scale prediction of four types of shield diseases. Finally, the positioning box of four types of disease are outputted.

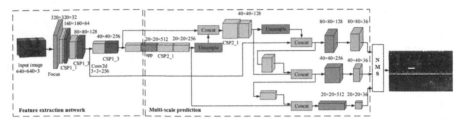

Fig. 1. YOLOv5 network structure.

4.2   Initial Anchor Box Optimization

YOLOv5 introduces the anchor box in the target detection process. Through analysis and comparison, we find that in the model training stage, the initial anchor box parameters affect the speed of target detection and the accuracy of anchor box position directly. The closer initial anchor box parameters are to the real bounding box, the faster the model converges, and the higher accuracy can be obtained.

In order to improve the speed and accuracy of disease detection, we propose an anchor box optimization approach based on the K-means clustering algorithm. We analyze and cluster the marked bounding boxes in the training set, using the metrics of width and height of the anchor boxes. We cluster 20000 disease bounding boxes in the sample set into 9 cluster centers through the K-means clustering algorithm, and use the average (width, height) values of each cluster as the parameters of the initial anchor box in the network configuration file.

The 9 bounding boxes are (173,123), (38,137), (257,319), (72,79), (24,304), (189,22), (23,69), (71,248), (10, 173), and the clustering results are shown in Fig. 2.

Where, the X-axis represents the width of the bounding box, and the Y-axis represents the height of the bounding box. The scattered dots represent 16,845 disease bounding boxes. They are clustered into 9 categories, which are represented by colors in Fig. 2. The black dots represent the centers of 9 clusters, which are the (width, height) of the bounding boxes. Experimental results show that after optimizing the prior anchor box, the average IOU of disease detection results has increased from 48.10% to 60.20%.

4.3   Loss Function Analysis and Optimization

The loss function is the basis for the evaluation of the mis-tested samples of the deep neural network. For different application fields, different loss functions may produce completely different effects, so it is extremely important to choose targeted loss functions

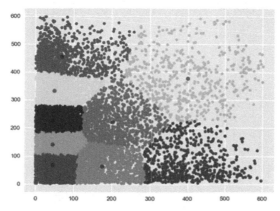

Fig. 2. 20,000 sample clustering results.

[17]. In 2019, H. Rezatofighi proposed generalized intersection over union (GIOU) based on IOU [18]. Assuming that the areas of two anchor-boxes are marked as A and B respectively, and the minimum enclosing area of the two anchor-boxes is C, the expression of GIOU is shown in Eq. (6).

$$GIOU = IOU - \frac{|C/(A \cup B)|}{|C|} \qquad (6)$$

It can be seen from Eq. (6) that GIOU does not consider the distance between the centers of the predicted box and the ground-truth box. Actually, the smaller distance between the centers of the predicted box and the ground-truth box, the more accurate the prediction. Therefore, in 2020, Zheng proposed distance intersection over union (DIOU) based on GIOU [19], as shown in Eq. (7).

$$DIOU = 1 - IOU + \frac{\rho^2\left(b, b^{gt}\right)}{c^2} \qquad (7)$$

where, b and b^{gt} represent the centers of the predicted box and the ground-truth box. ρ represents the Euclidean distance between the two centers. c represents the diagonal distance of the smallest closed area that can contain the ground-truth box and the predicted box.

DIOU takes into account the Euclidean distance between the center of ground-truth box and predicted box. It solves the problem introduced by GIOU, which occurs when one of the boxes is inside of another box. In this situation, GIOU does not change when the distance between these two boxes changes. So the gradient cannot be passed through back to the backend network, and learning and training cannot be carried out.

We train the YOLOv5 network with the Loss function using CIOU and DIOU, and compares the performance of the model with the original GIOU. Figure 3 shows the mAP of the model after being trained with four types of diseases.

In Fig. 3, the model training repeats 8000 times and the IOU threshold is less than 0.7, the mAP of the model by using DIOU is the highest. When the IOU threshold is higher than 0.7, the mAP of the model by using GIOU is the highest. Since the primary

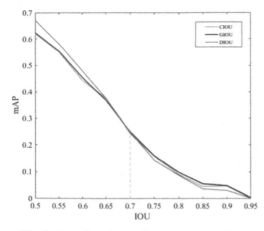

Fig. 3. Loss function performance comparison.

goal of this paper is to achieve the higher call-back rate, and the certain deviation of the proposal box position is allowed, so we set IOU threshold as 0.5, and choose DIOU as the loss function.

5   Experimental Results and Analysis

5.1   Experimental Environment

We use 6 heterogeneous servers to build a 6-node Spark cluster. The cluster consists of 1 master node and 5 slave nodes. The operating system of each node is centos6.8, and

Table 1. Node configurations for the distributed cluster.

Server ID	Server brand	Server model	CPU model	CPU cores	Memory	SSD + HD
master	Dell	PorwerEdge R420	E5–2670 v2 2.5 Ghz	10	40G	279 + 3.6T
ltis001	Lenovo	Systen x3650 m4	E5–2609 v2 2.5 Ghz	4	16G	279 + 1.8T
ltis002	IBM	Systen x3650 m4	E5–2609 v2 2.5 Ghz	4	16G	279 + 1.8T
ltis003	Lenovo	Systen x3650 m4	E5–2609 v2 2.5 Ghz	4	16G	279 + 1.8T
ltis004	Lenovo	Systen x3650 m4	E5–2609 v2 2.5 Ghz	4	16G	279 + 1.8T
ltis005	Dell	PorwerEdge R420	E5–2670 v2 2.5 Ghz	10	40G	279 + 3.6T

the configurations and the functionalities deployment in each node is shown in Table 1 and Table 2. All nodes in the cluster can be used as data nodes.

Table 2. Functionalities deployment on the distributed cluster.

Node name	Master	ltis001	ltis002	ltis003	ltis004	ltis005
HDFS	Name Node Data Node	Data Node	Data Node	Data Node	Data Node	Secondary NameNode DataNode
YARN	Node Manager	Node Manager	Node Manager	Node Manager	Node Manger	Node Manager
OTHER	Security Manager	Resource Manager	SPARK History sever	Node Manager	Zookeeper	Kafka

5.2 Performance Comparison Between the Single Sever and the Cluster

We use 40 LAS files of 1.5 km metro shield tunnel in our experiment, to compare the performance of our system on the cluster and the existing system on the single server. The existing system implements the coordinates projection, OPCS images generation, CSCS graphics generation excepting of locating and extracting the cross sections data which is done manually. The existing system executes on the single server with the configuration parameters as follows: the CPU is i7-8550u, and the frequency is 1.8 GHz, the memory is 16 GB, and the hard disk is a solid-state disk with 256 GB.

As shown in Table 3, We spend 1043 min on processing the data of 1 km on the single server, including 69 min on coordinates projection, 752 min on generation of the CSCS graphics, and 221 min on generation of the OPCS images. Because we locate cross sections in the existing system manually, so we cost more time in the CSCS graphics generation.

We spend 210 min on processing the data of 1 km on the cluster, including 57 min on coordinates projection, 57 min on generation of the CSCS graphics, and 96 min on generation of the OPCS images. and spend 210 min on processing the same data on the cluster. We locate cross sections on the Spark distributed parallel framework and generate CSCS data with 7.5% time of that of the existing system.

Comparing these the results, we can get the acceleration ratio of 4.96 of performance by the cluster to the single server.

5.3 Dataset of Metro Shield Diseases Construction

In order to train the disease detection model, we need to construct the metro shield disease dataset. We propose an approach for generating the disease samples automatically. On step 1, we extract the location information of the diseases from the manually-marked OPCS image file in the AutoCAD software. On step 2, we extract the image areas of the

Table 3. Time cost for data processing for 1 km data on the single server and the cluster.

Time cost	Single server (min)	Cluster (min)
Total time	1043	210
Coordinates projection	69	57
CSCS graphics generation and writing	752	57
OPCS images generation and file writing	221	96

diseases from the image file using the location information we extracted by the step1, and save each image area to the single image file. On step 3, we generate the label file for each disease sample in the format of PASCAL VOC data set. The label files and the disease sample image files are generated in batches to construct the data set of metro shield diseases. The disease sample image file are shown in Fig. 4.

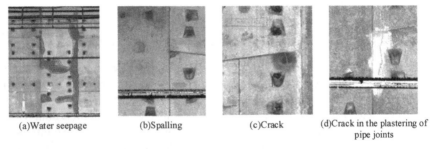

(a)Water seepage   (b)Spalling   (c)Crack   (d)Crack in the plastering of pipe joints

Fig. 4. Examples of disease sample image file for four types of diseases.

Due to the water seepage diseases are more common, and the cracks, spalling and cracks in the plastering of pipe joints disease are rare, we got imbalance samples of four types diseases. However, deep learning is based on a large number of balanced data sets for training, so we need enhance the sample data firstly.

We use optional online enhancement methods CutMix and Mosaic of YOLOv5, as showed in Fig. 5. We obtain a batch of data and then enhance them. These two methods can be achieved by setting *cutmix = 1* and *mosaic = 1* in the yolov5.cfg file.

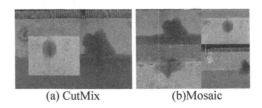

(a) CutMix   (b)Mosaic

Fig. 5. Examples of disease sample image enhancement.

By this approach, we archive a data set of about 5,000 for each disease type. We take 85% of the data set as the training set and 15% as the test set, the specific division of the sample data set is showed in Table 4.

Table 4. Experimental environment configuration.

Disease type	Training sets	Testing sets
Water seepage	4206	782
Spalling	4193	807
Cracking	4228	794
Cracking on joints	4218	772

5.4 Experiment and Analysis on Disease Detection Model

We use the above training set train the YOLOv5 model, the Loss curve and IOU curve obtained in the training process is shown in Fig. 6, the Loss curve goes downward and stabilizes when the training batch reaches 16000, and the IOU curve goes upward and reaches 0.8.

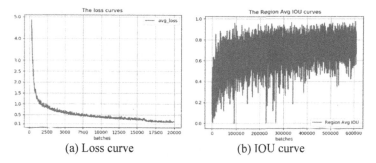

(a) Loss curve   (b) IOU curve

Fig. 6. Loss curve and IOU curve.

Using the above testing set, we test the disease detection model. The prediction boxes of the different types of disease are drawn on the image with different colors, and the confidence score are indicated in the upper left corner of the prediction box, as showed in Fig. 7.

We calculate the IOU of the predicted disease box and the ground-truth box, and analyze the detection accuracy under different IOU thresholds, which are shown in Table 5. We can see that, when the IOU threshold is 0.1, the accuracy of the water seepage and spalling detection box is higher than 90%, and that of the cracks and the cracks on joints is higher than 80%.

| (a)Crack | (b)Water seepage | (c)Crack at the plastering of structural joints | (d)Spalling |

Fig. 7. Disease detection results of the metro shields.

Table 5. Precision and accuracy of detection accuracy rate for four types diseases.

Threshold	Metrics	Water seepage	Spalling	Cracks	Cracks on joints
0.04	Precision	100%	100%	100%	100%
	Accuracy	92.19%	92.71%	82.40%	89.77%
0.1	**Precision**	**100%**	**100%**	**100%**	**99.87%**
	Accuracy	**91.56%**	**92.07%**	**80.01%**	**88.08%**
0.3	Precision	100%	100%	84.26%	91.83%
	Accuracy	88.79%	86.18%	65.92	81.86%
0.5	Precision	92.82%	88.36%	58.36%	75.70%
	Accuracy	77.58%	70.46%	45.22%	68.78%

6   Conclusions

This paper proposes an approach of distributed parallel point cloud data processing and metro shield disease detection based on the LiDAR scanning tunnel point cloud data. The approach is based on HDFS and Spark, and converts the LiDAR point cloud data into orthographic projection space, generating OPCS images and CSCS graphics efficiently. By the experiment using 1.5 km of measured data and a distributed cluster of 6 computing nodes, a speedup ratio of 4.96 compared to single server is achieved.

The approach for detecting shield diseases is based on deep neural networks, aiming at four types of metro shield diseases: cracks, water seepage, spalling and cracks in the plastering of pipe joints. We construct a metro shield disease data set using the enhanced sample data, and optimize the disease detection model based on YOLOv5. The experimental results show that by optimizing the prior anchor box, the average IOU of disease detection results has increased from 48.10% to 60.20%. When the IOU threshold is set to 0.1, the accuracy of the water seepage and spalling detection box is higher than 90%, and that of the cracks and the cracks on joints is higher than 80%.

In summary, our approach can process the LiDAR scanning point cloud data and detect the metro shield diseases efficiently and automatically, and satisfy the accuracy requirements of the current metro operation. For the future work plan, we plan to design a more effective approach to increase the generalization ability of the model to improve the accuracy of cracks disease identification. We also plan to improve the performance of the metro shield disease detection system by optimizing the distributed parallel framework.

References

1. Elaraby, W., Hamdy, M.: Alruwaili: optimization of deep learning model for plant disease detection using particle swarm optimizer. Comput. Mater. Continua **71**(2), 4019–4031 (2022)
2. Xu, P.J., Li, C., Zhang, L.G., Yang, F., Zheng, J.: Underground disease detection based on cloud computing and attention region neural network. J. Artif. Intell. **1**(1), 9–18 (2019)
3. Zaharia, M., Chowdhury, M., Das, T.: Resilient distributed datasets: a fault-tolerant abstraction of in-memory cluster computing. In: Proceeding of NSD, USENIX Association, pp. 15–28 (2012)
4. Ebada, A.I., Elhenawy, I., Jeong, C., Nam, Y., Elbakry, H.: Applying apache spark on streaming big data for health status prediction. Comput. Mater. Continua **70**(2), 3511–3527 (2022)
5. Aydoan, M., Karci, A.: Spam mail detection using naive bayes method with apache spark. In: Proceeding of IDAP, Inonu Univ (2018). https://doi.org/10.1109/IDAP.2018.8620737
6. Semberecki, P., Maciejewski, H.: Distributed classification of text documents on apache spark platform. In: Rutkowski, L., Korytkowski, M., Scherer, R., Tadeusiewicz, R., Zadeh, L.A., Zurada, J.M. (eds.) ICAISC 2016. LNCS (LNAI), vol. 9692, pp. 621–630. Springer, Cham (2016). https://doi.org/10.1007/978-3-319-39378-0_53
7. Lee, H., Song, S.: Distributed moving objects management system for a smart black box. Int. J. Contents **14**(1), 28–33 (2018)
8. Valença, J., Dias-Da-Costa, D., Júlio, E., Araújo, H., Costa, H.: Automatic crack monitoring using photogrammetry and image processing. Measurement **46**(1), 433–441 (2013)
9. Attard, L., Debono, C.J., Valentino, G., Valentino, G., Castro, M.: Vision-based change detection for inspection of tunnel liners. Autom. Constr. **91**, 142–154 (2018)
10. Wu, C.R., Huang, H.W.: Laser scanning inspection method and application for metro tunnel leakage. J. Nat. Disasters **27**(4), 61–68 (2018)
11. Gong, Q., Wang, Y., Yu, Z.: A tunnel crack identification algorithm with convolutional neural networks. In: Proceeding of ITOEC, IEEE, pp. 175–180 (2018)
12. Makantasis, K., Protopapadakis, E., Doulamis, A.: Deep convolutional neural networks for efficient vision based tunnel inspection. In: Proceeding of ICCP, IEEE, pp. 335–342 (2015)
13. Protopapadakis, E., Doulamis, N.: Image based approaches for tunnels' defects recognition via robotic inspectors. In: Proceeding of International Symposium on Visual Computing, pp. 706–716. Springer (2015)
14. Huang, H., Li, Q., Zhang, D.: Deep learning based image recognition for crack and leakage defects of metro shield tunnel. Tunn. Undergr. Space Technol. **77**, 166–176 (2018)
15. Redmon, J., Farhadi, A.: YOLOv3: An Incremental Improvement. arXiv:1804.02767 (2018)
16. Ashraf, A.H., Imran, M., Qahtani, A.M., Alsufyani, A., Almutiry, O.: Weapons detection for security and video surveillance using CNN and yolo-v5s. Comput. Mater. Continua **70**(2), 2761–2775 (2022)
17. Wang, J., Feng, S., Cheng, Y., Al-Nabhan, N.: Survey on the loss function of deep learning in face recognition. J. Inf. Hiding Priv. Protection **3**(1), 29–45 (2021)
18. Rezatofighi, H., Tsoi, N., Gwak, J.Y.: Generalized intersection over union: a metric and a loss for bounding box regression. In: Proceeding of CVP, IEEE, pp. 658–666 (2019)
19. Zheng, Z., Wang, P., Liu, W., Li, J., Ye, R., Ren, D.: Distance-IoU loss: faster and better learning for bounding box regression. In: Proceedings of the AAAI Conference on Artificial Intelligence, vol. 34, no. 07, pp. 12993–13000 (2020)

BlockFAD: A Federated Learning Based I/O Anomaly Detection Method for Blockchain Domain Name System

Haotian Wang[1,2], Dongyi Zheng[1], Fang Liu[2(✉)], and Nong Xiao[1]

[1] National University of Defense Technology, Changsha 410073, Hunan, China
[2] Sun Yat-sen University, Guangzhou, 510275 Guangzhou, China
liufang25@sysu.edu.cn

Abstract. Anomaly detection in storage systems of blockchain domain name service is a challenging problem due to the high dimensional sequential data involved, lack of labels, and privacy data protection issues in distributed storage. To find anomalies in the massively distributed domain name servers, we present BlockFAD, a federated learning based I/O anomaly detection method for blockchain DNS. The distributed model aggregation scheme based on the blockchain ensures the security of the model sharing and storage. And we use the two-channel Transformer encoder to detect anomalies in DNS I/O. Experiments on datasets such as server anomaly detection demonstrate the effectiveness and rationality of the method.

Keywords: Domain name service · Anomaly detection · Blockchain

1 Introduction

DNS (Domain Name System) is one of the most critical infrastructures of the Internet. It connects domain names to IP addresses to each other. DNS is a globally distributed, loosely consistent, scalable, reliable and dynamic database. With the emergence of blockchain technology, its tamper-evident, decentralized, de-trusted, and multi-party maintenance features provide a new design for decentralized domain name system ideas. Blockchain is essentially a distributed database [4], which is a combination of peer-to-peer networks, cryptographic algorithms, consensus mechanisms, and other The application of blockchain technology to DNS system can give the system decentralized, traceable and other characteristics, which can help to resist various attacks.

Blockchain-based distributed storage systems are a crucial and ubiquitous part of blockchain DNS. While failures of components like hard disks, etc. are typically easily detectable, changes in performance require more involved knowledge about the system. For example, systems can suffer from abnormally long response times which leads to a loss in productivity and ultimately impact the client. The performance of a system is gauged by a set of key performance indicators, each of which measures a particular system characteristic. These indicators are made available via a data collection tool and are collected at the system level. Example indicators are Overall Back-end Response Time ms/op, Port Send I/O Rate ops/s, and Read Data Rate MiB/s.

In addition to this, another issue with distributed storage in DNS is the protection of private data. Due to privacy protection, DNS data exists in "data silos" between different countries or enterprises, making it impossible to train more robust anomaly detection models.

This paper proposes BlockFAD, a federated learning based I/O anomaly detection method for blockchain domain name system. The method uses federated learning for privacy-preserving distributed model training. Since blockchain DNS is a decentralized distributed storage, we integrate federal learning with blockchain technology. Meanwhile, we use the two-channel Transformer encoder to detect anomalies in DNS I/O data.

2   Related Work

DNS I/O data is a kind of time-series data, so we investigated the current methods of time series data anomaly detection. Current time series data anomaly detection methods can be broadly classified into two categories: prediction-based methods and reconstruction-based methods.

Prediction-based methods predict the normal values of indicators based on historical data and detect anomalies based on prediction errors. LSTM-NDT [2] proposes an unsupervised and non-parametric thresholding approach to interpret predictions generated by an LSTM network. It builds up an automatic anomaly detection system to monitor the telemetry data sent back by the spacecraft. DAGMM [8] focuses on anomaly detection of multivariate data without temporal dependencies. The input of DAGMM is just single entity observation (with multiple feature dimensions) instead of a temporal sequence. But in complex real-world systems, some indicators may be inherently difficult to predict.

Reconstruction-based methods learn low-dimensional representations, reconstruct "normal patterns" of the data, and detect anomalies based on reconstruction errors. LSTM-VAE [5] integrates an LSTM and a variational self-encoder to fuse the signals and reconstruct the expected distribution. For encoding, it uses an LSTM-based encoder to project the multivariate observations and their time dependence at each time step into the potential space. For decoding, it estimates the expected distribution of the multivariate inputs from the latent representation. OmniAnomaly [6] argues that deterministic methods may be misled by unpredictable instances and proposes a stochastic model for domain name system anomaly detection. It captures the normal pattern behind data by learning robust representations of multivariate time-series with stochastic variable connection and planar normalizing flow. Their model considers patterns with low reconstruction probability as anomalies. However, such methods are poor at modeling temporal correlation.

Additionally, Cheng et al. [1] observe that the autoencoder generalizes so well on the training data that it can reconstruct both the normal data and the anomalous data well, leading to poor anomaly detection performance. Besides, we find that anomaly detection performance is not stable when using reconstruction error as anomaly score, which is unacceptable in the unsupervised scenario. Because there are no labels to guide on selecting a proper model. To mitigate these drawbacks for autoencoder-based anomaly detection methods, we propose an Improved AutoEncoder for unsupervised Anomaly Detection (IAEAD). Li et al. [3] propose a novel unsupervised fast and accurate anomaly detection (FAAD) method which includes three algorithms. First, a method called "information calculation and minimum spanning tree cluster" is adopted to reduce redundant dimensions. Second, to speed up model construction and ensure the detection rate for the sequence over the data stream, we propose a method called "random sampling and subsequence partitioning based on the index probabilistic suffix tree." Last, the method called "anomaly buffer based on model dynamic adjustment" dramatically reduces the effects of concept drift in the data stream.

3   Proposed Approach

3.1   Overview

As shown in the Fig. 1, we propose a blockchain-based federated anomaly detection framework to solve the server single-point-of-failure problem of federated learning by incorporating the blockchain mechanism into federated learning. As shown in the figure, the steps of DNS I/O data anomaly detection are as follows:

1. The task publisher creates the Genesis block (first block) based on the training task, which contains: model initialization parameters, number of training rounds and random number seeds (for consensus phase election of the leader). Broadcast to all nodes via a secure link.
2. The node trains the anomaly detection model on the local DNS I/O data and iterates n times before the resulting local gradient is updated.
3. A leader is elected from the nodes based on random number seeds and is responsible for computing the global gradient and generating new blocks.
4. After the new block is verified for legitimacy, the ledger is synchronized across the network via broadcast.
5. After the node updates the ledger, the global gradient is obtained from it to update the local model. And start the next round of training from step 2 until the model converges or reaches the maximum number of training rounds.

3.2   Problem Formulation

Assume that $x^{(t)} \in R^M$ denotes the DNS I/O data at time step t, where M is the number of sensors or any data measurement nodes within the same entity, i.e. the number of features or variables. In the prediction-based approach, we predict the value of the time series data at time step t base on the historical data $\mathcal{X}^{(t)} = \{\mathbf{x}^{(t-n)}, \cdots, \mathbf{x}^{(t-1)}\}$ of n time steps. In the reconstruction-based

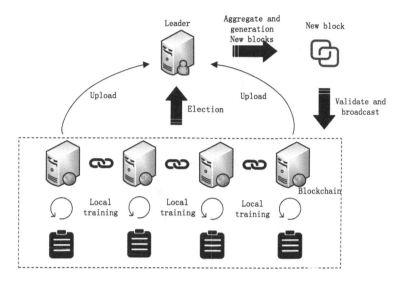

Fig. 1. The architecture of BlockFAD

approach, we reconstruction the input data $\mathbf{x} = \left\{ \mathbf{x}^{(t-n)}, \cdots, \mathbf{x}^{(t-1)} \right\}$. The sum of the prediction error and the reconstruction error is used as the anomaly score, and the points exceeding the threshold value are considered anomalies according to the magnitude of the threshold value.

3.3 Data Preprocessing

For DNS I/O data, the dimensionality of different series is completely different, and the difference in values affects the subsequent prediction and threshold selection. Therefore, we preprocess the data using normalization methods for the data:

$$\widetilde{x} = \frac{x - \min\left(X_{\text{train}}\right)}{\max\left(X_{\text{train}}\right) - \min\left(X_{\text{train}}\right)} \tag{1}$$

where $\max\left(X_{\text{train}}\right)$ and $\min\left(X_{\text{train}}\right)$ are the maximum value and the minimum value of the training set respectively.

3.4 Two-channel Transformer Encoder

For DNS I/O data, learning temporal and variable features is key to the study. Unlike other work using Transformer for time series classification and prediction, we use a two-channel encoder for extension, where two channels of the encoder capture the correlation between time and variables separately. The input data are processed by simply transposing the two input data time and variable dimensions to each other to satisfy the input requirements.

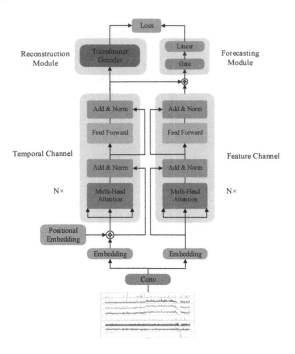

Fig. 2. Anomaly Detection Model

Temporal Encoder. As in the original Transformer encoder architecture, the time steps are encoded by computing paired attention weights over all time steps, using a self-attentive mechanism to focus on each point of the time step. In the multi-headed self-attention layer, the scaled dot product attention forms an attention matrix over all time steps. Fully connected feedforward network layers are stacked on top of each multi-headed attention layer for enhanced feature extraction. The residuals passed between two sub-layers are connected as information and gradient flow channels and then layer normalization is performed.

Variable Encoder. The variable encoder calculates the attention weights between all variables. There is no relative or absolute correlation between the positions of the variables in the DNS I/O data; therefore, we only add position encoding to the time encoder. Correlations between variables are captured at each time step using the same self-attentive layer. By transposing the variables and time dimensions of the input time series, they can be output to the two encoders separately.

3.5   Joint Optimization

In the prediction module, we use a gating mechanism to fuse the feature information from the two encoders. First, the two feature information T and V are connected and input to the linear layer to obtain d, and then the Softmax function calculates the two weights g_1 and g_2. The final input to the prediction and reconstruction modules is the connected values of the time and variable feature vectors with weights y.

$$
\begin{aligned}
d &= \mathbf{W} \cdot \text{Concat}(T, V) + b \\
g_1, g_2 &= \text{Softmax}(d) \\
y &= \text{Concat}\,(T \cdot g_1, V \cdot g_2)
\end{aligned}
\tag{2}
$$

As mentioned above, the prediction and reconstruction methods each have different advantages and they complement each other. Our model includes a prediction-based module to predict the value of the next time step and a reconstruction-based module for capturing the data distribution of the entire time series.

In the reconstruction module, as shown in the Fig. 3, the input of the Transformer decoder includes the output from the encoder and the output from the embedding layer. Since these two tensors have different dimensions after feature fusion, feature fusion cannot be performed in the reconstruction module, and we only use the feature tensor of the Transformer encoder in the temporal dimension as the input of the decoder. Meanwhile, the original Transformer decoder is a self-attentive mechanism with masking, which aims to mask the effect of posterior data on anterior data in sequence data prediction and natural language translation tasks. In contrast, our reconstruction module integrates the temporal correlation of all fields in the temporal data with the aim of reconstructing the original input information to the maximum extent, so no masking mechanism is added to the decoder.

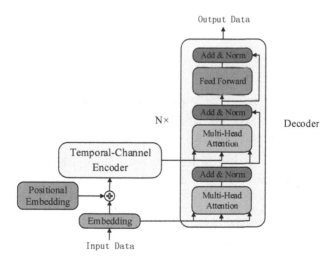

Fig. 3. Reconstruction Module

During the training process, the parameters of both models are updated simultaneously. The loss function is defined as the sum of the two optimization objectives, $Loss = Loss_{for} + Loss_{rec}$, where $Loss_{for}$ and $Loss_{rec}$ represent the loss functions of the prediction-based and reconstruction-based models, respectively.

Prediction Module. A prediction-based model is used to predict the value of the next time step. We use a fully connected network as the prediction module and the loss function uses the Root Mean Square Error:

$$Loss_{for} = \sqrt{\sum_{i=1}^{k} \left(x_i^{(t)} - \hat{x}_i^{(t)} \right)^2} \tag{3}$$

where $x^{(t)}$ denotes the true value at t-th time step, $x_i^{(t)}$ denotes the i-th variable value, k denotes number of variables, $\hat{x}_i^{(t)}$ denotes the predicted value of the prediction module for t-th time step.

Reconstruction Module. Reconstruction-based models are used to reconstruct the input data $\mathcal{X}^{(t)} = \left\{ \mathbf{x}^{(t-n)}, \cdots, \mathbf{x}^{(t-1)} \right\}$. We use the Transformer decoder as the reconstruction module, and the output is $\hat{\mathcal{X}}^{(t)} = \left\{ \hat{x}^{(t-n)}, \cdots, \hat{x}^{(t-1)} \right\}$. The loss function is expressed in the second paradigm as $\| \mathcal{X}^{(t)} - \hat{\mathcal{X}}^{(t)} \|_2$. Again using the Root Mean Square Error, the formula is as follows:

$$Loss_{rec} = \sqrt{\sum_{t=t-n}^{t-1} \sum_{i=1}^{k} \left(x_i^{(t)} - \hat{x}_i^{(t)} \right)^2} \tag{4}$$

4   Experiment

4.1   Dataset

To demonstrate the effectiveness of BlockFAD, we conducted experiments on three datasets, namely SMD, SMAP and MSL, where SMD is the server monitoring data and SMAP and MSL are spacecraft detection data.

1. SMD is a dataset published in KDD19 by Tsinghua University. SMD contains monitoring data of servers of a large Internet company, such as disk utilization, CPU utilization, etc. The dataset has a total of 5 weeks of data, divided into two subsets of equal size: the first half is the training set and the second half is the test set. Anomalies in the SMD test set have been flagged by domain experts based on anomalous event reports.
2. SMAP and MSL are the data collected by NASA's from the Curiosity Mars rover and Mars Science Laboratory. Each dataset has a training subset and a test subset, and anomalies in both test subsets are flagged.

Table 1. The details of datasets

Dataset	Number of entities	Dimensions	Training sets	Test sets	Anomaly rate(%)
SMAP	55	25	135183	427617	13.13
MSL	27	55	58317	73729	10.72
SMD	28	38	708405	708420	4.16

4.2 Evaluation Metrics

We evaluate the performance of BlockFAD and the baseline model using precision, recall, and F1 score (denoted F1):

$$\text{Precision} = \frac{\text{TP}}{\text{TP} + \text{FP}} \tag{5}$$

$$\text{Recall} = \frac{\text{TP}}{\text{TP} + \text{FN}} \tag{6}$$

$$\text{F1} = \frac{\text{Precision} \times \text{Recall}}{\text{Precision} + \text{Recall}} \tag{7}$$

where TP represents positive samples predicted by the model (True Positive), FP represents negative samples predicted by the model (False Positive), and FN represents negative samples predicted by the model (False Negative). The precision rate refers to the percentage of positive samples among all the samples predicted by the model, and the higher the precision rate represents the inference performance of the model, the better the model performance. The higher the recall, the higher the sensitivity of the model.

In reality, temporal sequence anomalies usually occur consecutively, forming consecutive anomaly segments. If the anomaly detection of the sequence by the model occurs within any subset of the anomaly-tagged segments, it is acceptable for the anomaly detection in the present. Therefore, we use the point adjustment [7] method to calculate the anomaly detection performance, i.e., for a segment of continuous anomalous timing data, if the model detects an anomaly for the value of any of its points, then the entire anomaly segment is considered to be correctly detected and all timing points in that anomaly segment are detected as anomalous.

4.3 Baseline

To demonstrate the overall performance of BlockFAD, we compared it with four unsupervised methods for domain name system anomaly detection.

1. LSTM-NDT [2] The model uses an LSTM network for the prediction of time-series data while using a nonparametric approach to determine dynamic thresholds.

2. DAGMM [8] The model combines the Estimation network and Gaussian Mixture Model (GMM) to jointly optimize the downscaling and density estimation, solving the problem of ignoring key information when downscaling multidimensional data.
3. LSTM-VAE [5] The model implements a combination of LSTM and VAE by replacing the feedforward network in Variational Auto-Encoder (VAE) with LSTM for anomaly detection by reconstruction-based methods.
4. OmniAnomaly [6] The model combines GRU and variational autoencoder, considering both time dependence and stochasticity, to learn potential representations of time-series data in normal mode for their reconstruction.

4.4 Results and Analysis

As shown in Table 2, BlockFAD outperforms the other algorithms on all three datasets.

Table 2. Performance comparison

Dataset	SMAP			MSL			SMD		
Metrics	P	R	F1	P	R	F1	P	R	F1
LSTM-NDT	0.8965	0.8846	0.8905	0.5934	0.5374	0.5640	0.5684	0.6438	0.6037
DAGMM	0.5845	0.9058	0.7105	0.5412	0.9934	0.7007	0.5951	0.8782	0.7094
LSTM-VAE	0.8551	0.6366	0.7298	0.5257	0.9546	0.6780	0.7922	0.7075	0.7842
OmniAnomaly	0.7416	0.9776	0.8434	0.8867	0.9117	0.8989	0.8334	0.9449	0.8857
BlockFAD	0.9114	0.9725	**0.9410**	0.9498	0.9542	**0.9520**	0.9055	0.9125	**0.9019**

LSTM-NDT is a prediction-based method, however, some time-series data are inherently unpredictable, and at the same time, uncontrollable factors can lead to inaccurate data prediction. In contrast, the BlockFAD algorithm combines the advantages of both prediction and reconstruction methods and has better generalization ability even when the data is unpredictable.

DAGMM algorithm is based on the reconstruction of multivariate data values at one moment in time and ignores the time correlation of the time series data itself. In contrast, our model considers both temporal correlation and correlation between variables, so it outperforms DAGMM.

LSTM-VAE uses LSTM and VAE to model the temporal correlation of the data without considering the dependence between variables, so the performance is worse than BlockFAD.

OmniAnomaly treats each time variable as a random variable for learning reconstruction, and this algorithm has better performance on all three datasets. However, its drawback is also that it does not consider the correlation between multiple variables.

Figure 4 shows the histogram of F1 scores of the five methods on the three datasets, and it can be seen that our method exhibits the highest F1 scores on all datasets. Compared with the other four methods, the mean F1 scores of the BlockFAD model on the three data sets are 22.3%,32.8%,25.6%,9.4% higher, respectively.

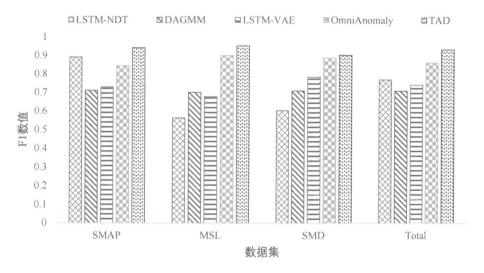

Fig. 4. F1 Score Comparison

4.5 Ablation Experiments

As shown in Table 3, we demonstrate the necessity of each component in the BlockFAD model by ablation experiments, and the components considered for removal separately include temporal encoder, variable encoder, Transformer decoder, and linear output layer.

1. w/o temporal: This part removes the input of the Transformer temporal encoder to the prediction module, leaving only the output of the variable encoder in the feature fusion part of the model. However, the input to the reconstruction module, the Transformer decoder part of our design, still comes from the temporal encoder, and this part cannot be removed, so the model still has the ability to model temporal context. The data shows that this part does not have a significant impact on the model.

2. w/o feature: This section removes the Transformer variable encoder input to the prediction module, leaving only the output of the temporal encoder in the feature fusion section of the model. It can be seen that the performance of the model on the SMAP and SMD datasets shows a decline, while the performance on MSL does not fluctuate much, indicating that there is less correlation between the variables in the MSL dataset.

3. w/o forecast: The prediction module is removed from this part, making the model an anomaly detection method based on temporal correlation reconstruction. It can be seen that the reconstruction module does not have the

ability to model variable correlation, while the model does not have the output of the prediction module, making the performance of this part the worst.

4. w/o recons: The reconstruction module is removed from this part and the output of the model is based on the prediction method after the fusion of temporal and variable features. It can be seen that the performance of this part degrades on all three datasets, indicating that it is necessary for us to design the reconstruction module as an auxiliary anomaly detection tool.

Table 3. Results of ablation experiments

Dataset	SMAP			MSL			SMD		
Metrics	P	R	F1	P	R	F1	P	R	F1
w/o temporal	0.9490	0.8984	0.9230	0.9193	0.9348	0.9270	0.8748	0.9395	0.8951
w/o feature	0.9425	0.8601	0.8994	0.9537	0.9312	0.9423	0.8806	0.9071	0.8860
w/o forcast	0.7092	0.9564	0.8144	0.8391	0.9443	0.8886	0.8578	0.8814	0.8594
w/o recons	0.9623	0.7176	0.8222	0.9240	0.9542	0.9389	0.8815	0.8889	0.8811
BlockFAD	0.9114	0.9725	**0.9410**	0.9498	0.9542	**0.9520**	0.9055	0.9125	**0.9019**

5   Conclusion

This work proposed a federated anomaly detection method for blockchain DNS. The proposed scheme achieved the final higher F1 model aggregation and sharing through multi-party aggregation training. To improve the quality of the model, this work proposed a two-channel Transformer encoder model to detect anomalies in DNS I/O data.

Our experiments on the ablation of the four parts of the BlockFAD model show that BlockFAD integrates temporal and variable correlations, and aids the temporal context reconstruction method based on the prediction method, which enables the model to adapt to the different characteristics of different temporal data sets, and the absence of any of the modules leads to the degradation of the anomaly detection performance, indicating the necessity of the existence of each part of the BlockFAD method and the validity.

Funding Information. This work is supported by The National Key Research and Development Program of China (2019YFB1804502)

References

1. Cheng, Z., Wang, S., Zhang, P., Wang, S., Liu, X., Zhu, E.: Improved autoencoder for unsupervised anomaly detection. Int. J. Intell. Syst. **36**(12), 7103–7125 (2021). https://doi.org/10.1002/int.22582

2. Hundman, K., Constantinou, V., Laporte, C., Colwell, I., Soderstrom, T.: Detecting spacecraft anomalies using LSTMS and nonparametric dynamic thresholding. In: Proceedings of the 24th ACM SIGKDD International Conference on Knowledge Discovery & Data Mining, pp. 387–395 (2018)
3. Li, B., Wang, Y., Yang, D., Li, Y., Ma, X.: FAAD: an unsupervised fast and accurate anomaly detection method for a multi-dimensional sequence over data stream. Front. Inf. Technol. Electron. Eng. **20**(3), 388–404 (2019). https://doi.org/10.1631/FITEE.1800038
4. Li, X., Zheng, Z., Dai, H.N.: When services computing meets blockchain: challenges and opportunities. J. Parallel Distrib. Comput. **150**, 1–14 (2021)
5. Park, D., Hoshi, Y., Kemp, C.C.: A multimodal anomaly detector for robot-assisted feeding using an LSTM-based variational autoencoder. IEEE Robot. Autom. Lett. **3**(3), 1544–1551 (2018)
6. Su, Y., Zhao, Y., Niu, C., Liu, R., Sun, W., Pei, D.: Robust anomaly detection for multivariate time series through stochastic recurrent neural network. In: Proceedings of the 25th ACM SIGKDD International Conference on Knowledge Discovery & Data Mining, pp. 2828–2837 (2019)
7. Xu, H., et al.: Unsupervised anomaly detection via variational auto-encoder for seasonal KPIS in web applications. In: Proceedings of the 2018 World Wide Web Conference, pp. 187–196 (2018)
8. Zong, B., et al.: Deep autoencoding gaussian mixture model for unsupervised anomaly detection. In: International Conference on Learning Representations (2018)

Density and Viscosity Prediction of Mixtures Based on Multitasking and Attentional Mechanism

Yabin Xu[1(✉)], Lulu Cui[2], and Xiaowei Xu[3]

[1] Beijing Advanced Innovation Center for Materials Genome Engineering, Beijing Information Science and Technology University, Beijing 100101, China
xyb@bistu.edu.cn
[2] School of Computer, Beijing Information Science and Technology University, Beijing 100101, China
[3] Department of Information Science, University of Arkansas at Little Rock, Little Rock, USA

Abstract. The density and viscosity data of the mixture is an important basis for chemical calculation and design. However, there are some problems in obtaining these data, such as complexity, time consuming, low precision, and no-universality. To solve these problems, a prediction model based on multitasking and attention mechanism with the idea of materials genome engineering is proposed. With it, the density and viscosity of the mixture at different components and different experimental environments can be quickly and accurately predicted based on the existing experimental data. The predictive model introduces a Multi-task Learning (MTL) framework on the basis of the Deep fully connected Neural Network (DNN) to fully consider the associated features, and trains the density and viscosity of the mixture in parallel. In addition, an attention mechanism is introduced for each task, so that each task can focus on the most relevant features to itself. In the J. Chem. Eng. Data magazine of the American Chemical Society, with "organic mixture, density, viscosity" as the key word, 10158 experimental data of mixture density and viscosity are collected in 69 documents, including 336 mixture density systems and 331 mixture viscosity systems. The effectiveness of the model on this data set is verified and compared with other methods. Contrast experiment results show that, the model can effectively improve the prediction accuracy and reduce the prediction time at the same time.

Keywords: Mixture density · Mixture viscosity · Materials genome engineering · Multi-task learning · Attention mechanism

1 Introduction

The physical properties of mixtures contain many necessary information for engineering design, which is an important basis for chemical design. In general, the most reliable way to obtain density and viscosity data of mixtures is by experimental measurements. However, the density and viscosity of the mixture are constantly changing with the change of temperature and pressure, so the experimental measurement is subject to many restrictions such as manpower, material resources, reagent sources and experimental conditions. Therefore, the amount of data obtained by experimental measurement is often limited, which is difficult to meet the actual demand.

At present, many mathematical models, such as strict equations, empirical equations and mixing rules have been proposed to estimate the density and viscosity data of mixtures. However, due to the complexity and diversity of mixtures in chemical production, these estimation methods are very complicated and time-consuming, and the accuracy of estimation is also low. In addition, these methods are not universal for all mixtures of systems, so different estimation methods need to be designed for different mixtures of systems, which has great limitations.

Material genetic engineering is a disruptive frontier technology emerging in the international material field in recent years. Its basic idea is to integrate high-throughput material computing, high-throughput experiment and material big data technology, accelerate the development process of materials from discovery, manufacturing to application through collaborative innovation, and reduce costs [1]. Data + artificial intelligence is the core of material genetic engineering. Through the application of big data and artificial intelligence technology, the association between structure, performance and process of new materials and process optimization can be realized to improve the performance of materials.

Based on the concept and method of material genetic engineering, a prediction model of density and viscosity of mixtures based on multi-task and attention mechanism without relying on any specific expression is proposed. It can quickly and accurately predict the density and viscosity of arbitrary mixtures under arbitrary experimental conditions. It is of great theoretical significance and application value to promote chemical calculation, engineering application, industrial process and process design of new products.

The main contributions of this paper are as follows:

(1) A prediction model of mixture density and viscosity based on multi-task learning is proposed. By training the density and viscosity of mixture in parallel, the model learns the common features applicable to different tasks, which improves the prediction accuracy of the model and reduces the time required for training the two models.

(2) in order to solve the same characteristic parameters of mixture density and viscosity influence degree of different problems, and in the model for each task is introduced into a particular attention mechanism, through the calculation of attention weighting of different characteristics, to achieve the purpose of highlight main characteristics for each task, and thus improve the accuracy of model prediction.

(3) In view of the problem that the mixture of different systems should have different prediction models, the components of the mixture of different systems are taken as the input characteristics of the model, and the content of the components that do not contain this component is set to 0, so as to distinguish different mixtures and improve the universality of the model for the mixture of different systems.

2   Related Work

Machine learning methods have been widely used in the past two decades to predict physical properties in various areas of chemical engineering. Mostafa et al. [2] constructed a three-layer back-propagation artificial neural network to predict the density of binary mixtures. In literature [3–5], a three-layer artificial neural network was constructed to predict the viscosity of mixtures, and the prediction results were compared with experience-based models and equations. Experimental results showed that the prediction results of artificial neural network were more consistent with experimental measurement results. Julien Molina et al. [6] predicted the viscosity of unsaturated resin by establishing a three-layer artificial neural network, and found the descriptors that could not improve the performance of the neural network by adding descriptors and calculating NSE in sequence during the training of the neural network, so as to reduce the number of descriptors and prevent over-fitting. Cao et al. [7] trained two density and viscosity neural network models composed of components and temperature of ternary mixtures respectively based on the experimental data of binary systems by using back propagation algorithm. Diego et al. [8] used feedforward neural network and Support Vector Regression (SVR) to make different combinations between the two selected descriptors MD and FGCD respectively to predict density and viscosity at different temperatures. Liu et al. [9] proposed a general machine learning framework based on support vector regression to predict the thermodynamic properties of pure fluids and their mixtures, and compared the prediction results of the model on the training set and test set with three equations of state (PR, SRK, DMW). Experimental results show that the machine learning method has better fitting performance.

In conclusion, with the traditional empirical equation or compared model methods, machine learning methods in the field of mixture density and viscosity prediction obtained better results, which fully demonstrated in the case of not dependent on any specific expression, using data driven method to forecast the density and viscosity of mixture is feasible. However, all the above methods adopt traditional single-task machine learning methods such as support vector machine and artificial neural network, which excessively rely on human experience to select characteristic parameters and ignore the rich correlation information between the two related tasks. For the two related tasks of density and viscosity of mixture, if the two models are trained separately by single task learning, not only the training time is increased, but also the rich correlation information between the two tasks is ignored.

Cheng Jin et al. [10] constructed a prediction model of converter terminal temperature based on multi-task neural network according to BPNN structure, and optimized the learning ability of the model by using two sub-tasks of total blown oxygen and ore replenishment, and assisted in optimizing the terminal temperature task at the same time. Compared with the traditional neural network, this model can effectively improve the prediction accuracy of terminal temperature, and also shows strong generalization ability. Su Yun et al. [11] proposed a multi-task learning method based on low-rank representation to predict load at multiple locations. This method can extract the shared low-dimensional representation of load prediction models at different locations during the learning process, so as to mine the association relationship between multiple tasks and effectively improve the accuracy of load prediction. Zheng Jinghua et al. [12] proposed a big five personality prediction model based on multi-task learning, which regarded the prediction of five personality dimensions as five types of tasks, and made full use of the potential correlation information between tasks through parallel learning of these five types of tasks to improve the prediction effect of the model. Shen Xiaohai et al.

[13] designed a multi-task deep network model based on the Faster RCNN network, introduced three different tasks into the detection framework, and optimized each task by taking advantage of the information sharing between tasks.

In conclusion, the multi-task-based learning method has a better prediction effect than the traditional single-task learning method. Multi-task learning model improves the prediction effect of the model by sharing the potential association information between tasks to optimize the model for each task. In recent years, attention mechanism has been applied in various fields to improve the prediction effect of models through automatic learning and adjusting the attention of input features.

Zhang Quangui et al. [14] proposed a deep music recommendation algorithm based on attention mechanism on the basis of DNN algorithm of deep learning, which allocates different weights of music preferences to users through the attention mechanism to improve the accuracy of the recommendation algorithm. Xie Enning et al. [15] proposed a deep collaborative filtering model based on attention mechanism, which effectively extracted potential features from implicit feedback data by combining deep neural network and attention mechanism, so as to improve the recommendation performance of the model. Shen Dongdong et al. [16] introduced attention mechanism into the model to solve the problem that traditional item-based collaborative.

Above, by assigning weight coefficients to different features, the model can pay more attention to the extraction of important features in the hidden layer and improve the prediction effect of the model.

In order to solve the shortcomings of existing methods in predicting mixture density and viscosity, a multi-task learning framework and attention mechanism were introduced to improve the quality of hidden layer feature extraction based on deep fully connected neural network (DNN), so as to improve the prediction accuracy of the model.

3 Model Construction

3.1 Model Architecture

The existing prediction methods of mixture density and viscosity are difficult to fully mine the implied information between data. And, the single-task learning method cannot share the potential correlation information between the two related tasks of mixture density and viscosity [17]. Based on the idea and method of materials genetic engineering, a prediction model of mixture density and viscosity based on multi-task and attention mechanism is proposed in this paper. Its overall architecture is shown in Fig. 1. There is input layer, parameter sharing layer, attention mechanism layer and multi-task layer in it.

3.2 Parameter Sharing Layer

In the prediction of density and viscosity of mixture, the characteristic matrix of density and viscosity of mixture is composed of each component of mixture, temperature and pressure. Then, the feature matrices of the two tasks are combined and input into the deep neural network, so that the two tasks share the parameters of the deep neural network, and the feature vector $H = [h_1, h_2, ..., h_n]$ of the shared hidden layer is obtained.

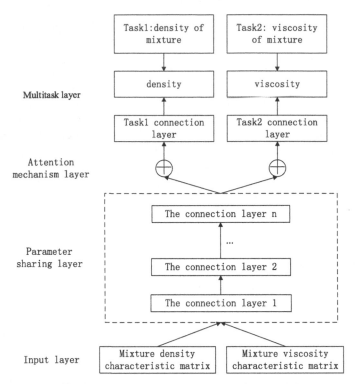

Fig. 1. Overall architecture diagram of the model.

3.3 Attention Mechanism Layer

The attention mechanism draws on the processing mode of human vision to focus attention on key areas [18]. The essence of this mechanism is to select the information that plays a key role in the task from many kinds of information, and improve the accuracy of the model while reducing the complexity of the task. Considering the different effects of the same characteristic parameters on the density and viscosity of the mixture, an attention mechanism module was introduced for each task in the model, so as to find the most critical features for each task. In this model, the shared hidden layer feature vector H obtained by deep neural network is used as the input of the respective attentional mechanism module of the two tasks, and the new hidden layer feature vector $a_1 = [a_{1\_1}, a_{1\_2} \ldots a_{1\_n}]$, $a_2 = [a_{2\_1}, a_{2\_2} \ldots a_{2\_n}]$ of the two tasks are obtained.

3.4 Multitask Layer

Multi-task Learning is an inductive transfer mechanism. The main idea is to make full use of domain-specific information hidden in the training signals of multiple related tasks to promote the model to learn common features applicable to different tasks in the process of parallel training, so as to improve the prediction accuracy of the model.

In this model, we treat the density and viscosity of the mixture as two different tasks (task1: mixture density, task2: mixture viscosity). Then input the new hidden layer vectors a_1 and a_2 of the two tasks obtained from the attention mechanism layer into the fully connected layer of the two tasks respectively. Through the calculation of activation function sigmoid of the two tasks, the output results Y_1 and Y_2 of the two tasks are obtained, as shown in Eq. (1) and (2):

$$y_1 = W_{y1}a_1 + b_1 \tag{1}$$

$$y_2 = W_{y2}a_2 + b_2 \tag{2}$$

Where, W_{y1} and W_{y2} are the weight matrices of task1 and task2 respectively, b_1 and b_2 are the bias items of task1 and task2 respectively.

During model training, the model is trained by jointly optimizing the loss values of the two tasks. The total loss function of the model is defined as formula (3): L_{loss} is minimized to train the network, Adam optimizer is selected to optimize the loss function, and λ is used to weigh the relative importance between the two tasks.

$$L_{loss} = \lambda \cdot L_{loss\_task_1} + (1 - \lambda) \cdot L_{loss\_task_2} \tag{3}$$

Where, $L_{loss\_task_1}$ represents the loss function of task1, which is calculated with Eq. (10). $L_{loss\_task_2}$ represents the loss function of task2, calculated with Eq. (4):

$$L_{loss\_task_1} = \frac{1}{n} \sum_{i=1}^{n} \left| y1i - y1i^p \right| \tag{4}$$

$$L_{loss\_task_2} = \frac{1}{n} \sum_{i=1}^{n} \left| y2i - y2i^p \right| \tag{5}$$

Where, $y1i$ and $y2i$ represent the real values of task1 and task2 respectively, $y1i^p$ and $y2i^p$ represent the model predicted values of task1 and task2 respectively.

4   Experiments and Analysis

4.1   Experimental Data and Experimental Environment

Experimental Data and the Pretreatment. First of all, the experimental data of 69 articles were collected in j. Chem. Eng. Data of American Chemical Society with "Organic mixture, Density, viscosity" as the key words. After cleaning, 10,158 pieces of density and viscosity Data were obtained respectively. There were 336 mixture density systems and 331 mixture viscosity systems [19].

Then, the collected data are preprocessed. Firstly, the collected density and viscosity data of all the mixtures were statistically analyzed, and it was found that there were 156 different components. These components were then combined with experimental conditions (temperature and pressure) to form a 158-dimensional data feature set. In addition, because of the same material under the same experimental conditions do not necessarily contain the mixture density and viscosity data at the same time, namely the mixture density and viscosity data is not one-to-one, so the data input for the mixture density and viscosity respectively introduces a characteristic matrix, forming two 158 d of the characteristic matrix, and the null value in each of the data for zero padding operation; Finally, in order to eliminate the dimensional influence among indicators, the data are normalized to the maximum value and all data are mapped to 0 and 1, as shown in Eq. (6):

$$X_{scale} = \frac{X - X_{min}}{X_{max} - X_{min}} \tag{6}$$

where, X_{scale} is the normalized value, X is the original value, X_{max} and X_{min} are the maximum and minimum value of the original data set respectively.

Finally, 10158 data of 158-dimensional mixture density and viscosity obtained after pretreatment were randomly divided into training set and test set according to the ratio of 8:2.

Experimental Environment. The CPU model of this experiment is Intel(R) Core(TM) I7-7700HQ CPU @ 2.80 GHz, and the memory size is 8 GB.

4.2 Evaluation Indicators

The mean absolute error MAE, root mean square error MSE, relative error MRE and determination coefficient R2 were selected as the evaluation indexes of this experiment, as shown in Eqs. (7), (8), (9) and (10). The smaller MAE, MSE and MRE values are, the better the prediction effect of the model is. R2 is used to measure how close the data is to the regression line. The closer the value is to 1, the better the prediction effect of the model is.

$$MAE = \frac{1}{n} \sum_{i=1}^{n} \left| yi - yi^p \right| \tag{7}$$

$$MSE = \frac{1}{n} \sum_{i=1}^{n} \left(yi - yi^p \right)^2 \tag{8}$$

$$MRE = \frac{1}{n} \sum_{i=1}^{n} \frac{\left| yi - yi^p \right|}{yi} \tag{9}$$

$$R^2 = 1 - \frac{\sum_{i=1}^{n} (yi - yi^p)^2}{\sum_{i=1}^{n} (yi - \bar{y})^2} \tag{10}$$

Where, n represents the total number of samples, yi represents the true value, and yi^p represents the predicted value of the model.

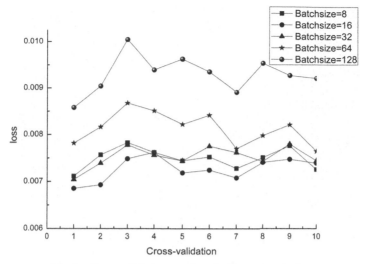

Fig. 2. Cross-validation results of different batch sizes.

4.3 Model Parameter Selection

In order to select the optimal batch size (batch size), 5 batch sizes (8, 16, 32, 64 and 128) were selected for 10-fold cross-validation respectively. In the same experimental environment, changes in the loss values of the model under different batch sizes were observed, and the experimental results are shown in Fig. 2.

As can be seen from Fig. 2, when batch size is 16, the model has the minimum loss value. Therefore, we choose batch size of this model as 16.

As mentioned in [20, 21], the loss function of this model is jointly determined by the respective loss functions of the two tasks, and λ is used to weigh the relative importance of the two tasks. Here, we determine the value of λ through experiments, and the results of the weight coefficient selection experiment are shown in Fig. 3:

As can be seen from Fig. 3, when the weight coefficients of task1 and task2 are 0.5 respectively, the overall loss of the two tasks is the smallest. Therefore, we choose the value of λ as 0.5, and the experiment also shows that the density and viscosity of the mixture are of the same importance.

In addition, the number of hidden layers, number of neurons and training rounds are selected through cross validation. The final parameter Settings are shown in Table 1.

We trained the model on the basis of the above parameters, and compared the predicted value of the model with the real value on the test set to evaluate the prediction effect of the model on the density and viscosity of the mixture. Due to the large number of test sets, it is difficult to clearly show the model predicted values and real values in all test sets by means of graphs. Thus, we randomly select a part of continuous test sample numbers from the test set (the test sample numbers selected here are 500–549) for display. The results are shown in Fig. 4 and Fig. 5.

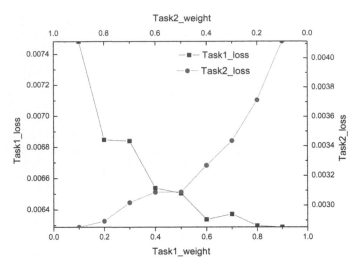

Fig. 3. Comparison of predicted and real values of mixture density in part of the test sample.

Table 1. Model parameter.

Task	Parameter
Parameter shared part	Dense (128)
	Dense (64)
task 1: Density	Attention_1
	Dense (32)
	Dropout (0.2)
	Dense(1)
task 2: Viscosity	Attention_2
	Dense (32)
	Dropout (0.1)
	Dense(1)
Training rounds (epoch)	150

It can be seen from Fig. 4 and Fig. 5 that the model can well fit the predicted values of mixture density and viscosity in randomly selected test samples with the real values. In addition, in order to show the prediction effect of the proposed model on all test sets, the evaluation indicators of the proposed model on all test sets are presented in the form of tables, as shown in Table 2.

As can be seen from Table 2, the model proposed in this paper has a good prediction effect on the density and viscosity of mixtures in all indicators.

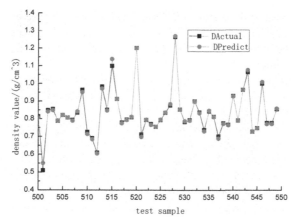

Fig. 4. Comparison of predicted and real values of mixture density in part of the test sample.

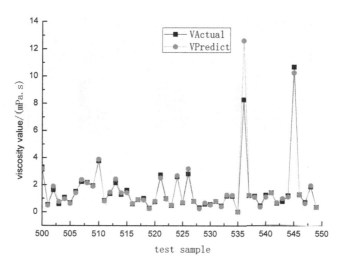

Fig. 5. Comparison of predicted and real values of mixture viscosity in some test samples.

Table 2. Evaluation index values of this model on all test sets

	MAE	MSE	MRE	R^2
task1: Density of mixture	0.00583	0.00015	0.00701	0.99164
task2: Viscosity of mixture	0.15414	0.28216	0.09427	0.97846

4.4 Comparative Experiment

The comparison results of the model proposed in this paper (A-DNN + MTL) with the support vector regression model, deep fully connected neural network (DNN) model and DNN fusion multi-task learning (DNN + MTL) model in reference [8] on various indicators are shown in Fig. 6 and Fig. 7. In order to display the changing trend of each indicator more clearly in the figure, the R2 index value of the mixture density in Fig. 6 is reduced by 100 times.

It can be seen from Fig. 6 and Fig. 7 that, the model proposed in this paper has the optimal performance in the two tasks of mixture density and viscosity.

The reasons are as follows:

Firstly, in the two tasks of mixture density and viscosity, the interaction between components can not be simply described by mathematical model. In this model, a deep fully connected neural network is used as the mapping between the inputs and outputs of the whole model. Compared with support vector regression (SVR), the interior of deep fully connected neural network can be understood as a black box. A large number of input and output mappings can be learned and stored without having to describe the mappings beforehand. The internal mathematical model of SVR is strict, and it is difficult to describe the mapping relationship between input and output.

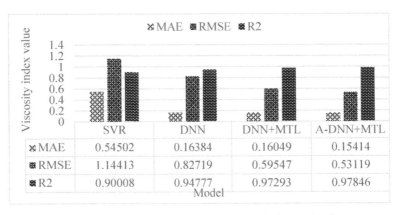

Fig. 6. Comparison of prediction results of mixture density.

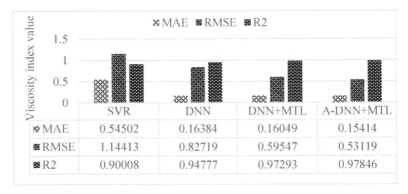

Fig. 7. Comparison of predicted results of mixture viscosity.

Secondly, based on DNN, a multi-task framework was introduced to train the density and viscosity of mixture in parallel. In this way, the model can learn the common features hidden in the two tasks to help optimize the model and improve the prediction effect of the model. In addition, based on the multi-task learning framework, this model adds an attention mechanism for each task, so that each task can pay attention to the features most relevant to its own task while sharing the features of other tasks, which further improves the prediction effect of the model.

In order to illustrate the advantages of the proposed model in time, there will be training time also compares the different model. The results are shown in Table 3:

Table 3. Comparison of training time for different models

Model	DNN		DNN + MTL	DNN + MTL + A
task	task1	task2:	task1 + task2	task1 + task2
Training time	82 s	78 s	104 s	128 s

It can be seen from Table 3 that, it takes more time to train two single-task models separately than to train one multi-task learning model. Therefore, the model proposed in this paper can not only improve the prediction accuracy of mixture density and viscosity, but also reduce the time required for training the model and improve the efficiency.

The above experimental results show that the proposed model (DNN + MTL + Attention) can not only improve the prediction accuracy of mixture density and viscosity, but also shorten the training time of the model.

5 Conclusion

In order to improve the prediction accuracy and efficiency of mixture density and viscosity and the universality of the prediction model for mixtures of different systems, a prediction model of mixture density and viscosity based on deep learning is proposed and verified by using the concept of material genetic engineering. Firstly, the deep fully connected neural network is used as the mapping between the input and output of the whole model. Then, considering the correlation between the two tasks of mixture density and viscosity, a multi-task learning framework was introduced for the model to train the two tasks of mixture density and viscosity in parallel on the basis of deep fully connected neural network, so that the model could learn the common features related to each task. Finally, in order to enable each task to focus on the features most relevant to its own task, a specific attention mechanism module is introduced for each task in the model.

The experimental results show that the proposed model has the best performance in predicting the density and viscosity of mixtures in each index while reducing the time required for training the two models, and the model has a certain universality for mixtures of different systems, which will effectively improve the scope of application of the model. Although the prediction model contains more kinds of mixtures than the existing methods, it is not comprehensive enough. The next step will consider using smaller molecular structural units (such as groups and chemical bonds) as input features, so as to reduce the complexity of the model and improve the application range of the model.

References

1. Hong, W., Xiaodong, X., Lanting, Z.: Data+Artificial Intelligence is the core of material genetic engineering. Sci. Technol. Rev. **36**(14), 15–21 (2018)
2. Mostafa, L., Ali, Z., Hezave, A.Z., Aziz, B.: Correlation of density for binary mixtures of methanol + ionic liquids using back propagation artificial neural network. Korean J. Chem. Eng. **30**(1), 213–220 (2013)
3. Lashkarblooki, M., Hezave, A.Z., Alajmi, A.M.: Viscosity prediction of ternary mixtures containing ILs using multi-layer perceptron artificial neural network. Fluid Phase Equilib. **326**(1), 15–20 (2012)
4. Bahiraei, M., Hosseinalipour, S.M., Zabihi, K., et al.: Using neural network for determination of viscosity in water-tio2 nanofluid. Adv. Mech. Eng. **14**(5), 677–683 (2012)
5. Jatinder, K., Ajay, B., Jha, M.K.: Comparison of statistical and neural network techniques in predicting physical properties of various mixtures of diesel and biodiesel. Lecture Notes in Engineering and Computer Science **2167**(1), 95–98 (2007)
6. Molina, J., Laroche, A., Richard, J.: Neural networks are promising tools for the prediction of the viscosity of unsaturated polyester resins. Front. Chem. **7**(1), 375–389 (2019)
7. Yi, C., Qing, L., Shu, Y.: Neural networks for predicting density and viscosity of ternary molecular mixtures. Comput. Appl. Chem. **14**(2), 133–138 (1997)
8. Saldana, D.A., Starck, L., Mougin, P.: Prediction of density and viscosity of biofuel compounds using machine learning methods. Energy Fuels **26**, 2416–2426 (2012)
9. Liu, Y., Hong, W., Cao, B.: Machine learning for predicting thermodynamic properties of pure fluids and their mixtures. Energy **30**(188), 116–121 (2019)
10. Jin, C., Jian, W.: Steelmaking end point prediction method based on the multitasking study. J. Comput. Appl. **5**(3), 889–895 (2017)
11. Yun, S., Fanpeng, P., Naiwang, G.: Multiple tasks based on low rank said short-term power load forecasting research. J. Mod. Electric Power **4**(3), 58–65 (2019)
12. Jing, Z., Shi, G., Liang, G., Nan, Z.: Based on the number of big five personality task learning. J. Univ. Chin. Acad. Sci. **35**(4), 550–560 (2018)
13. Xiao, S., Ze, S., Min, L.: Aluminum surface defect detection based on multitasking depth study. Laser Optoelectron. Progress **57**(10), 283–292 (2020)
14. Quan, Z., Xin, Z., Zhi, L.: Depth of music recommendation algorithm based on attention mechanism. Comput. Appl. Res. **4**(8), 2297–2299 (2019)
15. En, X., Ling, H., Xiu, W.: The depth of collaborative filtering model based on attention mechanism. J. China Univ. Measure. **30**(2), 219–225 (2019)
16. Dong, S., Hai, W., Ying, J., Xing, C.: Recommended project similarity model based on attention mechanism. J. Electron. Measure. Technol. **8**(15), 150–154 (2019)
17. Peng, J., Xia, C., Xu, Y., Li, X., Wu, X.: A multi-task network for cardiac magnetic resonance image segmentation and classification. Intell. Autom. Soft Comput. **30**(1), 259–272 (2021)
18. Li, Y., Liu, J., Shang, S.J.: WMA: a multi-scale self-attention feature extraction network based on weight sharing for VQA. J. Big Data **3**(3), 111–118 (2021)
19. Cui, L., Xu, Y.: Research on copyright protection method of material genome engineering data based on zero-watermarking. J. Big Data **2**(2), 53 (2020)
20. Xu, Y., Chen, S., Xu, X.: Research on viewpoint extraction in microblog. Intell. Autom. Soft Comput. **30**(2), 495–511 (2021)
21. Xu, Y., Cui, L., Xu, X.: A prediction method of fracture toughness of nickel-based superalloys. Comput. Syst. Sci. Eng. **42**(1), 121–132 (2022)

Author Index

Printed in the United States
by Baker & Taylor Publisher Services